ENTRYWAYS OF MILAN

INGRESSI DI MILANO

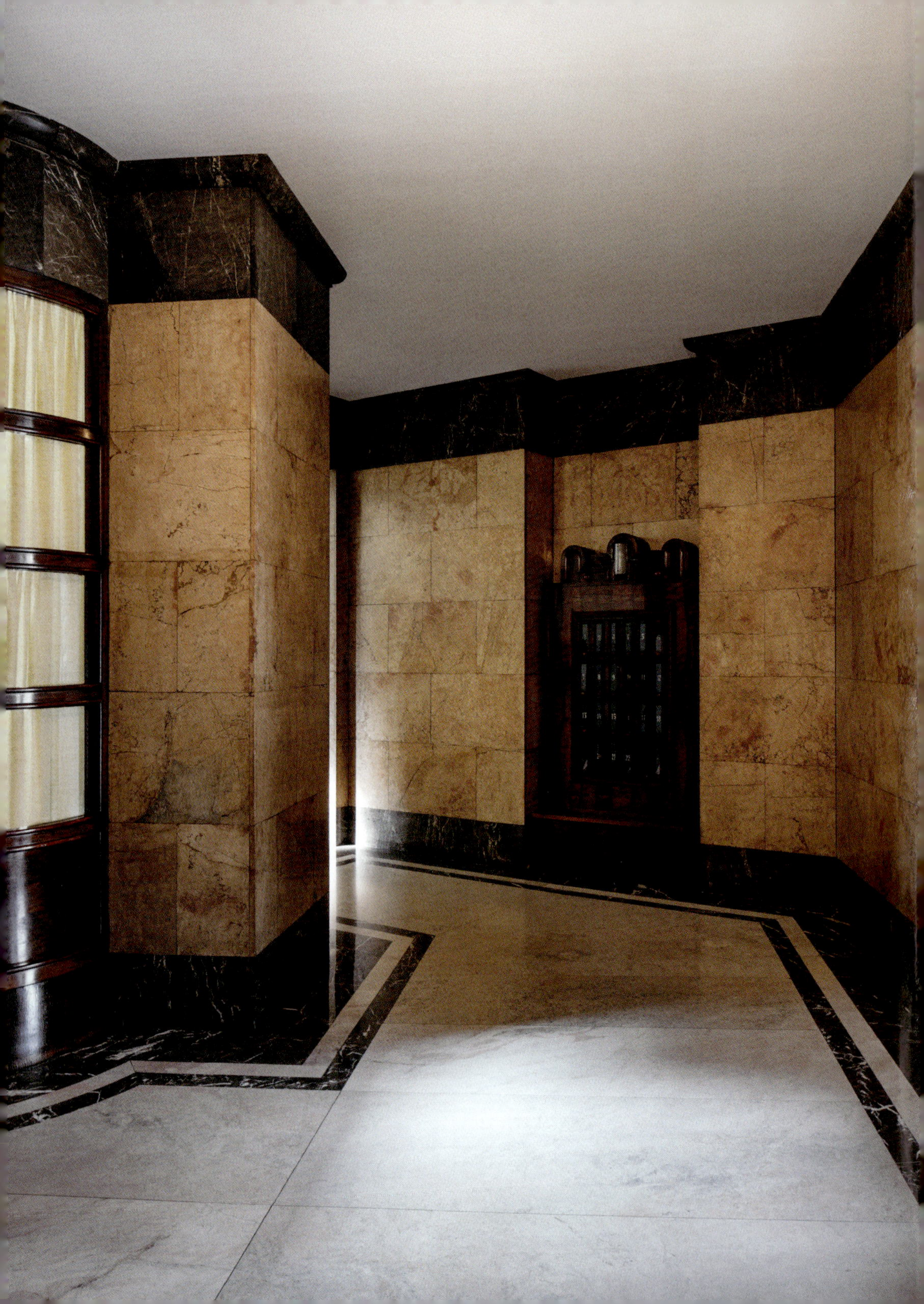

ENTRYWAYS OF MILAN
INGRESSI DI MILANO

TASCHEN

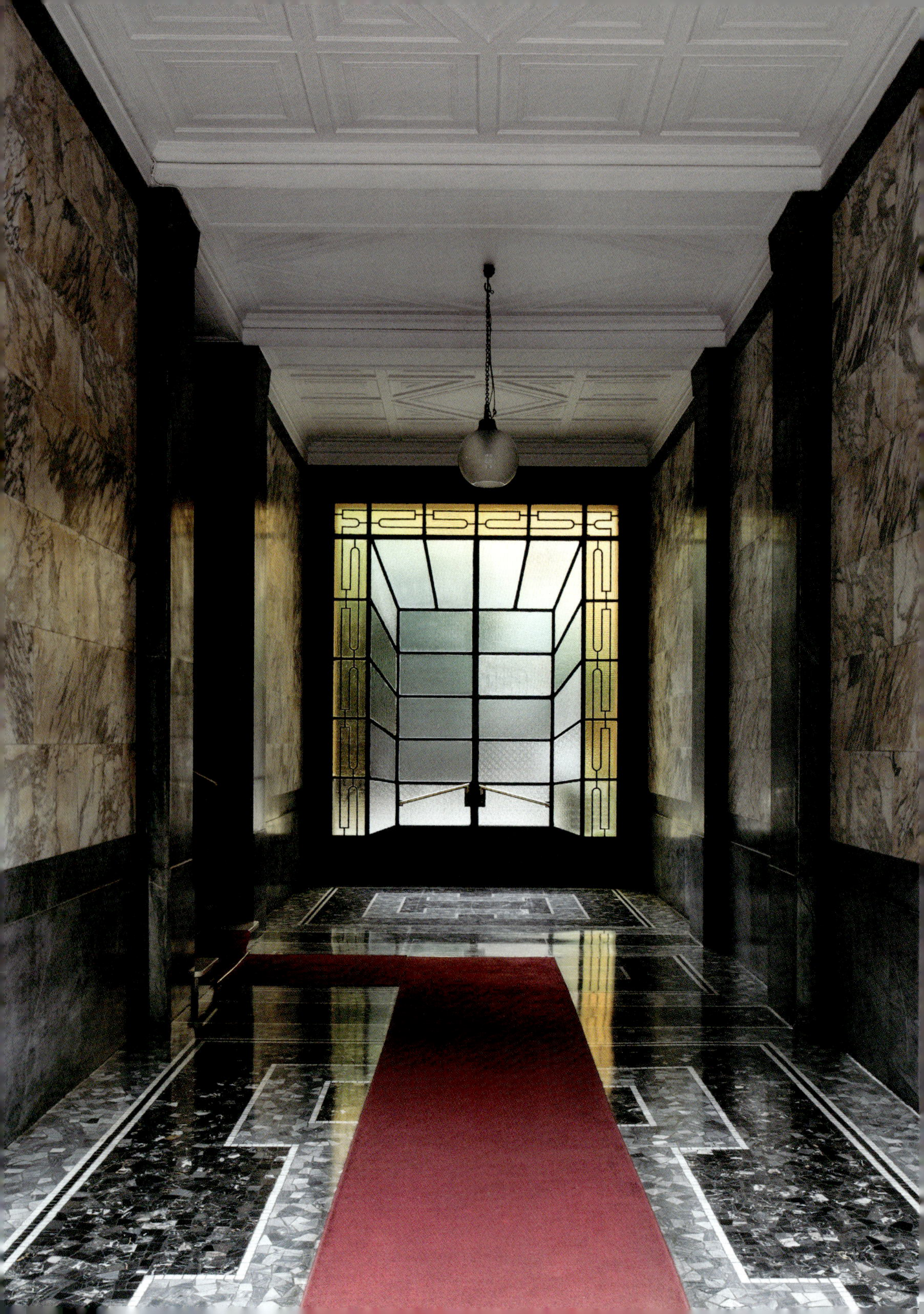

Edited and Directed by

KARL KOLBITZ

Photographs by

MATTHEW BILLINGS
DELFINO SISTO LEGNANI
PAOLA PANSINI

Texts by

FABRIZIO BALLABIO
LISA HOCKEMEYER
DANIEL SHERER
PENNY SPARKE

Stone Identification by

ANGELA EHLING
GRAZIA SIGNORI

Stone Commentary by

GRAZIA SIGNORI

Design Identification and
Commentary by

BRIAN KISH

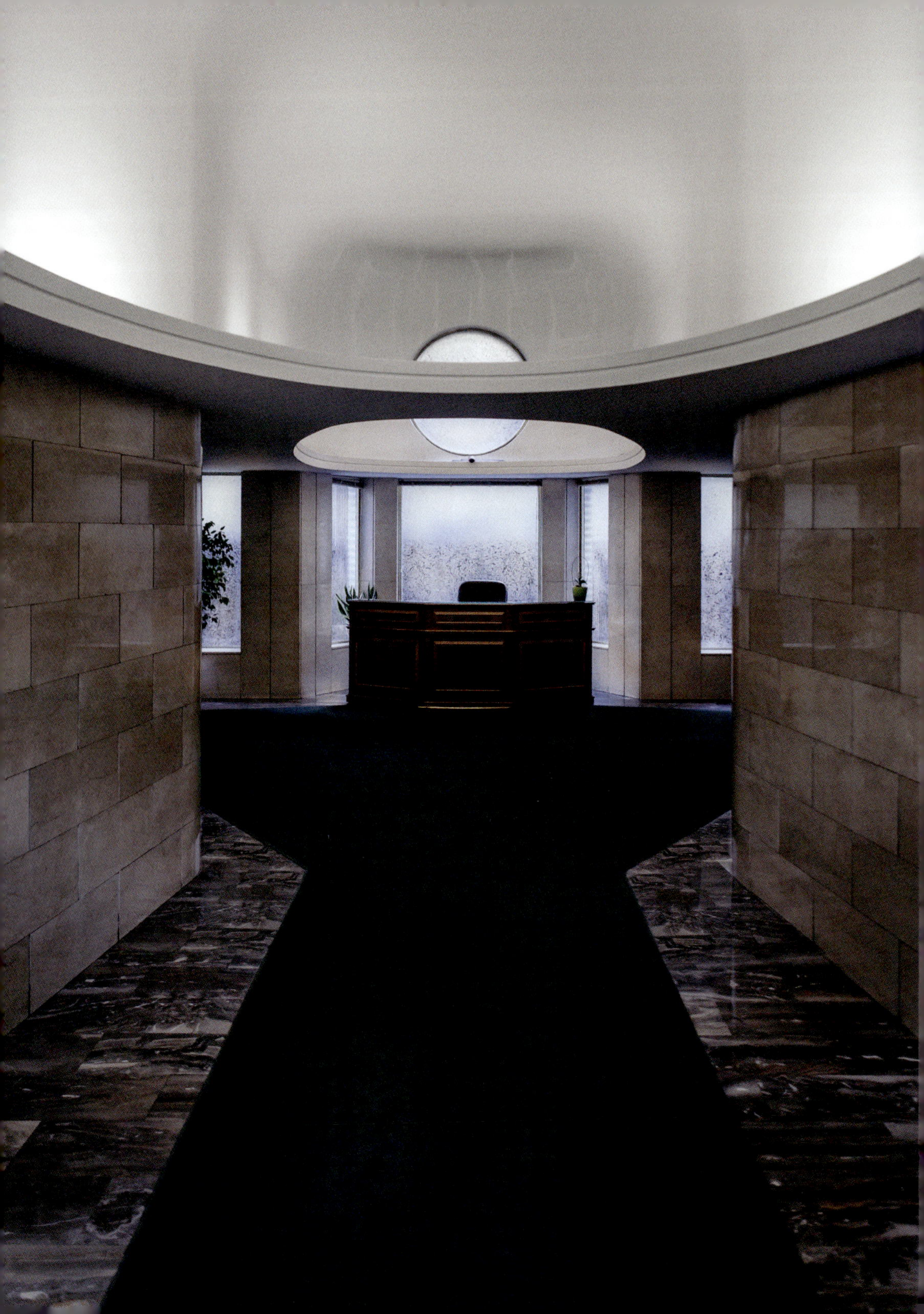

viale Abruzzi 16 · Luigi Mattioni, 1959–65
floor: Arabescato Orobico Grigio limestone · walls: Botticino limestone

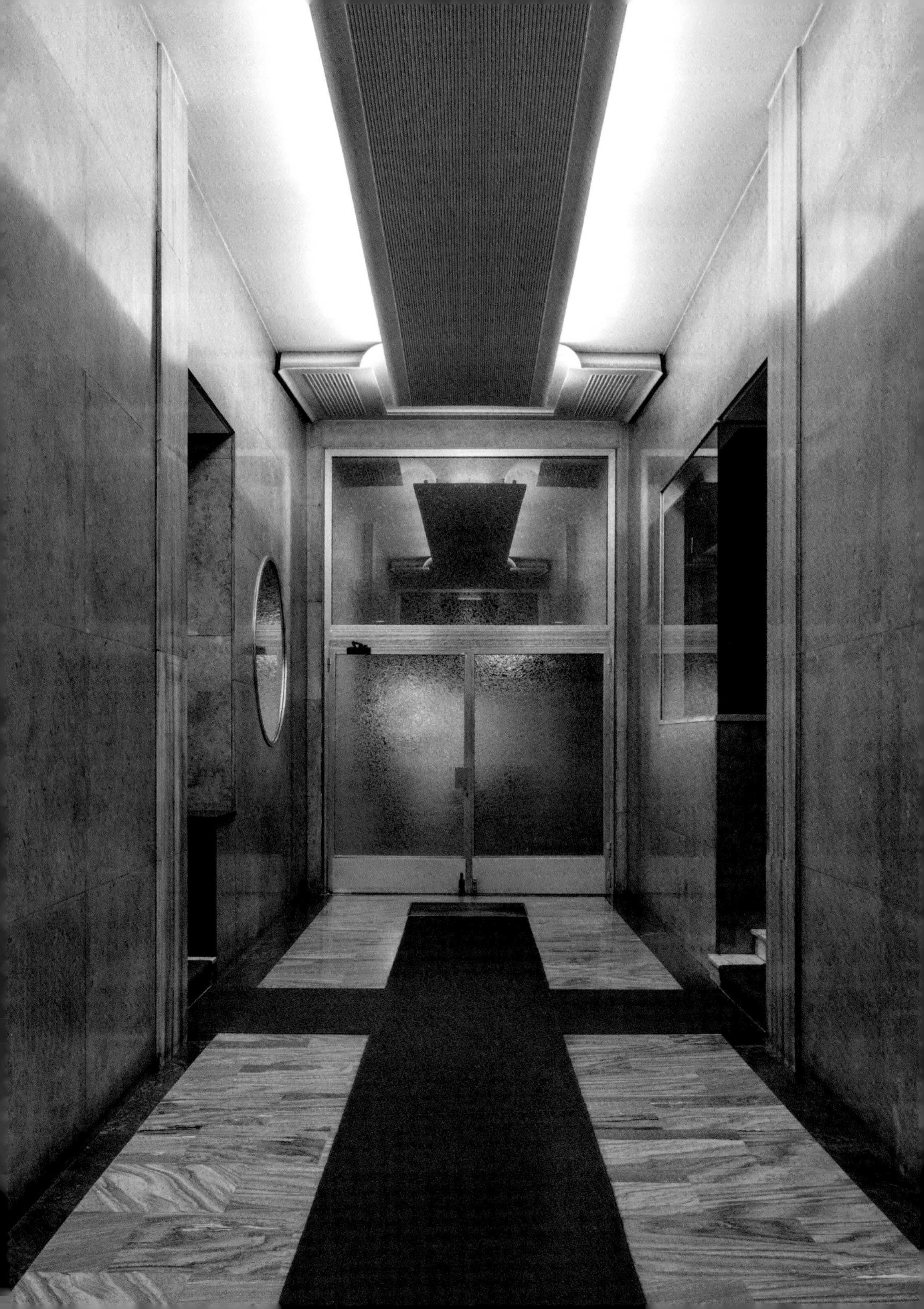

Karl Kolbitz

Foreword

I started traveling to Milan as a teenager and ever since I have been intrigued by the beauty of this city, even though its allure is not as effervescent as that of Paris, nor as ancient as that of Rome. As a kid growing up in reunited Berlin, surrounded by Socialist housing blocks and unkind re-construction efforts, Milan felt like a place where the twentieth century had grown both effortlessly and elegantly.

I found myself exploring the city's perimeters, set on a relentless search for its treasures. What struck me most were the places that spoke of the everyday—train stations, piazzas, residential areas. These were the true emblems of Milan's urban splendor. Cast in precious building materials, their design solutions and variations asked me to linger, to return, to enter, and to experience. Milan is a city that draws you in, that shows itself while screening itself at the same time. It is at once private, grandiloquent, and refined.

How can it be that this city, which has exported its design all over the world, has kept so silent about its exuberant and profuse entryways? The city's complex Modernist heritage is documented and reproduced in countless publications, yet this very Milanese singularity, the *ingressi*, has gone almost unnoticed.

The entryways to all kinds of residential buildings—the city's most hidden treasures—present themselves in plain sight to the eye. Not only to their residents, or visitors, but to anyone who endeavors to discover them. Every day, heavy wooden portals swing open while others, fitted with large glass panels, forever invite our gaze.

Looking through these portals, I witness sublime interiors that speak to me about how architecture shapes our lives. Thus I fantasize about who the people who inhabit them might be, what their lives may be like. The *ingressi* reveal these nuances of lives and living to us in the most subtle and allusive ways.

Italy is constantly presenting and representing itself. Wherever we look, we are met by a unique way of dancing with a material, of creating something as perfectly as it can be made. This book wishes to represent for its readers the way in which the *ingressi* stand as a piece of punctuation to the architectural and design accomplishments of the city's modern history.

viale Tunisia 48 · Giannino Testori, 1936–37

Rectangular inset panels, in acid-etched tempered glass, by Fontana Arte.
floor: Cipollino Verde marble and serpentinite · lesene: Rosa Valtroce marble · walls: Repen limestone

Karl Kolbitz

Prefazione

Le prime volte che ho visitato Milano ero adolescente. Da allora, la bellezza di questa città ha catturato la mia attenzione. Non è una bellezza effervescente come quella di Parigi, né antica come quella di Roma. In quanto bambino cresciuto nella Berlino riunificata, circondato dall'edilizia dell'era socialista e dagli sforzi inclementi di ricostruzione, Milano mi era parsa un luogo nel quale il Novecento si era sviluppato con leggerezza ed eleganza.

Mi sono ritrovato a esplorare i perimetri della città, alla ricerca continua dei suoi tesori. A colpirmi maggiormente erano i luoghi che ne narravano la quotidianità – le stazioni ferroviarie, le piazze, i quartieri residenziali. Erano questi gli indicatori più autentici dello splendore urbano di Milano. I preziosi materiali impiegati, le poliedriche soluzioni progettistiche mi chiedevano di indugiare, di tornare, di entrare e assaporarne l'esperienza. Milano è una città coinvolgente, che si mostra ma contemporaneamente si cela. È al tempo stesso intima, magniloquente e raffinata.

Com'è possibile che una città che ha esportato il suo design in tutto il mondo abbia taciuto delle copiose ed esuberanti entrate dei suoi palazzi? La sua complessa eredità modernista è documentata e riprodotta in innumerevoli pubblicazioni, eppure questa peculiarità che la contraddistingue, gli ingressi, sono passati quasi del tutto inosservati.

Gli ingressi di edifici residenziali di ogni genere – i tesori più nascosti delle città – si offrono allo sguardo non solo degli abitanti, o dei visitatori, ma anche di chiunque ne vada in cerca. Giorno dopo giorno, i pesanti portoni di legno si aprono, mentre le grandi vetrate sono un invito continuo a scrutare all'interno.

Attraverso questi varchi, avevo modo di vedere interni sontuosi che mi facevano percepire fino a che punto l'architettura plasmi la nostra esistenza. E fantasticavo su chi potessero essere le persone che transitavano in quegli androni, su come potessero essere le loro vite. Erano queste sfumature di vita vissuta ciò che gli ingressi mi mostravano, nella maniera più allusiva e penetrante.

L'Italia presenta e rappresenta se stessa costantemente. Dovunque si posi lo sguardo, ci troviamo davanti quel modo unico di danzare con un materiale, di fare qualcosa al meglio delle possibilità. Questo volume aspira a illustrare ai lettori come gli ingressi costituiscano una sorta di interpunzione nella sintassi architettonica e progettuale della moderna storia della città.

via Monviso 37 · Arnaldo di Lenna, 1931–34

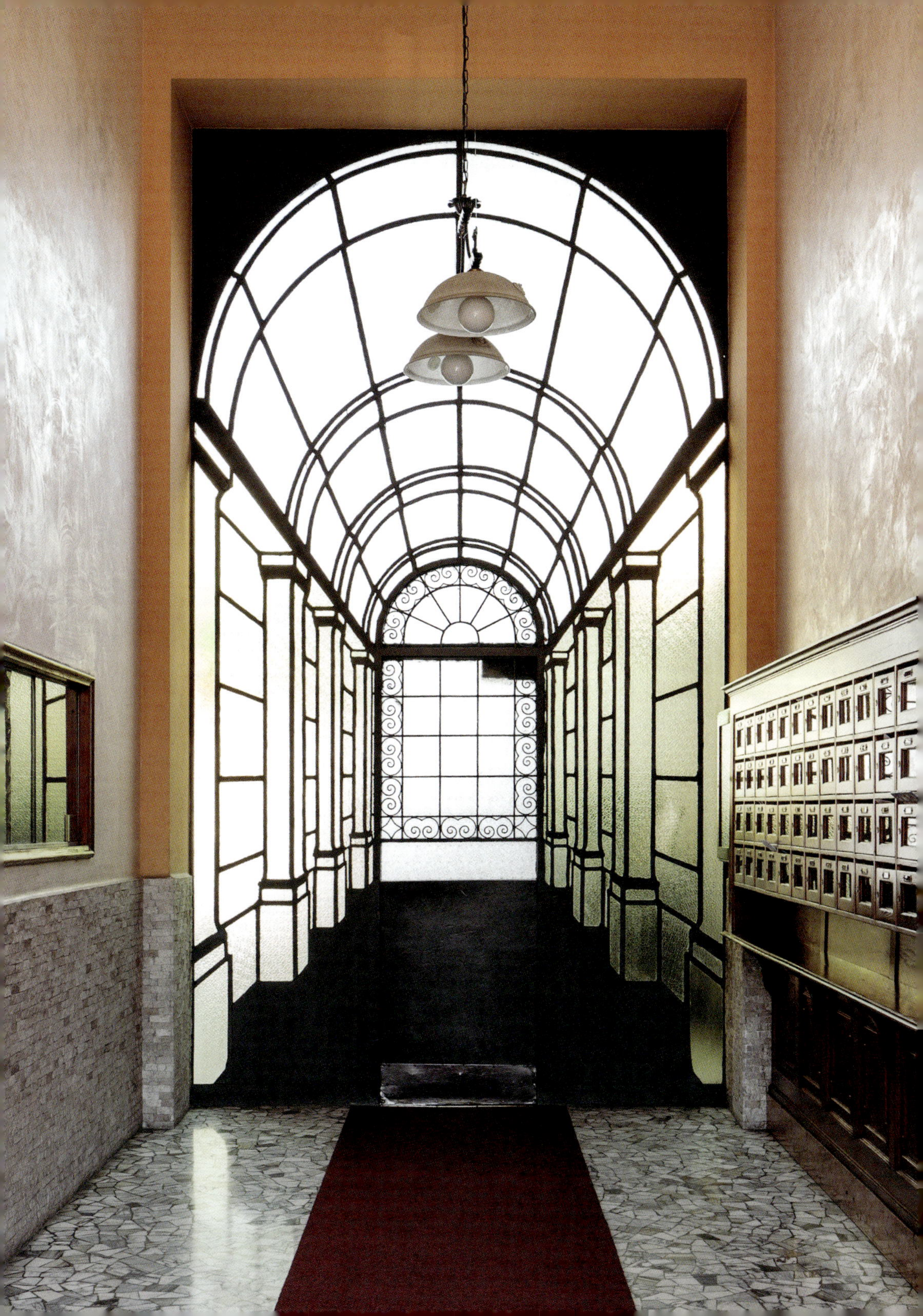

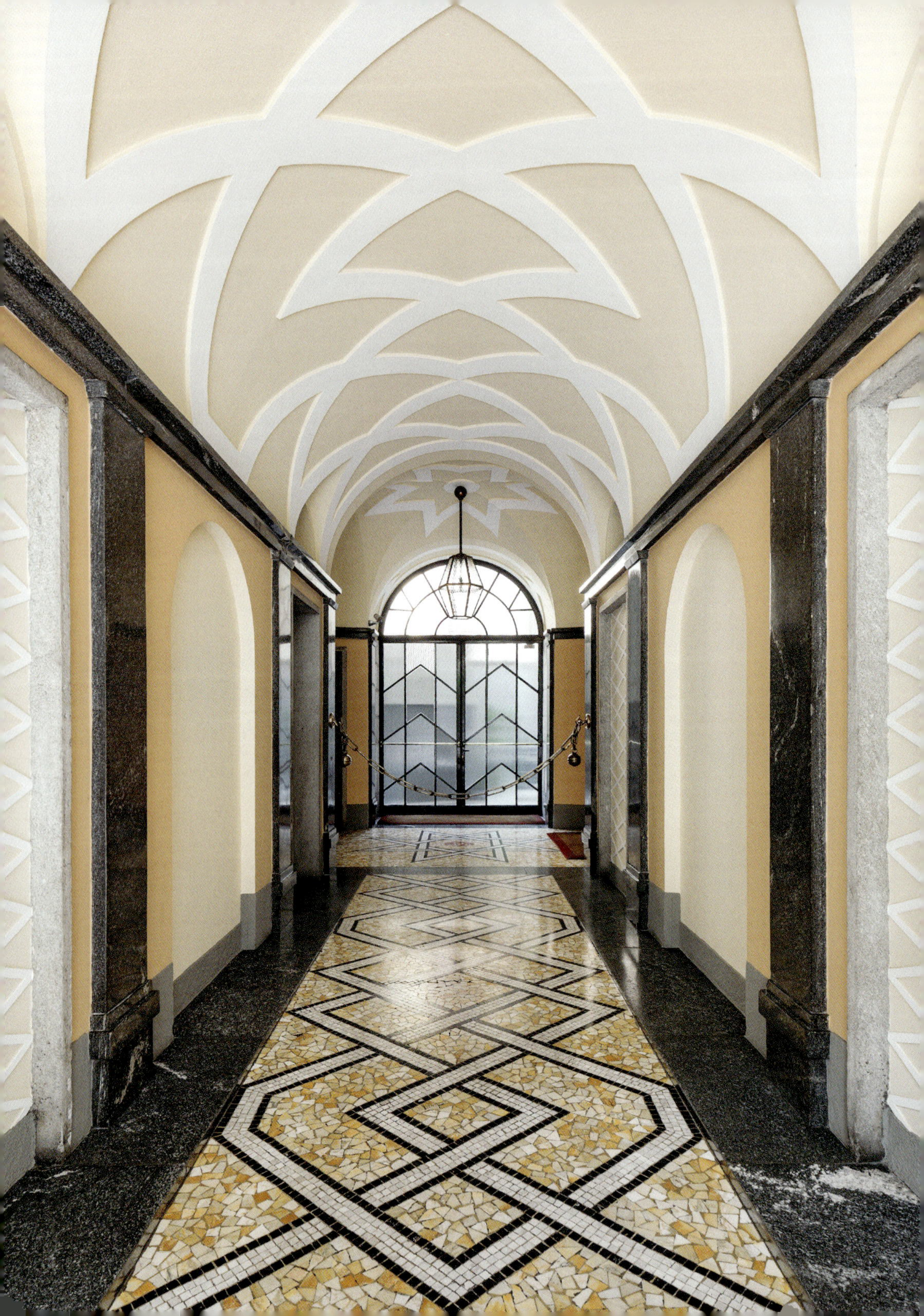

Fabrizio Ballabio

Behind Closed Doors

MILAN'S *INGRESSI* AS LIMINAL SPACES FOR ARCHITECTURAL EXPRESSION

Milan Is an Ugly City—In an essay published in the Italian magazine *Emporium* in 1921, Novecento architect Giovanni Muzio begins with the regretful recognition of an enduring stereotype that, at the dawn of the twentieth century, had characterized a vast amount of visual and literary accounts of his beloved place of origin. It might sound idle, he argues, to write of Milanese architecture given the repute of "ugly city" Milan had earned over the turn of the century. At the time Muzio was writing, the city's derogatory fame was in fact firmly rooted in the radical transformations it had been subject to since vigorously establishing itself as a leading industrial center.[1] And yet, by Muzio's own subtle admission, accounts of Milan's "ugliness" in reference to the quality of its buildings date back to at least the 1500s, when renowned chroniclers and those on the first Grand Tours would inform the common view. Writing in 1546, for instance, the biographer of Ferrante Gonzaga, Giuliano Goselini, deemed the city "ungrateful to its onlookers" both for the neglected state in which its architecture appeared and for its poor quality of construction. In 1609 local historian Paolo Morigia, in his *Sommario delle cose mirabili della città di Milano*, admitted that the palazzi of the Milanese (although copious in number) were guilty of relatively scarce interest to those who observed them, despite their being equipped with all the necessary comforts. According to Italian scholar Marzia Capello,[2] this condition endured up to the early eighteenth century when, in the eyes of foreign visitors, Milan's houses and streetscapes were considered all the more disappointing given the wealth of their inhabitants.[3] The unimpressiveness of Milan's residential architecture has historically been even further paled when confronted with that of other Italian cities. Grand Tourist Michel Eyquem de Montaigne writes as early as 1581 about a city rich in craftsmanship, with intense mercantile activities and the most populated in Italy that nonetheless lacked the magnificent palaces of Rome, Naples, Genoa, and Florence.[4] In all accounts, and leaving aside those eulogies that were most likely to have been motivated by either political or social favors, the enduring narrative is one of a city with immense and distributed wealth that nevertheless consistently resisted rendering it architecturally manifest within the urban realm.

via Mario Giuriati 5 · Giovanni Muzio, 1930–31
floor: Palladiana of Giallo Siena marble and mosaics, Nero di Anzola diorite
lesene: Nero di Anzola diorite

Milan is an ugly city, or so it may "appear." Underwhelming as it may have presented itself in its outward appearance, narrators from the time, in fact, also unanimously recounted a rather different situation beyond the city's many thresholds. Morigia himself, for instance, while dismissing their elevations, spares no words in comparing the interiors of Milan's aristocratic residences to true "paradises on earth"—an observation that has endured to become something of a cliché in the majority of subsequent descriptions of Milan, or the "Città Meneghina" as it is sometimes nicknamed. Yet it is precisely through such ponderings that one can gauge the peculiar hierarchy denoting the layering of Milan's expressive structure that so often inverts or even reshuffles conventional architectural schemata. Precisely during the years when the local historian had been writing, the court would, in fact, affirm itself as the key space of architectural expression in the city's urban fabric and at the expense of the façade, which, contingent as it was to the many vicissitudes of Milan's medieval building structure (consider that Palazzo Marino was for a long time the only palazzo to entirely occupy its plot), would often be left unfinished.[5] Much in the Cinquecento tradition of a space with porticoes on all four of its symmetrically arranged sides, these enclosed universes—exempt for their very nature from the severe ethical and moral norms prevailing in the street[6]—allowed for the ambitions of their inhabitants to be duly expressed to illustrious guests, independently of questions of context and propriety. This was of course valid for the city's nobility but even more so for its bourgeoisie, the status of which swiftly rose in Milan's years under the Borromeo bishops—so much so that by the end of the seventeenth century, that a house should be built "bela de denter, pei padroni, brutta de foera, pei mincioni" (beautiful on the inside for its owners and ugly on the outside for the fools) was much more than a mere dictum and indeed became a distinctive characteristic of most of the private construction built in Milan at that period.

Peeping Through an Ugly House—Within this narrative, the fact that Muzio's first built work would be concertedly dubbed Ca' Brütta (the Ugly House) entails a curious atavism, particularly when accepting that the rage in its reception was unlikely to have been prompted by the casual aversion to so-called modernism. In presenting it in the early numbers of his *Architettura ed arti decorative* in 1922, Marcello Piacentini himself wondered why the project had been received with such strong hostility given the modesty and propriety of its outer form. Regardless of its repute (which, after all, has changed over the years), the temptation to discuss the project in correlation with its sixteenth- and seventeenth-century forebears is all the more appealing in view of the stark contrast that exists between the building's bland and flattened outer elevations and the decorative richness of its inner representative spaces. Walking along the northern sidewalk of Via della Moscova, one need only peep deep within the portal of No. 12, arguably the most prominent of the building's entrances (see pp. 236–239), to be immersed within a cosmos of polychrome marble and gilded moldings, ornate plastering, and elaborate mosaic floor-tiling. To the foreign gaze, the dialectic tension that is established with the building's adjoining, quasi-hermetic, two-story travertine base is unexpected to say the least.

In the case of the Ca' Brütta, the curious friction between the building's street presence vis-a-vis one's experience of it upon entering is somewhat colored by Muzio's whimsical use of classical motifs on the building's elevations; perhaps this is why Muzio would later refer to this building as a juvenile compromise. However, in his later endeavors this motif would find even stronger uses. Already in the façade of the house in Via Giuriati (1930) (see p. 12), the animated horizontal striation of Ca' Brütta gives way to a more conventional, tripartite solution in which, with the exception of the ground floor, the stone string courses and the quoining pilasters at each of the façades' terminals are washed out under a thick coat of marmoreus white plaster. Crossing the threshold of the portico, the visitor is funneled into a deep vaulted passageway which, for the vividness of its decorations and for its spatial qualities, could be comfortably sited among the Roman engravings of the nineteenth-century French scholar Paul Marie Letarouilly. Notice how the marble floor's design motif is elegantly echoed in the stuccoed lozenges denoting the articulation of the ceiling; or how the partitioning of the side walls cadences one's way toward the oval crossing leading to the building's main staircase. In Muzio's later Palazzo Bonaiti in Piazza della Repubblica (1935–36) (see pp. 172–177), the traditional references characterizing the façades of the two earlier projects seem to dissolve entirely in favor of a more abstract *parti* around the motif of the grid. The development is compact and economically profitable; the cheap building material (brick) is exposed without shame. Again though, within the homogenous mineral base on which the complex sits, the neatly placed portals sculpted by Giacomo Manzù lead four steps up into a world of reflective colored marble and other precious facings. The architectural resolution of the three featured *androni* is undoubtedly more abstract; the arrangement of materials is less reliant on composition than it is on effect—and yet in their airy elegance, their alignment of portal and staircase within a seamless spatial continuum, and finally in their contrasting relation with the building's quasi-hermetic exterior, one can easily envision them in relation to the former schemes.

In instances such as these one can gauge the representative significance of the space of the *androne* (a space of passage typically leading from the portal to the main stairway or the portal to the court) in the residential complexes of Muzio as much as in the many building endeavors of interwar Milan. The *androne* was a space in which the aspirational sentiments of the rising middle class would find apt architectural expression, apart from the public gaze—behind closed doors, so to say. Imbued with comfort and décor, and discretely hidden behind unglamorous building fronts, these *ingressi* can be deemed as tangible embodiments of a penchant for reception so typical of the industrial bourgeoisie, which nonetheless still summons up the spatial cerimonialism of late Renaissance and Baroque palatial architecture.

Of course, by the time the modern condominium had risen as the "last and most recent chapter in the development of European cities," with its multiple ownership schemes and numerical efficiency, the defining elements of its antecedent architectural typologies (the court, the façade, the means of circulation) would be entirely re-articulated in their morphology and meaning. After all, on more than one occasion, Muzio himself would clarify that neither he nor his comrades took the "palazzo" or the "chatelet" as references while responding to the challenges posed by the modern building industry. And yet, in experiencing these spaces in their suave scenic grandeur, their material and decorative richness, and in the particular attention given to the sequencing of both those architectural and artistic episodes that mark one's experience on entering, it is hard not to recall the perspectival and pictorial effects that throughout the whole of the seventeenth century and into the eighteenth would be deliberately sought after in palazzi across Italy to turn the space of the *androne* into the first picture frame within a highly choreographed spatial sequence.[7]

In Milan, this particular motif—prompted by the new patterns of reception[8]—still remains visible today in the palazzi of the Clerici, the Gallarati Scotti, or the Olivazzi Trivulzio where, via successions of colonnades, the axial arrangement of multiple courts and accelerated perspectives into sculptural or pictorial apparatuses, the experience of entering was conceived as an ingeniously choreographed promenade toward the main apartments. As with Muzio and his colleagues, the sought-after effects were rendered even more dramatic in contraposition to the façades that, much in the local Milanese Cinquecento and Seicento tradition, would remain relatively spare in both their formal articulation and decorative schemes. If the reminiscence is not obvious as one enters the Ca' Brütta, around the corner, the *androne* of No. 1 Via Andrea Appiani[9] features a *trompe l'oeil* backdrop of linear metal profiles that for its composition, its relation to the portal, and its capacity to evoke depth is almost pedantic in its referencing the above-mentioned tradition (see p. 231). Curiously, this particular solution would become highly popular among practitioners from the 1930s and shows a poised uninhibitedness in dealing with the typological and contextual contingencies encountered on site, which becomes even more significant if understood in an apt context. Is it not in the same spirit that in Santa Maria presso San Satiro Donato Bramante devised his notorious faux choir to overcome the impossibility of realizing it in the "real"?

Of "Paradises on Earth"—The above observations apply almost invariably to the larger part of Milan's interwar residential architecture that, for a number of different reasons (let us not forget that the rhetoric of Fascism was formed precisely at that time), saw the values of local architectural traditions as a fertile repertoire from which to draw new canons. Even with the advent of so-called "Rationalism" in the early 1930s (of which Muzio's Palazzo Bonaiti is somewhat paradigmatic) and the consequent overcoming of the literal borrowings that characterized the previous decade, the indebtedness to the typological findings that marked the city's Novecento years remains discernible throughout. It is by no means accidental that a large number of the *ingressi* from this time are located along the urban axis that crosses today's Viale Tunisia. Ever since the drafting of Milan's first urban development plan in the late 1880s (Piano Beruto), and even more so with the relocation of the main train station from Porta Nuova to its current location in Piazza Duca d'Aosta (1910–30s), the area became one of the most active building sites in the construction of the modern city.

As Italian historian Fulvio Irace explains when writing of the postwar Milanese condominium,[10] with the end of World War II and the dawn of the Italian Miracle, for different reasons, the typological variety of the city's residential architecture would increase exponentially when compared to that of the previous wave. The aberrations reflected the diversification in the nature of building commissions as well as the swiftly changing lifestyle of the city's inhabitants. They were also contingent on the emergence of new architectural leanings that, regardless of their belonging or kinship to the earlier generation, would lead practitioners to experiment outside of the accepted repertoires (the metamorphic character of Gio Ponti's work as both architect and writer is exemplary in this sense). Innovations of both a technological and an aesthetic nature would steadily make their way within the city's urban fabric, which came to grow ever more unconscious of its pre-modern legacy.[11] Still, and it is again Irace that comes to our assistance, Milan's industrial bourgeoisie remained the sound protagonist of the building endeavors of the 1950s and 1960s, perpetuating that concealed longing for internal comfort and decorum that so typically, and timelessly, has been associated with *milanesità*.

Clearly, it is impossible to draw direct formal parallels between the *ingressi* of the second generation and those that had preceded the global conflict. In place of the symmetrical arrangements of Muzio, Portaluppi, Martinenghi, and the like, the later generation (Ponti, Asnago & Vender, BBPR, and so on) makes deliberate attempts to move the visitor off center—be that via the disposition of architectural elements, the articulation of stairs, the accentuation of diagonals in the decorative motifs, or the sporadic introduction of flower beds and ponds. An intelligibile example of this that (typologically at least) remains faithful to the elongated, rectilinear hall can be appreciated in the *ingresso* of Via Pinturicchio 11 (see p. 89), where the asymmetrical layout of the stair, the carpet, the wall claddings, the handrail, and the artwork in the distance throws the otherwise tube-like character of the room off balance. In more drastic departures from this established model (for example, Via Marcona 49, see pp. 246–247, in BBPR's Piazza Sant'Erasmo 5, see pp. 214–215 or even Via Francesco Ferrucci 6, see p. 297), the boundaries of theses spaces seem to dissolve entirely to form a hybrid internal/external zone that acts as a threshold to the condominiums' multiple cores.

The material qualities of this more recent group also reflect a rising interest in exploiting the skills and artistry of local industries, be that in the development of cladding solutions or in the production of highly bespoke fittings. The range of practices involved in the "curation" of the *ingressi* found in postwar Milan had come to encompass more traditional know-how, such as stone cutting, metalwork, and ceramics, to more ambitious ventures into the devising, for example, of ad hoc lighting components. Anyone familiar with the work of Gio Ponti might recall his frequent collaborations with ABET LAMINATI or with porcelain manufacturers such as Richard Ginori and La Riggiola. Caccia Dominioni and Gardella went as far as founding their own company, Azucena, producing furnishings and fittings to be featured in their own projects as well as those of other contemporary practices.

And yet, while the formality of the "central axis" made way for drifting promenades, and as an aura of disengaging saturation replaced the solemn overtones of the previous endeavors, these liminal passages through which life (theatrically) swept continued to be treated as sites of vivid architectural expression. Collectively invested upon, owned, and ultimately maintained, Milan's *ingressi* were culturally significant in ways that, in the current climate of financial self-interest and social distrust, are almost inconceivable. They have also become one of the city's enduring leitmotifs, making the "simple" act of entering a timeless and geographically pervasive ritual so dear to the Milanesi. If well into the 1940s it was the turn of Giuseppe Pogatschnig, also known as Pagano, the editor of *Costruzioni-Casabella*, to grant the Lombard capital its discreditable "primacy of ugliness," the photographs that follow show, if anything, that Morigia's observations written five centuries earlier hold true in many ways. In Milan, behind closed doors, there are still "paradises on earth."

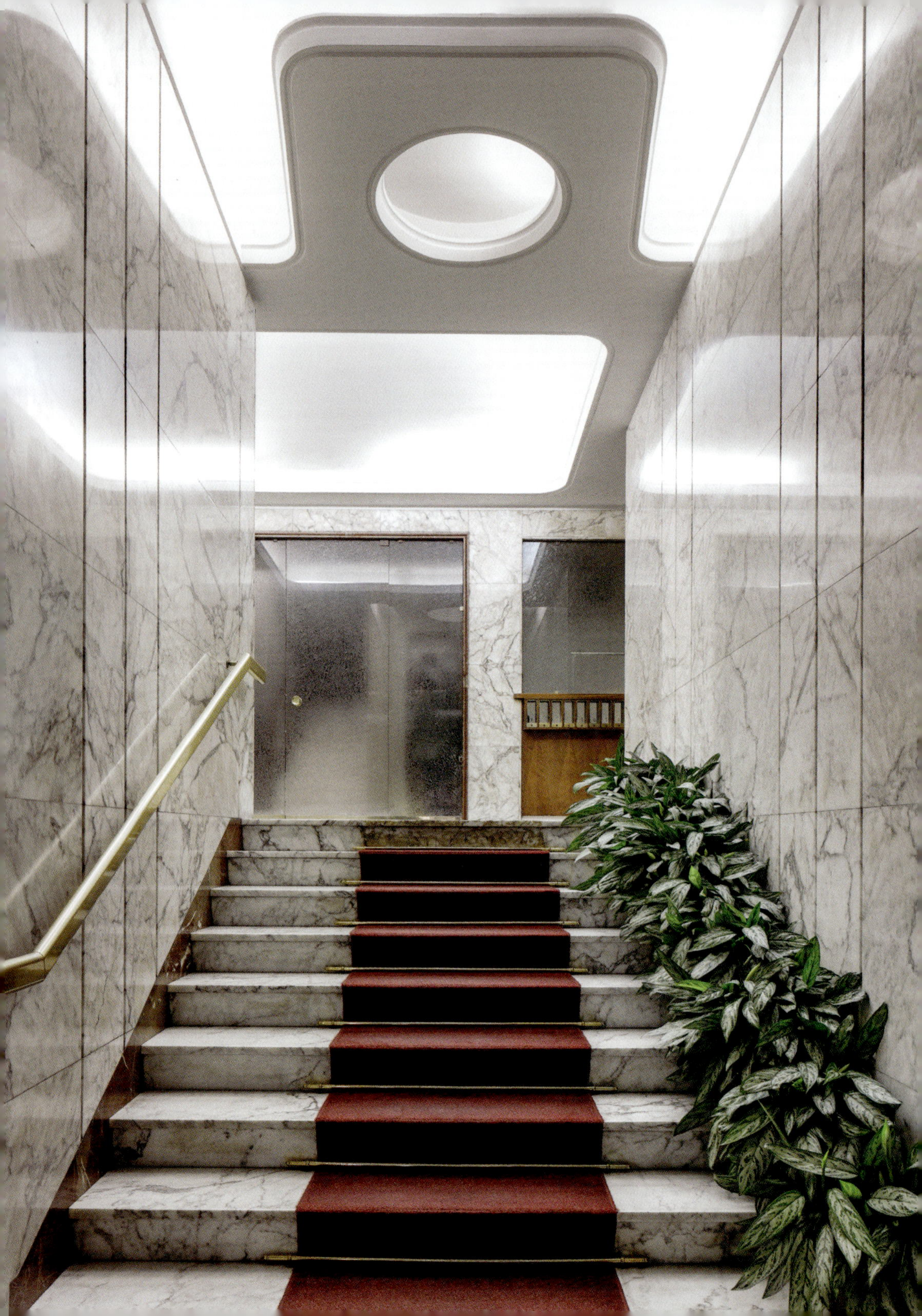

Fabrizio Ballabio

Dietro le porte chiuse

GLI INGRESSI DI MILANO O UN'ARCHITETTURA DELLA LIMINALITÀ

Milano è una città brutta – In un saggio sull'architettura dell'Ottocento milanese, apparso nella rivista italiana *Emporium* nel maggio 1921, l'architetto "novecentista" Giovanni Muzio esordisce acconsentendo a un famoso stereotipo che dagli albori del ventesimo secolo ha contraddistinto in modo quasi univoco la miriade di narrazioni visive e letterarie sulla sua amata città natale. "Può sembrare a taluno ozioso," spiega Muzio, "scrivere di architettura milanese dei tempi trascorsi [...] data la diffusa nomea che ha Milano di città brutta". In quegli anni, la cattiva reputazione di cui godeva la città era principalmente dovuta alle radicali trasformazioni che, come è noto, stravolsero il tessuto urbano della Milano storica sin dal suo affermarsi in quanto importante polo industriale.[1] Eppure, Muzio stesso ammette che i resoconti narranti la "bruttezza" di Milano, in particolar modo quelli relativi alla scarsa qualità del suo patrimonio edilizio, non erano affatto circoscritti al suo periodo "moderno", ma risalivano almeno al sedicesimo secolo, quando furono cronisti e "Grandtouristi" italici e stranieri a plasmare il pensiero comune intorno ai più importanti centri urbani della penisola. Ad esempio, nel 1546, il biografo di Ferrante Gonzaga, Giulio Gosellini, reputò la città "poco a' riguardanti grata" sia per lo stato di trascuratezza in cui giaceva la sua architettura, sia per il suo essere "mal fabbricata". Nel 1609, fu lo storico milanese Paolo Morigia, nel suo *Sommario delle cose mirabili della città di Milano*, ad ammettere che le dimore dei milanesi, sebbene fossero in larga misura equipaggiate di tutti "quei commodi che si possono desiderare", non presentassero "diletto alcuno" a chi si fosse fermato a osservarne i fronti urbani. A dir di Marzia Capello,[2] questa condizione permase fino al diciottesimo secolo, quando all'occhio del forestiero le case e le strade di Milano parevano tanto più deludenti vista la ricchezza diffusa degli abitanti della città.[3] E che dire dei confronti con l'architettura delle altre maggiori città italiane, dove le classi benestanti facevano teatro di piazze e strade per manifestare la grandezza dei loro casati? Già nel 1581, Michel Eyquem de Montaigne descrive Milano come una città ricca di artigianato, con fruttuose attività mercantili, tra le più popolate d'Italia, alla quale mancano però i magnifici palazzi di Roma, Napoli, Genova o Firenze.[4] Nella quasi totalità dei casi, e fatta esclusione di quegli encomi che solevano essere motivati da favori politici o sociali, i resoconti su Milano (e sui milanesi) narrano di

via Plinio 55 · L. Kovacs, 1957–62
skirting: Rosso Collemandina limestone · walls and stairs: Arabescato marble

una città dove immense e distribuite ricchezze raramente si palesano nel tessuto urbano.

Pertanto, Milano è una città brutta, o se non altro in apparenza. Per quanto deludente nel suo aspetto esteriore, infatti, va specificato come la situazione fosse, notoriamente, alquanto diversa al di là delle soglie dei suoi numerosi palazzi. Lo stesso Morigia, critico severo delle facciate di questi ultimi, non si risparmiò affatto nel paragonare i loro interni a veri e propri "paradisi in terra": osservazione che, nel tempo, si affermerà volgarmente come uno dei più noti stereotipi della città meneghina ("Milano è una città da scoprire", come si suol dire). E sono proprio stereotipi di questo genere che ci permettono di captare la particolare stratigrafia espressiva dell'architettura milanese, che così spesso ha sovvertito, o ancor meglio invertito, i convenzionali schemi percettivi dell'architettura classica. Nel contesto storico in cui scriveva Morigia, erano le corti, infatti, a rappresentare il fulcro espressivo di questi grandi complessi, e a discapito delle facciate.[5] Queste ultime, soggette com'erano alle innumerevoli vicissitudini del tessuto medievale della Milano *intra moenia* (si consideri che il Palazzo Marino è stato per vari anni l'unico a occupare un lotto nella sua interezza), si lasciavano addirittura incompiute per diverse generazioni. Le corti, d'altra parte, concepite in quanto cosmi racchiusi, simmetrici e circondati da portici secondo le tradizioni cinquecentesche, consentivano di dare sfoggio alle più svariate ambizioni rappresentative della committenza lontano dagli occhi indiscreti del popolo e del clero. Per loro stessa natura, esse erano esenti dal severo codice etico e morale vigente in città sin dagli anni della Controriforma.[6] E se l'espediente risultava valido per la locale classe aristocratica, lo era ancor più per la borghesia, il quale status fiorì rapidamente nella Milano borromaica. Tanto che, alla fine del diciassettesimo secolo, il fatto che una casa dovesse esser costruita "bela de denter, pei padroni, brutta de foera, pei mincioni", ovvero, bella dentro per i padroni e brutta fuori per gli stolti, fu molto più di un semplice detto, ma un carattere distintivo della più grossa parte dell'edilizia privata costruita a Milano in quell'epoca.

Sbirciando in una casa brutta – In questo contesto, che l'opera prima di Muzio fosse soprannominata la "Ca' Brütta" assume un significato particolare, ancor più se si constata che lo scandalo che suscitò aveva poco o nulla a che vedere con la consuetudinaria avversione del grande pubblico verso il linguaggio architettonico del modernismo. Nel recensirla in uno dei primi numeri della rivista *Architettura e Arti Decorative* nel 1922, lo stesso Marcello Piacentini si domandò come fosse possibile che un'opera così "silenziosa", così "a posto", venisse accolta con tanta ostilità. E infatti, seppure il soprannome le rimase, la sua nomea era destinata a cambiare negli anni a venire, tanto nel pensiero dei cittadini quanto in quello più arcigno della critica architettonica. Ma la tentazione di creare paralleli tra la Ca' Brütta e le architetture milanesi del sedicesimo e diciassettesimo secolo va al di là del valore aneddotico dell'appellativo. È il singolare rapporto tra i suoi sobri prospetti (dove i registri dell'architettura classica vengono, sì, liberamente riproposti, ma in veste spoglia e appiattita) e la ricchezza decorativa dei suoi spazi interni di rappresentanza a fare eco alla riservatezza formale che ha da sempre contraddistinto la tradizione architettonica milanese. Tradizione che Muzio stesso invoca nel lamentarsi del degenerato ecclettismo dell'architettura fineottocentesca. Camminando lungo il lato nord dell'attuale via della Moscova, basta sbirciare attraverso il portone del civico 12 (certamente il più sfarzoso tra i suoi ingressi) per ritrovarsi immersi in un mondo di marmi policromi e profili dorati, di intonaci a sgraffito ed elaborati pavimenti di mosaico (vedi pp. 236-239). La tensione dialettica che va a instaurarsi tra questi ultimi e l'esteriore basamento di travertino (una fascia di due piani quasi ermetica per la sua mancanza di rilievo) è un dato sorprendente per chiunque abbia il piacere di varcare le sue soglie.

E se, nel caso specifico della Ca' Brütta, il rapporto di contrasto è in qualche modo mitigato dai motivi classicheggianti che ne popolano i prospetti, questo carattere singolare dell'architettura di Muzio (ma non solo) si manifesterà in modo ancor più netto nei suoi progetti a venire. Già nella facciata della casa di via Giuriati (1930) (vedi p. 12), le striature orizzontali che animavano i prospetti della Ca' Brütta lasciano spazio a una soluzione di facciata decisamente più convenzionale dove, fatta eccezione per il basamento, i marcapiani e le paraste di chiusura, i timidi riferimenti all'architettura classica svaniscono dietro uno spesso strato di intonaco marmoreo. Varcata la soglia del portico, il visitatore è incanalato in un profondo spazio voltato che, per la vivacità del suo apparato decorativo e le sue caratteristiche spaziali, potrebbe comodamente sedere tra le incisioni romane di Paul-Marie Letarouilly. Si noti come il motivo ornamentale del pavimento in marmi policromi è riflesso nelle losanghe stuccate che animano il soffitto; o come la partitura delle pareti laterali detti il passo verso lo snodo ovale da cui si accede al vano scala. Nel più tardo Palazzo Bonaiti in piazza della Repubblica (1935-36) (vedi pp. 172-177), i riferimenti all'architettura classica che caratterizzarono le facciate dei due progetti antecedenti sembrano sparire del tutto lasciando spazio a una soluzione più astratta, secondo il motivo geometrico della griglia. Lo sviluppo è compatto ed economicamente redditizio; il materiale povero che riveste il complesso (ovvero il mattone) è esposto senza ritegno alcuno. Tuttavia, i tre portali scolpiti da Giacomo Manzù conducono il visitatore oltre l'austero basamento in granito e marmo di Musso ed entro un mondo di colorati riflessi lapidei e ulteriori finiture preziose. Lo spartito architettonico che caratterizza i tre rispettivi androni è indubbiamente meno classico; l'utilizzo dei materiali esalta le superfici, piuttosto che rifarsi a tradizionali schemi ornamentali; eppure, nella loro soave raffinatezza, negli allineamenti portone-scala entro un unico percorso, e infine nel rapporto di contrasto con i sobri prospetti dell'edificio, è innegabile la relazione con i modelli precedenti.

Ancor più, è in istanze come queste che si intende il valore rappresentativo dello spazio dell'androne (il passaggio che tipicamente conduce dal portone alla scala principale o dal portone alla corte), non solo nei complessi residenziali di Muzio, ma nella grandissima parte dell'edilizia residenziale eretta nella Milano interbellica. Uno spazio in cui le brame di prestigio dei nuovi membri della classe agiata avrebbero trovato le appropriate declinazioni architettoniche, lontano dalle indiscrezioni dei concittadini meno fortunati: "a porte chiuse", per così dire. Emblema di raffinatezza, di comfort, di decoro, l'ingresso milanese fu la manifestazione tangibile del vezzo borghese per il ricevimento che, seppur celato entro monotone fabbriche "moderne", protraeva in forme più o meno attuali le modalità tipiche dell'architettura rinascimentale e barocca.

Certamente, con l'instaurarsi del moderno condominio in quanto "ultimo, più recente capitolo dello sviluppo della città", con i suoi nuovi schemi proprietari e la sua ostinata efficienza numerica, gli elementi tipologici caratterizzanti le architetture residenziali dei secoli addietro (la corte, la facciata, gli schemi distributivi) avrebbero assunto forme e significati completamente nuovi. In più di un'occasione, Muzio stesso precisò come, nel rispondere alle esigenze della nuova committenza, non furono né il palazzo, né lo *châtelet* che lui e i suoi contemporanei ambivano a emulare. Eppure, nell'attraversare gli ingressi costruiti in questi anni, per il loro carattere scenico, per la cura nelle decorazioni e nell'uso dei materiali, e in particolare per l'attenzione rivolta al susseguirsi di episodi architettonici e artistici, è difficile non richiamare gli effetti prospettici e pittorici che, dal diciassettesimo secolo, venivano volutamente ricercati nei palazzi di tutta Italia per rendere lo spazio dell'androne il primo fotogramma entro un'ardita coreografia spaziale.[7]

A Milano questi schemi (emersi con l'instaurarsi di nuove pratiche legate al cerimoniale del ricevimento[8]) permangono ancora oggi nei palazzi dei Clerici, dei Gallarati Scotti e degli Olivazzi Trivulzio, dove le successioni di colonne, la disposizione assiale delle corti e le prospettive accelerate verso suggestivi apparati pittorici e scultorei facevano dell'esperienza dell'ingresso una vera e propria *promenade* che dal portone conduceva l'ospite sin negli appartamenti principali. Come con Muzio e i suoi colleghi, l'esperienza era resa ancora più drammatica in contrapposizione alle facciate, i cui apparati ornamentali, secondo la tradizione locale cinque e seicentesca, erano trattati con relativa modestia rispetto ai contemporanei esempi romani o fiorentini. E se il confronto può sembrare forzato nel caso specifico della Ca' Brütta, dietro l'angolo, l'androne di via Andrea Appiani 1[9] dispone di un *trompe-l'oeil* di fondale, il cui disegno, la cui relazione con il portale d'ingresso e la cui capacità di moltiplicare di diverse lunghezze la profondità del lotto sono quasi pedanti nel rifarsi ai dettami espressivi della tradizione sovramenzionata (vedi p. 231). La popolarità che ebbe questa particolare soluzione tra i progettisti della Milano degli anni Trenta è quanto mai sintomatica. In qualche modo, dimostra la bilanciata disinibizione con cui questi ultimi si confrontarono con le innumerevoli angustie contestuali e tipologiche inerenti al costruire nel contesto della città storica. Non è con simile arguzia che in Santa Maria presso San Satiro, Donato Bramante ideò il suo celebre "finto" coro lì dove non gli fu permesso di realizzarlo dal "vero"?

Di "paradisi in terra" – Le osservazioni di cui sopra valgono in modo quasi indistinto per la più grande parte dell'architettura residenziale costruita nella Milano interbellica, dove, per diverse ragioni (non dimentichiamo che la retorica del fascismo si formava proprio in quegli anni), i valori delle tradizioni architettoniche locali costituirono un vasto repertorio da cui attingere. Anche con l'avvento del cosiddetto "razionalismo" nei primi anni Trenta (di cui il Palazzo Bonaiti di Muzio si può considerare paradigma), e la conseguente "emancipazione" dai richiami letterali all'architettura classica che caratterizzarono il decennio precedente, rimasero valide le innovazioni tipologiche che si apportarono all'architettura residenziale durante gli anni del Novecento. Non è a caso che la maggioranza degli ingressi appartenenti a quest'epoca sia saldamente ancorata lungo l'asse urbano che attraversa l'attuale viale Tunisia, area che, sin dalla prima stesura del famoso Piano Beruto (1880) e ancor più con lo spostamento della stazione da Porta Nuova nell'attuale piazza Duca d'Aosta (1910-30), si affermava tra i più importanti centri nella moderna costruzione della città.

Come spiega Fulvio Irace nello scrivere del condominio milanese nel secondo dopoguerra,[10] con la fine del conflitto e agli albori del cosiddetto miracolo economico, la varietà tipologica delle nuove committenze sarebbe incrementata drasticamente. La natura di questi cambiamenti rifletteva quasi linearmente la diversificazione nella domanda, nonché il rapido cambiamento dello stile di vita degli abitanti della città. Si assisteva anche all'imporsi di nuove tendenze in campo architettonico che portarono i progettisti locali a sperimentare al di fuori dei repertori ormai consuetudinari della generazione precedente (il carattere metamorfico del lavoro di Gio Ponti, che pure operò tra le due guerre, è esemplare in questo senso, sia come architetto che come scrittore). Innovazioni di natura tecnologica quanto estetica si diffusero prontamente nel tessuto urbano, il quale, a sua volta, si riproduceva in modo sregolato e noncurante della sua eredità premoderna.[11] Eppure, ed è ancora una volta Irace che ce lo fa notare, come accadde in precedenza fu la locale borghesia industriale a essere il motore principale degli appalti edili tra gli anni Cinquanta e Sessanta. E con essa si perpetuò quell'innato senso di comfort e decoro che in molti hanno definito tratto caratteristico della milanesità.

Chiaramente, è difficile stabilire paralleli diretti tra gli ingressi della seconda generazione e quelli che hanno preceduto il secondo conflitto globale. È palese, ad esempio, come in luogo delle composizioni simmetriche di Muzio, Portaluppi, Martinenghi e i loro coetanei, la generazione successiva (Ponti, Asnago e Vender, BBPR ecc.) usasse deliberatamente spostare lo spettatore al di fuori di un ipotetico centro. Ciò avveniva tramite la disposizione di elementi architettonici, l'articolazione delle scale, l'accentuazione delle diagonali nei motivi decorativi quanto nella disposizione puntuale di fioriere e vasche d'acqua. Tra questi ultimi casi, un ingresso che (nell'impianto, almeno) rimase fedele alla classica tipologia dell'androne interbellico può essere apprezzato in via Pinturicchio 11 (vedi p. 89), dove il posizionamento asimmetrico della scala, del tappeto, dei rivestimenti alle pareti, del corrimano e infine del dipinto di fondale crea un piacevole squilibrio entro l'ingombro generico dello spazio. In altre istanze, più drastiche nel discostarsi dai modelli consuetudinari (ad esempio in via Marcona 49, vedi pp. 246-247, nell'edificio BBPR in piazza Sant'Erasmo 5, vedi pp. 214-215, o anche in via Francesco Ferrucci 6, vedi p. 297), l'ingresso sembra perdere i suoi limiti formando uno spazio ibrido (al contempo interno ed esterno) che agisce meramente in quanto soglia, oltre la quale sono ubicati i diversi nuclei del sovrastante condominio.

La materialità di questi ultimi androni rifletteva inoltre un crescente interesse per le industrie locali, creando il contesto per vere e proprie collaborazioni, siano esse state volte allo sviluppo di un particolare materiale di rivestimento o alla produzione di finiture *ad hoc*. Nella realizzazione di questi spazi, maestranze locali (come il taglio della pietra, il lavoro del metallo e la ceramica) e avanzati processi industriali (volti, ad esempio, alla produzione di sistemi d'illuminazione) si trovavano a far parte di un'unica impresa in cui l'architetto era al contempo progettista e curatore. Chiunque abbia familiarità con le opere di Gio Ponti ricorderà facilmente le frequenti collaborazioni con Abet Laminati o con Richard Ginori e La Riggiola, ad esempio, nella produzione di porcellane. Luigi Caccia Dominioni e Ignazio Gardella fondarono addirittura un'azienda propria, Azucena, dedicata alla produzione di arredi e finiture per i loro progetti, ma non solo.

Tuttavia, per quanto ai solenni assi di simmetria tipici degli androni interbellici seguirono animati percorsi obliqui, e pur se il rigore formale dei primi lasciava spazio ad atmosfere di vivace disimpegno, gli ingressi a Milano continuarono a rappresentare un importante luogo di espressione architettonica. Collettivamente finanziati, gestiti e infine mantenuti, questi avevano un importante valore culturale che, nell'attuale clima di diffidenza dove su tutto prevale l'interesse personale, risulta quasi incomprensibile. Si sono per di più affermati come un vero e proprio *Leitmotiv* della città, testimonianza del continuato valore che il "semplice" atto di entrare ha a lungo avuto presso i milanesi. E se negli anni Quaranta inoltrati era la volta dell'allora direttore di *Costruzioni-Casabella*, Giuseppe Pogatschnig, noto anche come Pagano, a concedere alla città meneghina il disdicevole "primato di bruttezza", se non altro, nelle fotografie che seguono, le parole di Morigia scritte cinquecento anni fa continuano a dimostrarsi attuali: a Milano, dietro le porte chiuse, vi sono ancora "paradisi in terra".

Following spread:
piazza Eleonora Duse 2, Palazzo Civita · Gigiotti Zanini, 1927–33
base: Bardiglio marble · pilaster: Cipollino marble · walls: travertine

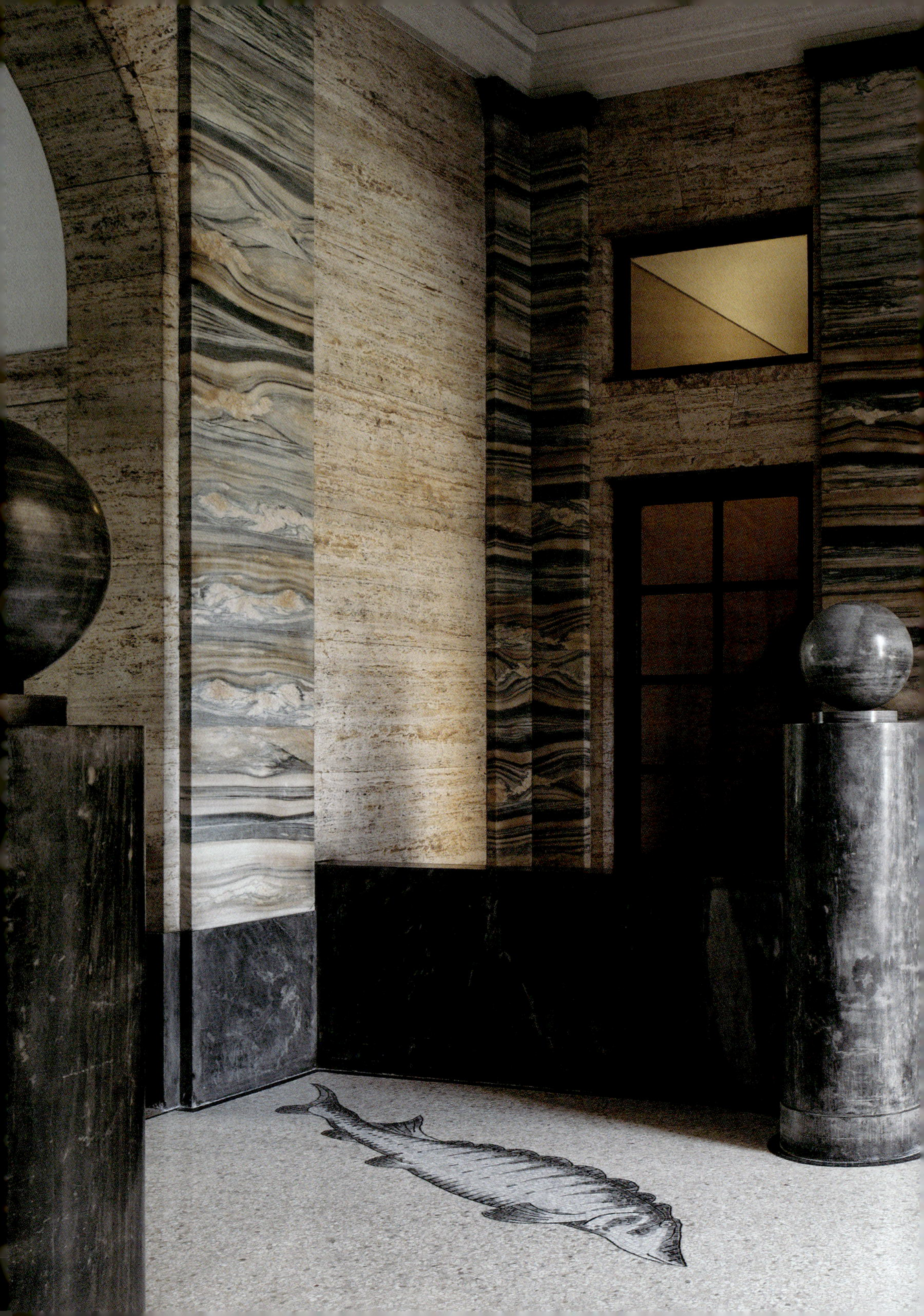

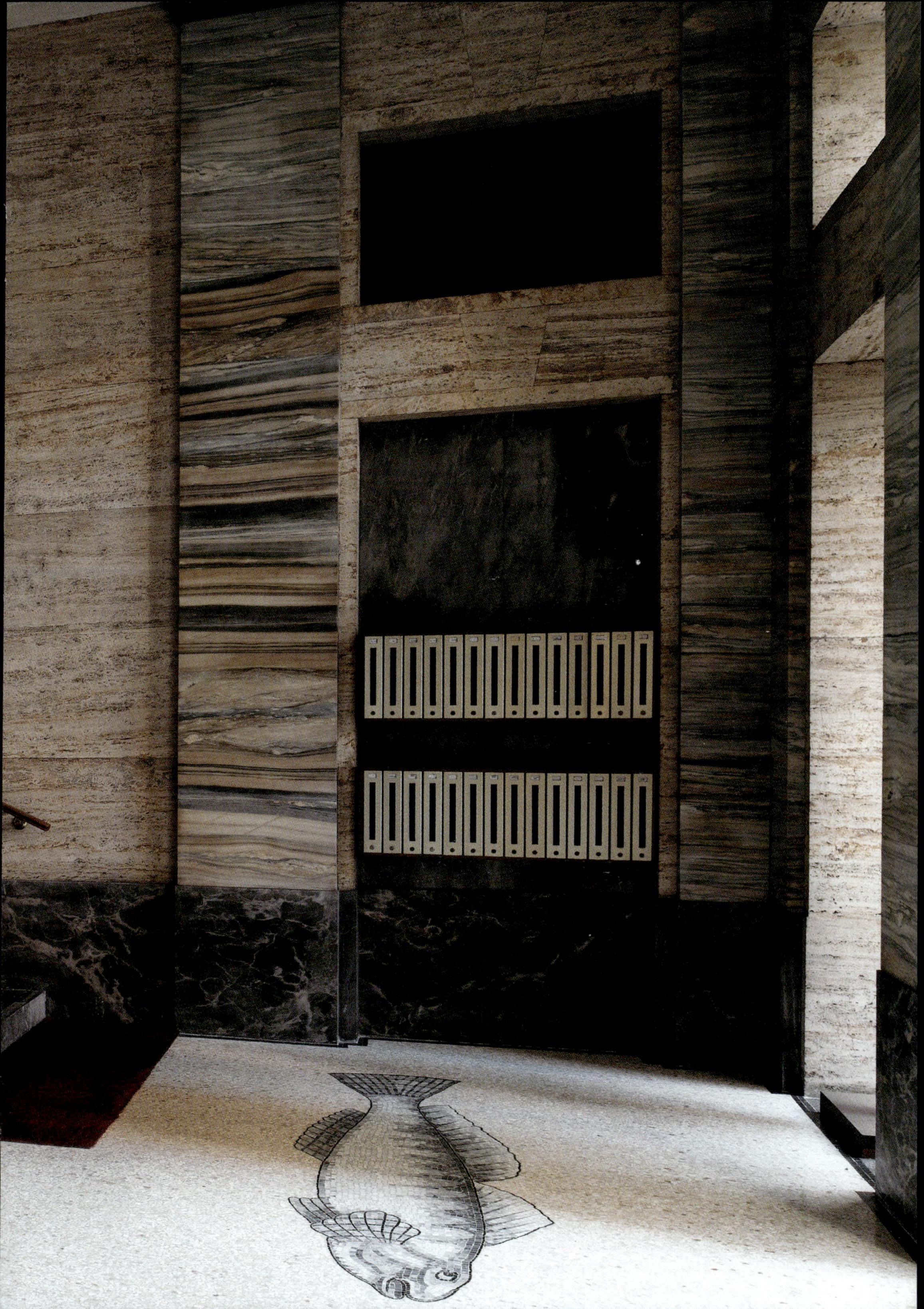

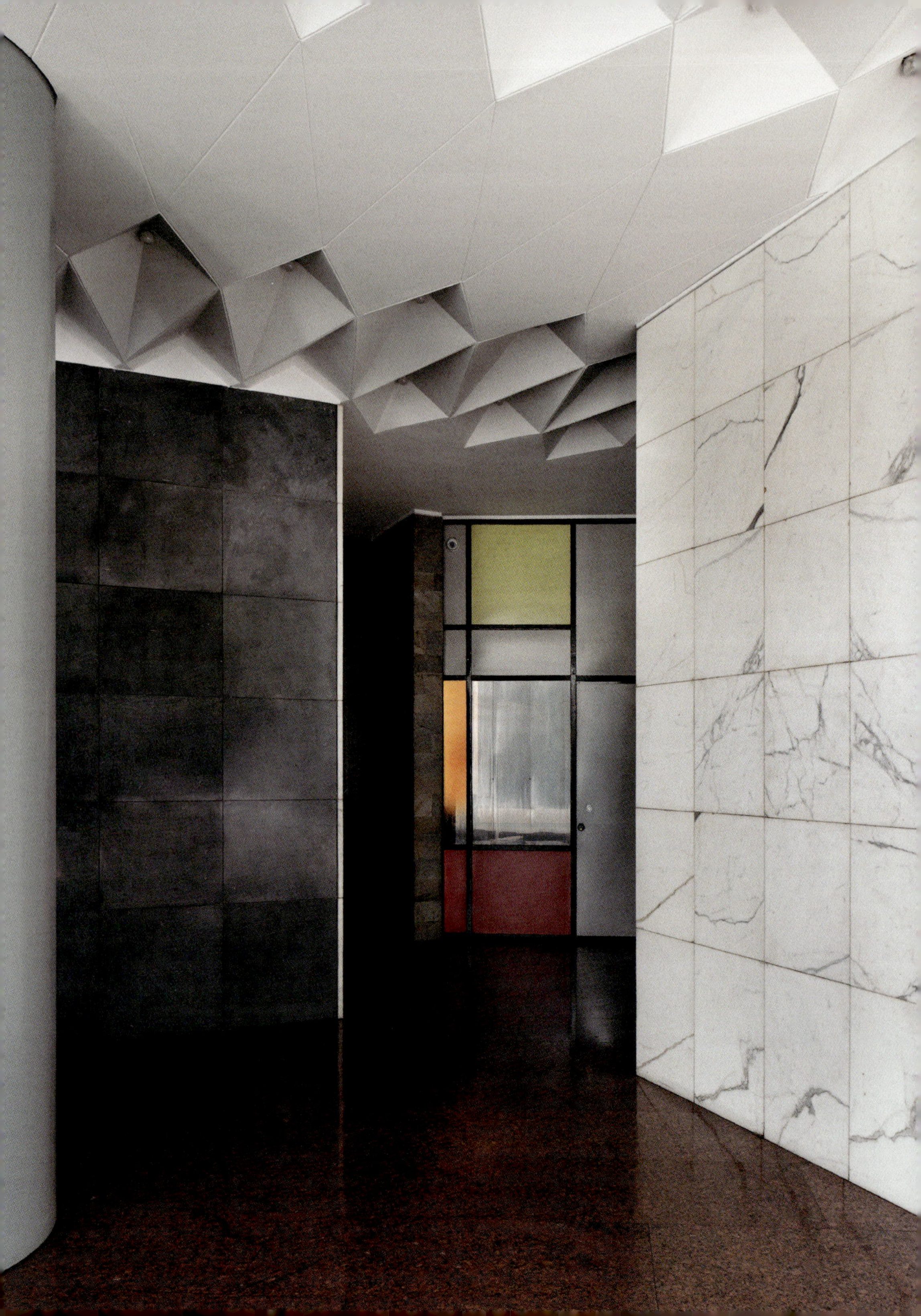

Daniel Sherer

The Discreet Charm of the Entryway

ARCHITECTURE, ART, AND DESIGN IN THE MILANESE *INGRESSI*, 1910–70

"Every beginning is cheerful;
the threshold is the place of expectation."
—Goethe

Few conventions of architecture are as omnipresent, and at the same time as taken for granted, as the threshold. The purpose of the threshold seems straightforward enough: to allow passage between interior and exterior while establishing a formal demarcation between the two domains. However, it should be remembered that the threshold, as a liminal zone—indeed, as a decisive paradigm of liminality itself—is riven by ambiguity: simultaneously joining and separating, it generates a space that is neither inside nor outside, but partakes of both. In this respect, the threshold, which might seem to sanction a clear-cut spatial division, actually disrupts any unequivocal categories of interior and exterior.

These places of mediation developed in a unique way in Italy, and nowhere in Italy is as replete with functionally articulated, formally complex, and spatially orchestrated thresholds as Milan. These are the *ingressi*: extended threshold areas in residential buildings that are veritable laboratories of architectural form, use, and meaning. Given their singularity one might venture to claim something at once plausible and paradoxical about these "signature spaces": for just as Bologna has her *portici*, Naples her palatial staircases, and Venice her *androne* and *portego* in the palazzi on the Grand Canal and elsewhere in the maritime city, Milan may be said to have her most characteristically porous feature of entry, access, and passage: the *ingressi*.[1]

This hypothesis is plausible because no other feature of Milanese modern architecture exhibits such a clear typological character as the *ingresso*. It is paradoxical because, unlike the other architectural "signatures" just mentioned, the splendor and conspicuousness that mark the *ingressi* are largely visible from the inside, or are due to the interplay between interior and exterior, and for this reason are less

via Legnano 4 · Gigi Ghò, 1956–57
floor: Red Balmoral granite · right wall: Carrara Statuario Venato marble

well known. In this regard one might call the *ingressi* Milan's best-kept secret, the architectural equivalent of Poe's purloined letter: a secret that is "prominently hidden" for all to see, and for a more restricted number to enter. With the *ingressi*, in fact, we are dealing with spaces that, by a peculiar logic of representation, start as passages to a given place but end up becoming their own destinations.

Crucial to this process is the way that the *ingressi* orchestrate a triple encounter between art, architecture, and design. Artists, designers, and architects contributed to these spatial "*concerti*" in different ways: testing the limits of collaboration, they renewed inherited forms of representation and related modes of spatial transformation.

If the *ingressi* occupy an intermediate zone between divergent aesthetic domains, they also mark out a liminal area between inside and outside. This dual power of mediation underscores what is lacking in other, less well-appointed entry environments. The *ingressi* can thus be said to operate as signifiers of this privilege, but also as repositories of the aesthetic values they consecrate and draw upon, in contrast to those spaces that are incapable of fulfilling this partly ideological, partly artistic, and in any case characteristically Milanese cultural role.[2] This jostling, competitive quality, made evident both by the plurality and relative proximity of some of the most lavish *ingressi*—which bring the entire universe of Milan's architecture and art down to the measure of their own scale—is a dimension of their form and function that has been only partly explored by historians and critics.[3]

Mediation and Representation—To orient the reader on his or her visit to the *ingressi*—one that is highly selective in any case—the analysis will center on the intersection of two specific hermeneutic axes. If the first refers to the unique role played by the *ingressi* in the urban context of Milan, the second designates the diversified strategies of mediation and representation they deploy to transform liminal space into a site that stands out both in the building and the city.

From this angle the *ingressi* can be seen as a spatial and formal means of announcing and maintaining a high level of social distinction. Like the use of colored ceramic cladding on the exterior of Milanese apartment buildings (*Klinker*), which, as a recent study has shown, exercises a specific role as a marker of the social status of those who live there, the *ingressi* enable new modes of social ascent for a haut-bourgeoisie torn between the emulation of established aristocratic modes of comportment and the most up-to-date amenities of the modern metropolis.[4]

Ultimately, the novelty and verve of these entryways not only derives from their deployment of modern forms, but from their radical rewriting of tradition. If the axialized stairways and symmetrical as well as oblique modes of entrance and circulation have deep roots in Renaissance and Baroque palatial and theatrical architecture, and more particularly in Palladio's emphasis on the axial synthesis of the façade and central stairway and its various seventeenth- and eighteenth-century progeny, the engagement with new materials and technical forms (ferroconcrete frames, plate glass skins, elevator shafts) registers a commitment to modernity and its universe of technological innovation. Although this synthesis of retrospective and prospective impulses is characteristic of Italian modernism, it becomes particularly intense in the *ingressi*, where it assumes its most concentrated form, both as a privileged locus of the most varied stylistic hybridizations or, alternatively, of the distillation of single stylistic codes.

The* Ingresso *as a Traversable Boundary—This last observation leads us to ask: is there such a thing as an identifiably Rationalist *ingresso*? The perfection of the Rationalist language of the residential and office building, the Casa Rustici, on Corso Sempione 36 of 1934 by Giuseppe Terragni and Pietro Lingeri (see pp. 292, 295) would seem to suggest an affirmative answer to this question, as this language marks it as one of the milestones of the Rationalist idiom in the history of modern housing, and not only in Milan. As one approaches the building, which is inserted into an angled site, one immediately notes the floating volumes of an ideal grid that frame the entire structure, lending it the feel of a composition both planar and abstract and yet also bridge-like in its inner connectivity.[5] Here, Thomas Schumacher's observation that Terragni (along with Lingeri) developed the structural language of the exo-skeleton, with clear effects of tectonic expression, applies in exemplary fashion.

Consistent with this overall skeletal and frame-like character is the austere pathway of stone flooring, which presents the *ingresso* as an ideal condition or transfiguration of the boundary zone. It at once lays down the threshold with Rationalist rigor and encourages us to cross it while recognizing its mixture of manifest openness and a certain air of mystery, a hint of opacity connected with the labyrinthine character of the hallway. This blend of opposed qualities spurs our curiosity so that we desire entry, even as it lends a very modern tension to an ancient Roman theme, the *limen*. In certain ways this complex treatment anticipates one of the most important projects, and certainly the greatest unbuilt work of Terragni, the Danteum.[6]

This is the case because, as in the Danteum, the hallway is of an unusual height, is clad entirely with the same marble revetment of off-white marble with gray intrusions, and has a labyrinthine character emphasized by the lack of windows, a feature it shares with some works of Le Corbusier, such as the Mundaneum and the late Museum of Infinite Growth in Japan. An archaic, almost primordial feeling, appropriate to the theme of Daedalian ingenuity, presupposing a basic, classical simplification of elements, prevails, giving rise to a Rationalist ethos whose metaphysical affiliations are only compounded by the shadows that emanate from the large door surround. Completing the composition is the bright central vestibule whose gridded ceiling, in which the theme of the space-frame reaches its zenith in this work, is strongly reminiscent of the soffit of the central space of the Casa del Fascio in Como—one whose inherent rational order is only reinforced, through a logic of contrast, by the apparent randomness of the assembled puzzle-like marble chips of the *terrazzo* flooring beneath.

Symmetries Unbound—The most memorable *ingressi* strike a subtle balance between opposed impulses and, above all, between diverse spatial vectors and their axial and formal features. An exemplary case of this is provided by the celebrated entry onto Piazza Velasca of BBPR's Torre Velasca (see pp. 265–266), in which the entire ensemble of symmetrical planimetric elements is offset by the hanging, pod-like forms of the quadripartite brass chandelier and the shimmering outlines and specks of light tonalities of the mosaics that extend up the polyhedral piers into the double-height space. The elevator banks are clad with bespoke veneer strips of dark mahogany, each of a slightly different shape, which overlap in random fashion, creating unique patterns of wood grain that seem to strive upward and whose production impresses the eye as having been unusually labor intensive. Here the eye is invited to search the boundaries of the visible in the higher reaches of the *ingresso* itself, as if to underscore the soaring, tectonically articulated vertical thrust of the residential tower from the inside as well as the outside, from the near view and the far in a unique dialectic of proximity and distance.

An earlier, more dramatic instance of this dialectic is provided by the strictly symmetrical *ingresso* of Giulio Ulisse Arata's Stile Liberty *tour de force*, the Casa Berri-Meregalli at Via Cappuccini 8, of 1911–14, whose main axis directs the gaze, through a formidable *fer forgé* metalwork grille by Alessandro Mazucotelli, to a sculpture located at the far end of the hallway (see pp. 120–123).[7] This is the *Winged Victory* by the Symbolist sculptor Adolfo Wildt, a floating female bust of remarkable strangeness. The head of gleaming, caramel-colored marble with an open, protruding mouth and socketless, almond-shaped eyes, is covered by a light-green wimple flanked by a pair of insect-like wings with deeply etched bronze insets and is supported—or rather impaled upon—a simple metal rod. Floating in the semidarkness, the bust is directly aligned with a stained-glass window that serves as its backdrop. An unsettling presence within the radiating, apse-like (and crypt-like) hallway, this highly polished head becomes visible through a setting framed by rusticated neo-Romanesque squat arches and shimmering, vitrified mosaics by Piero Adamo Rimoldi, manufactured by the firm of Villeroy & Boch, with color schemes and patterning reminiscent of Gustav Klimt.[8]

The entire ensemble is nothing short of visionary, aimed at beating the Secession at its own game by constructing a symphony of color and texture within a crepuscular atmosphere fusing classical, Byzantine, and medieval elements. Marked by carefully calculated contrasts of light and dark, the entire passage is intimately associated with themes of death and resurrection embodied in the eerie, almost totemic image of the winged spirit. As such it partakes as much of the Viennese *fin de siècle* sensibility of Richard Strauss and Gustav Mahler as it does in the everyday life of an *haut bourgeois* Milanese apartment building.

Effectively worked out in advance by the strategic placement of the bust along the central axis of vision, the complex interaction of art, design, and architectural space that transpires in this *ingresso* is such that one can scarcely imagine the *Winged Victory* in any other place besides her particular habitat, where she greets the comings and goings of the astonished visitor with an air of strained detachment. Guardian of her chosen abode, she transmits the anxieties of her time like no other comparable artistic figure, except possibly for her more celebrated, barely less androgynous "cousin," the protagonist of Edvard Munch's *The Scream*, one version of which was completed around the same time. Both bear witness to a crisis of culture to which neither can give voice, though both are shown in the act of striving to do precisely that through the enactment of a psychic struggle of unbearable intensity.[9] Yet, unlike Munch's sufferer, Wildt's, in a sort of artistic recasting of Zeno's paradox, is at once depicted as hurtling headlong through infinite space (notice the clusters of stars that fall away at the sides of her prow-like neck) and as being rooted to this particular spot in Milan, at once bodiless and embodied: the passageway itself being the approximation of her extended, violent, and immaterial body, so that we can hardly avoid a shudder as we pass through her domain to the metropolis beyond.

Wildt's tormented *Victory*, shaken by a turbulence that, being at least partly latent, may be seen as a distinguishing feature of repression, reminds us in equal measure of Freud and Breuer's *Studien über Hysterie* (1895), with its concept of the hysteric who, burdened by strangulated affect, cannot give voice to her pain—the pain of *haut bourgeois* Woman, here projected backward into some archaic or primordial world of mythical figuration—and of the collective hysteria and ensuing mass sacrifice of World War I, which was beginning just as the *ingresso* was nearing completion.[10] Partly because of her unsettling presence, the *ingresso* she inhabits is moreover the very image of an "other" space that Michel Foucault speaks about, the complex site of heterotopia and hence of also of a liminality where the

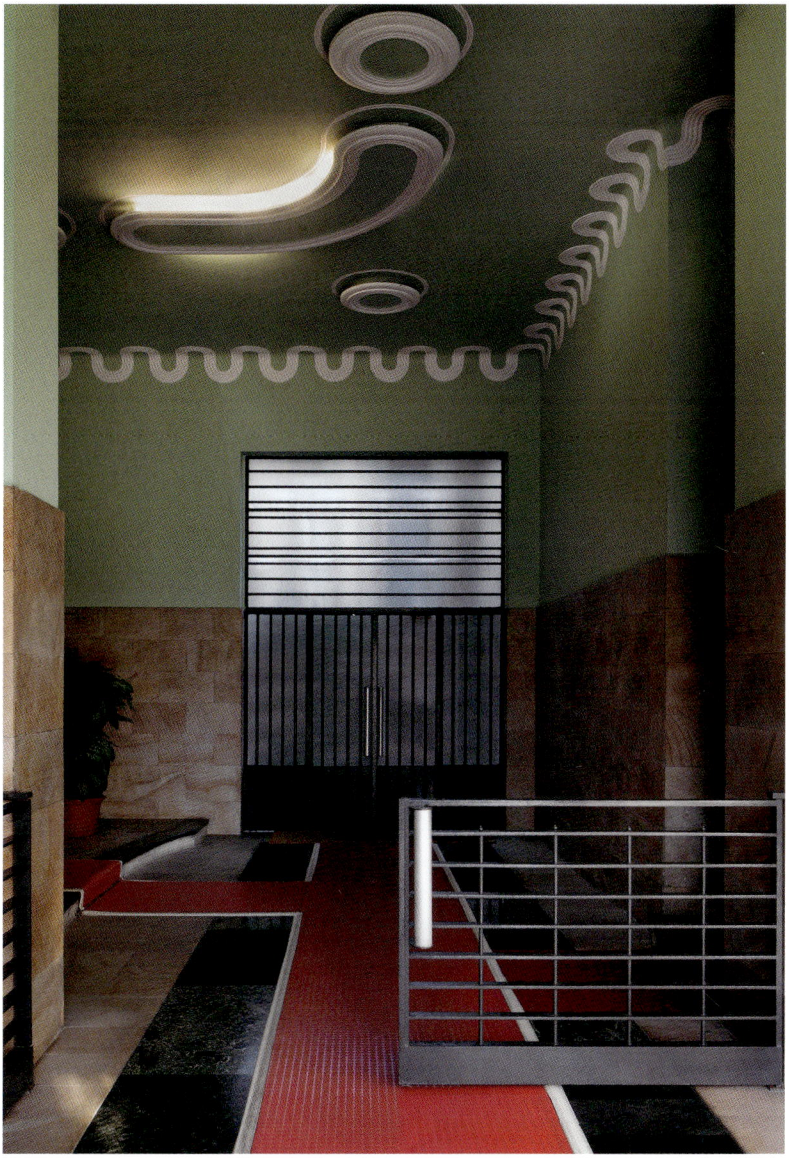

piazza Lavater 3 · P. Masera, L. Canzi, 1933–36

floor: alabaster, serpentinite and Verde Alpi ophicalcite · walls: alabaster

normal rules of urban and territorial space are provisionally suspended. It is striking that it is precisely on this site that the conversation between the two forms of genius, the sculptural and architectural, of Wildt and Arata, whose collaborative effort creates the first important *ingresso*, brings about the apotheosis of this space of otherness through a play of hidden oppositions—the very same oppositions that Foucault utilizes to explicate the logic of alterity that is at the heart of the heterotopia:

"And perhaps our life is still governed by a certain number of oppositions that remain inviolable, that our institutions and practices have not yet dared to break down. These are oppositions that we regard as simple givens: for example between private space and public space, between family space and social space, between cultural space and useful space, between the space of leisure and that of work. All these are still nurtured by the hidden presence of the sacred."[11]

Wildt and Arata show us this hidden face, at once alluring and destructive, of the Sphinx of their time: and it is no accident, surely, that this revelation erupts precisely at the point of juncture, the liminal point of inflection, between private and public realms, between the domains of domestic architecture and the modern city.

Another exploration of these contiguous domains is evident in the only figure in the prewar era of the *ingresso* who can stand comparison with Arata in complexity, audacity of formal and spatial invention, and sheer imaginative intensity: Aldo Andreani. Like Arata, Andreani is the only architect who feels confident enough to be able to join forces with a visionary of Wildt's caliber.[12] And like Arata's, Andreani's daring linguistic concatenations seem to elude classification. In fact, the inquiries of both architects, in different ways, represent Stile Liberty tendencies attempting to come to terms with those moments of the classical tradition where the exception is elevated to the rank of the norm (Peruzzi, Serlio, Giulio Romano) and with the radicalism and sense of experiment that characterizes the Baroque. To be more precise, Andreani, in two separate instances, invents an entryway characterized by a heady combination of florid cinquecentismo and neo-Baroque eclecticism that resurrects the actual Baroque trope of the *concetto*.[13]

In the Palazzo Fidia of 1926–30 (see pp. 118–119), the *concetto* in question is spatial in character, and is based on the premise of a radical axial shift toward the oblique in two respects: on the one hand, the oval of the entryway vestibule is entered at a sharp angle from the chamfered open corner of the polygonal plan of the entry to the apartment block. This last is richly rusticated in a grotesque manner, in a twentieth-century interpretation of Serlio's portals cross-pollinated with references from late nineteenth- and early twentieth-century architectural culture as varied as Frank Furness, Joseph Maria Olbrich, Edwin Lutyens, and the same Giovanni Muzio, whose more restrained classicizing Novecento aesthetic rejected the excesses of Andreani himself.[14]

Just as one enters the heart of the oval by following the diagonal axis at the corner, so too one reaches the helicoidal stair tower—one of the most dramatic in all of Milan, and not only during the prewar period—as well as the porter's lodge, from a diagonal axis branching off from another corner of the polygonal plan in which the oval is inscribed. The inside/outside interplay is enhanced by the emerging volumes of the marble revetment, which give way to a receding mass of brick, chamfered to extend the thrust of the diagonal side entrance upward, as they rise above the entrance. Entry and service areas thus take center stage in a reversal of the normative logic of entry in neoclassical or classicizing contexts. Equally striking is the complex inlay of colored marbles juxtaposing yellow, cream, dark emerald, and near-black tones, fitted together in a pattern reminiscent of seventeenth-century Florentine *intarsia* in the floor design that extends to the edge of the extruded oval.

Andreani, like Arata before him, does not hesitate to pull out all the stops in this monumental *tour de force* in which *fin de siècle* aestheticism celebrates its nuptials with late Renaissance and Baroque classical vocabularies. Yet he had not exhausted his taste for virtuosic expression. In the second intervention, located around the corner at Via Serbelloni 10 (see pp. 38, 43), the visitor is confronted by a massive entrance portal to the Palazzo Sola-Busca, the right side of which is adorned with a large human ear in the form of a sculpted bronze inset by Andreani, who was, in addition to being an architect, a sculptor trained in the Brera by Wildt.[15] Here the *concetto* does not center on the play of space, vision, and directed movement as in the Palazzo Fidia, but on an enigmatic figuration of the sense of hearing that enters into a complex relation with the sense of sight. Known to the Milanese as Ca' de Oreggia (House of the Big Ear)—just as the nickname of Muzio's Ca' Brütta (the Ugly House) stuck, so did this one—this work, comparable in its strangeness to the *Winged Victory*, dates to 1924/5. Accurate to the smallest detail, the ear is complete with stirrup, tympana, and hammer bones. Well into the 1930s, due to the transmission of sound through a pipe embedded in the wall, it actually served as a highly original, if not bizarre, form of communication, in what might seem to be an updating of the architectural fantasies of transmitting sound through sculptural elements by the seventeenth-century Jesuit polymath Athanasius Kircher, who dreamed of inserting speaking tubes in statues to be located in Baroque palaces.[16]

In Andreani's case the trope is reversed: instead of being spoken to by a formerly mute sculpted mouth, one speaks into a sculpted ear that is open to all vocalizations. (One might also plausibly see Andreani's sculpture as an anatomically accurate, Milanese answer to the Roman Palazzo Zuccari of Federico Zuccari, now the residence of the Bibliotheca Hertziana, which is entered by means of an enormous sculpted grotesque mouth.) Here the conceit analogizes building and body: by means of this inserted ear, we enter into a curious situation in which we speak to the building, and it speaks back, adding a new level of awareness to the modern experience of the technological amenities associated with the porter's lodge. These are elevated to an allegorical level unheard of previously in the architectural experience of its era. By means of this conceit, sound is not only visualized, but also spatialized: the neo-Baroque *concetto* thus extends its sway over two of the senses simultaneously in a sort of built synesthesia.

Spaces of Synthesis: The Integration of Design and Art—As we make our way through the *ingressi*, we move through spaces shaped in different ways by the architect, the artist, and the designer, and at times by all three equally. Diverse strategies of synthesis condition these spaces, modulated by effects of illusion and underlying structural and tectonic realities. These include, on the architectural level, modes of conjunction and disjunction, evident in such devices as the syncopation of apertures and passageways, the rhythmic alternation and juxtaposition of materials, the use of spatial caesuras and techniques of formal and historical quotation, and the evocation and transformation of precedents and codes.

In this respect a key role is assigned to the interplay of surfaces and the actual depth of the space as a means of lending an impression of unity or, on the contrary, effects of discontinuity to the interior. Take for instance, the *ingresso* by Giannino Testori in Viale Tunisia 48 of 1936–37 (see p. 8), one of a series of dramatic entryways that help define the character of this major thoroughfare connecting the Piazza della Repubblica to the area around Corso Buenos Aires. At first

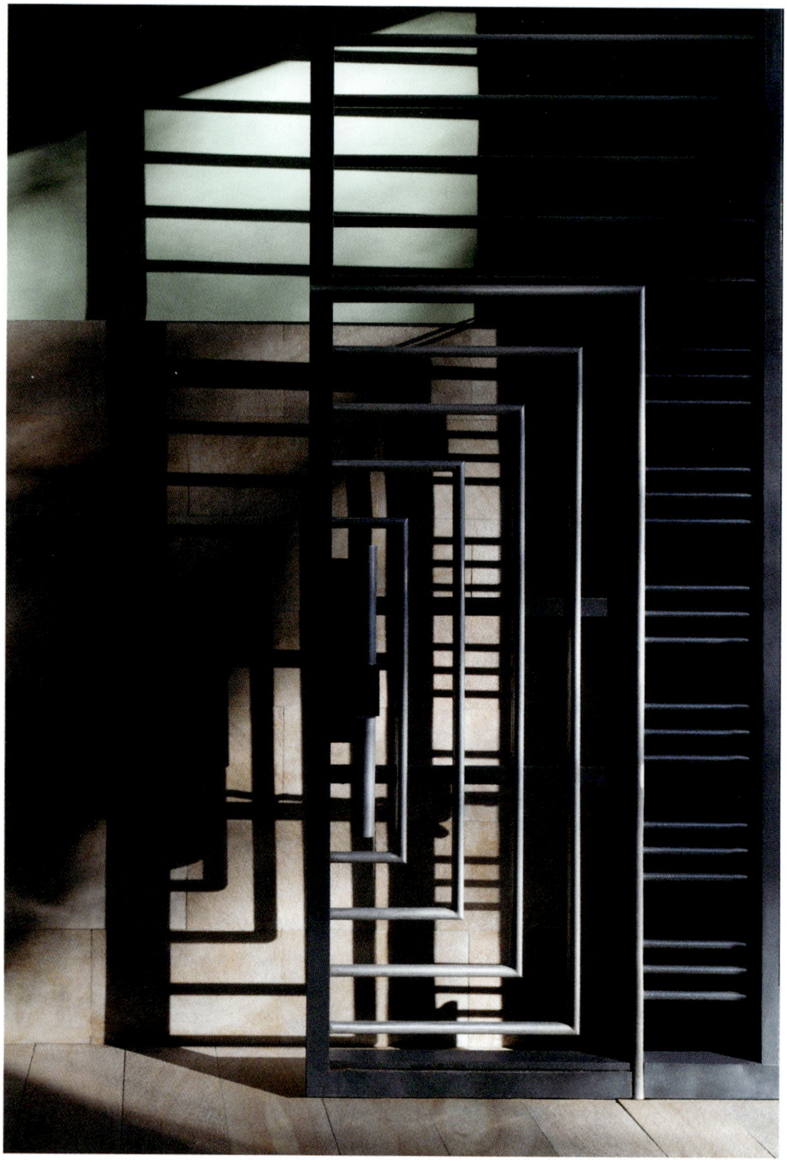

piazza Lavater 3 · P. Masera, L. Canzi, 1933–36

floor: alabaster, serpentinite and Verde Alpi ophicalcite · walls: alabaster

glance we are confronted by a single long axial and symmetrical hall with pink marble revetment on the walls. These offer a stark contrast with the gray-veined marble of the floor, which is framed by a darker inlay with milky intrusions. The visual telescope of the axialized passage sets up a distinct path of directed movement that is especially clear to the visitor who enters, more so than for those who exit, given the symmetries of the T-shaped door, and the hovering glass elements above it, that captures the gaze of the visitor with all the force of a traffic signal.

A closer look reveals yet another layer of complexity. This is apparent not simply in the strategic placement of asymmetrical elements, such as the circle of the inner window on the left side, which stands opposite the dramatically turned corner, entirely glazed, of the porter's lodge, but also in the illusionistic reflections and visual "noise" that is established by the frosted glass of the centralized door, split into two symmetrical halves. This last set of elements unleashes a sort of perceptual interference with the sunken ceiling, which contains a hidden light source, and which mirrors, in its basic shape, the perspectively organized depth of the sunken receding pattern of the soffit beyond the door.

A third set of observations would have to include the interplay of two cruciforms: the attenuated T-shape cruciform of the metal doorframe and the more complex one made by the soffit itself; both indicate different options of circulation and different kinds of spatial interaction with the visitor. In its play of functionalist and purely aesthetic elements, the entire composition evokes Bauhaus precedents, nautical motifs of Art Deco provenance, and an idea of spare luxury, much like that of an ocean liner, in accordance with a carefully realized scenographic idea. In short, this small space spells out the triumph of representation in a *mise-en-scène* with nautical, theatrical, and ceremonial associations. In this sense, the impression of unity is created as much by a network of highly orchestrated design elements, conceived of as surpassing the usual level of simple architectural décor or surface effects, in tandem with the illusion generated by specific material strategies (i.e., frosted glass, metal and marble inlays) as much as by the testing of specific formal conventions (i.e., the precarious balancing act of symmetry and asymmetry).

The Kovacs entryway in Via Plinio 55 of 1957 (see p. 18) reads like a deliberate critique of the Testori *ingresso* carried out through a novel dialogue of space and surface. The critique carries more weight because many of the same devices and even some similar conventions and materials are mobilized in antithetical ways. In sharp contrast to the Testori, the first impression one obtains of this space is that of a dramatically articulated asymmetrical shift to the right, a move that becomes legible against the symmetrical backdrop of a bipartite composition consisting of a frosted rectangle of internal window glass and its identical counterpart, found in the window, clear this time, of the porter's lodge, which rises above the wooden mailbox. The steps, which are made of a milky gray marble, are similar to Testori's, yet, this time, the scenographic quality of the entryway is enhanced by the upward flight of the stair that runs parallel to the continuous brass handrail on the other side above the stairway. And in sharp contrast to the doubled lighting elements above and beyond the doorway visible from the entryway foyer in the Testori, in the Kovacs ingresso the ceiling is fitted with a *moderne* asymmetrical soffit with chamfered biomorphic edges of a roughly keylike shape, with light pouring in from an off-center circle that emphasizes the thickness of the *poche*. The most striking feature of the entire entryway is this partly luminous, partly contoured unitary body, at once hovering, artificial, and cloudlike, outlined against a higher ceiling above. The dramatic viewpoint that is emphasized from the street, together with the variable illumination within the *ingresso* as a whole, completes the scene, which bespeaks a cold elegance appropriate to the postwar period. This was an era expressive of the values of the economic miracle, eager to include modernist tropes of asymmetrical character along with Italian grandeur and lusso in one single space.[17] This tendency goes hand in hand with what Manfredo Tafuri has identified as the recovery of the representational value of the image typical of Italian architecture of the 1950s: a development that links Kovacs, a Hungarian architect who emigrated after the war to Milan from Austria-Hungary, to more prominent native figures such as Caccia Dominioni, Gio Ponti, Vico Magistretti, and Marco Zanuso, despite significant differences between their approaches.[18]

In some of the other *ingressi* the play of surfaces dominates the visual field upon entry, and the placement of light sources assumes a diminished role. Take, for instance, the densely articulated, multicolored mosaic in Gigiotti Zanini's Palazzo Civita in Piazza Duse (see pp. 24–25), which makes the floor and walls cohere within a single organic statement; or the idea of differentiation obtained by the use of pink granite mosaic tiles, ranged against the gray of the floor, in the Torre Velasca; or the swirling, wavelike forms, made of strips of brown, black, white, and sepia marble tile, by Francesco Somaini, in the entrances of Corso Italia 22/1 and 22/2 of 1957–61 by Luigi Caccia Dominioni (see pp. 282–285), which, due to its internal dynamism, stands out as an individualized work of art and simultaneously acts to unify the perceptual field of the hallway as one moves deeper into the *ingresso*.

In this last entryway, formal unity is achieved through a subtle orchestration of disparate materials and a highly organic yet at the same time clearly premeditated deployment of design elements. These are inscribed within the architectural space as sensitively as the latter's inscription within the urban space: the sinuous hallway that marks out the passage of the ingresso is at once oriented toward the *giardino/cortile* and is part of a larger curving itinerary with the nearby church of Sant'Eufemia, and is flanked by tall aquamarine glass panels at the perimeter. The passage itself is lit at the top by a basin-like shallow dome punctured by small skylights and at the sides by bespoke triple lamps by Azucena. Despite their traditional, candelabra-like form, in their texture and shape these lighting fixtures are clearly meant to evoke those emblems of modernity, car headlights, that Achille Castiglioni—the same Castiglioni who was also a collaborator of Caccia's—exploited in his lamp designs too. Moreover, this *ingresso* not only may be said to be one of the most characteristic and brilliant of Caccia's achievements in the field of residential architecture, but also constitutes an object-lesson in his theory of human movement in built space: for, according to him, people, left to their own devices, tend to move in meandering lines, rather than in straight ones, wandering in accordance with circular, oval, or some other kind of curvilinear vectors. Whether or not this is actually the case, this specific idea of a modern Baroque pattern of movement is clearly exemplified in the Somaini/Caccia collaboration in the Galleria Strasburgo.[19]

***Echoes of International Modernism in the Postwar* Ingressi**—Moreover, in the *ingressi* a particular place is reserved—in a tendency that becomes particularly evident in the postwar era, to the point of approximating a kind of "delirium of quotation"—for the transposition of motifs taken over from the historical avant-gardes: ranging from Russian Suprematism, De Stijl, Czech Cubism, Scandinavian Empiricism, Aalto's Organicism, Bauhaus, and other modalities of European Functionalism, these resonances are sometimes unobtrusive and in other cases more obvious. In fact, at this point in their development, "citations" make their presence felt in different ways as part of the ambient scenography, instead of being integrated into any inherent structural logic. In this regard, the allusions in question are not only alienated from their original context, but are put to uses that are frequently antithetical to their original modernist ideals, which tend to stress tectonic lucidity, formal austerity, and truth to materials.

This is clearly illustrated by a number of different features that shaped the entryways, above all, the lucid spatial relationships evoked by the wall of glass brick in Asnago and Vender's Condominio XXI Aprile in Via Lanzone 7 of 1950–53 (see pp. 368–369), a modernist trope echoing Pierre Chareau's aesthetic of glazed construction, whose abstract elegance is underscored by an inflected porte cochere clad in chrome strips; or by the abstract, diamond-shaped ceiling and wall treatment, of a startling chromaticism, reminiscent of the Café Aubette of Theo van Doesburg and Hans Arp and Sophie Taeuber-Arp of 1926–28; or by Gio Ponti and Alberto Rosselli of the Casa Melandri in Viale Lunigiana 44, of 1954–57, where harlequin-like patterns establish a dialectic of flatness and spatiality that only assists the perception of depth as one ascends the stairwell (see pp. 194–197).

Conclusion—As it moved through the successive phases of prewar Stile Liberty, Art Deco, Novecento, Rationalism, Bauhaus Functionalism, and postwar Scandinavian Empiricism, Organicism, and Brutalism, the Milanese *ingresso* experienced a dual process of expansion and aestheticization. This multifaceted evolution presents intriguing problems of synthesis and mediation that, for their part, presuppose the elimination of certain formal and spatial concepts and the elaboration of others. If what is being synthesized are competing formal languages, what is being mediated is the dichotomy of interior and urban space. Indeed, the first thing one notices when moving through Milan's dense weave of streets, parks, piazzas, and palazzi, is the sheer variety of architectural idioms that intersect in the city, generating, and, in the end, leaving open the possibility of multiple readings. The *ingressi* play a decisive role as privileged points of articulation within this network.

From this perspective the *ingressi* take up their rightful position within the Milanese metropolis as a unique set of architectural paradoxes: for while they clearly operate as servant spaces, they also tend to dominate, formally, spatially, and functionally, the architectures they ostensibly serve. The *ingressi* thus lead a curious double life: if they are integral parts of their buildings, they are also set apart from them. As a result the *ingresso* becomes what has been called, in another context, "an in-between destination."[20] This is tantamount to a fundamental reversal of foreground and background, of architectural space and vestibule space. All of the *ingressi* exhibit in this respect an ingenious and in some ways insidious theatricality. As such they are at least partly analogous to stage sets, and it is no accident that their heyday is situated between the flowering of late-nineteenth-century opera, which was just coming to a close as they began to proliferate, and the 1960s, when Italian Neorealist cinema, and the suspended tonalities of Antonioni in particular, featured them as part of their existential *mise-en-scène*.[21] In the final analysis, the most apt representational analogue for the *ingressi* is not the fixed stage of the theater, nor the uninterrupted flow of the cinematic image, but the dynamic unfolding of the drama itself, with its variable rhythms, sudden plot turns, and lively interplay of opposed protagonists. For the ingressi are nothing if not dramatic: like powerful *dramatis personae* who upstage the other actors caught up in the theatrical process, they tend to outshine their respective built environments from the moment that the visitor places his or her foot upon the threshold.

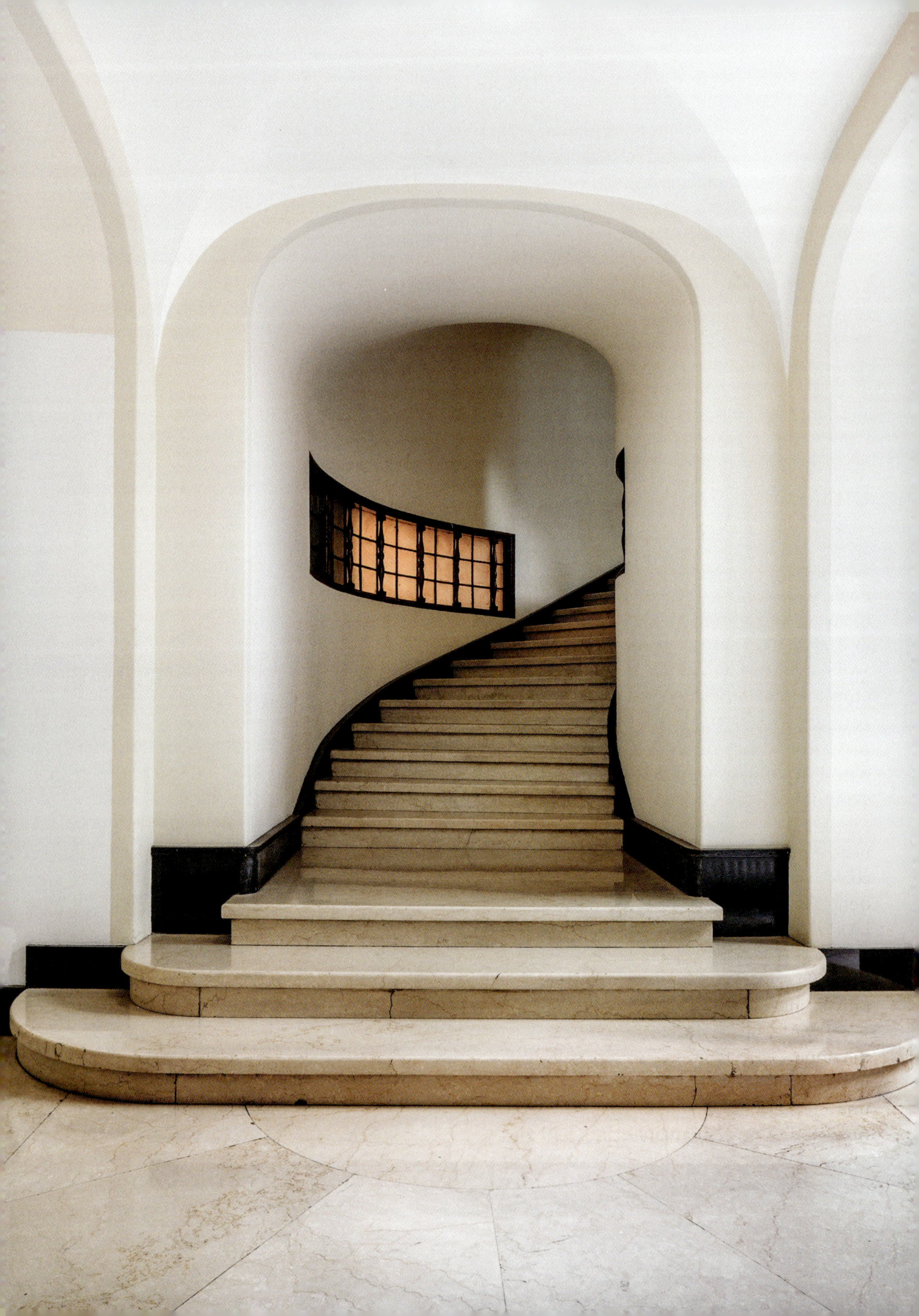

Daniel Sherer

Il fascino discreto della soglia

ARCHITETTURA, ARTE E DESIGN NEGLI INGRESSI MILANESI, 1910–70

"Ogni inizio è lieto,
la soglia è il luogo dell'attesa."
—Goethe

Poche convenzioni architettoniche sono così onnipresenti, e quindi così date per scontate, come la soglia. A prima vista lo scopo di quest'ultima sembra ovvio: facilitare il passaggio tra spazi esterni e interni stabilendo una netta distinzione tra loro. Al tempo stesso va però ricordato che la soglia, considerata come zona liminale, se non come paradigma essenziale della liminalità stessa, ha un carattere fortemente ambiguo: coniugando e simultaneamente separando i vari momenti del percorso, essa genera uno spazio che non è né dentro né fuori, bensì partecipe di entrambi. La soglia, dunque, benché sembri sancire una chiara distinzione di spazi, in realtà sovverte qualsiasi categoria che separi in maniera definitiva l'interno dall'esterno.

Non c'è dubbio che tali luoghi di mediazione si siano sviluppati in modo unico in Italia, e in nessuna città italiana mostrano una complessità formale, un'articolazione funzionale e un'elaborazione spaziale come a Milano. Tali sono gli "ingressi": ampie zone di transizione in palazzi residenziali che fungono da veri e propri luoghi di sperimentazione architettonica. Data la loro singolarità, si può constatare che c'è qualcosa di verificabile e al tempo stesso di paradossale nel loro ruolo come episodi chiave dell'esperienza architettonica milanese. Possiamo dire, infatti, che, se Bologna ha i suoi portici, e Napoli le sue scale inserite nei cortili dei palazzi, e Venezia i suoi *porteghi* e androni nei palazzi affacciati sul Canal Grande e altrove nella città lagunare, Milano contribuisce a questa serie di luoghi di accesso e passaggio con i suoi tipici ingressi.[1]

La plausibilità di tale ipotesi deriva dal fatto che nessun altro tratto dell'architettura milanese del periodo moderno possiede un'impronta tipologica più palese. Ciò è paradossale, perché è facile isolare altri caratteri architettonici milanesi più visibili e manifesti, dato che lo splendore e il lusso, per non parlare della complessità spaziale e formale,

via Gabrio Serbelloni 10, Palazzo Sola-Busca · Aldo Andreani, 1924–30
stairs: Botticino limestone

degli ingressi diventano evidenti soltanto all'interno o, al limite, guardando dall'esterno verso l'interno, attraverso grandi finestre, vetrate o scaloni. Considerati in questa luce, gli ingressi diventano uno dei segreti più gelosamente custoditi della città di Milano: un segreto che, come la lettera rubata di Edgar Allan Poe, è per tutti "nascosto in bella vista", e accessibile solo a un numero assai ristretto di persone. Con gli ingressi, siamo di fronte a spazi che, per una loro peculiare logica di rappresentazione, cominciano come passaggi per raggiungere un determinato luogo e finiscono per trasformarsi nella destinazione stessa.

Un ruolo decisivo è giocato in questo processo dal modo in cui gli ingressi rendono possibile un triplice incontro fra architettura, arte e design. Artisti, architetti e designer hanno contribuito all'organizzazione formale di questi spazi in modi diversi, esplorando i limiti della collaborazione artistica e rinnovando le forme della rappresentazione e le relative modalità di trasformazione spaziale. Si potrebbe dire, infatti, che gli ingressi occupano una zona intermedia tra campi estetici diversi così come occupano uno spazio liminale tra esterno e interno. Questa doppia capacità di mediazione enfatizza non solo il loro specifico contributo, ma anche ciò che manca in altri spazi di transizione che non hanno elaborazioni estetiche e formali paragonabili. Gli ingressi fungono da significanti di questa discrepanza, ma anche da veicoli dei valori estetici che rafforzano il ruolo di questi spazi liminali nei vari contesti in cui compaiono.[2] D'altronde, data la loro alta qualità estetica, e la minuta attenzione riservata ad articolazioni formali, materiali e spaziali, gli ingressi più noti si distinguono dagli altri che, in questi campi, non possono competere con loro. Questo fattore di rivalità concentra tutte le forze delle varie tendenze architettoniche e artistiche milanesi negli spazi più o meno ristretti degli ingressi stessi, e costituisce una dimensione della loro forma e funzione che storici e critici, finora, non hanno studiato in modo adeguato alla ricchezza e all'importanza del tema.[3]

Mediazione e rappresentazione – Per orientare il lettore nella sua "visita" agli ingressi che si dispiega in queste pagine (una visita, in ogni caso, molto selettiva e ristretta agli *exempla* più eloquenti del genere), l'analisi è focalizzata sull'intersezione di due assi ermeneutici. Il primo corrisponde al ruolo singolare svolto dall'ingresso nell'universo urbano milanese; il secondo è invece più articolato, e corrisponde alle strategie diversificate di mediazione e rappresentazione assunte dagli ingressi per trasformare lo spazio liminale in un sito eccezionale che si distingue sia dal contesto architettonico che da quello urbano.

In quest'ottica, gli ingressi sono intesi come mezzi formali e spaziali che annunciano un elevato livello sociale in determinati contesti residenziali. Come l'uso del *Klinker* quale elemento chiave della tipologia residenziale e della tecnica di costruzione dei palazzi altoborghesi milanesi,[4] l'ingresso svolge un ruolo simbolico e ideologico cruciale: quello di segnalare la necessità del lusso, l'uso dello sfarzo come mezzo sociale di autorappresentazione e di valorizzazione dello spazio domestico (o, più precisamente, del *vestibulum* pubblico di questo spazio), in una prospettiva di ascesa sociale ancora sospesa tra l'emulazione del modello aristocratico consolidato e le nuove attrattive della moderna metropoli.

In ultima analisi, la forza innovatrice e la vitalità degli ingressi deriva non solo dall'uso delle forme moderne, ma anche dalla trasformazione radicale della tradizione. Se gli scaloni assiali e le modalità di ingresso e di passaggio simmetriche od oblique nella loro organizzazione spaziale hanno radici profonde nei modelli rinascimentali e barocchi, domestici e teatrali, e soprattutto nell'enfasi palladiana sul ruolo dello scalone in asse con la facciata, l'uso di nuovi materiali, forme e strategie tecniche (pannelli di calcestruzzo armato, trombe d'ascensore, superfici esterne totalmente vetrate) riflette una volontà di affrontare le innovazioni del moderno e di assimilare, al livello più profondo, le mutazioni tecnoscientifiche dell'universo della razionalizzazione. Sebbene la sintesi di tendenze retrospettive e prospettive sia tipico dell'architettura italiana moderna, questa sintesi diviene particolarmente evidente negli ingressi, dove assume la sua forma più concentrata, e forse anche più eloquente, come luogo privilegiato per verificare le più estreme ibridizzazioni o, al contrario, la distillazione di singoli codici stilistici.

L'ingresso come confine attraversabile – Le ultime osservazioni sollevano una domanda specifica: si può parlare di un ingresso prettamente "razionalista"? L'esemplarità del linguaggio razionalista nella Casa Rustici, un palazzo residenziale e per uffici in corso Sempione 36 realizzato nel 1934 da Giuseppe Terragni e Pietro Lingeri (vedi pp. 292, 295), tende a favorire una risposta affermativa a una tale domanda, poiché questo linguaggio lo identifica come pietra miliare del lessico razionale nella storia dell'architettura residenziale moderna, e non solo a Milano. Avvicinandosi al palazzo, inserito in un sito irregolare, la disposizione dei volumi levitanti diventa immediatamente evidente, ed è chiaro che questi volumi appartengono a una griglia ideale che inquadra l'edificio, conferendovi un senso di planarità e astrazione e insieme un carattere tettonico che evoca una struttura "a ponte".[5] Nella sua analisi di questo elemento del palazzo, Thomas Schumacher sostiene che Terragni (qui insieme a Lingeri) ha sviluppato un apparato strutturale a esoscheletro, una constatazione che è persuasiva e apre nuove vie di lettura del lessico di questi architetti.

Il percorso austero del corridoio, che ha un pavimento di pietra, trasforma l'ingresso in una condizione ideale e quasi purificata di passaggio, congruente con il carattere elementale dell'espressione tettonica esteriore. Si può dire, dunque, che l'ingresso e l'esterno sono animati dallo stesso impulso formale. Quest'ultimo stabilisce le pretese architettoniche dell'ingresso con rigore, attributo altamente razionalista. Ci permette anche di attraversarlo riconoscendo che in esso si può verificare una strana compresenza di ampiezza palese e opacità misteriosa: il carattere labirintico dell'ingresso, senza finestre, dotato di un altissimo soffitto, rinforza questo senso di mistero nonché il carattere enigmatico dell'insieme. Un simile coacervo di qualità opposte suscita la nostra curiosità, cioè il desiderio di entrare in questo luogo, attraversarlo fino in fondo, e per questo motivo si può dire che aggiunge una nuova tensione moderna all'antico *topos* romano del *limen*. D'altronde, questo trattamento complesso, per certi versi, prefigura uno dei progetti più importanti, e certamente il più importante tra quelli non realizzati, nell'iter di Terragni, il Danteum.[6]

Tale ipotesi deriva la sua legittimità dal fatto che, come nel Danteum, il corridoio di corso Sempione è insolitamente alto, è rivestito dello stesso marmo biancastro e ha un carattere ambiguo e labirintico, accentuato dalla mancanza di finestre, un tratto che lo accomuna a certi lavori di Le Corbusier come il Mundaneum e il Museo della Crescita Infinita in Giappone. In questo spazio un sentimento arcaico, quasi primordiale, si unisce a una fondamentale semplificazione classica degli elementi: coerente, quest'ultima, con l'idea di ingenuità dedalica che prevale nell'insieme. Tale sentimento genera un ethos razionalista con associazioni metafisiche sottolineate dalle ombre prodotte dalla modanatura del portale che sbocca nello spazio centrale. A completare la composizione è il luminoso vestibolo centrale, il cui soffitto a griglia, che annuncia il trionfo del tema del telaio monumentale, richiama l'intradosso dello spazio centrale di un altro lavoro di Terragni: la Casa del Fascio a Como, con la differenza che qui, in corso Sempione, il pavimento consiste di centinaia di pezzi di pietra inseriti in modo apparentemente irregolare, formando un insieme che, tramite una logica di contrasto, sottolinea l'impressione di un ordine razionale inerente che pervade tutte le altre componenti dello spazio.

Simmetrie scatenate – Spesso gli ingressi sono, generalmente parlando, i luoghi più memorabili dell'edificio; e quando si cerca il fattore predominante che ne determina tale straordinarietà una risposta plausibile non è difficile da trovare: i più memorabili, infatti, esibiscono un equilibrio precario tra impulsi opposti, e soprattutto tra diversi schemi spaziali, elementi formali e direzioni assiali. Un caso esemplare si trova nel famoso ingresso della Torre Velasca del BBPR (vedi pp. 265-266), in cui l'insieme di elementi planimetrici forma un ordine simmetrico comprensivo che apre su piazza Velasca. Questo ordine entra in dialettica con le lampade pendenti a forma di baccello che fanno parte di candelabri d'acciaio quadripartiti e con i contorni iridescenti dalle tonalità variopinte che si estendono sui pilastri poliedrici nello spazio a doppia altezza. Le trombe dell'ascensore sono rivestite con un impallacciatura fatta di pezzi di mogano di varia misura, con differenze spesso quasi impercettibili, costituendo un insieme che sorge in alto, fatto con minuta attenzione artigianale. In questo spazio esteso di un'ampiezza grandiosa, l'occhio è invitato a esplorare i limiti del visibile nelle zone più alte dell'ingresso, sottolineando così la spinta verticale della torre residenziale all'interno e all'esterno, in un dialogo singolare tra prossimità e distanza.

Più clamoroso, e al tempo stesso ermetico, è un ingresso realizzato parecchi decenni prima della Torre Velasca, nell'ambito di quello che può essere considerato il *tour de force* dello stile liberty di Giulio Ulisse Arata: la Casa Berri-Meregalli in via Cappuccini 8, del 1911-14, il cui asse centrale guida il nostro sguardo, tramite una formidabile griglia di *fer forgé* concepita da Alessandro Mazzucotelli, verso una scultura posta alla fine di un lunghissimo corridoio (vedi pp. 120-123).[7] Quest'opera, la *Vittoria alata* del maestro simbolista Adolfo Wildt, è un enigmatico busto femminile che sembra levitare nello spazio. Una testa di marmo di color caramello lucidato, con la bocca protrusa semiaperta e gli occhi socchiusi a forma quasi di mandorla, la Vittoria è raffigurata coperta di un soggolo color smeraldo. Affiancata da un paio di ali di insetto in bronzo intagliato, quest'opera è una delle più misteriose di Wildt. Di fatto, il mistero è intensificato non solo dall'inserzione del busto in questo contesto stranamente rarefatto, ma anche dal suo sostegno semplicissimo e quasi brutale: una verga di bronzo su cui la scultura è impalata. Sospesa nello spazio semibuio del corridoio, la figura è posta in asse rispetto alle finestre interne di vetro colorato che fungono da quinte. Presenza inquietante nell'absidale, funerario e radiante vestibolo, la testa alata è inquadrata da basse arcate neoromaniche e mosaici scintillanti disegnati da Pietro Adamo Rimoldi ed eseguiti dalla ditta Villeroy & Boch, con effetti cromatici che evocano quelli di Gustav Klimt.[8]

Decisamente visionario, l'insieme di design, scultura e architettura di questo ingresso tenta di rivaleggiare con la cultura visiva della *Sezession* nell'orchestrazione di stilemi bizantini, medievali e classici che si fondono in un ambiente crepuscolare. Attraversati da contrasti di luce e ombra, le forme e gli spazi del corridoio sono intimamente connessi con temi di morte e resurrezione incarnati nella figura sovrannaturale, quasi totemica dello spirito alato. L'ingresso partecipa dunque in ugual misura della sensibilità estetica viennese *fin de siècle* di un Gustav Mahler o un Richard Strauss e della vita quotidiana di un palazzo residenziale dell'alta borghesia milanese.

Qui la interazione di arte, design e spazio architettonico è così complessa e comprensiva da far sì che sia impossibile immaginare

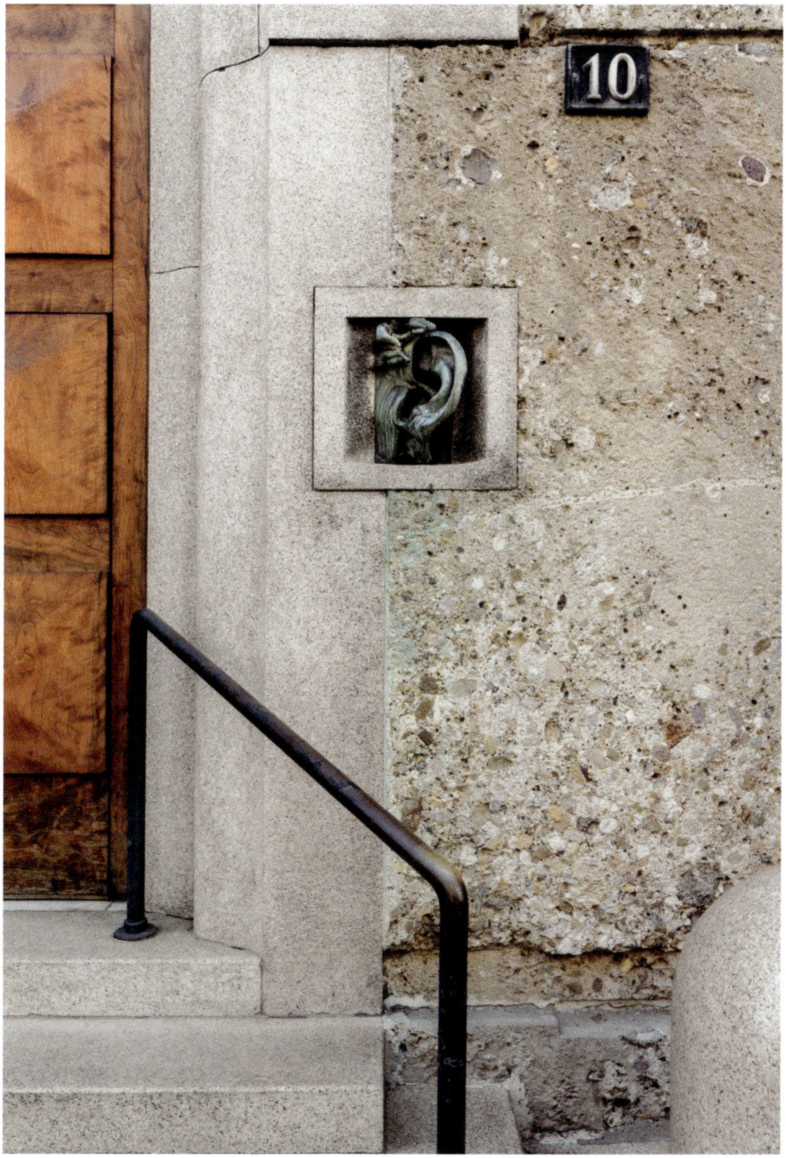

via Gabrio Serbelloni 10, Palazzo Sola-Busca · Aldo Andreani, 1924–30

Bronze sculpture/interphone by Adolfo Wildt.
stairs: Bianco Baveno granite · doorframe: Rosa Baveno granite · walls: Ceppo dell'Adda, mediano (i.e. medium coarse-grained)

la *Vittoria* in uno spazio più adatto di questo suo peculiare "habitat", dove assiste al via vai dei visitatori stupiti con un'aria di travagliato distacco. Guardiana della sua dimora, la figura trasmette le ansie del proprio tempo come nessun'altra invenzione artistica contemporanea, tranne forse il suo cugino certamente più famoso, ma a malapena meno androgino, *L'urlo* di Edvard Munch, opera realizzata negli stessi anni. Entrambi attestano la stessa crisi culturale alla quale né l'una né l'altro possono dare voce. Ed entrambi sono raffigurati nel tentativo di esprimere precisamente questo: un atto destinato, naturalmente, a fallire. La loro lotta interiore risulta quindi di un'intensità intollerabile.[9] Tuttavia, a differenza della figura di Munch, quella di Wildt, grazie a una sorta di riattivazione del paradosso di Zenone, è rappresentata nell'atto di sfrecciare attraverso l'infinità dello spazio (si notino le stelle raggruppate intorno al suo collo proteso come una prua) e contemporaneamente come radicata in questo specifico luogo di Milano. Essa è dunque corporea e incorporea: l'ingresso stesso è il suo corpo esteso, a un tempo immateriale e violento, tanto che non possiamo sopprimere un fremito d'inquietudine quando lasciamo il palazzo per addentrarci nella metropoli.

La figura tormentata della *Vittoria* di Wildt è agitata da energie che, essendo in gran parte latenti, possono a ben vedere essere considerate sintomi di repressione. Questa osservazione richiama non solo gli schemi psicoanalitici cui gli storici dell'arte e dell'architettura si sono ispirati negli ultimi decenni, ma un testo seminale spesso citato da questi stessi: gli *Studien über Hysterie* (1895) di Freud e Breuer e soprattutto il concetto di "stato affettivo strangolato" che questo testo esplica.[10] Tale concetto, infatti, ci fornisce un'ottima descrizione psicologica dell'incapacità dell'isterico di esprimere il dolore in modo aperto. Nel caso della statua di Wildt, questo dolore e la connessa difficoltà di manifestarlo liberamente vanno identificati con il dolore individuale della donna altoborghese, qui proiettata in un mondo di figurazione mitica e arcaica. Ma evocano anche, sebbene in modo allusivo, l'isteria collettiva scatenata dalla prima guerra mondiale, scoppiata quasi nel momento in cui questo ingresso veniva portato a compimento così come l'opera di Wildt (che in fin dei conti potrebbe anche essere vista come una raffigurazione, sebbene molto strana, della Vittoria militare). Data la sensazione conturbante generata dalla scultura, l'ingresso che la ospita diventa a tutti gli effetti l'immagine di uno degli *espaces autres* di cui parla Michel Foucault e, più precisamente, lo spazio dell'eterotopia e quindi della liminalità dove tutte le regole consuete dello spazio urbano e territoriale sono provvisoriamente sospese. Ciò che colpisce in questo contesto è il dialogo tra le due forme di genio qui presenti, quello dello scultore Wildt e quello dell'architetto Arata, specchio di una collaborazione che, è opportuno sottolineare, ha creato il primo ingresso milanese di importanza artistica. Questo dialogo, inoltre, ha determinato l'apoteosi dello spazio dell'alterità tramite un gioco di opposizioni latenti, le stesse opposizioni che Foucault utilizza per esplicare la logica dell'altro al cuore dell'eterotopia: "E forse la nostra vita è ancora governata da un certo numero di opposizioni che rimangono inviolabili, che le nostre istituzioni e pratiche non hanno osato ancora deporre. Sono opposizioni che consideriamo semplici dati di fatto: per esempio tra lo spazio pubblico e lo spazio privato, tra lo spazio della famiglia e lo spazio sociale, tra lo spazio della cultura e lo spazio della funzione, tra lo spazio del piacere e lo spazio del lavoro. Queste distinzioni sono ancora fondate sulla presenza nascosta del sacro."[11] Wildt e Arata ci mostrano questa faccia velata, simultaneamente seducente e distruttiva, della Sfinge del loro tempo; e non è per caso, certamente, che tale rivelazione irrompe precisamente nel punto di congiunzione liminale tra lo spazio pubblico e lo spazio privato, tra lo spazio domestico e quello della città moderna.

Un'altra esplorazione delle reciproche relazioni tra questi spazi è evidente nell'opera dell'unica personalità del periodo tra le due guerre nella storia dell'ingresso che sia paragonabile ad Arata per quanto riguarda il livello di complessità, audacia di invenzione formale e intensità immaginativa: Aldo Andreani. Come Arata, Andreani è l'unico architetto dotato di sufficiente sicurezza di sé per ricevere la lezione di un visionario come Wildt.[12] E, come Arata, le sue radicali combinazioni linguistiche resistono alle categorie storiografiche convenzionali. Infatti, le ricerche dei due architetti, in modi diversi, corrispondono a una singolare lettura dello stile liberty che cerca di raggiungere un accordo con quei momenti della tradizione classica in cui l'eccezione è elevata al rango della norma, della regola stessa (Peruzzi, Serlio, Giulio Romano) e con lo sperimentalismo formale, tipologico e spaziale che caratterizza il barocco. Si può essere più precisi su questo punto: Andreani, in due momenti della sua opera, inventa ingressi caratterizzati da una sintesi inebriante di cinquecentismo ed eclettismo neobarocco che resuscita il motivo, tipico della cultura barocca stessa, del "concetto".[13]

In Palazzo Fidia, opera chiave di Andreani del 1924-26 (vedi pp. 118-119), il concetto in questione è di carattere spaziale, e riguarda l'idea di un movimento obliquo in due sensi: da una parte, si entra nell'ovale del vestibolo d'ingresso dall'angolo smussato della pianta poligonale, dall'altra, c'è un percorso che ha una seconda tappa, anch'essa obliqua. Il portale stesso, l'inizio del percorso, è riccamente ornato col rustico in modo quasi grottesco, e rappresenta una reinterpretazione di modelli rinascimentali, essendo una ripresa delle porte di Serlio lette attraverso una vasta gamma di riferimenti della cultura architettonica di fine Ottocento e inizio Novecento. Tra questi si possono includere senz'altro Frank Furness, Joseph Maria Olbrich, Edwin Lutyens e lo stesso Giovanni Muzio, che ha creato un'estetica del Novecento più austera del lessico dell'Andreani, basando le sue scelte stilistiche, almeno in parte, su un ripudio dell'esempio neobarocco di Andreani stesso.[14]

Andreani, dunque, raddoppia l'idea di entrare "ad angolo", portando avanti il concetto di obliquo lungo il percorso e rilanciando l'asse diagonale nell'interno: l'unico modo per raggiungere lo scalone elicoidale (uno dei più impressionanti di Milano, e non solo del periodo tra le due guerre) e la portineria passa attraverso il lato opposto della pianta poligonale, in cui l'ovale è inscritto. Dunque l'obliquità dell'ingresso, o meglio, la diagonalità del suo attraversamento, è indispensabile per capire la logica dell'insieme. Inoltre, questo gioco tra interno ed esterno, mediato dal concetto di obliquità stessa, risulta arricchito dai volumi emergenti del rivestimento di marmo, che cedono al movimento della massa di mattone diradante, smussata per meglio trasmettere la spinta verso l'alto dell'ingresso stesso. In questo modo l'ingresso principale e le aree di servizio, insieme, occupano il centro dell'attenzione, in un rovesciamento della logica primaria dell'ingresso nei contesti classici o neoclassici. Ugualmente impressionanti sono i marmi colorati, che contrappongono oro, crema, smeraldo e nero, e sono disposti in modo tale da evocare le tarsie fiorentine del Seicento nel disegno del pavimento che si estende al perimetro dell'ovale stesso.

Come Arata, Andreani non esita a usare tutte le risorse formali a sua disposizione in questo *tour de force*, in cui l'estetismo *fin de siècle* si unisce ai linguaggi neo-rinascimentali e neobarocchi. Ma il suo virtuosismo non si è esaurito in questo lavoro. Nel suo secondo intervento, in Palazzo Sola-Busca di via Serbelloni 10 (vedi pp. 38, 43), si può ammirare un portale enorme, di carattere rustico, con bugnato fuori scala. In alto, a destra, è collocata una grande scultura in bronzo, un rilievo inserito nel muro, che rappresenta un orecchio umano, anch'essa fuori scala,

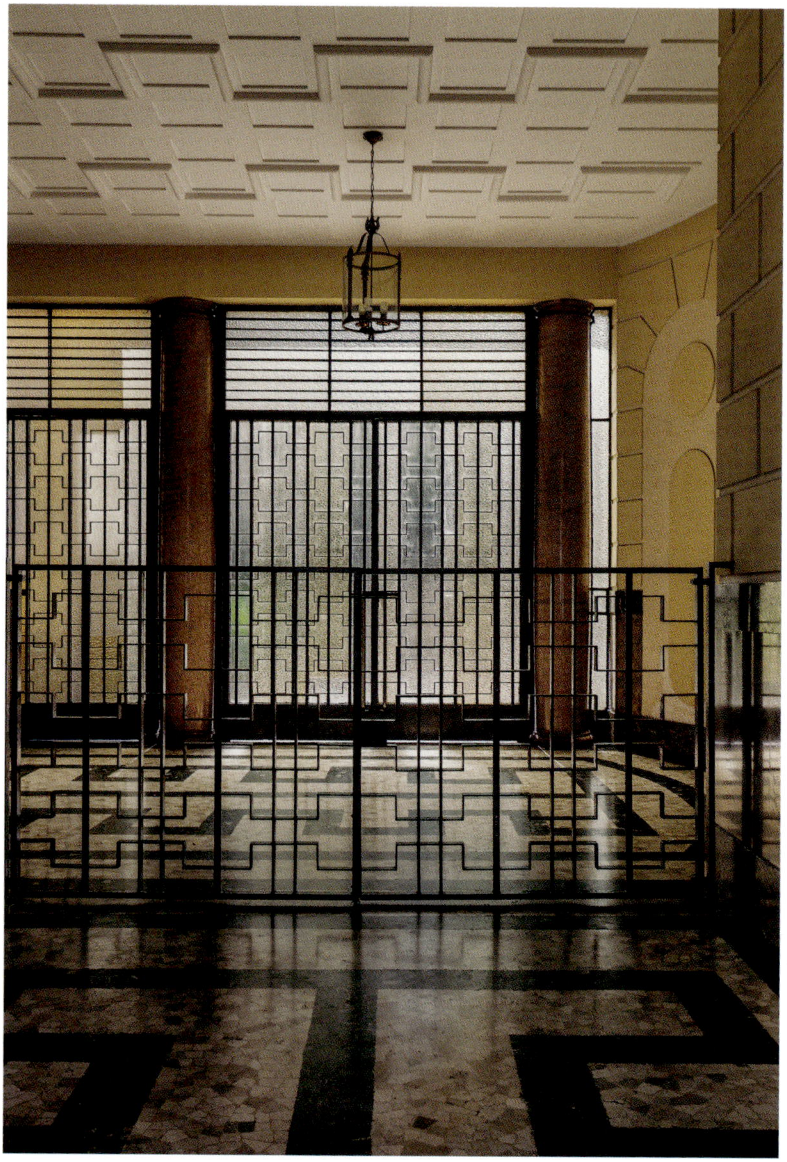

via Tonale 9 · Cesare Donini, A. Scala, 1935–36

floor: Palladiana of several stones · columns: Rosa Baveno granite

di un naturalismo sconcertante. È opera di Andreani stesso, che era non solo architetto, ma anche scultore, discepolo di Wildt a Brera.[15] In questo caso il concetto non verte sul rapporto fra spazio, visione e direzione del movimento, come in Palazzo Fidia, ma sulla figurazione enigmatica dell'udito nel suo rapporto complesso con la visione. Nota fra i milanesi come "Ca' dell'oreggia" (un soprannome che resiste nel tempo, analogamente alla "Ca' Brütta" di Muzio), quest'opera, paragonabile alla *Vittoria alata* per la sua qualità bizzarra, è del 1924-25. Accurata nella più minuta attenzione ai dettagli anatomici, fino agli anni Trenta la scultura trasmetteva suoni attraverso un tubo inserito nella massa muraria: un mezzo di comunicazione molto originale, se non bizzarro, in quello che può sembrare un aggiornamento della fantasia architettonica della trasmissione istantanea delle voci attraverso elementi scultorei sognata dal poliedrico erudito gesuita del Seicento Athanasius Kircher, che voleva inserire tubi nascosti nelle statue dei palazzi barocchi per comunicare a distanza.[16]

Nel caso di Andreani, il concetto è rovesciato: anziché una bocca che emette soltanto silenzio, qui ci si trova di fronte a una situazione in cui non solo si parla a un orecchio, ma a un orecchio aperto a tutte le vocalizzazioni. (È plausibile, inoltre, vedere la scultura di Andreani come una risposta artistica al portale di Palazzo Zuccari a Roma, ora sede della Biblioteca Hertziana, un ingresso che ha la forma di un'enorme bocca grottesca.) Qui si tratta di un concetto che stabilisce un'analogia tra edificio e corpo: tramite questo orecchio, il soggetto entra in una situazione curiosa in cui può addirittura conversare con l'edificio, e l'edificio gli risponde, una possibilità che aggiunge un nuovo livello di consapevolezza alla moderna gamma di tecniche di ascolto connesse alla portineria, le quali sono in questo modo elevate a un livello allegorico mai incontrato prima nell'esperienza architettonica dell'epoca. E, tramite questo concetto, il suono non è soltanto visualizzato, ma anche spazializzato: anche qui il concetto neobarocco opera estendendo il suo dominio in nuovi territori del regno dei sensi per creare una sorta di "sinestesia costruita".

Spazi di sintesi: l'integrazione di design e arte – Entrare negli ingressi significa attraversare spazi articolati in modi diversi dall'architetto, dall'artista e dal designer, e in certi casi da tutti e tre in modo uguale. Strategie diverse di sintesi condizionano tali spazi, che sono modulati da specifici effetti illusionistici e dalle realtà strutturali e tettoniche sottostanti. Queste ultime includono, a livello architettonico, strategie di congiunzione e disgiunzione, manifeste in dispositivi quali la sincopazione dei vani e dei passaggi, l'oscillazione ritmica e la giustapposizione dei materiali, l'uso di cesure spaziali e tecniche di citazione formale e storica, e l'evocazione e la trasformazione di modelli e codici.

In questo contesto un ruolo chiave è giocato dalle interazioni delle superfici e dalla profondità reale dello spazio come mezzo per dare un'impressione di unità o, al contrario, effetti di discontinuità all'interno. Prendiamo ad esempio l'ingresso di Giannino Testori in viale Tunisia 48 del 1936-37 (vedi p. 8), che fa parte di una serie di ingressi clamorosi che ci aiutano a definire i caratteri fondamentali di questa grande strada che connette piazza della Repubblica alle zone attraversate da corso Buenos Aires. Ci troviamo di fronte a un lungo corridoio organizzato assialmente, completamente simmetrico, le cui pareti sono rivestite di marmi rosa. Questi ultimi offrono un contrasto marcato col marmo grigio del pavimento inquadrato da un margine scuro. Il cannocchiale prospettico del passaggio assiale stabilisce un tracciato chiaro, date le simmetrie della porta a forma di T e gli elementi di vetro nel soffitto soprastante che catturano l'attenzione del visitatore con la stessa forza di un segnale stradale.

Ma uno sguardo attento rivelerà un altro livello di complessità, che si manifesta grazie non solo alla posizione strategica occupata da componenti asimmetrici come il circolo della finestra interna a sinistra, che sta di fianco all'angolo vetrato della portineria, ma anche per le riflessioni illusionistiche e la problematica visibilità del pannello di vetro della porta centrale, diviso in due parti simmetriche. Queste ultime scatenano una sorta di interferenza percettiva col soffitto che contiene una luce celata, e che rispecchia, nella sua forma, la profondità organizzata in prospettiva di un altro soffitto situato oltre la porta.

Una terza serie di osservazioni dovrebbe includere l'interazione di due cruciformi: si tratta del telaio della porta in metallo a forma di T e quello più complesso del soffitto, che indicano diverse opzioni di circolazione e diversi tipi di interazione spaziale. E infatti, mentre provoca un nuovo interagire di elementi funzionali ed estetici, l'intera composizione evoca modelli provenienti dal Bauhaus, accanto a motivi nautici connessi al lessico Art Déco, conforme a un'idea scenografica precisa. L'impressione di unità che ne risulta è generata in parte dall'insieme di elementi di design meticolosamente coordinati per superare ogni banale modalità decorativa o effetto di superficie, e in parte dall'applicazione illusionistica di strategie materiali (per esempio, la scelta del vetro satinato) e da una verifica dei limiti di specifiche convenzioni formali (per esempio, l'equilibrio precario tra simmetria e asimmetria).

L'ingresso in via Plinio 55 di Laszlo Kovacs del 1957 (vedi p. 18) può essere letto come una critica deliberata dell'ingresso di Testori espressa con un dialogo tra spazio e superficie. Tale critica pesa più di quanto potrebbe sembrare a prima vista, poiché tanti dispositivi, convenzioni e materiali, sono condivisi, ma utilizzati in modi antitetici. A differenza dell'ingresso di Testori, in questo ingresso la prima impressione è di un drammatico spostamento a destra, una mossa che diventa leggibile contro lo sfondo dato da una composizione bipartita e simmetrica costituita dal rettangolo di vetro satinato della prima finestra interna e da un'altra finestra corrispondente, quella della portineria, che sorge in asse sopra la cassetta delle lettere. La scala è di marmo latteo con venature grigie, assai simile a quella dell'ingresso di Testori: ma in questo caso il carattere scenografico è arricchito dalla rampa che corre parallela al corrimano d'acciaio continuo che sale dall'altro lato, di fianco. E, a differenza del soffitto simmetrico con luci raddoppiate oltre la scala, ma visibile dal corridoio esterno che si trova nell'ingresso di Testori, nell'ingresso di Kovacs il soffitto è "moderno" e asimmetrico, con un orlo smussato biomorfico illuminato da una luce singola che piove dall'alto tramite un'apertura fuori asse che enfatizza lo spessore del *poché*. Il tratto più manifesto dell'insieme è senz'altro questo corpo unitario pendente, luminoso e sagomato, un elemento che è al tempo stesso levitante, artificiale e nebuloso. Nella sua elegante astrazione, è visibile contro lo sfondo di un secondo soffitto più alto.

Il punto di vista della scala che sale in modo drammatico, già evidente dalla strada, e l'illuminazione abbagliante che piove dall'alto sono elementi distintivi di questo ingresso, che è caratterizzato da una fredda eleganza tipica del contesto postbellico e del "miracolo" economico,[17] un contesto avido di modernismi e tropi internazionali di carattere asimmetrico, pur di potervi includere elementi di grandiosa italianità e di "lusso". Tale tendenza, ricolma di energie quasi contraddittorie, va di pari passo con quello che Manfredo Tafuri ha identificato come il recupero del valore rappresentativo dell'immagine tipico dell'architettura italiana degli anni Cinquanta: uno sviluppo che unisce Kovacs, architetto ungherese proveniente dall'impero austroungarico, e protagonisti milanesi come Caccia Dominioni, Ponti, Vico Magistretti e Marco Zanuso, nonostante le significative divergenze dei loro linguaggi.[18]

In altri ingressi, e specialmente quelli del periodo prebellico, il gioco di superfici domina il campo visivo e agisce come fattore determinante dell'effetto totale: questo è già evidente dal momento in cui si attraversa la soglia, fattore innegabile della lettura d'insieme che non è affatto impedito dalla posizione delle fonti di illuminazione, che spesso assumono un ruolo secondario. Prendiamo, per esempio, il mosaico fittamente articolato di Palazzo Civita in piazza Duse, di Gigiotti Zanini (vedi pp. 24-25), in cui la coerenza di pareti e pavimento, intesi come insieme organico, è garantita proprio da questo elemento multicolore e iridescente; o, nella Torre Velasca, la differenziazione ottenuta dall'uso di piastrelle di granito di color rosa nel mosaico dei pilastri, che producono un effetto di contrasto se viste accanto al grigio del pavimento; o le forme ondulanti, create da piastrelle di marmo marroni, nere, bianche e seppia, nella composizione musiva di Francesco Somaini in corso Italia 22/1 e 22/2, realizzata da Luigi Caccia Dominioni nel 1957-61 (vedi pp. 282-285): qui, per il suo dinamismo interno, il mosaico campeggia come opera artistica individuale, ma allo stesso tempo unisce il campo percettivo dell'ingresso e offre un elemento cruciale di continuità nel momento in cui vi si entra.

In quest'ultimo ingresso, il senso di unità formale è raggiunto tramite un'orchestrazione sottile molto sensibile al contesto urbano, delineando così un approccio sintetico: il corridoio che segna il percorso dell'ingresso è al tempo stesso orientato verso il giardino/cortile e fa parte di un più vasto itinerario curvilineo con la chiesa di Santa Eufemia, è fiancheggiato lungo il perimetro da alti panelli di vetro color acquamarina, ed è illuminato dall'alto da una cupola forata con lucernari, a forma di vasca poco profonda, con ai lati applique appositamente realizzate da Azucena. Nonostante la loro foggia tipologicamente quasi tradizionale, a candelabro, la forma e la tessitura di queste applique evoca quegli emblemi di modernità, i fanali delle automobili, che, in un famoso esempio di design postbellico, Achille Castiglioni – lo stesso Castiglioni che ha anche collaborato con Caccia – ha usato per creare una lampada. Inoltre, questo ingresso è da porre tra le più caratteristiche e brillanti delle invenzioni di Caccia nel campo dell'architettura residenziale, costituendo un caso esemplare per la sua idea del movimento del corpo umano nello spazio architettonico, idea secondo la quale gli esseri umani, se lasciati a se stessi, spontaneamente tendono a muoversi secondo linee curve, ovali, circolari o sinuose, ma non rettilinee. Che tale principio sia vero o meno, quest'idea di uno schema di movimento ispirata a un "barocco moderno" appare chiaramente realizzata nella Galleria Strasburgo nella collaborazione tra il design di Somaini e lo spazio di Caccia.[19]

Risonanze del modernismo internazionale negli ingressi del dopoguerra – Inoltre, negli ingressi un posto particolare è riservato – in una tendenza che si manifesta soprattutto nel dopoguerra, fino a divenire una sorta di "mania citazionista" – alla trasposizione di motivi presi dalle avanguardie storiche. Suprematismo russo, De Stijl, cubismo ceco, empirismo scandinavo, organicismo di Aalto, Bauhaus e altre modalità del funzionalismo: tutti questi movimenti e impulsi, accanto a stilemi derivati da essi, hanno prodotto risonanze a volte esplicite, a volte più celate. Di fatto, in questa fase dello sviluppo degli ingressi, le "citazioni" moderniste fanno sentire la loro presenza nei modi più vari quando entrano a far parte degli ambienti scenografici, senza però contribuire a una logica strutturale inerente. A questo riguardo, le allusioni in questione non solo sono alienate dai loro contesti, ma sono adoperate in modi antitetici ai loro usi originali e quindi spesso contro gli ideali dell'architettura modernista nelle sue varie declinazioni, che tendono a porre l'accento sui valori di lucidità tettonica, austerità formale e pretese teoriche corrispondenti alle verità e proprietà delle materie.

Tutto questo è chiaramente illustrato da una svariata serie di tratti che connotano gli ingressi, primi fra tutti i lucidi rapporti spaziali evocati dalla parete di mattoni di vetro nel condominio XXI Aprile in via Lanzone 7 del 1950-53 di Asnago e Vender (vedi pp. 368-369), un tropo modernista che evoca l'estetica della costruzione in vetro di Pierre Chareau, la cui astratta eleganza è sottolineata dalla *porte cochere* rivestita in pannelli di cromo; o dall'astratto soffitto e dall'ornamentazione del muro in forma di diamante, di un cromatismo inaspettato, che cita il Cafè de l'Aubette di Theo van Doesburg e Hans e Sophie Tauber Arp del 1926-28; o da Ponti e Alberto Rosselli nella Casa Melandri di viale Lunigiana 44 del 1954-57, i cui schemi con motivo di arlecchino stabiliscono una dialettica tra spazio e superficie che si limita a segnare la percezione della profondità quando si salgono le scale dell'ingresso (vedi pp. 194-197).

Conclusione – Passando attraverso le successive fasi prebelliche dello stile liberty, Art déco, Novecento, razionalismo, funzionalismo Bauhaus, e quelle postbelliche dell'empirismo scandinavo, organicismo e brutalismo, l'ingresso milanese ha subito un doppio processo di espansione ed estetizzazione. Questa complessa evoluzione presenta affascinanti problemi di sintesi e di mediazione che a loro volta presuppongono l'eliminazione di certi concetti formali e spaziali e l'elaborazione più comprensiva di altri. Se a essere sintetizzati sono stati linguaggi e codici contrastanti e rivali, a essere mediata è stata la dicotomia fondamentale fra interni architettonici e spazio urbano. Infatti, la cosa che colpisce di più quando si cammina nella trama fitta di strade, parchi, piazze e palazzi milanesi è la varietà sorprendente di idiomi architettonici che si intersecano nella città, generando e, in ultima analisi, lasciando aperta la possibilità di molteplici letture. Gli ingressi giocano un ruolo decisivo come punti chiave di articolazione nella rete urbana.

In quest'ottica, gli ingressi possono essere letti come paradossi architettonici unici nel loro genere: fungendo chiaramente da spazi secondari che servono gli spazi primari, spesso dominano formalmente, spazialmente e funzionalmente le architetture che pretendono di servire. Gli ingressi menano così una curiosa doppia vita: parti integrali dei loro edifici, sono però anche zone ben distinte da essi. L'ingresso diventa quindi una specie di "infra-destinazione".[20] Questa doppia faccia, per quanto riguarda la logica interna dell'ingresso, equivale a un rovesciamento fondamentale di visione di sfondo e visione di primo piano, spazio architettonico e spazio liminale. Tutti gli ingressi esibiscono una teatralità ingegnosa e per certi versi insidiosa. In questa connessione sono almeno in parte analoghi alle scenografie teatrali, e non a caso il loro momento di massima fioritura coincide con la fine della grande stagione dell'opera lirica e l'ascesa del neorealismo cinematografico italiano, negli anni Sessanta: un fatto che rivela un nuovo livello di significato quando si ricorda, ad esempio, che Antonioni sovente introduceva gli ingressi nelle sue *mise en scéne* esistenziali.[21] In ultima analisi, però, l'analogia più adeguata non è né il palcoscenico fisso del teatro tradizionale, né il flusso continuo delle immagini cinematografiche, bensì lo sviluppo dialettico della narrazione drammatica stessa, con i suoi ritmi variabili, i punti di svolta e l'intenso scambio tra protagonisti e antagonisti. Gli ingressi sono in questo senso spazi teatrali per antonomasia: come potenti *dramatis personae* che mettono in ombra gli altri attori sulla scena, tendono a eclissare i rispettivi ambienti architettonici dal momento stesso in cui si varca la soglia.

This and following spread:
viale Regina Giovanna 35 · Mario Rodolfi, 1937–39

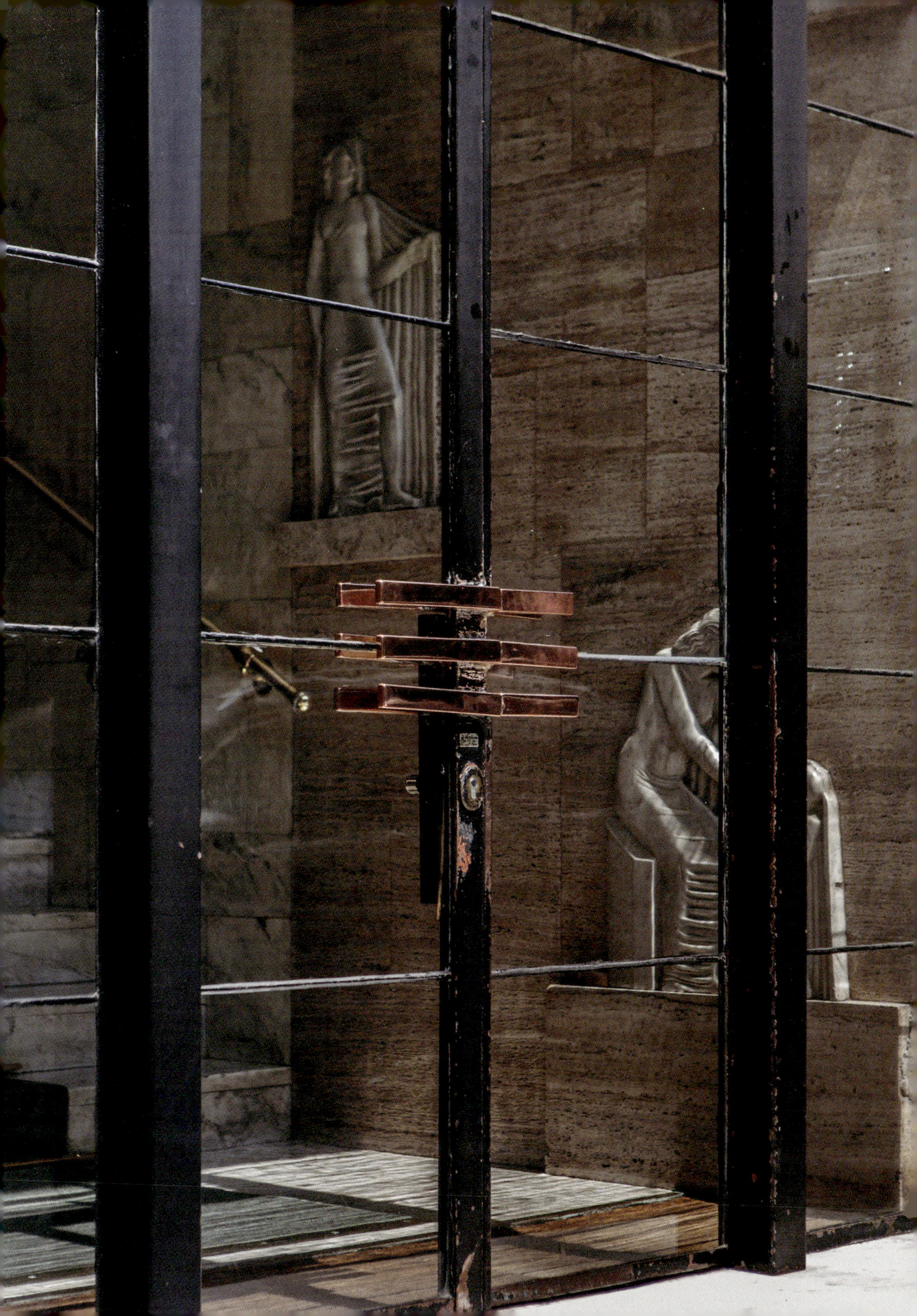

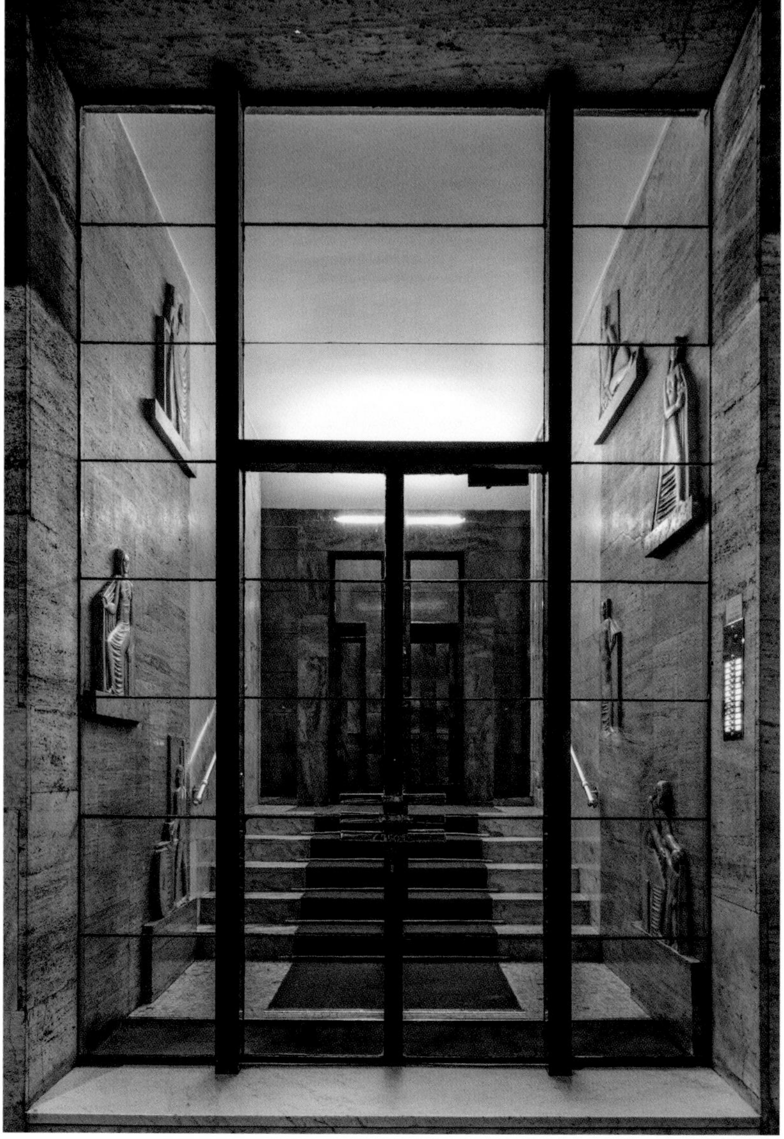

floor: Bianco Carrara marble · exterior walls: Tivoli travertine
interior walls: Carrara Calacatta marble · sculptures: Carrara Bianco Unito marble

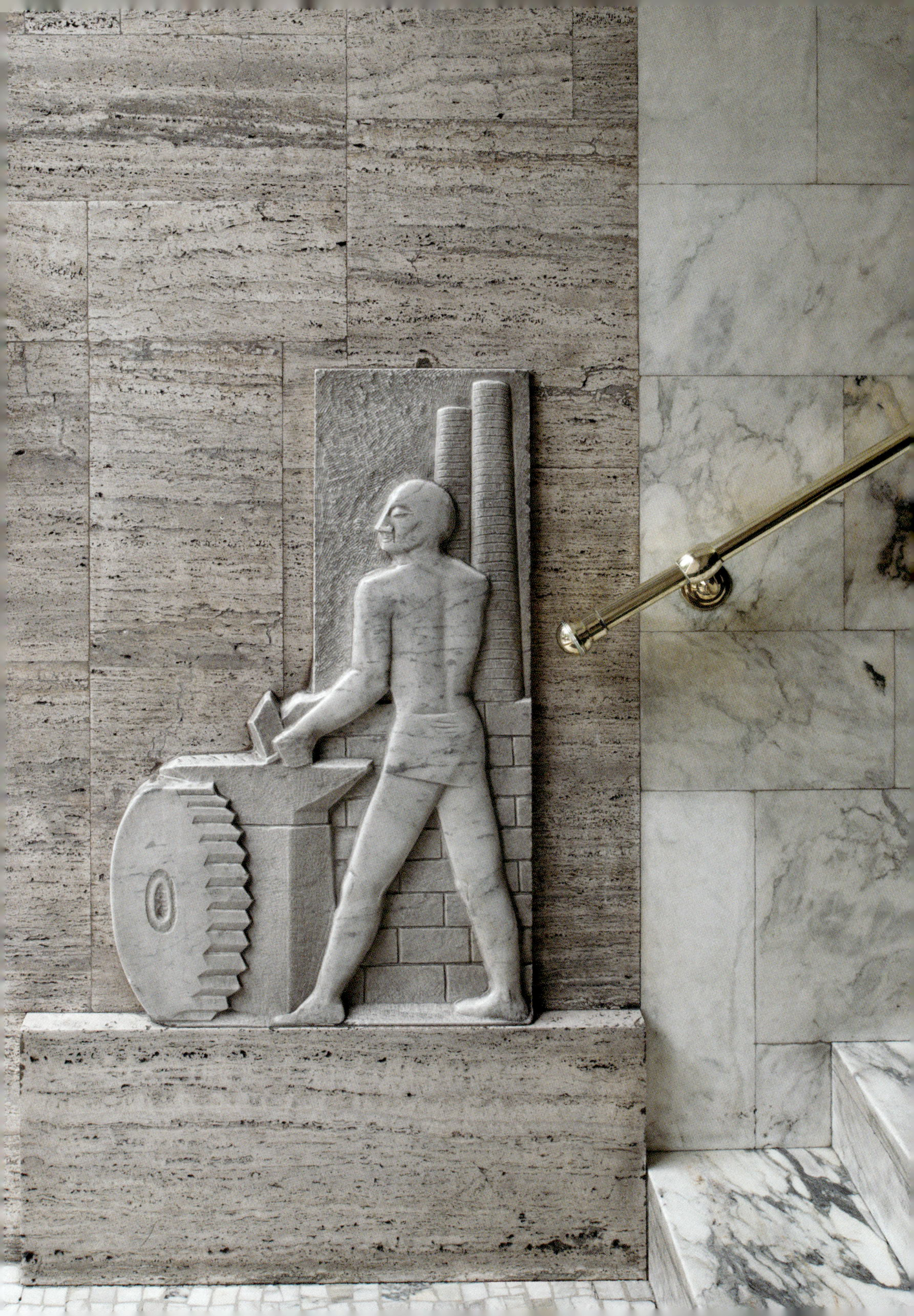

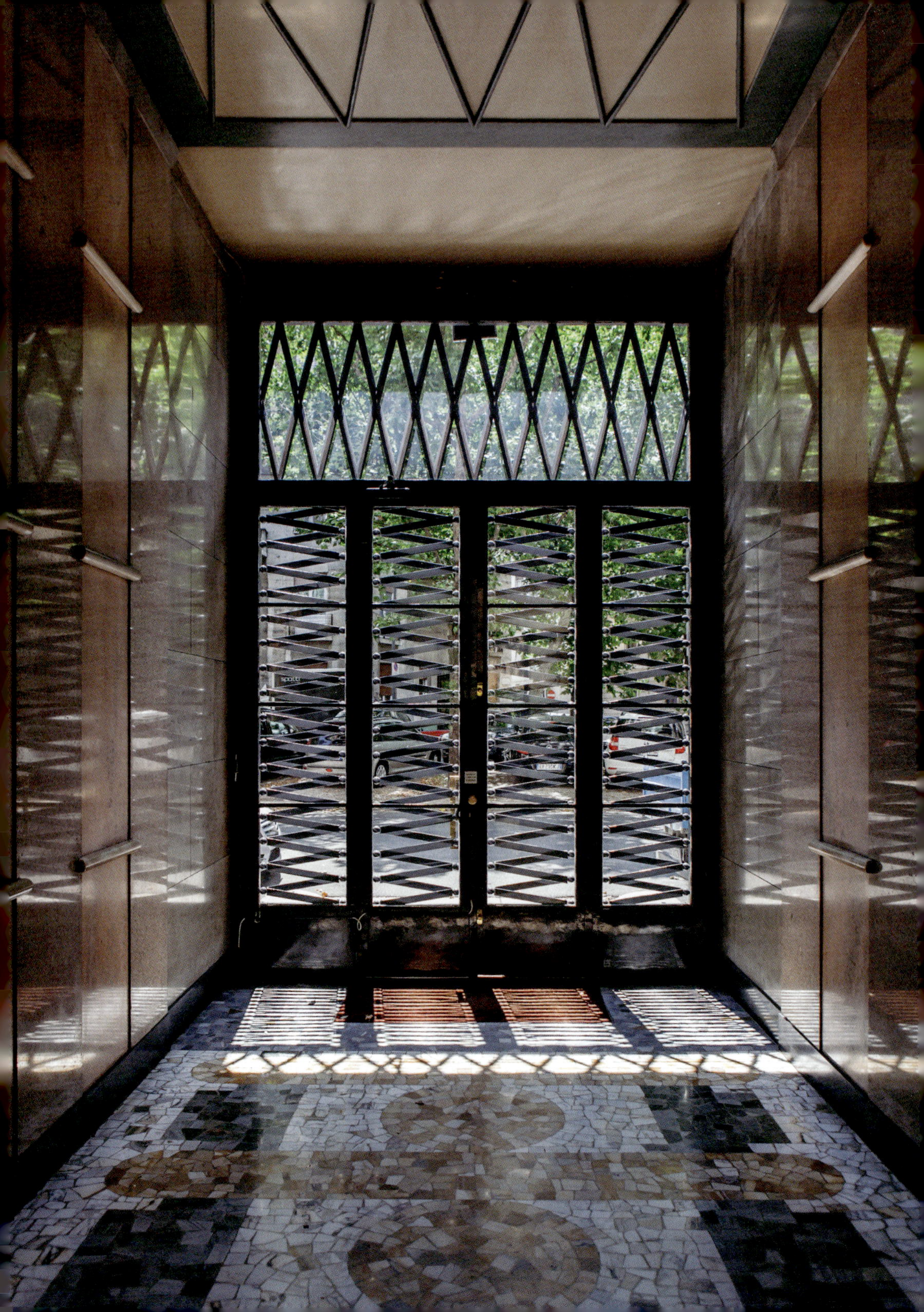

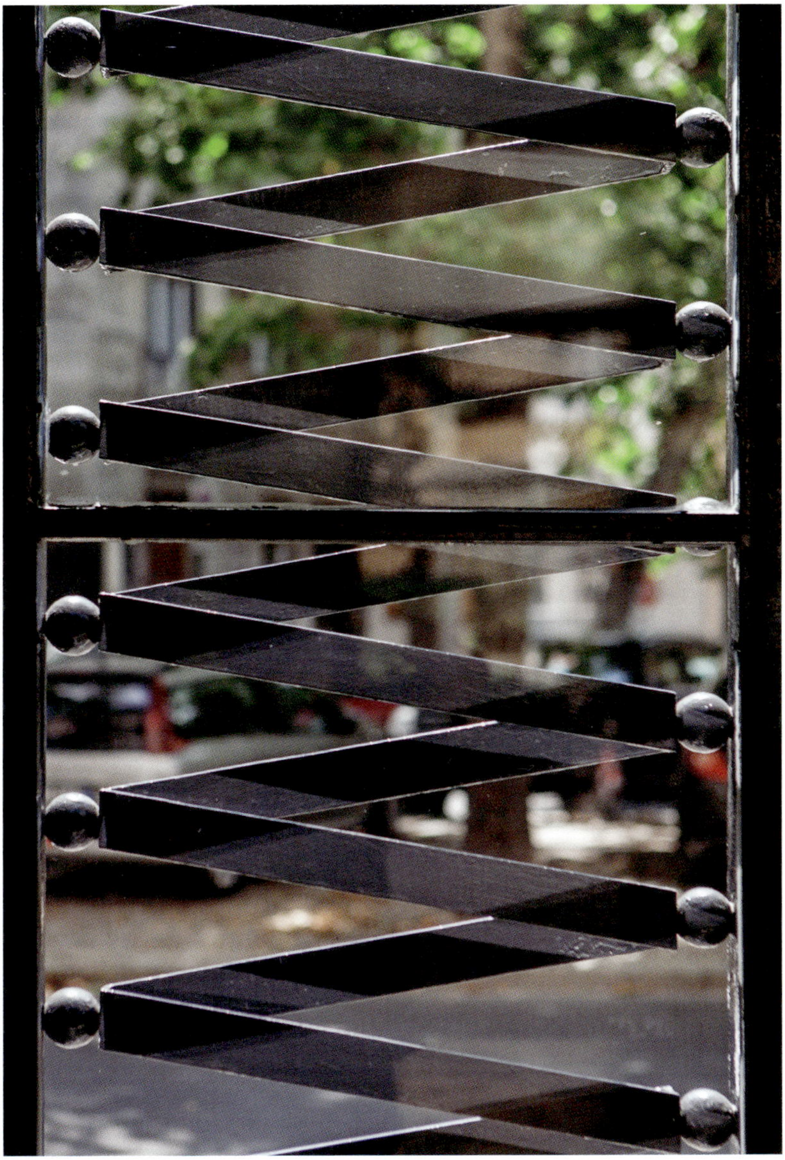

viale Giustiniano 5

BENEDETTO LIMESTONE

This polishable and durable Triassic limestone was quarried in the twentieth century in the Province of Bergamo beside an ancient Benedictine Abbey—hence its name. Dove gray in color, the stone is filled with white fossils (mainly corals) and white veining. Quarries closed after World War II.

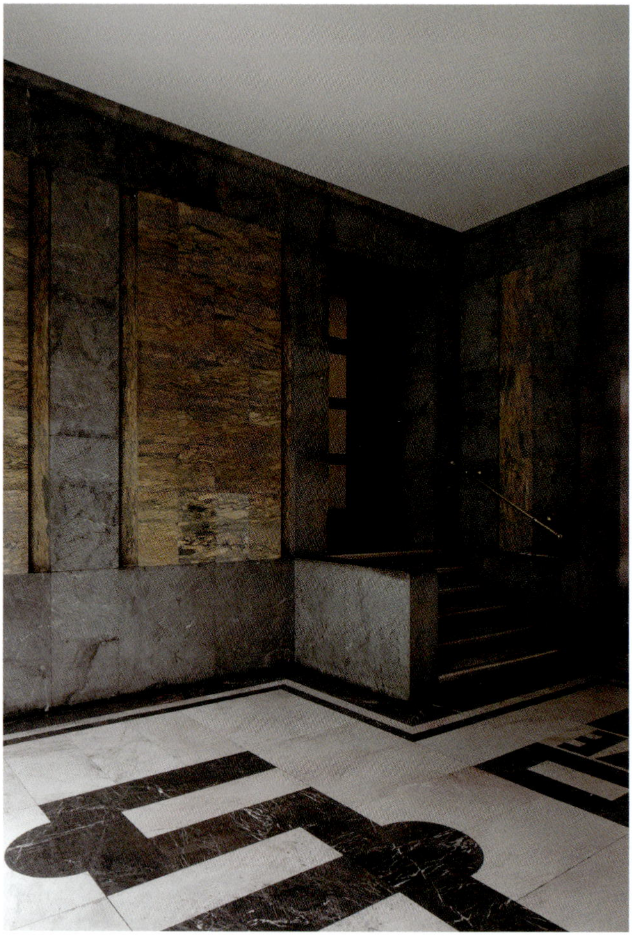

viale Giustiniano 2 · Giuseppe Roberto Martinenghi, 1935

floor: San Benedetto limestone, Zandobbio dolostone · skirting, lesene: San Benedetto limestone · walls: Calacatta marble

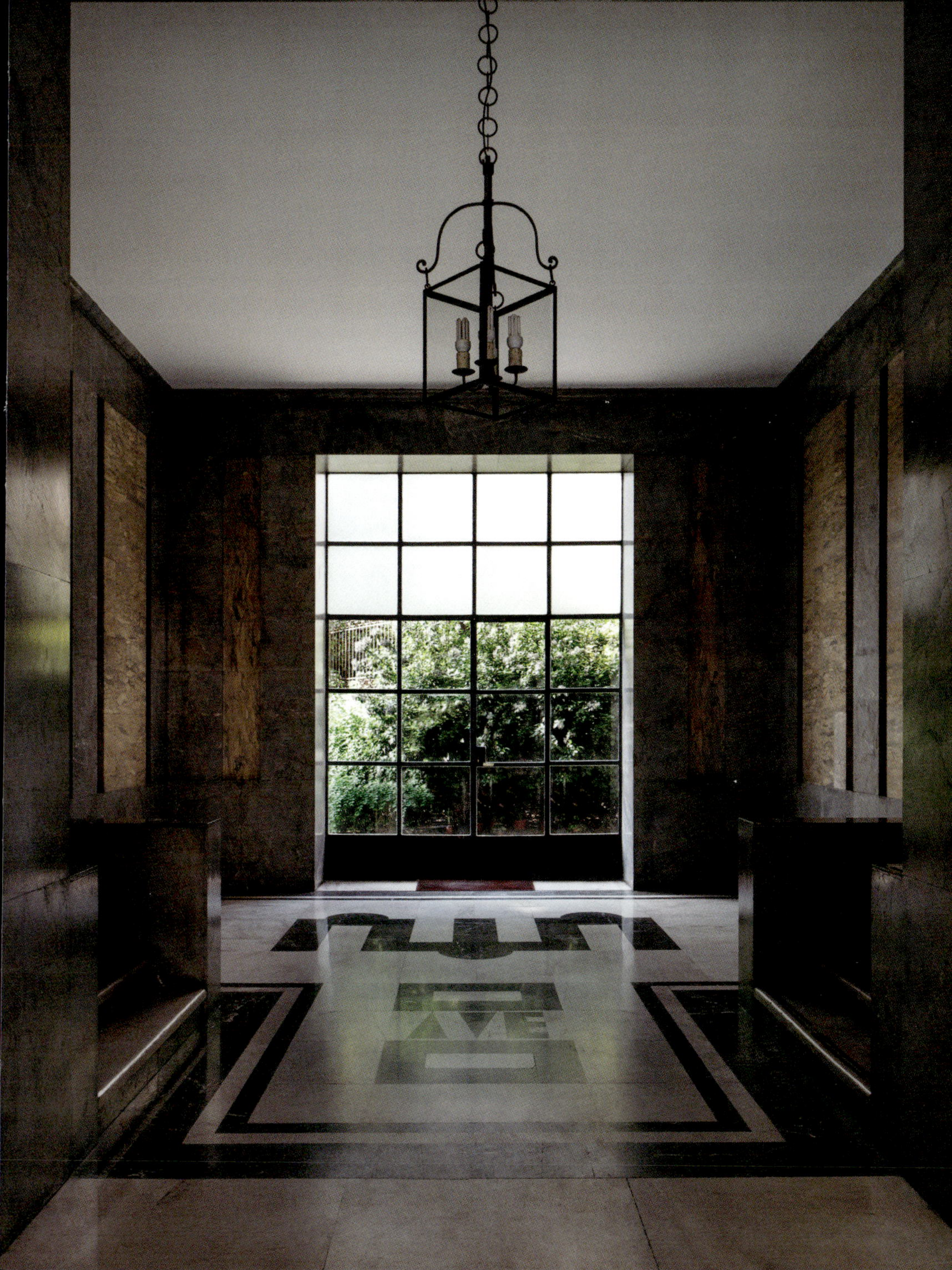
AVE

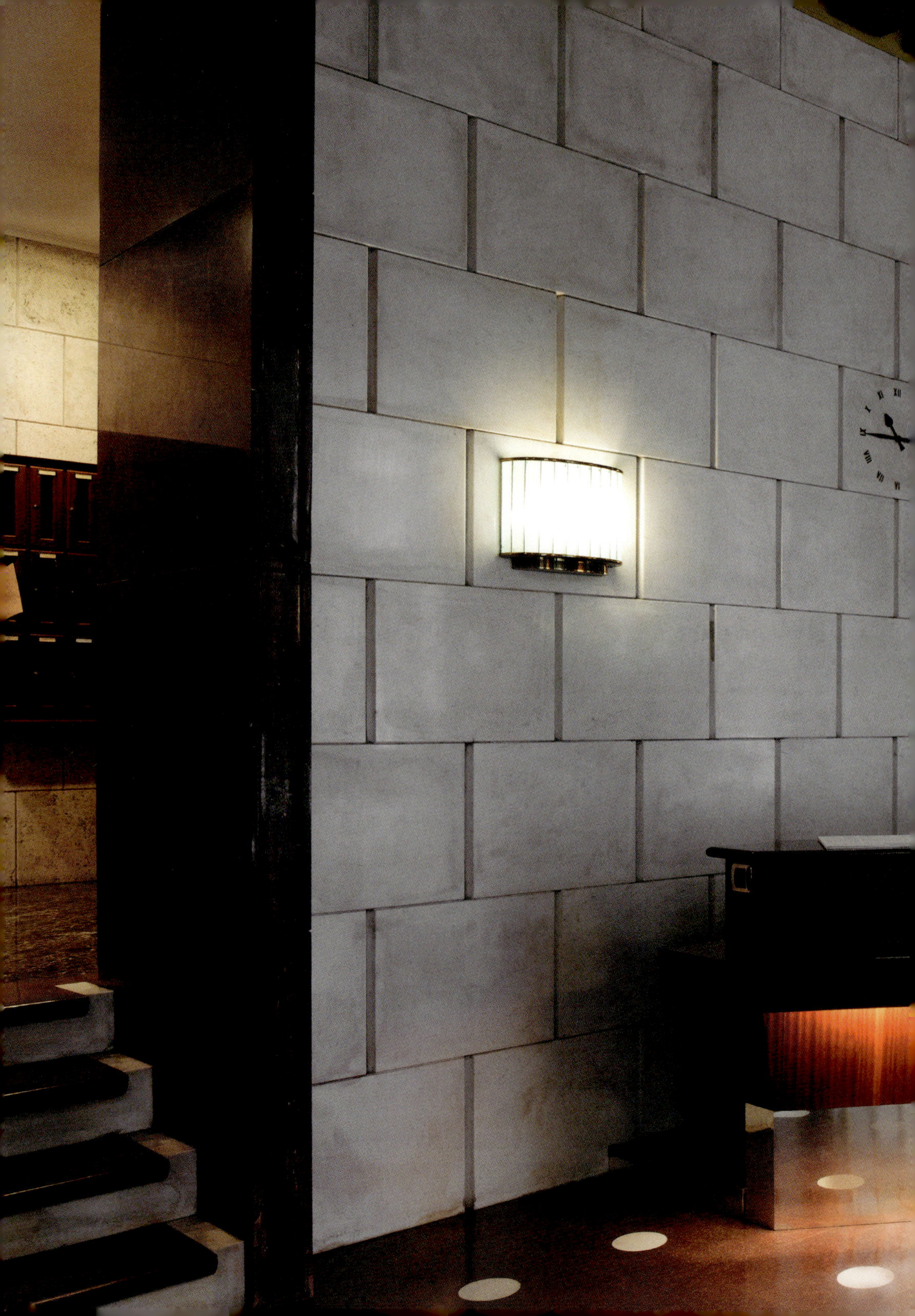

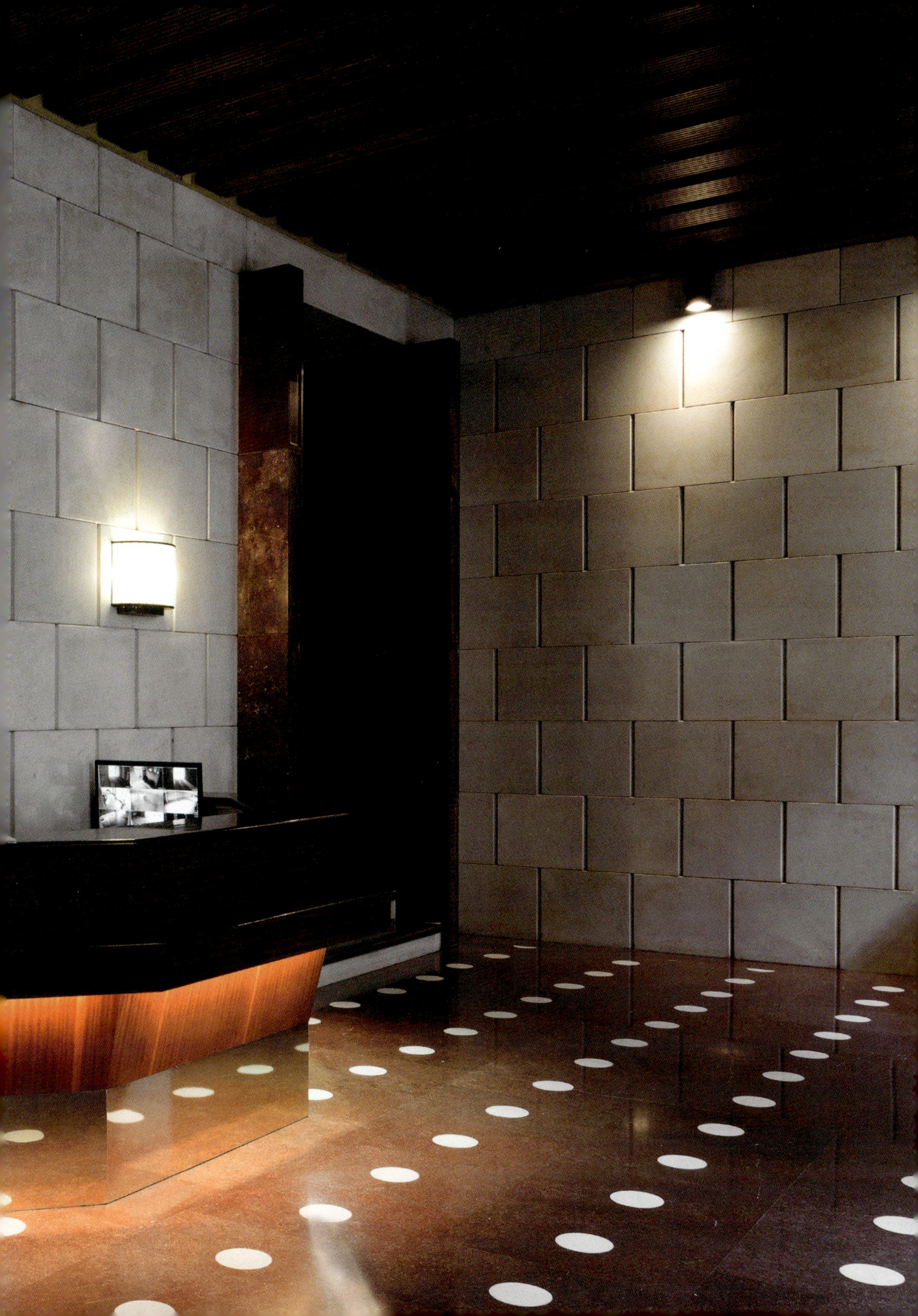

ROSSO PORFIRICO DI VERZEGNIS

Deep red in color with some small white grains, this limestone resembles porphyry, to which its name refers. Unlike porphyry stones, however, it can be polished. Quarried in the area of Udine, not far from places providing marbles such as Grigio Carnico and Fior di Pesco Carnico.

This and previous spread:
via Antonio Baldissera 5 · Giovanni Bertolaia, 1939–41
floor, stairs, doorframe: Rosso Porfirico di Verzegnis · walls: white marble · floor (upstairs): Rosso Levanto ophicalcite opus incertum *· walls (upstairs): travertine*

Following spread:
viale Regina Giovanna 32 · Giuseppe Roberto Martinenghi, 1936–38
Textured glass infill panels by Fontana Arte.
floor: Palladiana of Botticino limestone and Rosso Levanto ophicalcite · walls: Botticino limestone skirting, lesene: Breccia Aurora limestone

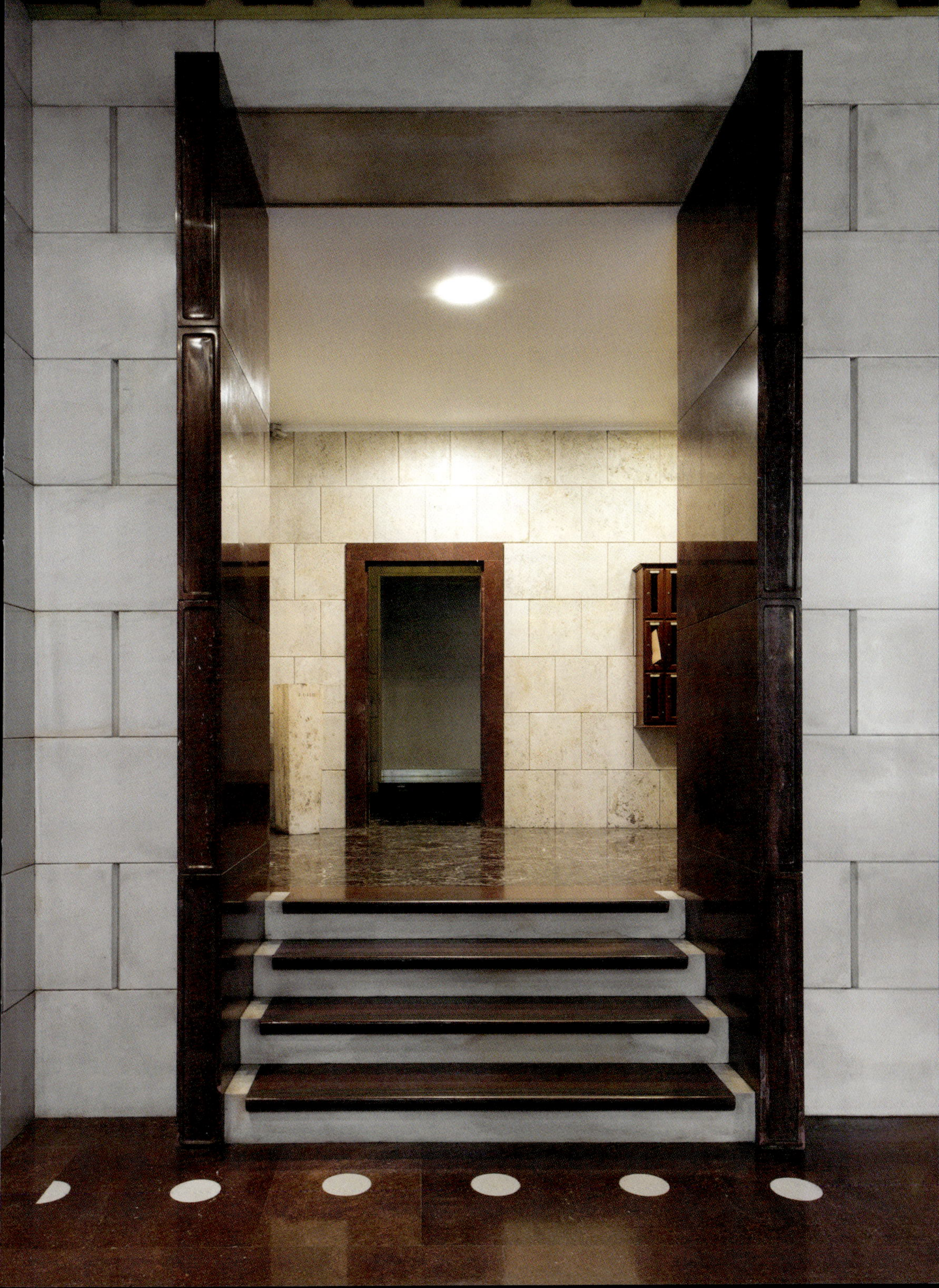

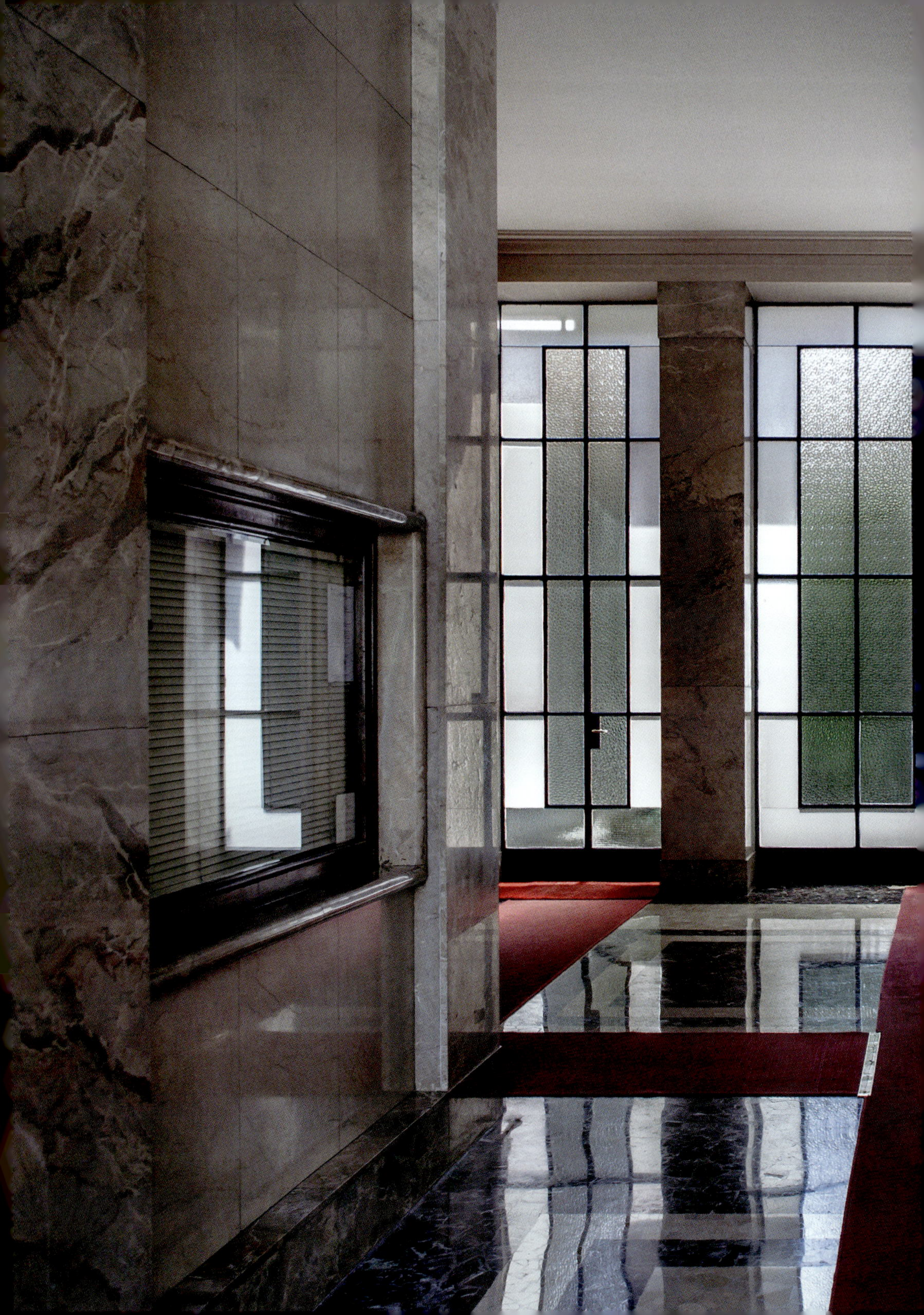

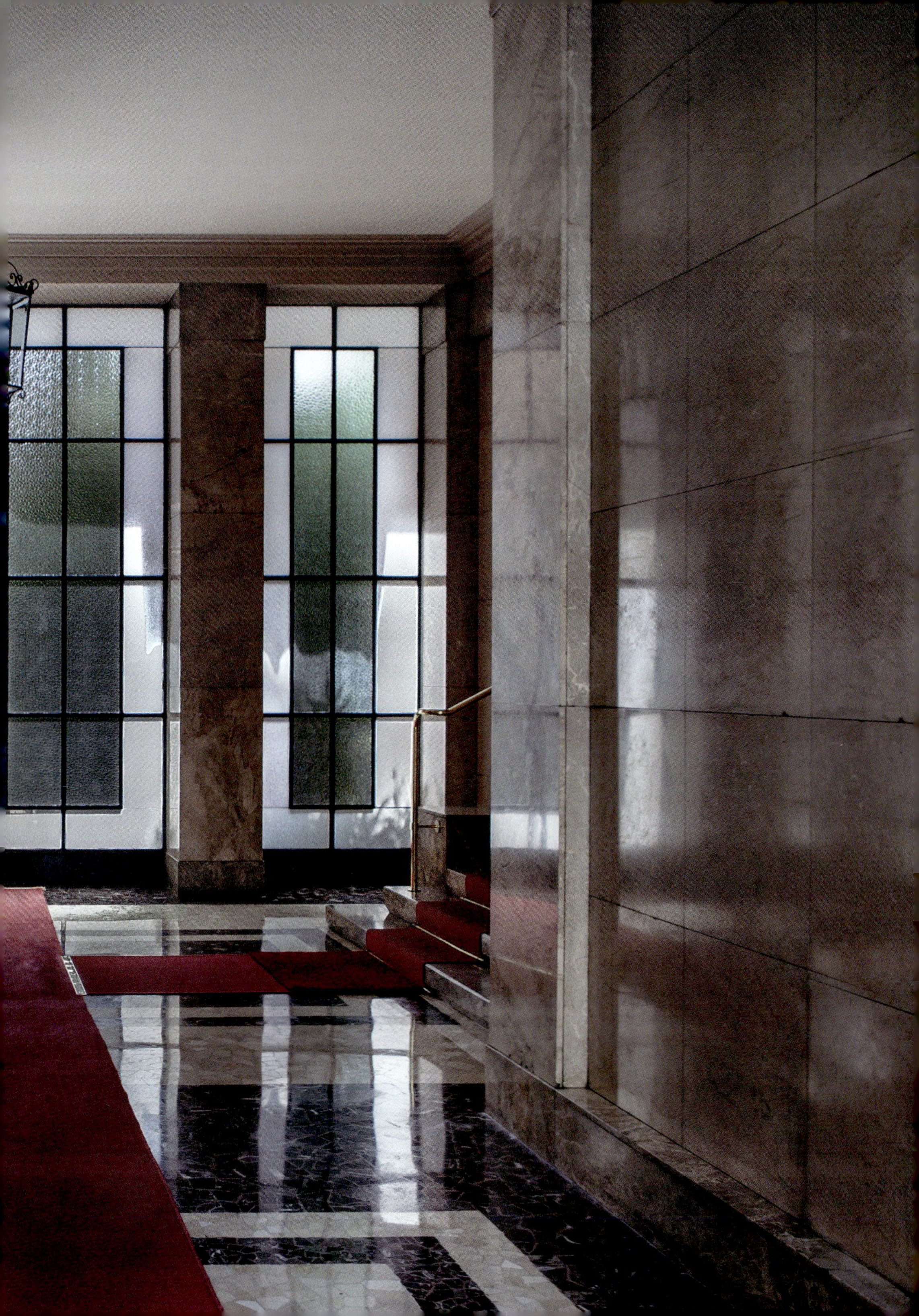

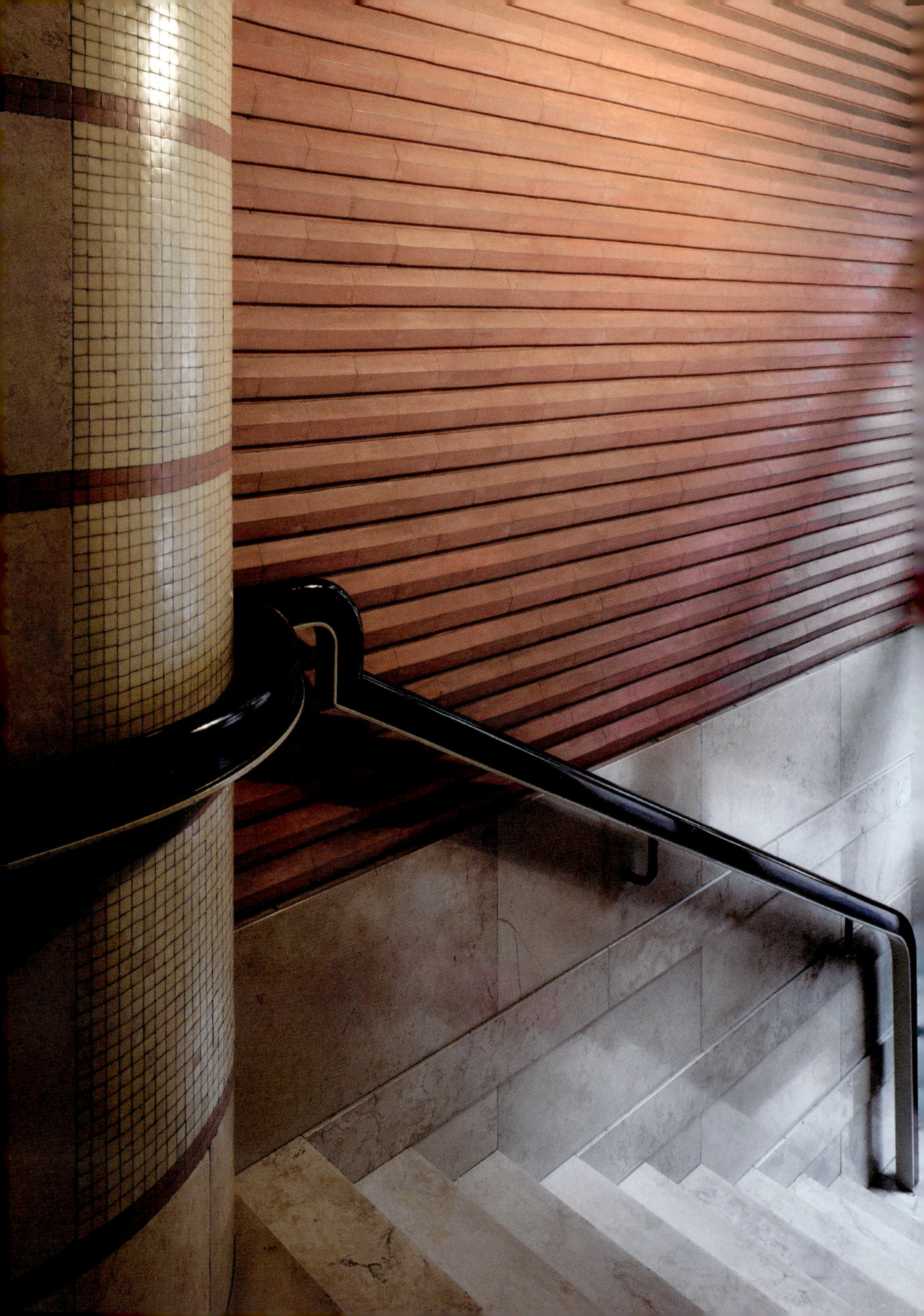

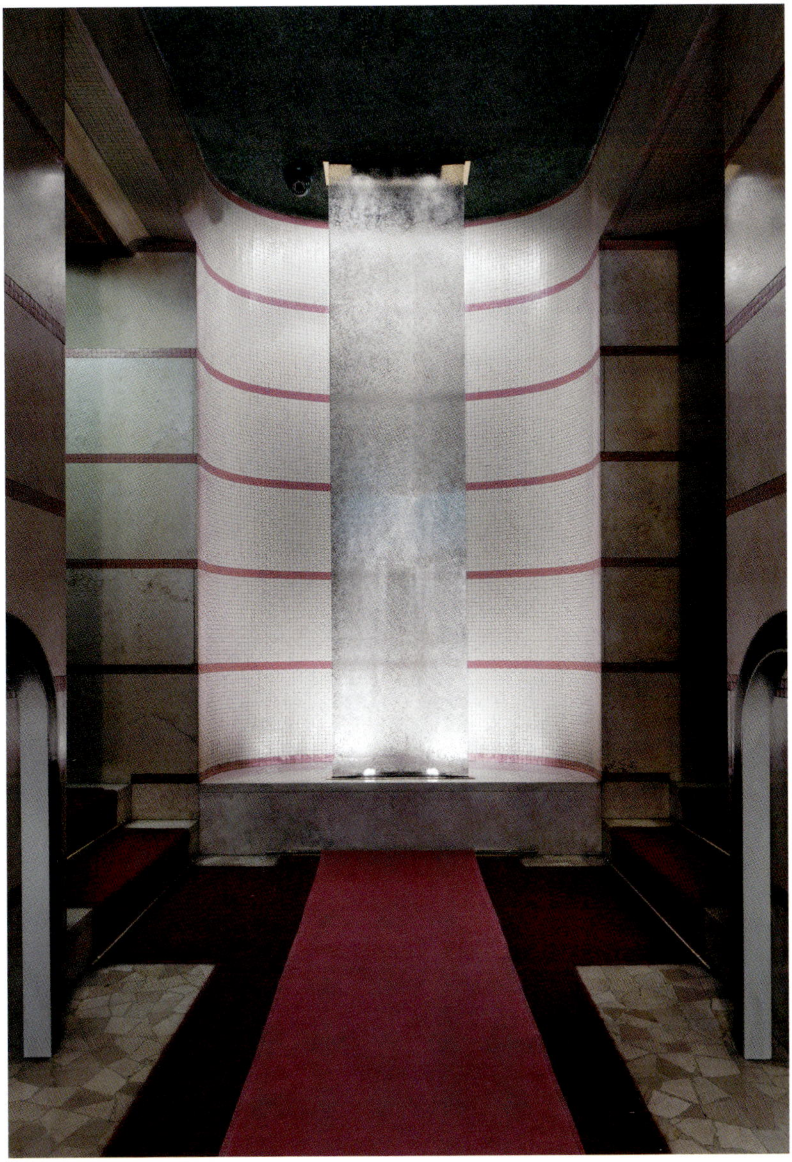

viale Regina Giovanna 8, 1938

floor, stairs and walls: Trani limestone

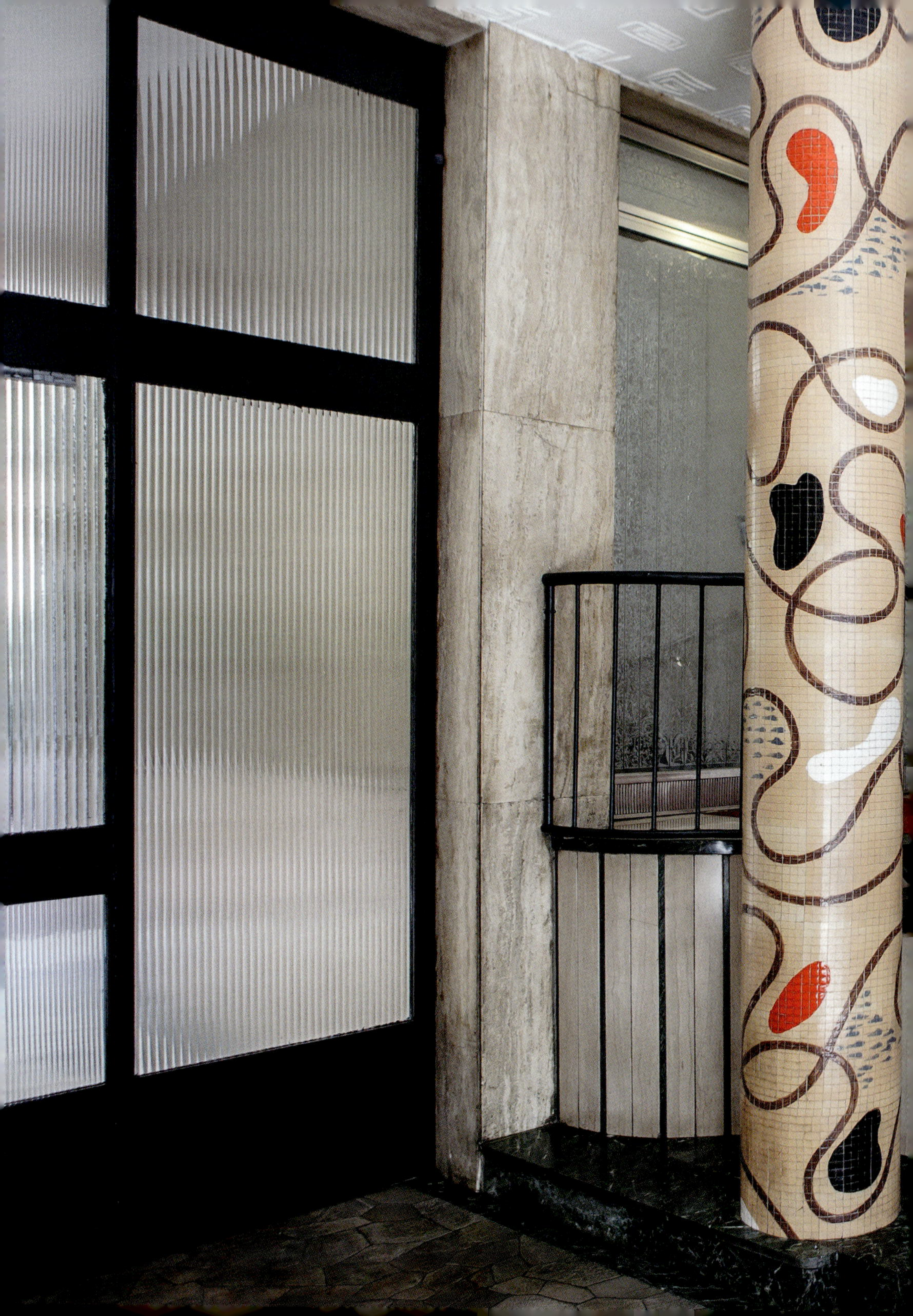

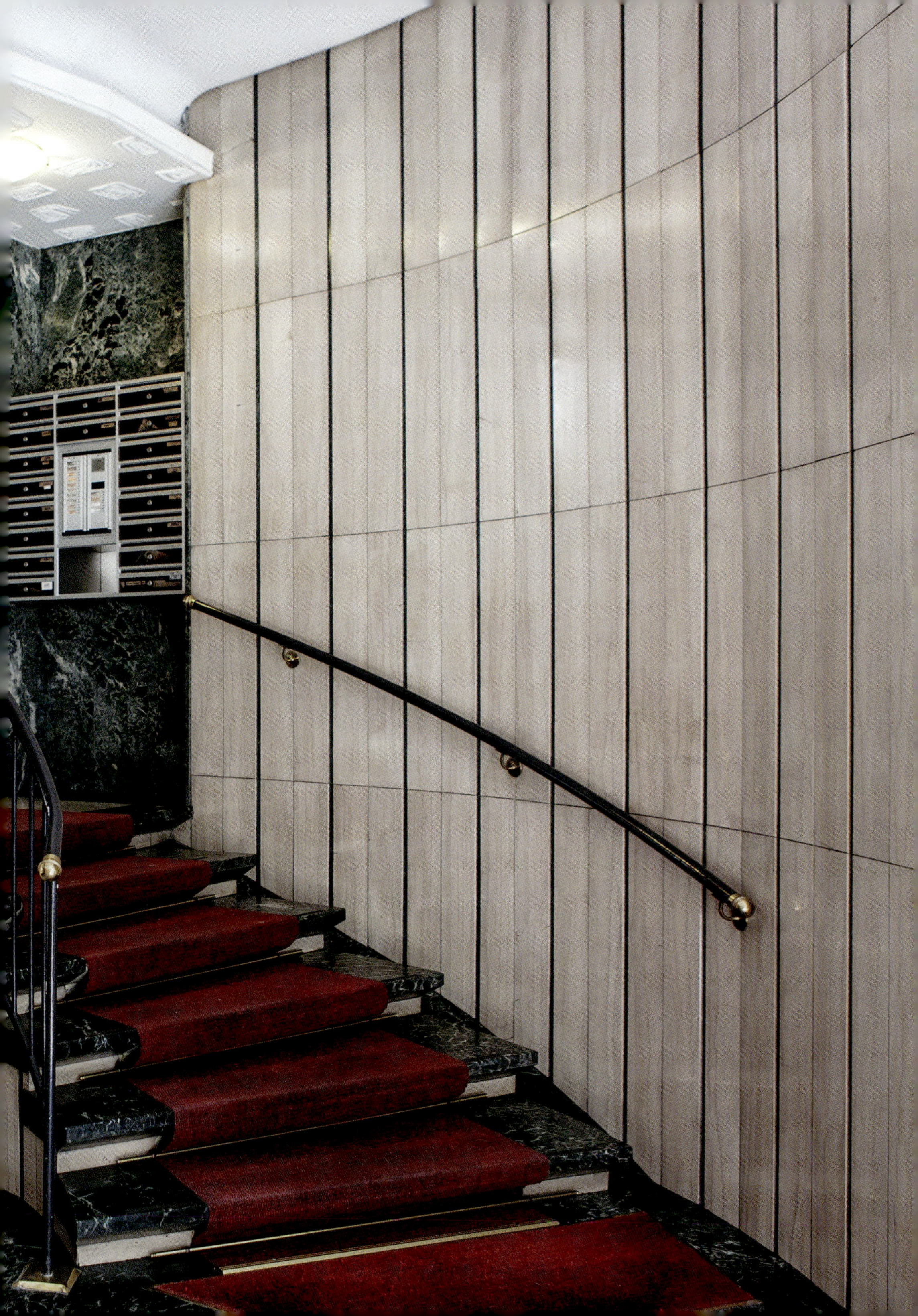

TERMINOLOGY

Over the centuries, the stone industry has developed its own language, which, in fact, is more related to manufacturing processes than to scientific definitions and petrological families. Consequently the industry's use of the terms "marble" or "granite" is different to the scientific or geological use of these terms. The term "marble" is derived from the Greek root "marmaros," meaning "shining stone." Commercially, any carbonate rock that has an ability to accept a polish is called "marble." The name is sometimes used for other soft rocks, such as polishable travertine, ophicalcites, serpentine, and many limestones. Petrologists and geologists refer to marble as a metamorphic crystalline carbonate rock, such as Carrara marbles. The term "granite" comes from the Latin "granum," or "grain," which refers to the grainy appearance of the rock. Commercially, any crystalline silicatic rock that has an ability to accept a polish is called "granite." The name is mainly used for magmatic rocks, meaning granites and other rocks such as syenites, tonalites, gabbros, diorites, and so on, and the corresponding metamorphic and polishable rocks such as gneisses, migmatites, and the like. The term "travertine" stems from Latin and refers to the region of Tivoli, where many hot springs formed huge deposits of layered and vacuolar carbonate rocks in the last million years. Romans quarried and named it Lapis Tiburtinum. Both the industry and petrologists agree with the name travertine as a designation. Polishing is a very important part of the stone processing dimension, as it makes the rock shine and enhances colors, patterns, and designs. Nevertheless, for some rocks polishing could be expensive or would not affect the final aspect. The industry classifies these rocks as stones. Whenever possible, stone identifications in this book refer to scientific denominations or to petrological families.

Previous spread:

via Achille Maiocchi 9 · Stefano Ferrario, 1955–57

floor: opus incertum *Quarzite di Barge, Verde Alpi ophicalcite · stairs: Verde Alpi ophicalcite · wall: travertine*

via Alvise Cadamosto 2 · Augusto Amatori, 1934

doorframe: Cardoso sandstone · threshold and external cladding: Bardiglio marble

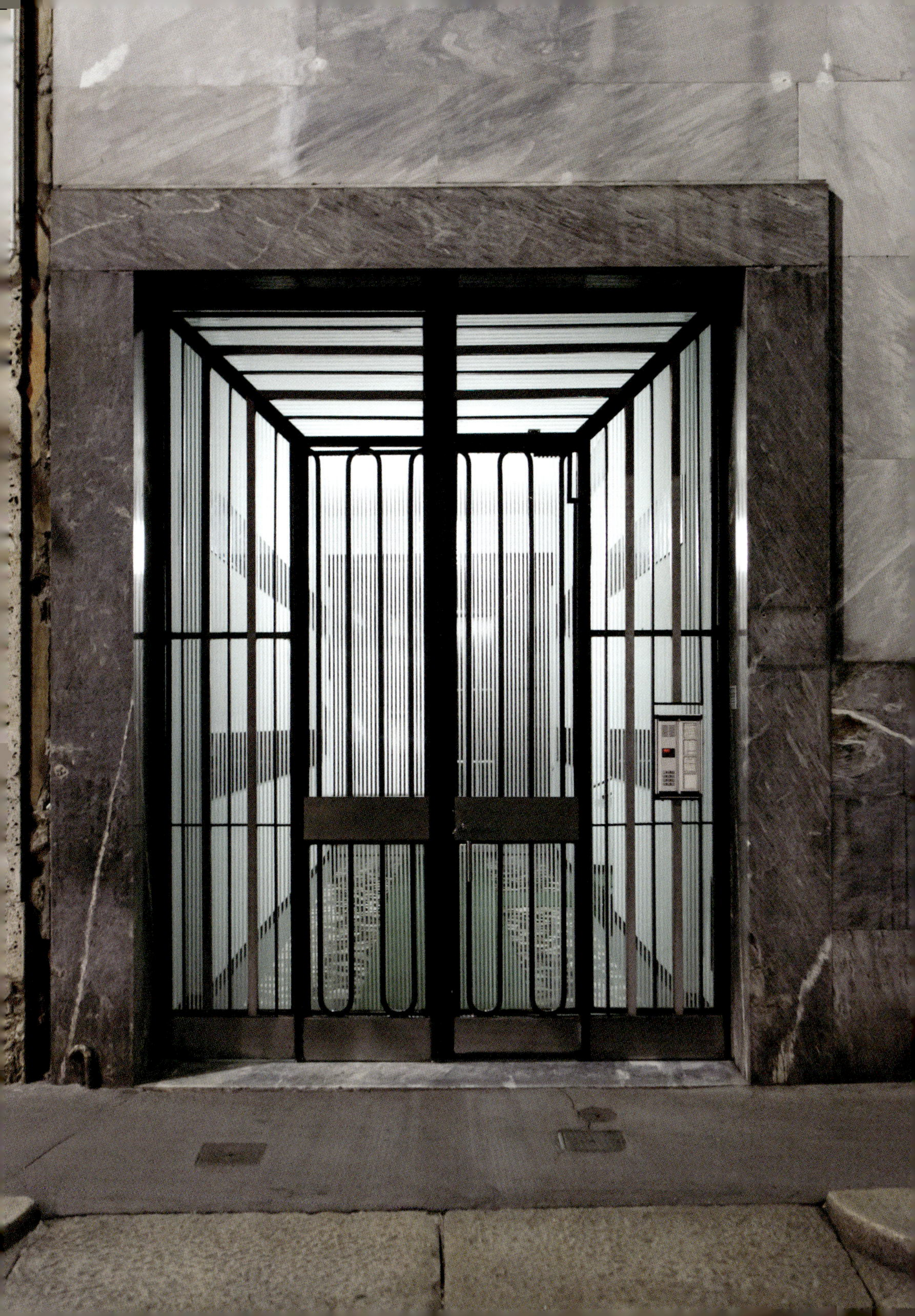

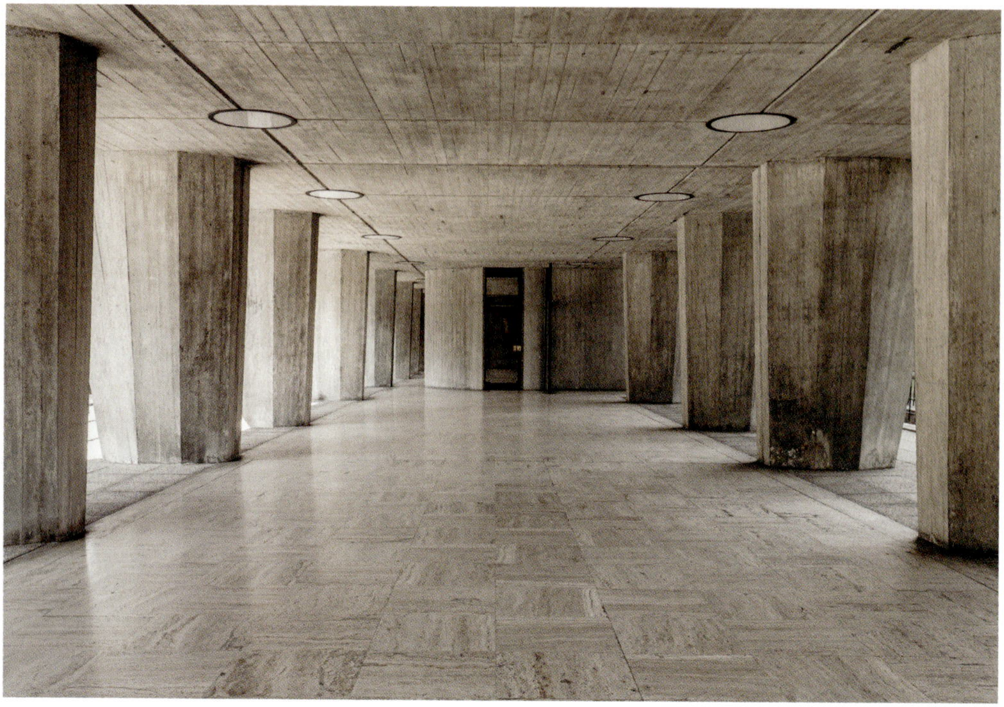

This and following spread:

piazza Leonardo da Vinci 3 · Giovanni Mistretta, 1966

Cascading Murano chandelier by Angelo Mangiarotti.

exterior floor: travertine

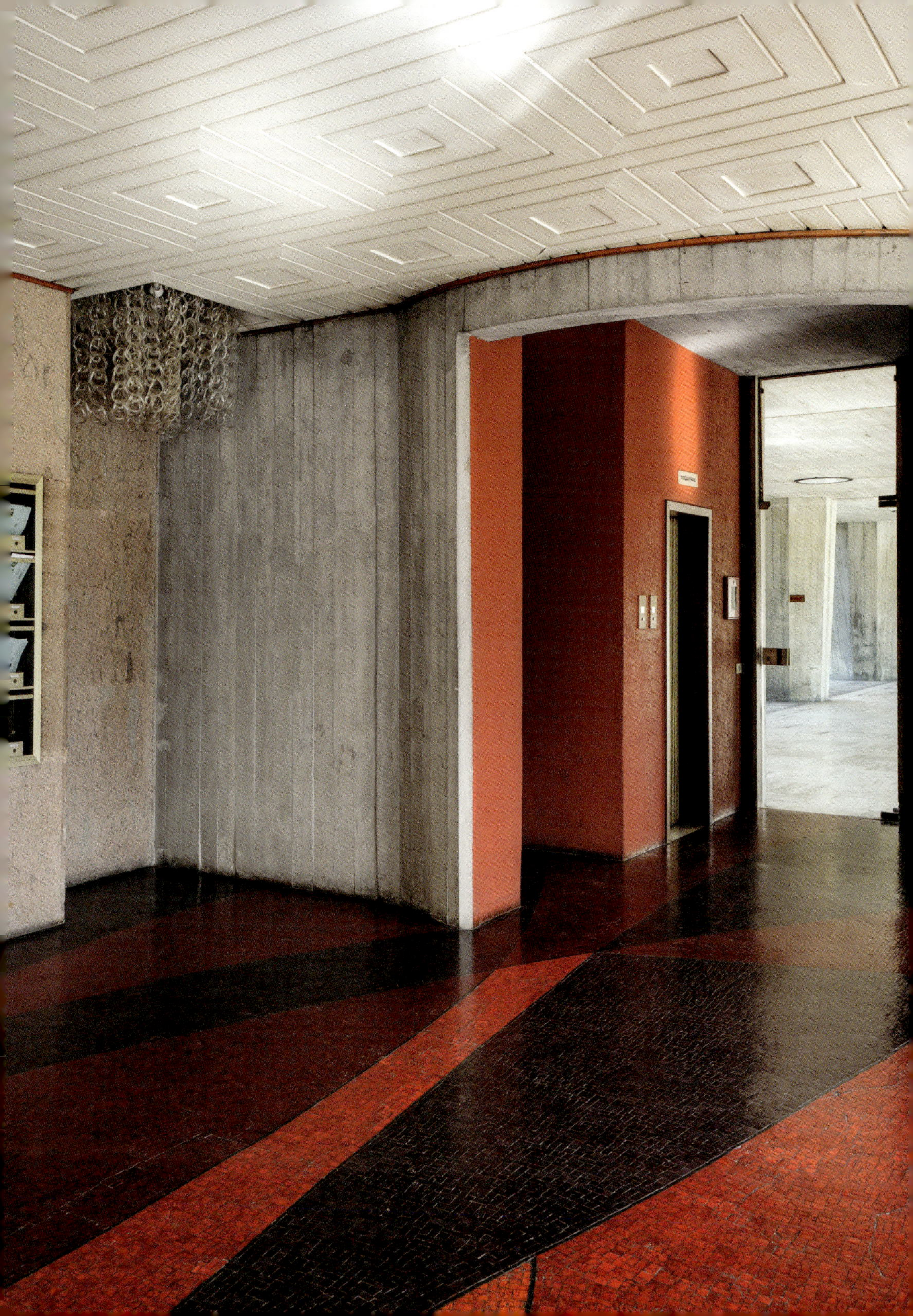

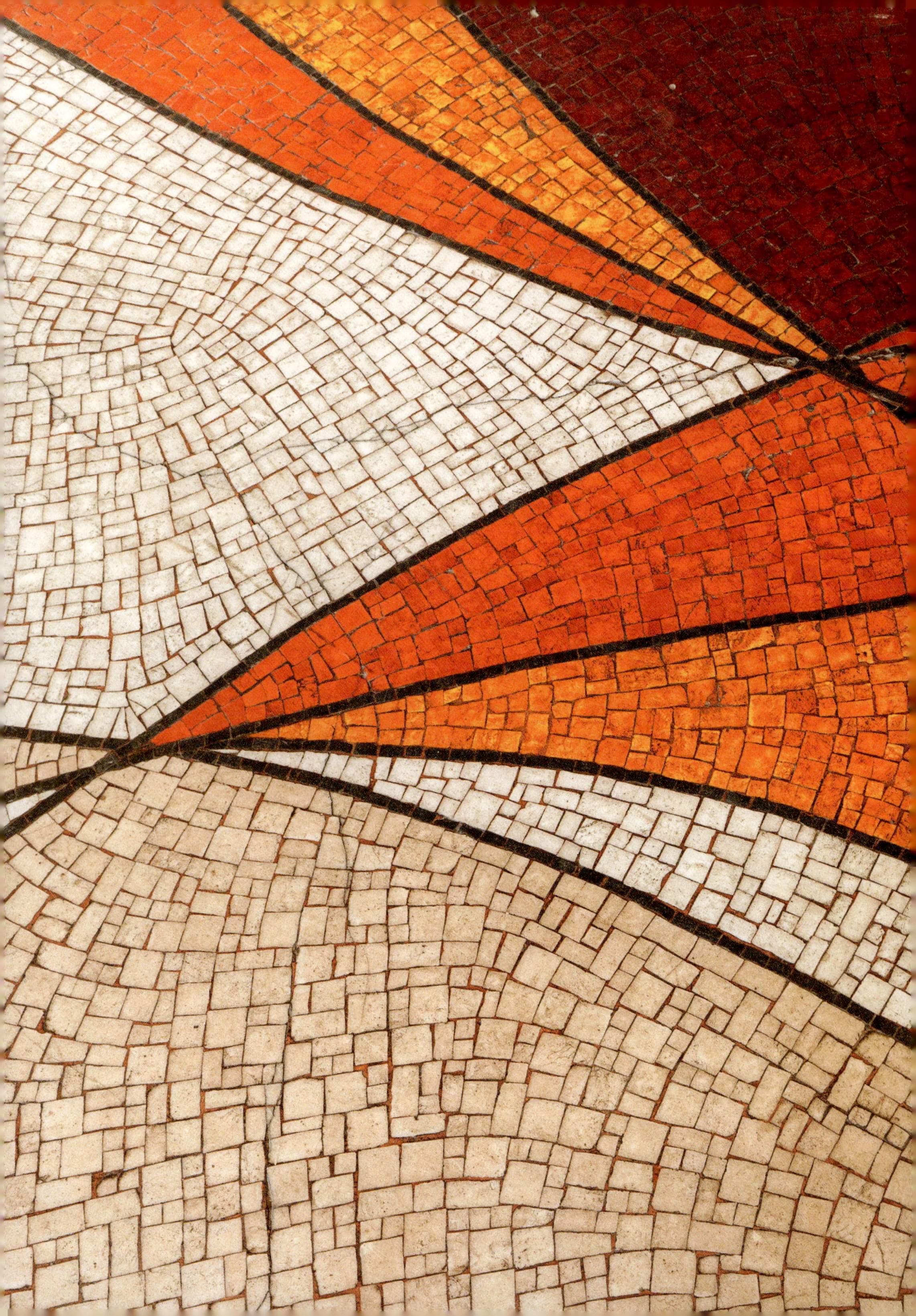

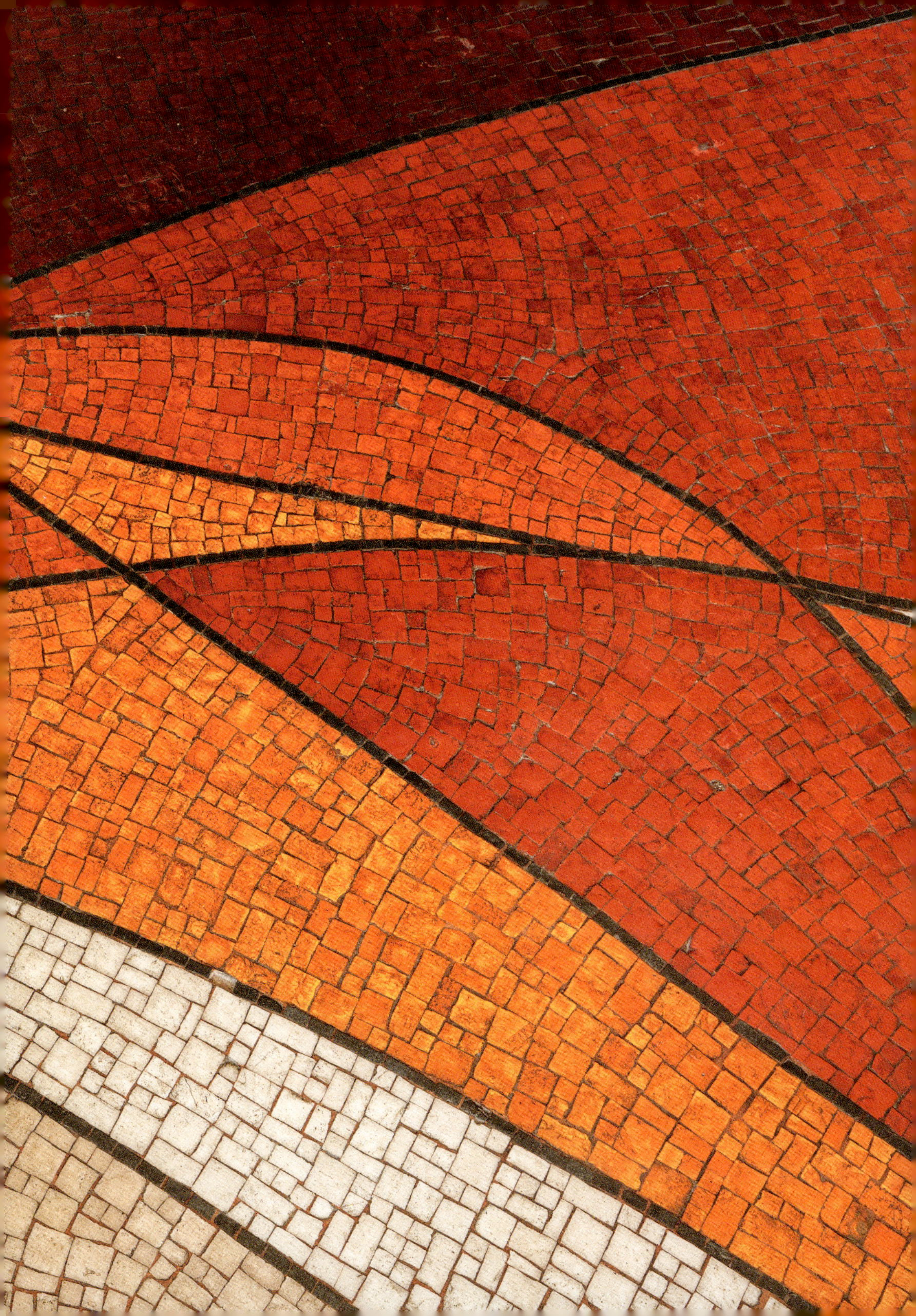

Trompe l'oeil devices were frequently used in 1930s Milanese apartment entrances: many were rendered in textured glass with iron tracery, unraveling endlessly diminishing vistas. These divertimenti were derived from Bramante's choir at Santa Maria presso San Satiro. That local matrix of future perspective designs in the city is plain to see in this example, though Borromini's Palazzo Spada in Rome could also be cited as a precedent.

via Renato Fucini 5 · Giuseppe Roberto Martinenghi, 1934–35

floor: Palladiana of white and dark marbles and limestones (Bardiglio and Portoro) · base: Nero Portoro limestone and graffiti · lesene: Macchiavecchia limestone breccia

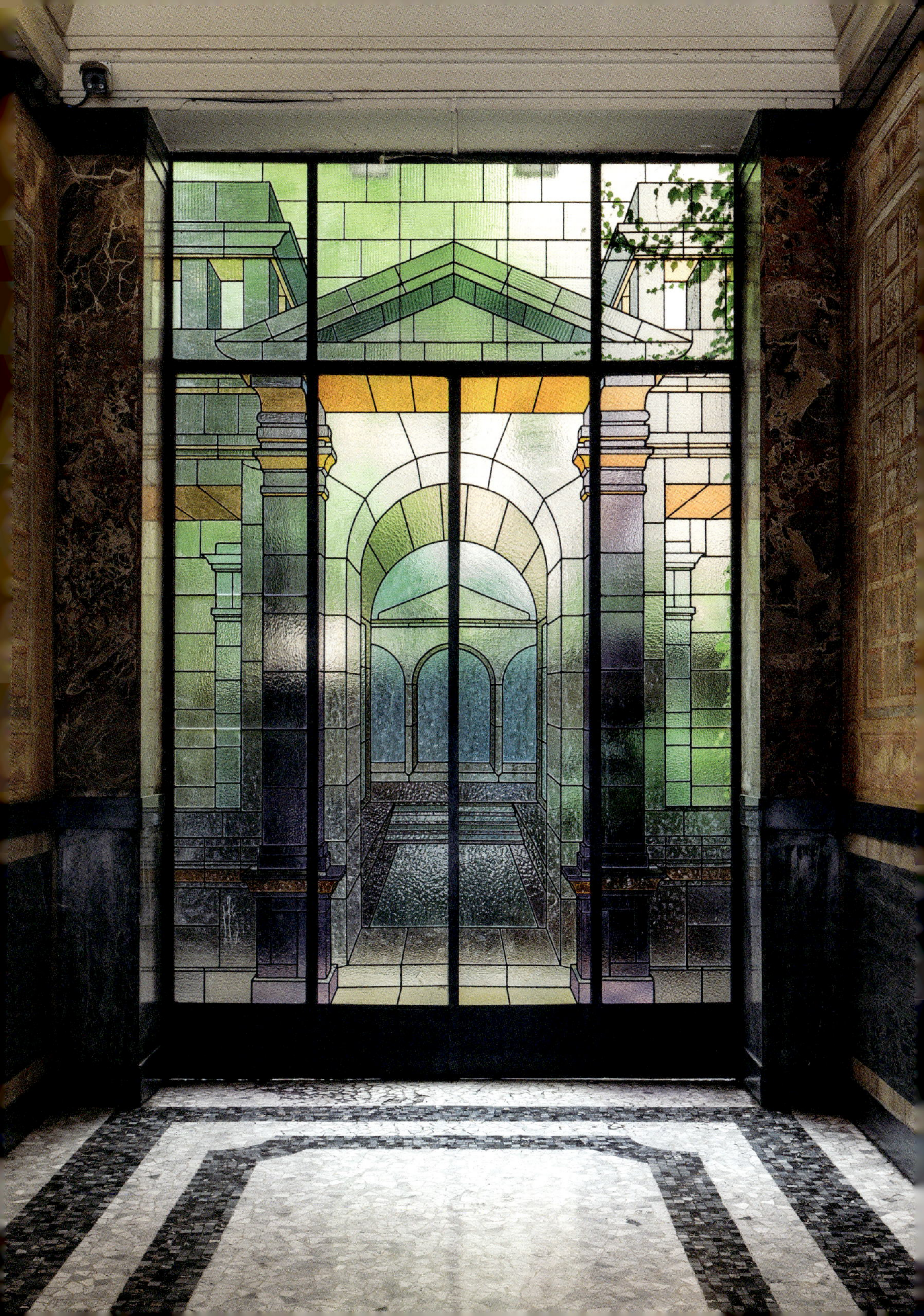

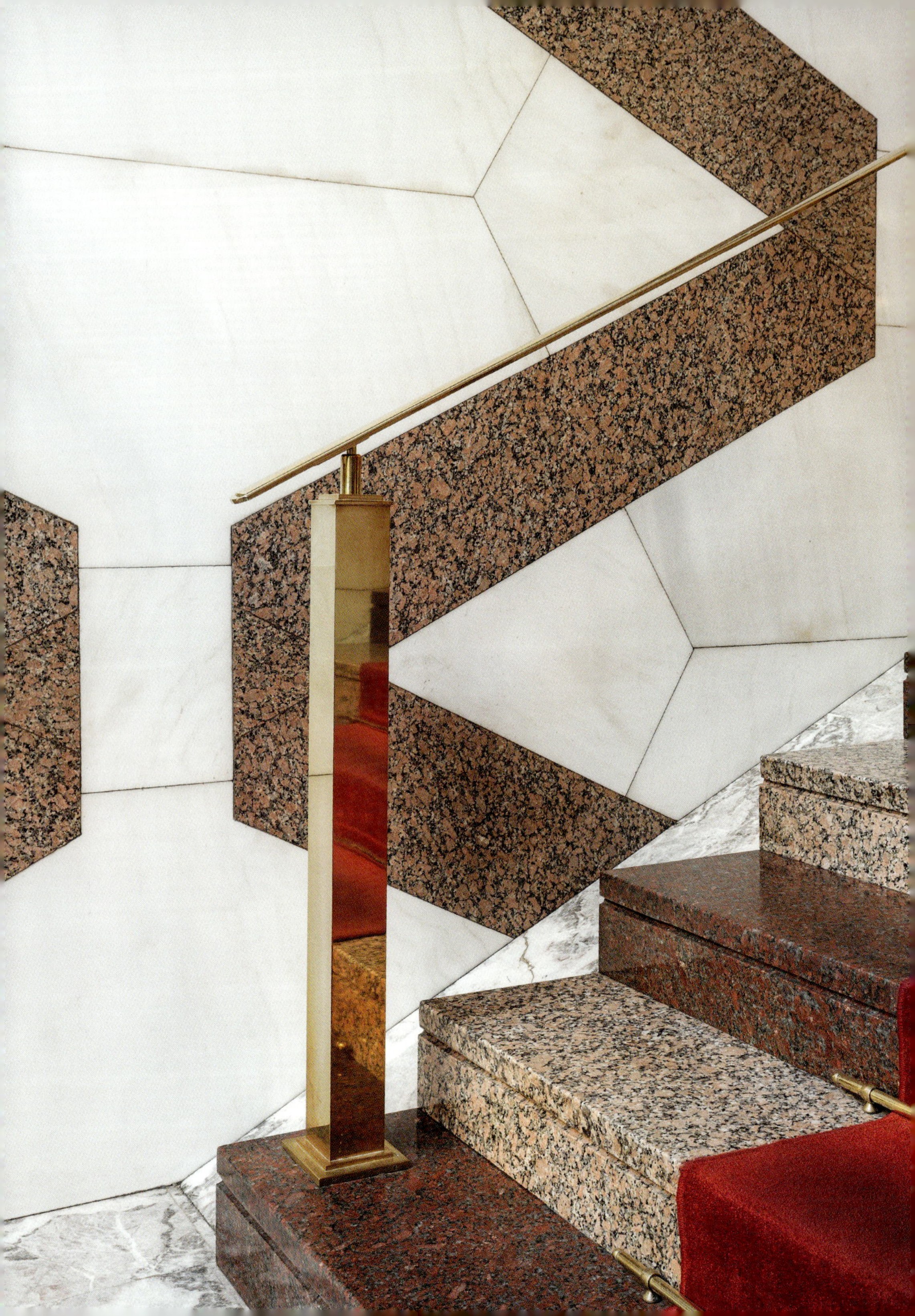

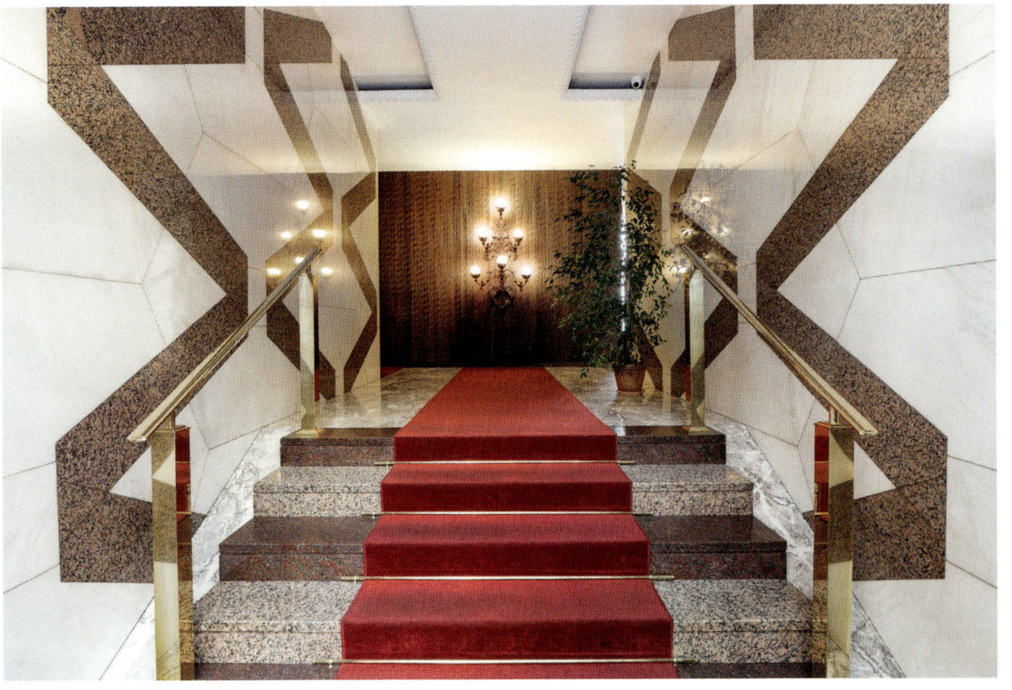

viale Lombardia 17, Casa Corbellini-Wassermann · Piero Portaluppi, 1935–36

floor: Fior di Pesco Carnico marble · stairs: Rosa Baveno granite and Rosso Imperiale della Svezia granite · walls: Lasa marble, Red Balmoral granite

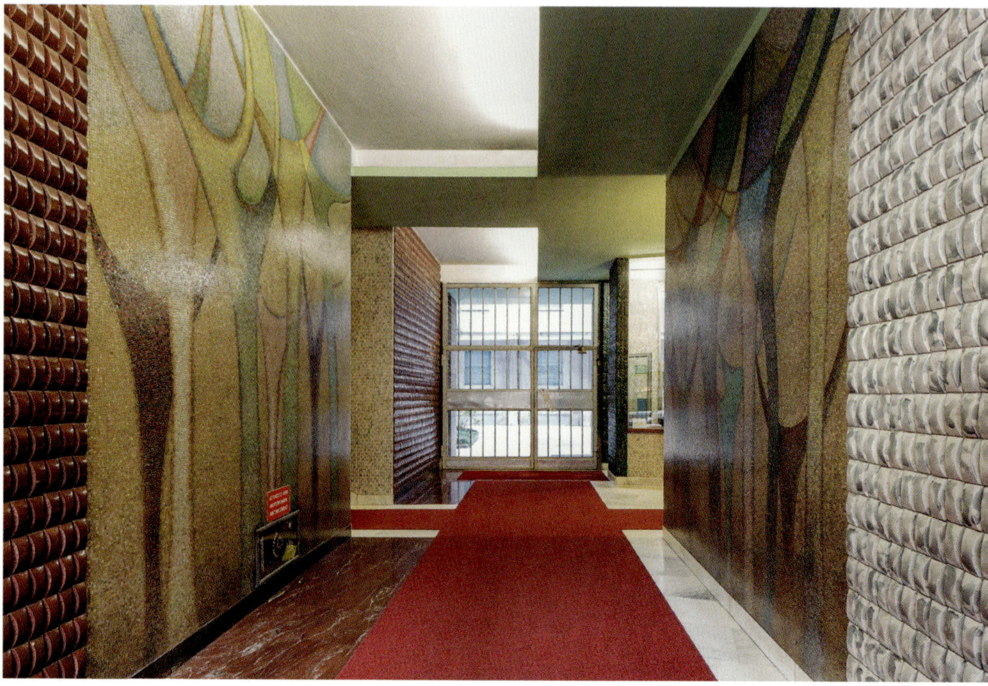

viale Lombardia 28

floor: Rosso Collemandina limestone and Carrara marble

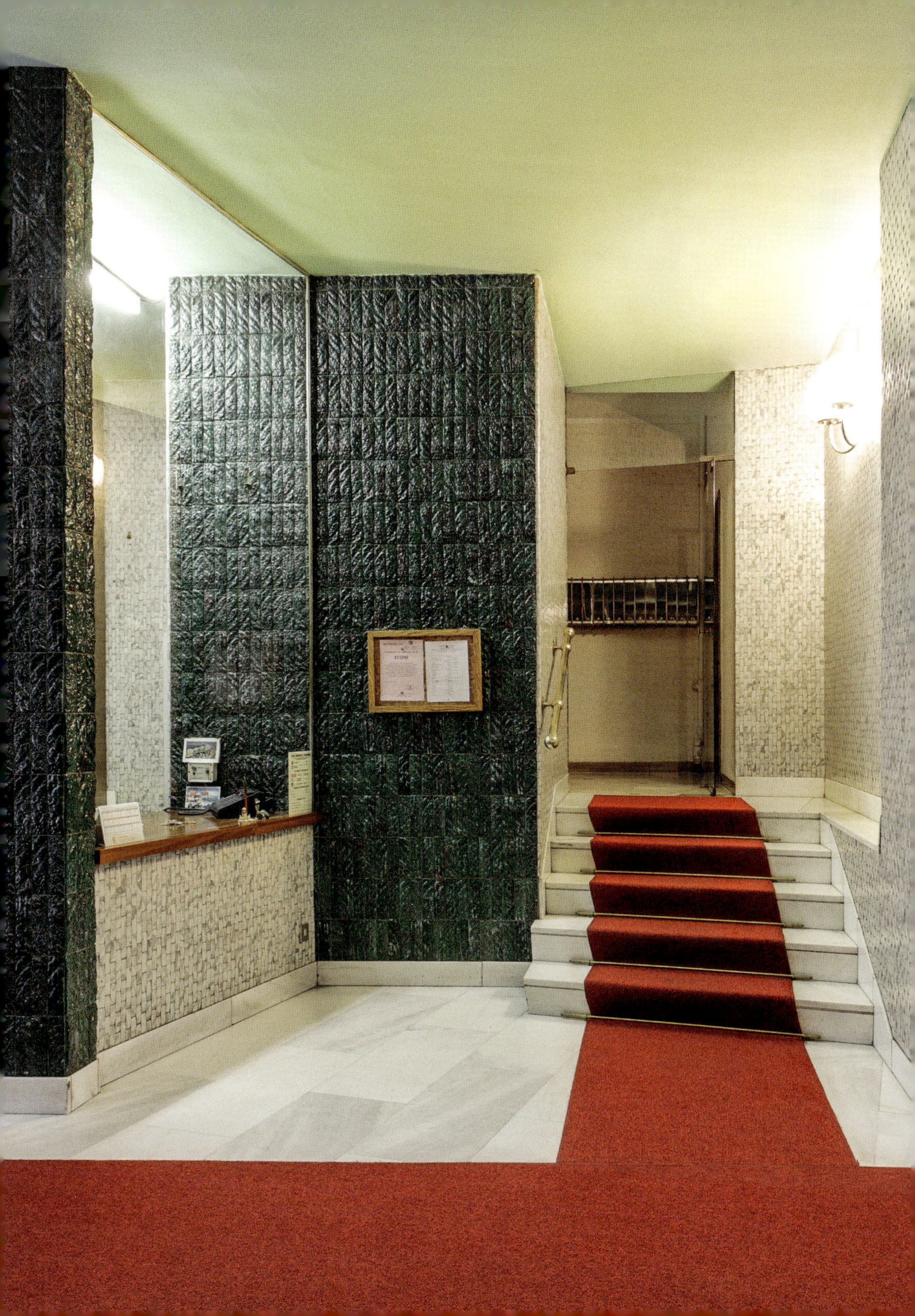

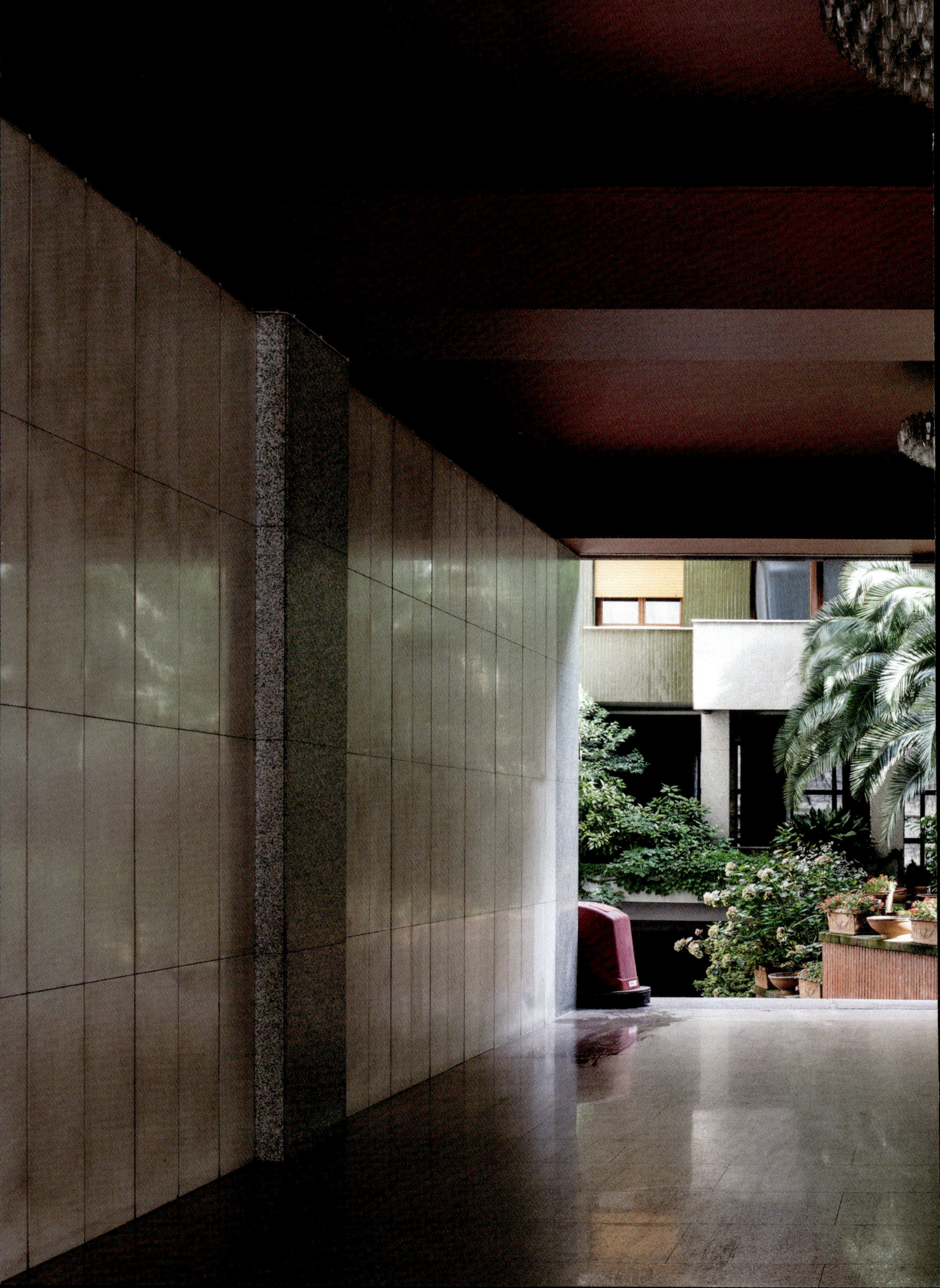

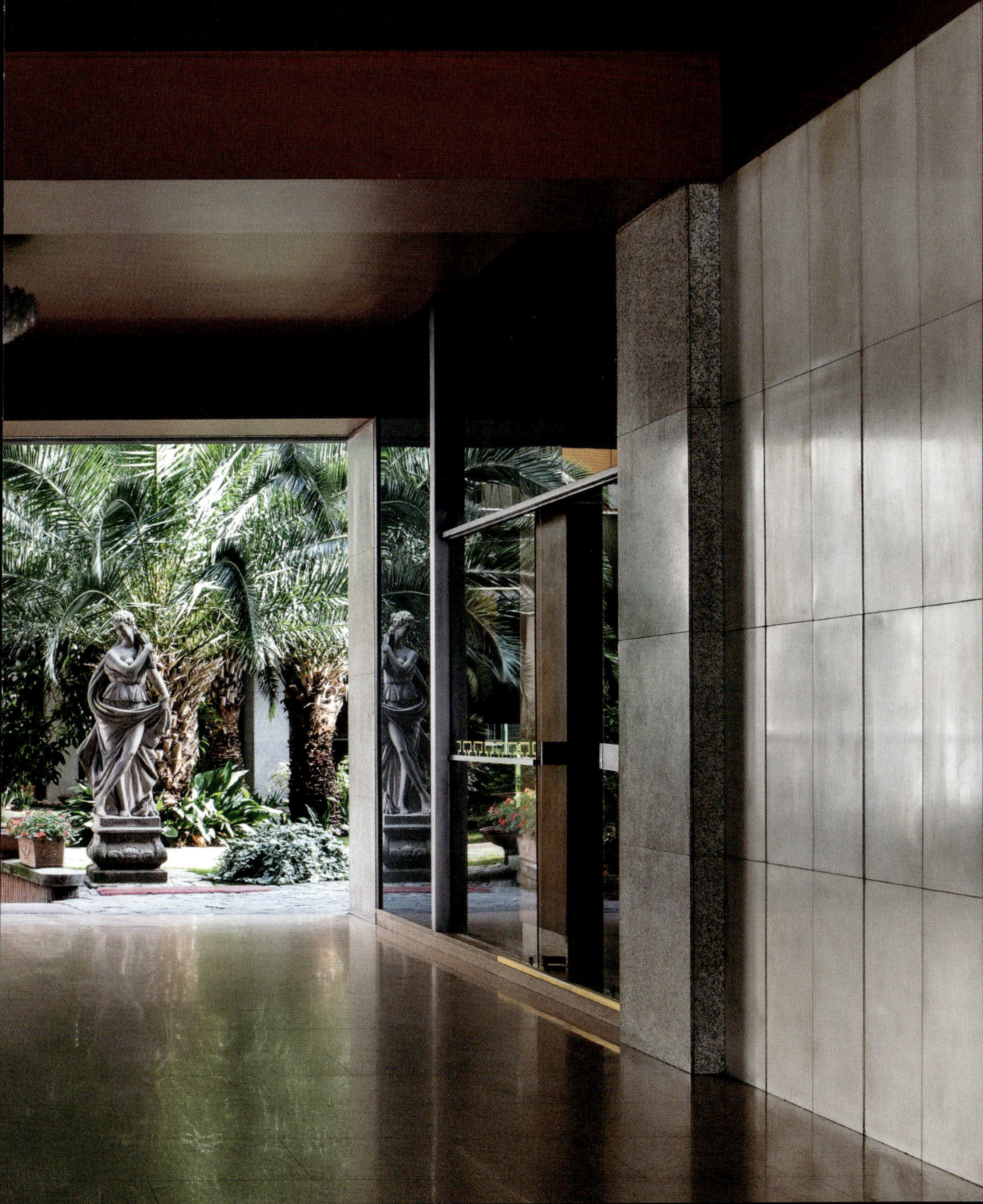

Previous spread:
viale Gran Sasso 3
Chandeliers by Venini · floor: Rosa Baveno granite
walls: Bianco Carrara marble and Bianco Montorfano granite

viale Gran Sasso 20
floor and stairs: Rosso di Svezia granite · walls: alabaster

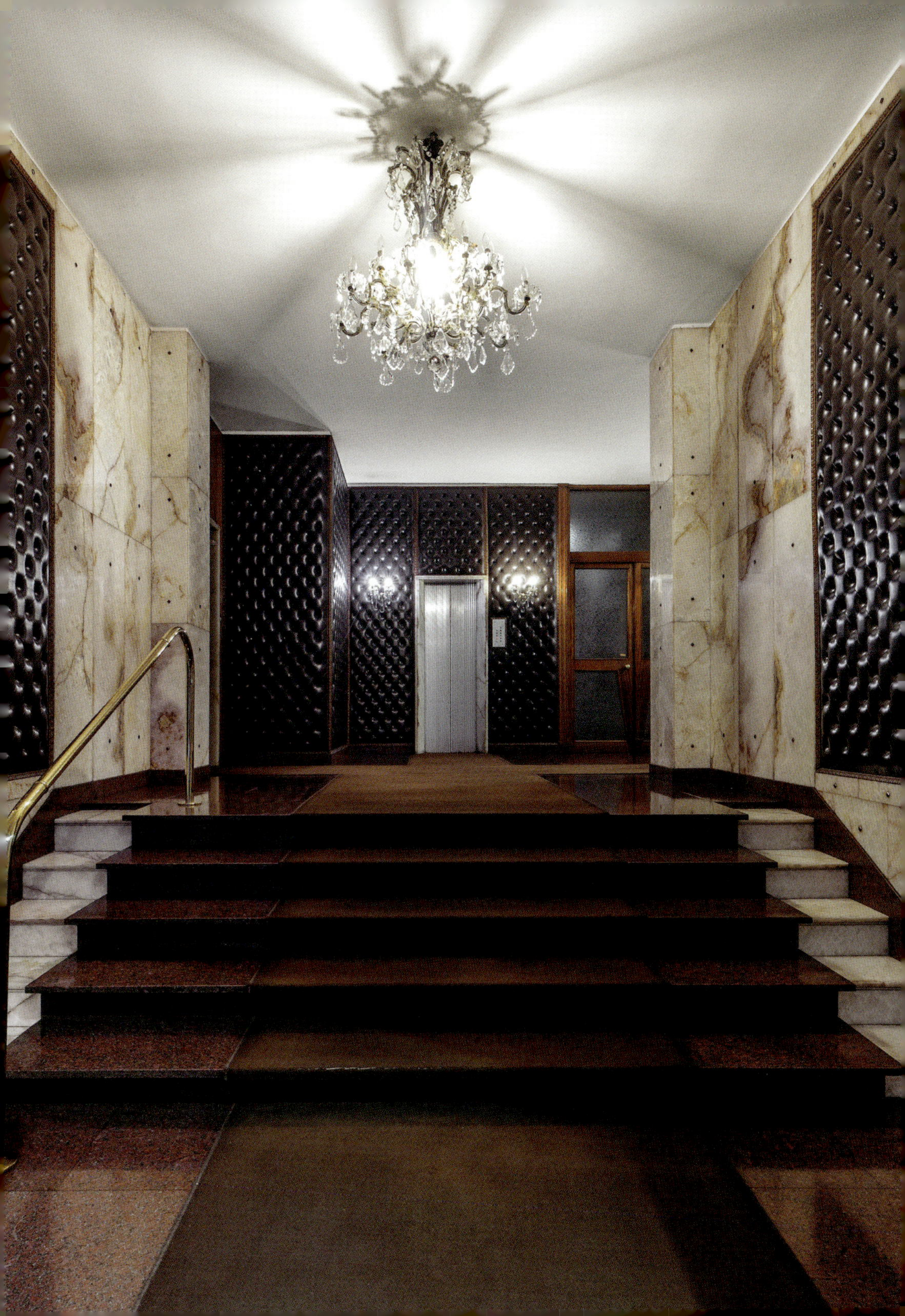

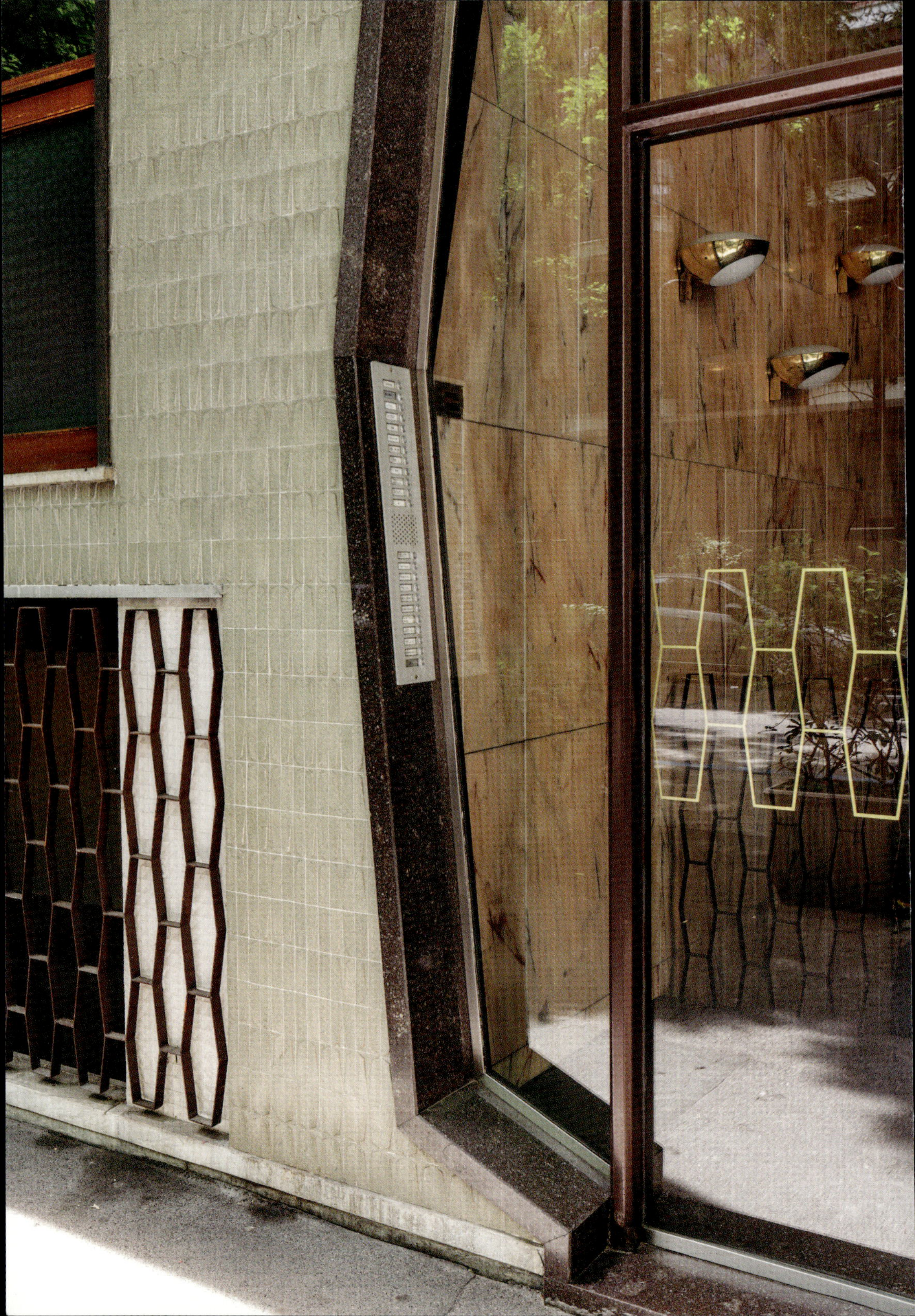

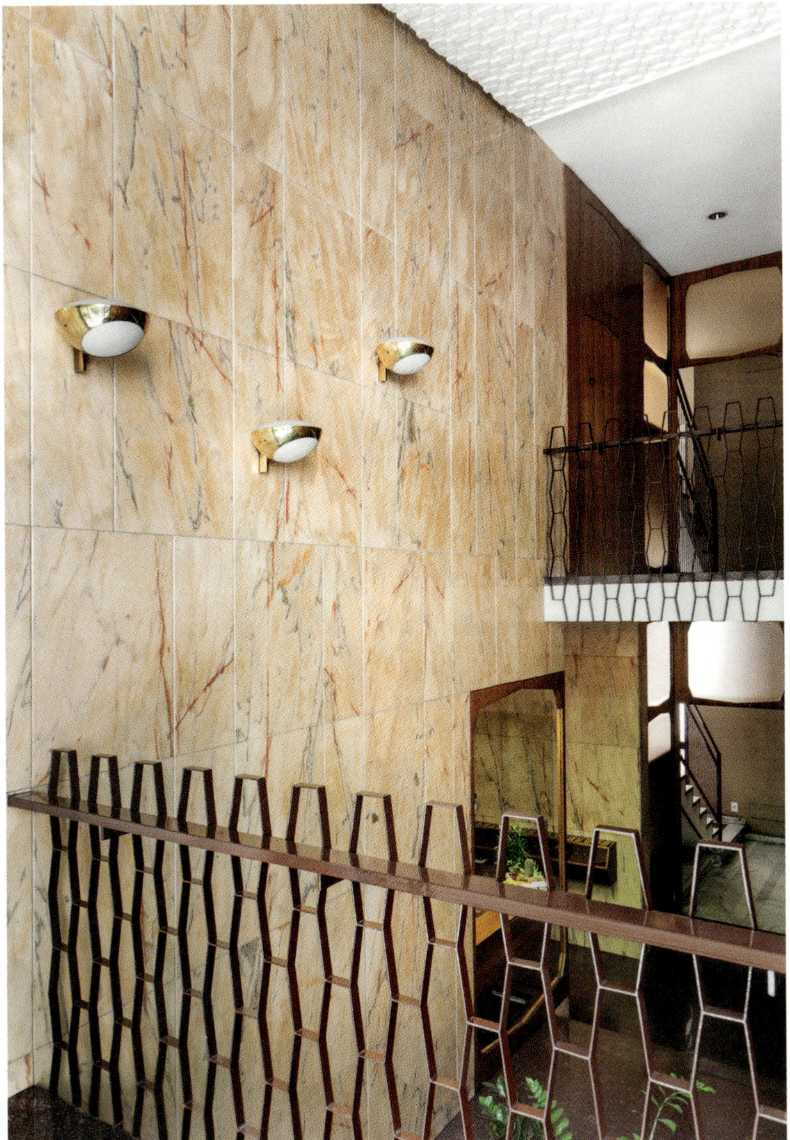

via Luigi Vanvitelli 3

Sconces by Stilnovo · doorframe: Porfido Monumentale di Bienno
interior walls: Rosa Portogallo Chiaro marble

via Luigi Vanvitelli 6A · Mario Hirsch, 1964–68

floor and stairs: Porfido Monumentale di Bienno

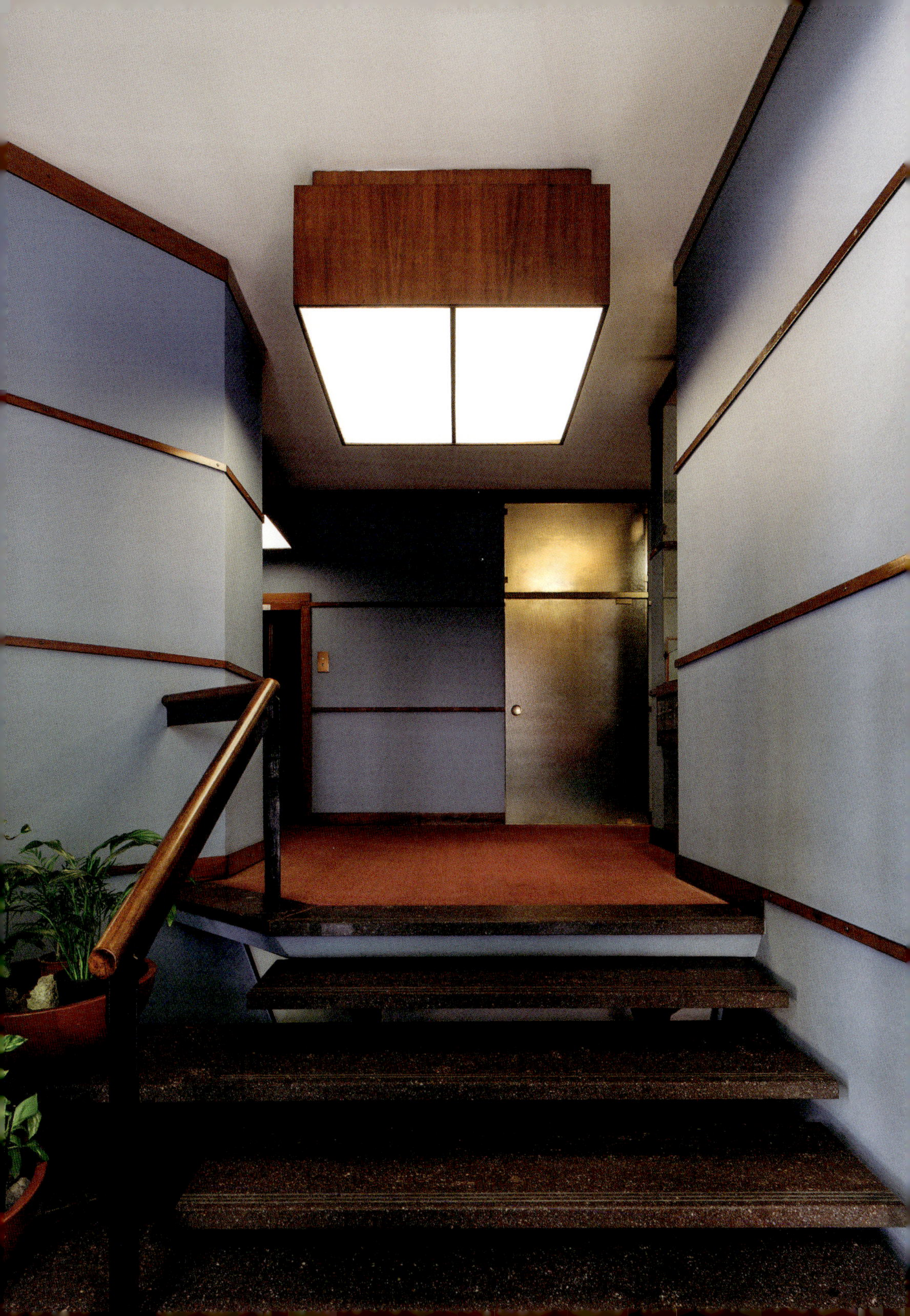

via Pinturicchio 11 · Pierluigi Requiliani, 1959–60

Pendant lamps by Artemide.
floor: Porfido Monumentale di Bienno with round Carrara marble inlays
skirting and stairs: Carrara marble, Porfido Monumentale di Bienno

Following spread:
via Plinio 59

Sconce by Luigi Caccia Dominioni.
floor: Verde Alpi ophicalcite · walls: Arabescato Carrara marble

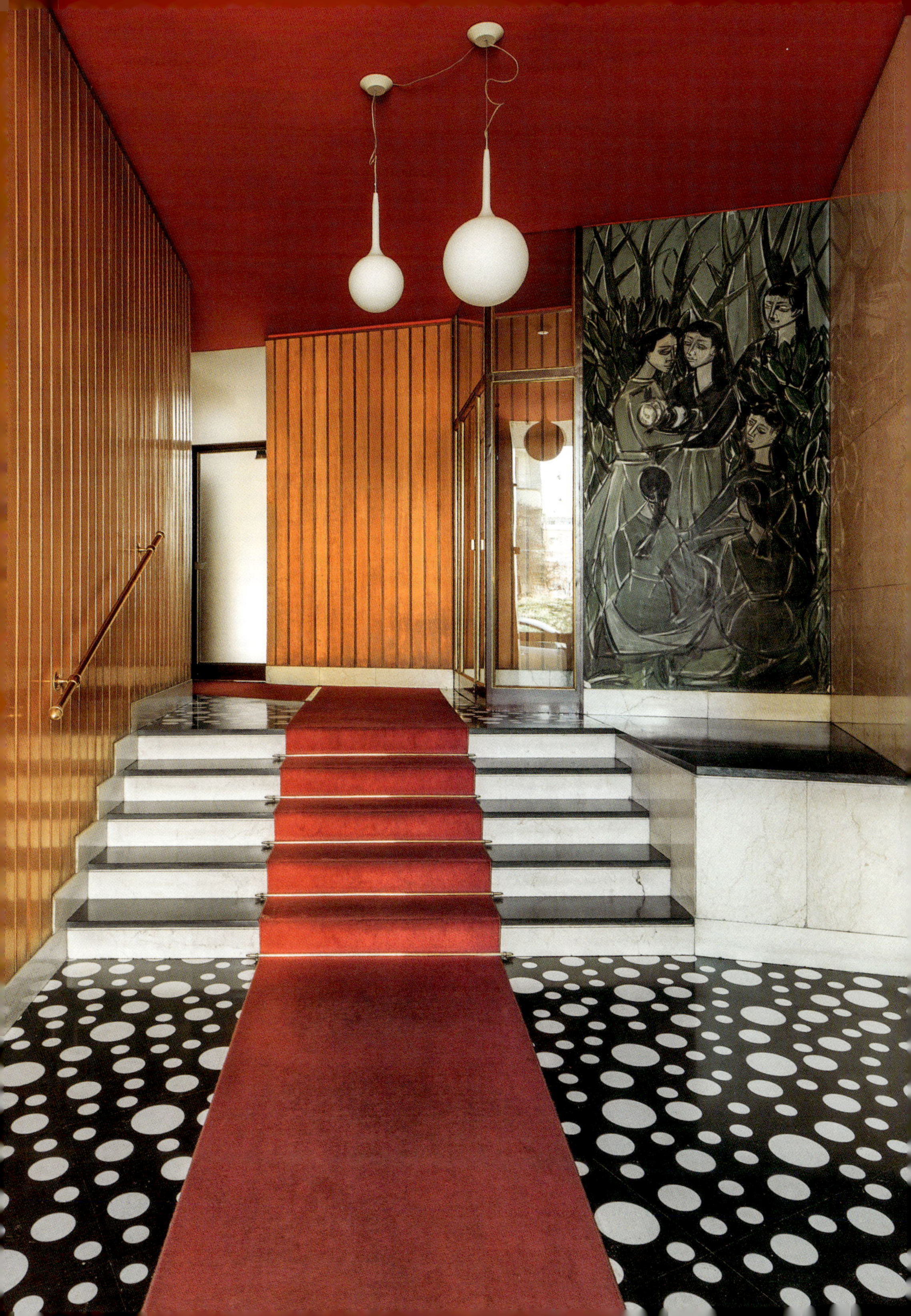

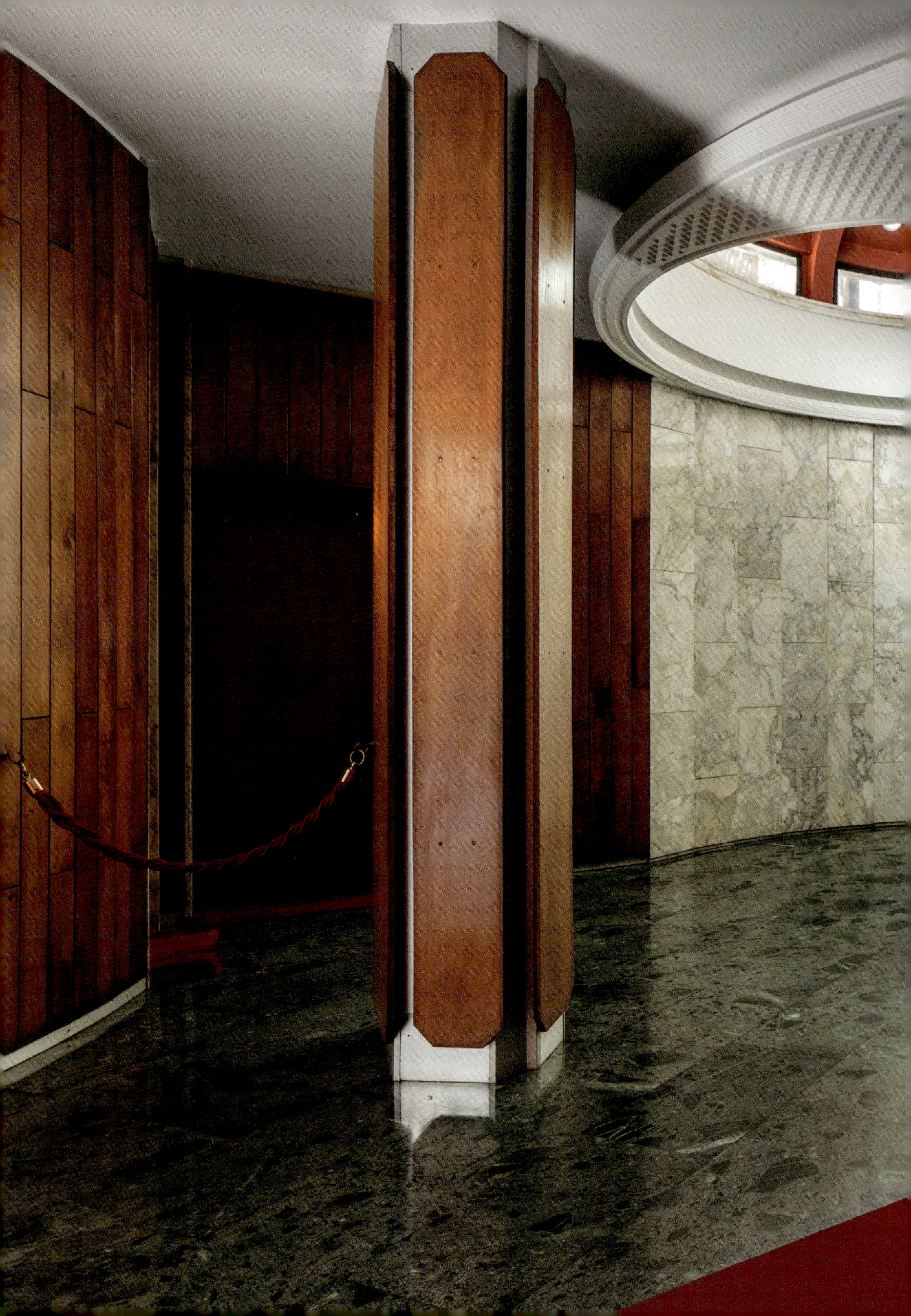

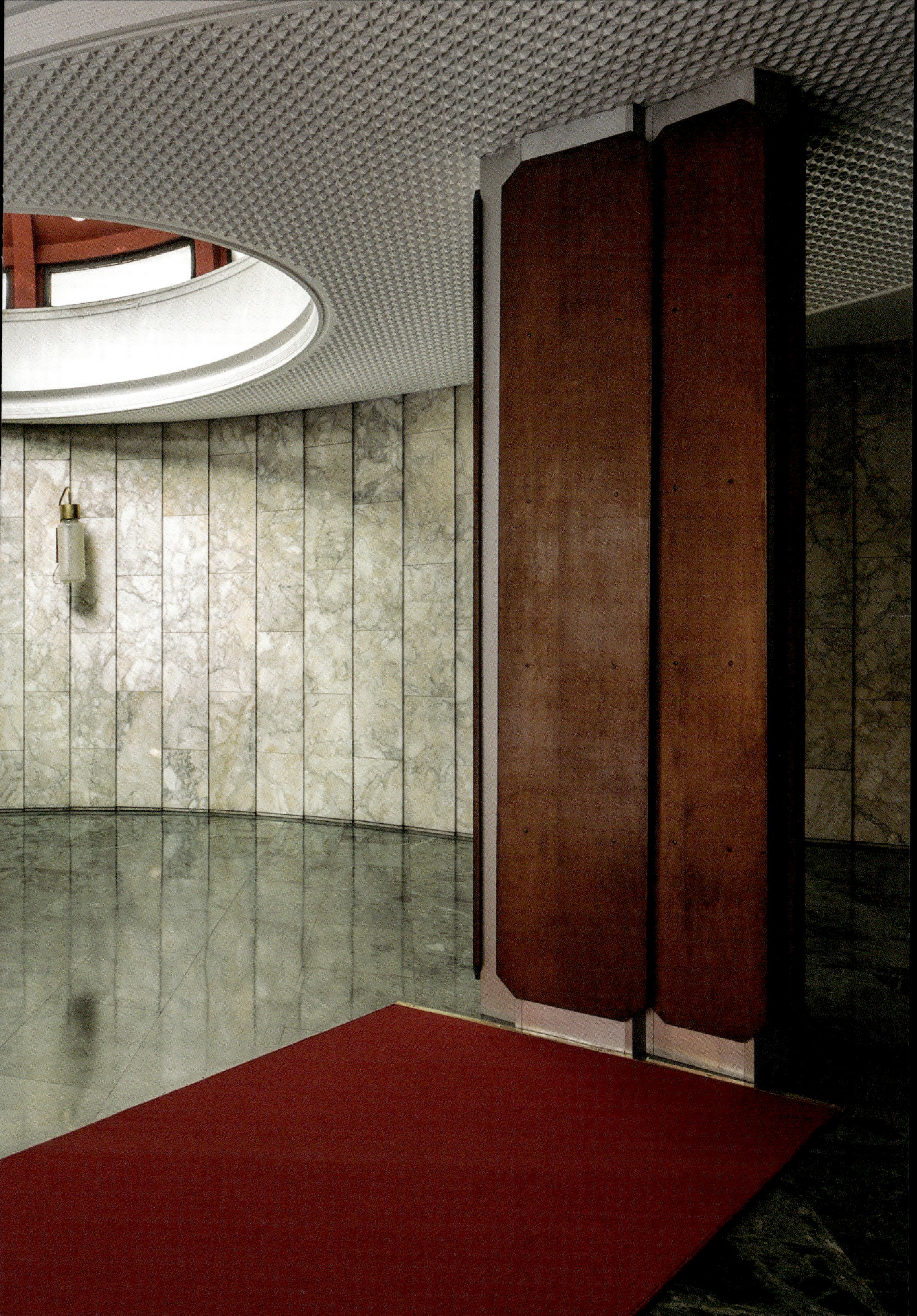

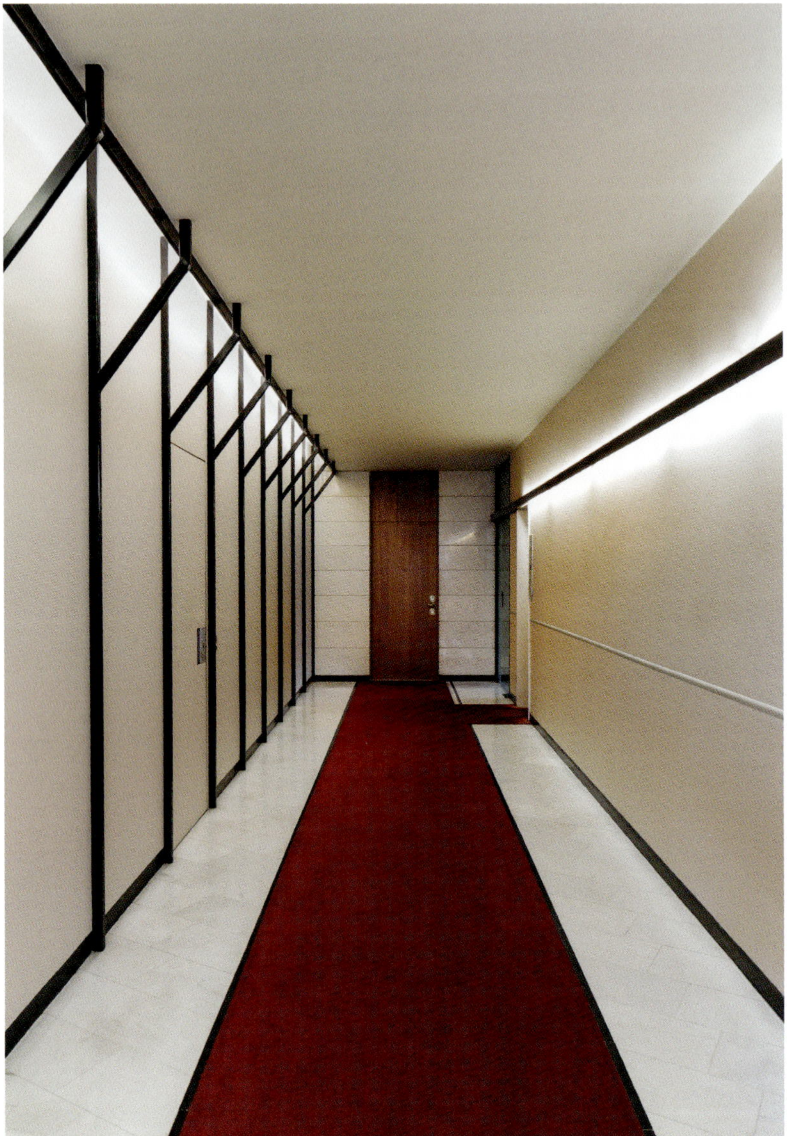

via Plinio 54

Artwork by Aldo Cerchiari.

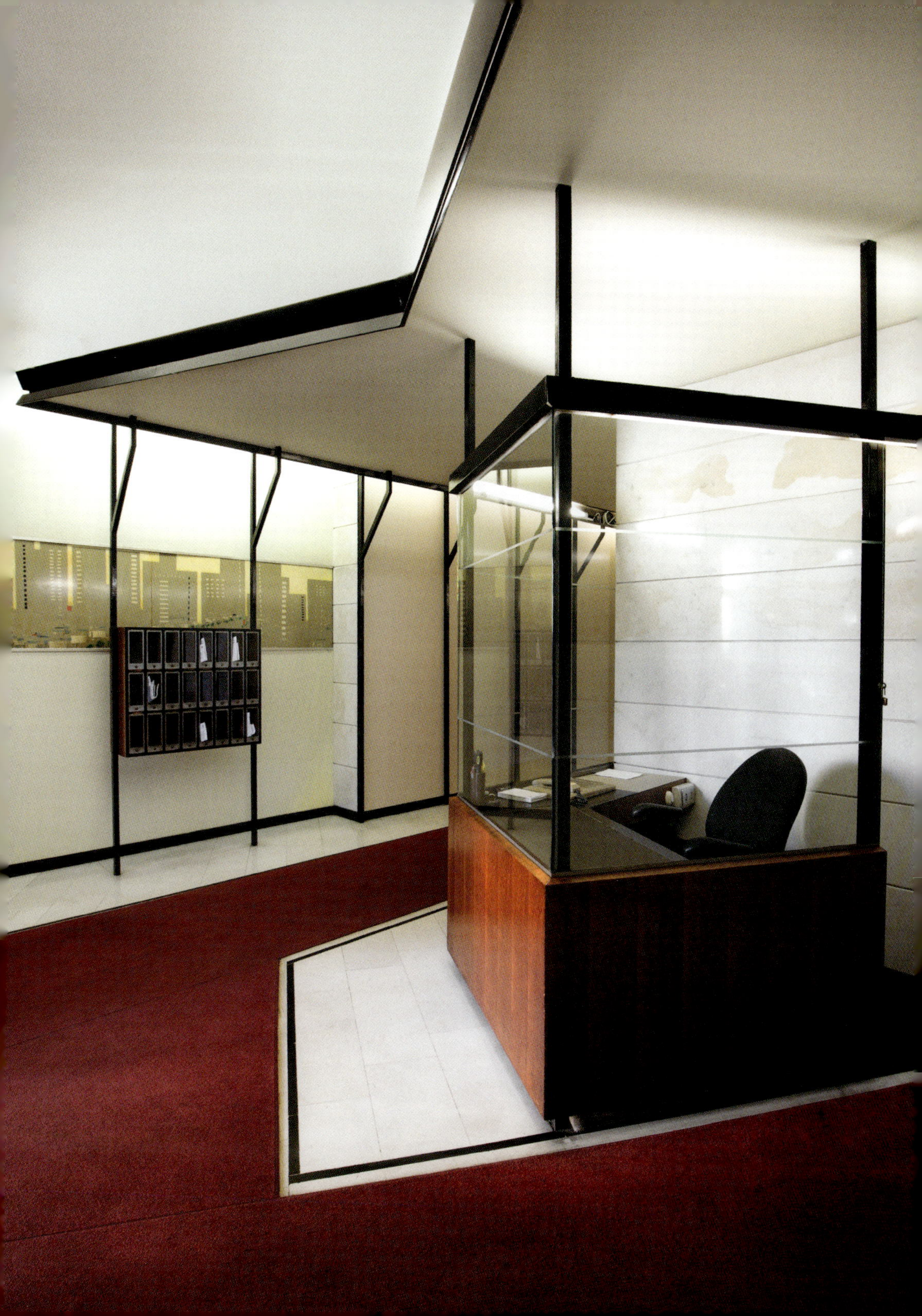

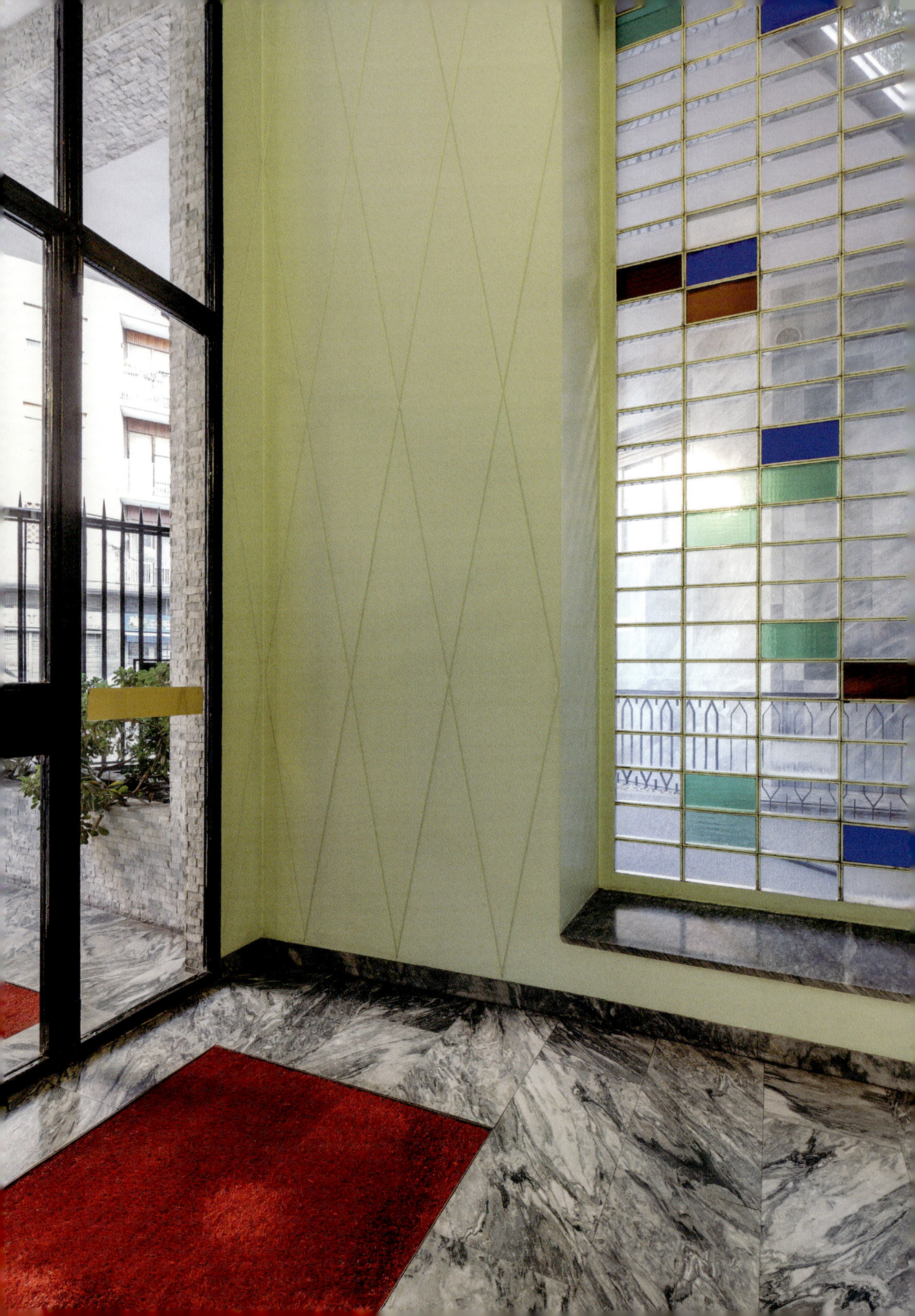

MARBLES FROM CARRARA AND LUCCA

In contrast to the contemporary market, many different types of Carrara marble have been used in the past: Cipollino Verde, Cipollino, Arabescato, Bianco Venato, Zebrino, Bardiglio, Bardiglio Nuvolato, Calacatta, and more.

via Plinio 52 · Gio Ponti, 1957–60

floor: Carrara Bardiglio Nuvolato marble

Numerous Milanese architects, throughout the mid-1950s into the 1960s, utilized the more than dozen ceramic tiles designs by Gio Ponti for their building façades as well as their interiors. In this entrance, two of his Renaissance-inspired motifs are employed both inside and out. Another classicist note is struck by a version of the traditional bronze and crystal chandelier that is split in half to create a singular sconce.

This and following spread:
via Bronzino 6
Ceramic tiles by Gio Ponti for Ceramica Joo.
planter: Bianco Montorfano granite

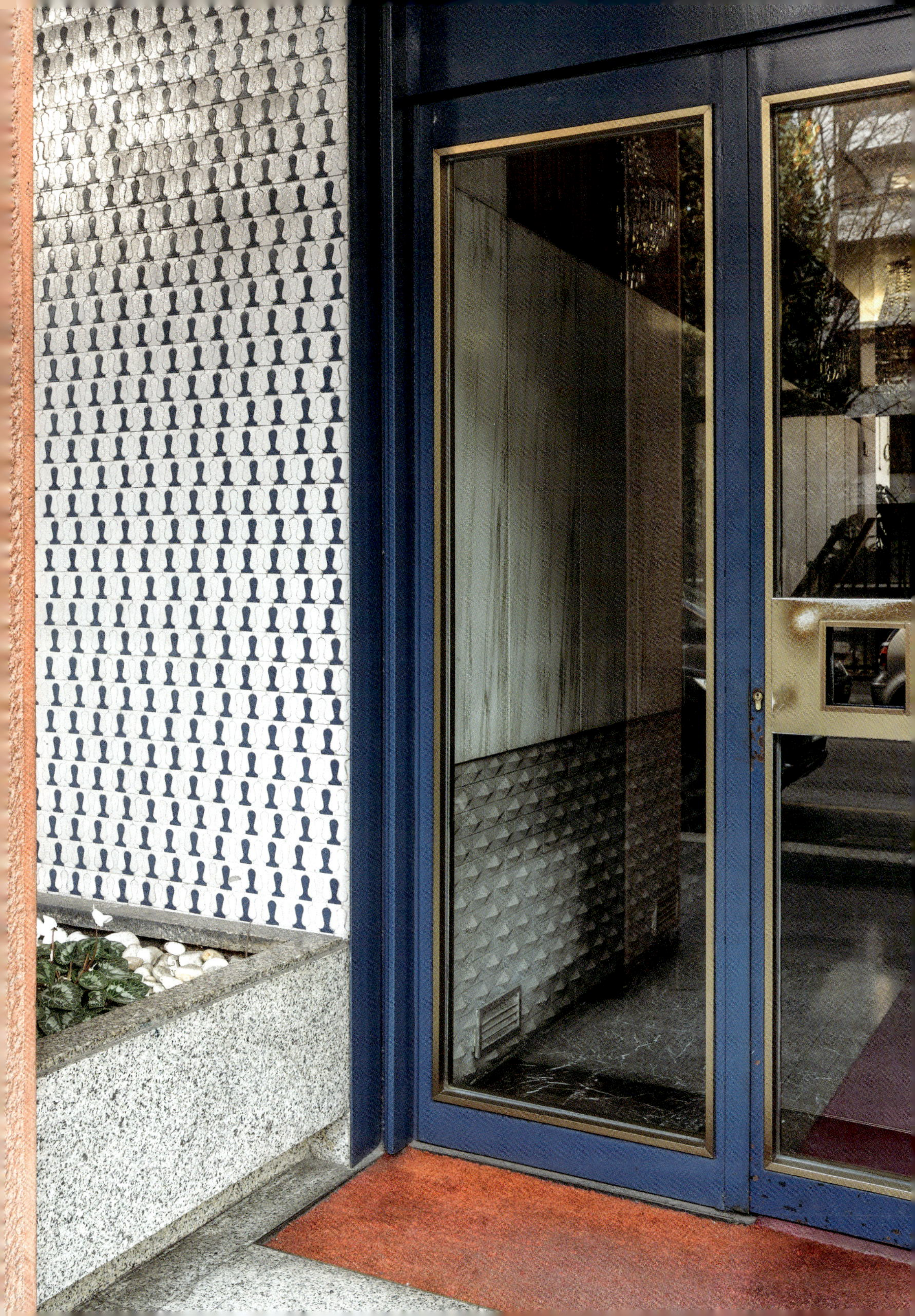

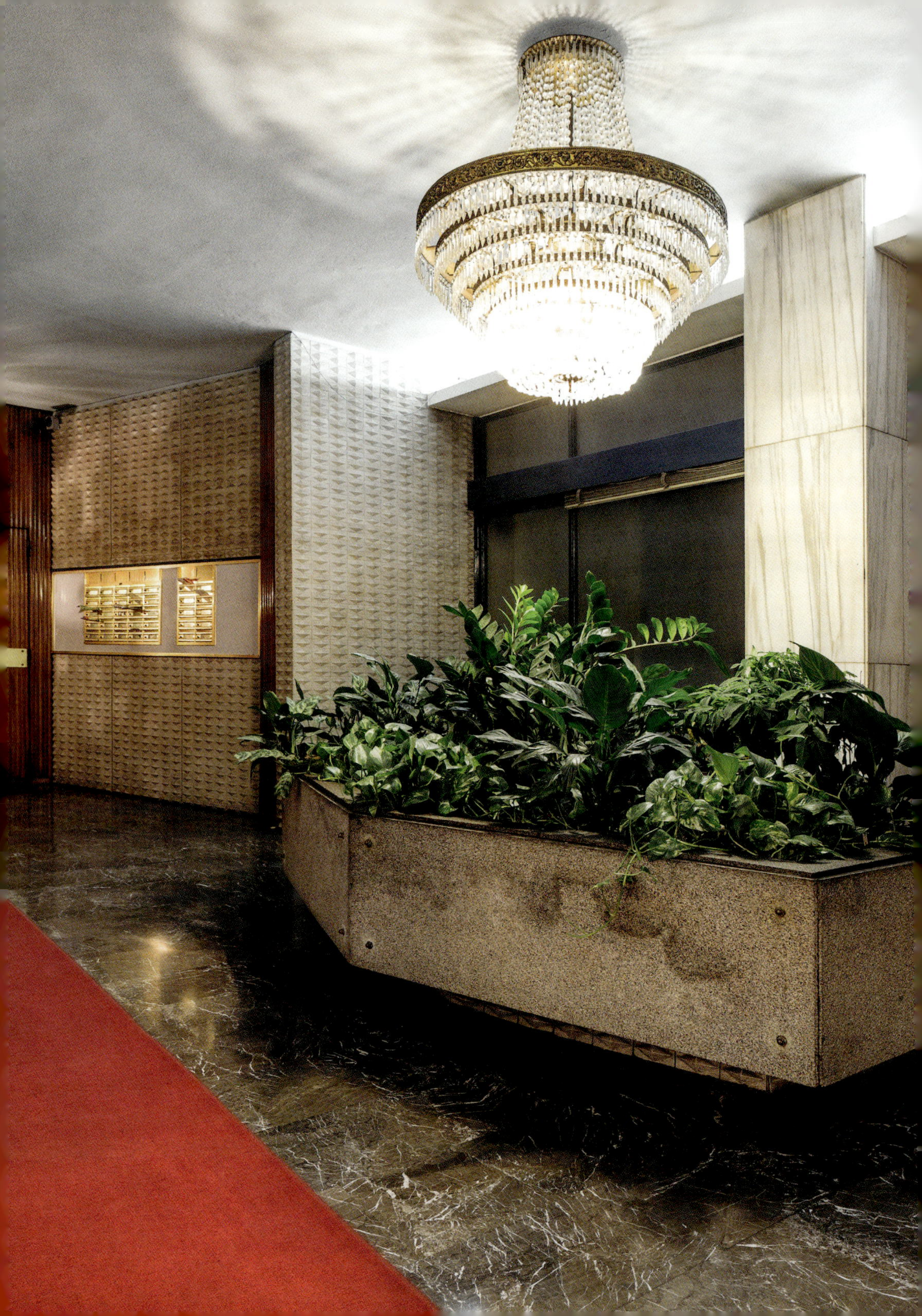

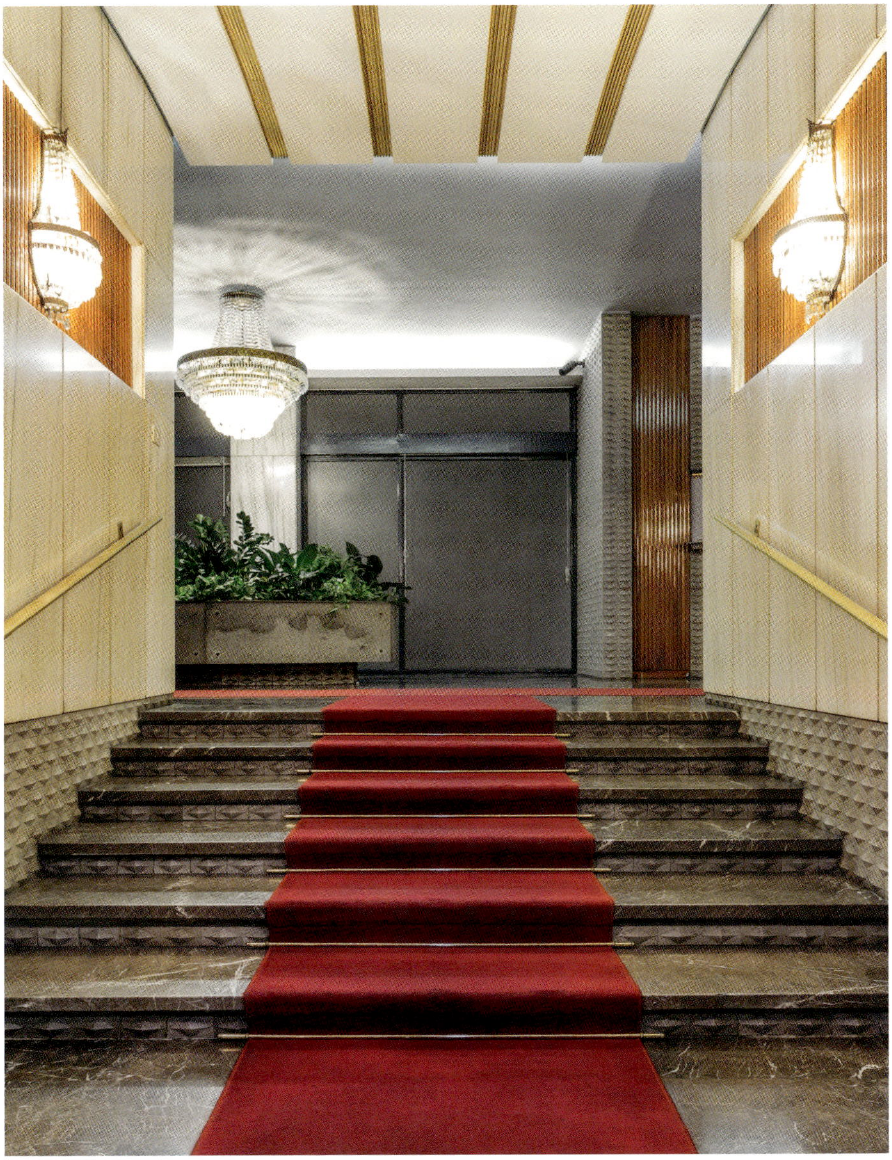

Diamond-shaped ceramic tiles by Gio Ponti for Ceramica Joo.
floor and stairs: San Benedetto limestone · walls: Palissandro marble

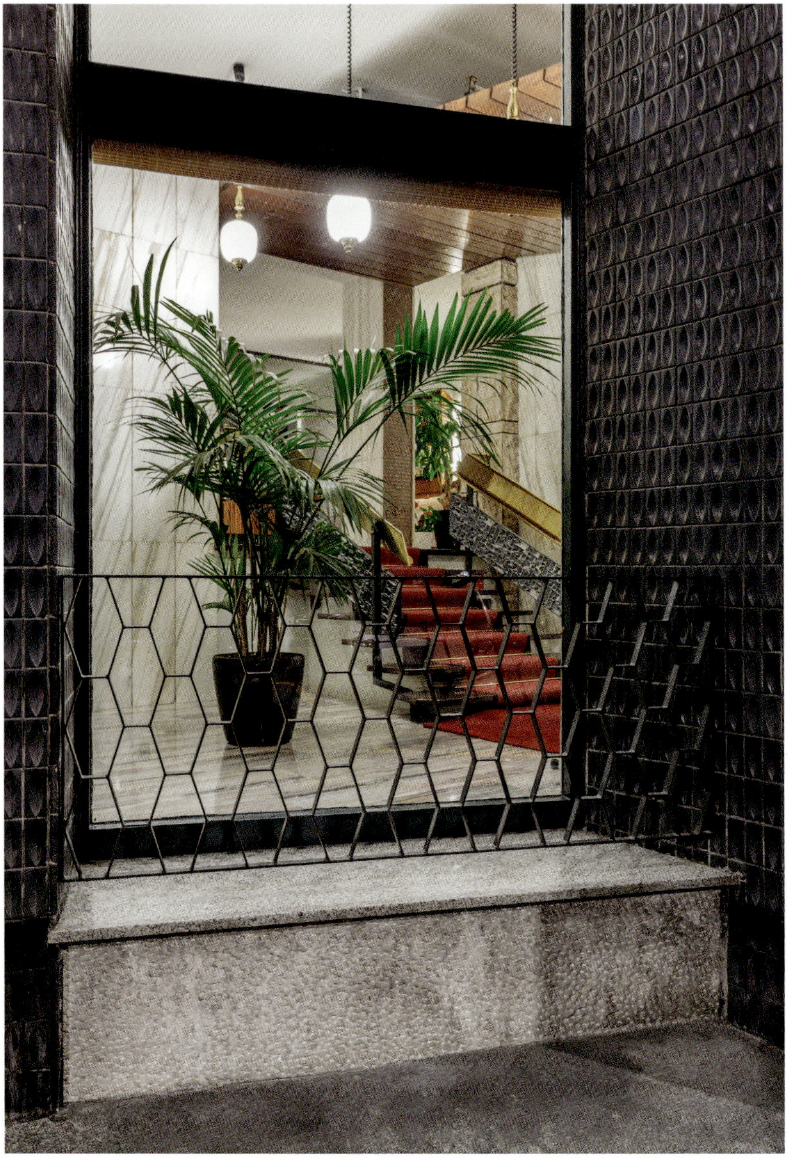

This and following spread:
via Amedeo D'Aosta 8
Ceramic tiles by Gio Ponti for Ceramica Joo · stairs: Bianco Montorfano granite

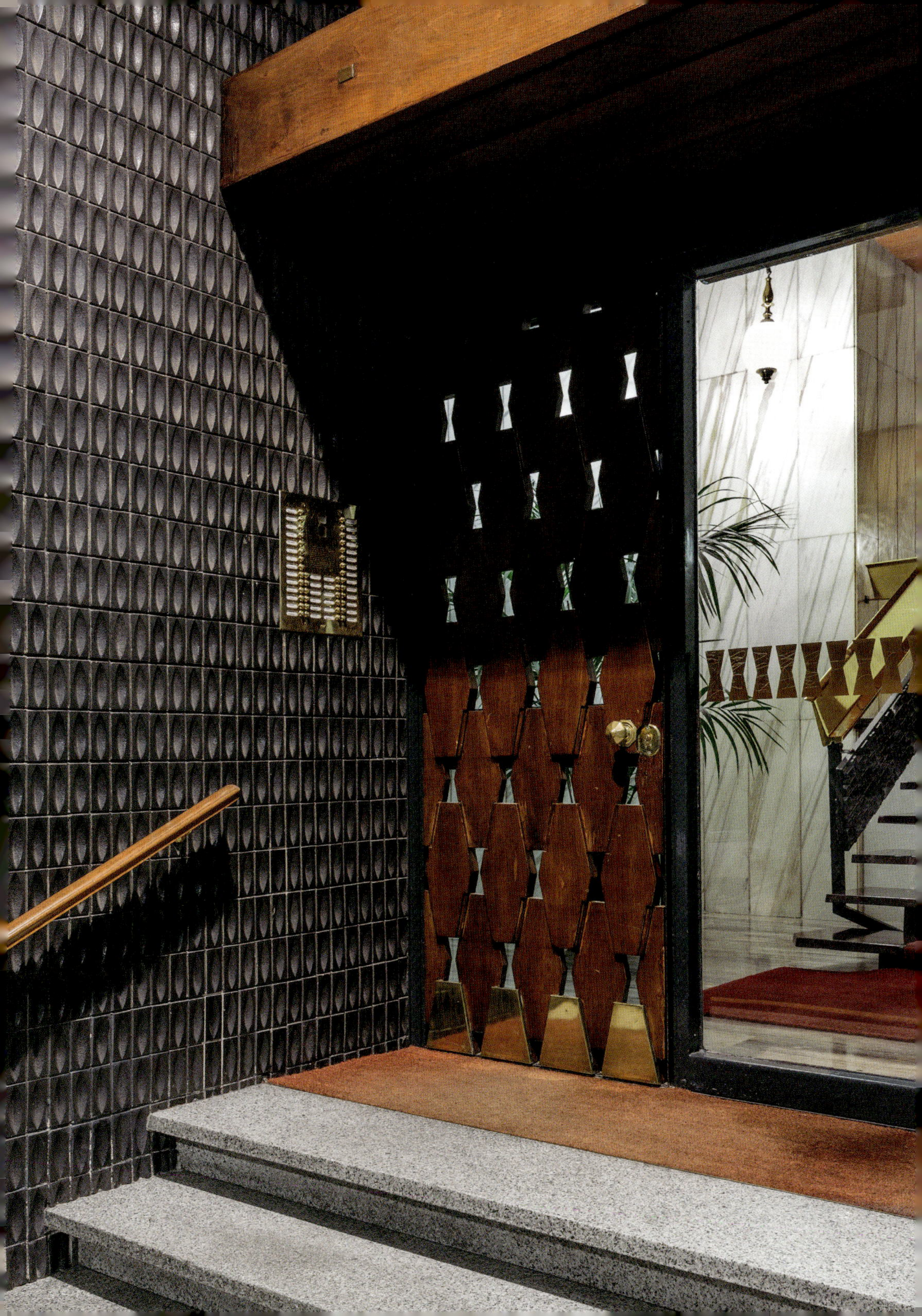

PORFIDO MONUMENTALE DI BIENNO

An Italian Permian porphyry. Unlike most such stones, and contrary to popular belief, this particular porphyry does not originate from Trento. It is world famous as one of the few porphyries that can be exploited in commercial blocks.

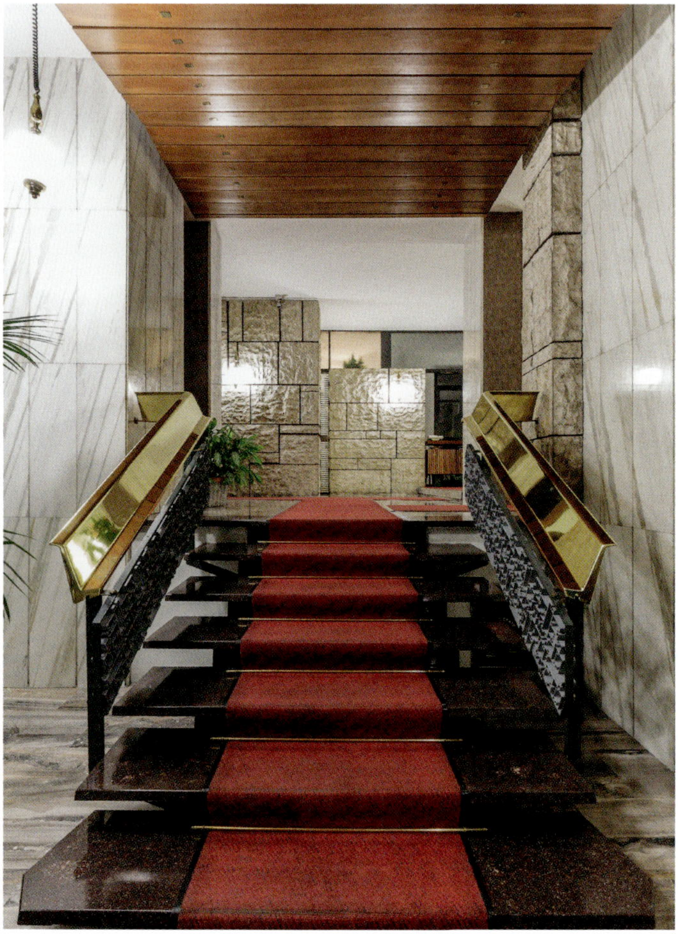

floor: Arabescato Orobico Grigio limestone · stairs: Porfido Monumentale di Bienno · walls: Calacatta marble

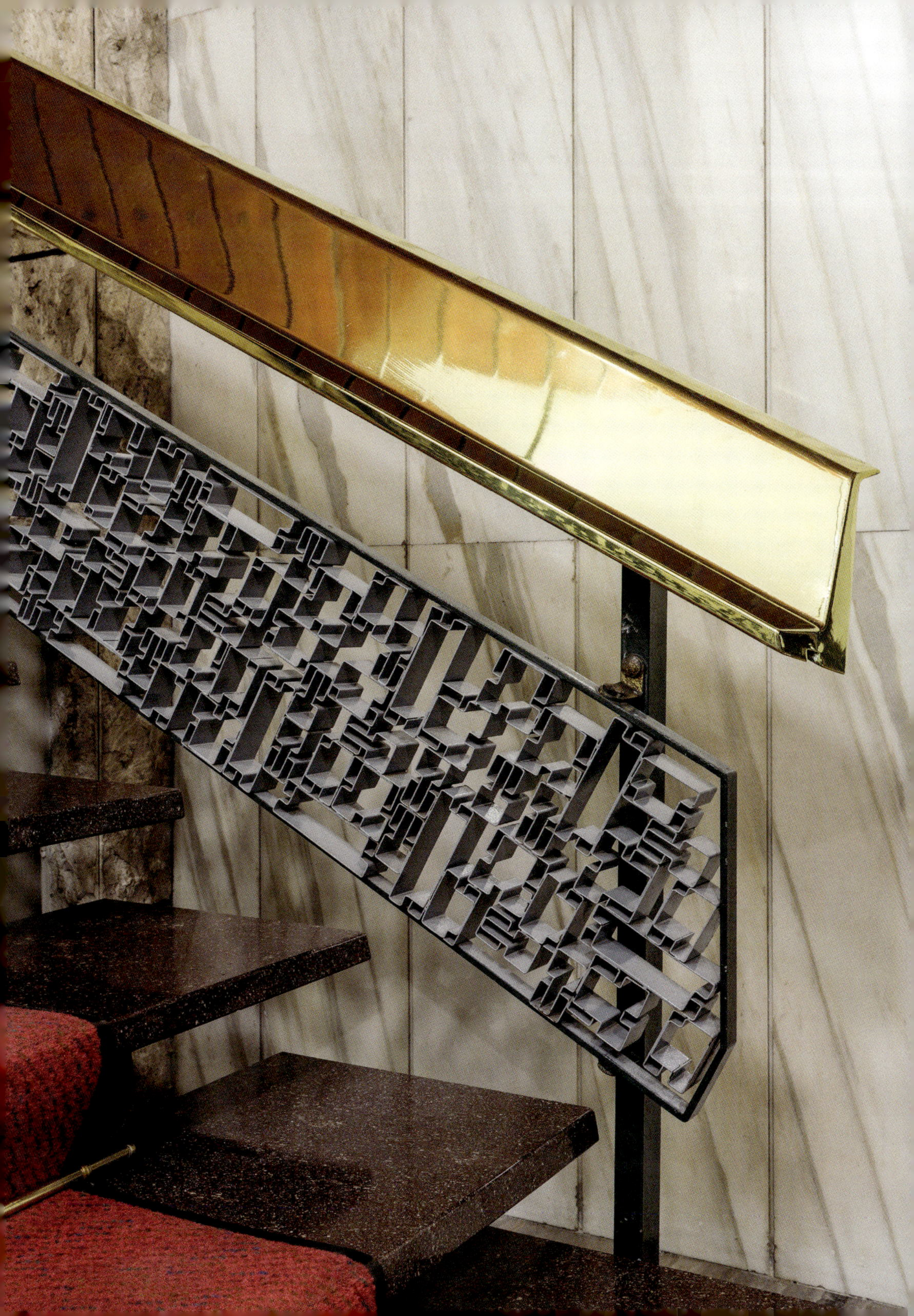

An adroit game that involves juggling Renaissance architectural codes, clearly invoking the spirit of Bramante. This erudite twist imparts a great variety to the experience of entering. All surfaces are both interrupted and conjoined in a lively caprice. The walls are an interlocking series of coined pilasters: alternating marbled "positives" and Pompeian-red "negatives." The flanking marble spheres, playing sentry to the steps, are in dialogue with their negative equivalents found in the upper frieze. The final note is struck in the meandering plaster patterning of the ceiling, which echoes the wall pilasters.

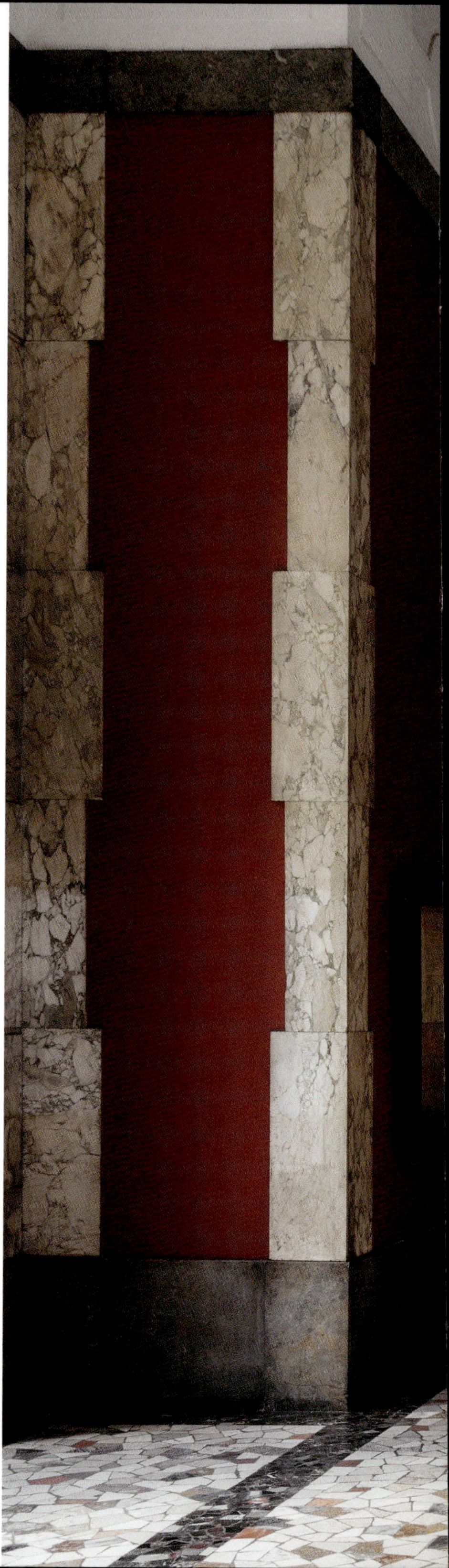

via Alessandro Stradella 11
Ferruccio Bigi, 1932–33
floor: Palladiana of several limestones and marbles
stairs: Bianco Carrara marble, Bardiglio marble
pilaster: Breccia di Stazzema marble

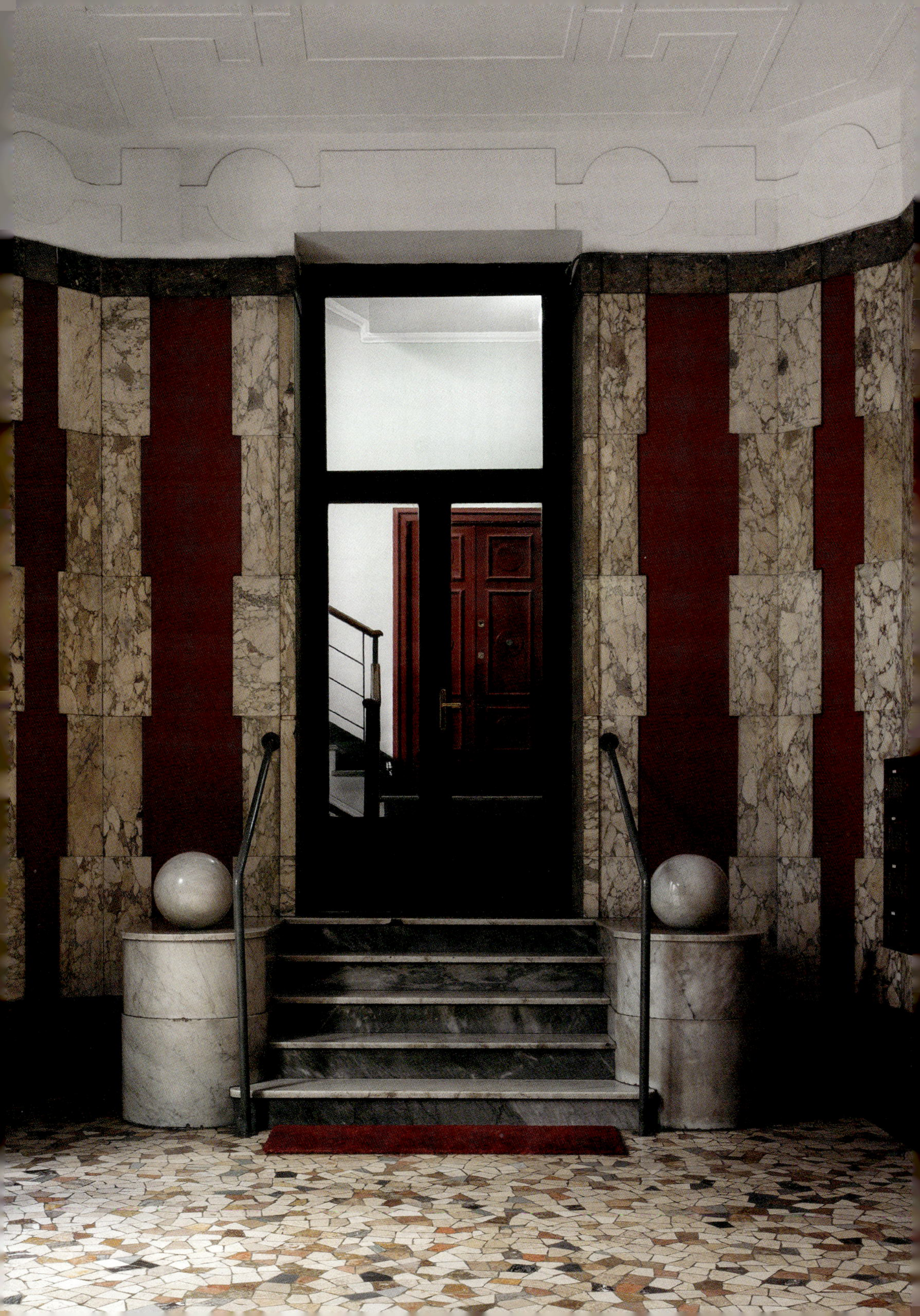

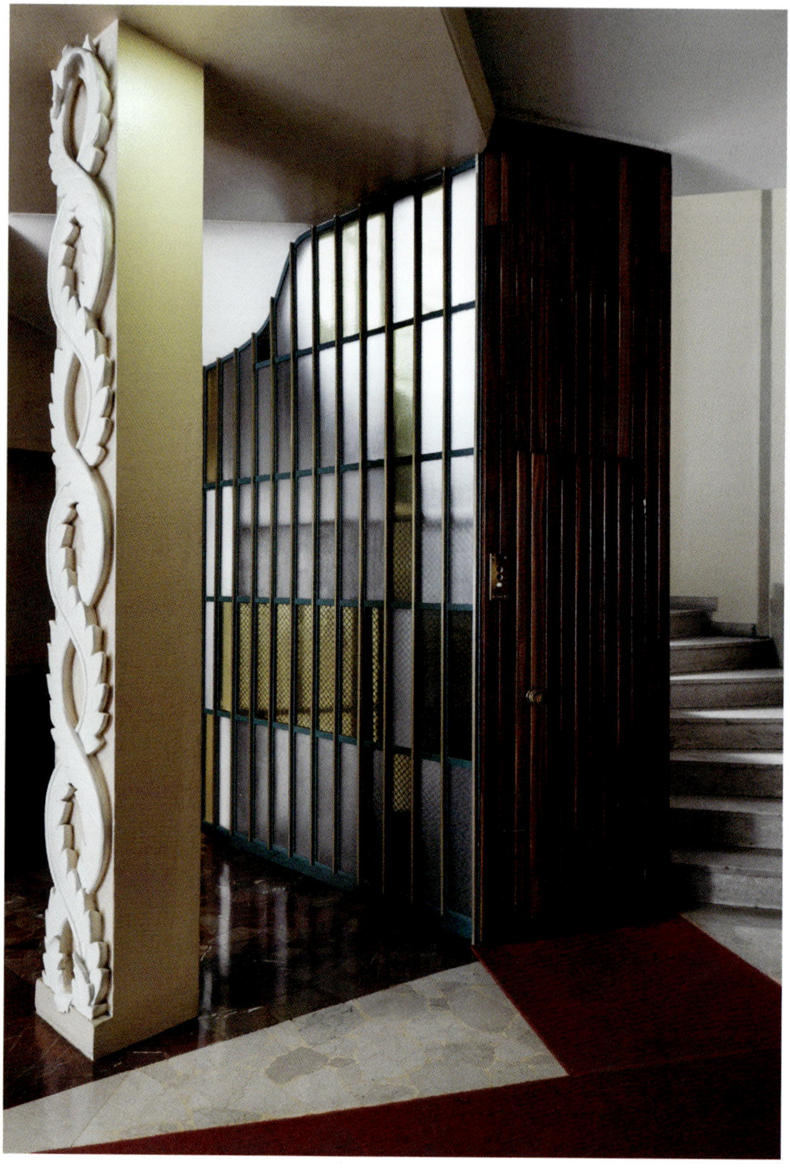

via Bronzino 21

Vertical plaster relief by Giovanni Gariboldi.
floors: slabs of Botticino limestone; Palladiana of Rosso Collemandina limestone · walls: travertine

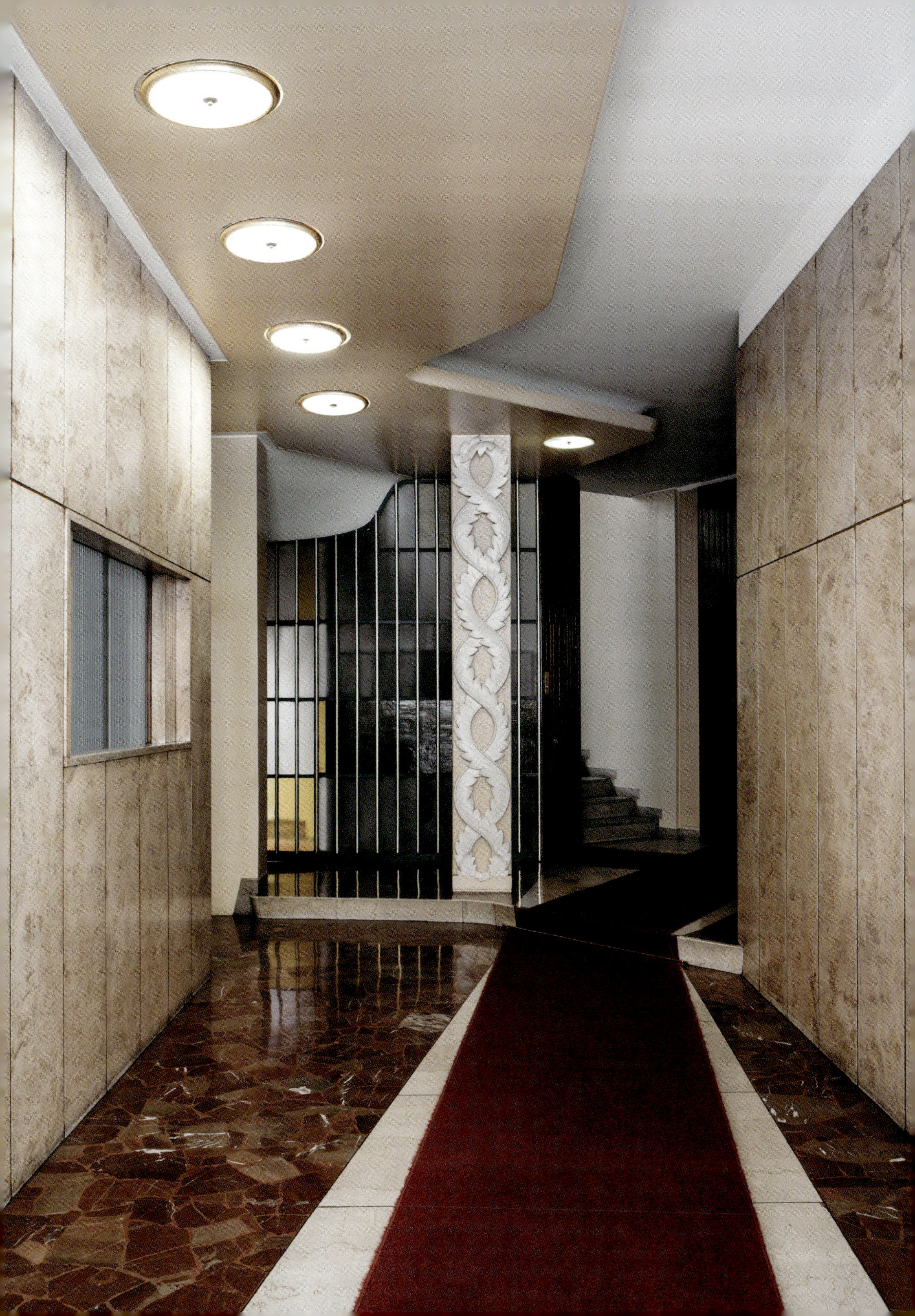

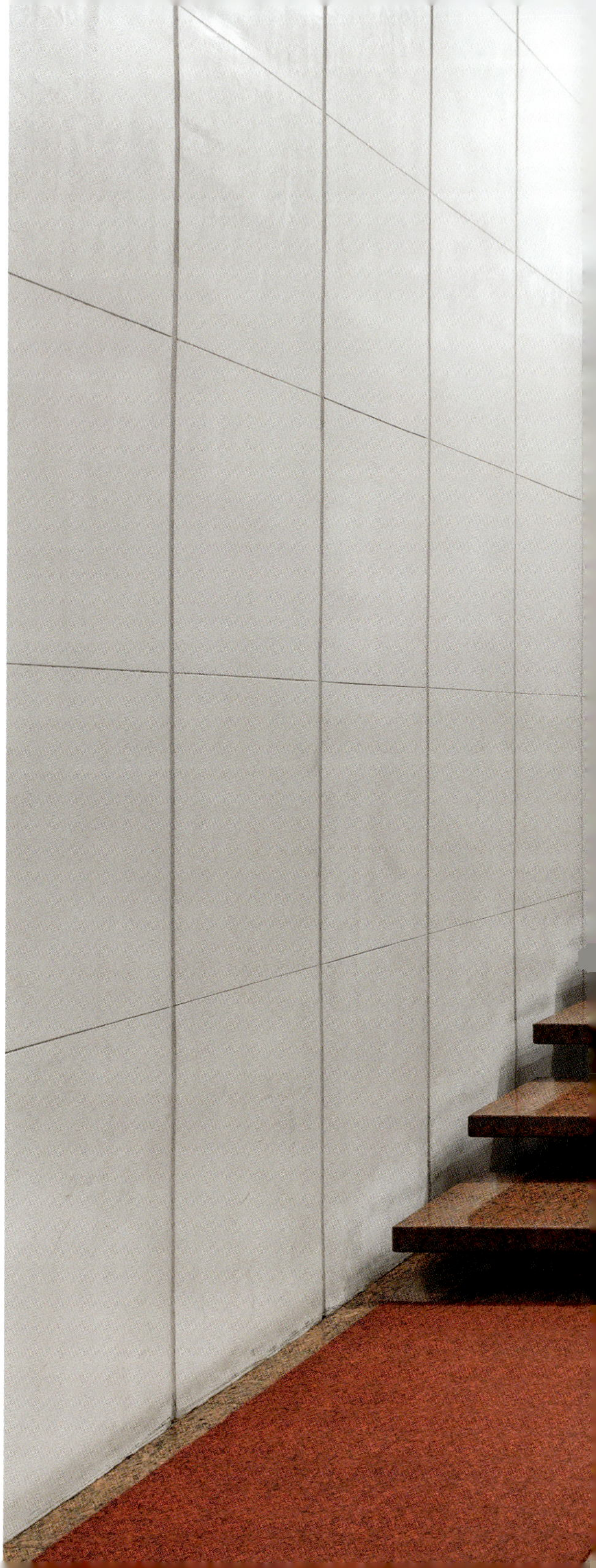

via Bronzino 7
Mario Arnaboldi, 1958–60
floor and stairs: Red Balmoral granite

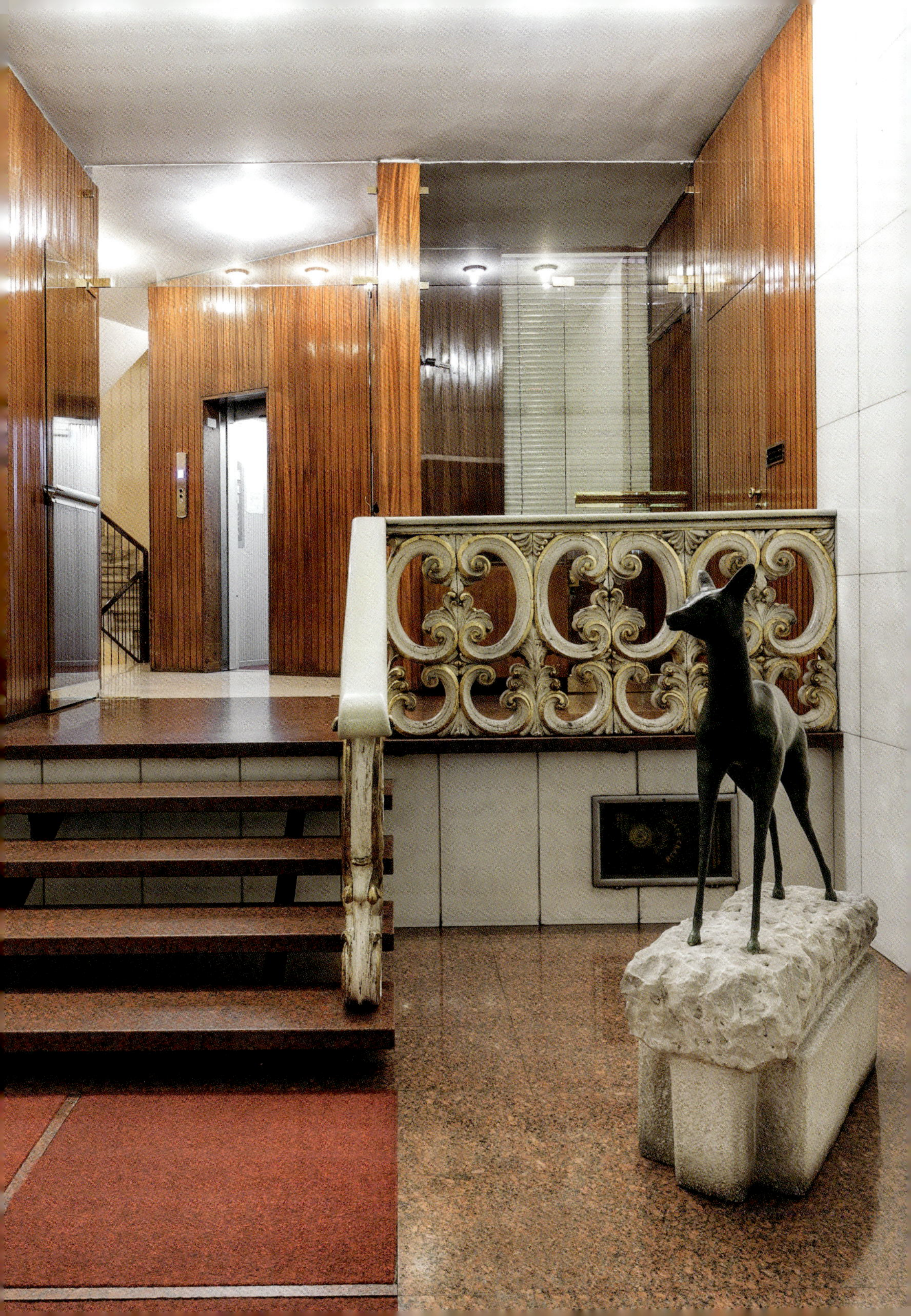

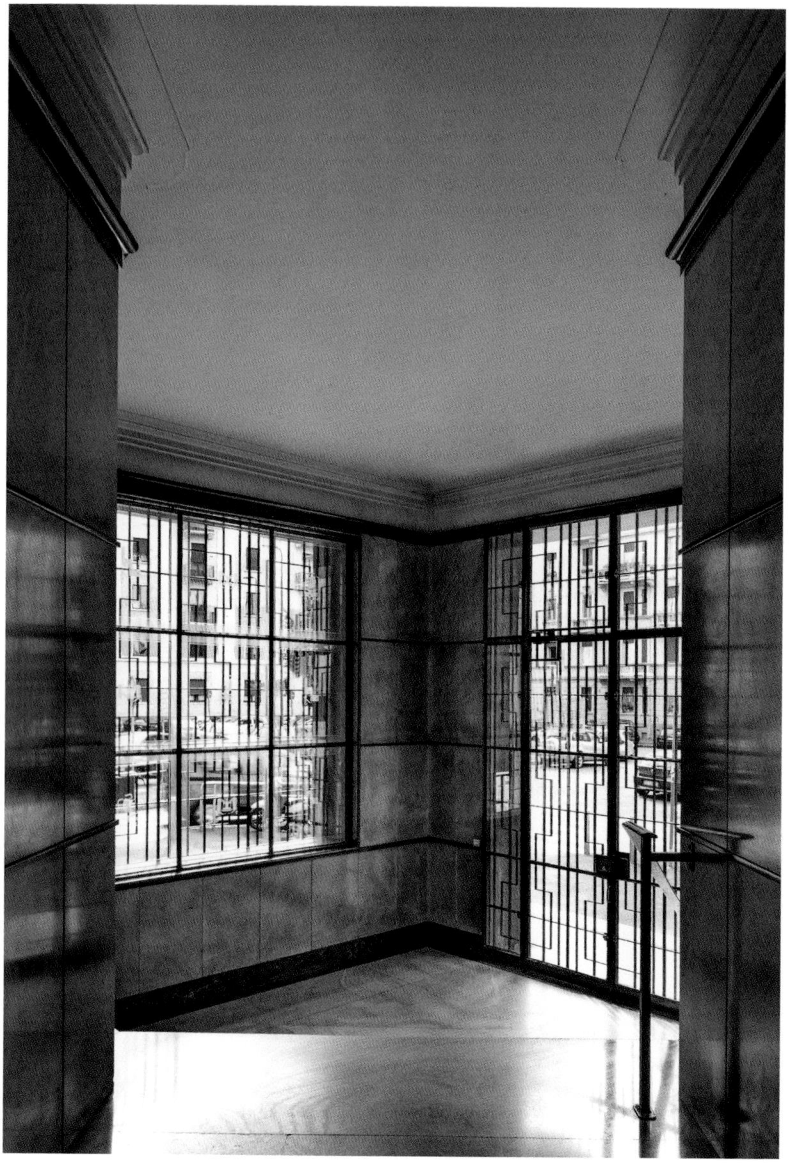

via Vincenzo Vela 19 · Carlo Schiavo-Campo, 1937

floor, stairs and walls: Musso marble and serpentinite

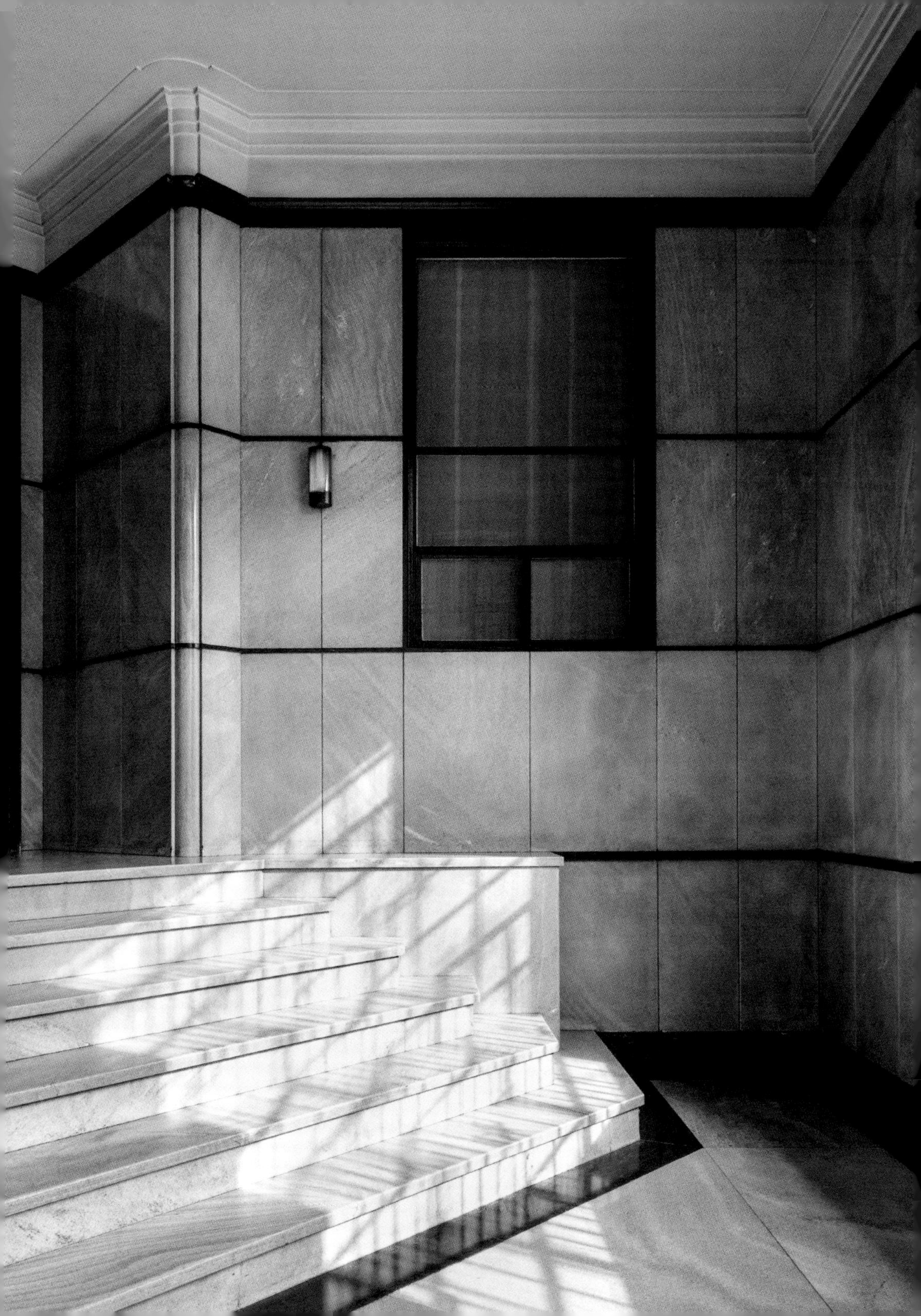

A compressed entrance is expanded at ceiling level, in alternating sections of channeled plaster, with hidden light sources, that evoke a taut tented space. The canting of the marble planter directs the visitor onward to a glass door that still retains to this day its emerald green, enameled metal door handle by Gio Ponti/Paolo de Poli.

This and following spread:
via Filippino Lippi 17 · Arutiun Kasangian, 1954–57
floor and stairs: serpentinite · walls: Breccia Damascata limestone

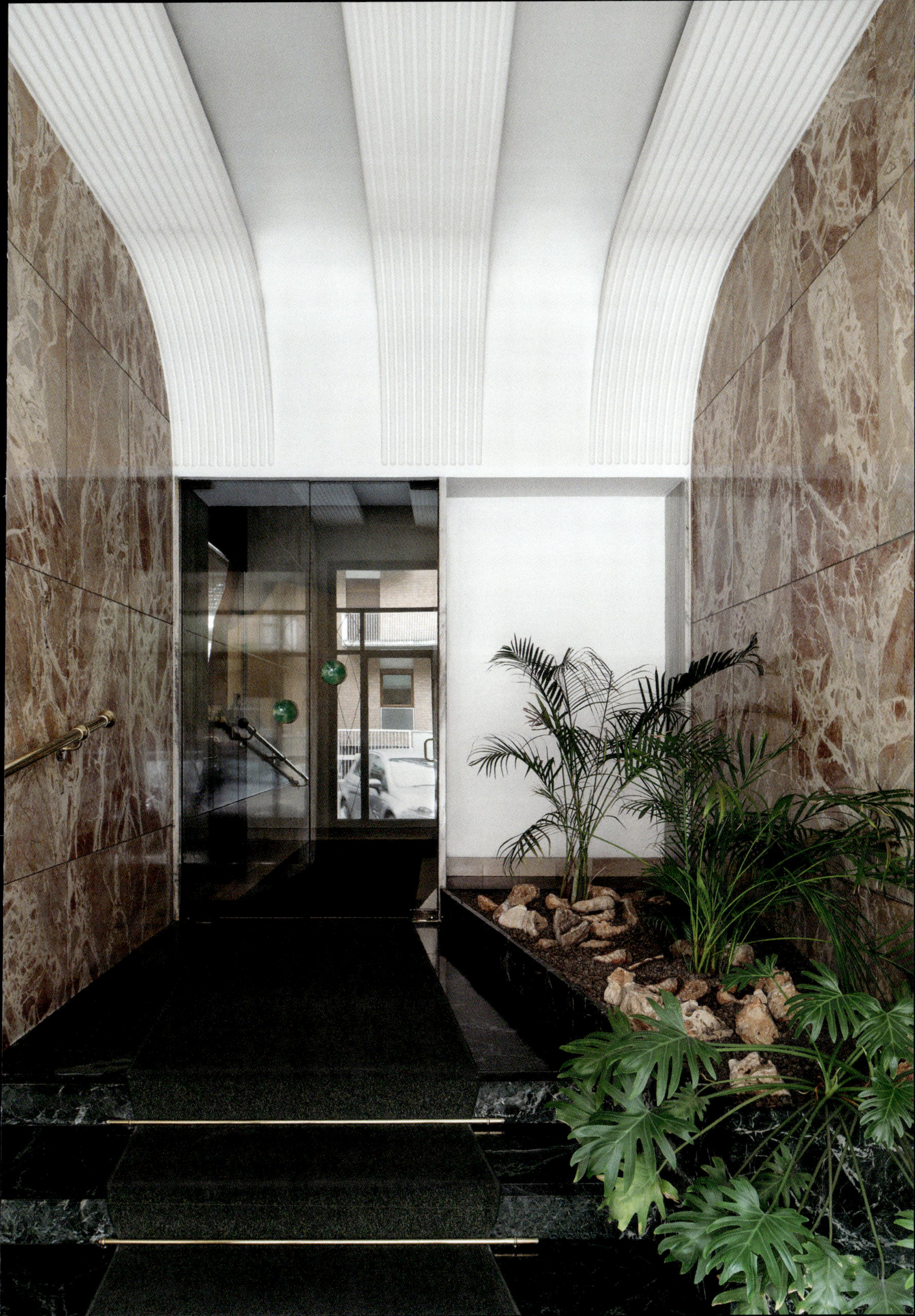

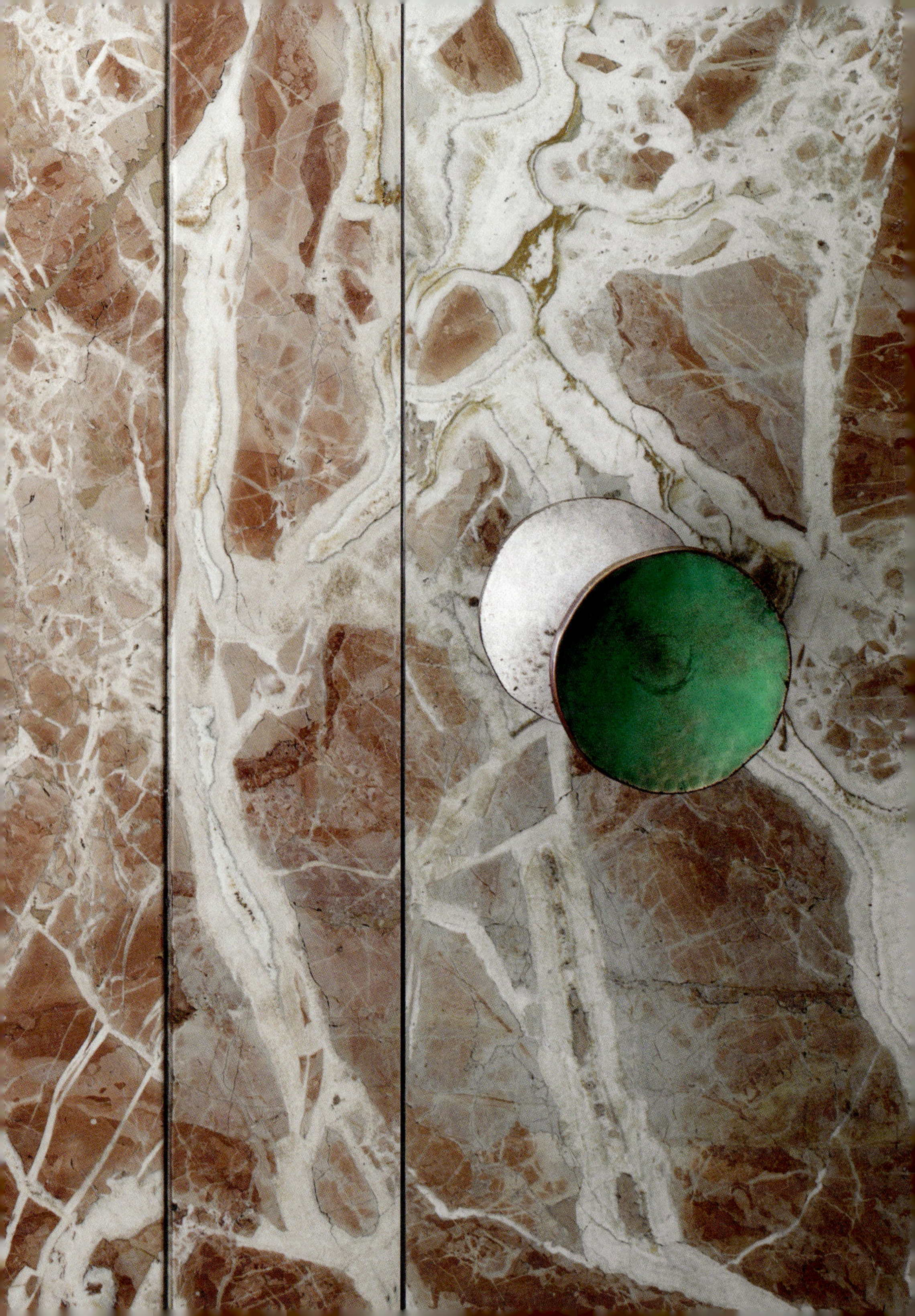

"The skin reads the texture, weight, density, and temperature of matter. The surface of an old object, polished to perfection by the tool of the craftsman and the assiduous hands of its users, seduces the stroking of the hand. It is pleasurable to press a door handle shining from the thousands of hands that have entered the door before us; the clean shimmer of ageless wear has turned into an image of hospitality. The door handle is the handshake of the building. The tactile sense connects us with time and tradition: through impressions of touch we shake the hands of countless generations."

—Juhani Pallasmaa

Door handle by Paolo de Poli from an idea by Gio Ponti.

Following spread:
viale Abruzzi 48
Sconces by Artemide.

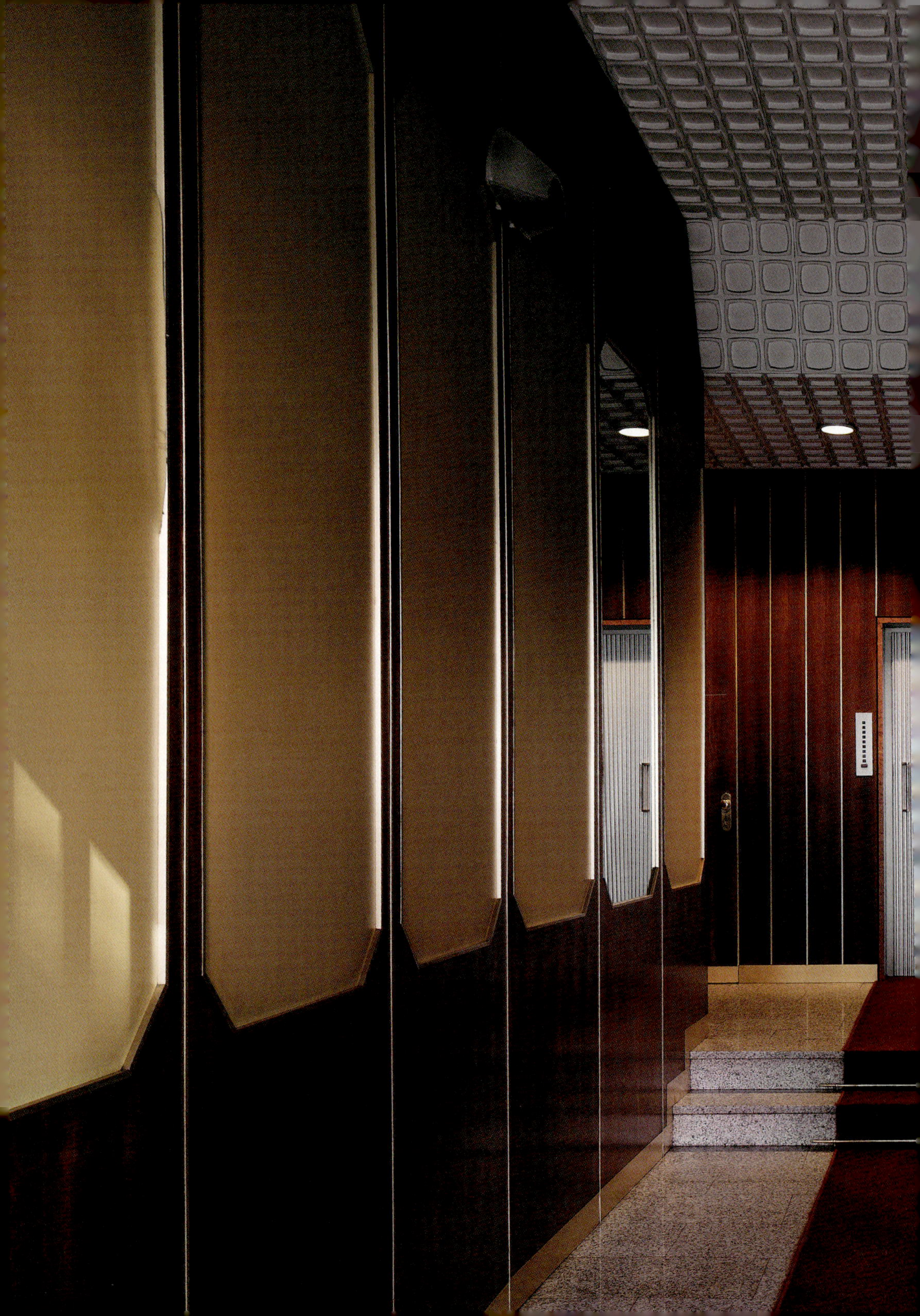

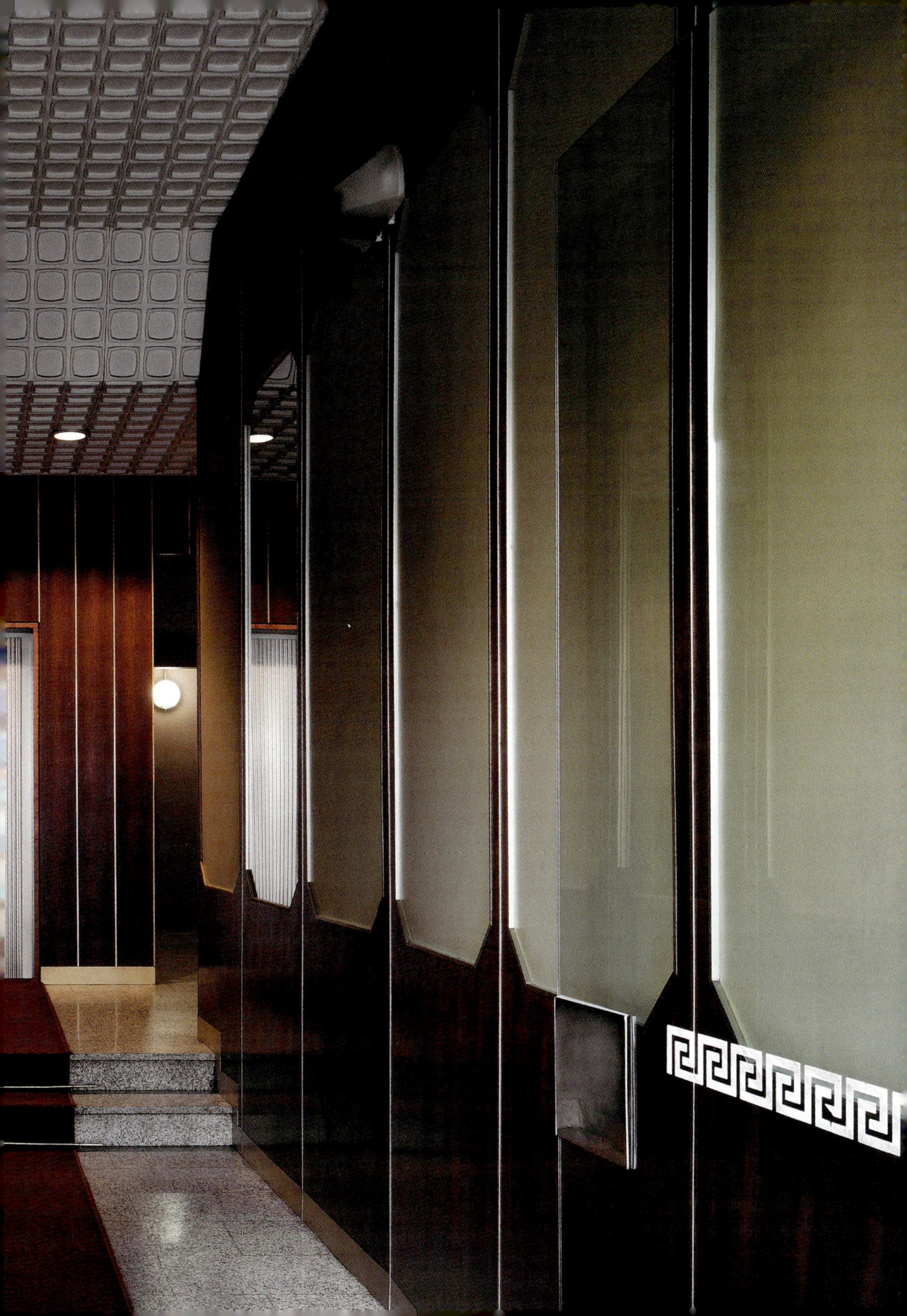

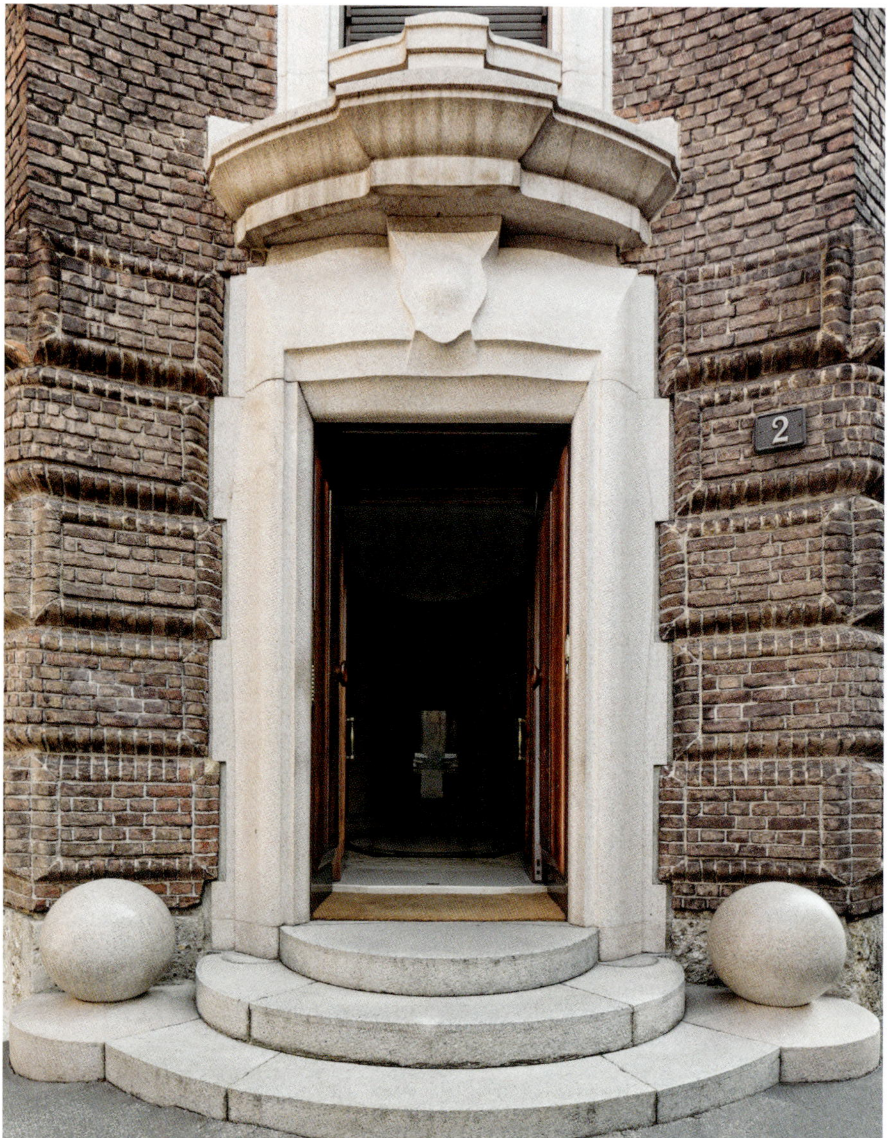

via Luigi Melegari 2, Palazzo Fidia · Aldo Andreani, 1926–30

doorframe, stairs: Rosa Baveno granite and Bianco Baveno granite · exterior base: Ceppo dell'Adda conglomerate
opposite page: floor: Carrara Arabescato marble, serpentinite, Verde Alpi ophicalcite, Giallo di Siena

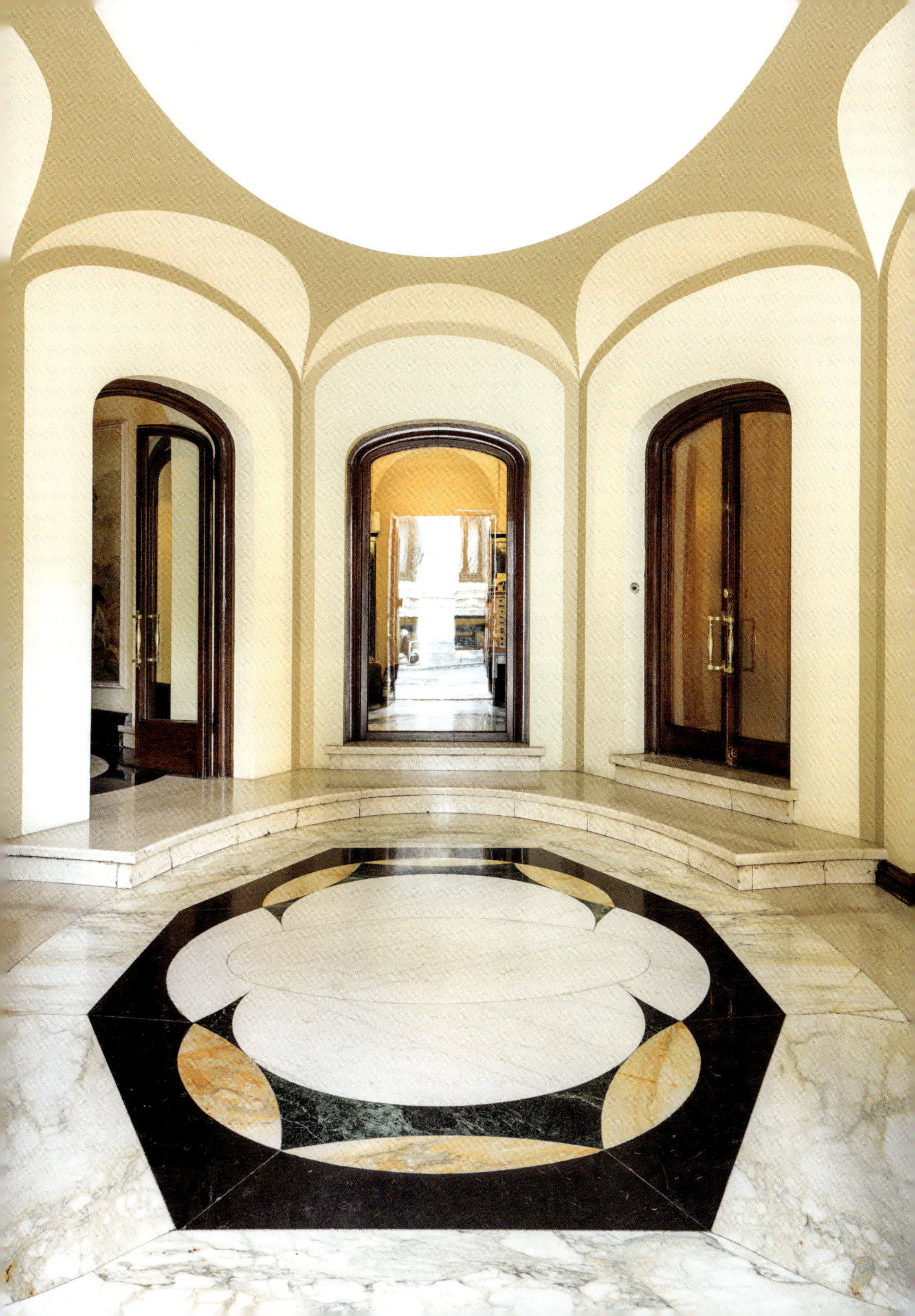

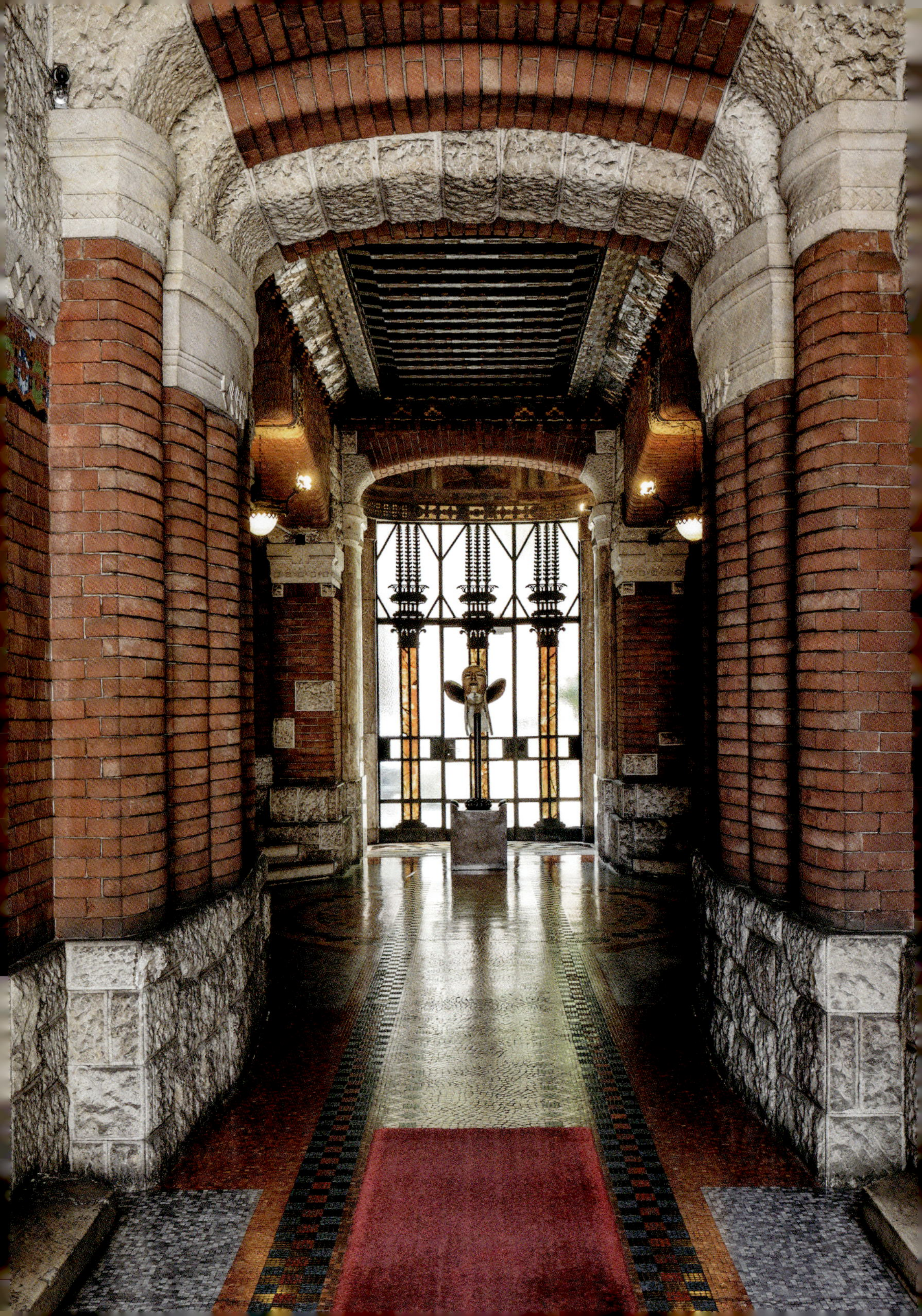

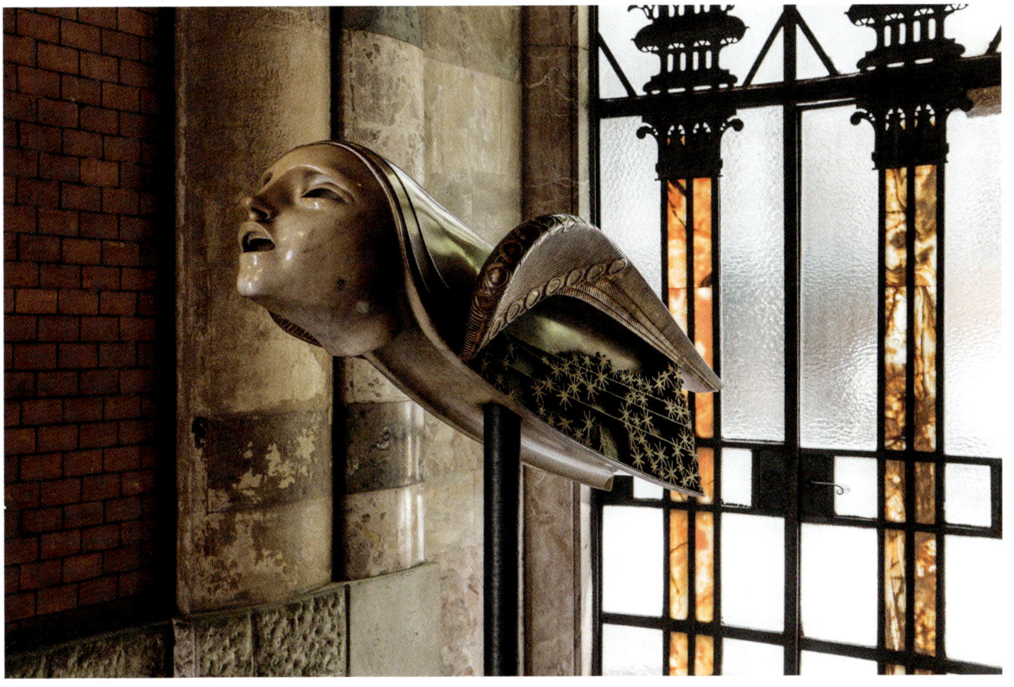

This and following spread:

via Cappuccini 8, Casa Berri-Meregalli · Giulio Ulisse Arata, 1911–14

Sculpture Winged Victory *by Adolfo Wildt.*
Wrought iron work by Alessandro Mazucotelli.
Vitrified mosaics by Piero Adamo Rimoldi manufactured by Villeroy & Boch.

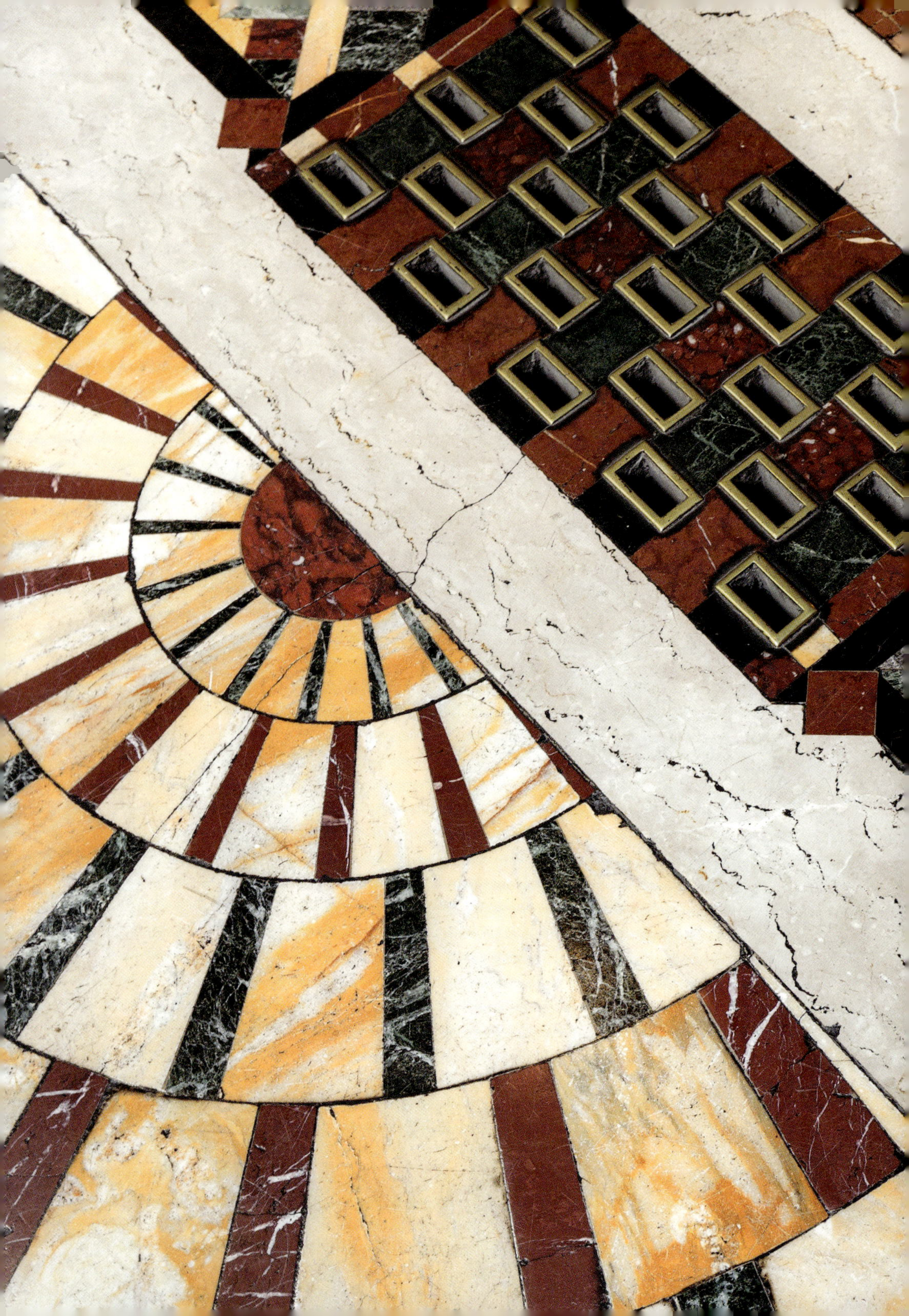

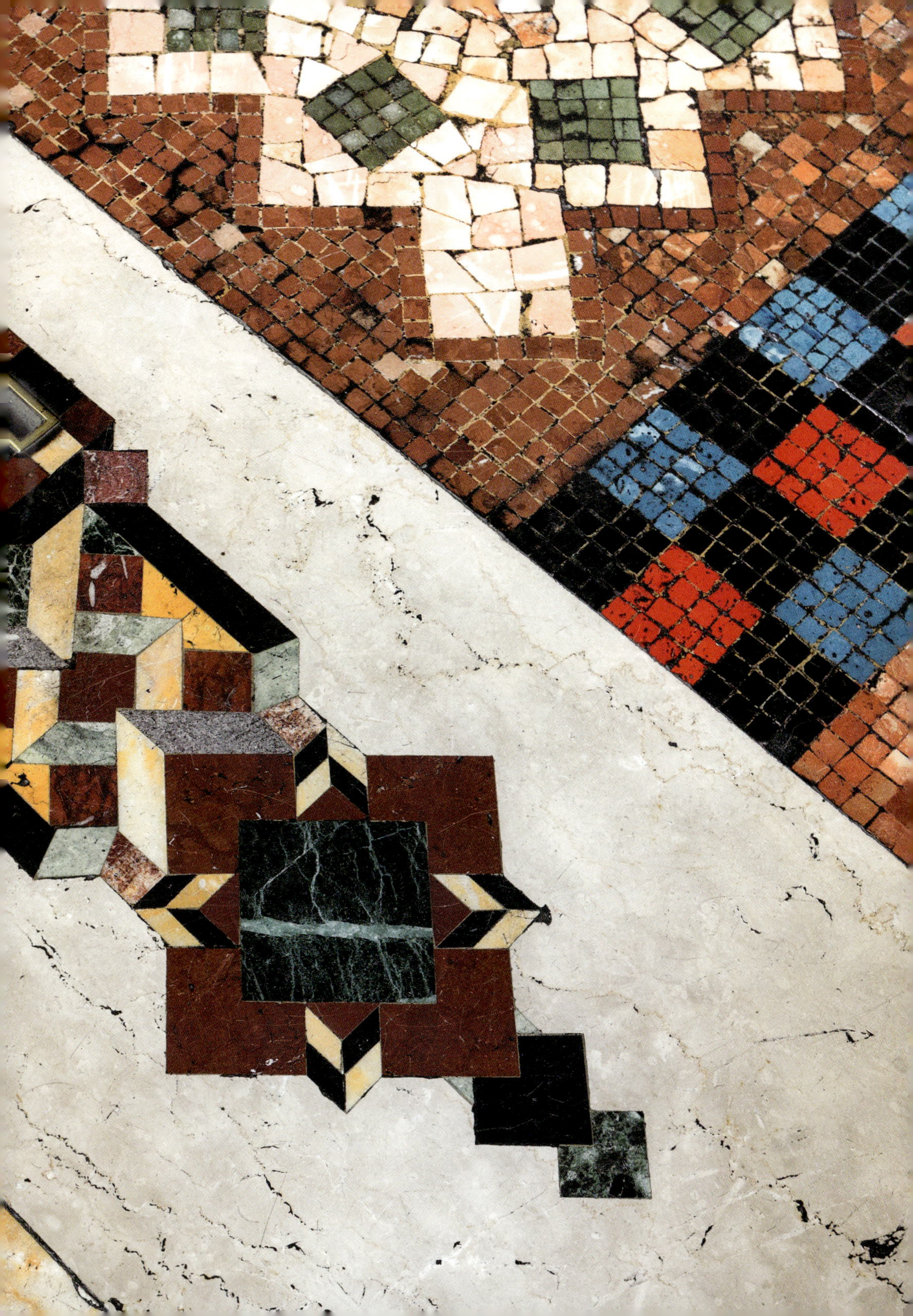

CEPPO

A local name used in Lombardy for heterogeneous, conglomeratic, or breccia-textured deposits that formed during the latter phases of the last glacial era along riverbanks (conglomerate types, such as Ceppo dell'Adda) or as the result of landslides (angular breccia types, such as Ceppo di Gré). As Ceppo dell'Adda outcrops are very accessible and lie along riverbanks, the stone has been exploited since Roman times and brought to Milan by river. Leonardo da Vinci designed a network of navigable channels in order to make its transport more efficient.

This and following spread:
viale Tunisia 10
external cladding: Ceppo di Gré

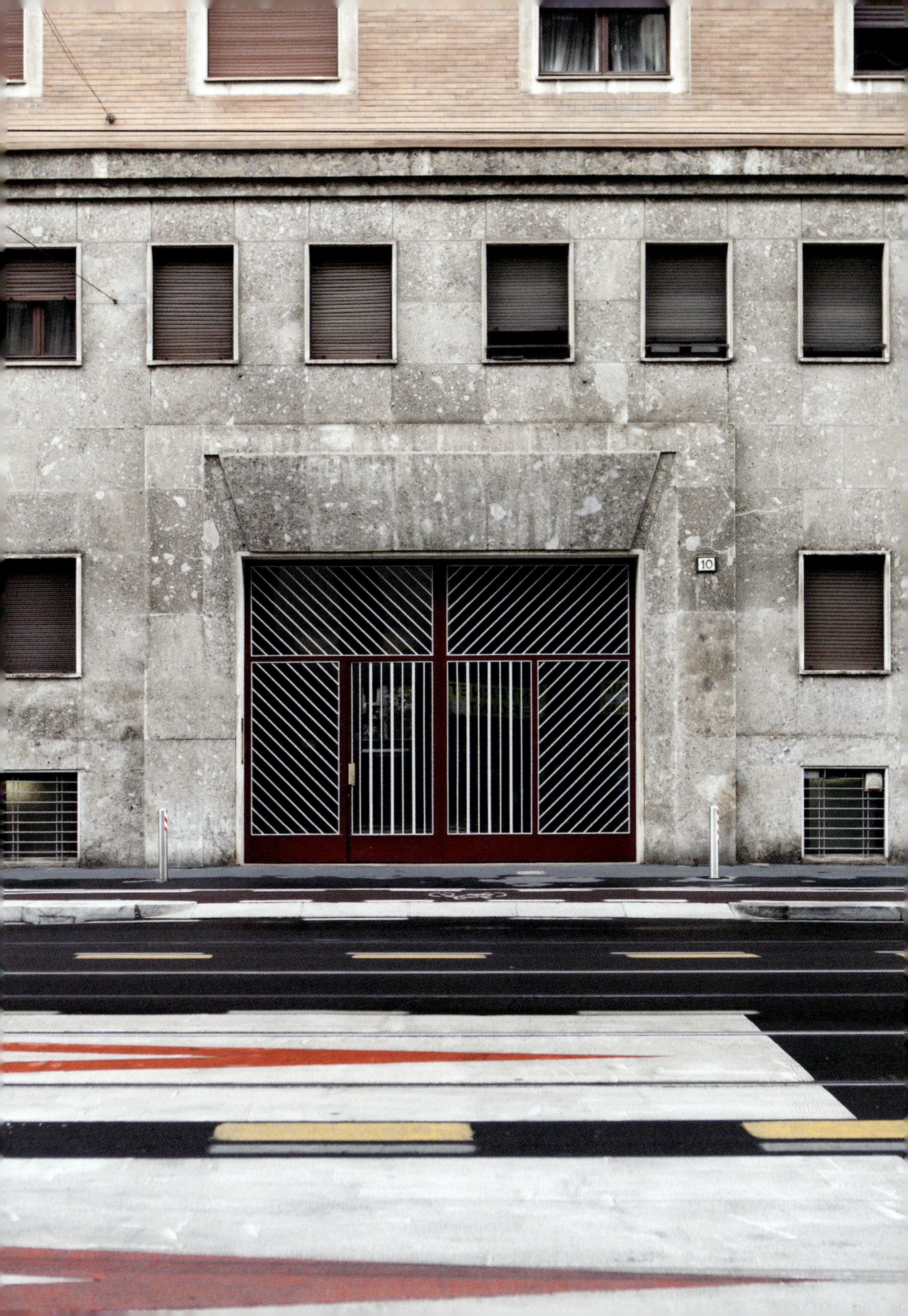
10

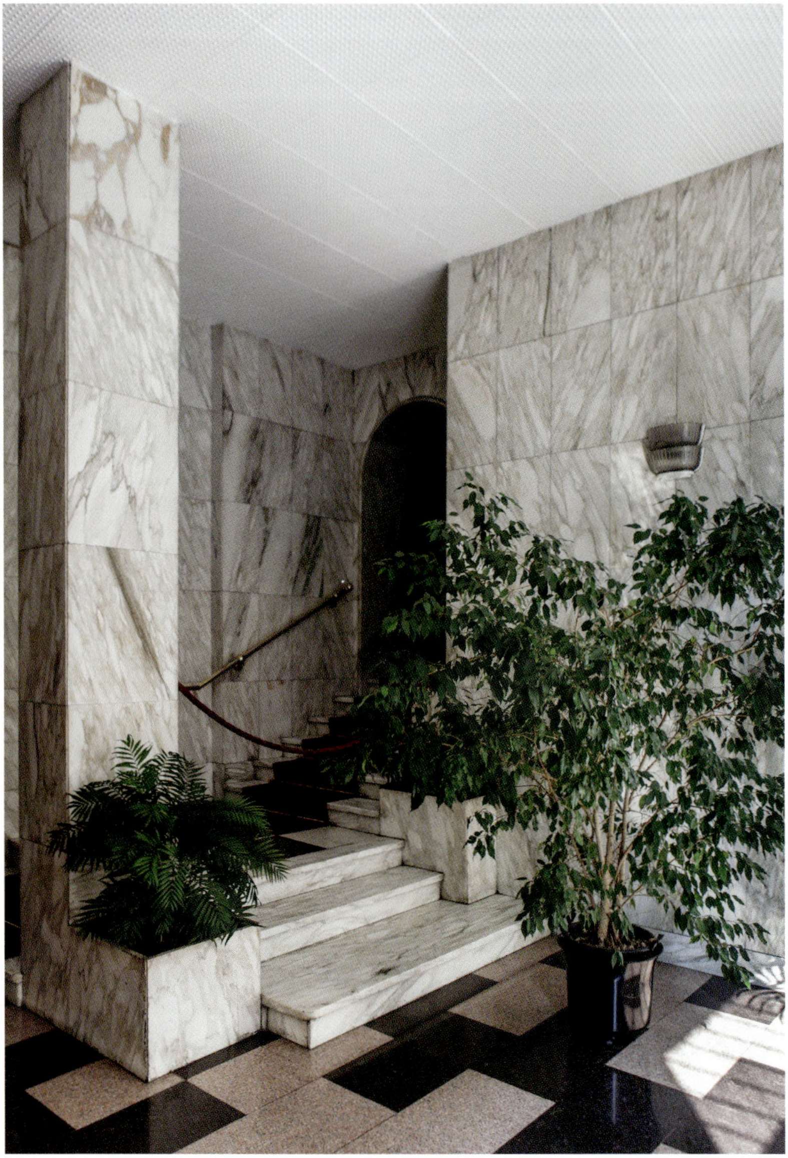

Sconce by Barovier & Toso.
floor: Rosa Baveno granite and Porfido Monumentale di Bienno · walls: Calacatta marble

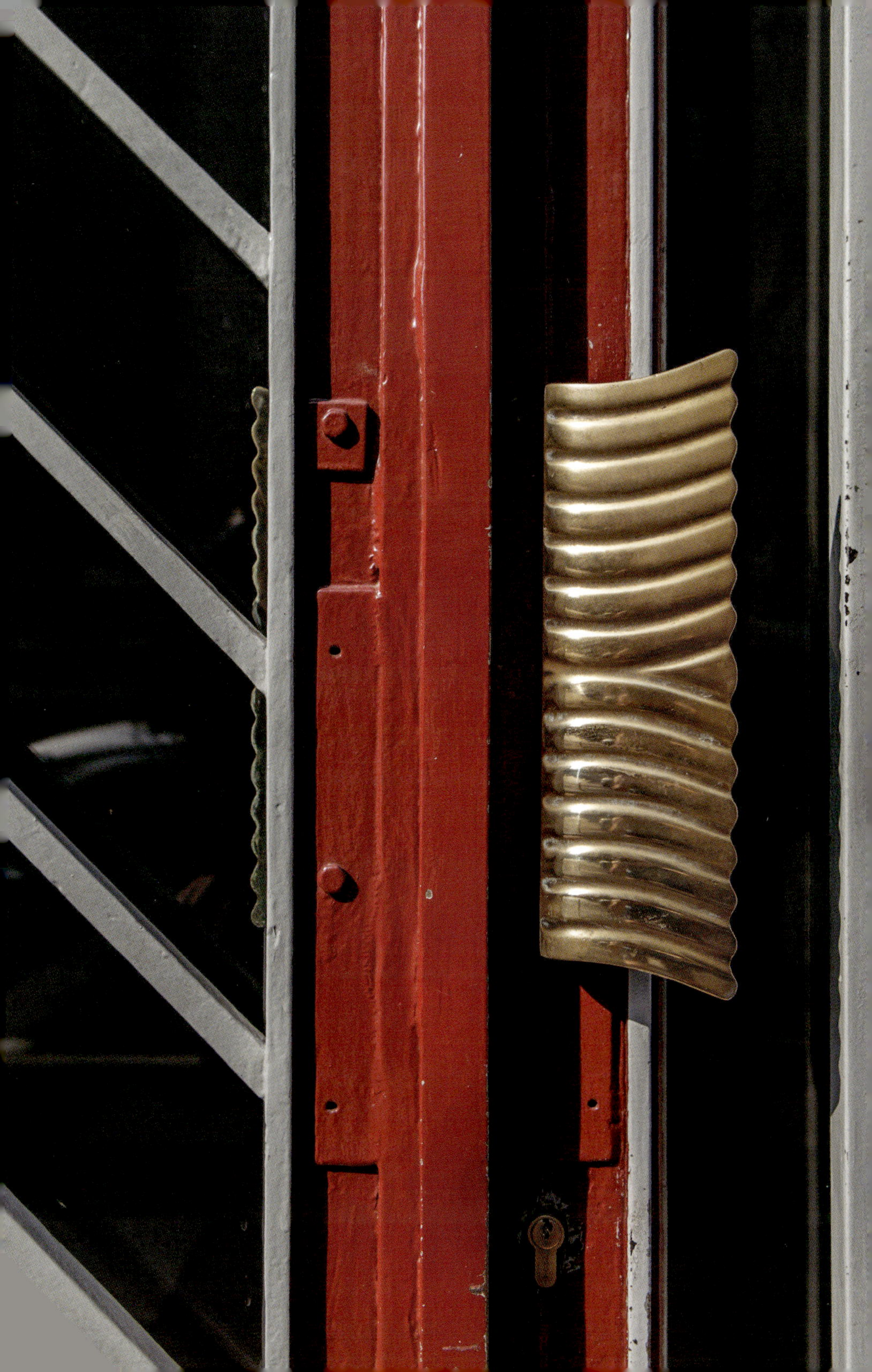

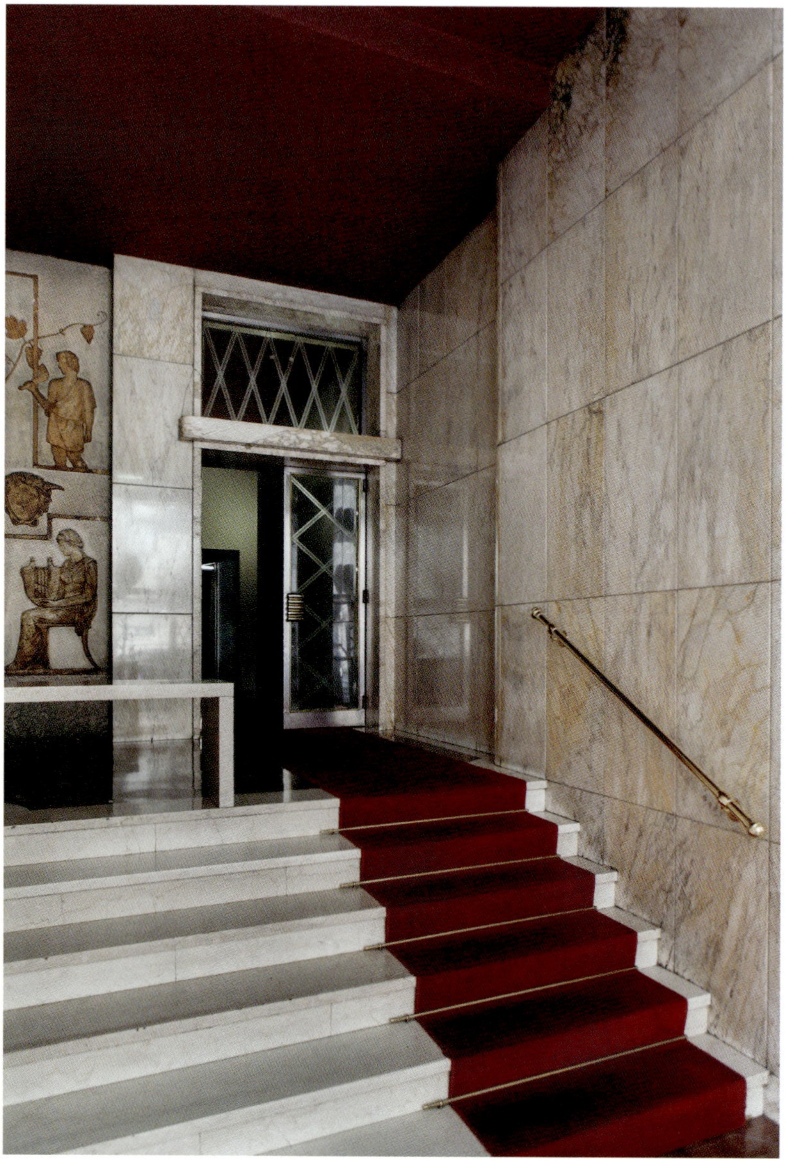

viale Tunisia 27 · Paolo Mario Lamborizio, 1938

floor: Rosso Collemandina limestone · stairs: Botticino limestone · walls: Arabescato Carrara marble

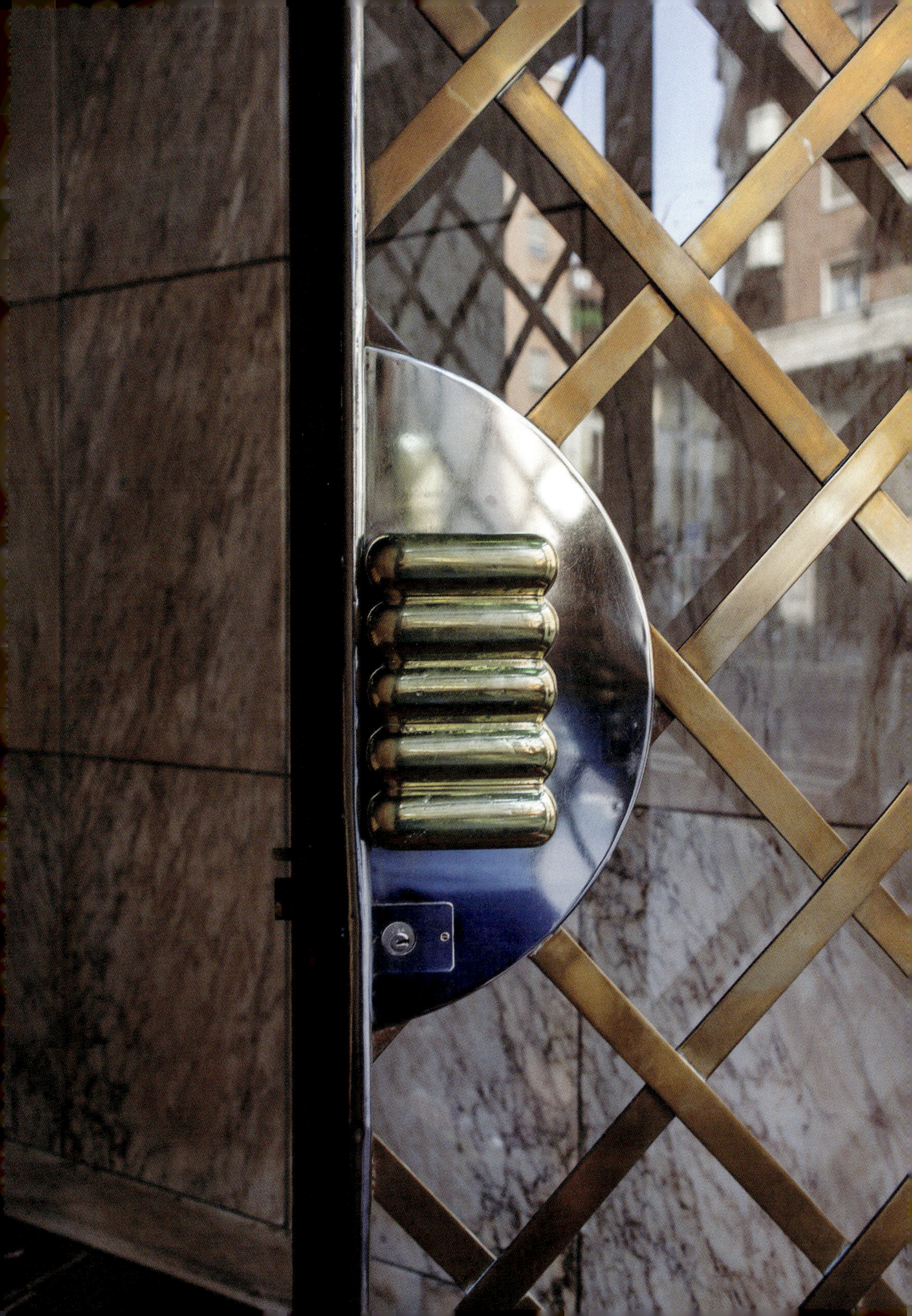

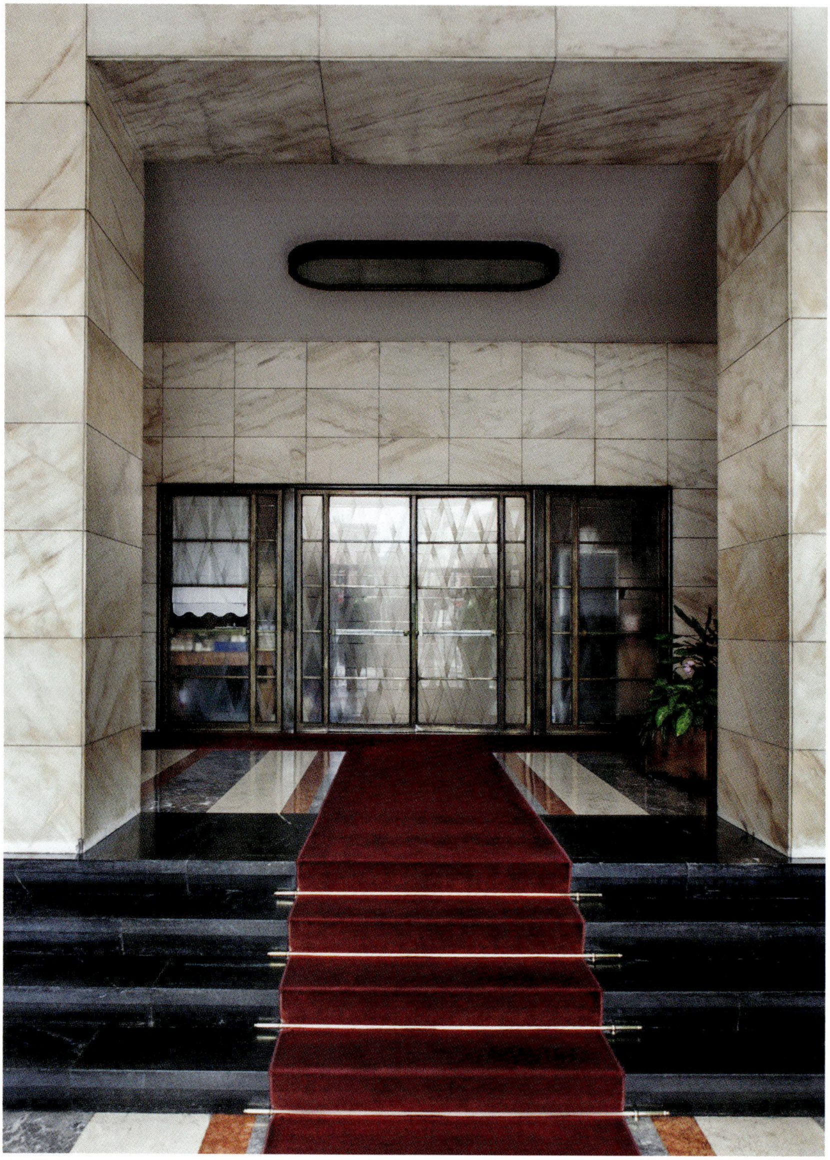

This and following spread:

viale Tunisia 42 · Paolo Mario Lamborizio, 1936–39

Ceiling lamp and door handles by Fontana Arte.

floor: Verona Rosso limestone, Occhialino Valcamonica limestone, Chiampo limestone

stairs: serpentinite · walls: Carrara marble

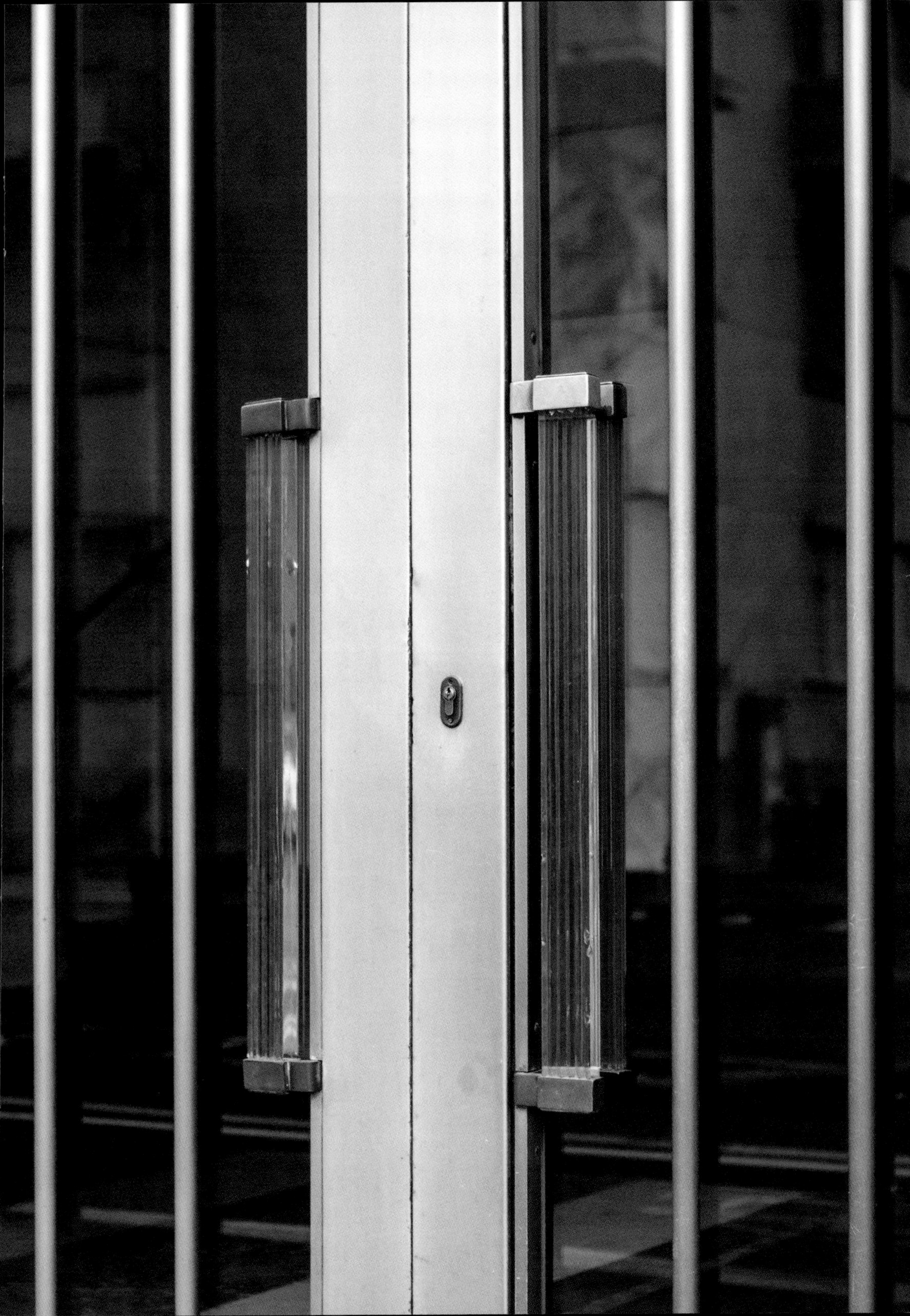

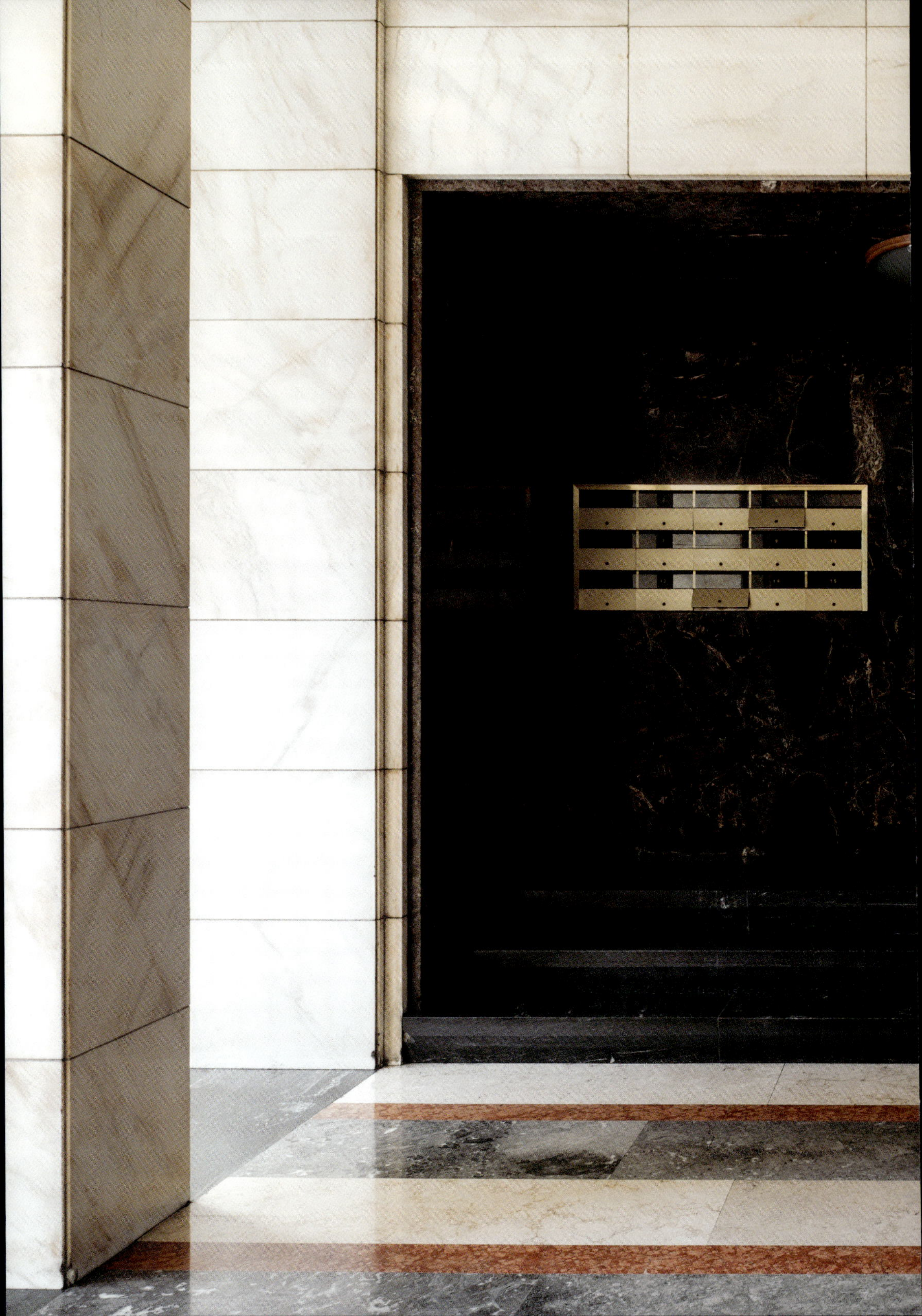

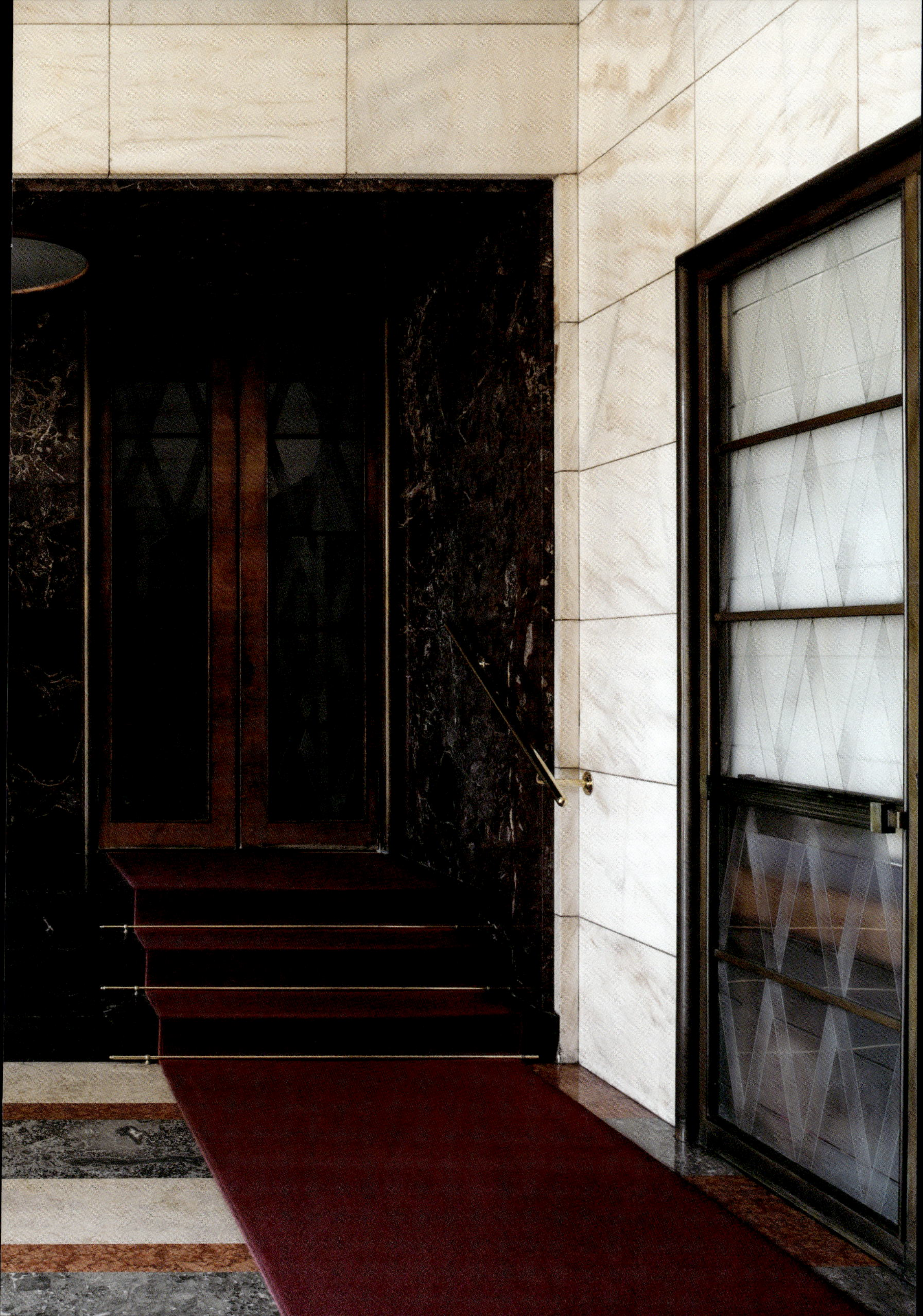

Previous spread:
floor: Verona Rosso limestone, Occhialino Valcamonica limestone, white limestone
stairs: serpentinite · doorframe: Rosso Levanto ophicalcite

viale Tunisia 11-13 · Pierluigi Requiliani, 1953–61
floor: Rosa Baveno granite, Beola Ghiandonata · stairs and upstairs floor: Rosa Baveno granite
wall: Calacatta marble

Following spread:
viale Tunisia 32 · 1938–40
Pendant lamp by Strada.
floor: Carrara statuario and Bardiglio marble

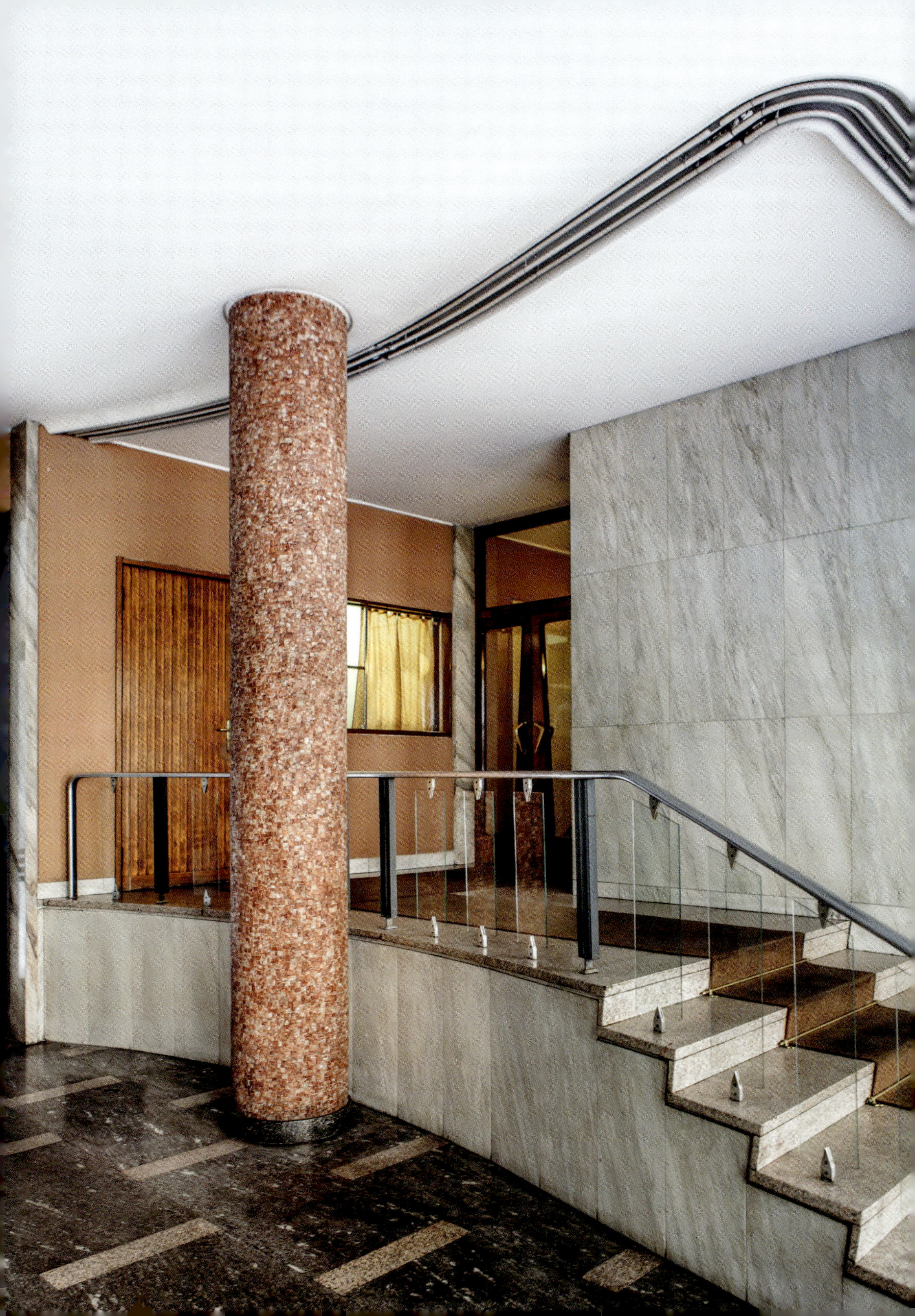

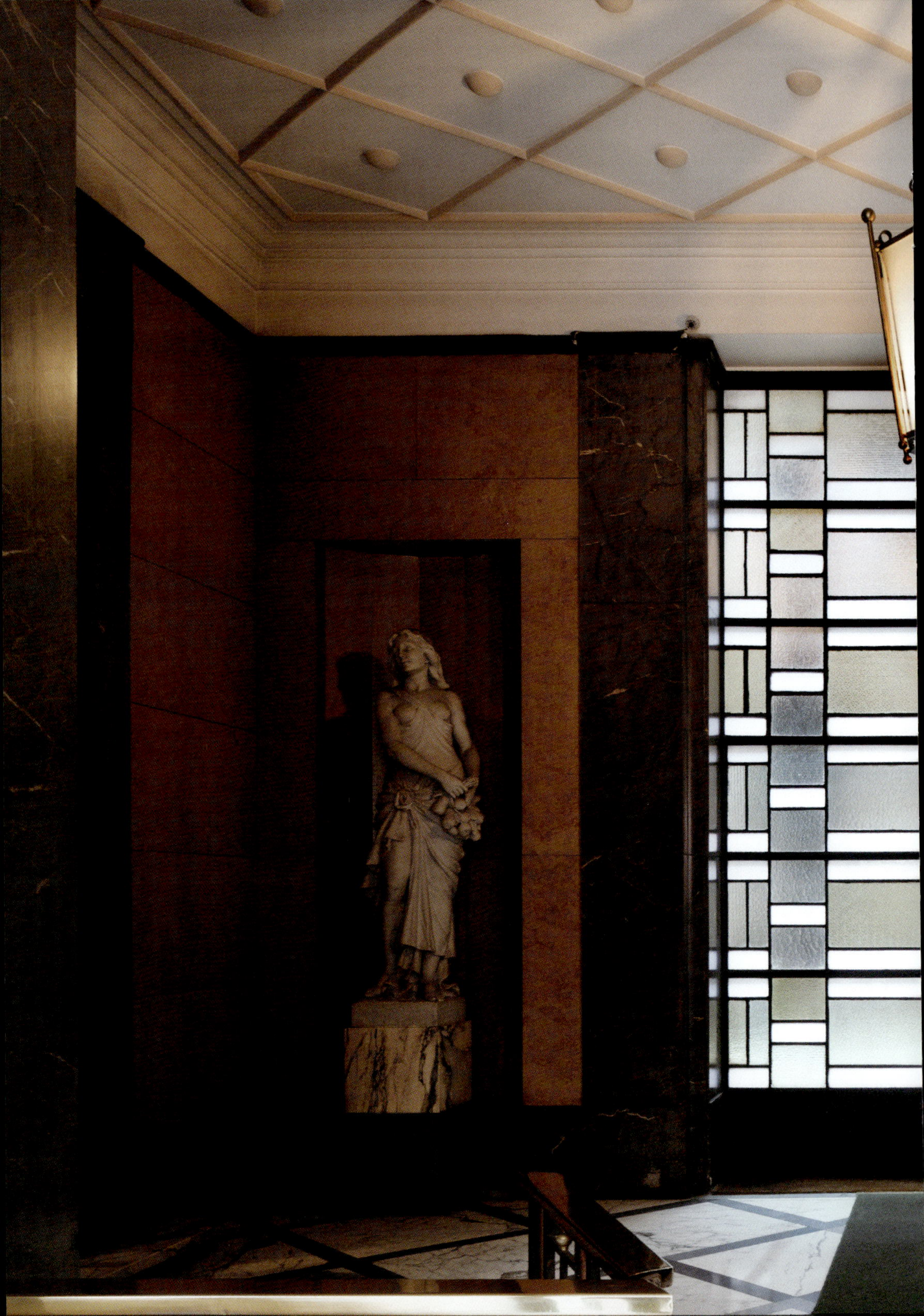

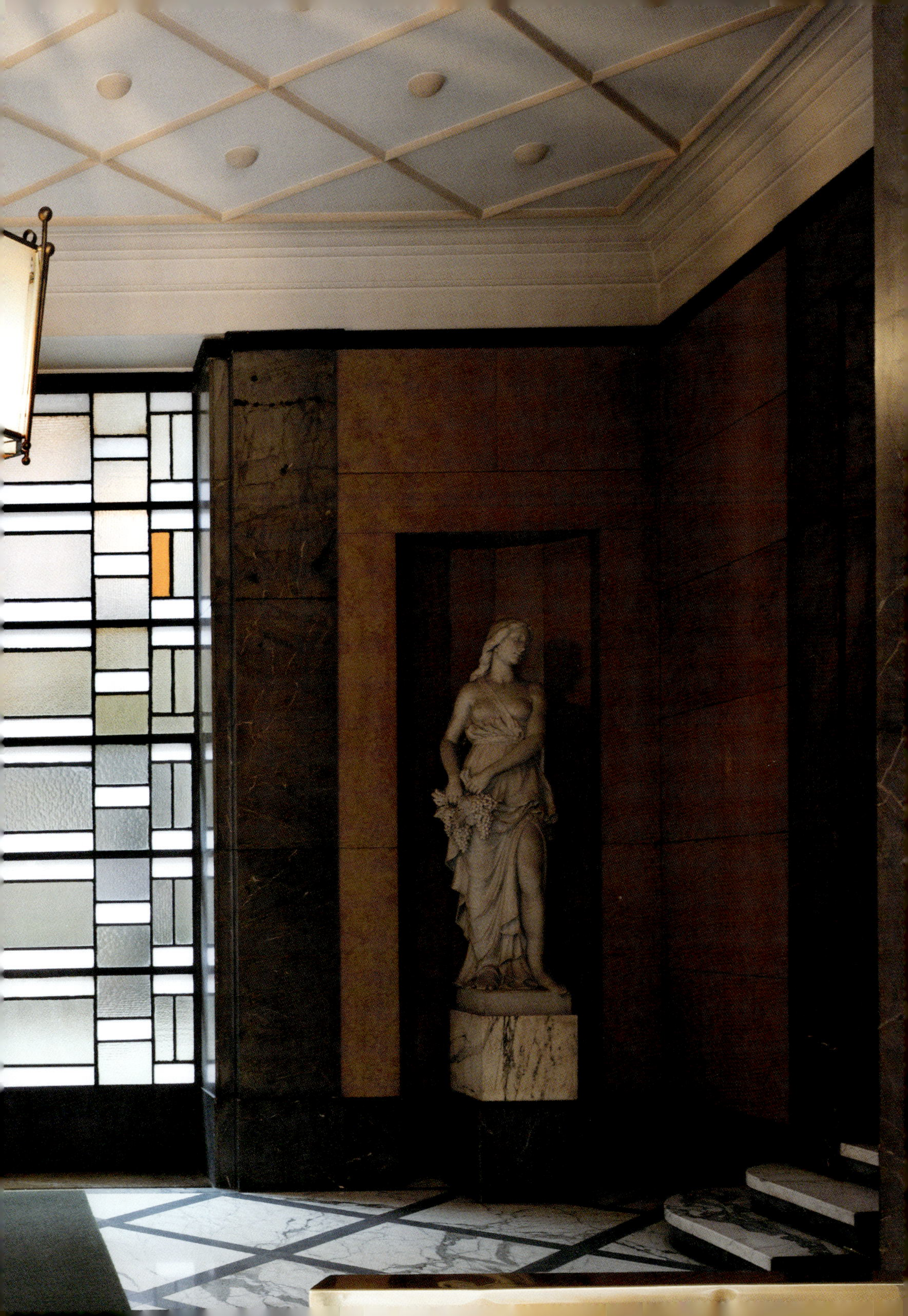

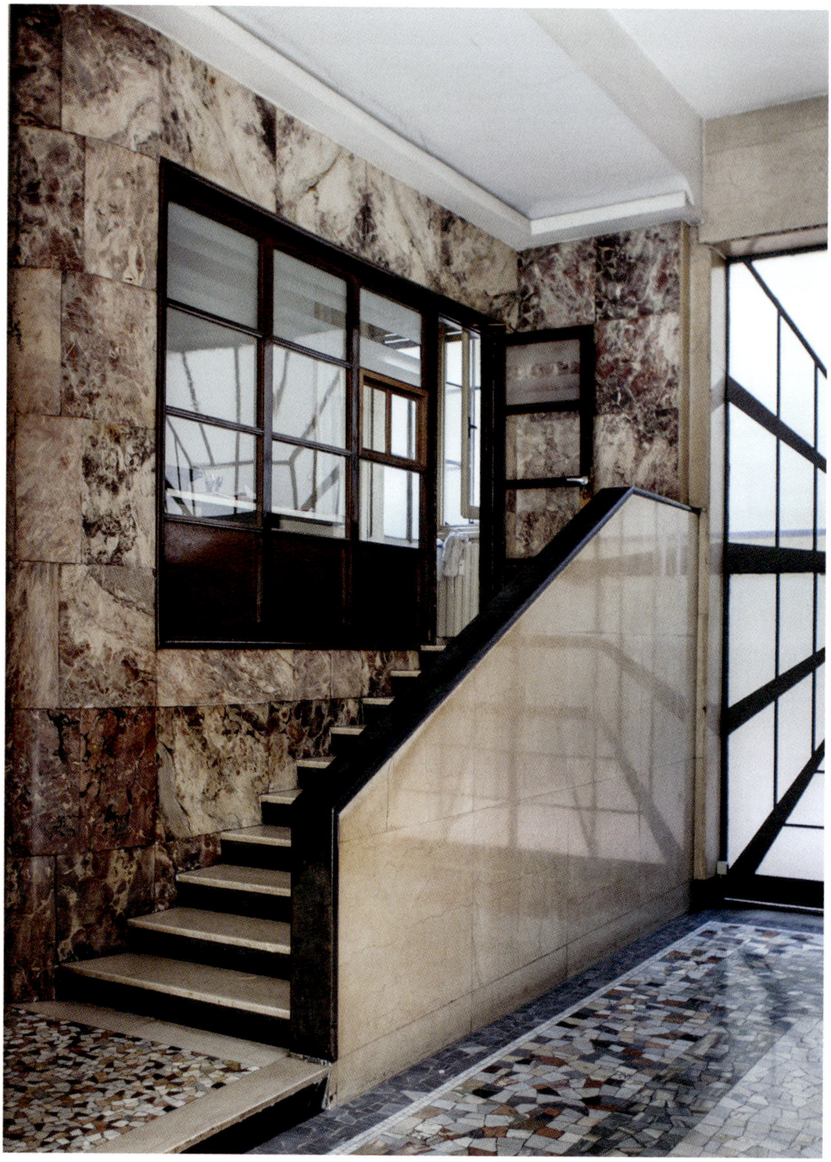

viale Tunisia 44

floor: Palladiana of several marbles and limestones · stairs: Botticino limestone and serpentinite
walls: Breccia Medicea marble and Botticino limestone

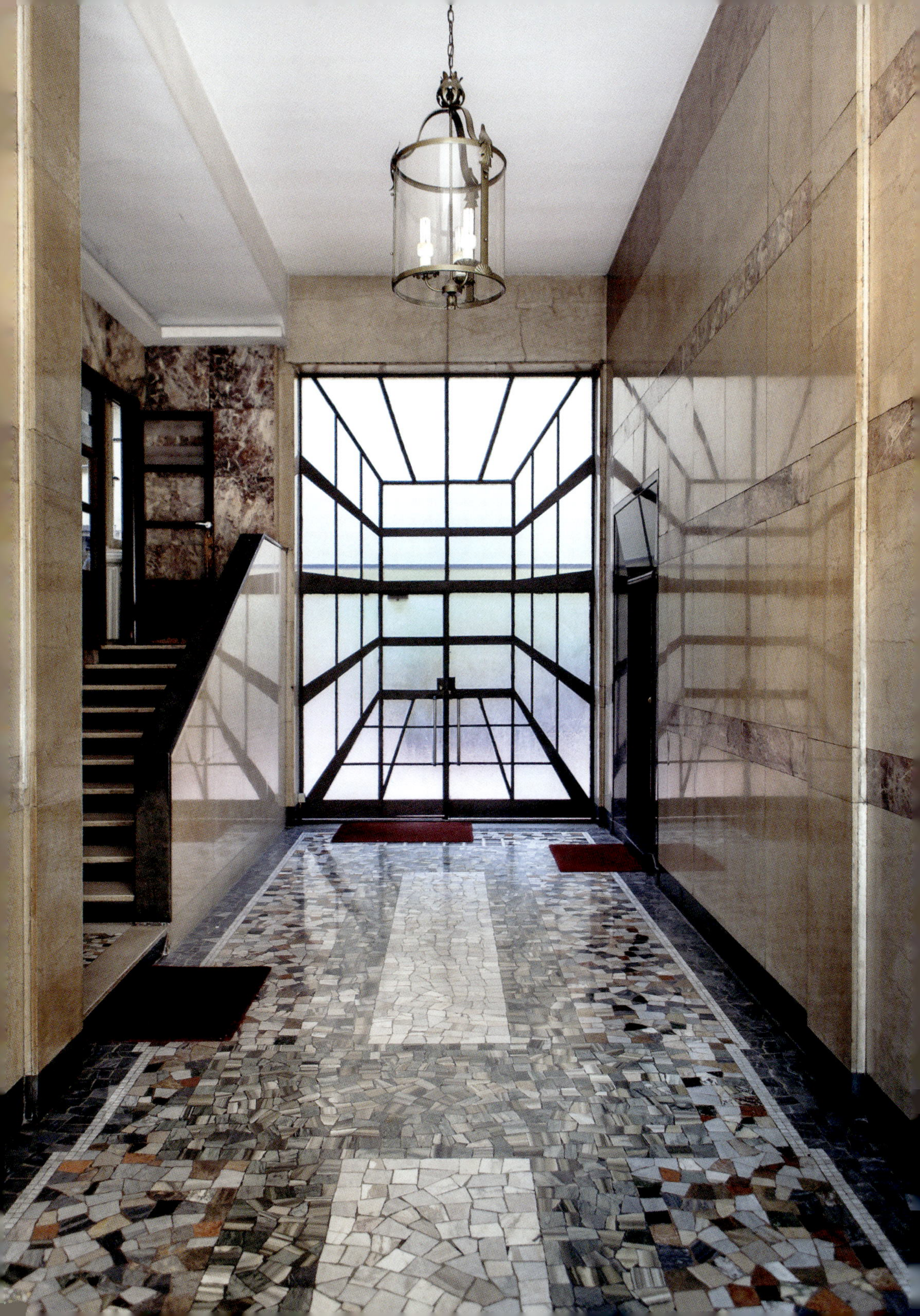

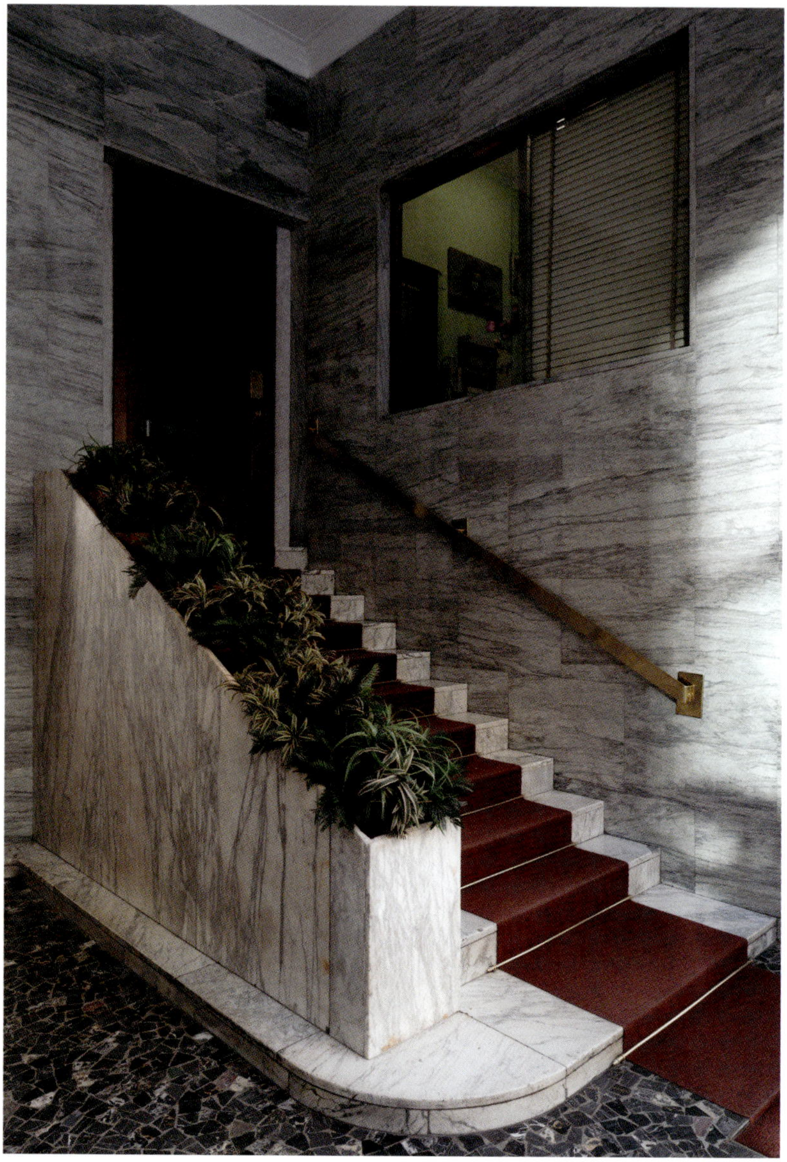

viale Tunisia 21 · Mario Rodolfi, 1939–49
floor: Palladiana of several marbles and limestones · stairs: Carrara Bianco Arni marble · wall: Cipollino marble

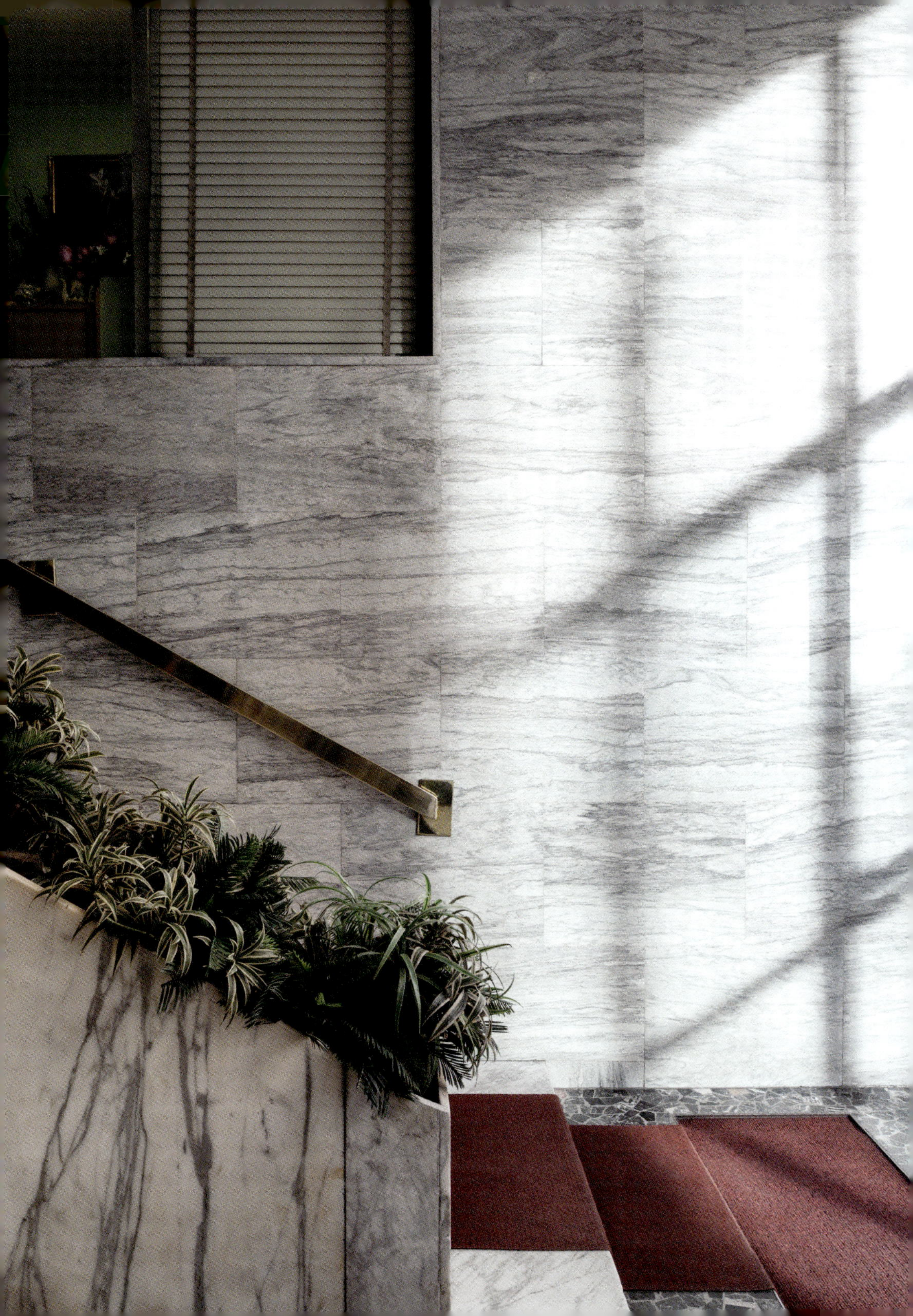

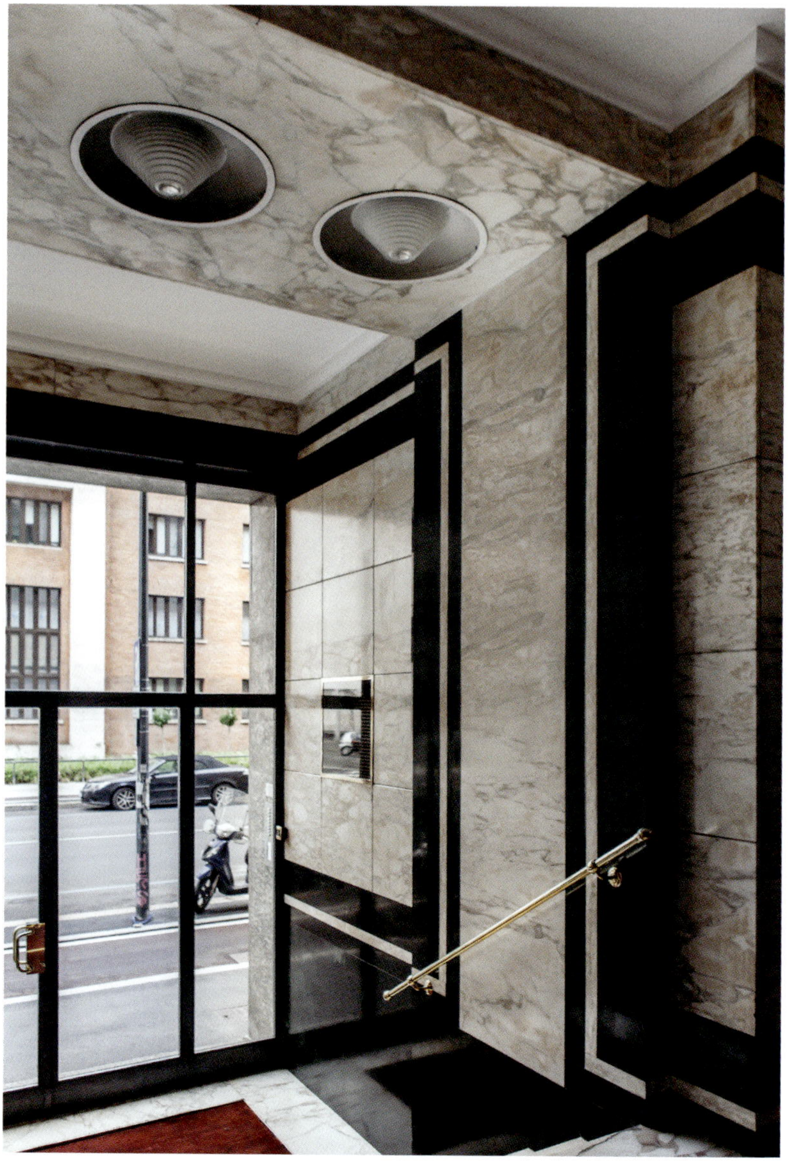

viale Tunisia 36 · Giuseppe Roberto Martinenghi, 1938

Ceiling lights by Angelo Mangiarotti.

stairs: Arabescato Carrara marble and serpentinite · walls and ceiling: Arabescato Carrara marble

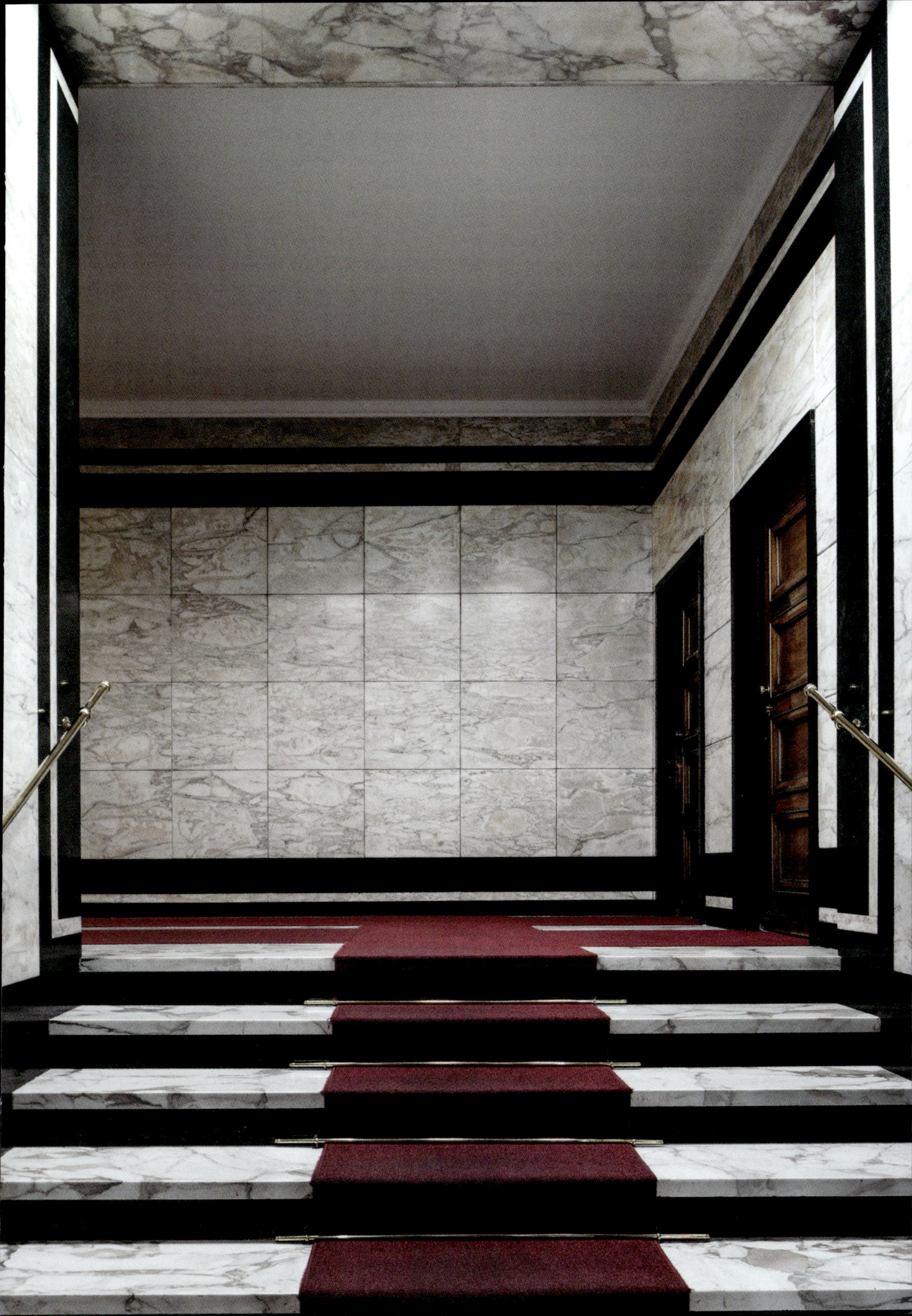

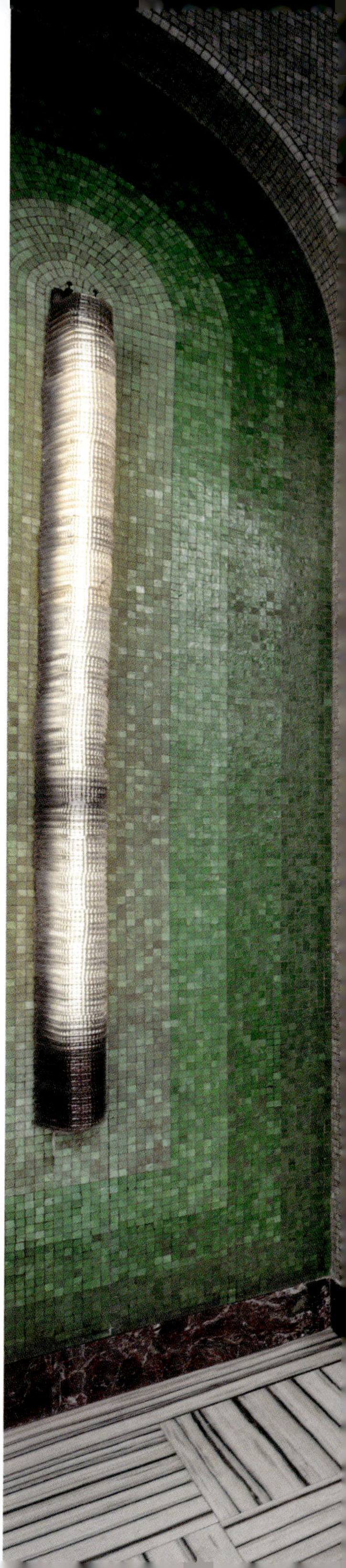

This and following spread:
viale Tunisia 39 · Aldo Avati, 1939
Ceiling light and two lateral sconces by Venini.
floor: Cipollino 900 marble, also known as Zebrino marble
skirting, doorframe: Rosso Levanto ophicalcite
stairs: Bianco Carrara marble, Rosso Levanto ophicalcite

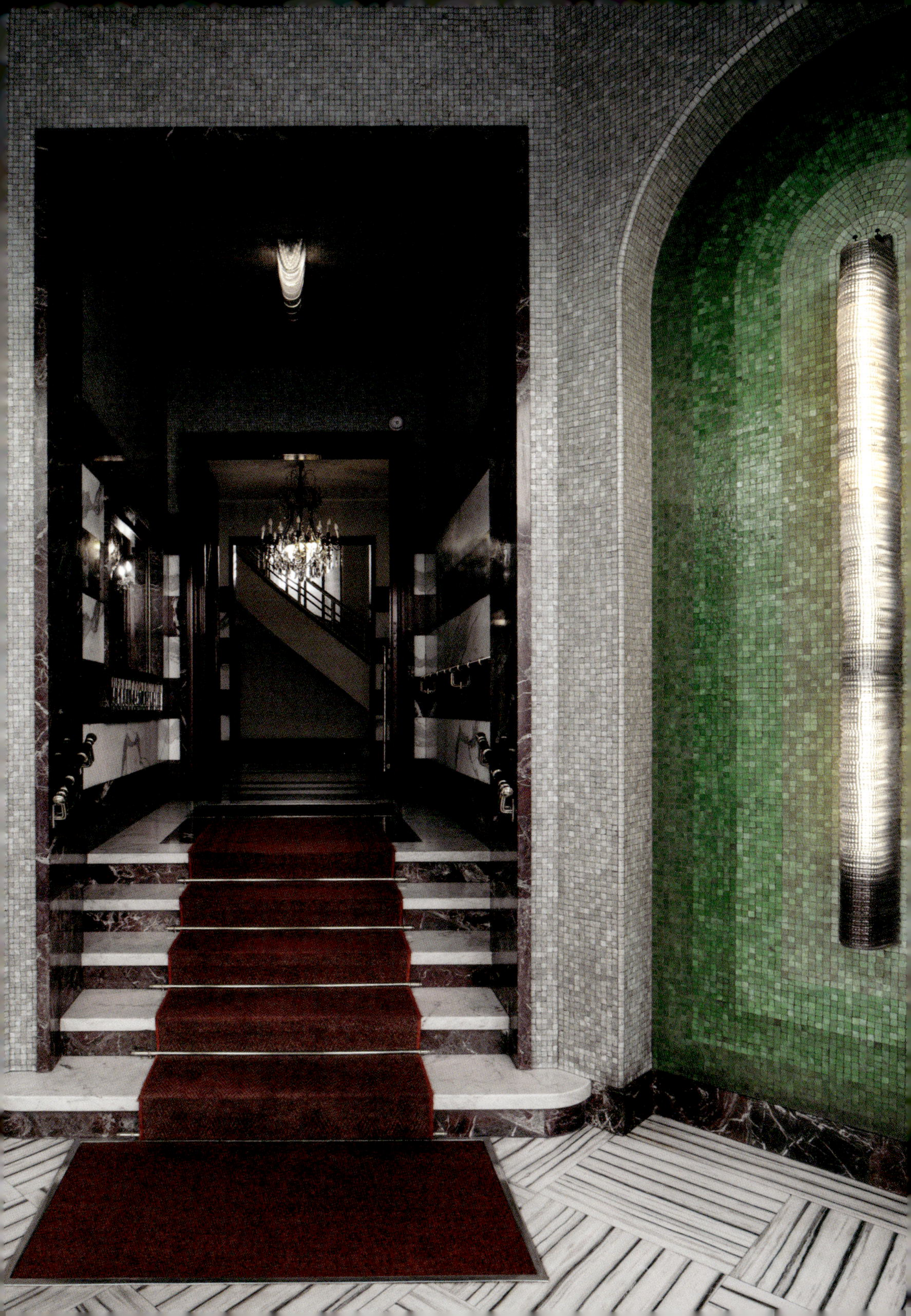

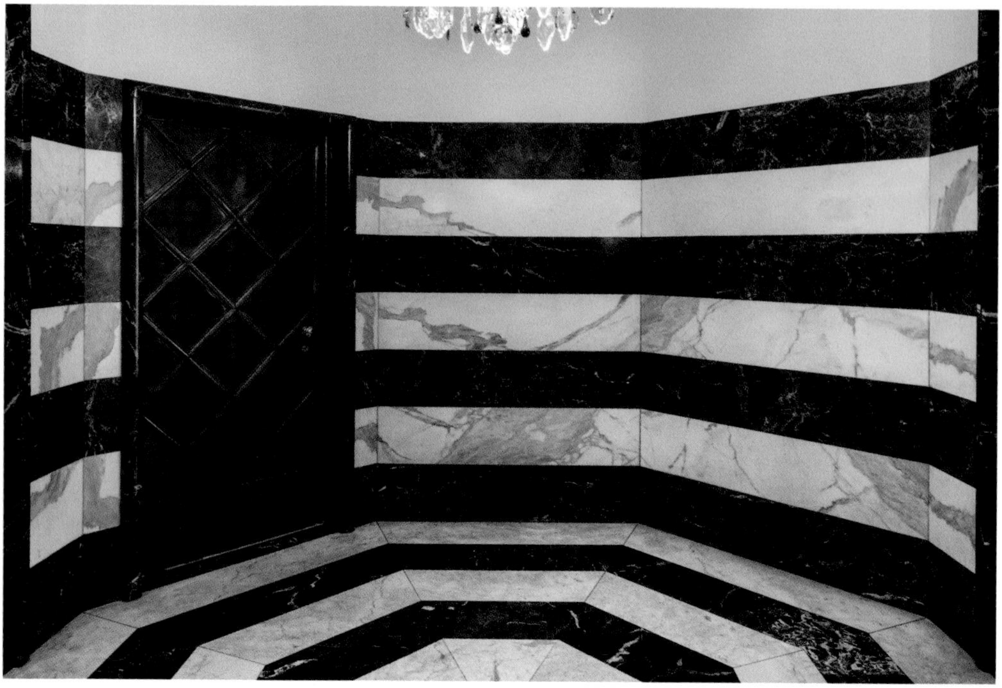

floor, walls, stairs and doorframe: Rosso Levanto ophicalcite and Carrara Statuario Veneto marble

Following spread:

via Raimondo Franchetti 3 · Domenico Poloni, 1937–39

floor: Palladiana of several marbles and limestones · walls: Cipollino marble and serpentinite · skirting, lesene: serpentinite

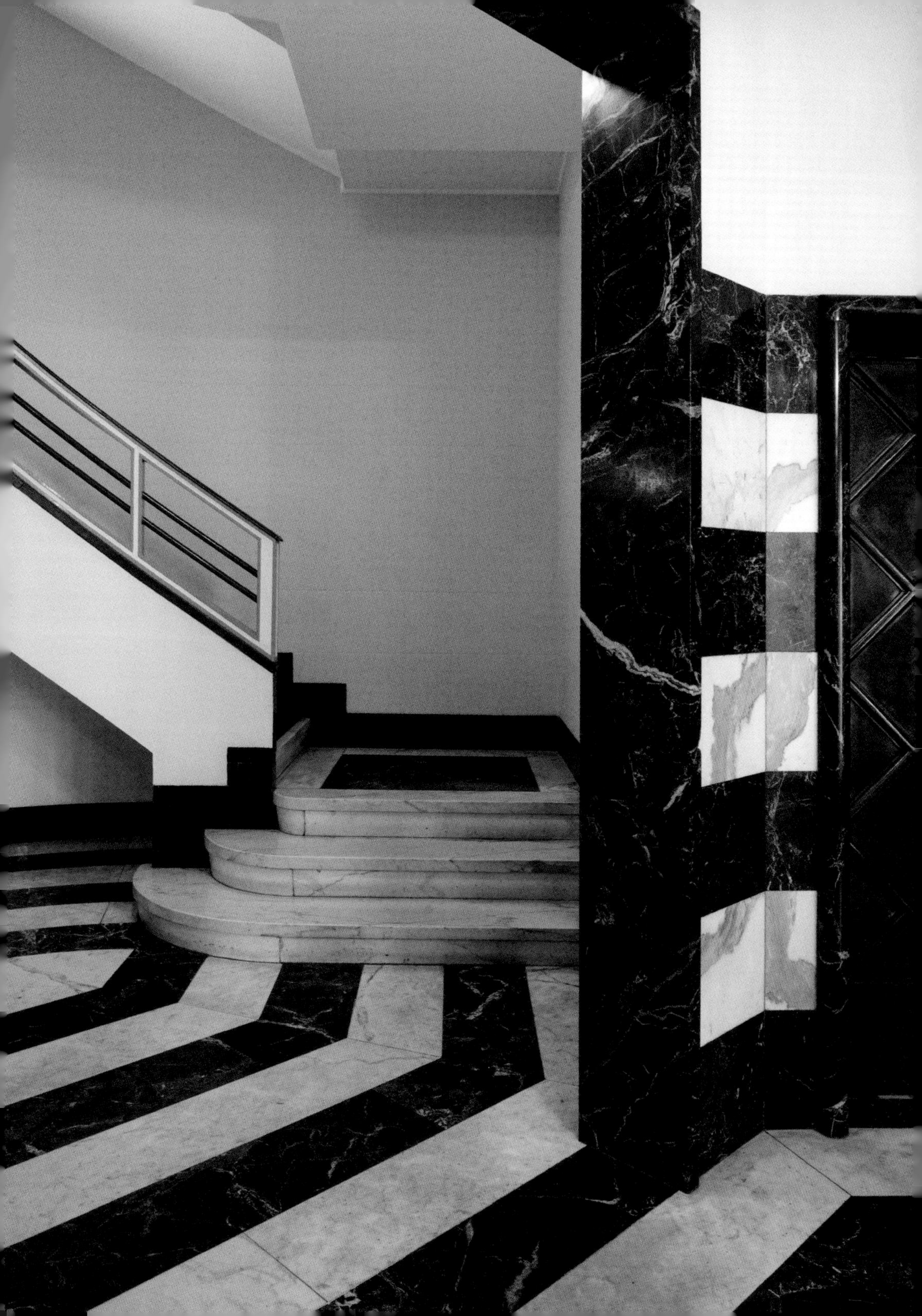

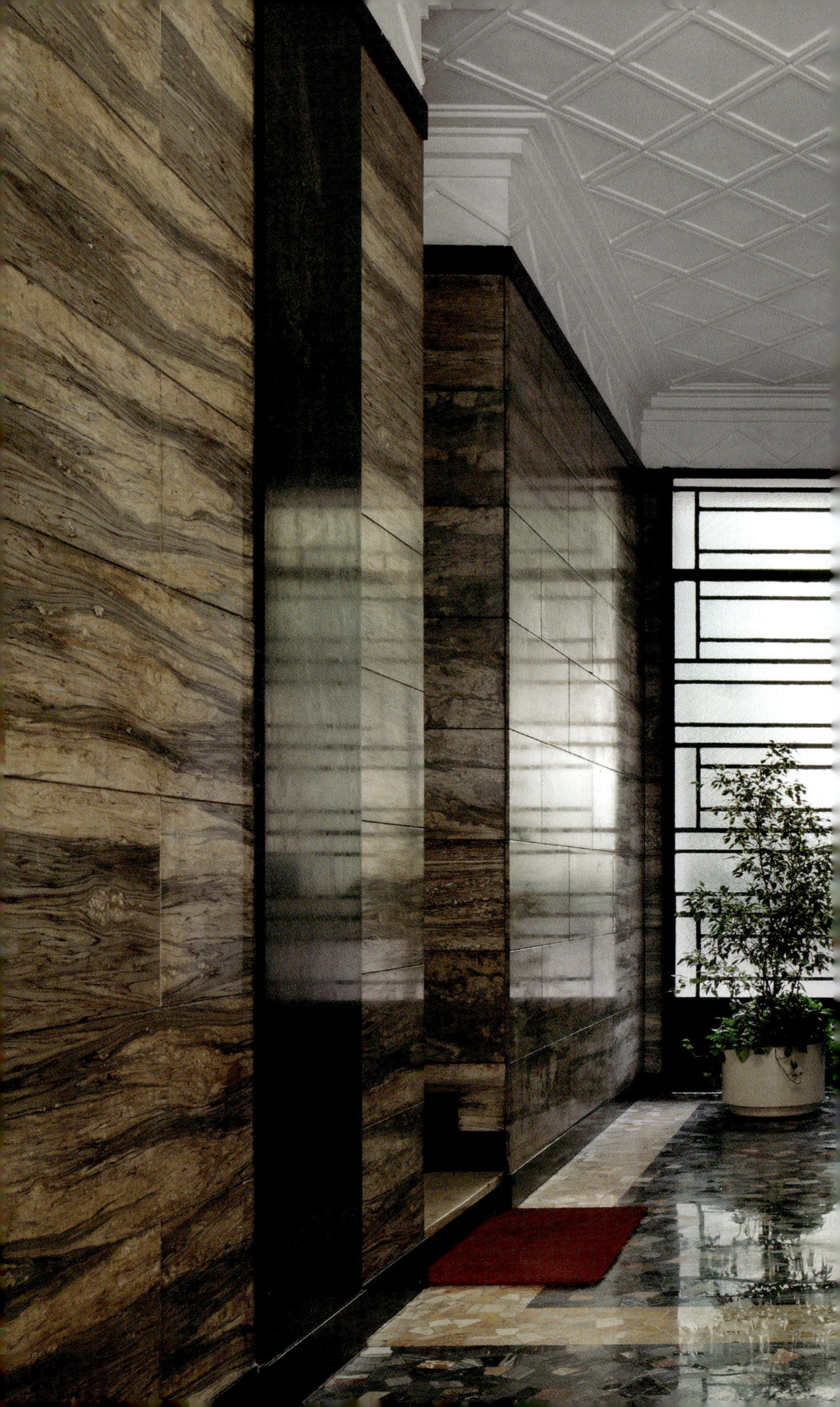

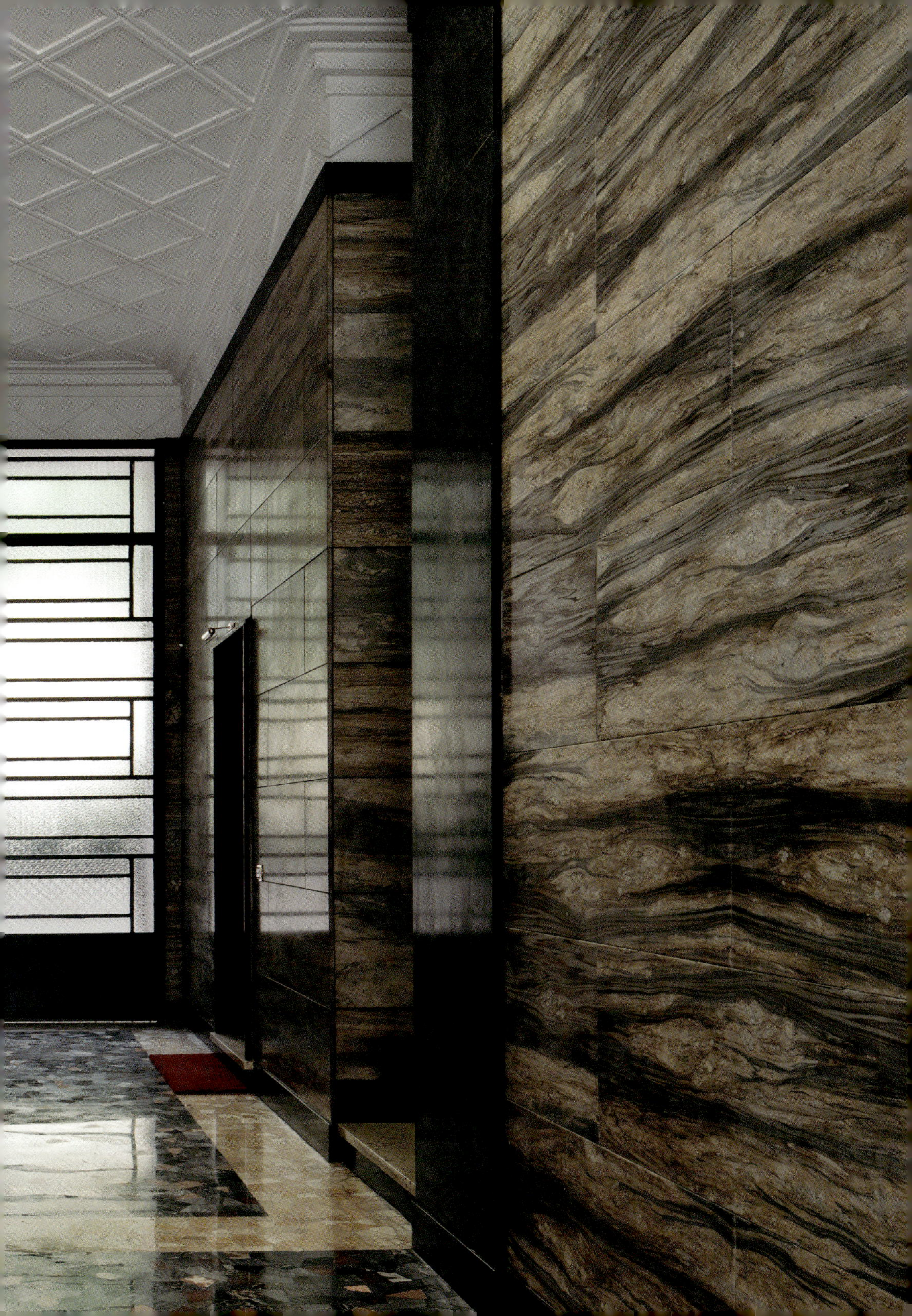

viale Vittorio Veneto 16 · Guglielmo Ulrich, 1952

Chandelier by Vico Magistretti.
floor and walls: Trani Serpeggiante limestone

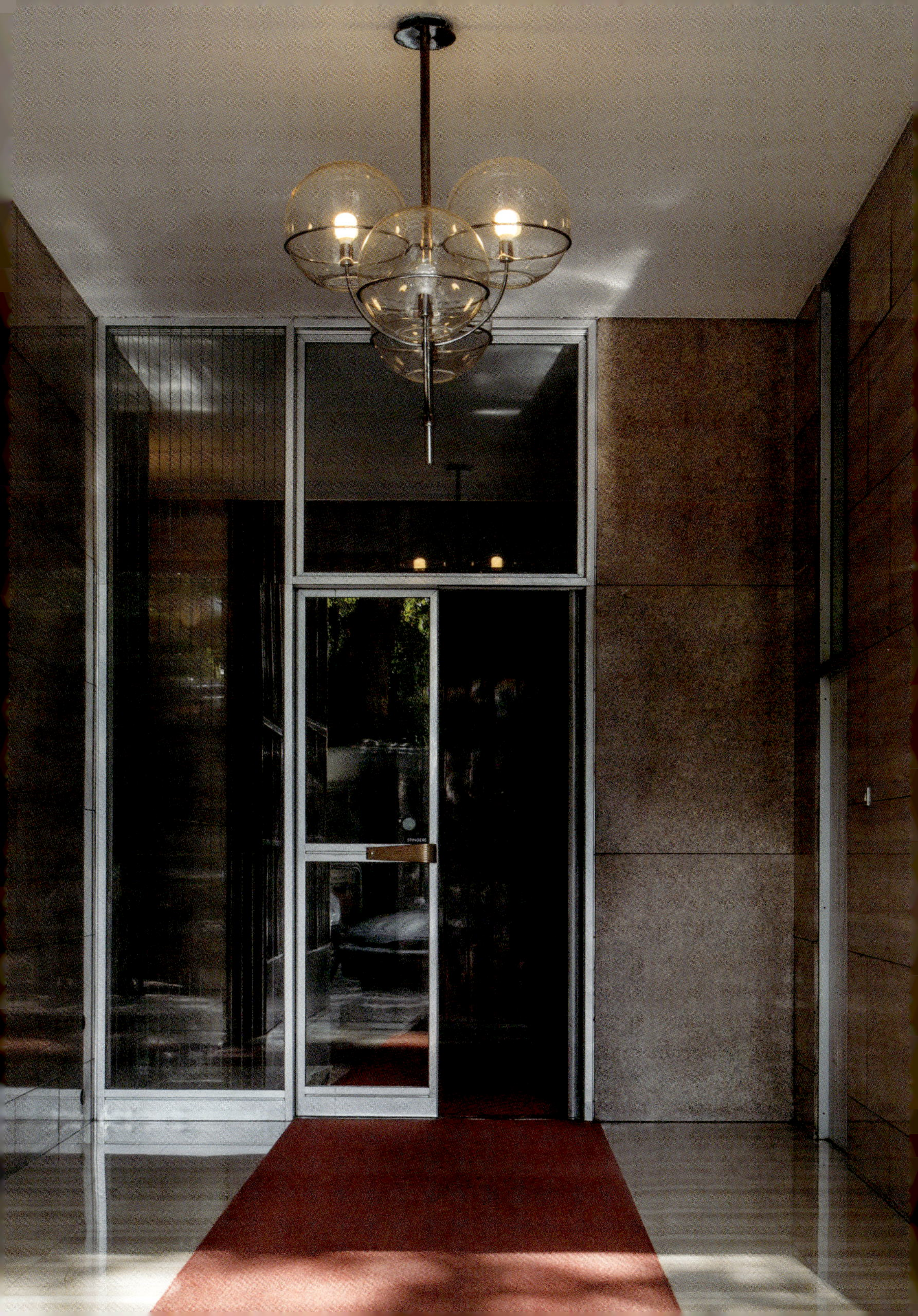

The entrance door with its porthole windows sets a maritime theme here, one that is accented by decorative elements made in Venice. A sconce with glass striations evokes the underwater world. There are also some notable ceramic details, such as a seashell-inspired door handle that leads to a stairway with a barnacled handrail.

This and following spreads:

viale Vittorio Veneto 20 · Achille Luigi Ferraresi, 1952–57

step: Verde Alpi ophicalcite (opposite page)

Sconce by Venini. Ceramic door handles by Ceramica San Paolo, Venice (pages 154–155).

Ceramic coverings for handrail by Ceramica San Paolo, Venice (pages 156–157).

floor: Botticino limestone and Verona Rosso limestone · walls: Botticino limestone

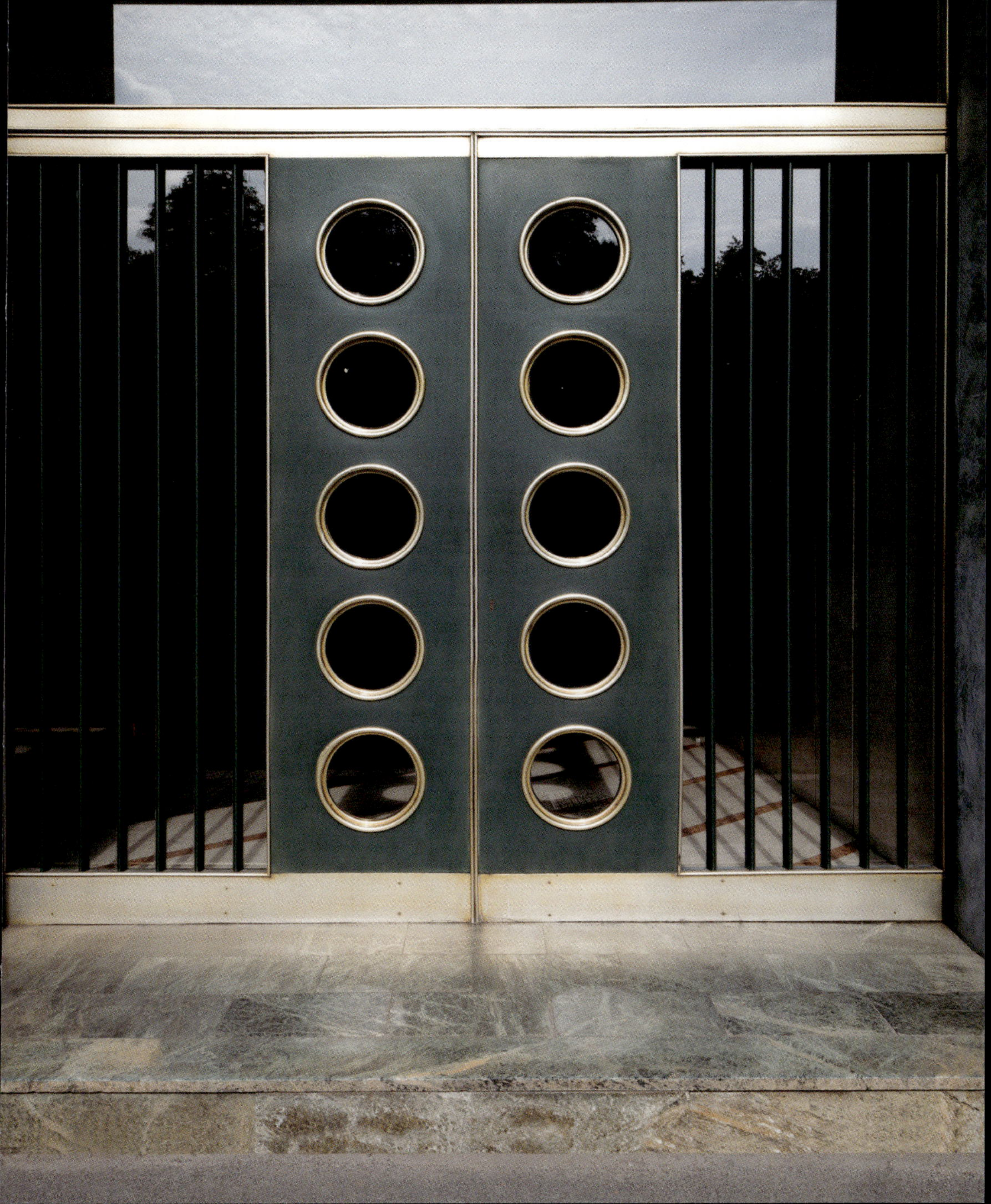

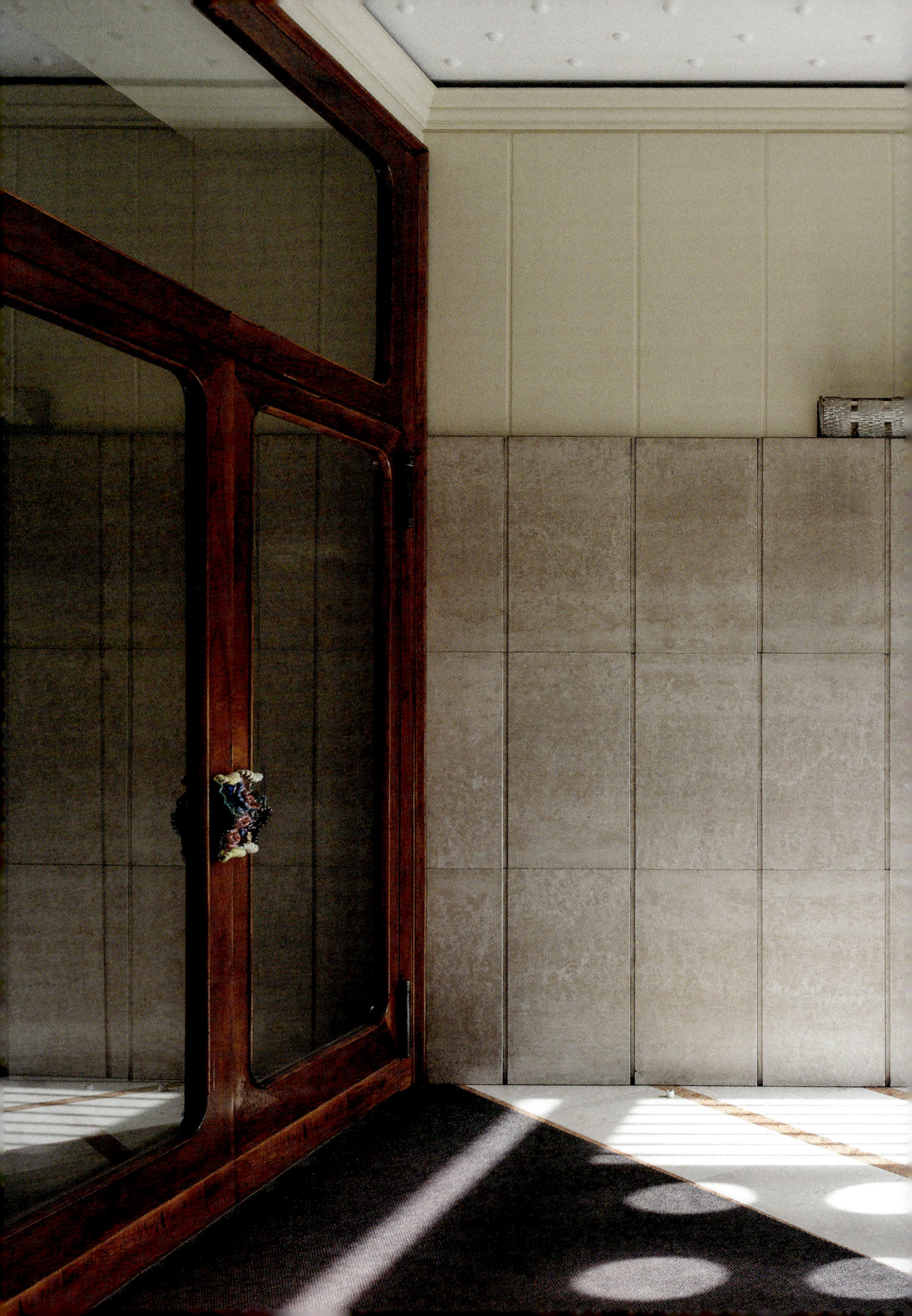

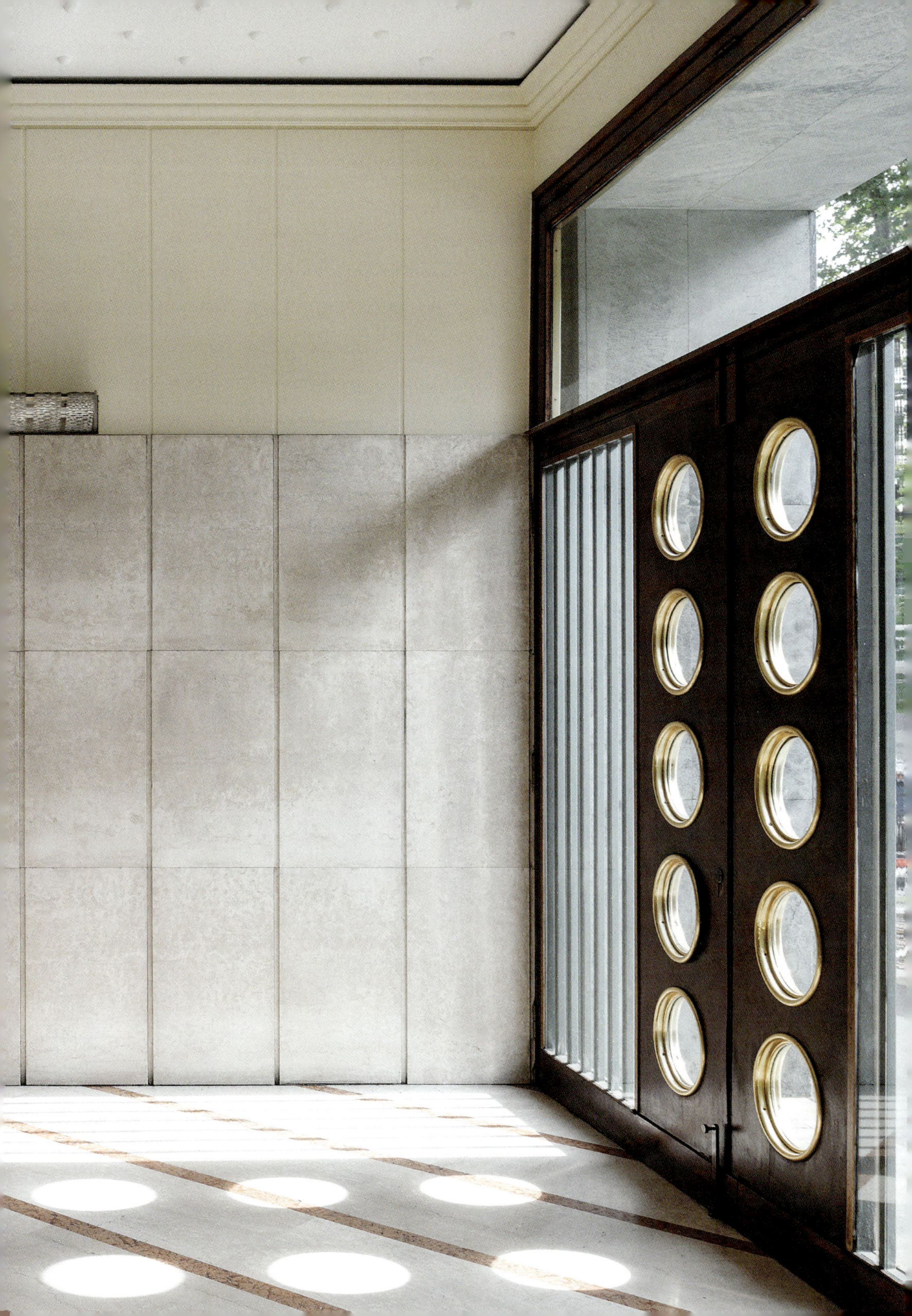

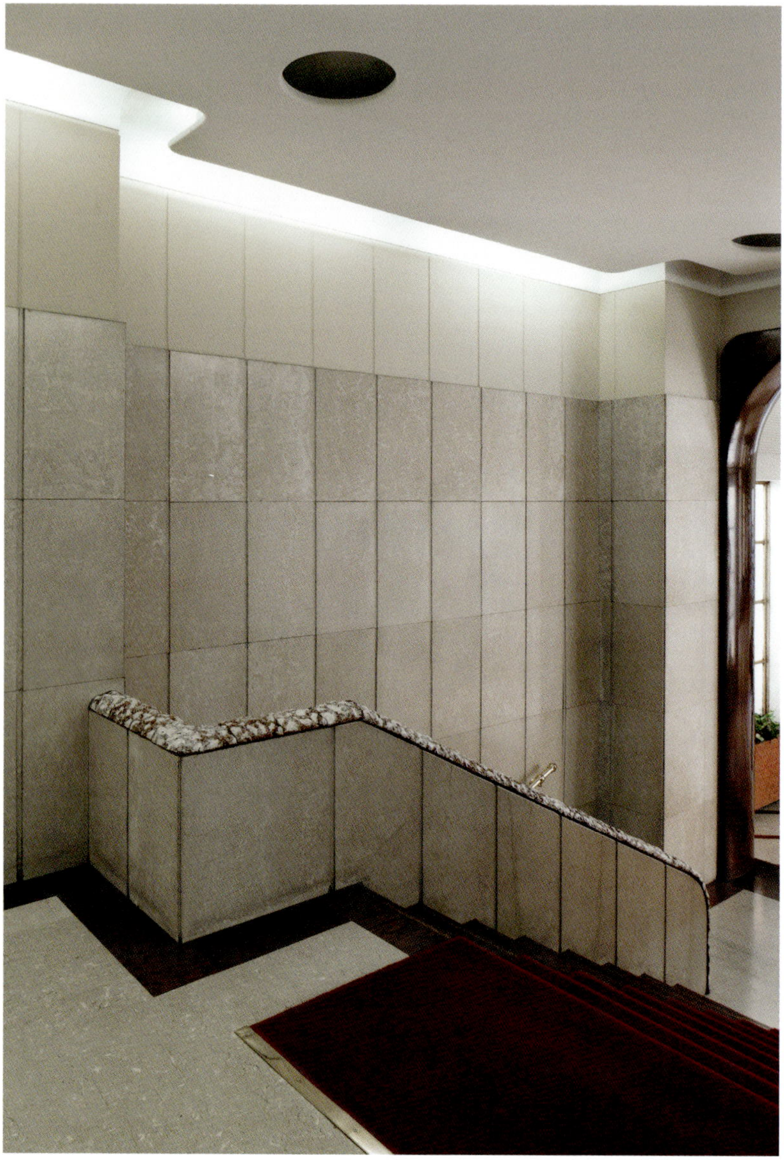

Following spread:
viale Vittorio Veneto 22 · Achille Luigi Ferraresi, 1952–57
floor: Botticino limestone and Verona Rosso limestone · pillars: Botticino limestone

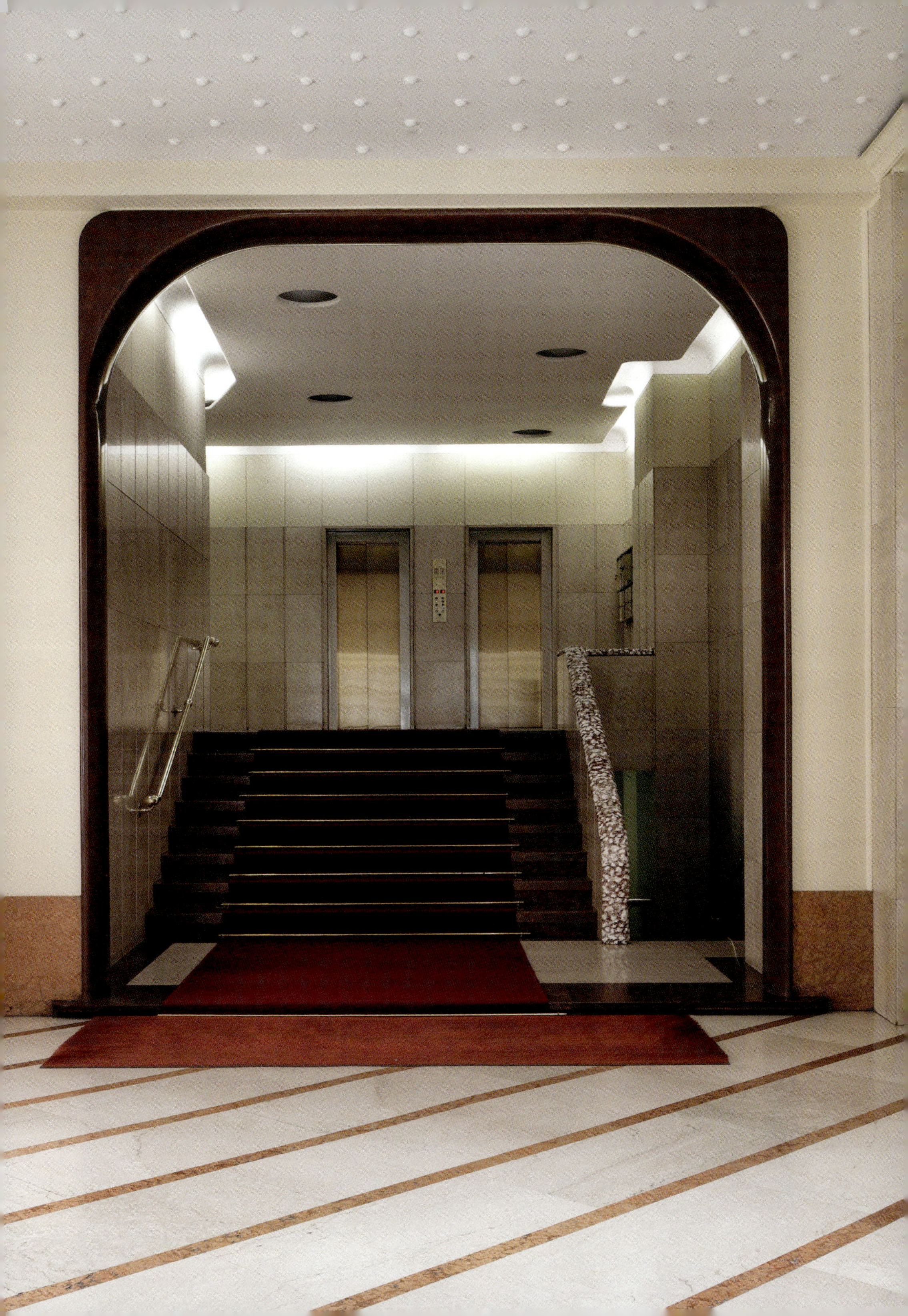

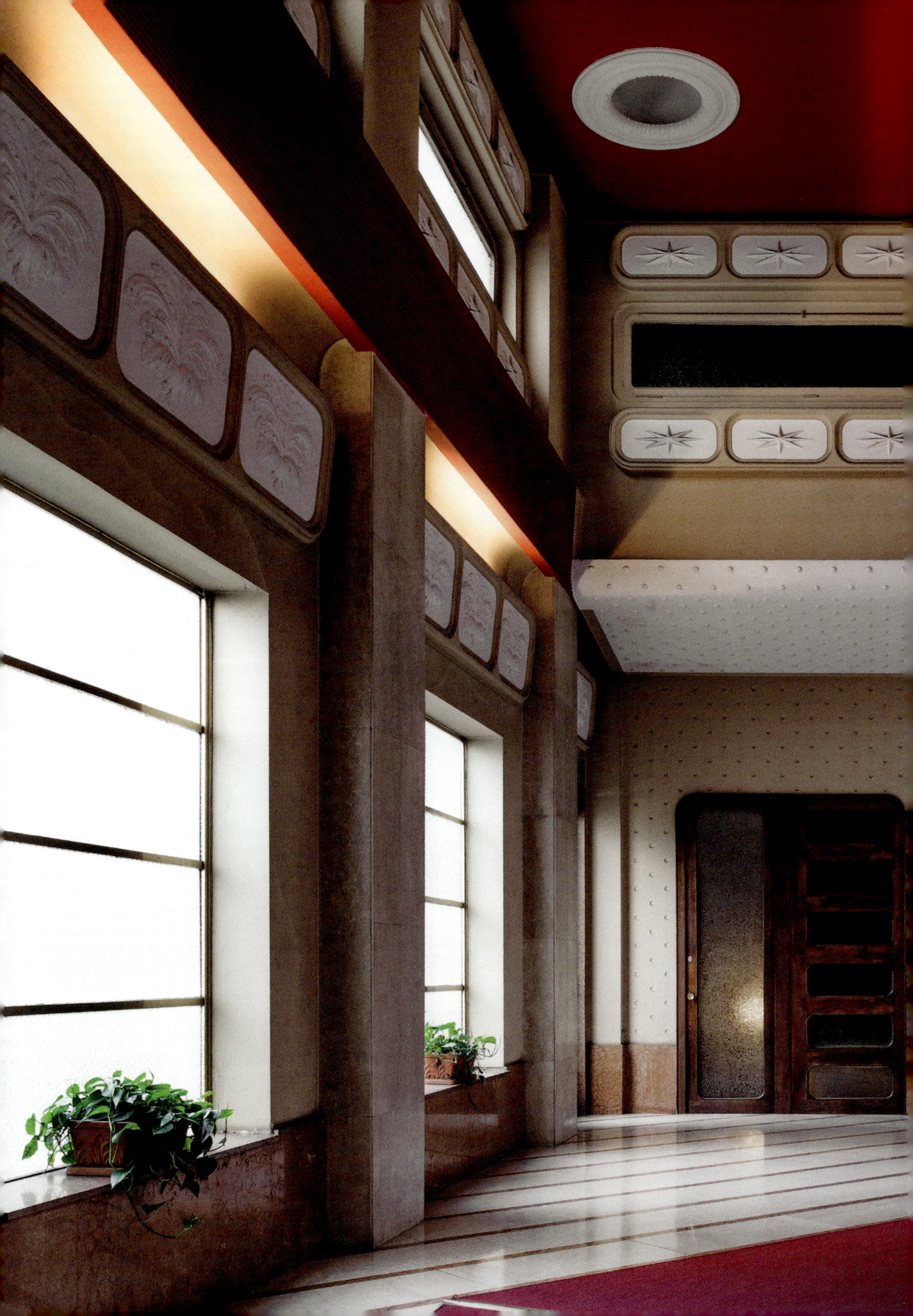

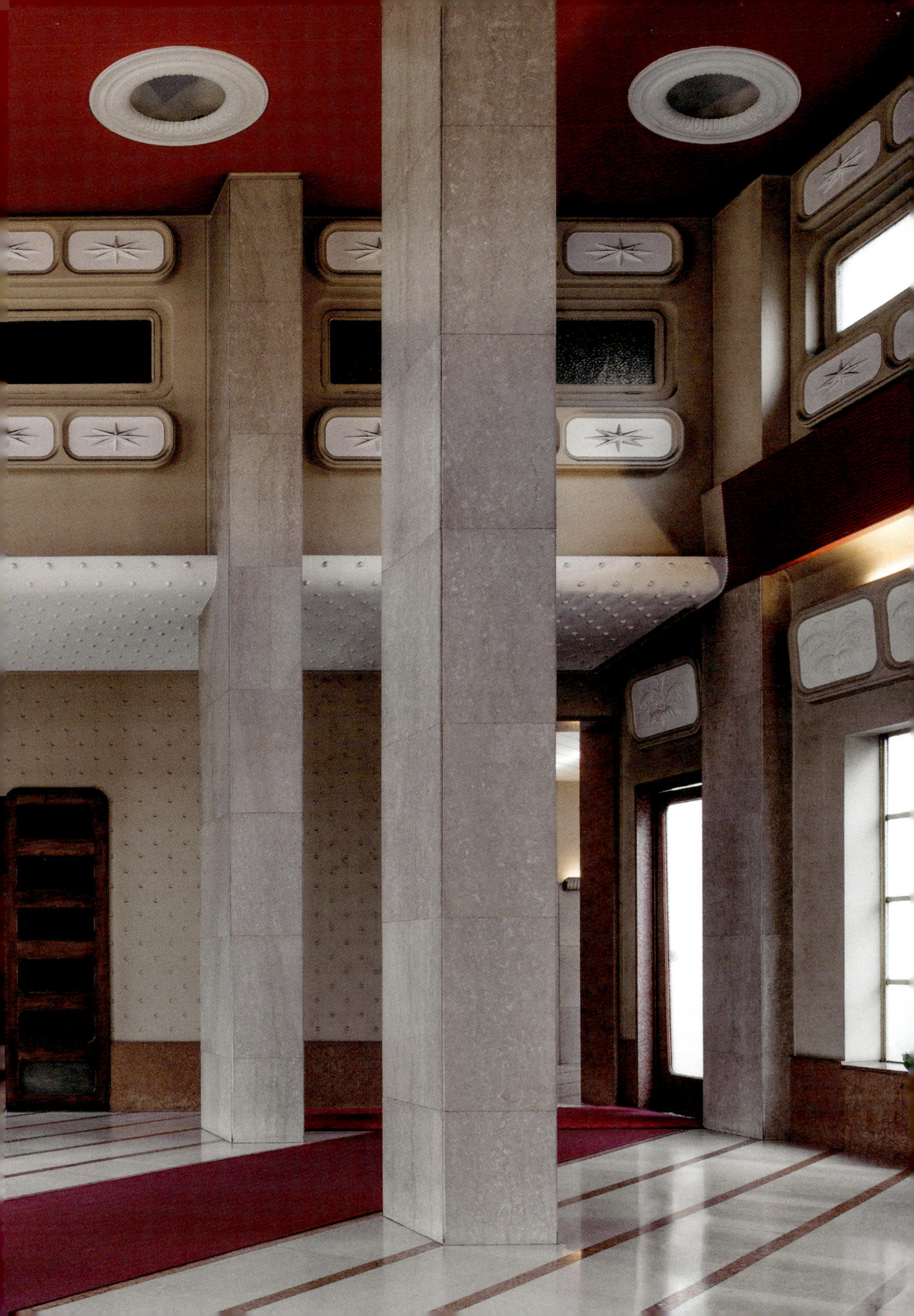

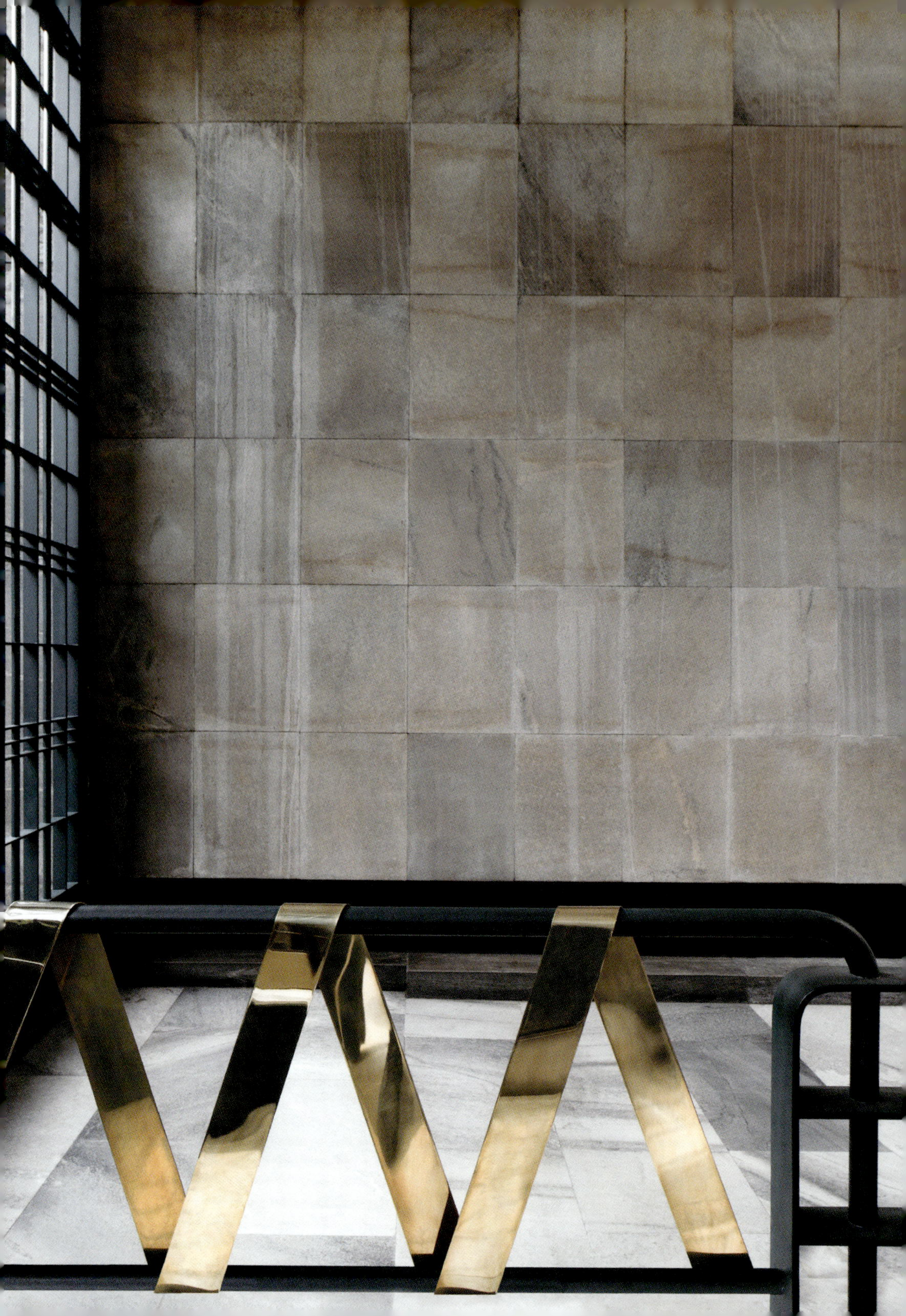

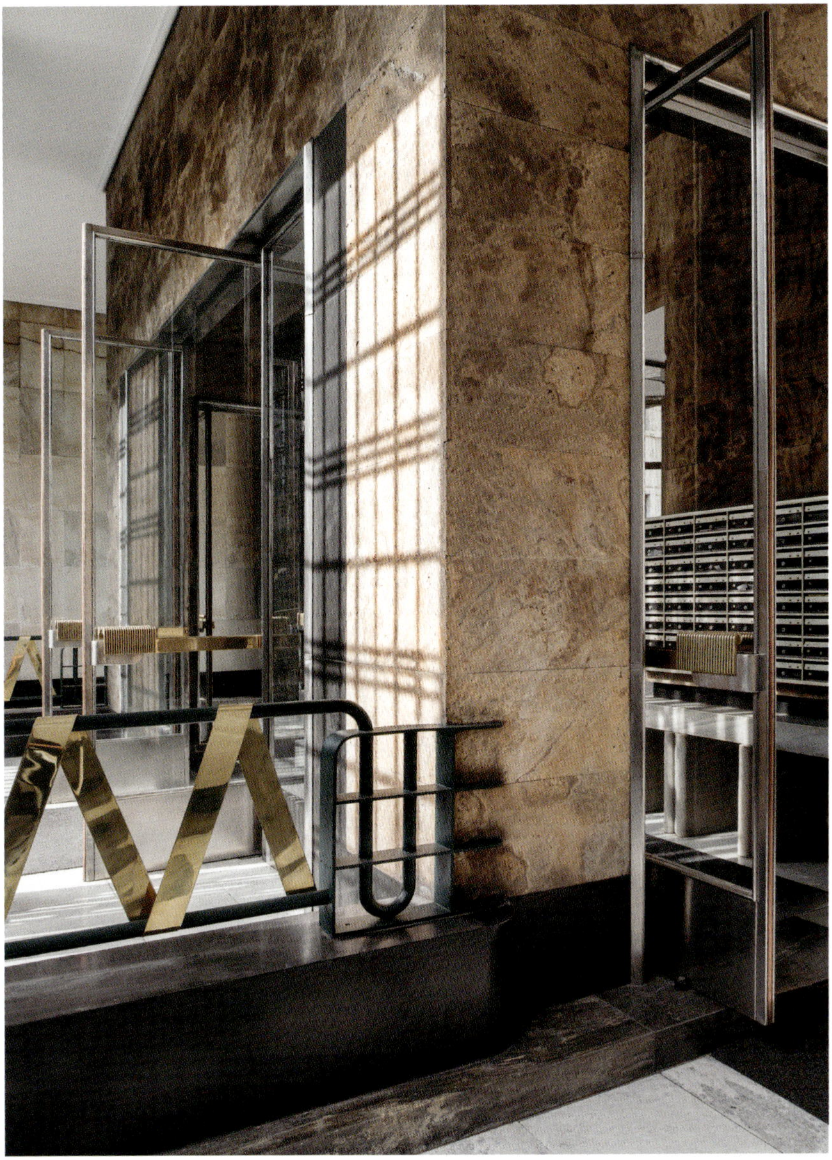

viale Vittorio Veneto 24, Casa della Fontana · Rino Ferrini, Franco Bruni, 1934–36
floor: Musso marble · skirting: Samolaco granite · walls (this page): alabaster

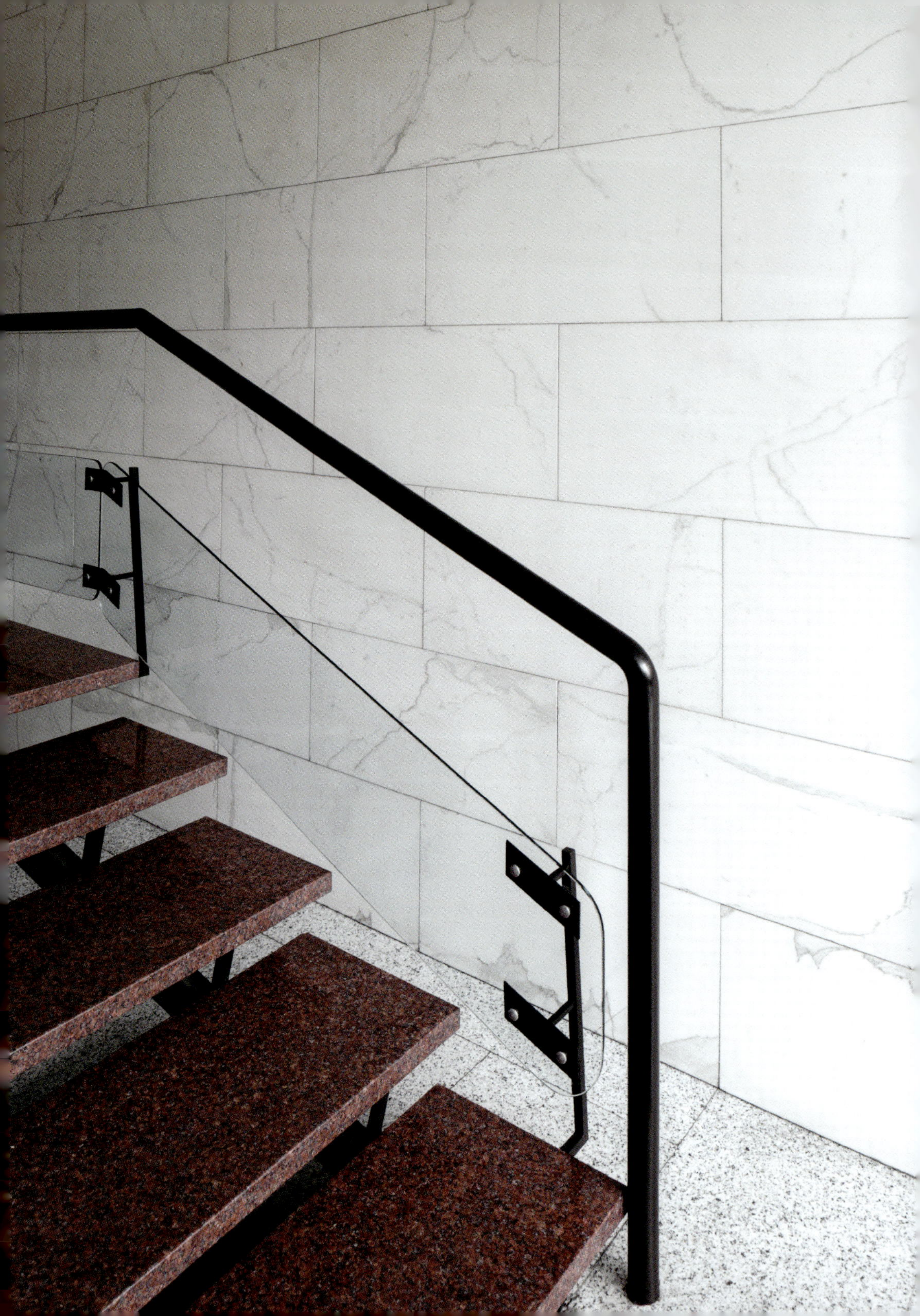

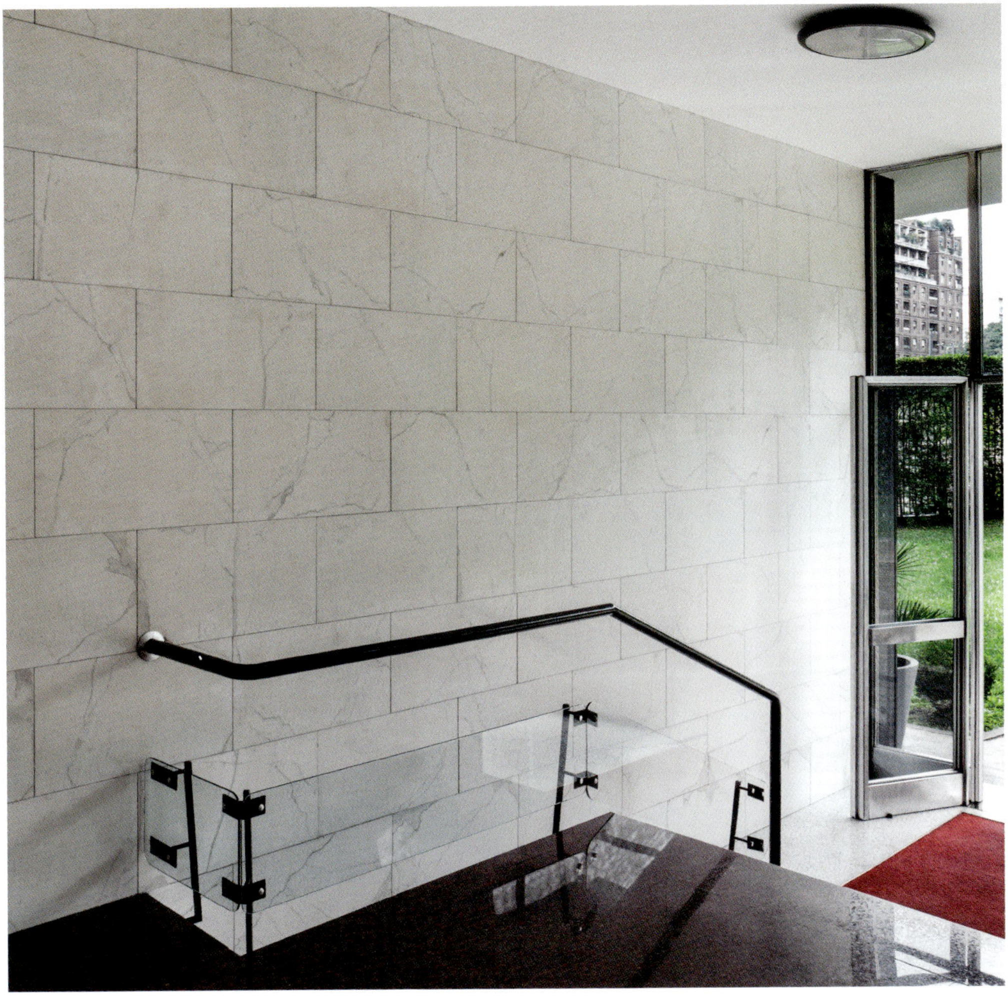

piazza della Repubblica 12 · Gigi Ghò, 1955

Ceiling lamp by Gino Sarfatti.

floor: Montorfano granite · stairs: New Imperial granite · walls: Carrara Statuario Venato marble

piazza della Repubblica 30 · Umberto Faccio, 1935–36

floor: Palladiana of Rosso Levanto ophicalcite · walls: Fior di Pesco Carnico marble

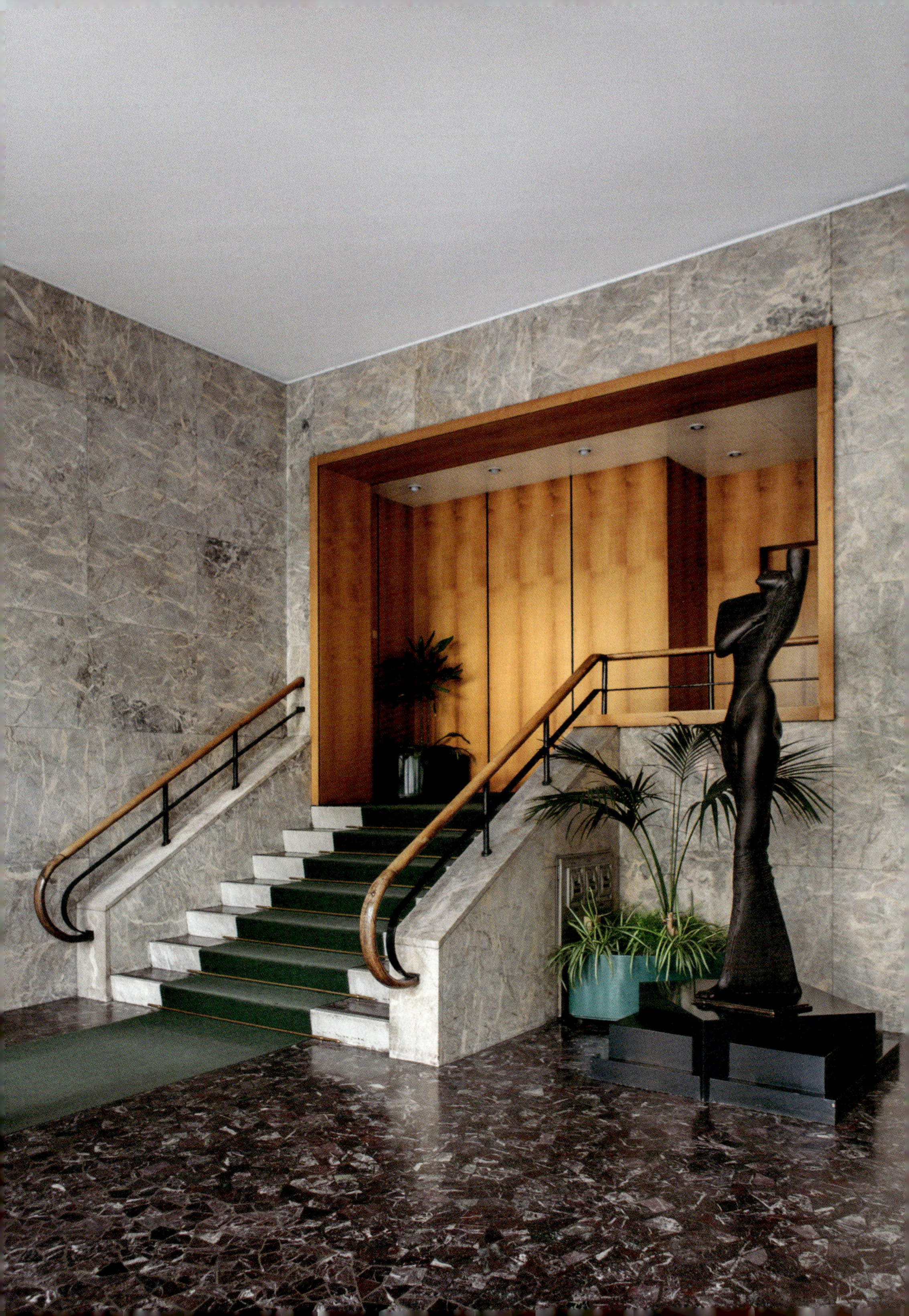

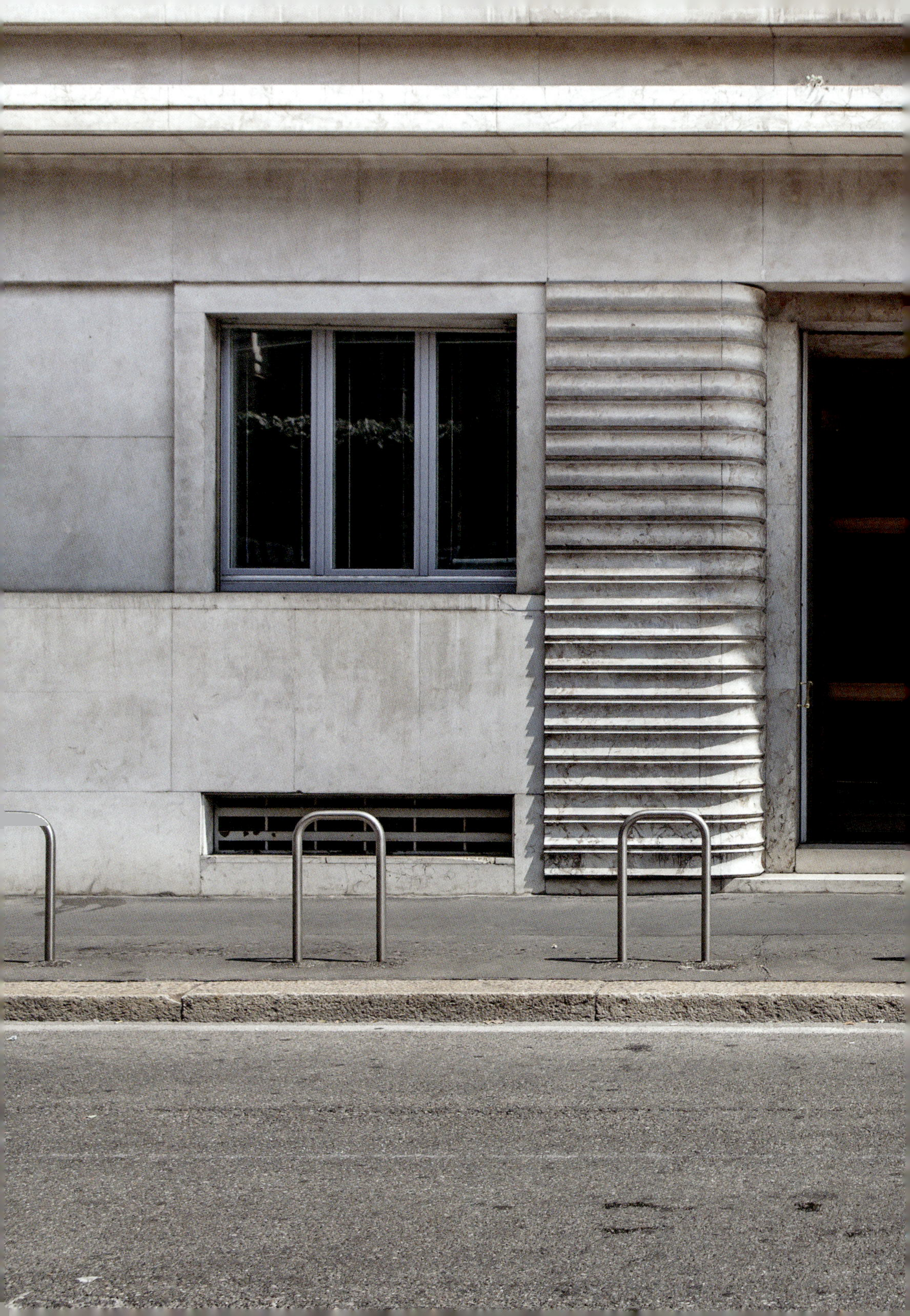

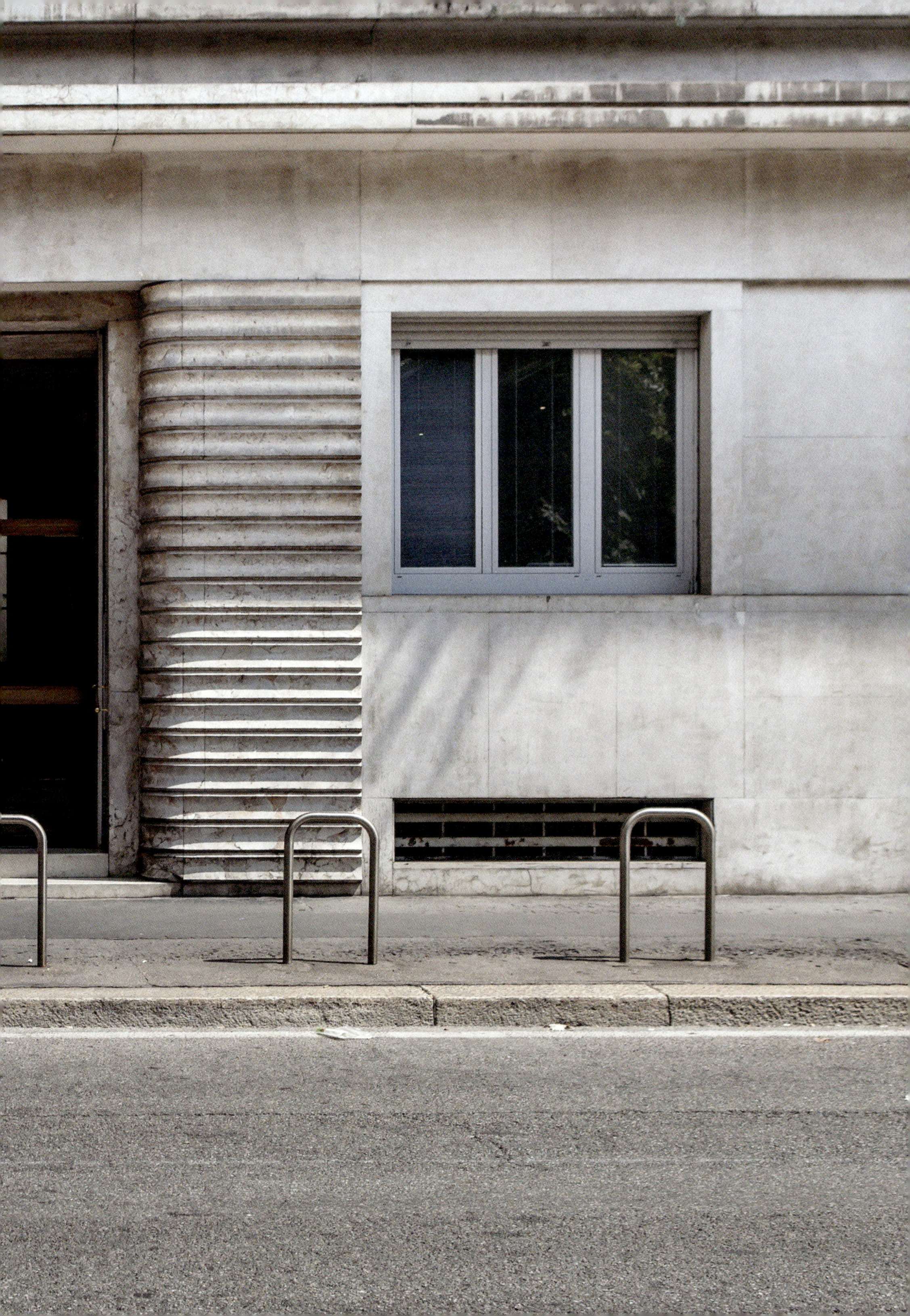

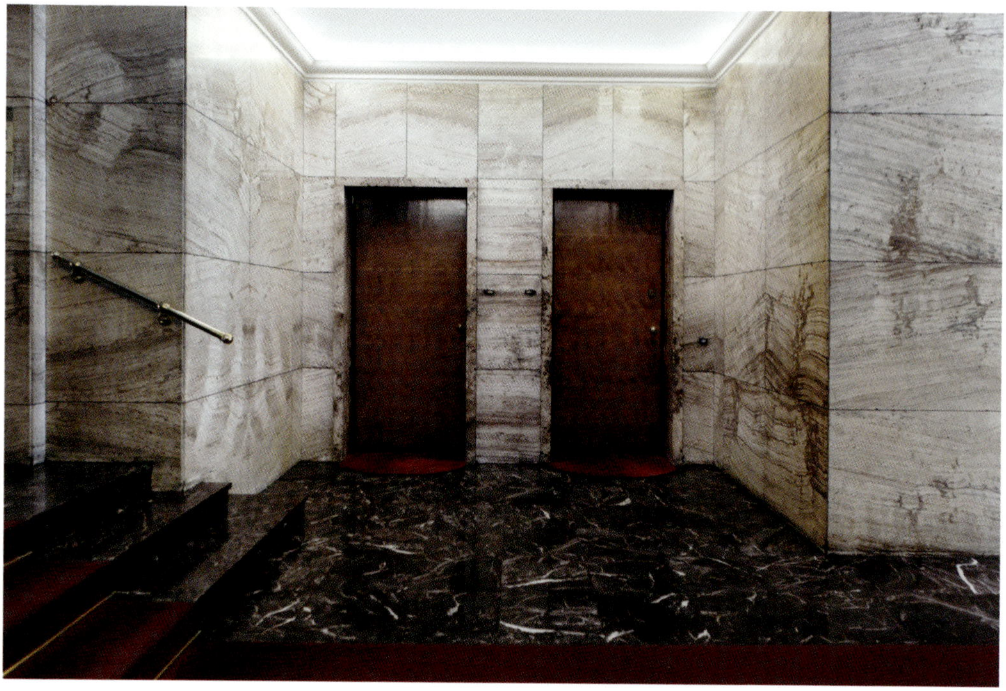

This and previous spread:
via Cartesio 19
floor: Rosso Levanto ophicalcite · walls: Oniciato travertine
doorframe (previous spread): Macchiavecchia Chiara limestone

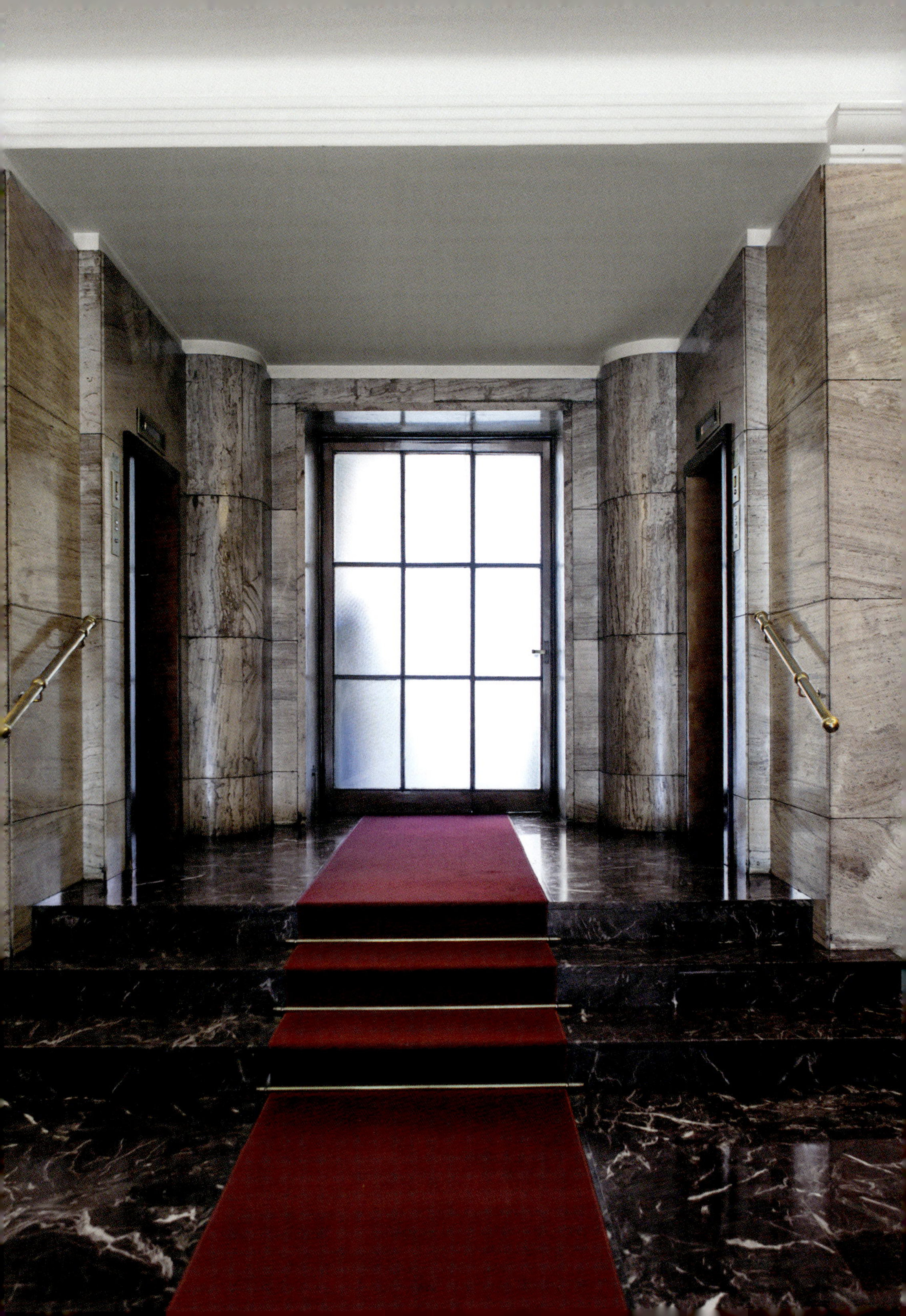

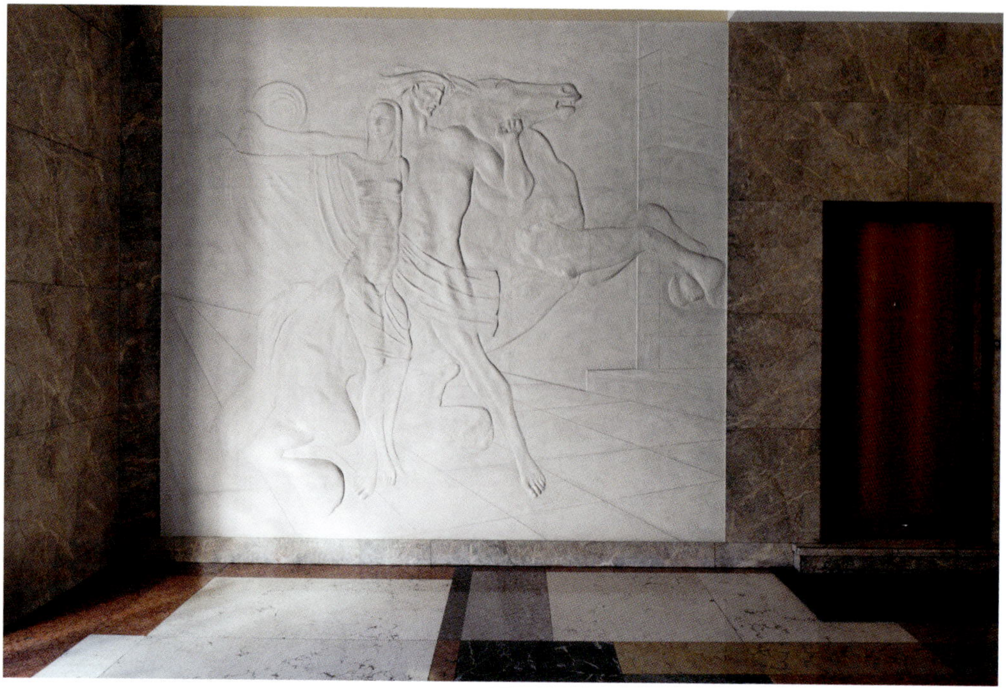

ROSSO AND GIALLO VERONA

Verona's world-famous limestones—such as Rosso Ammonitico, Nembro Rosato, and Giallo Torri—belong to the Jurassic series of Ammonitic limestones. They have been exploited since Roman times and, apart from Giallo Torri, are still quarried today.

piazza della Repubblica 23 · Camillo Bianchi, 1935–38

floor: Botticino limestone and serpentinite, Verona Rosso and Giallo Reale, Serpentino Rosso Levanto, Verde Alpi ophicalcite, Aurisina Fiorito limestone and Repen limestone, Giallo Torri, Chiampo skirting, column, walls: Fior di Pesco Carnico marble

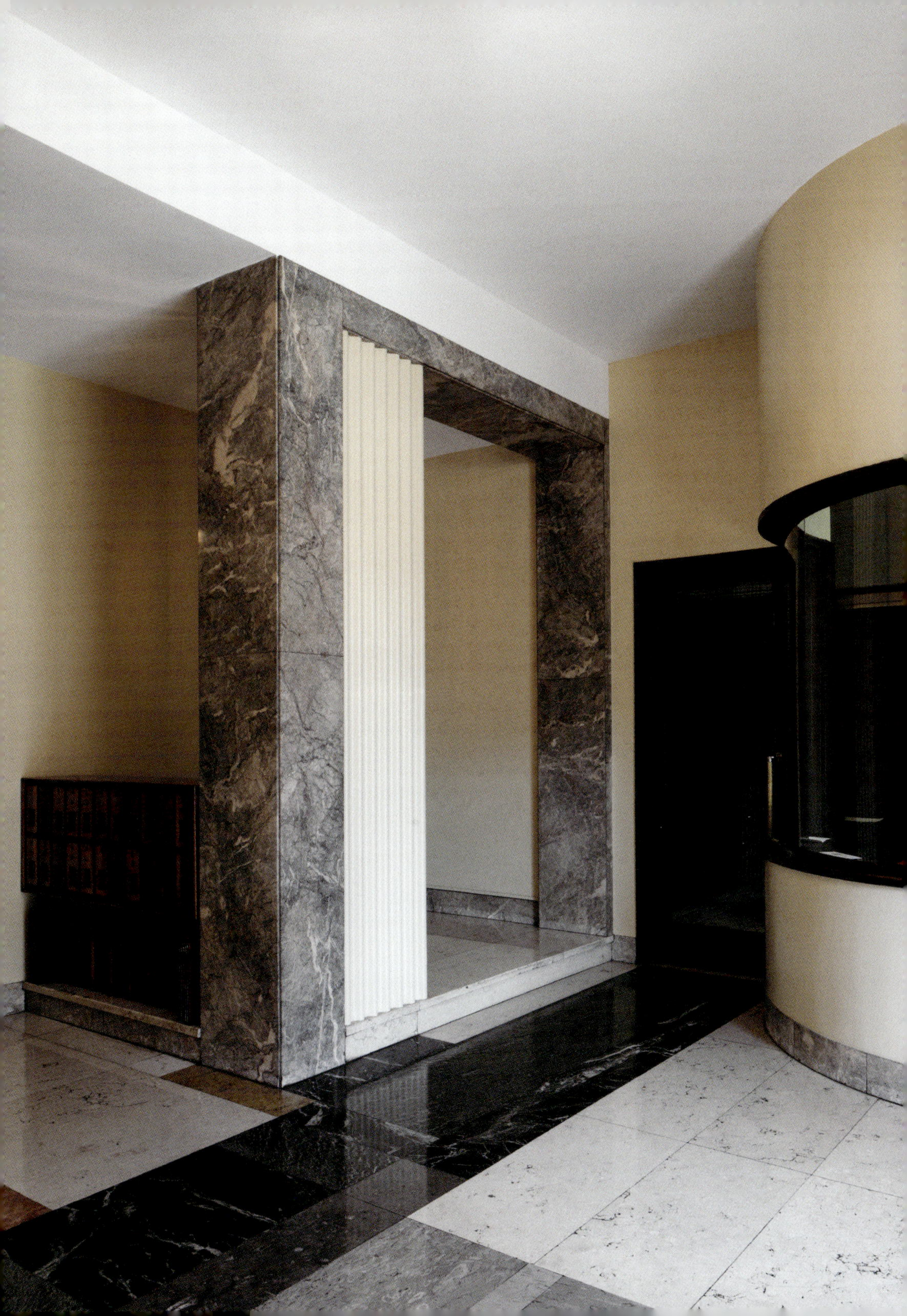

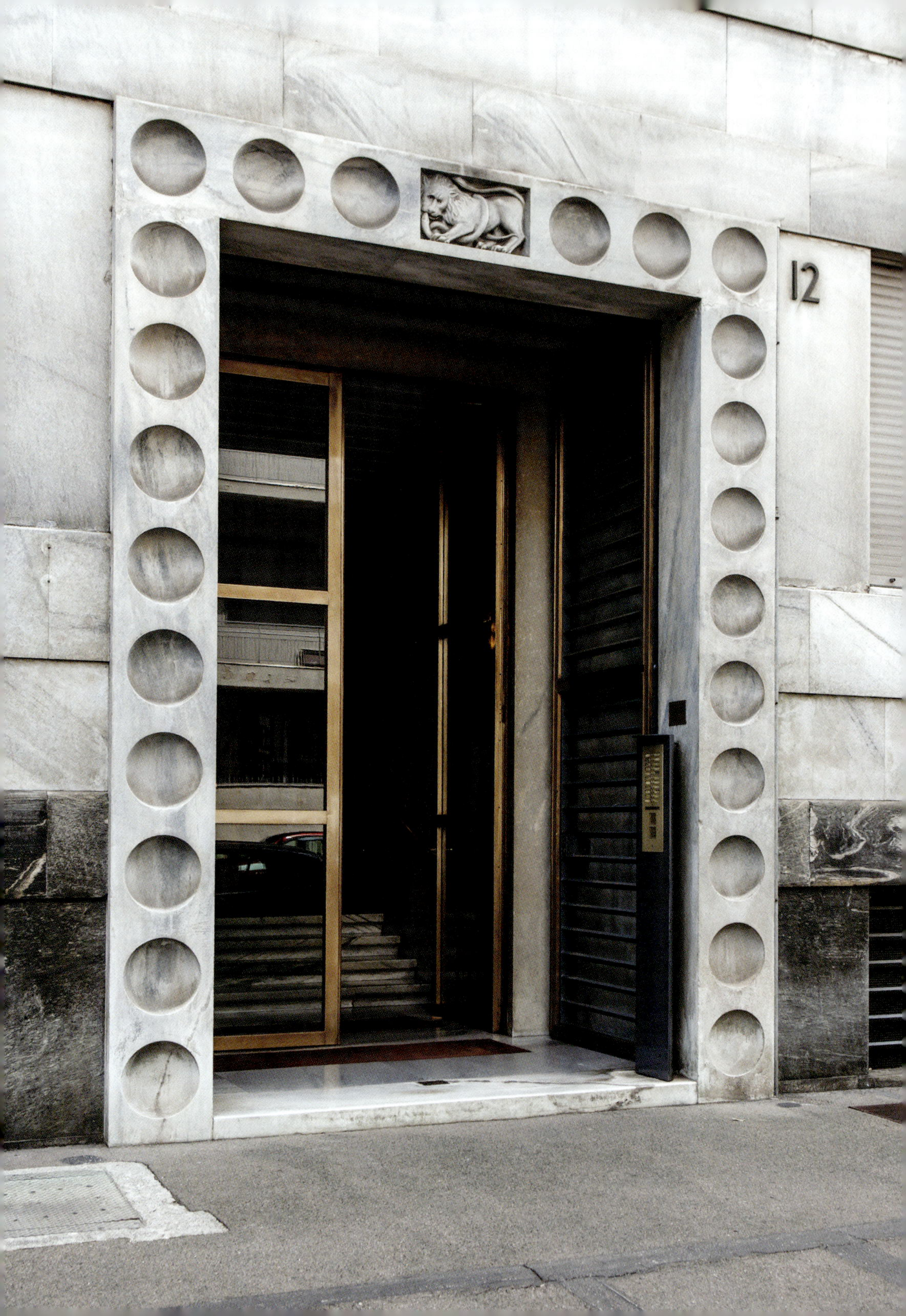
12

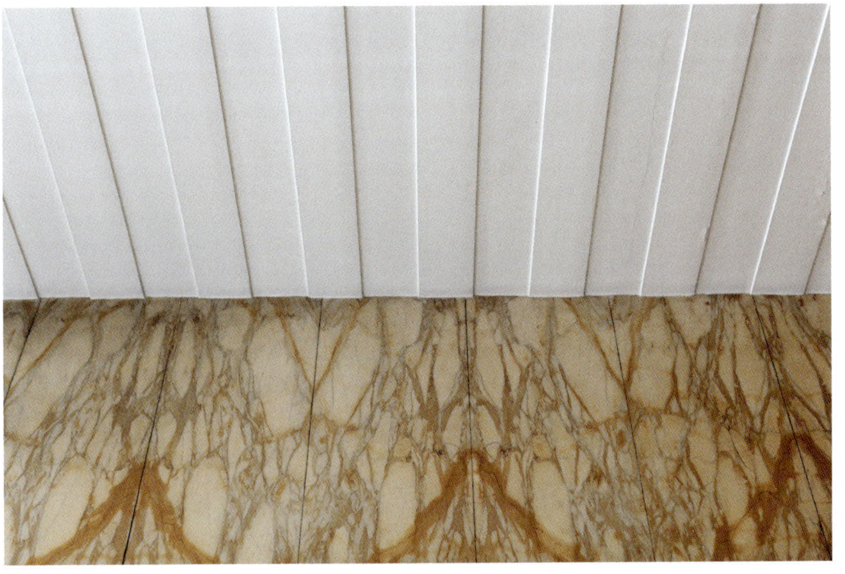

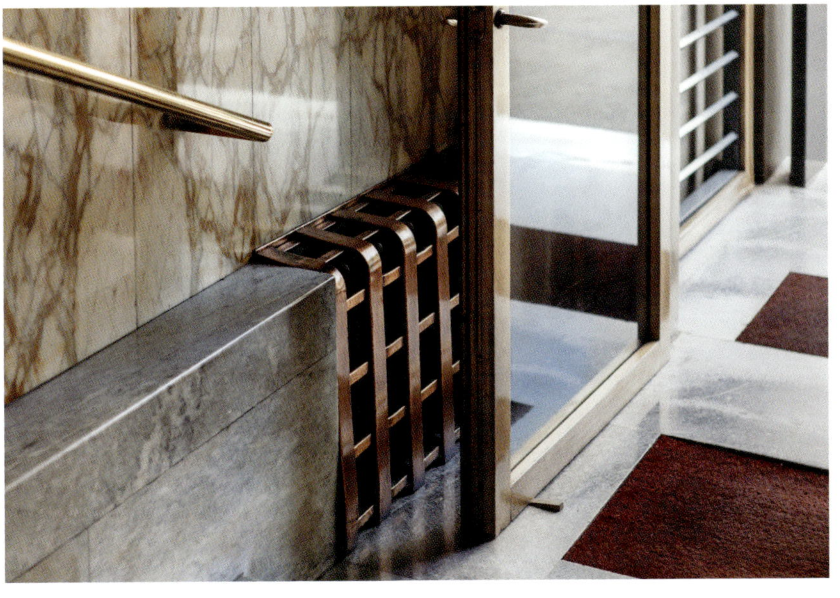

This and following spread:

via Giuseppe Marcora 12, Palazzo Bonaiti · Giovanni Muzio, 1935–37

Portal sculpted by Giacomo Manzù · stairs, doorframe, exterior cladding: Musso marble exterior base: Samolaco granite · interior walls: Giallo Siena marble

NERO VARENNA

A Triassic limestone from the eastern shores of Lake Como. Black limestone alternatives to Nero Belgio were once in great demand. The quarry is still in use, but only for restoration initiatives.

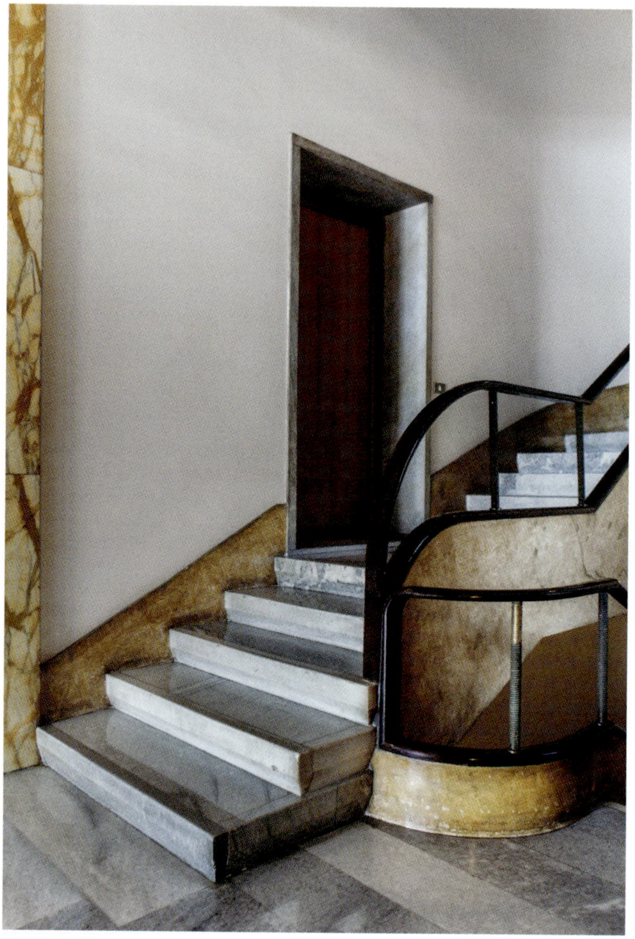

Sconces by Giovanni Muzio.
floor: Marmo di Musso and Palladiana of several red limestones
base: Nero di Varenna venato · lesene: Giallo Siena marble

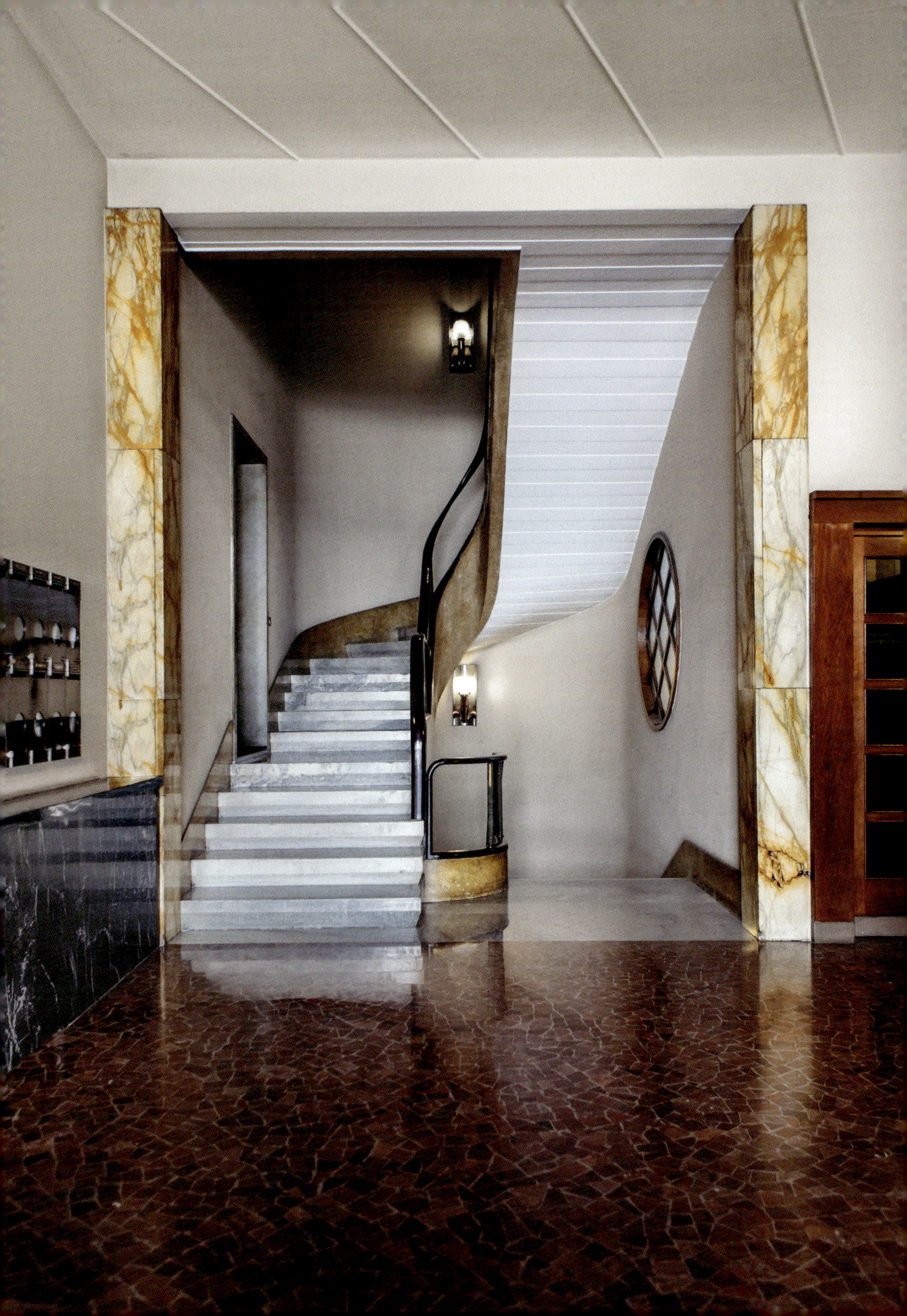

MACCHIAVECCHIA

A very typical and traditional stone used in Milan and surrounding Lombardy. Quarried just across the nearby Swiss border, in an area that was ruled over by Milan for centuries, it is a highly heterogeneous breccia stone consisting of brownish-gray phenoclasts and brick-red clusters. Since the Renaissance, it has been widely used in churches and palaces for such elements as doorframes, portals, altars, interior flooring, and cladding. In the twentieth century, its use also spread to other building types. The quarry is still active, mainly supplying material for restoration projects.

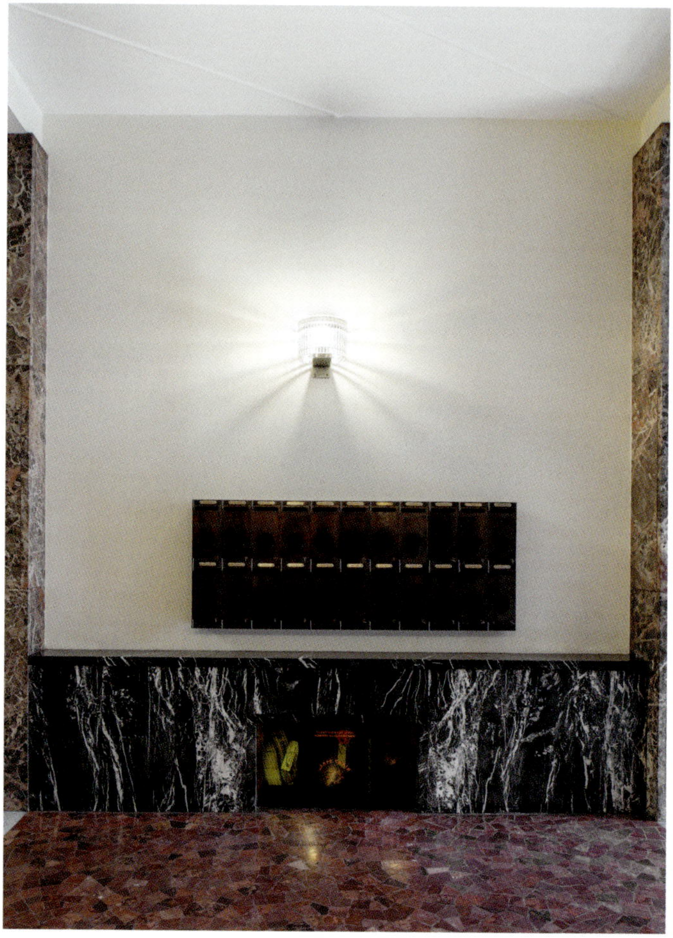

piazza della Repubblica 7, Palazzo Bonaiti · Giovanni Muzio, 1935–37

Sconce by Luigi Caccia Dominioni for Azucena.
floor and stairs: Marmo di Musso and Palladiana of several red limestones
base: Nero di Varenna venato · walls: Macchiavecchia limestone breccia

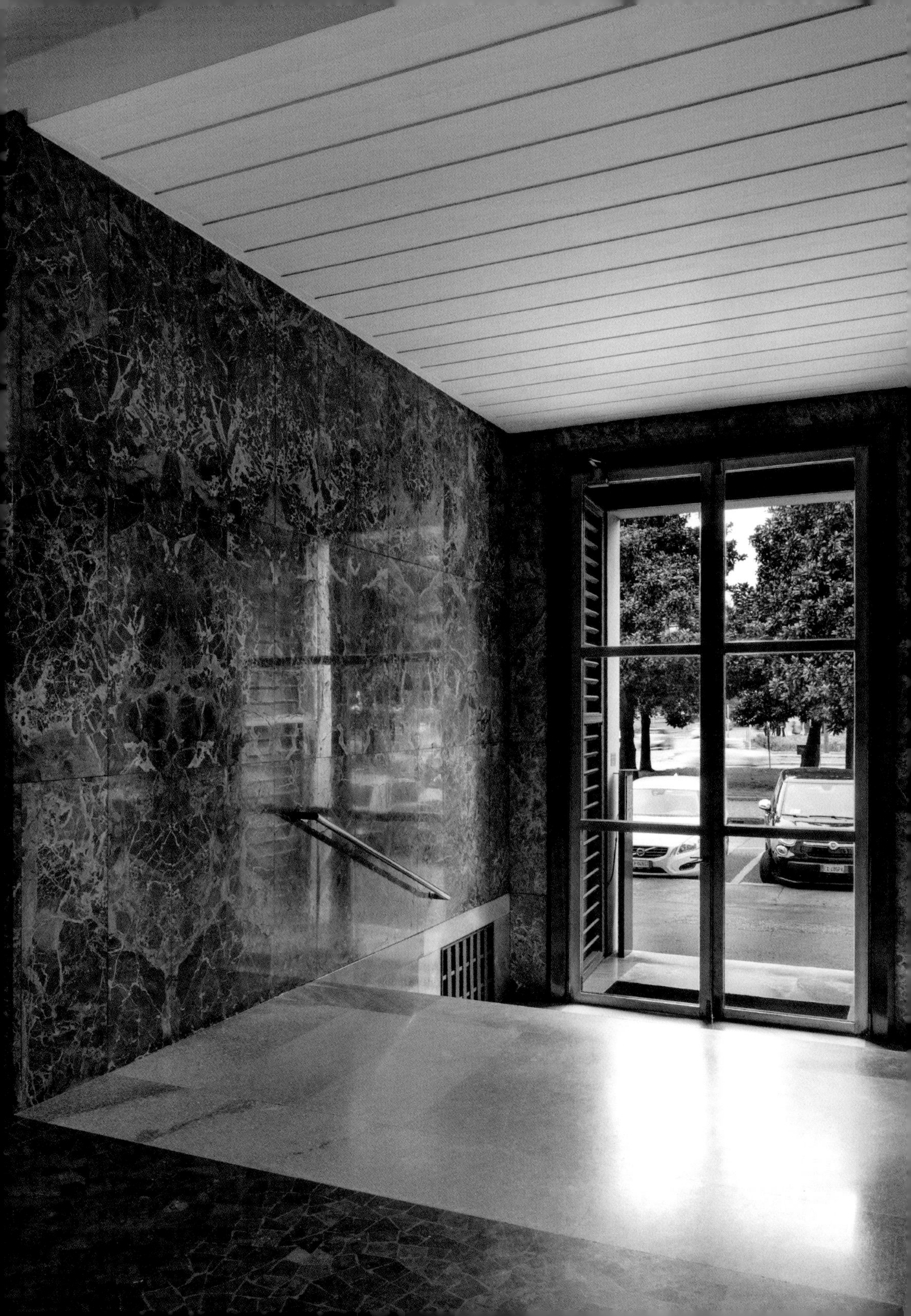

piazza della Repubblica 11 · Vito Latis, 1954–55

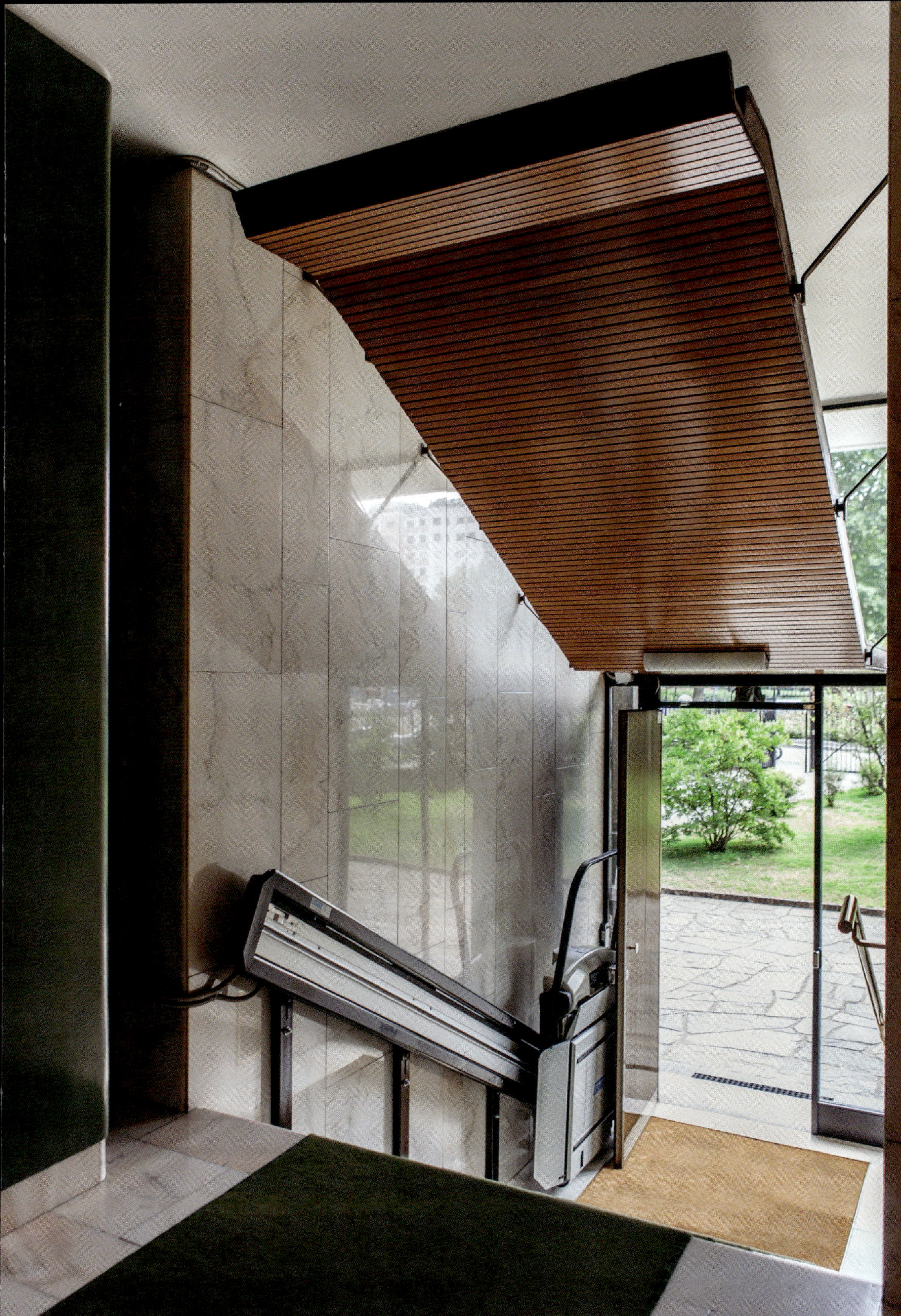

via Antonio Locatelli 1 · Mario Bacciocchi, 1936–39

floor: Grigio Carnico marble · walls: Lasa marble

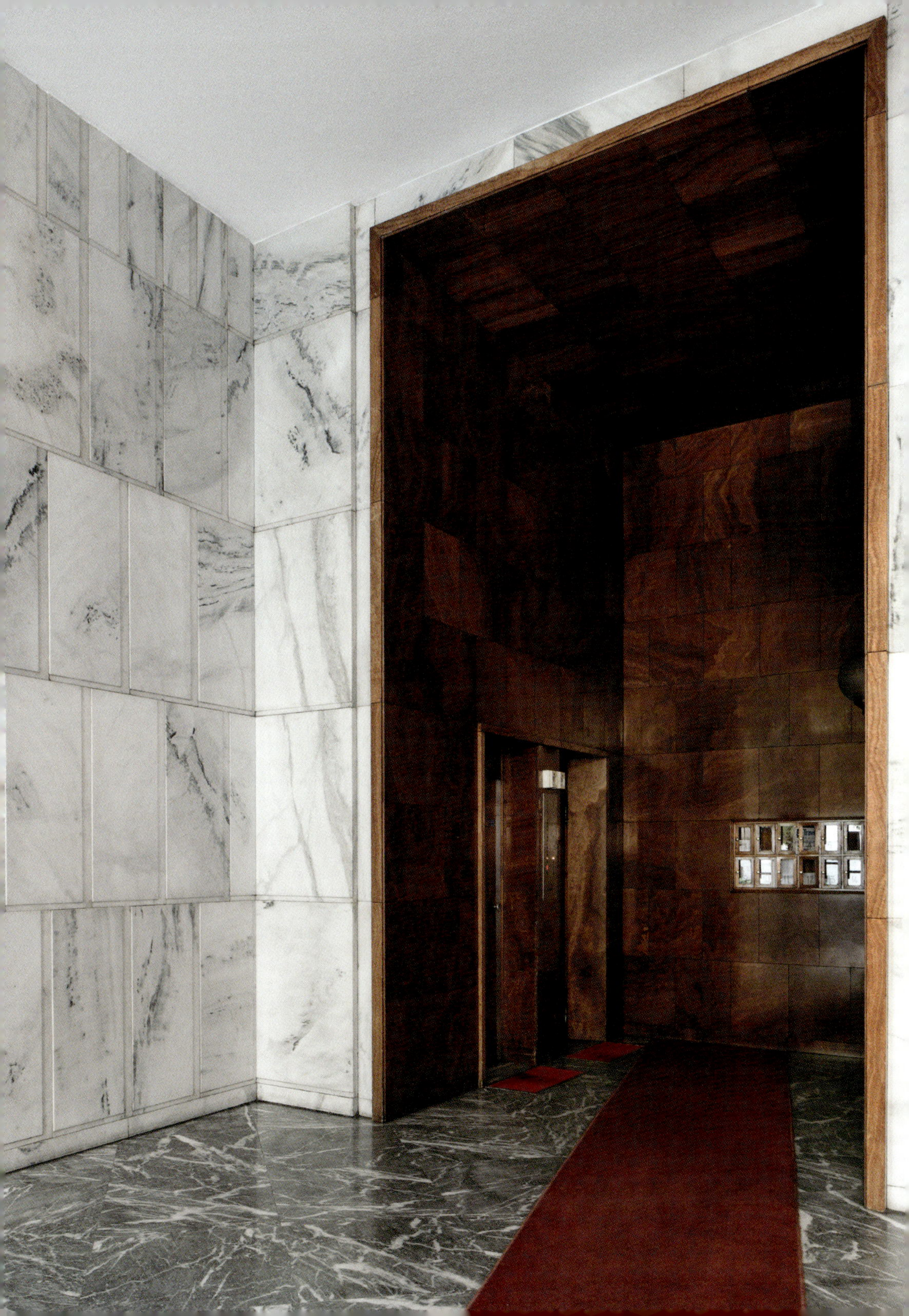

One arrives in the lobby through a long canopied entrance, where, underfoot, Lucio Fontana installed a hidden masterpiece, one of his *Concetto Spaziale* mosaics, rendered in diaphanous colors. In this restrained International Style lobby there is an early 1950s sofa, flanked on either side by two enormous ceramic sculptures from *commedia dell'arte* characters that impart a jarring note to an otherwise serene modernist space. These works are also Fontana's but they stem from his earlier neo-Baroque period, which deliberately recalls seventeenth- and eighteenth-century conceits, such as placing statuary cued to mythological themes at palace entrances.

This and following spread:
via Antonio Locatelli 5 · Roberto Radici, 1955–57
Floor mosaic and ceramic sculptures by Lucio Fontana.
Ceiling lamp by Gino Sarfatti.
stairs: Grigio Carnico marble · pilasters: Serizzo Ghiandone · exterior floor (not Fontana) and exterior walls: rectangular mosaic of travertine
Ceramic sculptures by Lucio Fontana.

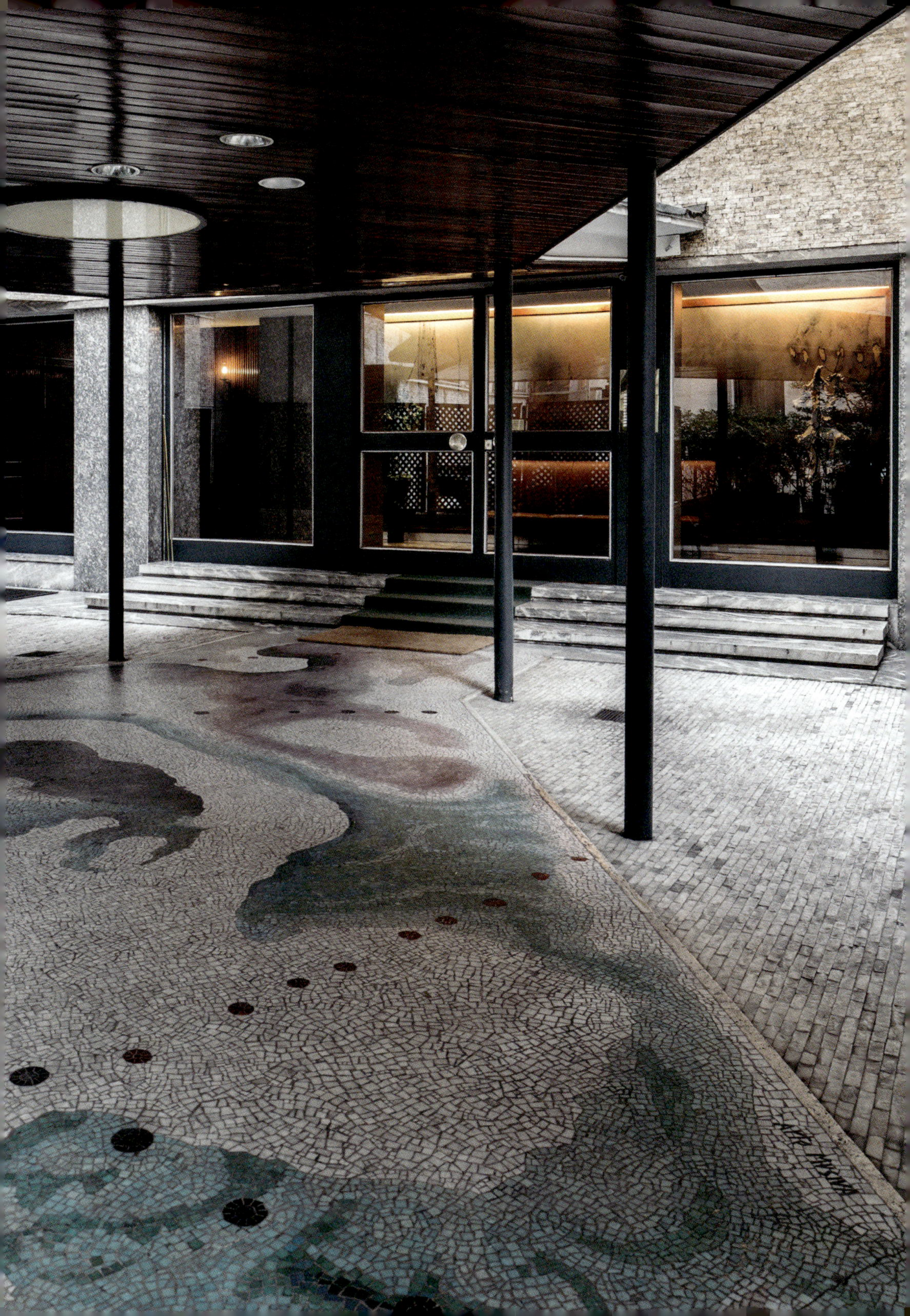

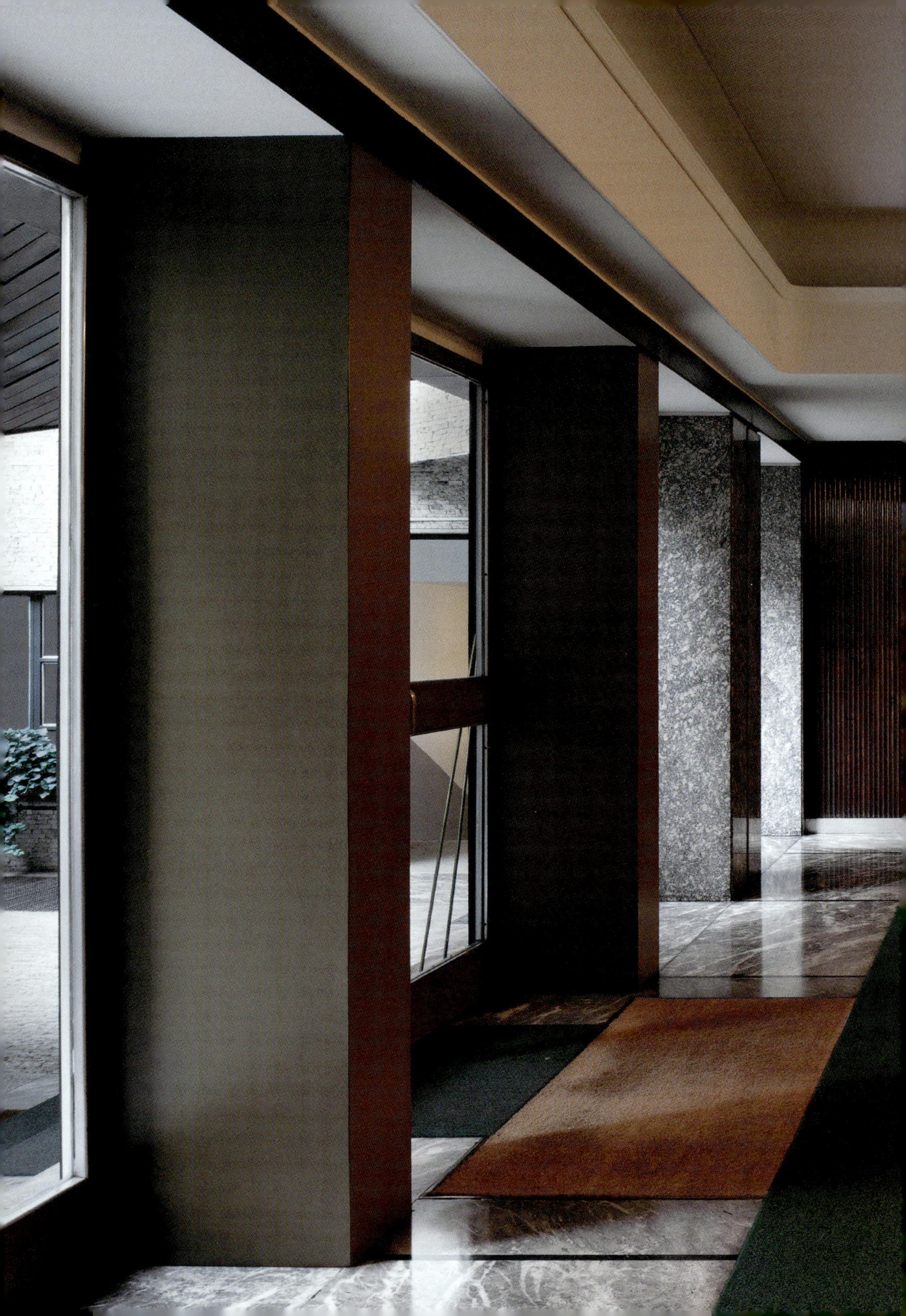

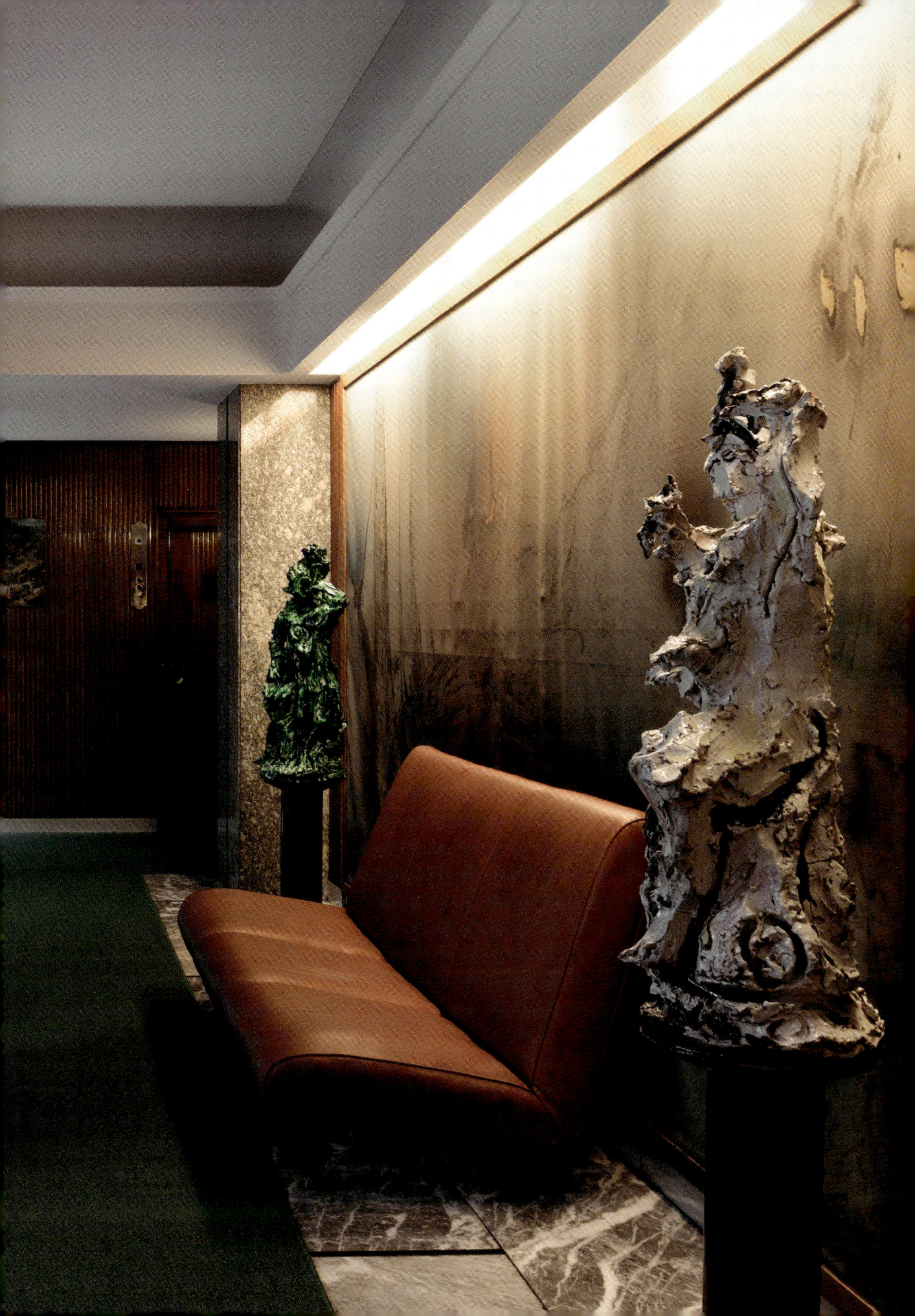

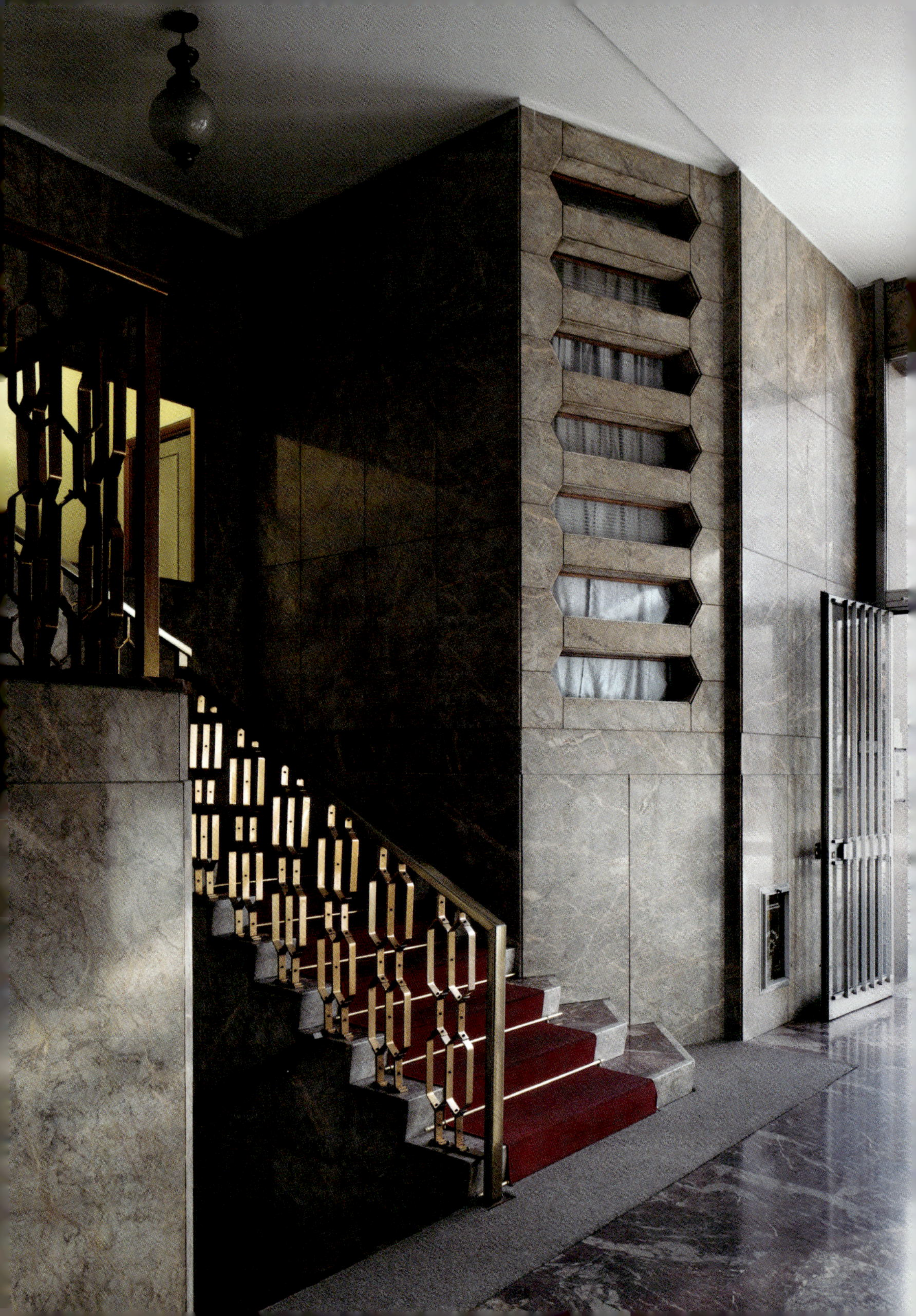

viale Monte Santo 4 · Giovanni Cesa Bianchi, 1961–64

Pendant lamp by Luigi Caccia Dominioni.
floor: Fior di Pesco marble · walls: Fior di Pesco Carnico marble

Following spread:

via Giuseppe Marcora 11, Casa Borgognoni · Gabriele Mucchi, G. Peraro, 1934–35

Stone fountain by Gabriele Mucchi.
stairs: Botticino limestone

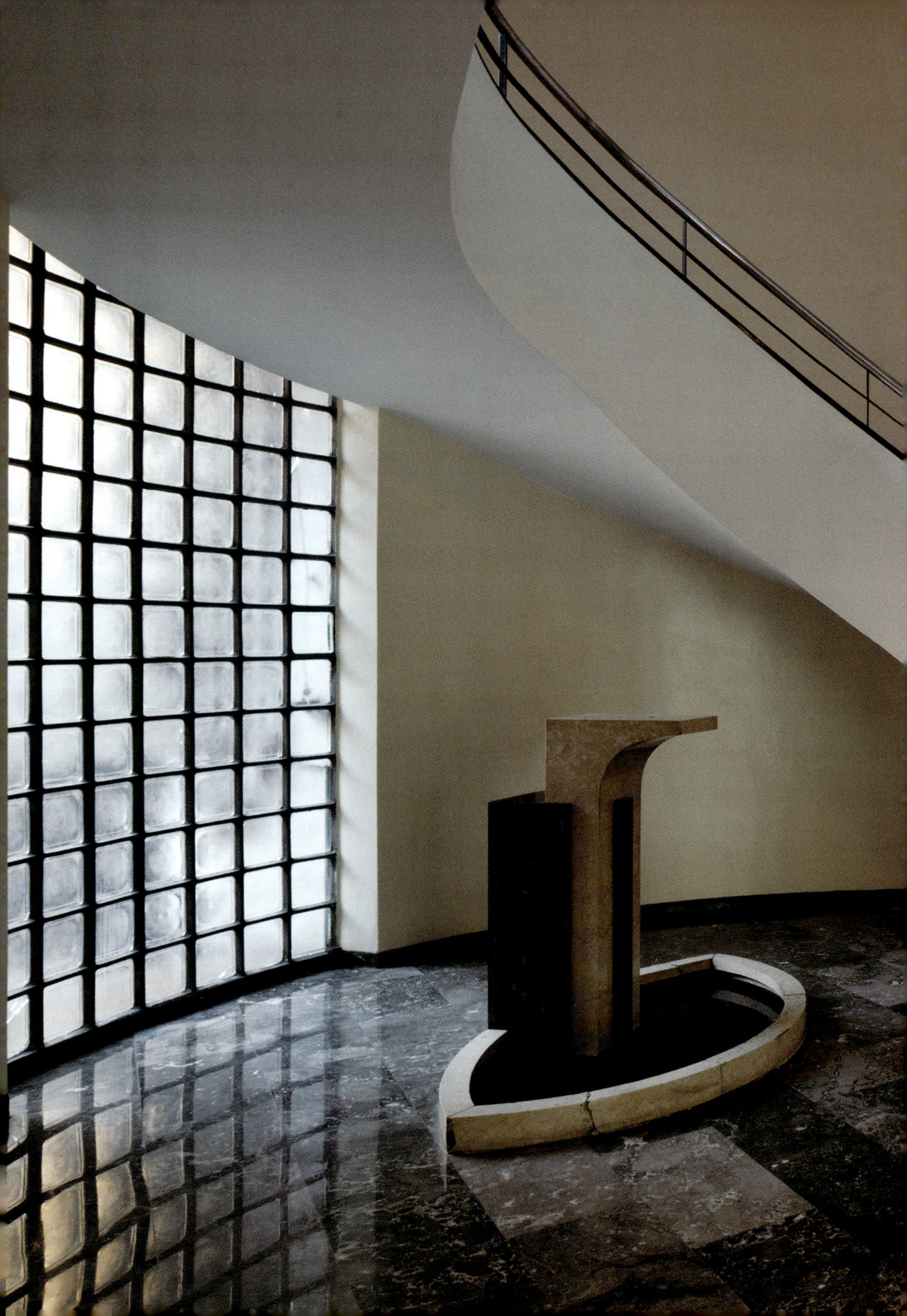

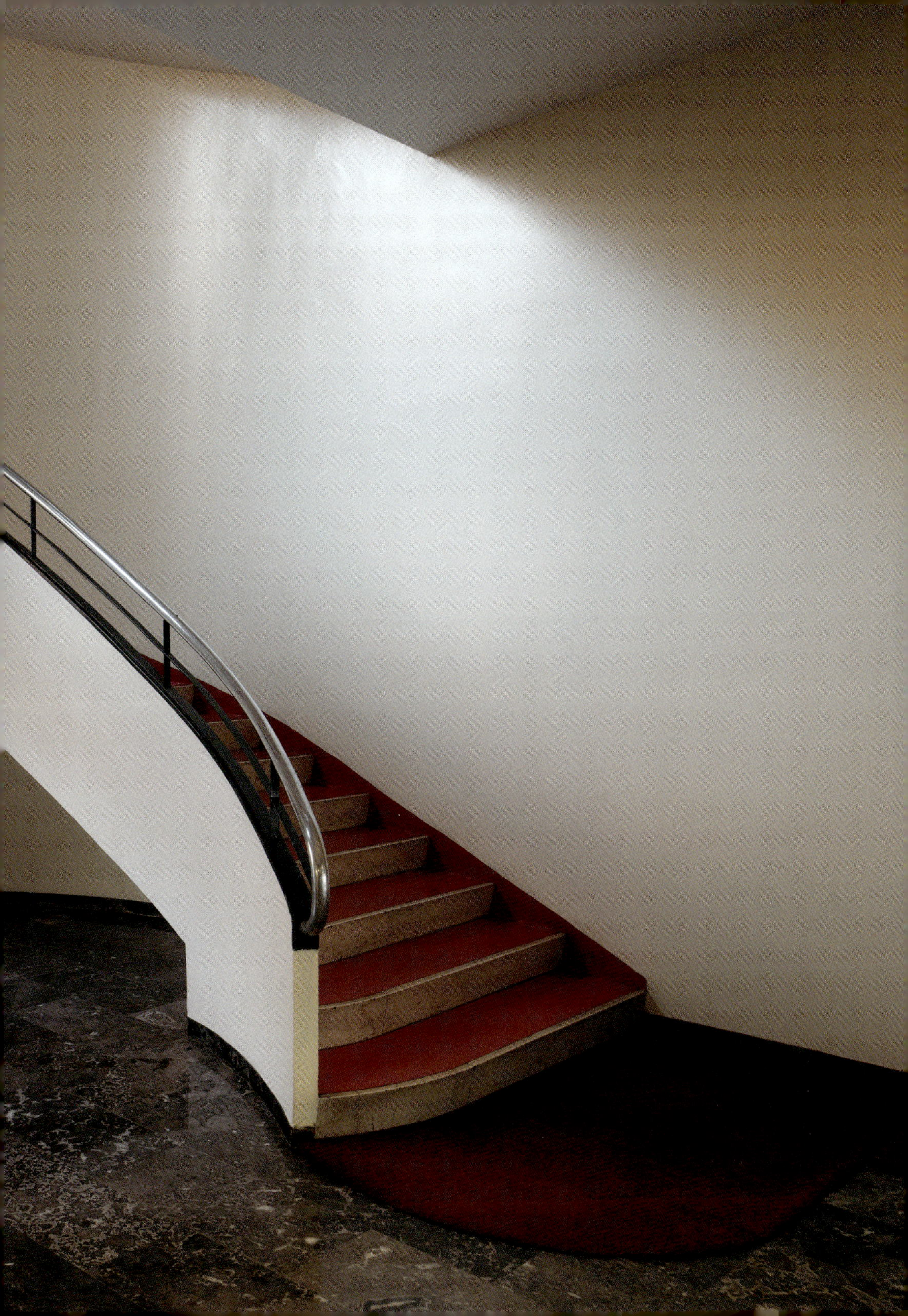

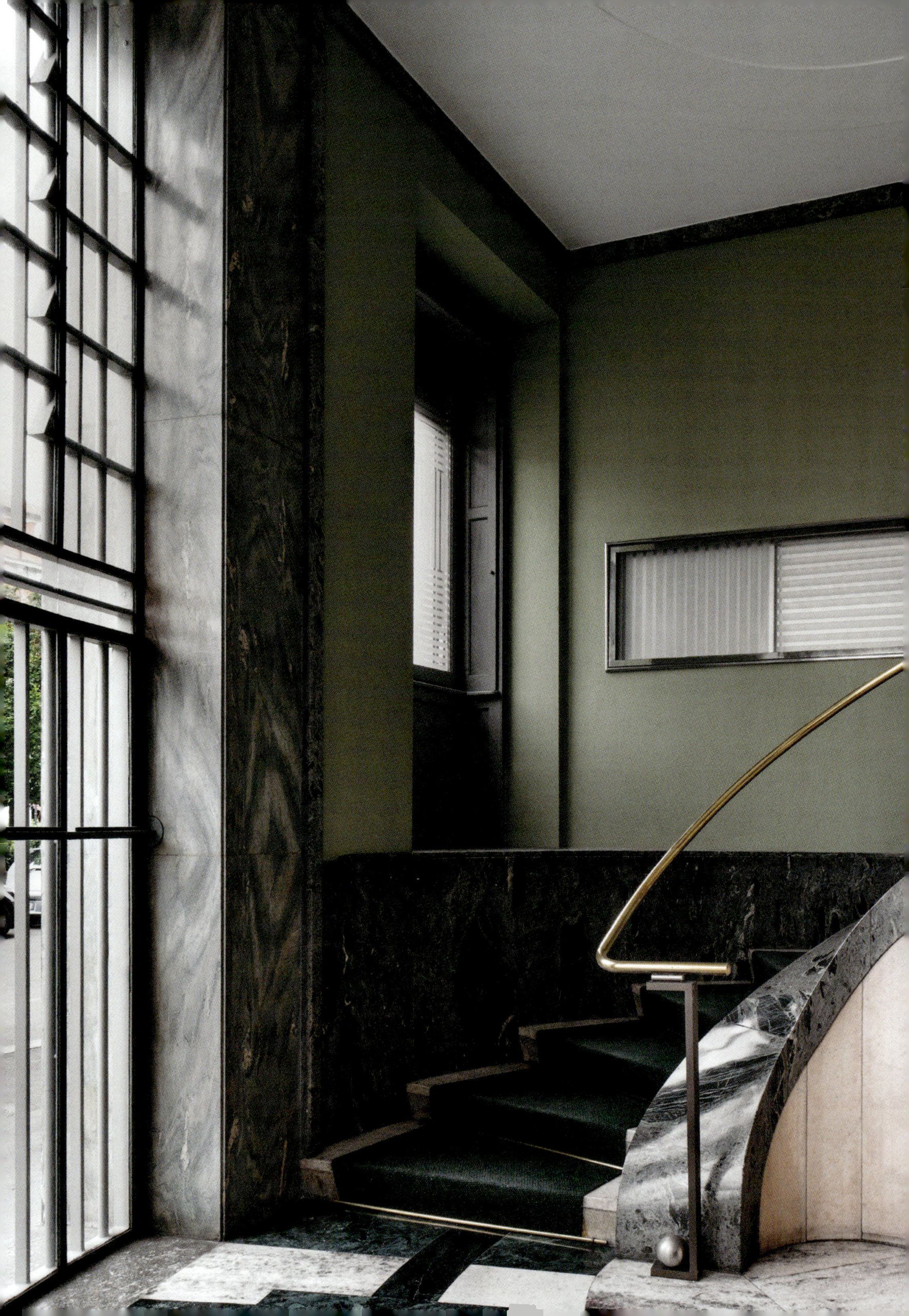

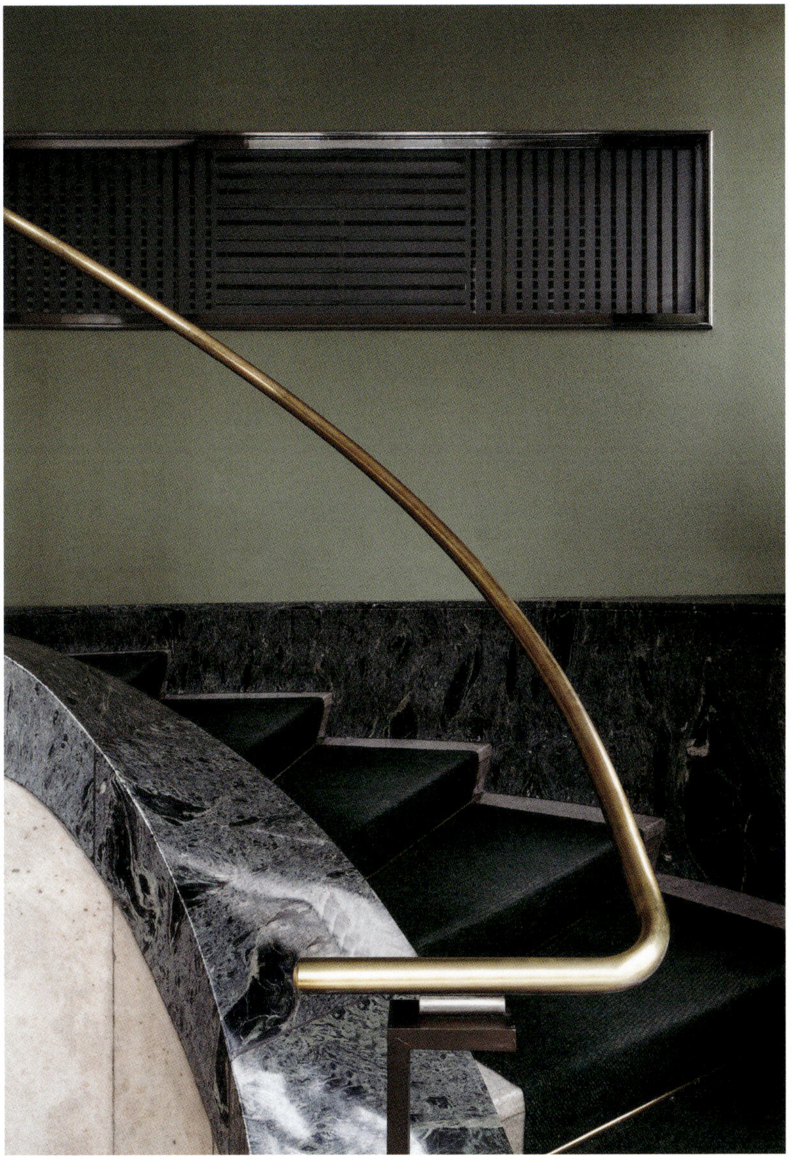

via Domenico Scarlatti 12

floor: Vallestrona marble and Verde Aver · rail: Verde Alpi ophicalcite

One of the standout elements in this entrance and one that imparts the most effect to this late 1930s ensemble is the large vertical mirror at the upper landing. Placed in the middle and almost congruent in size with two lateral doors, this is a metaphysical portal into a virtual space. Other architects insert this kind of space-expanding device among vast mirrored surfaces, but this particular example is an exquisitely elaborate design of 1939 with exaggerated chamfered framing using "rosambrato," a then newly patented mirror color from Fontana Arte.

viale Andrea Doria 32 · Mario Borgato, 1939

Mirror by Fontana Arte.
floor: Bardiglio nuvolato

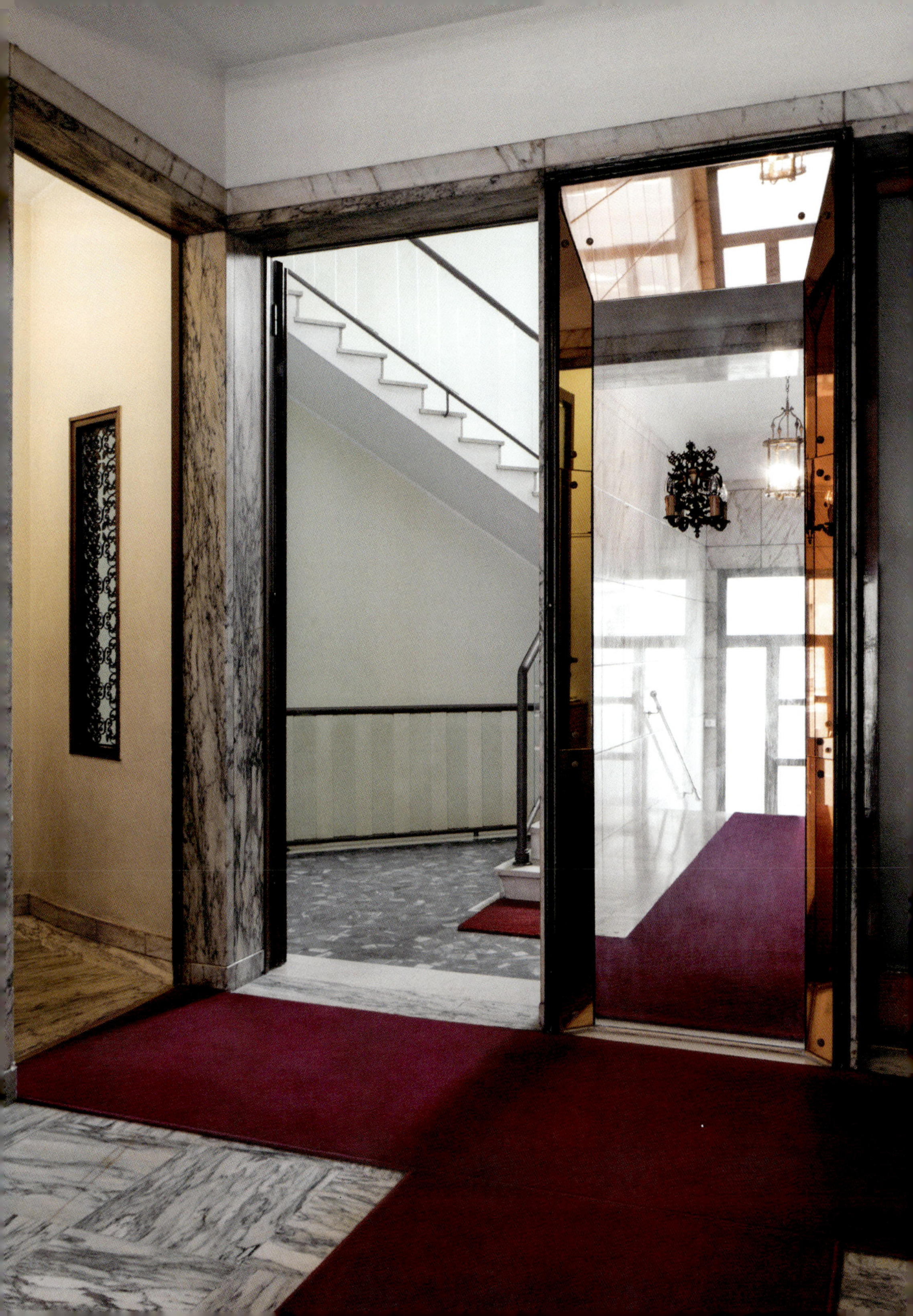

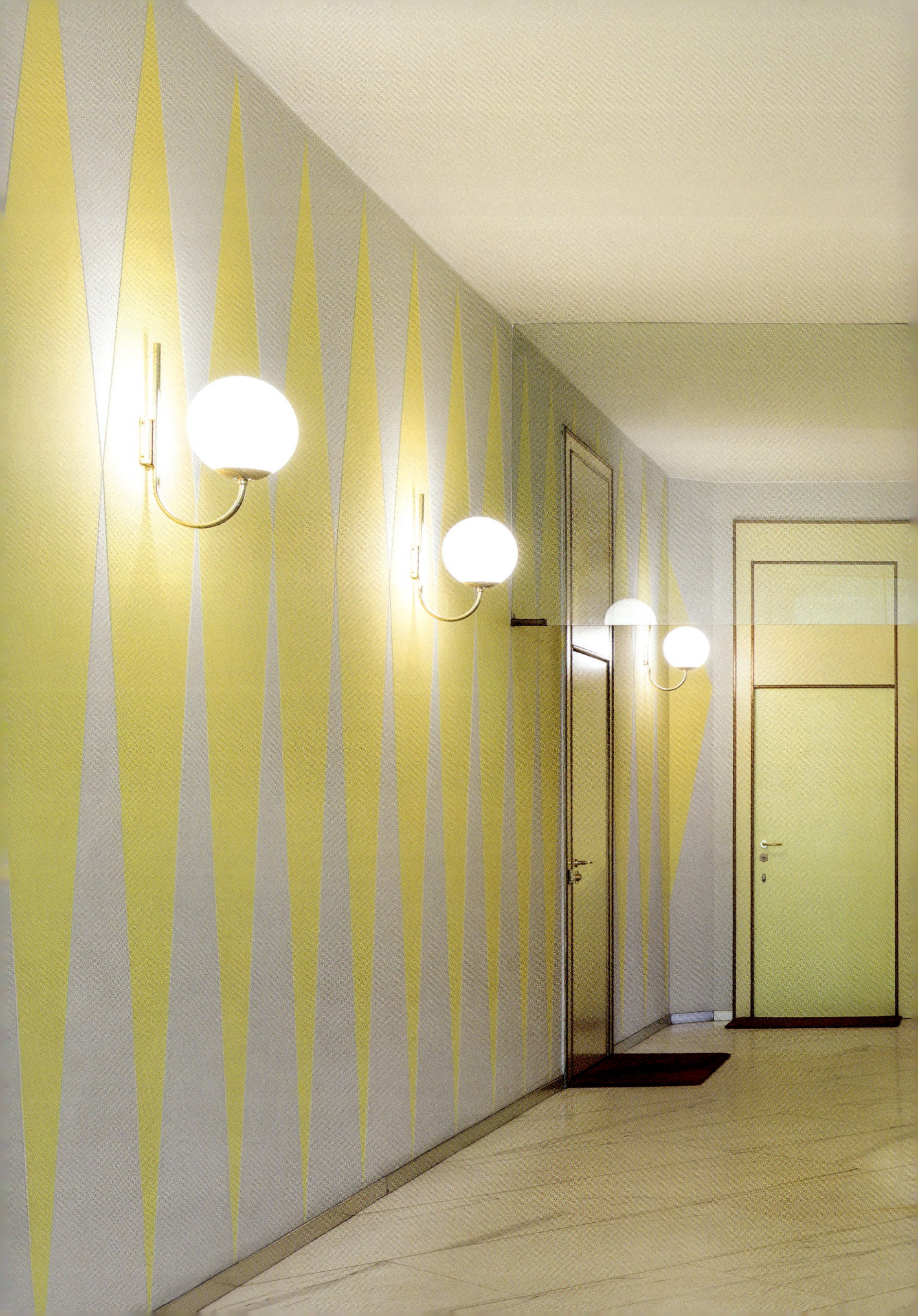

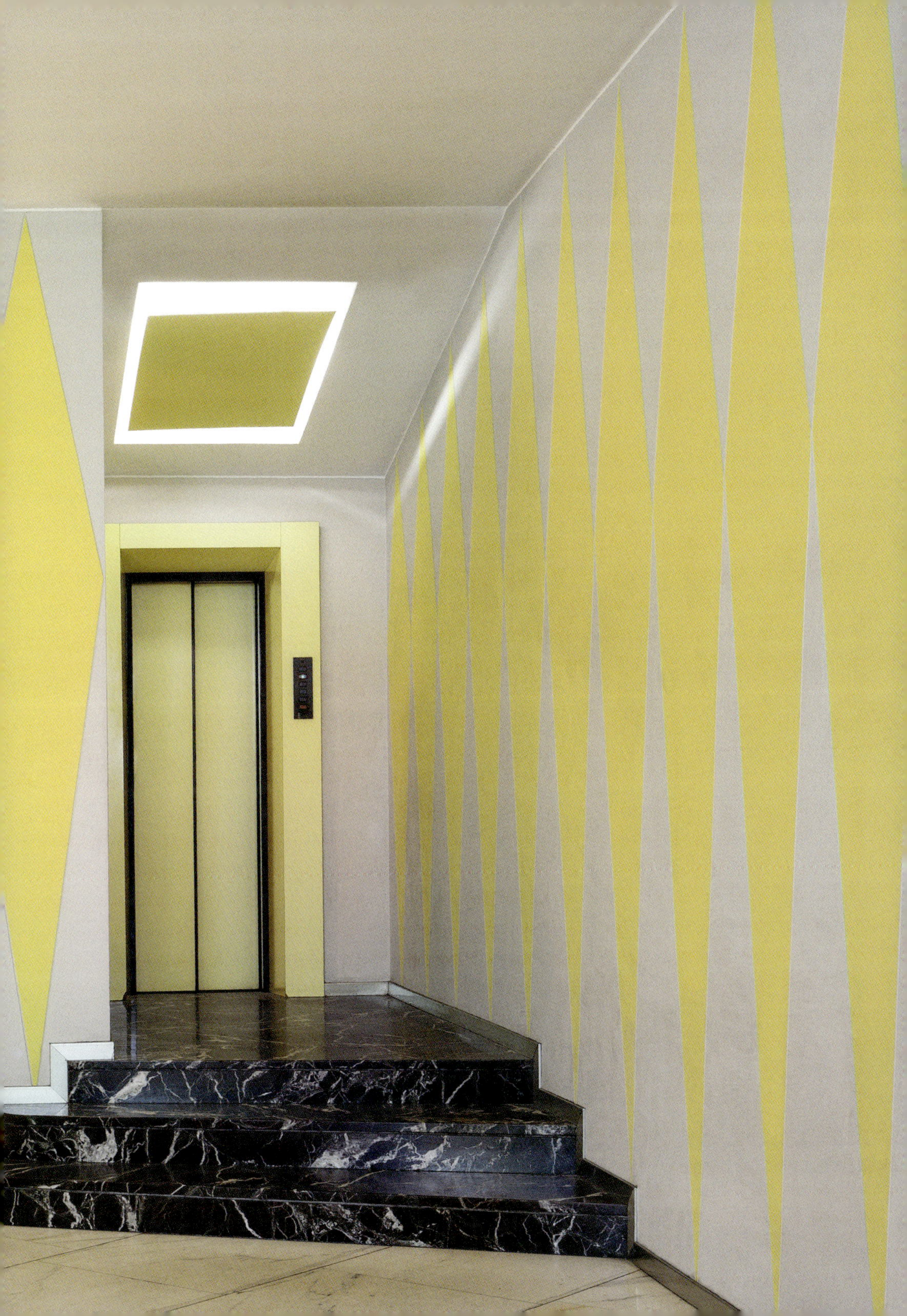

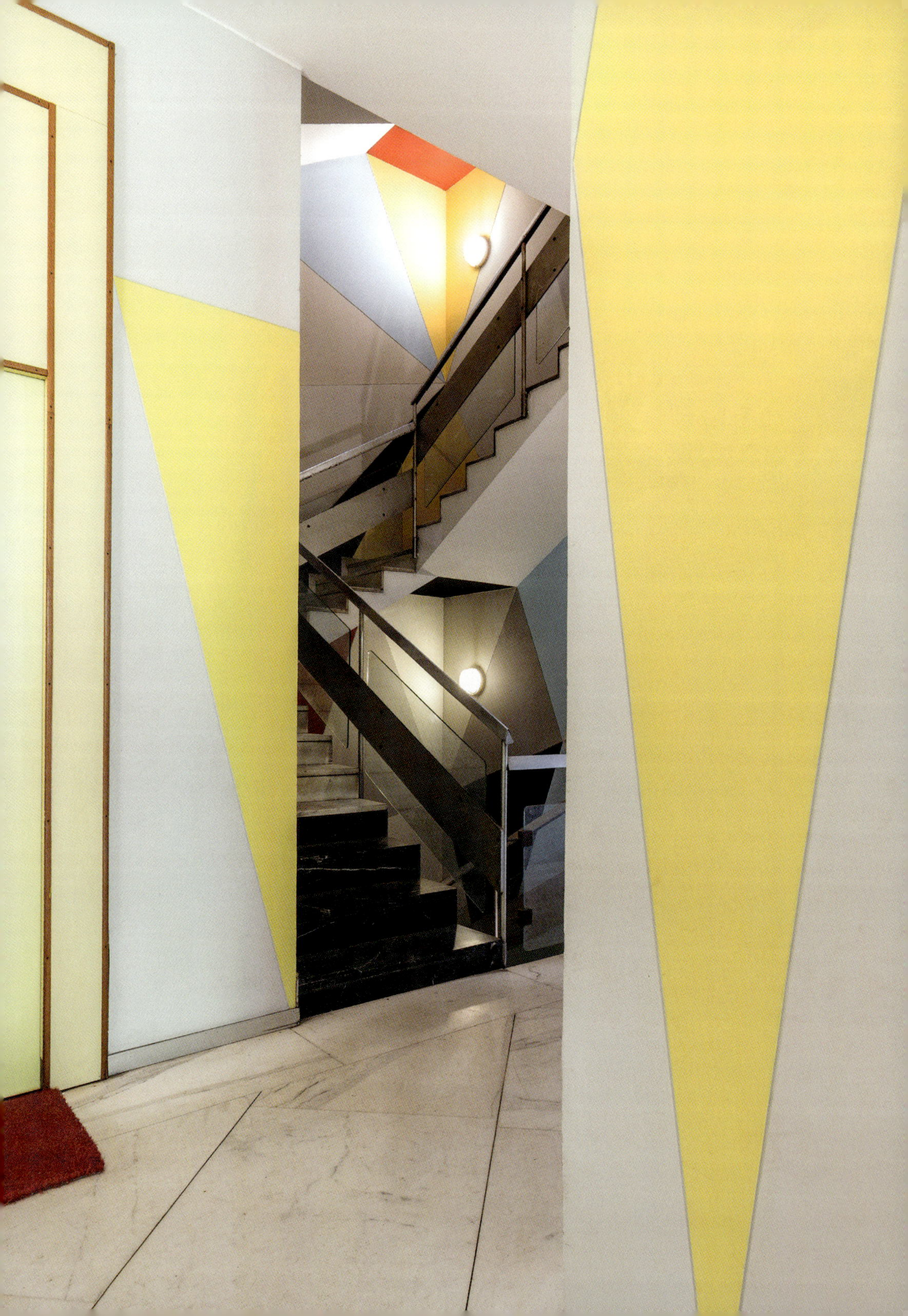

This 1954 interior by Gio Ponti is a *tour de force*, a catalyst for his vision of architecture as a crystal or as a diamond, one of his most treasured leitmotifs. Yet in this case he splits the diamond form into pyramidal and obelisk-like shards that are set in an uncanny constellation. This in turn can be understood as a kind of hermetic manifesto for his fascination with sharp-edged, pointed, crystalline forms. That approach is summed up in his own words: "The obelisk teaches architecture. It is perhaps the very symbol, the pure symbol, of architectural expression from which a song arises, the lines of which do not pause, do not sleep, do not merely stand but are statics in motion—the ecstasy of movement."

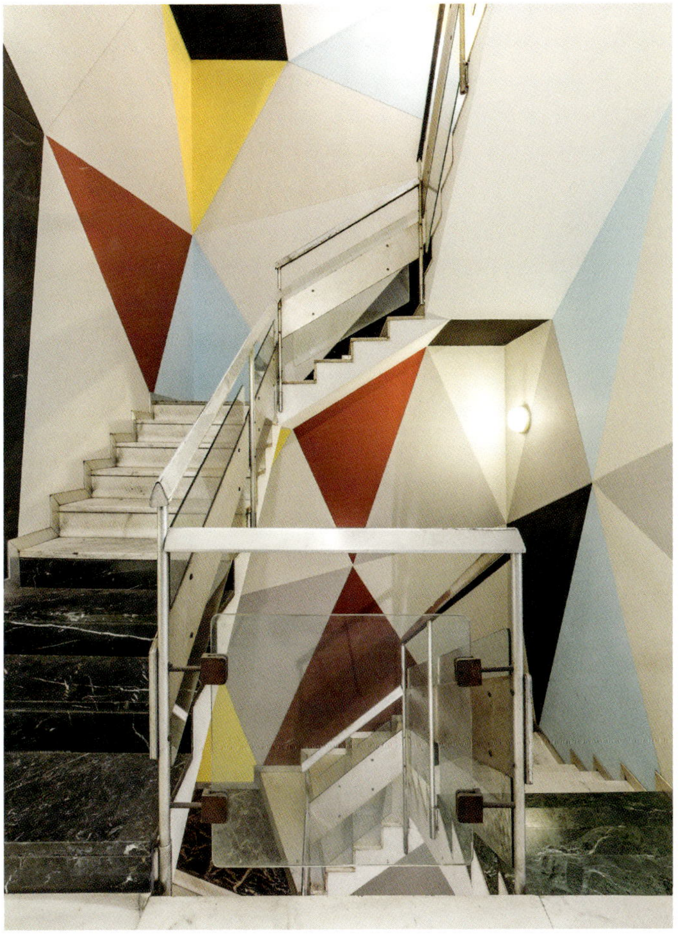

This and previous spread:
viale Lunigiana 44A · Casa Melandri · Gio Ponti, Alberto Rosselli, 1954–57
Sconces by Candle · floor: Carrara marble · stairs: Rosso Levanto ophicalcite

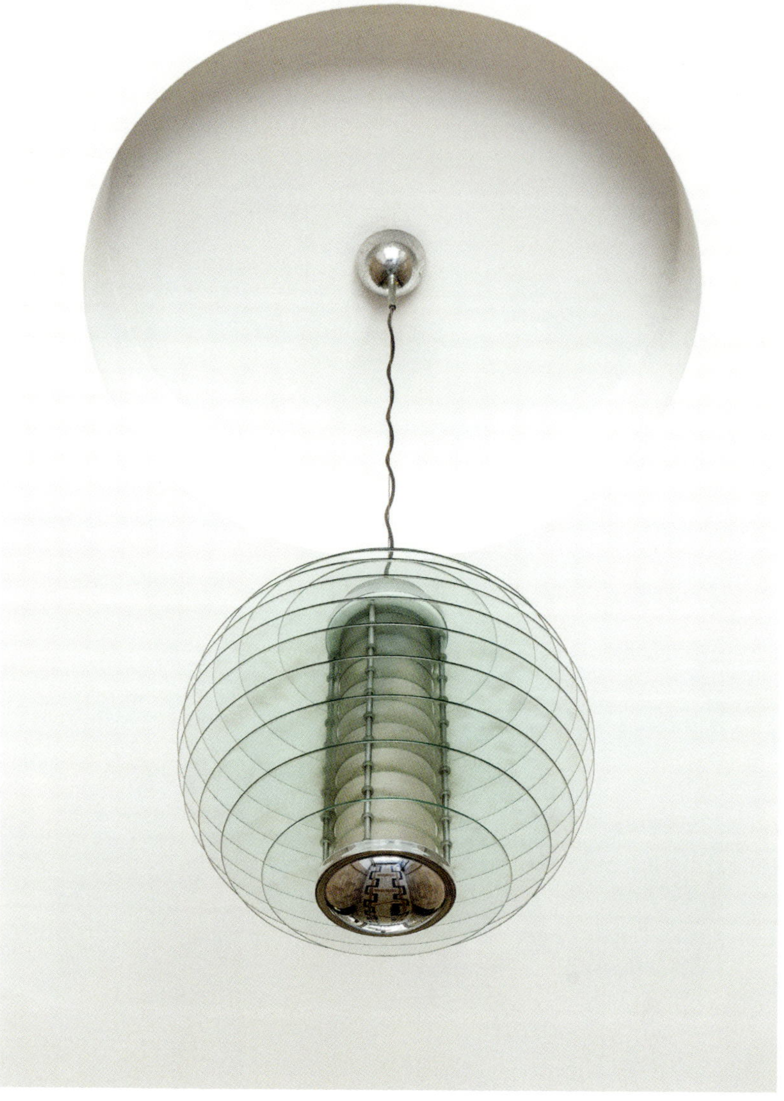

via Fabio Filzi 47

Pendant lamps by Gio Ponti.
floor: Palladiana of several limestones and marbles · skirting: Rosa Baveno granite
walls: travertine and Rosa Baveno granite

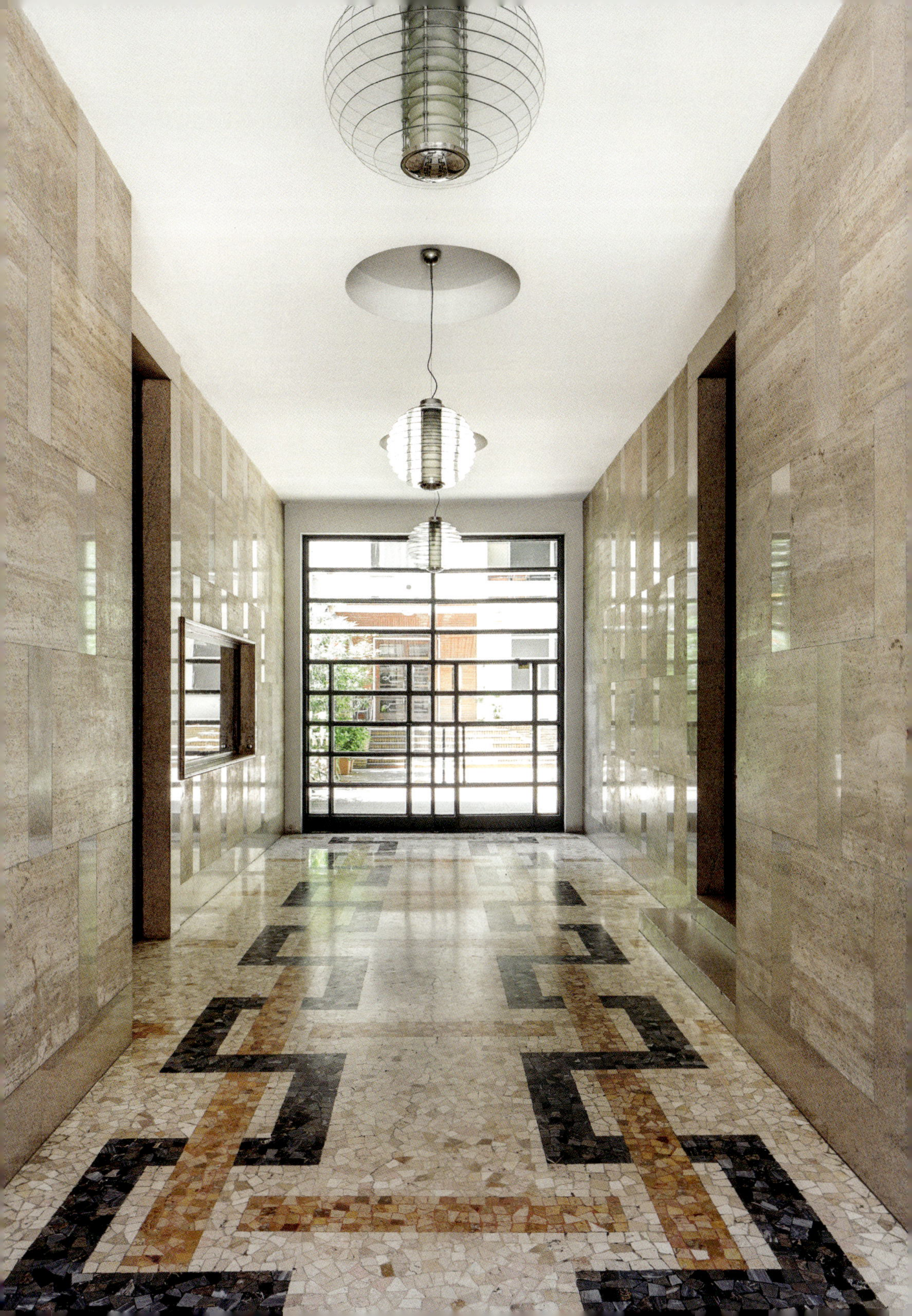

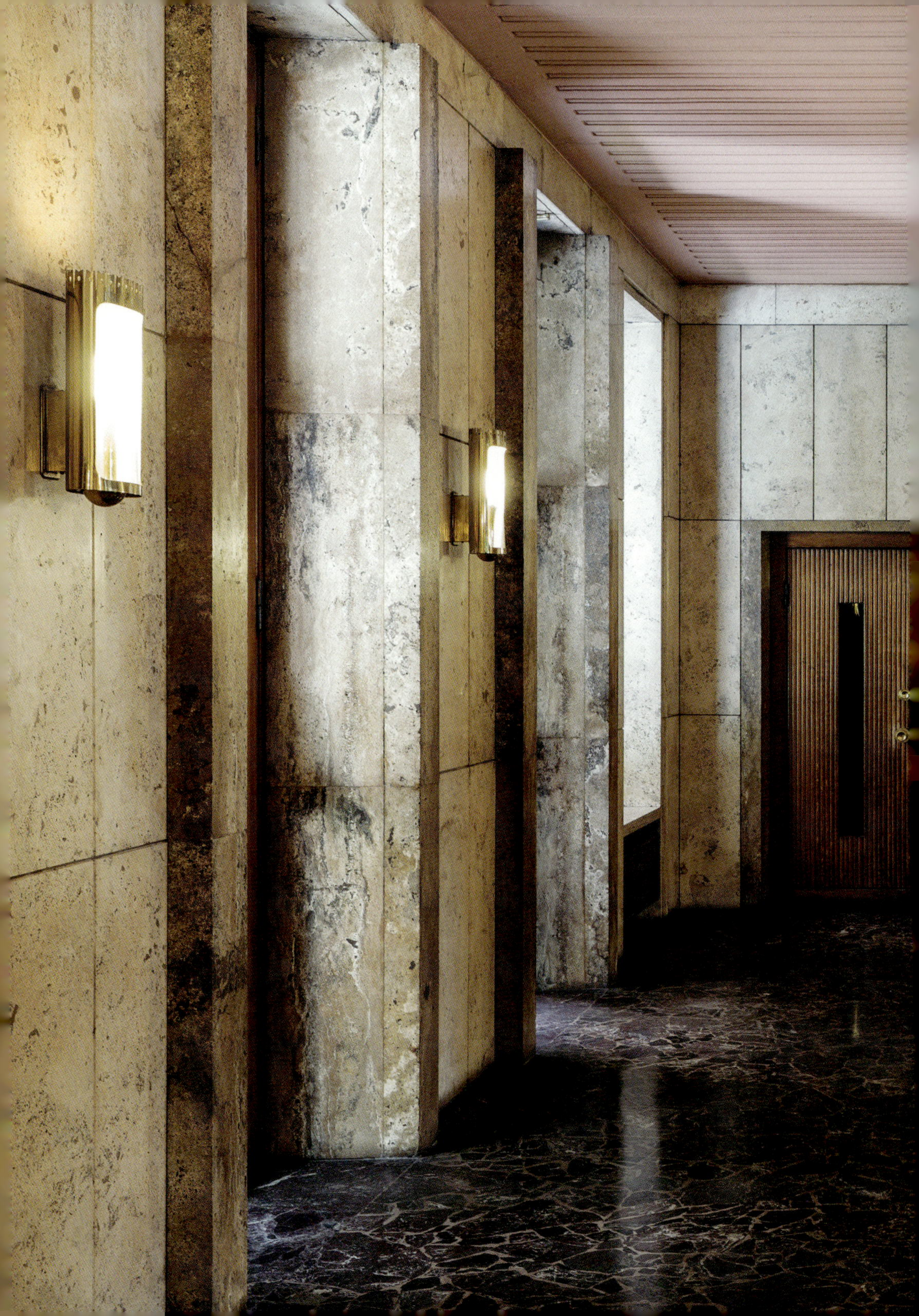

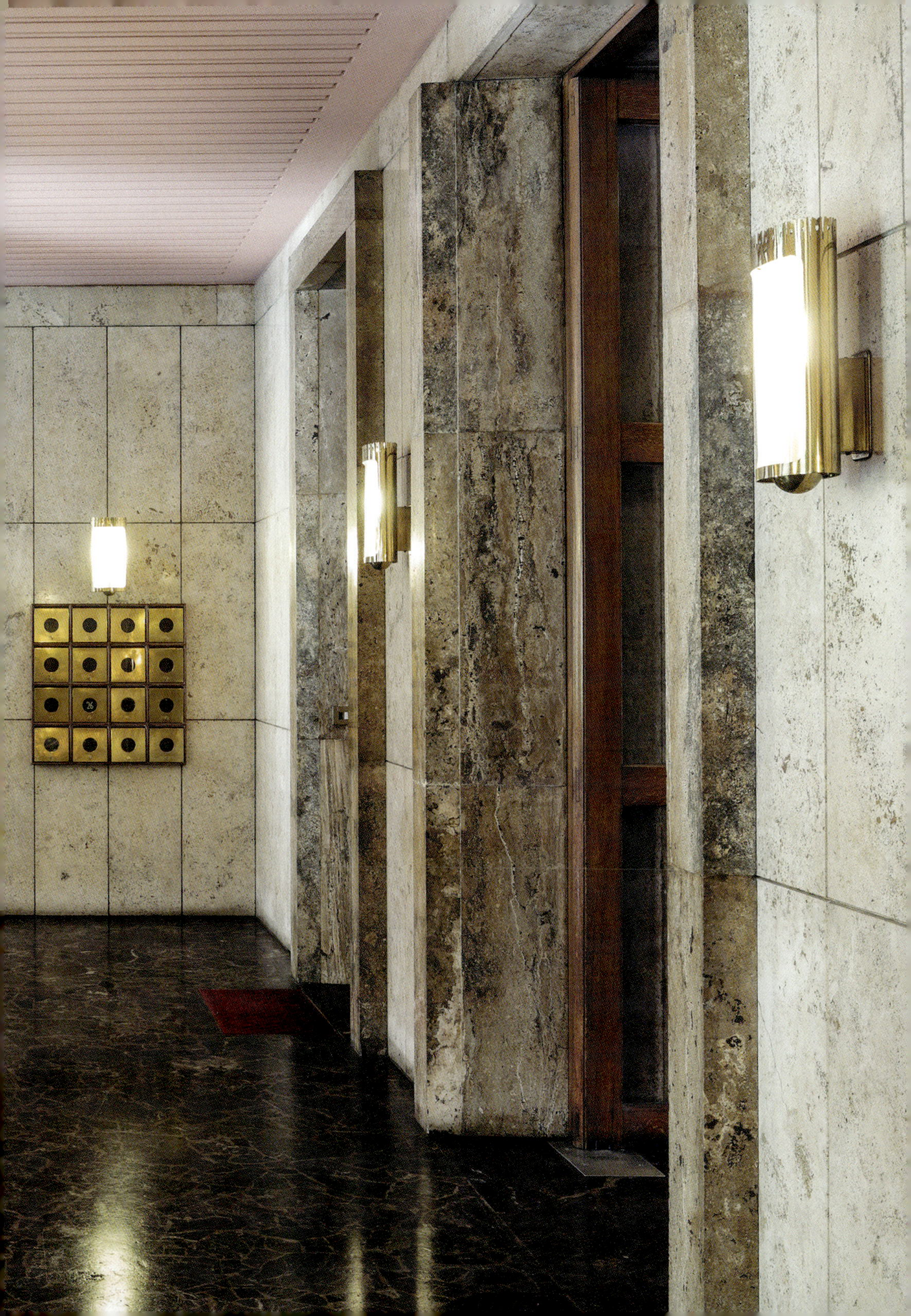

Previous spread:

via Mauro Macchi 42 · Paolo Buffa, 1946

Sconces by Paolo Buffa.

floor: Palladiana of Rosso Levanto · doorframes: Travertino noce · walls: travertine

This and following spread:

via San Marco 33 · Gigi Ghò, 1950–53

Sconce by Luigi Caccia Dominioni.

floor: Macchiavecchia limestone breccia · stairs: Macchiavecchia limestone breccia and Trani Serpeggiante limestone · walls: Trani Serpeggiante limestone

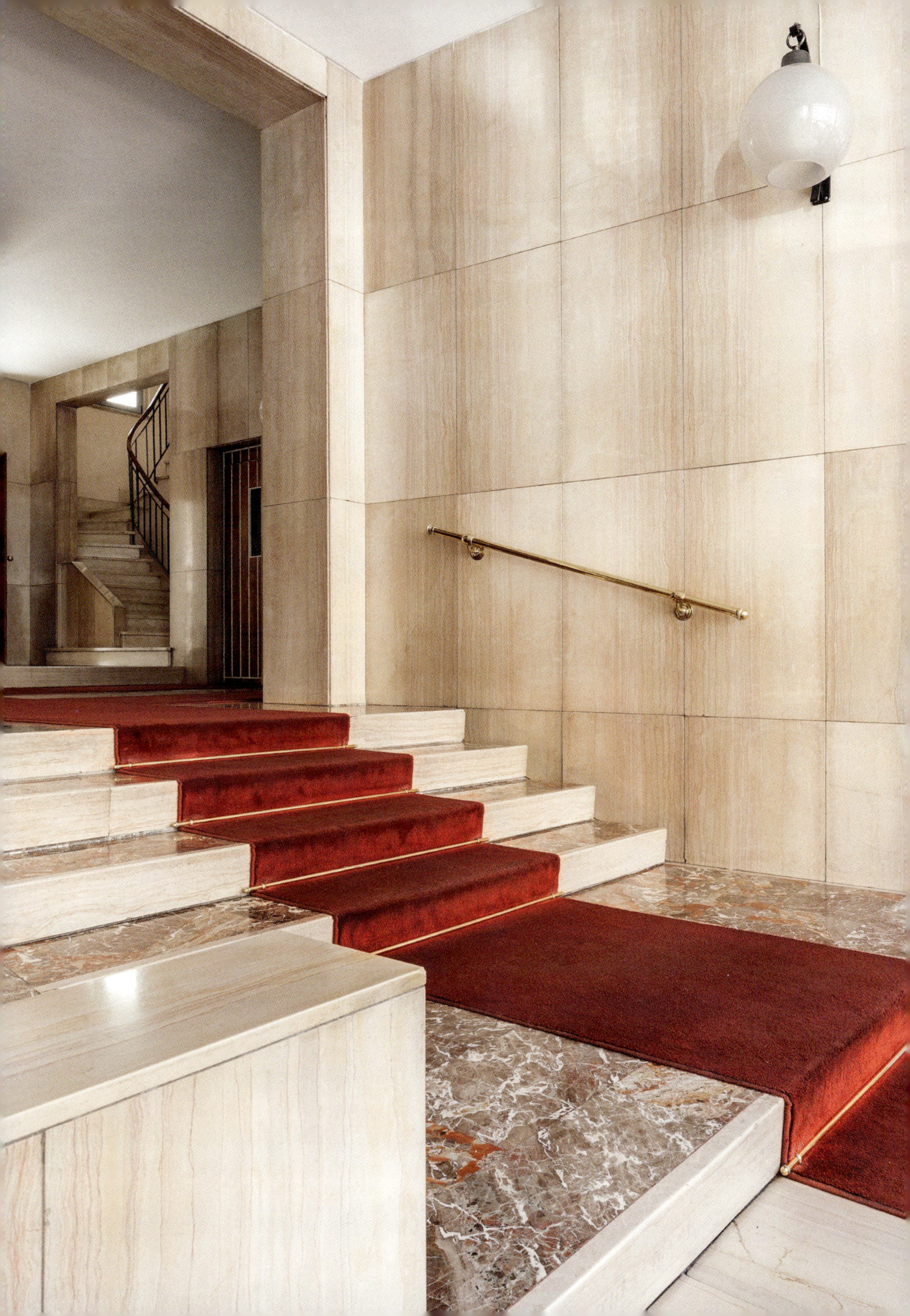

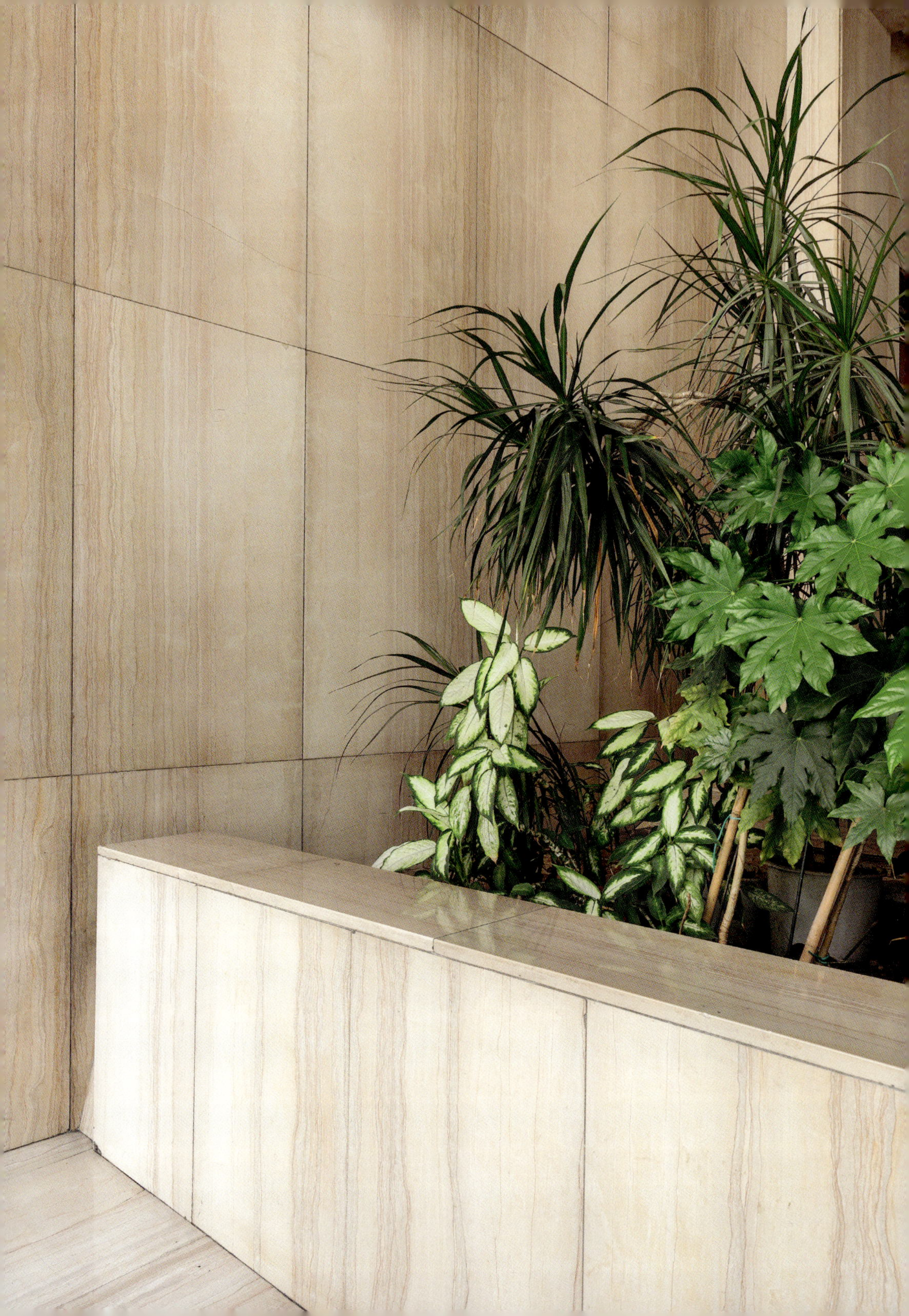

Penny Sparke

Nature Inside: Plants in Interior Spaces

Once one becomes aware of them, and starts looking for them, it quickly becomes apparent that potted plants are a recurrent feature in many of the entrance halls in Milan's mid-twentieth-century buildings. Nestling in corners, squatting on floors, delineating changes of levels and the meeting of planes, bordering stairways, emphasizing height, embellishing window sills, framing views, filling gaps, or simply adding highlights of variegated greenness, texture, and naturalness to what are otherwise hard, man-made, geometric spaces, they are silently ubiquitous. They are, at the same time, through that ubiquity, invisible and yet, through the striking visual contrast that they present to the other features they accompany, they are also highly visible.

Like pieces of sculpture that are sometimes also present, the texture of the marble so frequently used, and the other occasional *objets d'art*, plants add a level of sumptuous decoration to these otherwise minimally functional and, in terms of their purpose, somewhat mundane environments. Often they are contained in planters that have been built into the very architectural fabric of the spaces, so intrinsic are they to the decorative schemes envisaged by their designers.

Why are they really there though? Why, in these relatively small, transitional spaces, which, to the inhabitants of the buildings in question, are merely passages to take them from outside to inside, did anyone bother to insert a potted palm, or design and build a planter into the original plan? Given that they require work—potting and re-potting, dusting, and watering—there must be, one supposes, a significant benefit to be had from their presence. In the case of the Milanese entrance hall it is the role of the concierge—the only other living element of these spaces—to tend the plants. Like them he serves to soften the blow between the outside and the inside.

As well as providing the wide variety of practical, spatial roles described above—to which one could add their functions as screens and way-finders—plants play a highly symbolic role in these interiors. As already suggested, entrance halls mark the transition from outside to inside, from the public street to the private living space. Nature, as we normally experience it, is usually found outside, whether in the countryside or the garden. Brought inside, it can help us orient ourselves in the midst of that sudden shift. By blurring the boundary, plants can soften the blow and allow us to gently acclimatize ourselves in the new sphere.

Plants are more than that, though. Like the traditional materials sometimes used they add a level of familiarity to what are, partially at least, aggressively modern spaces. In these hybrid interiors, in which marble often vies with modern materials—a battle between tradition and modernity so familiar in mid-twentieth-century Italian material and spatial culture—plants provide a conservative, reassuring presence, comforting inhabitants who are confronted by the challenges of the modern world.

Plants are also welcoming in this context as they speak of domesticity, albeit in a modern guise. They tell the buildings' inhabitants that they are "at home." The story of how they acquired that particular symbolic meaning is rooted in the nineteenth century and the emergence of bourgeois culture. In Italy the love of greenery goes even further back. From the fifteenth century the garden was an important part of the aristocratic dwelling and the Italian garden influenced the developments in landscape design that occurred in both France and England. In the modern context, tamed nature first came into the home in the eighteenth century in the interior spaces of the upper classes, sometimes in the form of potted plants in conservatories attached to their houses and sometimes in examples that entered into the actual rooms of the homes themselves. Given that they were often imported from overseas, like so many of the other possessions of the aristocracy, these indoor plants were markers of their wealth and status.

With the rise of the urban middle class in the nineteenth century, and its overwhelming desire to emulate its social superiors and mark its arrival, indoor plants became increasingly popular at that level of society as well. The activity of "window gardening," seen as a feminine accomplishment, quickly became widespread and numerous advice books were published on the subject, helping middle-class housewives arrange potted plants prettily in their parlors as part of their responsibility for its décor. The greenery they introduced provided a visual foil for the dark woods that were used for nineteenth-century furniture and, along with textiles draped over surfaces, served to soften the appearance of the nineteenth-century home. Ferns were frequently positioned in the summer fireplace to cover that otherwise unused area; hanging baskets were suspended from the ceiling; and glazed boxes were added to the exterior of windowsills. Wardian cases, little horticultural ecosystems used to bring plants from the tropics, were often placed on tabletops, filled with ferns and other greenery.

In this newly-urbanized and industrialized context indoor plants took on many meanings. As well as maintaining the presence of the countryside in the city at a moment of traumatic transition, they also acted as an educational tool for children, a marker of God's presence on earth, and as a form of therapy for the elderly, the sick, and the bereaved. Certain plants, such as palms, which were hugely popular with those who could afford them, brought a level of exoticism into the everyday life of housewives reminding them, as well, of the imperial world of which they were a part.

Quite quickly plants became embedded not only in the physical spaces of the nineteenth-century middle-class home but also in the very concept of bourgeois domesticity itself. However, as nineteenth-century eclecticism gave way, in the subsequent century, to the uncluttered spaces of modernist architecture, that concept came to be despised by the latter movement's protagonists. They saw it as a marker of the bourgeois individualism that they rejected so absolutely and they questioned what they saw as the claustrophobic character of domesticity, seeking to replace it with unbounded, open-plan interiors. Plants did not disappear completely, however, but their earlier deep symbolism was sacrificed in favor of their capacity to perform a number of spatial functions.

In turn, by the middle years of the twentieth century, modernism had softened and a more humanistic modern architecture and interior design came to the fore, one in which plants once again played a key role. Nowhere was that more apparent than in the strikingly innovative "mid-century modern" homes built in California, where, in that benign climate, technology joined hands fully with nature and indoor plants were favored once again. In Europe, also, there were signs that modern architecture and domesticity were no longer at loggerheads with each other and that the symbolism of the latter could coexist with the spatial preoccupations of the former. Furthermore, that approach could be applied in buildings in both the private and the public spheres.

This brings us back to the Milanese entrance halls where that union between technology and nature can clearly be seen. Plants reinforce the important domestic nature of the spaces in question and help to articulate the ways in which they are to be negotiated physically and emotionally. Above all, though, they welcome inhabitants and remind them that they are back home.

Following spread:

via San Simpliciano 6

floor: Rosso Trento limestone · walls: Stucco Veneziano

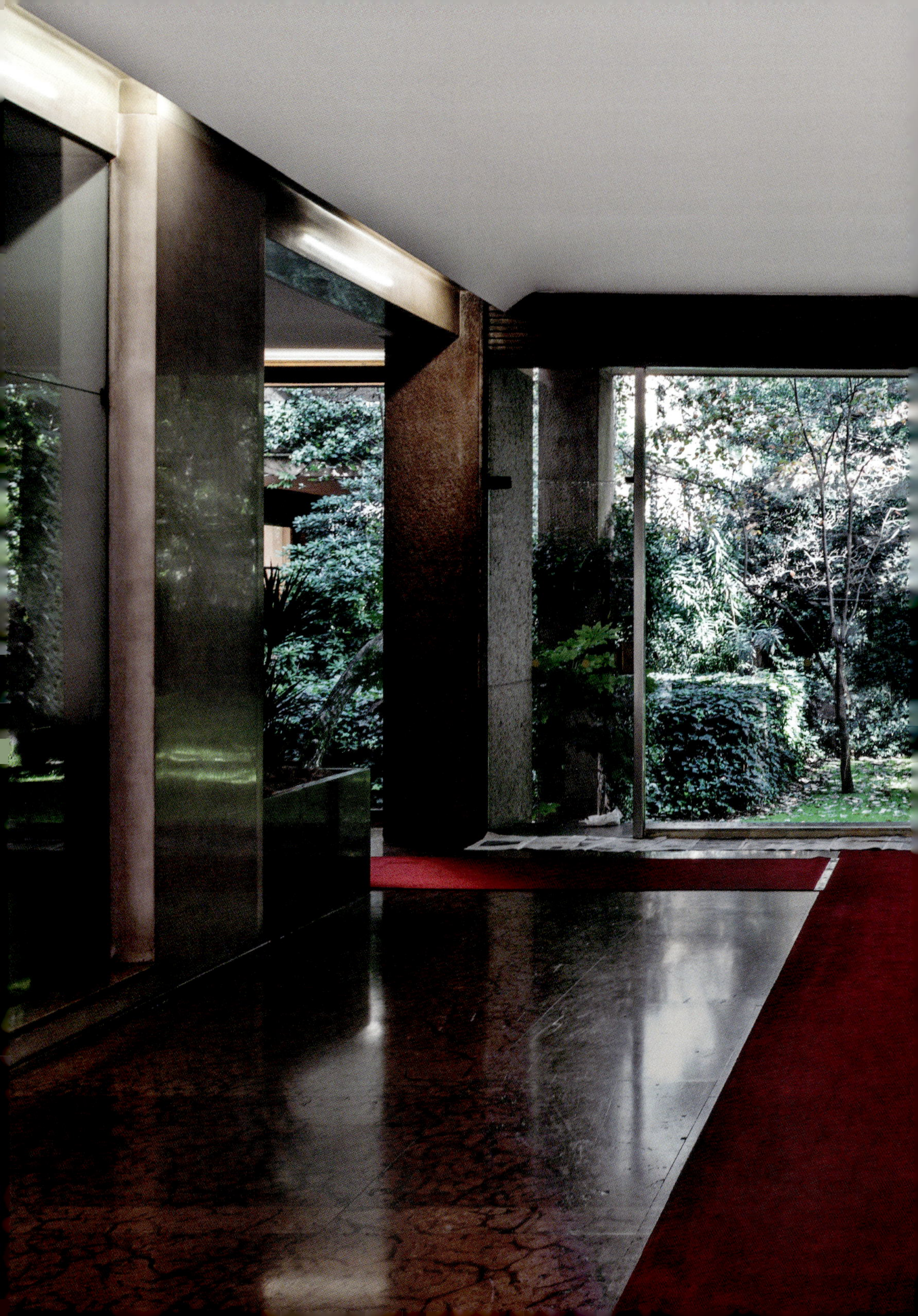

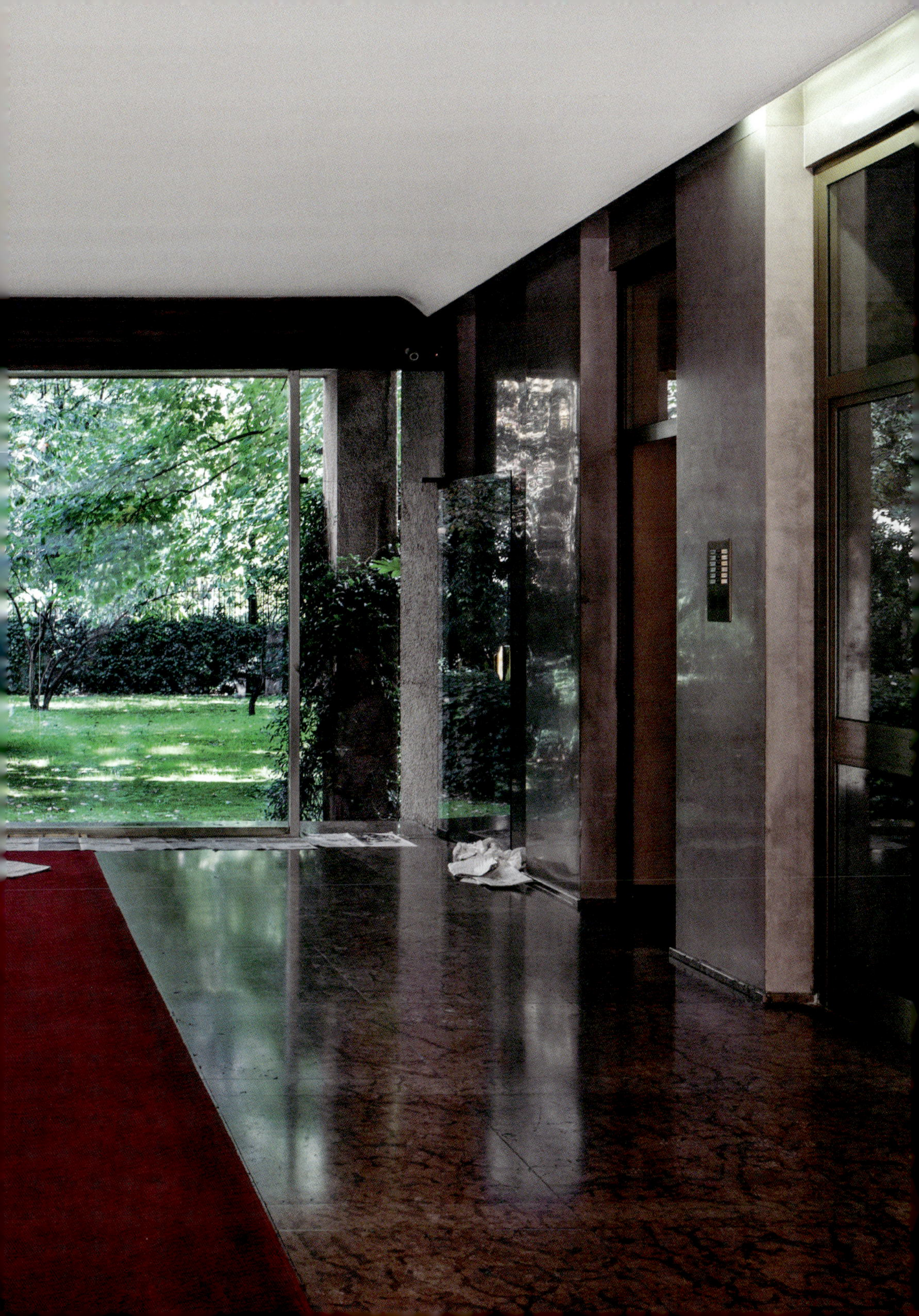

Penny Sparke

La natura dentro: piante negli spazi interni

Una volta che se n'è notata la presenza, e si comincia a cercarle, diviene subito chiaro che le piante in vaso sono un elemento ricorrente in gran parte degli ingressi degli edifici milanesi di metà Novecento. Nascoste negli angoli, allineate sui pavimenti, strategicamente collocate per segnare cambi di livello all'incrocio dei piani, o per fare da contorno alle scale, per sottolineare le altezze, abbellire i davanzali, incorniciare la veduta di una finestra, riempire vuoti, o semplicemente per dare un tocco di verde, di materia viva, di natura a quelli che di per sé sono spazi geometrici aspri, creati dalla mano umana, le piante sono silenziosamente ubique. Proprio per questa loro ubiquità sono invisibili ma, al tempo stesso, grazie ai forti contrasti visivi che generano con gli elementi cui sono accostate, sono anche molto visibili.

Come le sculture talvolta presenti negli androni, la tessitura dei marmi così spesso utilizzati e altri occasionali *objets d'art*, le piante aggiungono un livello di sontuosità alla decorazione di questi ambienti di per sé minimalisticamente funzionali e, in considerazione del loro scopo, talvolta banali. Spesso sono contenute in fioriere costruite nel tessuto architettonico stesso degli spazi che le accolgono, del tutto intrinseche all'intento decorativo prefigurato dai progettisti.

Ma perché sono così presenti? Perché, in questi spazi di transizione relativamente ridotti, i quali, per gli abitanti degli edifici in questione, costituiscono meri passaggi che portano dall'esterno all'interno, qualcuno si è preoccupato di inserire una palma in vaso, o di progettare fin dall'inizio la costruzione di una fioriera? Considerato il lavoro che le piante richiedono (invasare e rinvasare, pulire e innaffiare), dev'esserci, si sarebbe portati a pensare, un qualche vantaggio assai significativo derivante dalla loro presenza. Nel caso degli ingressi milanesi, è compito del portinaio – l'unico altro elemento vivo di questi spazi – prendersi cura delle piante. Come loro, anche il portinaio serve ad attenuare lo stacco tra il fuori e il dentro.

Oltre a rivestire l'ampia varietà di ruoli spaziali, pratici, descritti sopra (cui si potrebbero aggiungere le funzioni di schermatura e di indicazione del percorso), le piante svolgono un ruolo altamente simbolico in questi interni. Come già si è accennato, gli ingressi segnano la transizione dall'esterno

via Giovanni Pascoli 21

Sconce by Franco Albini for Venini.
floor and stairs: Verde Alpi ophicalcite · walls: Carrara marble

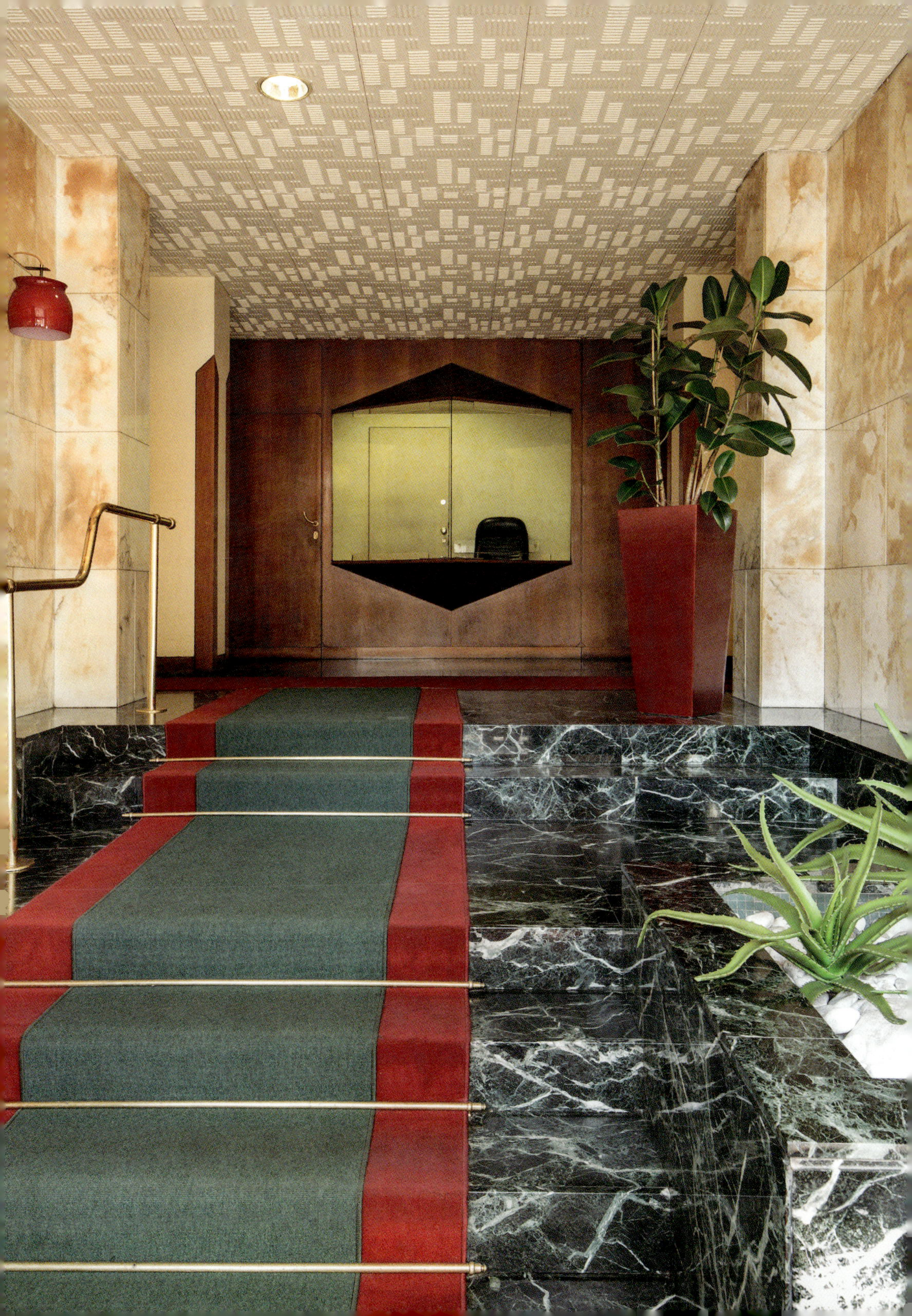

all'interno, dalla strada pubblica all'abitazione privata. La natura, per come normalmente la viviamo, si trova di solito al di fuori, che sia in campagna o in giardino. Portata dentro può esserci d'aiuto nell'orientarci in questo passaggio repentino. Rendendo più sfumato il confine, le piante possono attutire il colpo e permetterci di acclimatarci più dolcemente alla nuova sfera.

Tuttavia le piante sono più di questo. Come i materiali tradizionali talvolta impiegati, esse aggiungono un tono di familiarità a quelli che, almeno in parte, sono spazi connotati da una modernità aggressiva. In questi interni ibridi, dove sovente il marmo compete con materiali moderni, in una battaglia fra tradizione e modernità così tipica della cultura materiale e spaziale dell'Italia degli anni Cinquanta, le piante garantiscono una presenza conservatrice, rassicurante, che è di conforto ai residenti costretti ad affrontare le sfide del mondo moderno.

In questo contesto le piante sono bene accolte anche perché esprimono un senso di focolare domestico, pur se in versione contemporanea. Dicono agli abitanti dell'edificio che sono arrivati "a casa". La storia dell'acquisizione di questo particolare significato simbolico è radicata nel Novecento e nella nascita della cultura borghese. In Italia l'amore per il verde risale ancora più addietro nel tempo. Sin dal quindicesimo secolo il giardino era una componente importante della dimora aristocratica e il giardino all'italiana ha successivamente influenzato gli sviluppi della progettazione paesaggistica sia in Francia sia in Inghilterra. In tempi più recenti, nel diciottesimo secolo la natura addomesticata è entrata per la prima volta nelle case, negli interni delle classi più agiate, a volte sotto forma di piante in vaso poste in serre adiacenti alle abitazioni, a volte entrando letteralmente nelle stanze delle abitazioni stesse. Essendo molto spesso importate d'oltremare, come tanti altri beni dell'aristocrazia, anche le piante d'appartamento erano segni di ricchezza e di status.

Con la nascita, nel diciannovesimo secolo, della classe media urbana, e il suo travolgente desiderio di emulare le classi sociali superiori e affermare la propria esistenza, le piante da interni sono diventate sempre più popolari anche in quella fetta della società. Il "giardinaggio da balcone", visto come un'espressione della virtù femminile, si è rapidamente diffuso e numerosi libri sono stati pubblicati sull'argomento, per aiutare le casalinghe di classe media a disporre con grazia le piante in vaso nei propri salotti, come uno dei compiti connessi all'ornamento della casa. Le macchie di verde così introdotte facevano da contrasto visivo ai legni scuri usati per il mobilio ottocentesco e, insieme ai tessuti drappeggiati sulle superfici, servivano ad ammorbidire l'aspetto delle abitazioni dell'epoca. Spesso d'estate si collocavano delle felci nei camini, per dissimulare uno spazio in quel momento inutilizzato; si appendevano cesti di piante ai soffitti; e si esponevano vasi di porcellana sui davanzali esterni delle finestre. Ed era frequente vedere sui tavoli le cosiddette cassette di Ward, piccole scatole in vetro che, come micro-ecosistemi orticulturali, erano usate per trasportare le piante dai tropici, e contenevano felci e altre specie vegetali.

In questo nuovo contesto di recente urbanizzazione e industrializzazione, le piante da interni hanno assunto più d'un significato. Oltre a mantenere la presenza della campagna nella città in un momento di transizione traumatica, costituivano anche uno strumento per l'educazione dell'infanzia, un segno della presenza divina sulla terra e una forma di terapia per gli anziani, i malati, le persone in lutto. Certe piante, come le palme, che erano diffusissime tra coloro che potevano permettersele, portavano un tocco di esotismo nella quotidianità delle casalinghe, ricordando loro, al tempo stesso, il mondo imperiale di cui facevano parte.

Molto rapidamente le piante sono diventate un elemento inglobato non solo negli spazi fisici delle abitazioni della classe media del diciannovesimo secolo, ma anche nel concetto stesso di vita domestica borghese. Quando però, nel secolo successivo, l'eclettismo ottocentesco ha via via ceduto il passo agli spazi liberi da ingombri dell'architettura modernista, l'idea del verde da interni è stata disdegnata dai protagonisti di quel movimento, che la consideravano come un segno dell'individualismo borghese da rifiutarsi radicalmente, nel momento in cui mettevano in discussione quello che ai loro occhi appariva come il carattere claustrofobico della vita domestica, e tentavano di sostituirlo con progetti di interni aperti, senza confini. Tuttavia le piante non sono scomparse del tutto, però il loro simbolismo è stato sacrificato a favore della loro capacità di svolgere una serie di funzioni spaziali.

Intorno alla metà del ventesimo secolo, tuttavia, l'ideale modernista si era attenuato e saliva alla ribalta una versione più umanistica dell'architettura e del design moderni, nella quale le piante sono tornate a svolgere un ruolo chiave. Ciò si è reso manifesto in maniera eclatante nelle innovative abitazioni in stile "moderno di metà secolo" costruite in California, dove, grazie al clima mite, la tecnologia ha potuto sposarsi appieno con la natura, e le piante da interni hanno nuovamente trionfato. Anche in Europa si sono avuti segnali del fatto che architettura moderna e vita domestica non erano più necessariamente in disaccordo, e che i valori simbolici della seconda potevano coesistere con le istanze spaziali della prima. Inoltre, si trattava di un approccio applicabile in edifici sia privati che pubblici.

Questo ci riporta a Milano e ai suoi ingressi, dove quell'unione fra tecnologia e natura è chiaramente osservabile. Le piante rafforzano l'importante natura domestica degli spazi in questione e aiutano ad articolare i modi in cui essi andranno a essere negoziati fisicamente ed emozionalmente. Più d'ogni altra cosa, tuttavia, le piante danno il benvenuto agli abitanti dell'edificio e ricordano loro che si trovano a casa.

Following spread:
piazza Sant'Erasmo 5 · Studio BBPR, 1958
Sconces by Studio BBPR.
floor, stairs and pillars: Botticino limestone

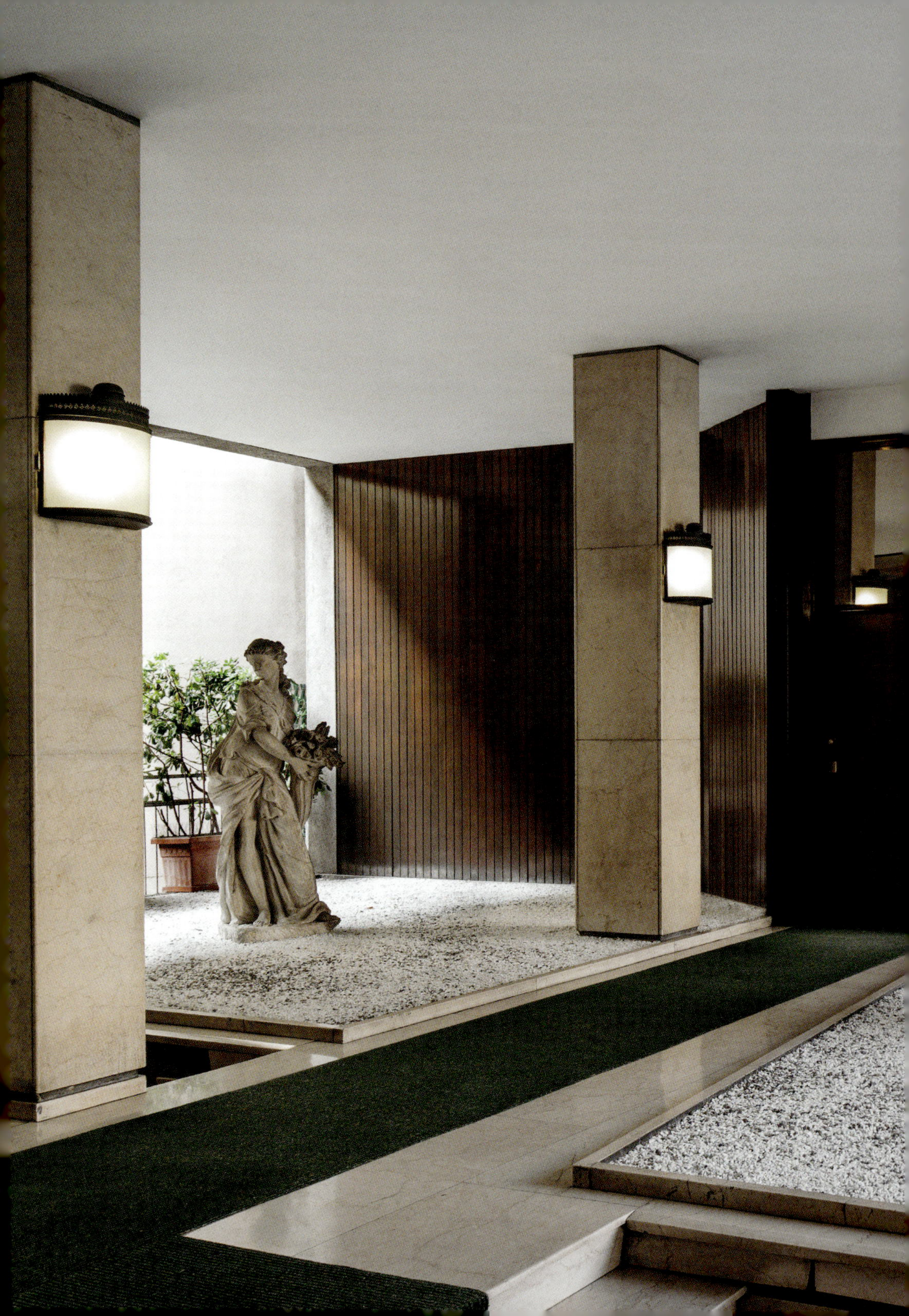

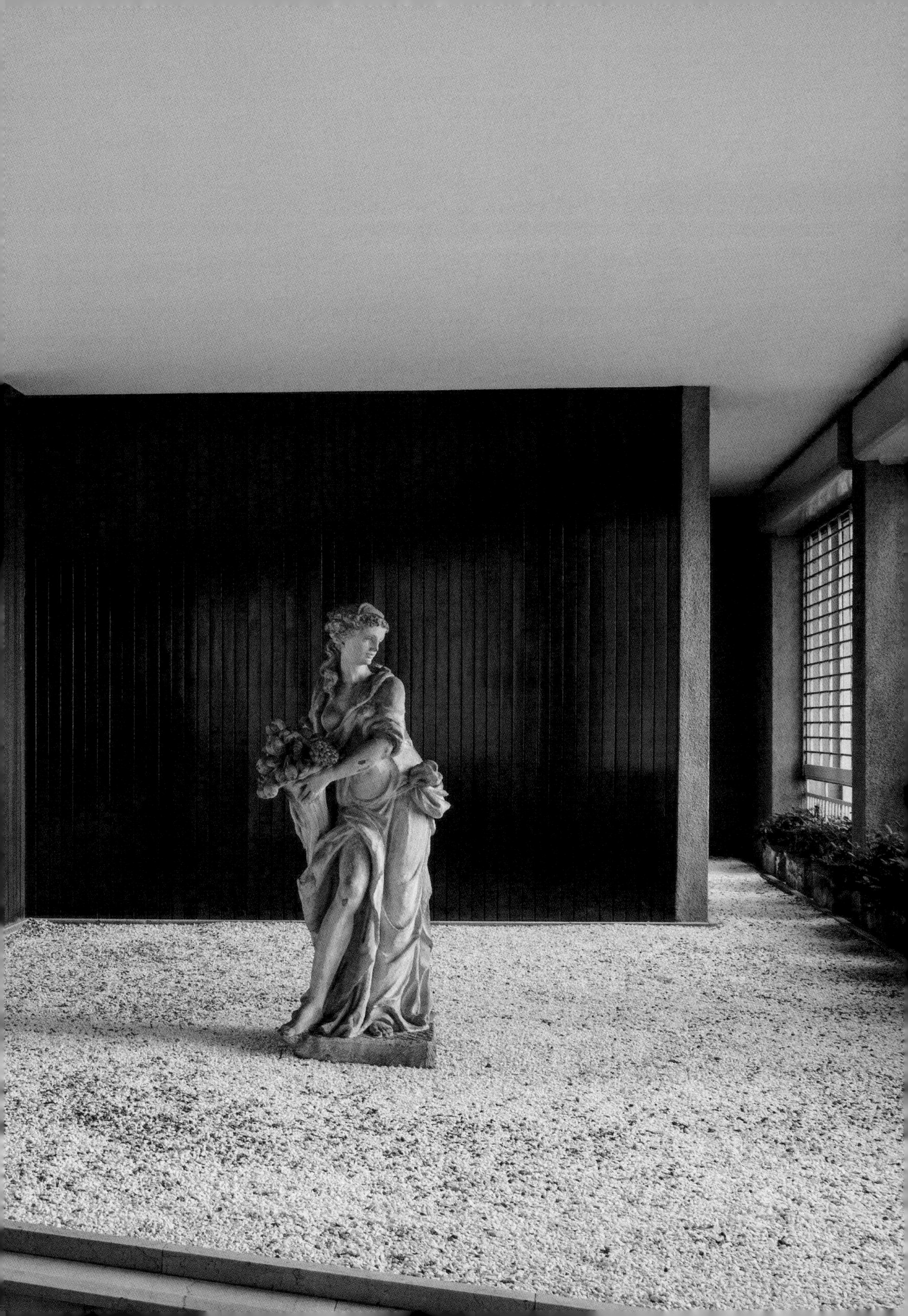

This entrance is graciously organized into three receding rooms. The telescoping effect gives a pictorial dimension to an otherwise uncomplicated succession of spaces. Paolo Buffa's distinctive design embellishments are highlighted by the continuous use of a star motif that appears in the iron entrance grill, recurs in the etched glass of the gilt sconces, and again on a coved plaster ceiling. Oddly, Buffa, one of Milan's most brilliant architects, is today remembered almost exclusively for his elegant 1930s and 1940s furniture designs.

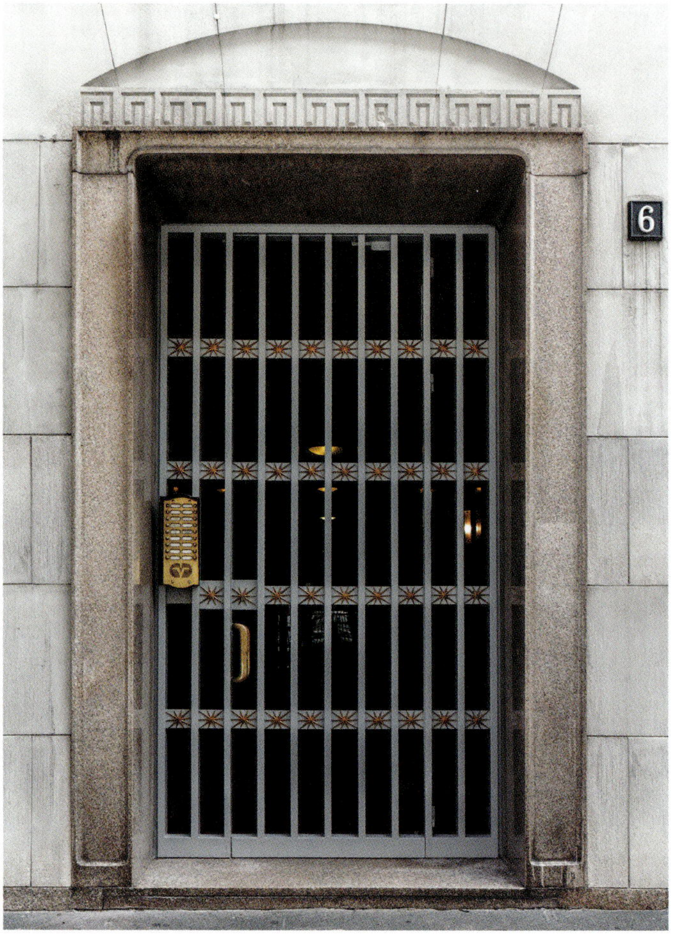

via Monte Napoleone 6 · Paolo Buffa, 1952

Sconces by Paolo Buffa.
doorframe: Rosa Baveno granite · interior floor: Musso marble · interior walls: travertine

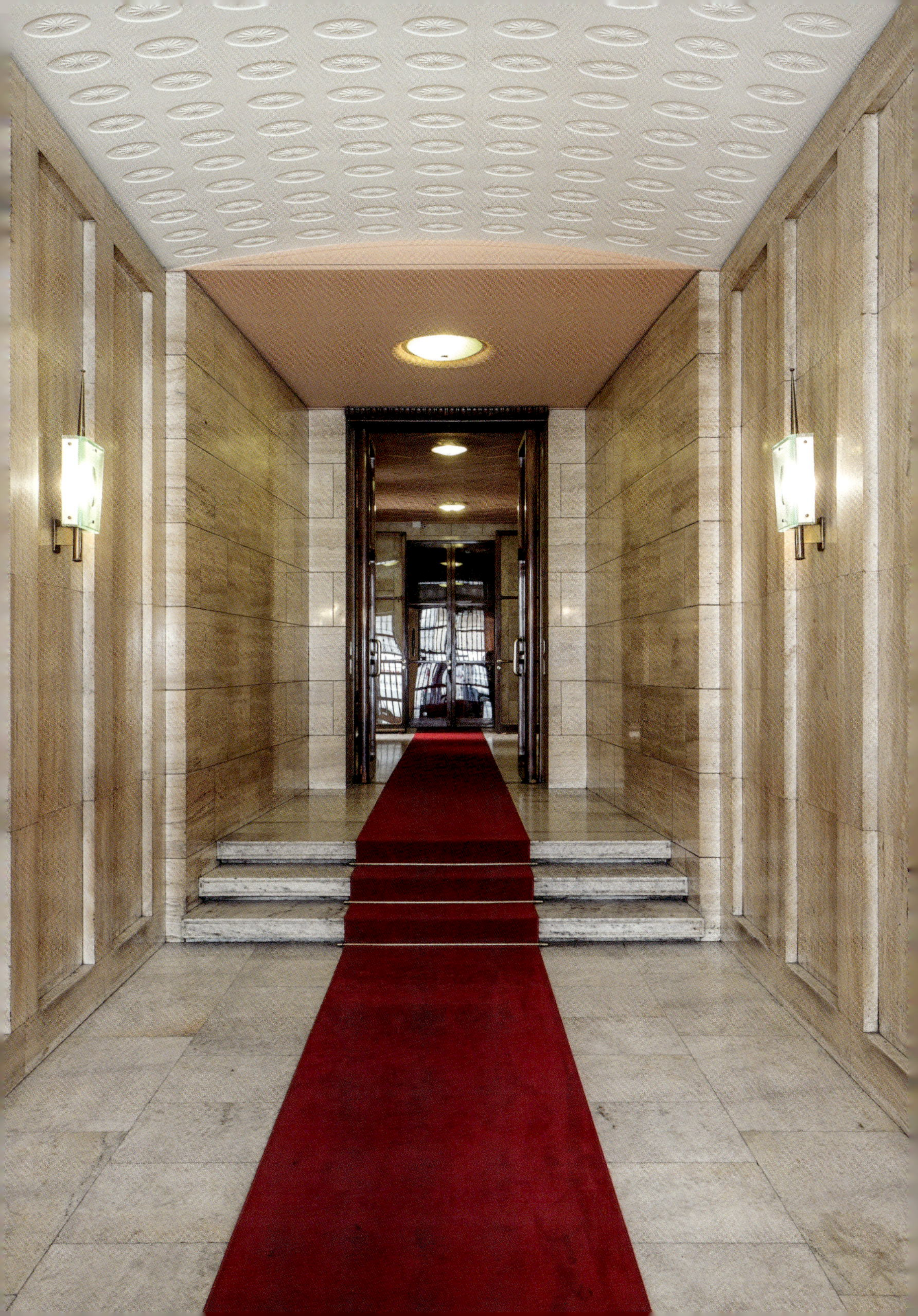

corso di Porta Nuova 2 · Giuseppe Roberto Martinenghi, 1937

floor: Arabescato Carrara marble · walls: Nero Assoluto d'Italia limestone and Calacatta marble

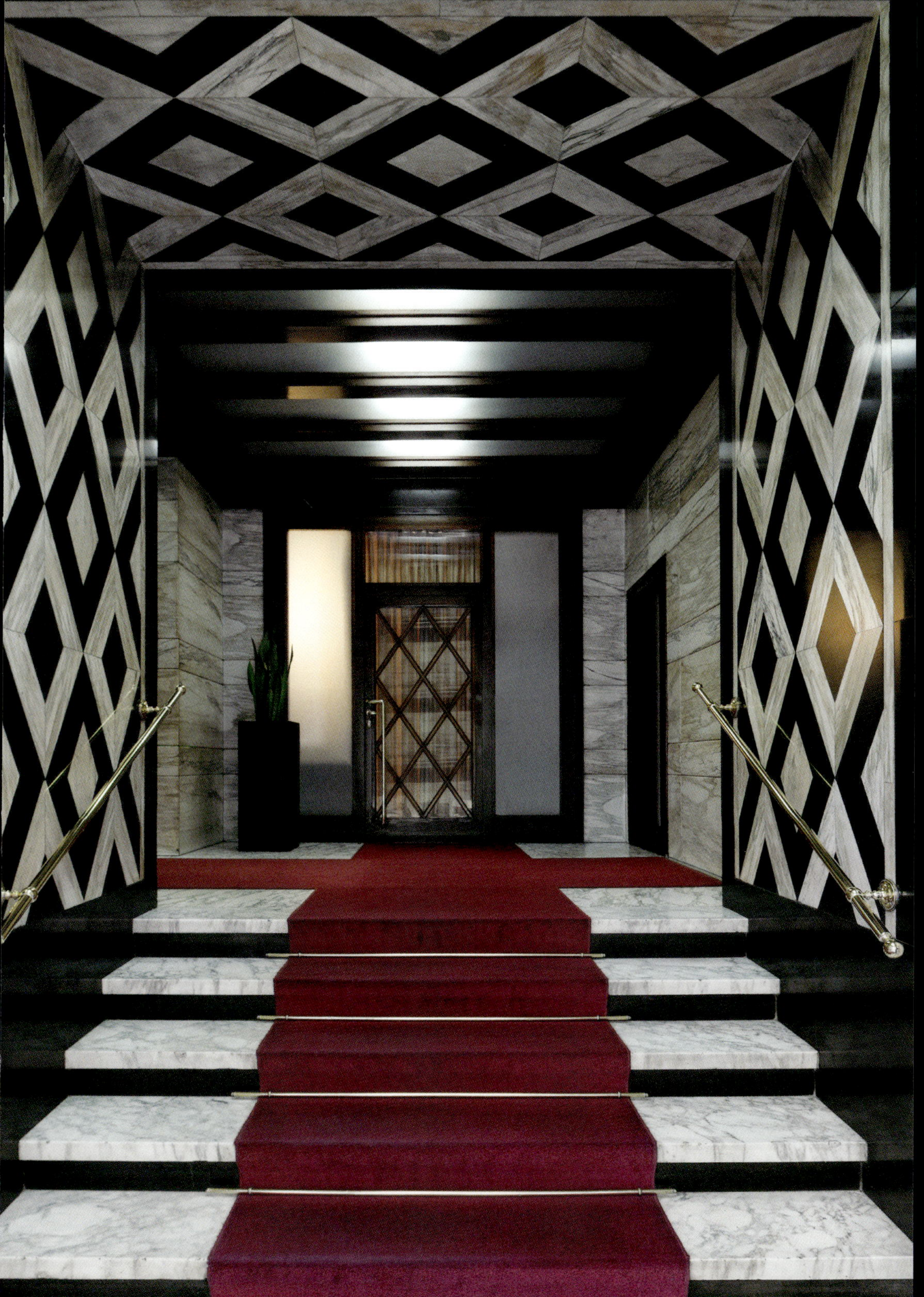

AUTARKY

At the start of the 1930s, in the face of an international embargo, Fascist authorities embarked upon a period of autarky ("self-sufficiency"), during which local industrial processes were greatly intensified. As part of this, the exploitation and manufacture of natural stone slabs was heavily encouraged, resulting in the wide-scale production and use of local dimension stones. For this reason, most of the stones and marbles used in Milan during the first half of the twentieth century are almost exclusively Italian in provenance. Due to the size of these quarries, most were either abandoned or exhausted after World War II.

corso di Porta Nuova 6 · Giuseppe Roberto Martinenghi, 1937
floor, stairs: Calacatta marble · walls: Calacatta marble, Portoro limestone

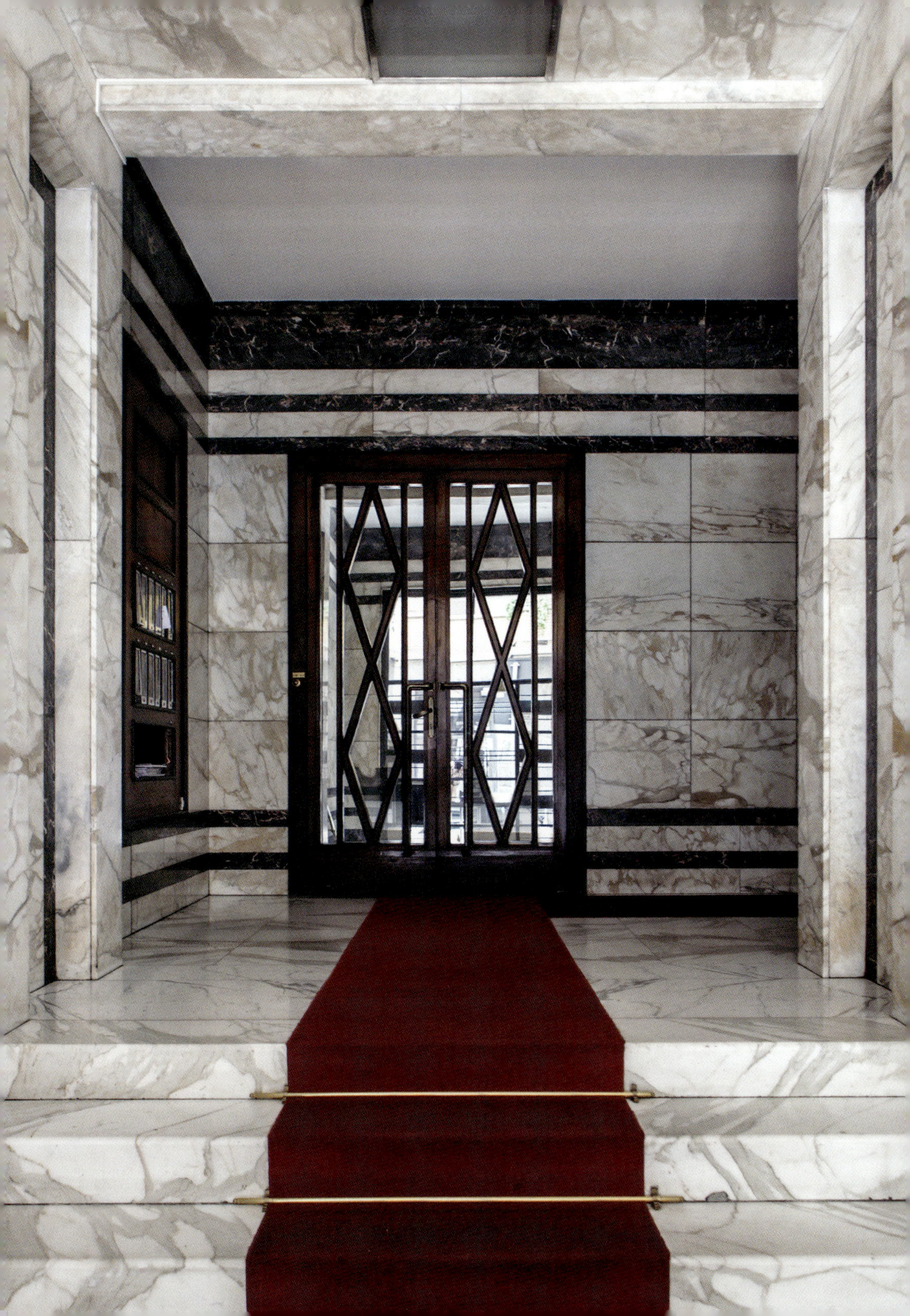

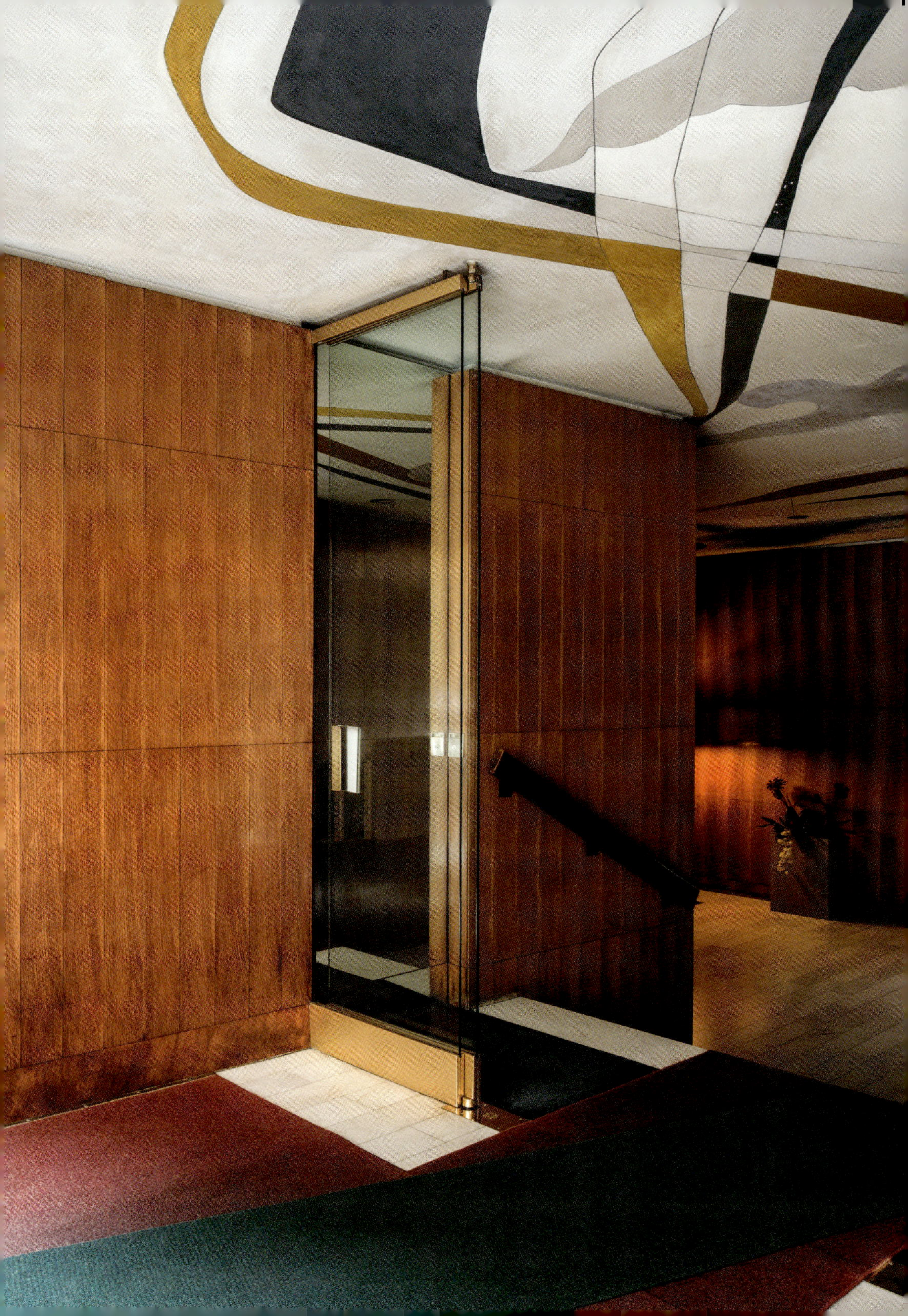

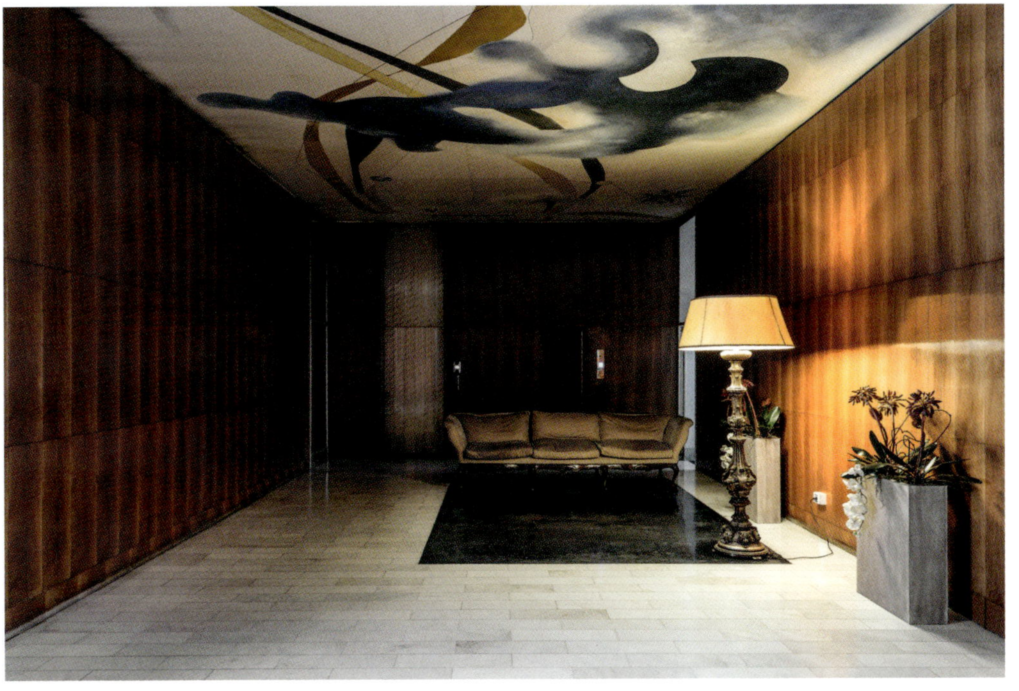

This 1951–55 interior lobby exerted an influence on many design concepts for other private residential entrances throughout Milan and beyond, in housing developments for every socio-economic level. Widely disseminated in Italian and foreign publications, Giulio Minoletti's work at the Casa del Cedro achieved the right balance in appealing to the different tastes prevalent in postwar Milan. It invented a building type that was appropriate for the historical center, without pandering to historical pastiche. Spatially unifying three walls to the lobby, a walnut low-lustre wood paneling in gradated tones is an omnipresent surface that adds great warmth and ushers in a domestic note into this large semi-public space. This nod to the private abode is also evident in the small clusters of interior artistic elements. The middle zone is marked out by a rectangular floor inlay of marble that functions as a substitute for, and a memory of, an absent carpet, where a Marco Zanuso 1951 Triennale sofa was installed, together with a monumental late Baroque ecclesiastical candelabra retrofitted as a floor lamp. Above, a ceiling painted by Antonia Tomasini covers this vast expanse with alternating geometric patterns and free-form gestural brushwork, alluding to passing clouds over a network of geometric ribbons. This derivation from Baroque frescoes, so resolutely Italian in evoking the past, is symptomatic of a then prevalent impulse to rethink the present built form within an ever wider historical context.

via Fatebenefratelli 3, Casa del Cedro · Giulio Minoletti, 1951–52

Ceiling decoration by Antonia Tomasini.
floor: Lasa marble · walls: satin-finished walnut

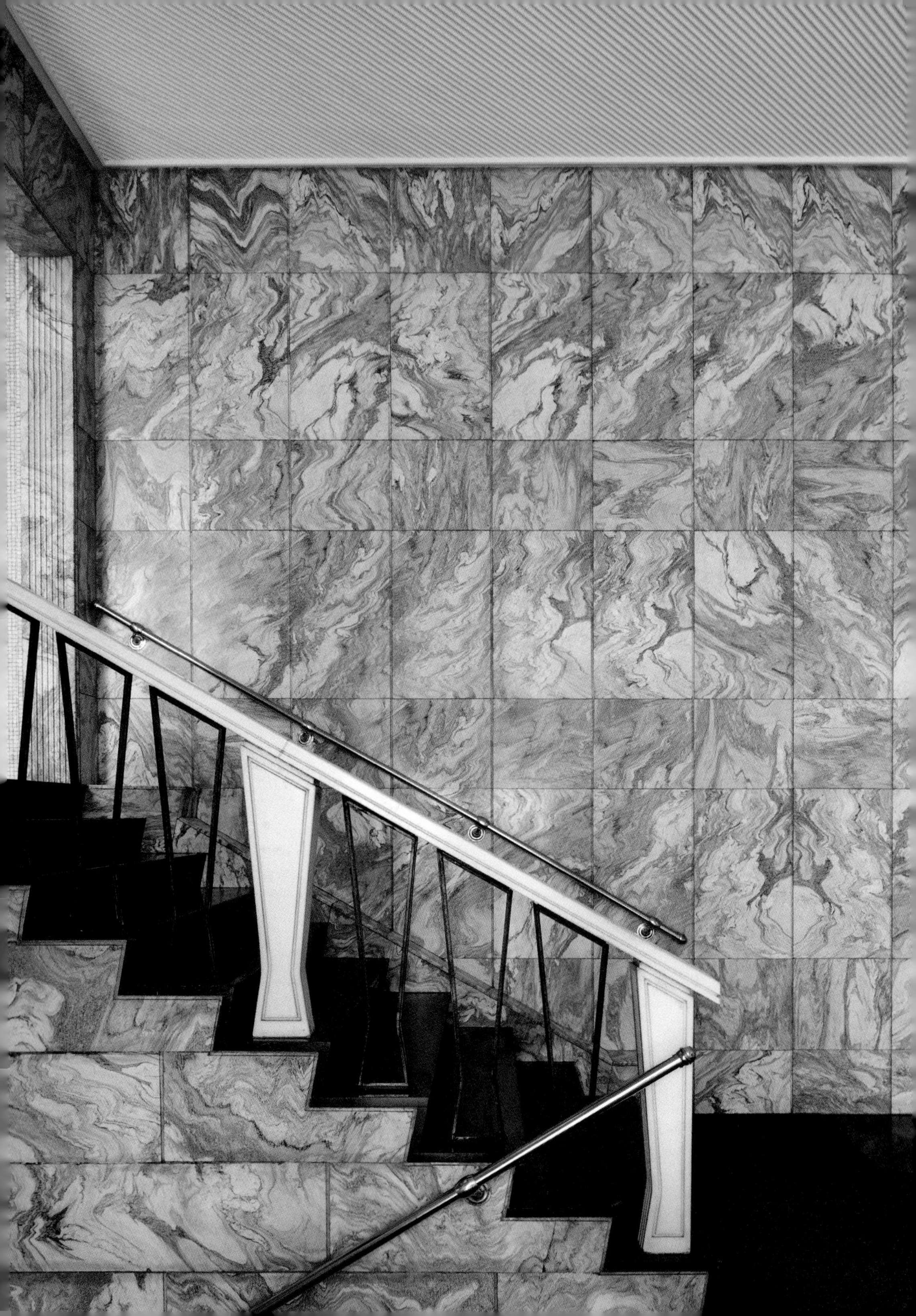

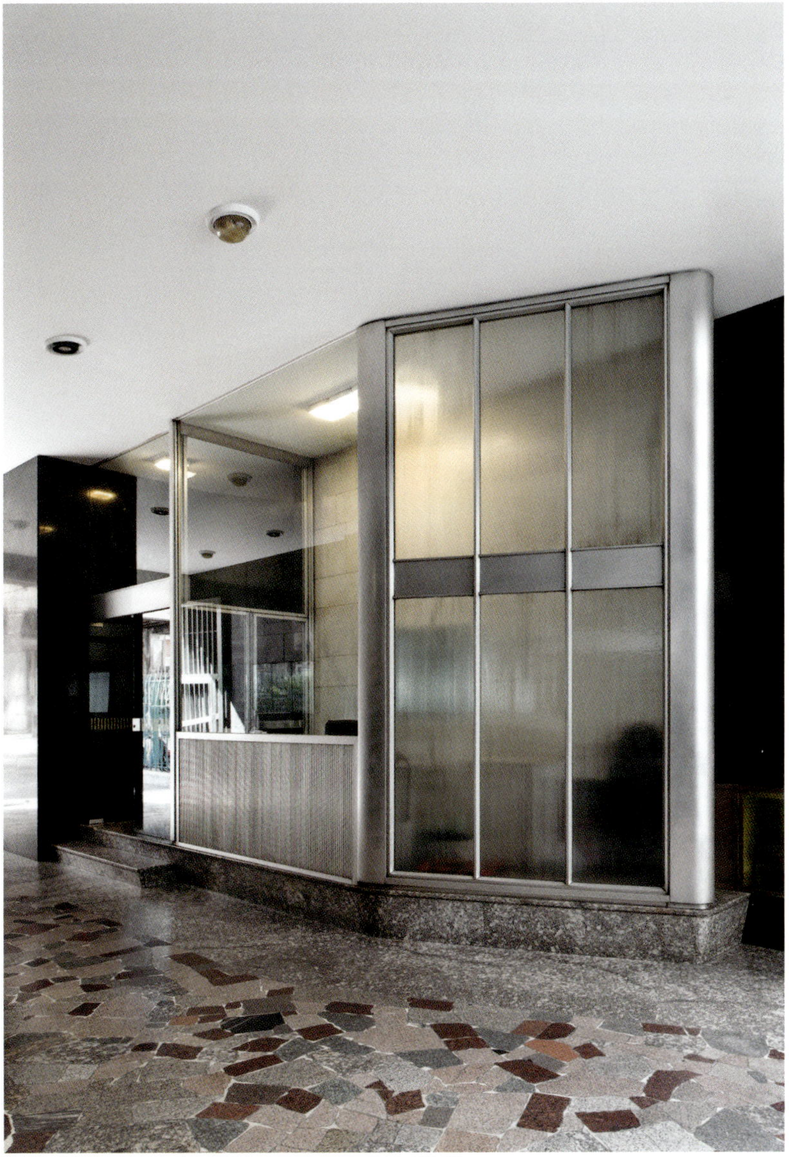

via Montebello 27 · A. Ronca, 1961–65

this page: floor: opus incertum *of several granites and Serizzo Ghiandone Valmasino*
opposite page: stairs: Black Serpentino Labrador · walls: Cipollino Verde marble

ARABESCATO OROBICO

A very peculiar layered limestone from the Province of Bergamo. It occurs in various forms, each named after its dominant color: Arabescato Orobico Grigio (gray), Arabescato Orobico Rosso (red), and Arabescato Orobico Rosato (pink). The quarries are still active.

corso di Porta Nuova 11

floor: Palladiana of white and gray marble (Musso marble) and Rosso Porfirico di Verzegnis · walls: Arabescato Orobico Rosso limestone

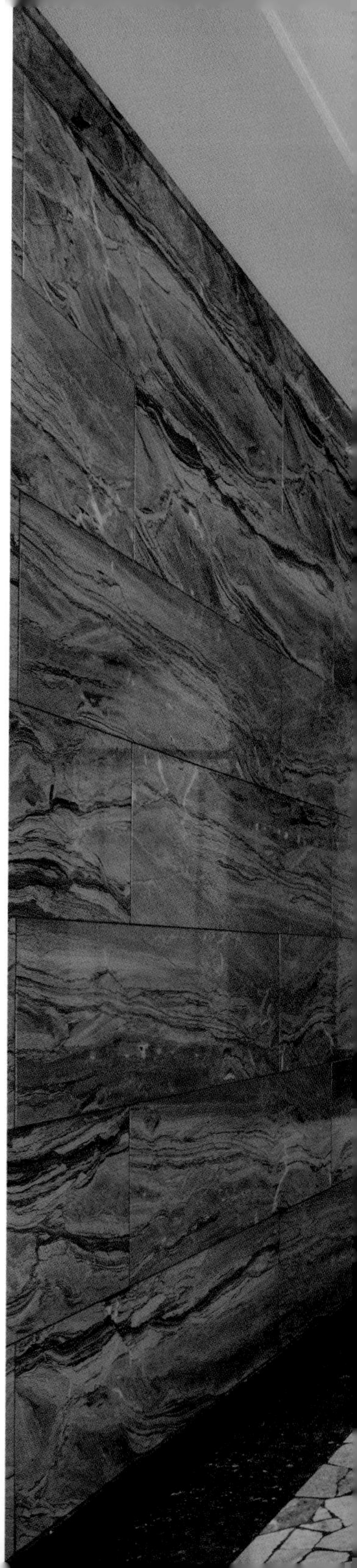

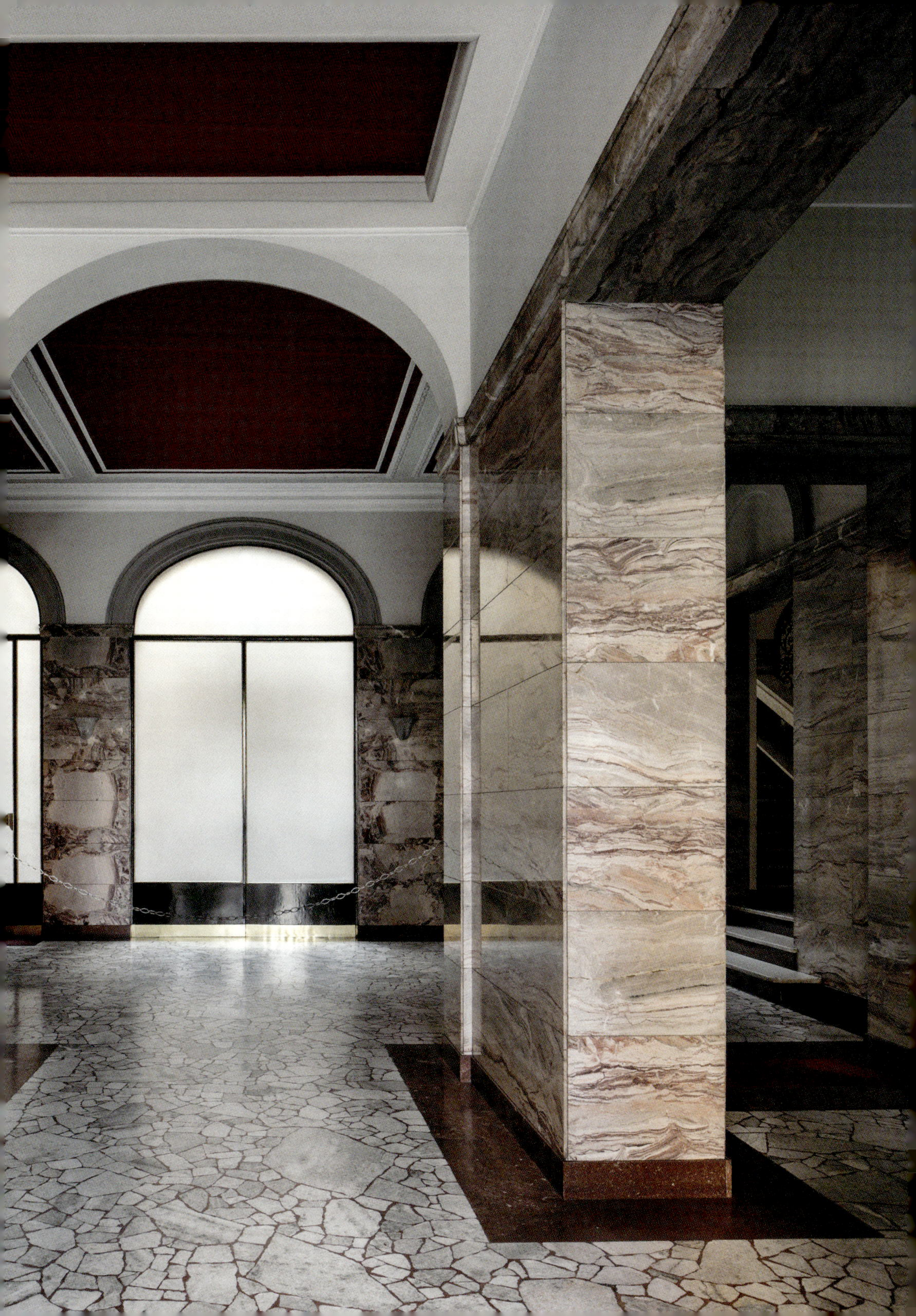

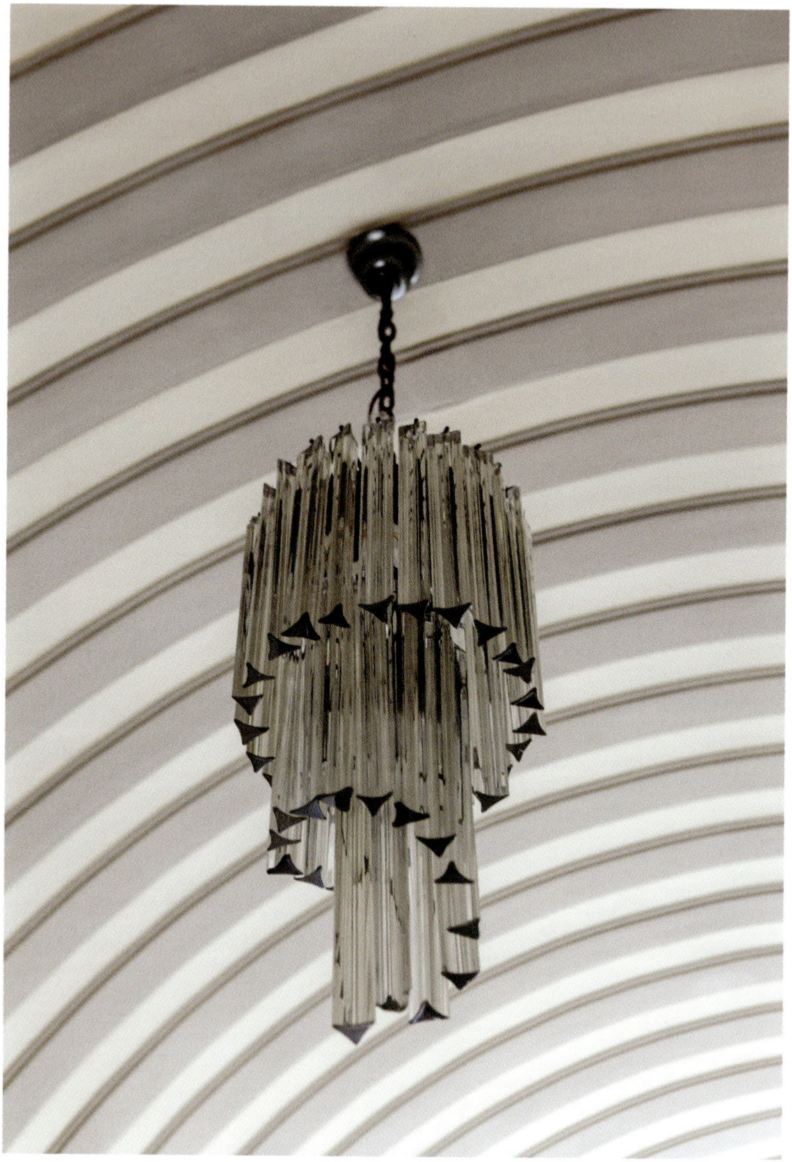

corso di Porta Nuova 46

Chandelier by Venini.

floor: Palladiana of white and gray marbles (Musso marble) · base: Botticino limestone

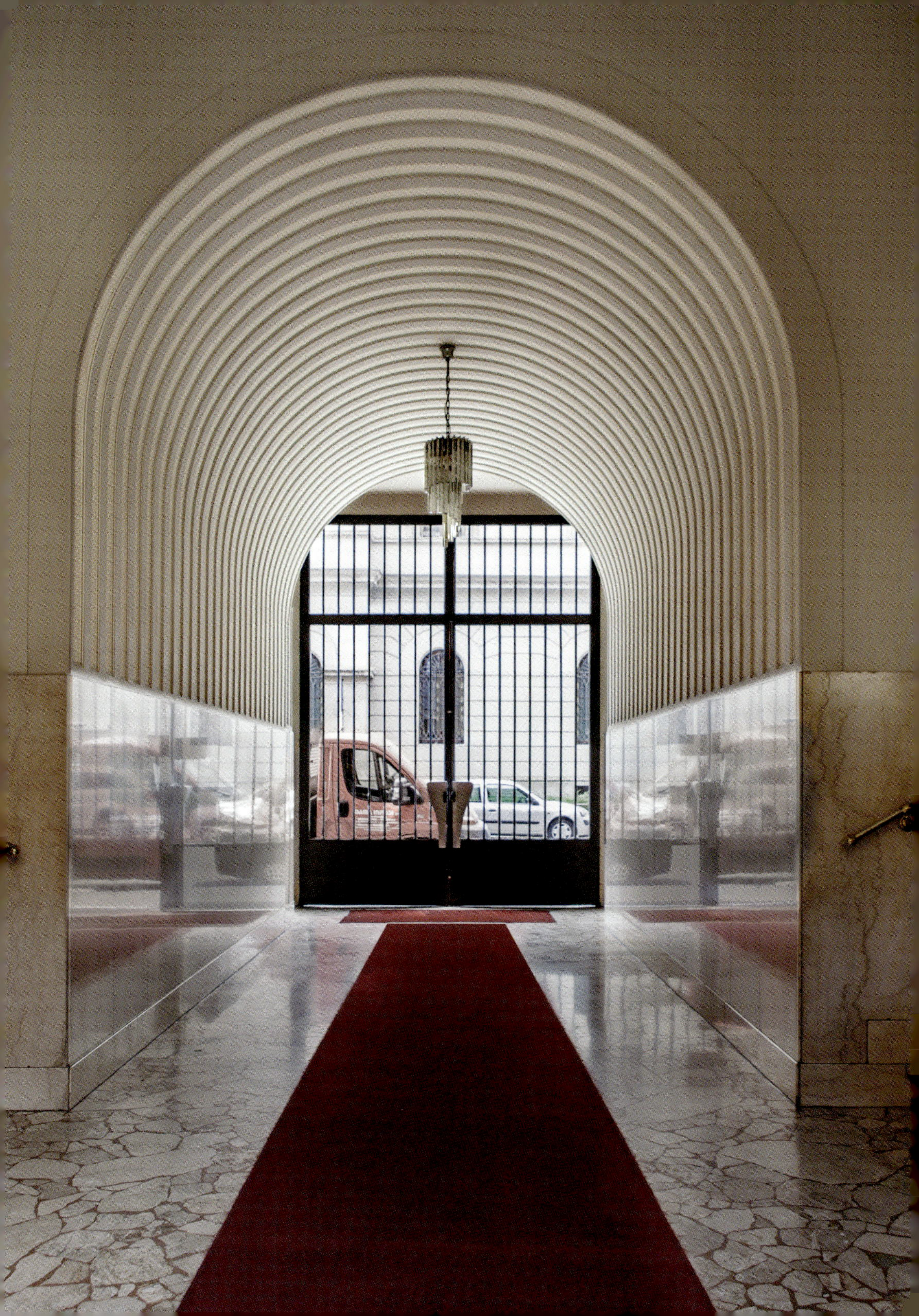

via Andrea Appiani 1 · Federico Rampazzini, 1947–49

floor: Botticino limestone slabs and Quarzite di Barge opus incertum
doorframe: Serizzo and black granite

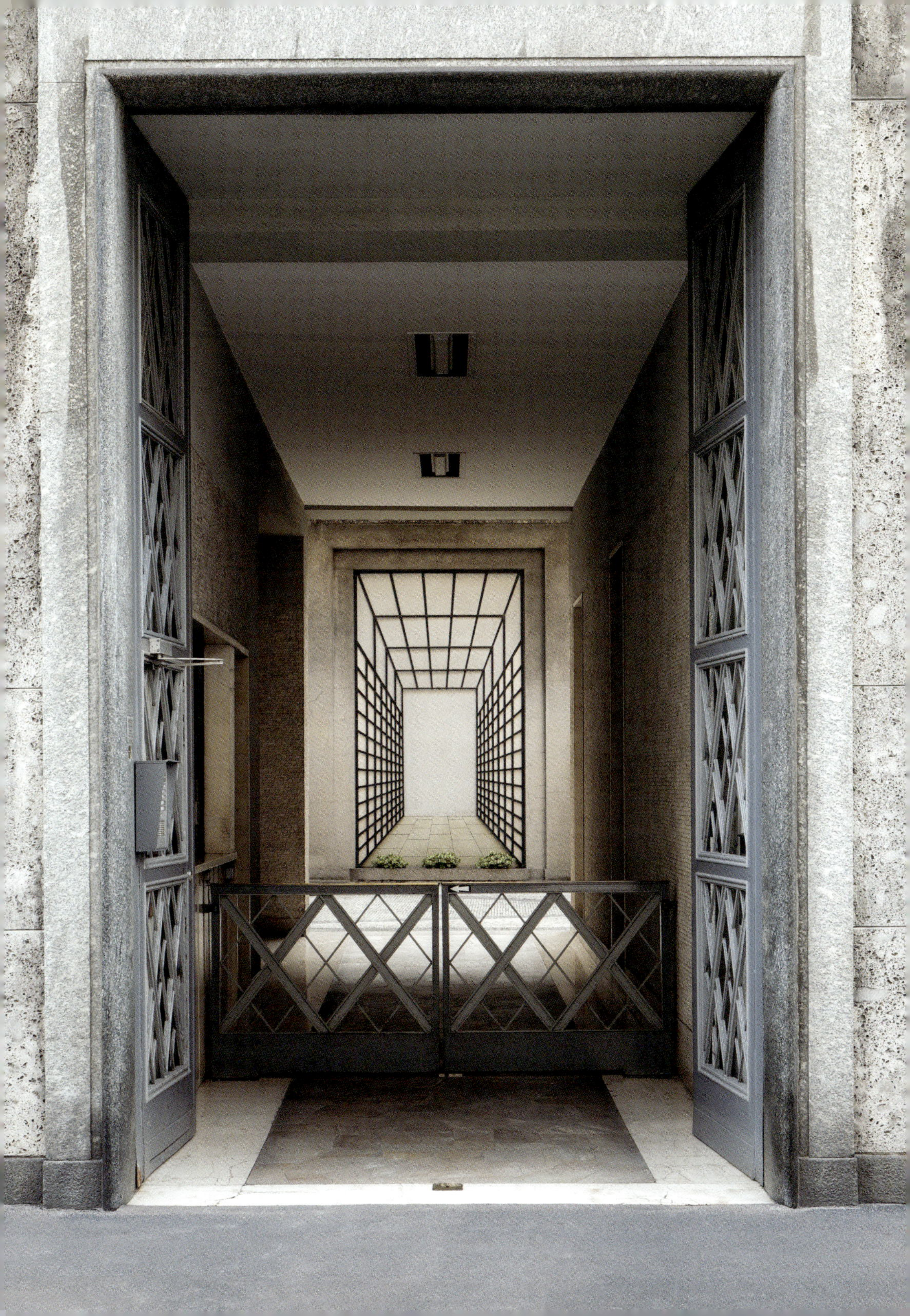

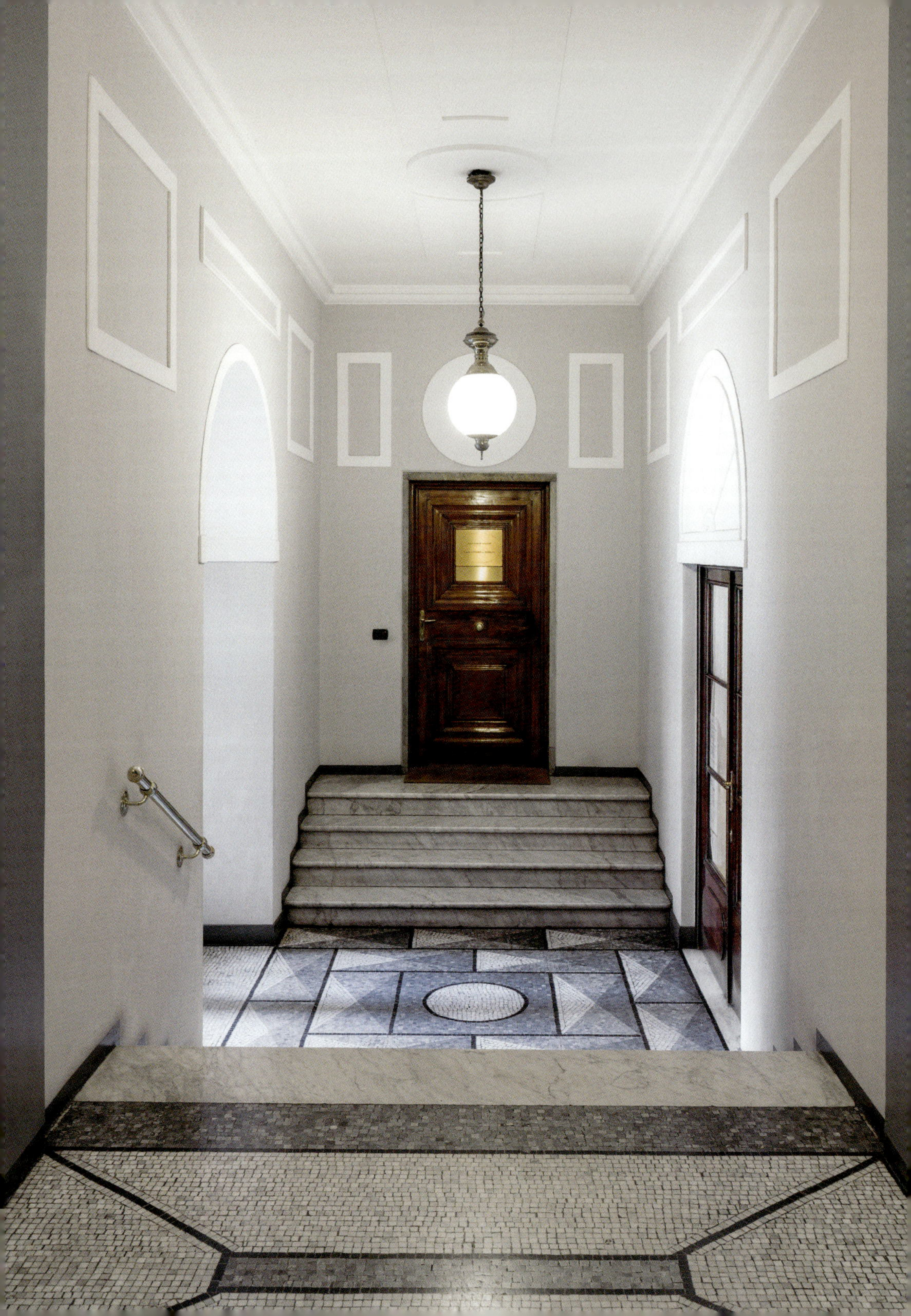

This and following spread:

via Privata Cesare Mangili 6, Ca' Brütta · Giovanni Muzio, Pier Fausto Barelli, Vittorino Colonnese, 1919–23

All plaster decorations by Giovanni Muzio · Pendant lamp by Luigi Caccia Dominioni. stairs: Bianco Carrara marble and Bardiglio marble

This early interior, at the heart of Giovanni Muzio's seminal building, essentially brought forth an entire new movement in early twentieth-century Italian architecture. That movement was then immediately termed Novecento. Right after the end of World War I in 1919, it was no coincidence that Muzio found inspiration and an equivocal comfort in the fine arts. The Italian Metaphysical movement, in particular the vision and concepts of Giorgio De Chirico, provided a decisive momentum to the new modern project in Italy between the twentieth-century wars. The design details on the walls and ceilings of the various interior entrances and foyers are taken from the exterior façade. Here Muzio builds upon a classical language repertory that is distilled down to an extreme flatness, verging on abstraction. All that is left is a memory of times past. The architect's inventions in this first large-scale work were the forerunners of endless variations by others in many buildings around the city for the following two decades.

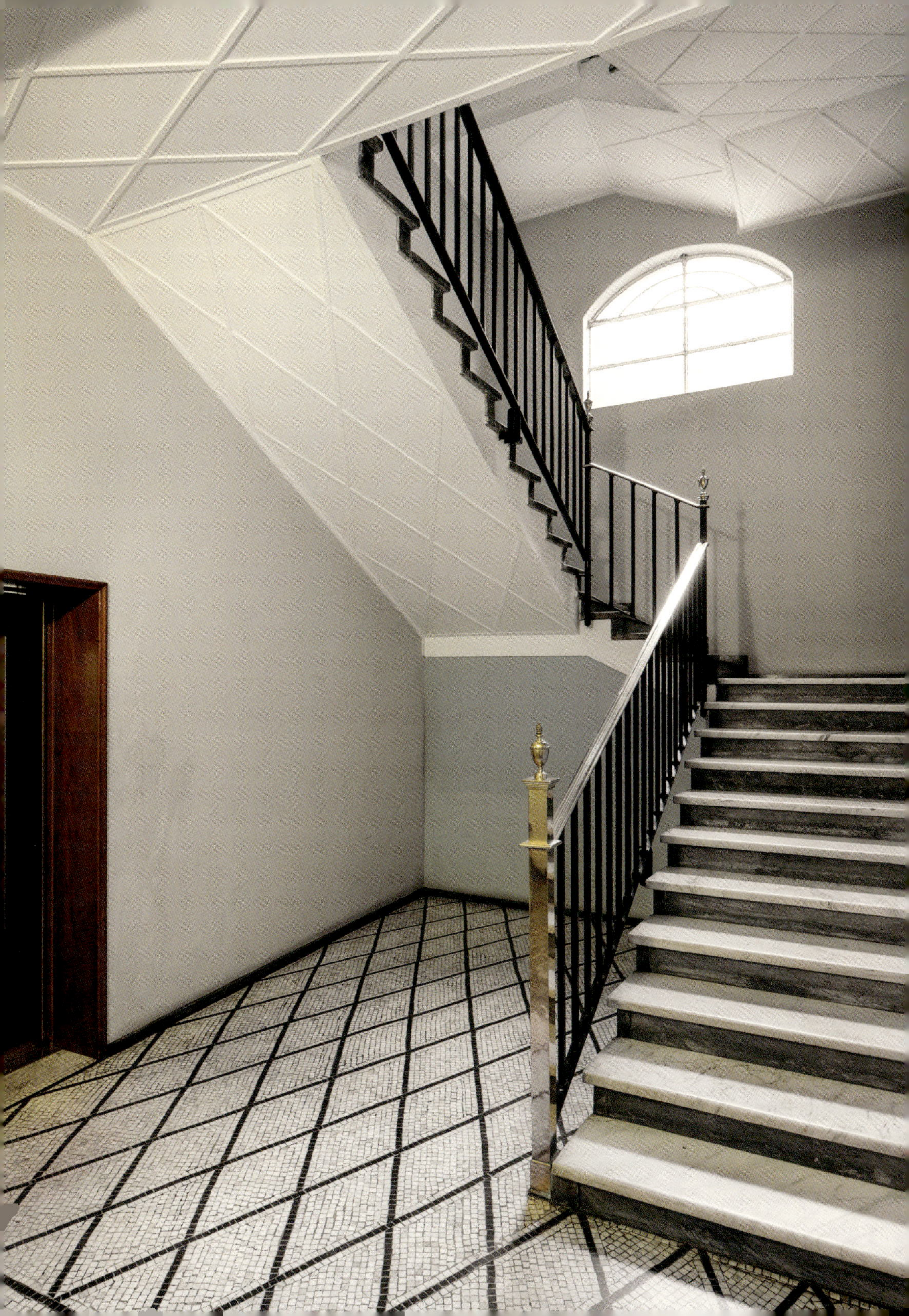

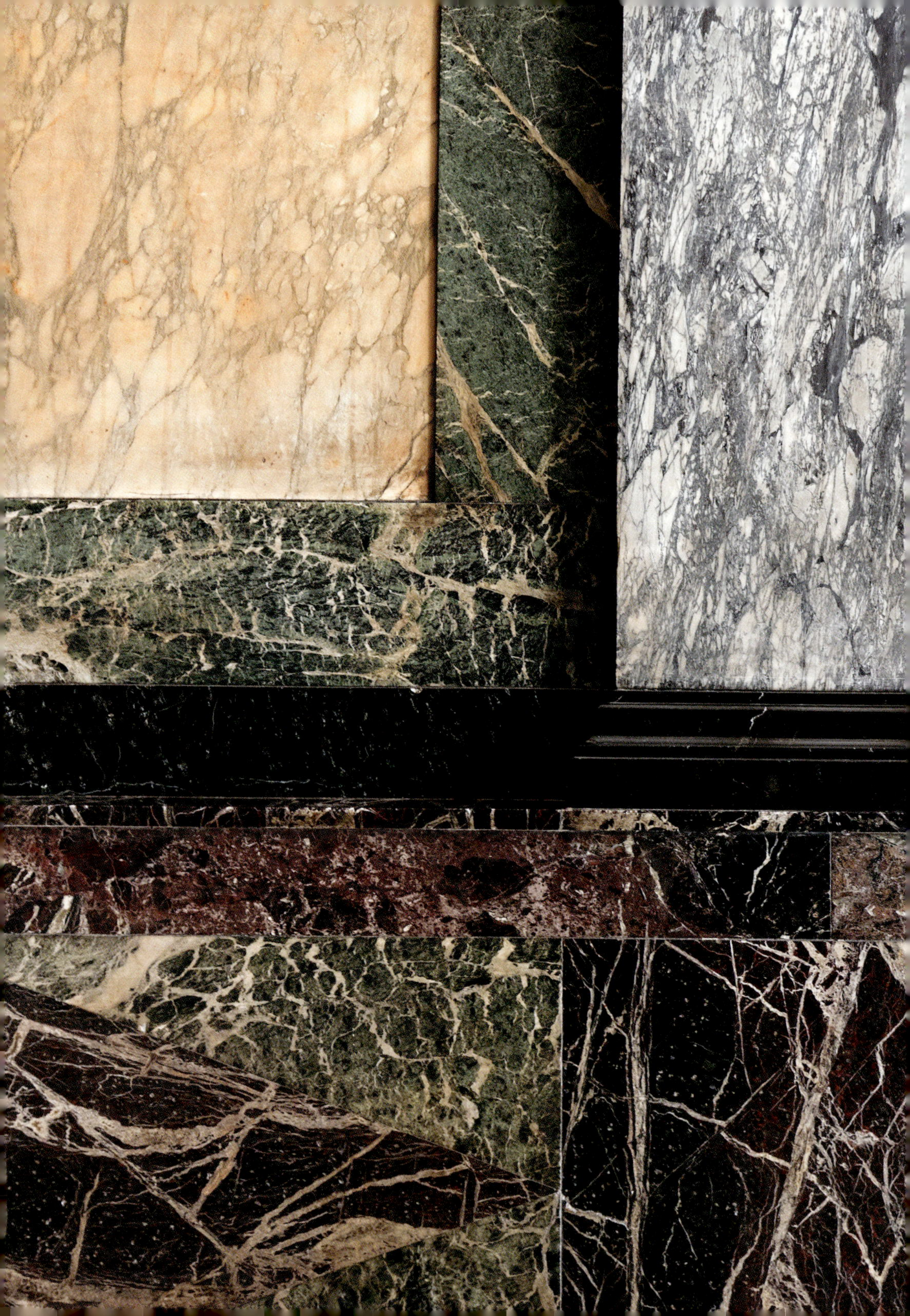

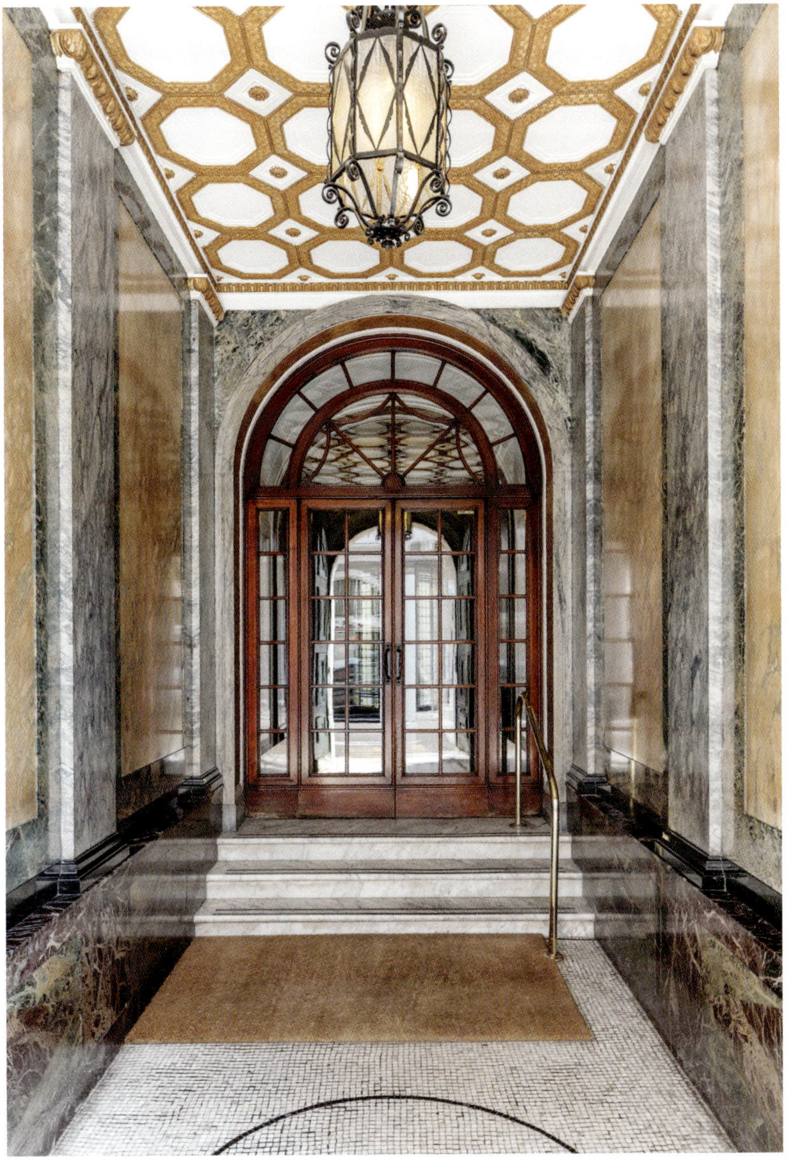

This and following spread:
via della Moscova 12, Ca' Brütta · Giovanni Muzio, Pier Fausto Barelli, Vittorino Colonnese, 1919–23
Lantern by Giovanni Muzio.
walls: Rosso and Verde Levanto ophicalcite, serpentinite, Bardiglio marble, Arabescato Carrara marble

Wall sgraffito and floor mosaics by Giovanni Muzio.
doorframes: Bardiglio marble

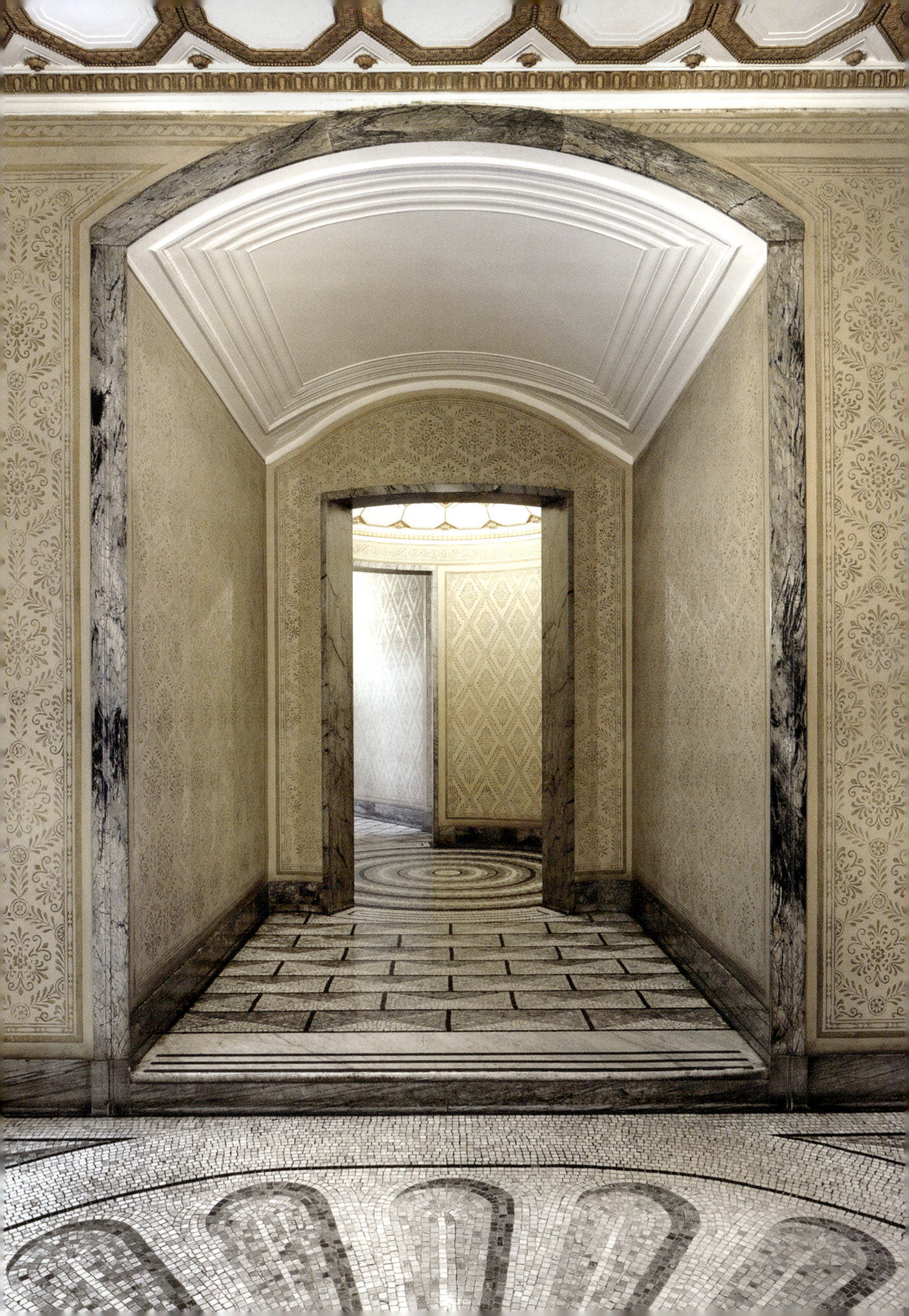

GIALLO DI SIENA

In the ancient world, from the time of the Pharaohs right down to the Romans, the colors red and yellow symbolized wealth and power. In the sixteenth century, the Medici family invoked such allusions once more when they began using Giallo di Siena as an alternative to the renowned Giallo Antico to decorate their chapels in Florence, and the marble has retained an air of luxury ever since. Golden yellow in color and with a breccia texture, this peculiar ornamental stone can be very striking, particularly when installed as book-matched slabs. Such claddings are of outstanding value because, up until the beginning of the twenty-first century, only very small blocks could be exploited due to the fragmentary nature of the stone's breccia texture. In light of their limited availability in the twentieth century, the slabs we see here are really quite large and show us that the designers of the day were sourcing top-quality precious marbles for their projects.

viale Piceno 36 · Giuseppe Bigontina, 1959–60

floors and stairs: Porfido Monumentale di Bienno
yellow wall: Giallo Siena marble

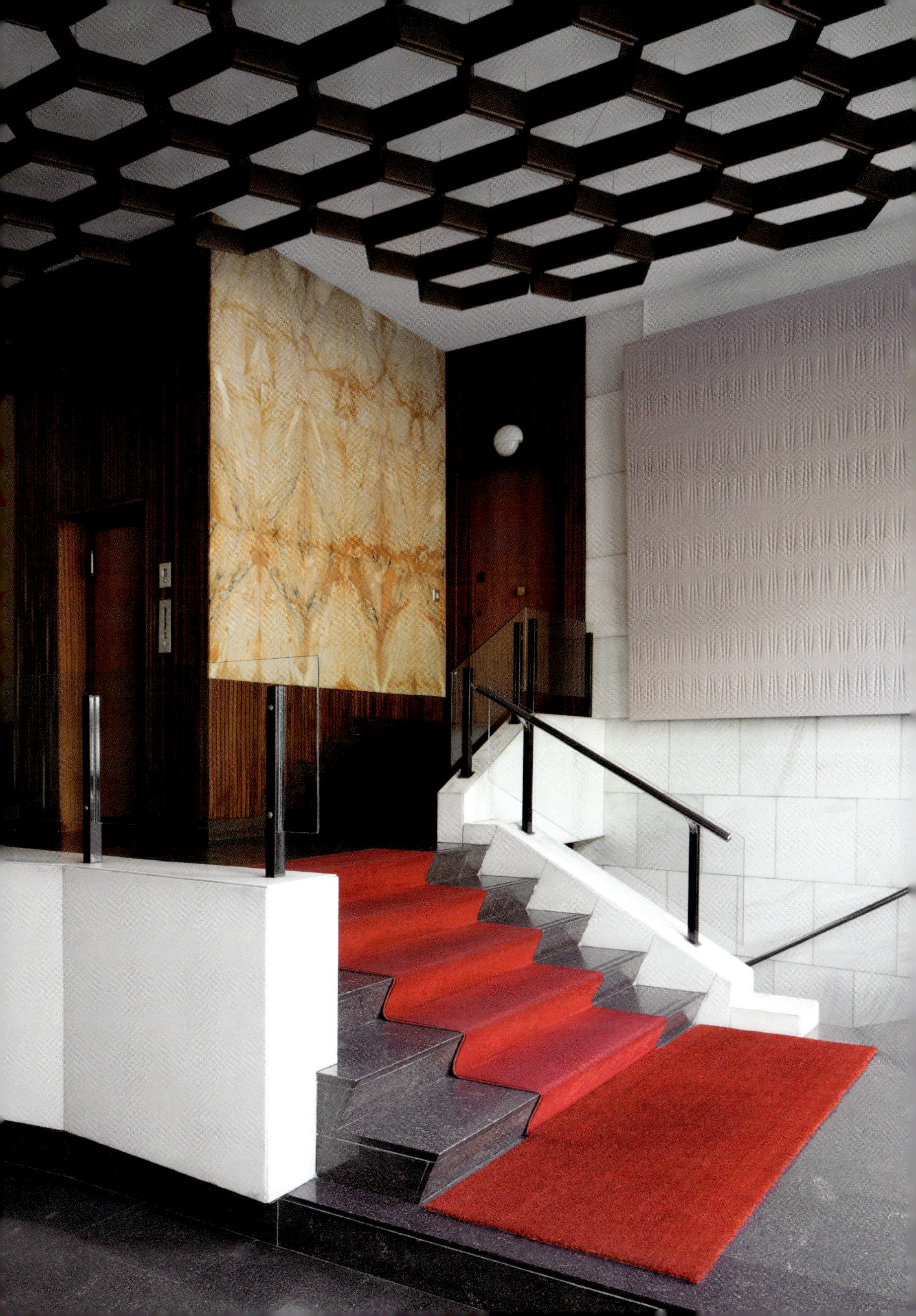

via Archimede 85 · E. Berté, F. Morini, 1963–68

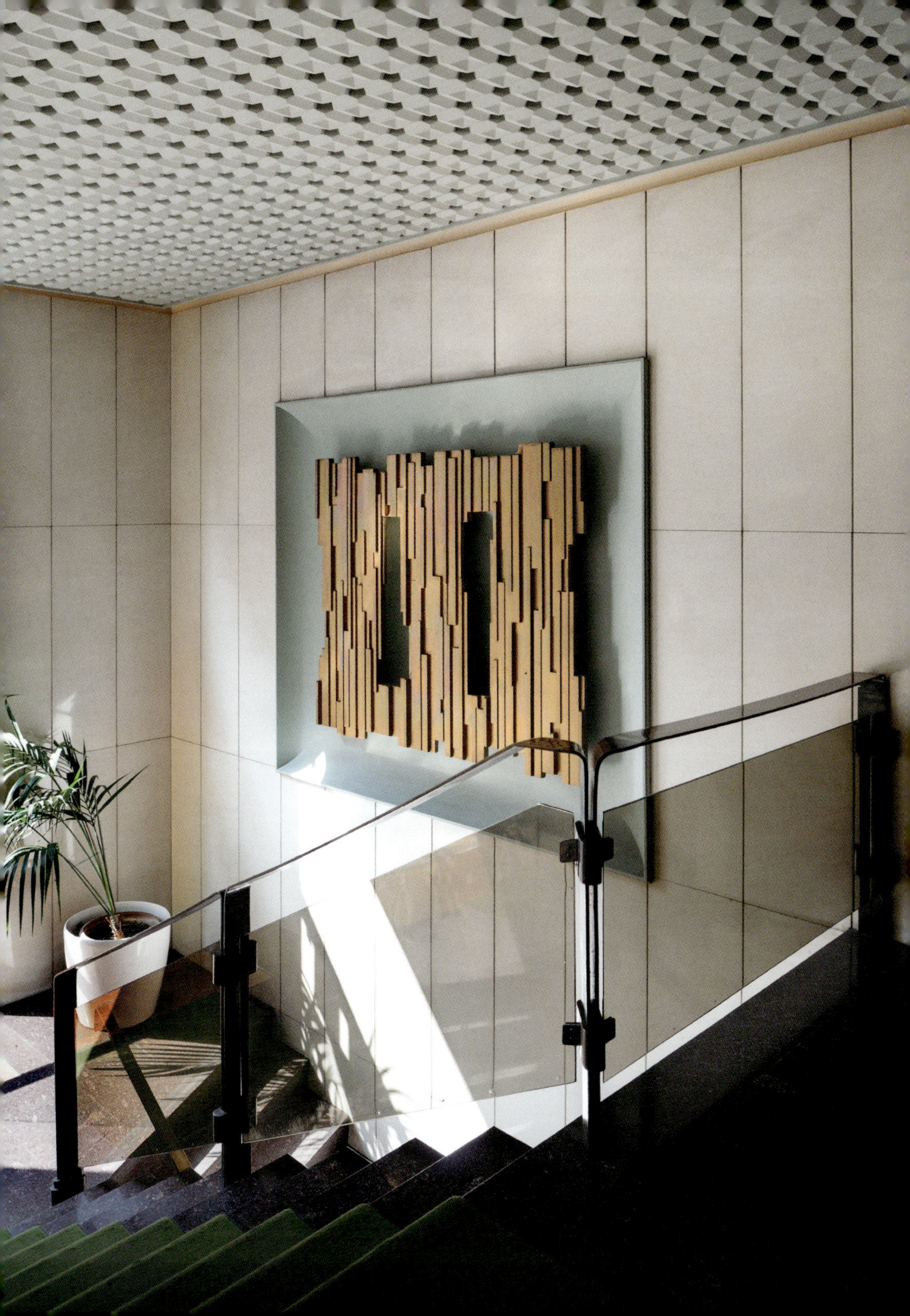

CIPOLLINO

A peculiar and traditional name for a specific kind of holo-crystalline marble exploited down the centuries for its ivory-white color streaked with green or greenish--gray stripes or winding veins, and for its typically silky sheen. The overall effect is reminiscent of the layered structure and skin texture of an onion, hence the name Cipollino, derived from the word "cipolla"—Italian for "onion." The most famous Cipollino marbles come from quarries in Greece that have been in use since ancient Greek and Roman times (Marmo Cipollino Antico) or from the Carrara area; they are still available today.

via Marcona 70 · Gustavo Bertini, 1952–54

walls: Cipollino Verde marble, book match

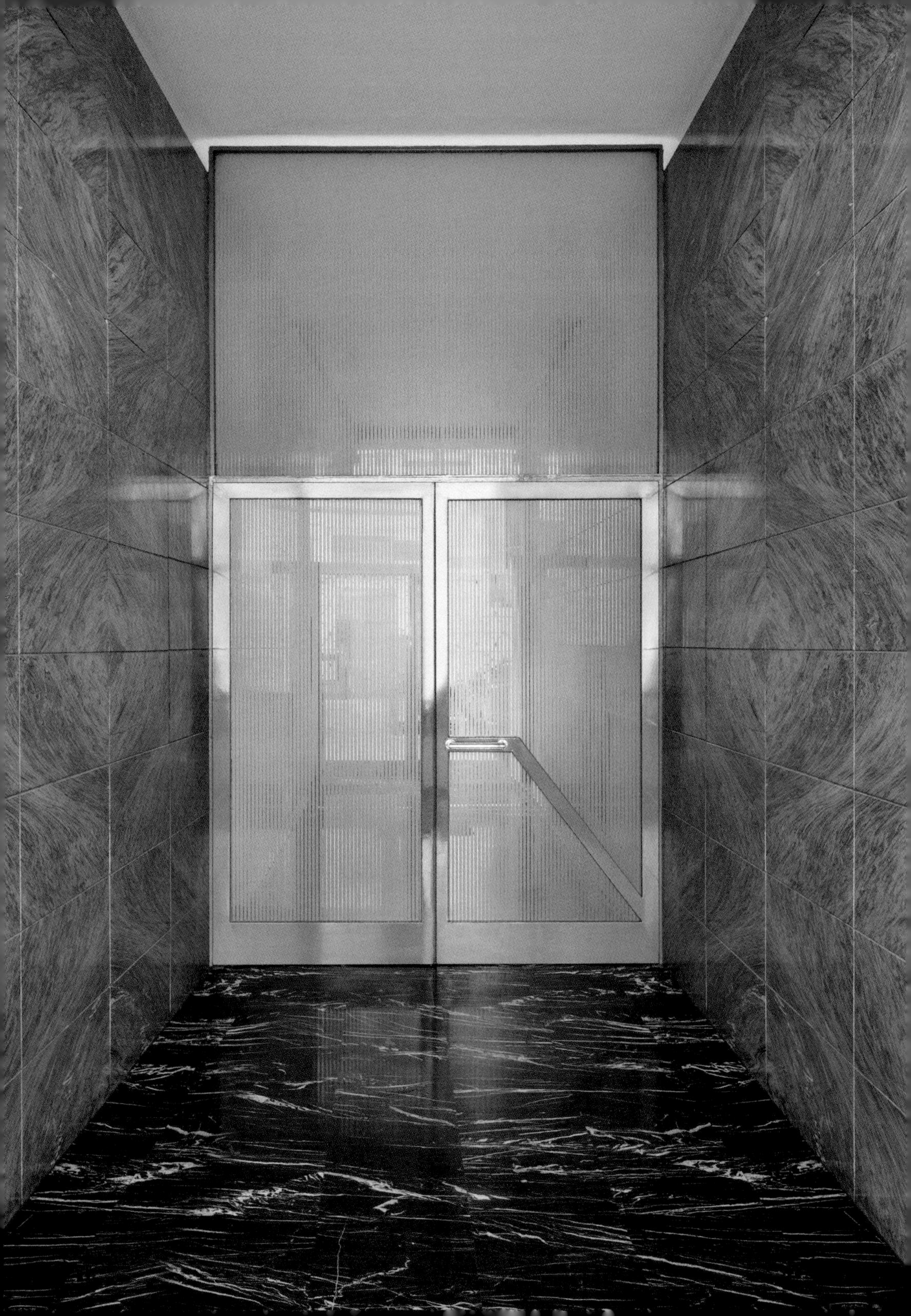

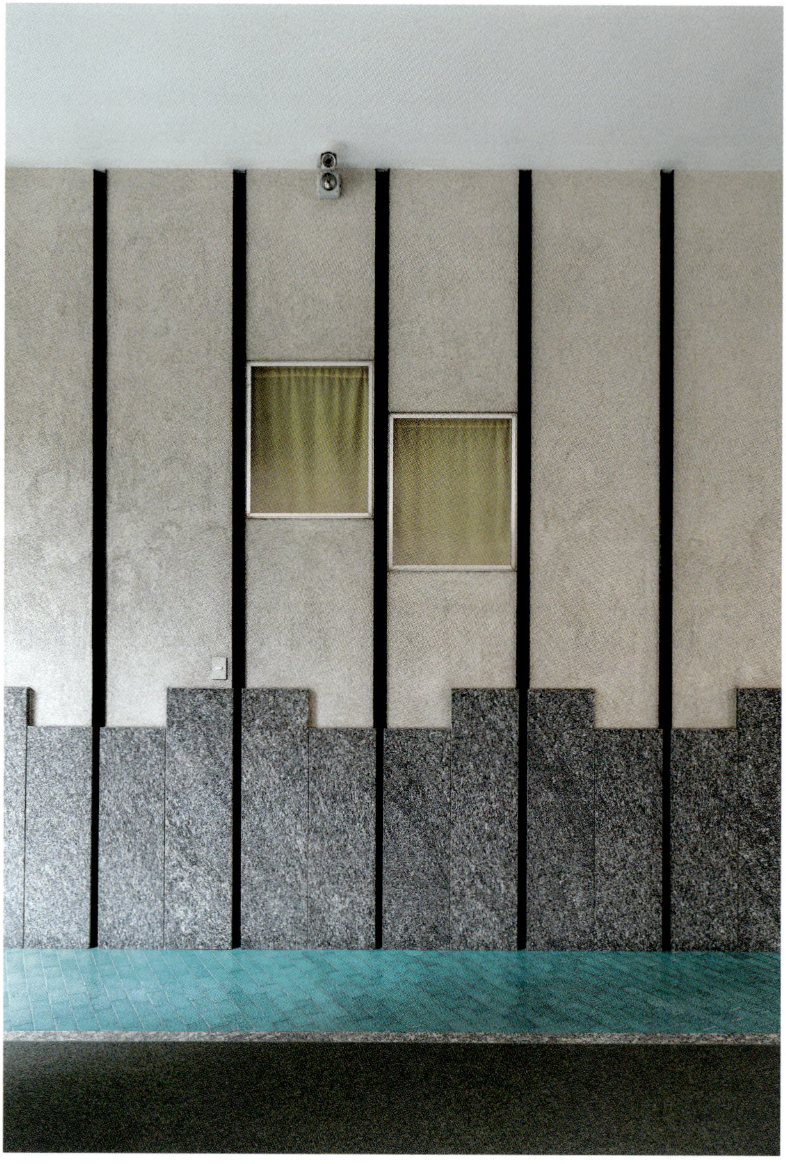

via Marcona 49 · Gian Angelini, 1960–62

wall: Serizzo granite

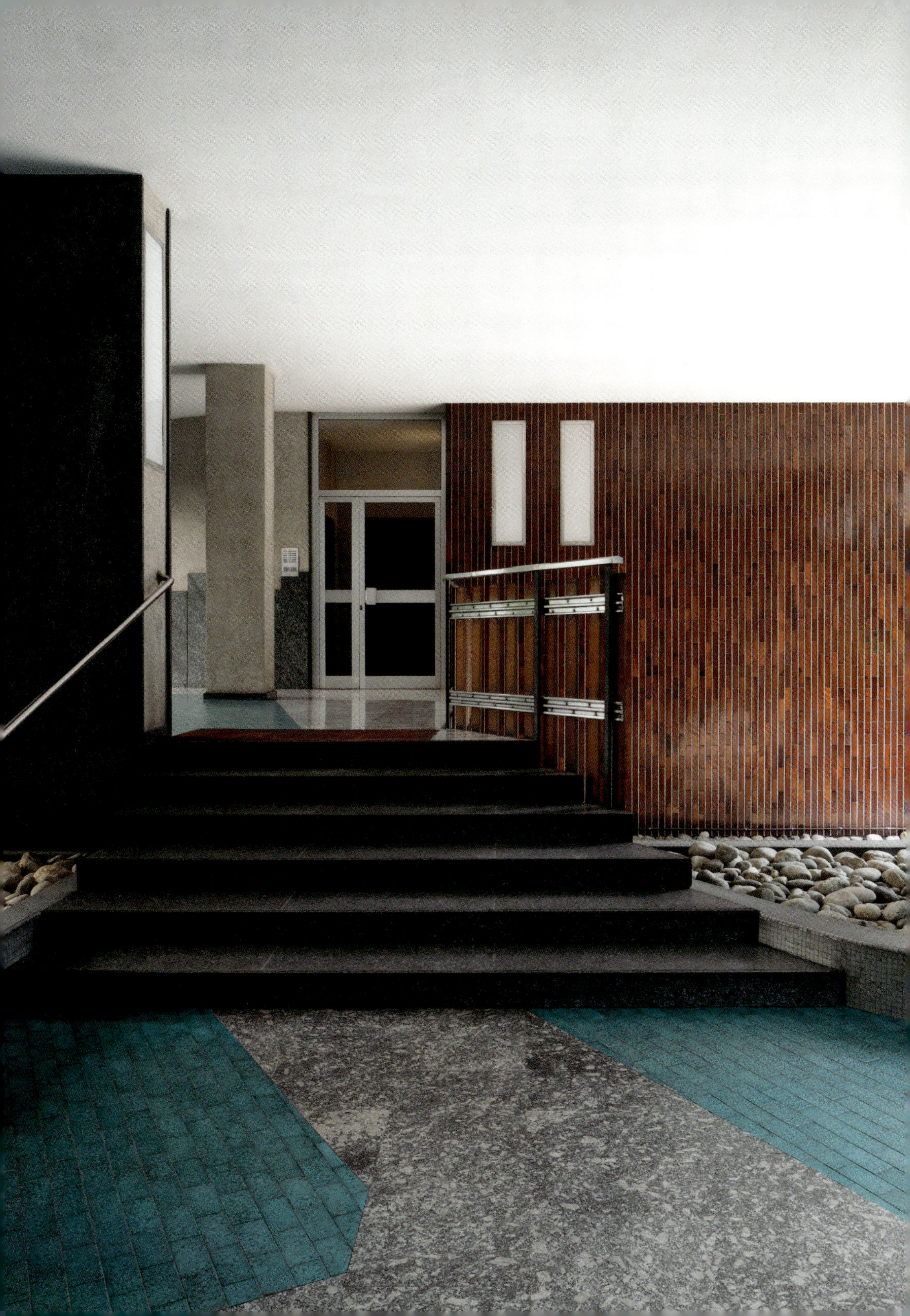

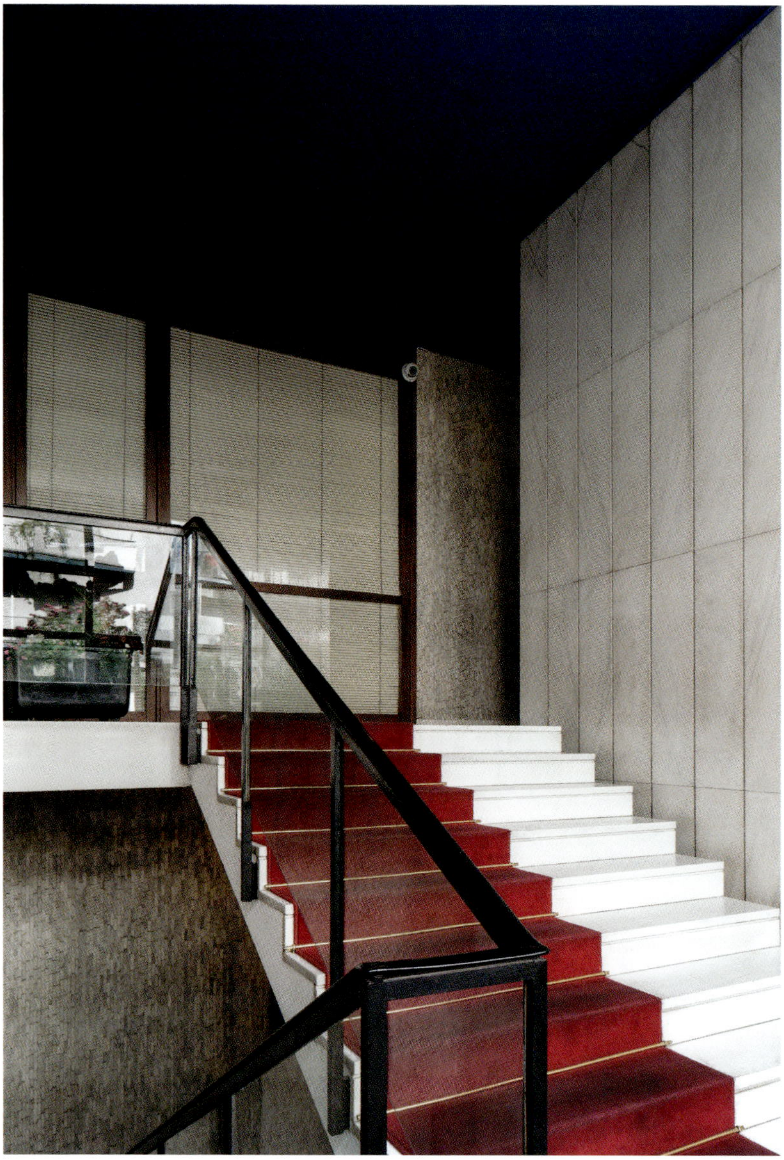

via Marcona 24 · Guido Gai, Giorgio Moro

floor: Palladiana of several white and gray marbles (Musso marble, Vallestrona marble, etc.) with light green joints · wall: Crevola marble

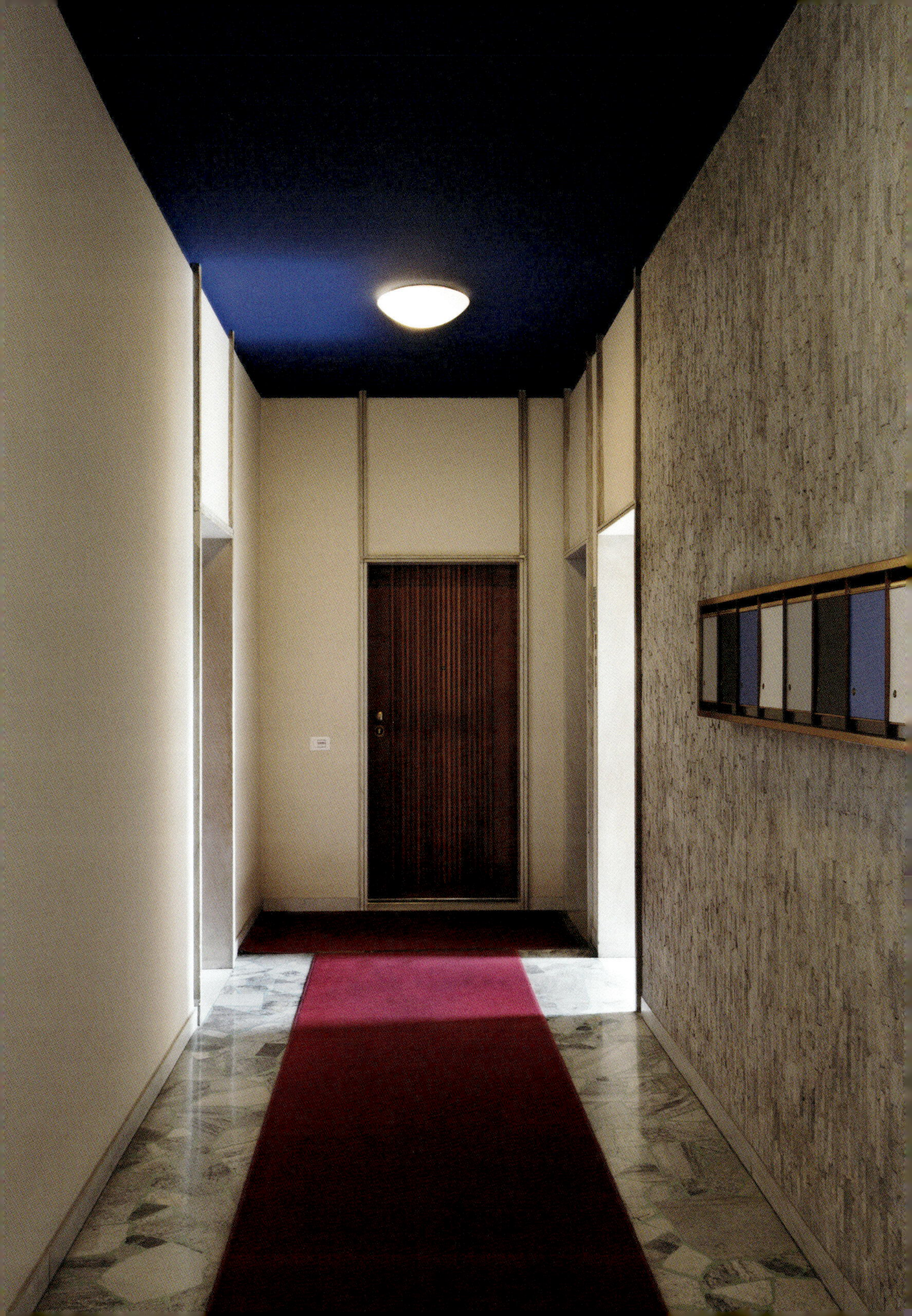

via Archimede 16 · Marcello Belleri, Mario Bianchini, 1949–52

Interior glass window panels by Fontana Arte.
floor: Valle Strona marble

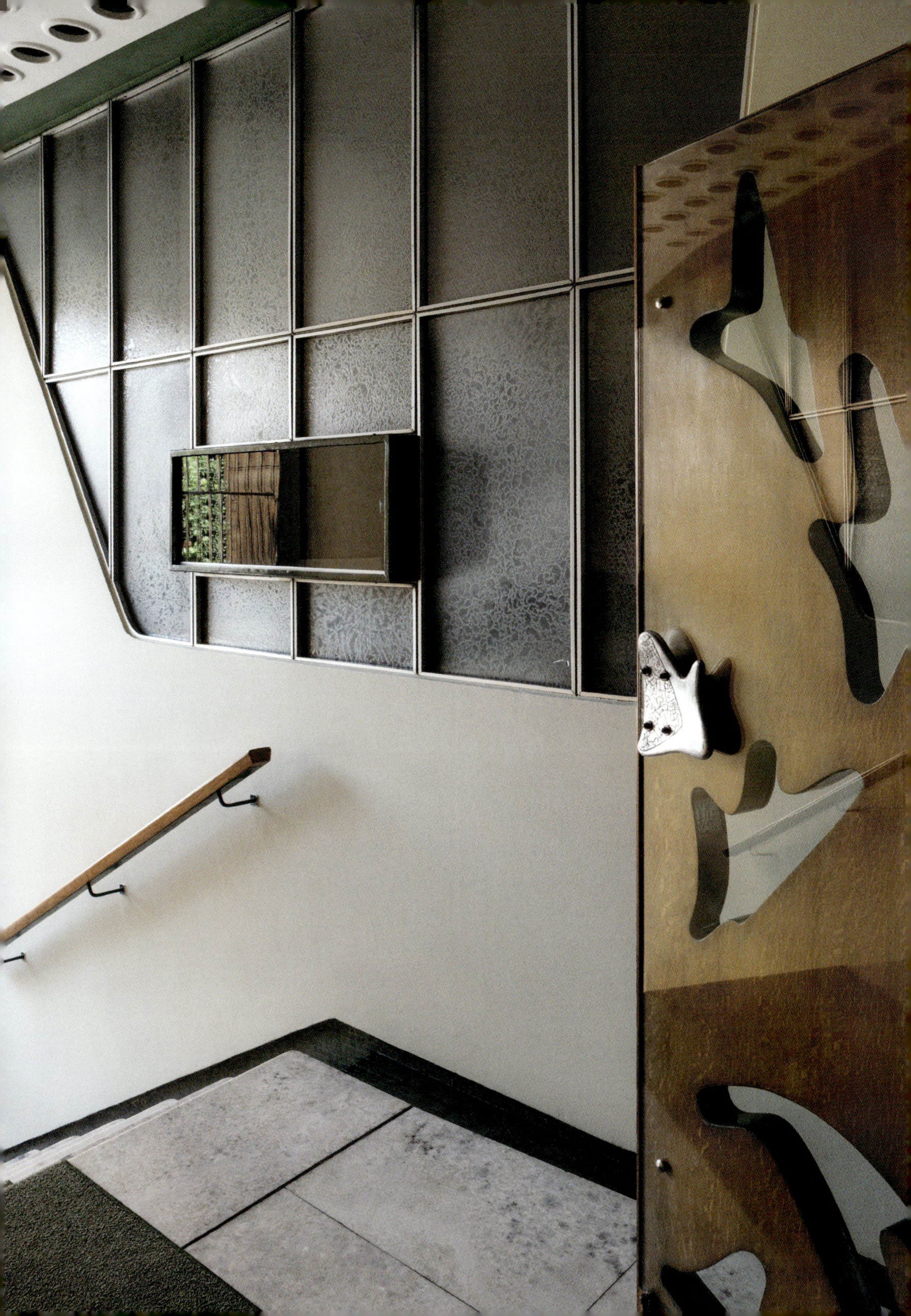

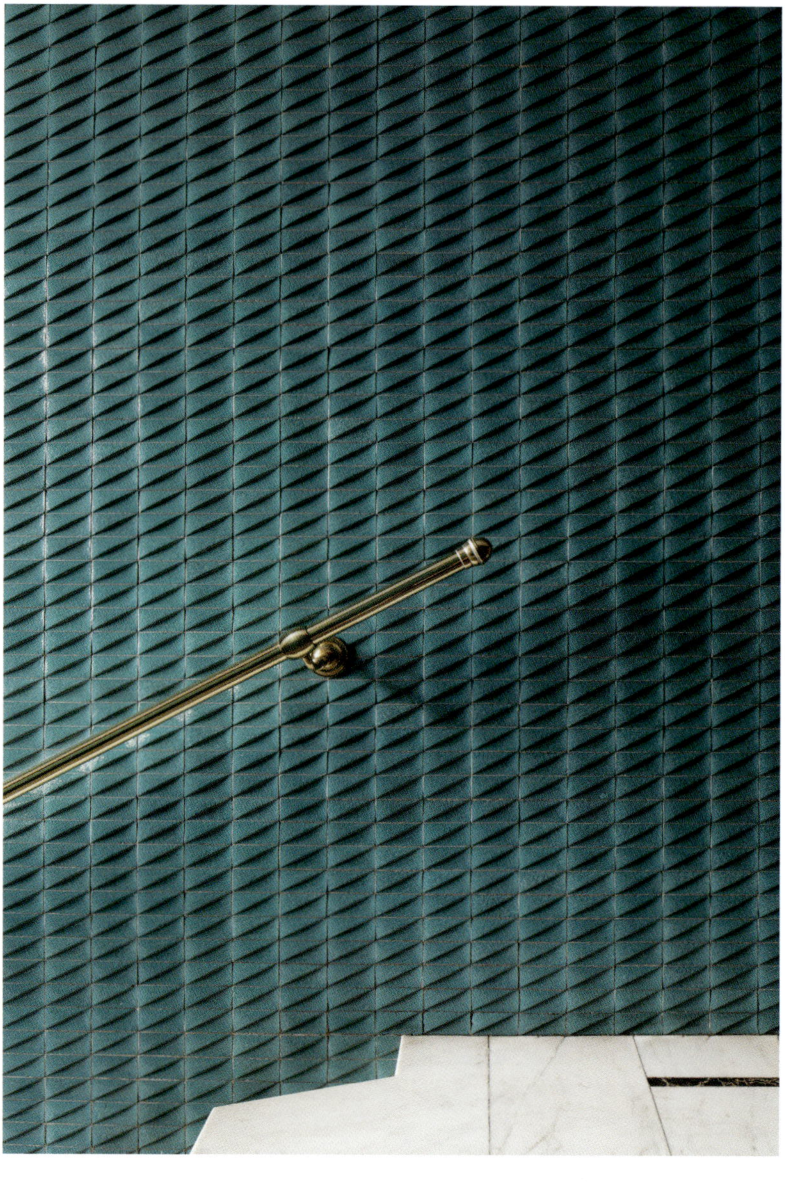

via Amatore Sciesa 24

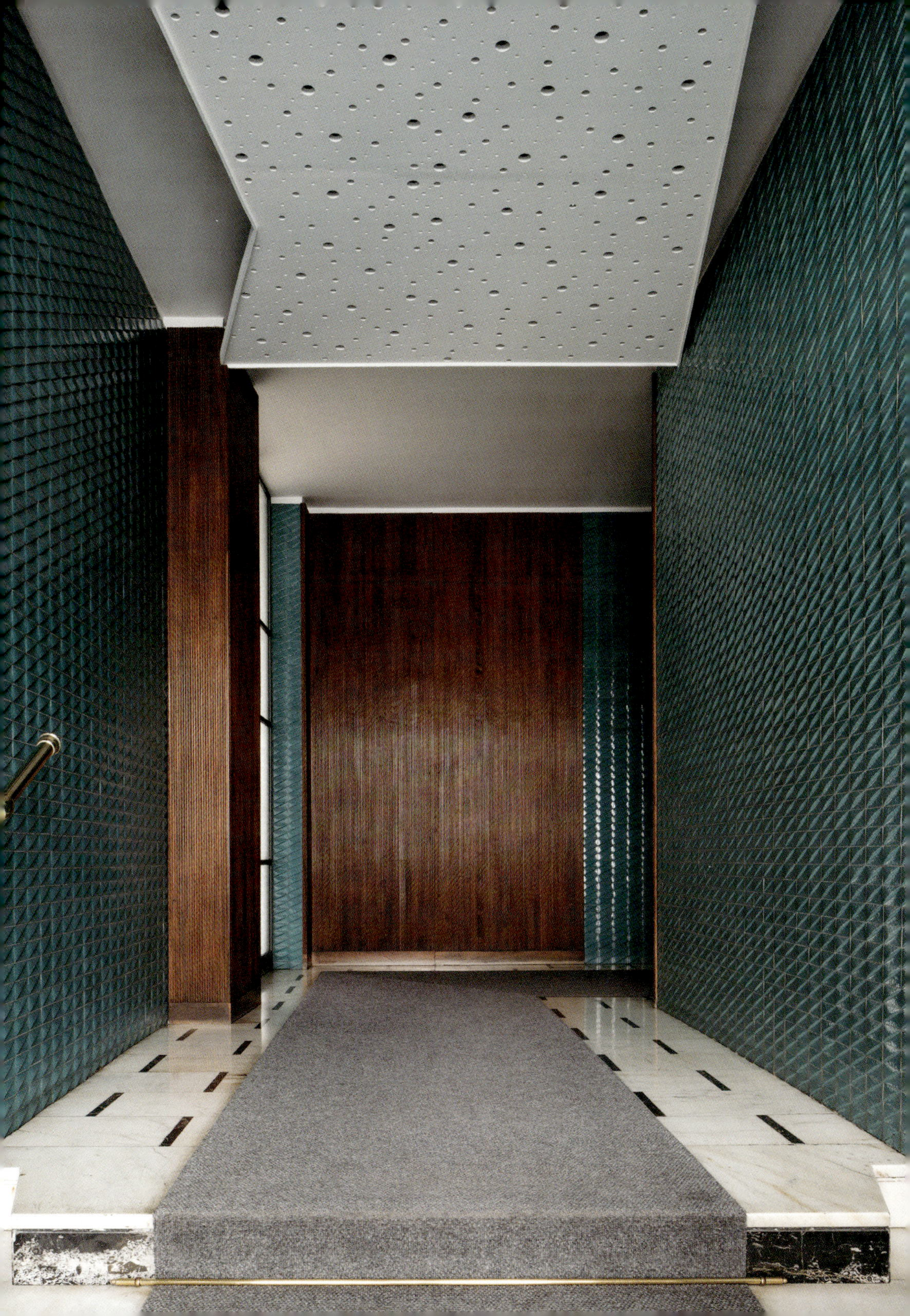

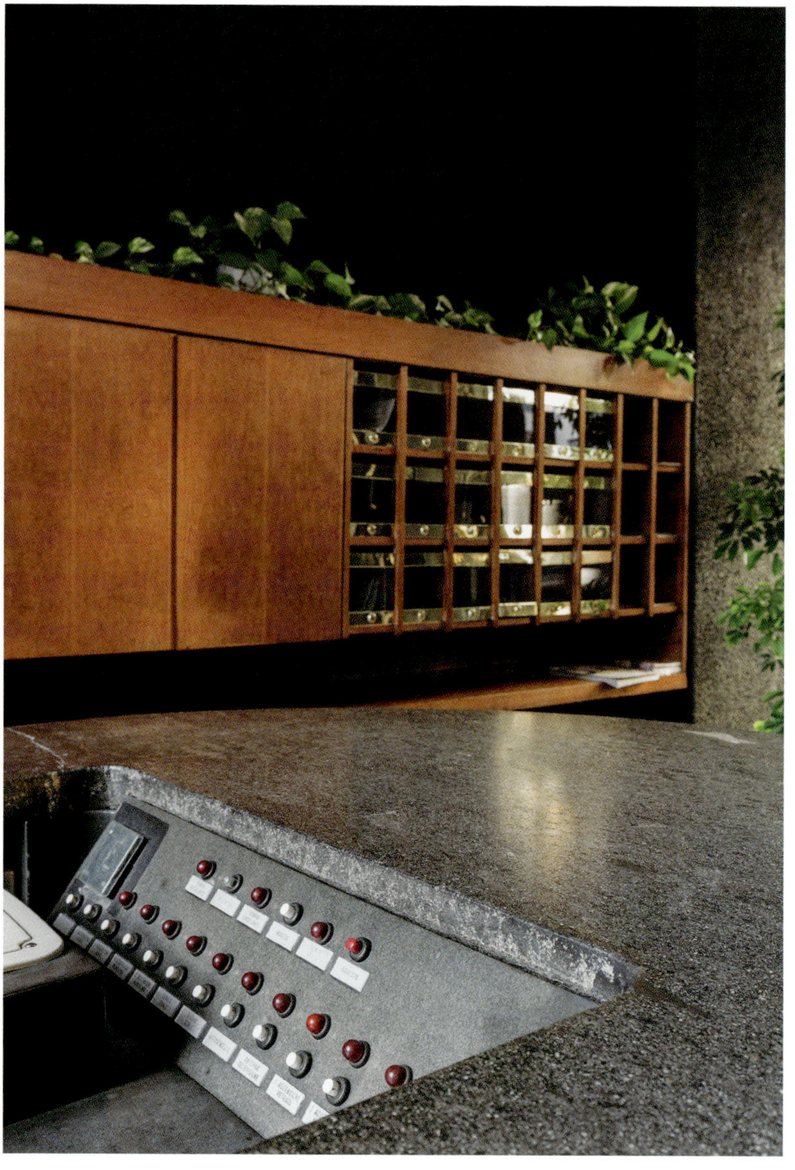

via Quadronno 24 · Angelo Mangiarotti, Bruno Morassutti, 1959–60

Mailbox made of walnut.
Reception desk made of black marble aggregate.

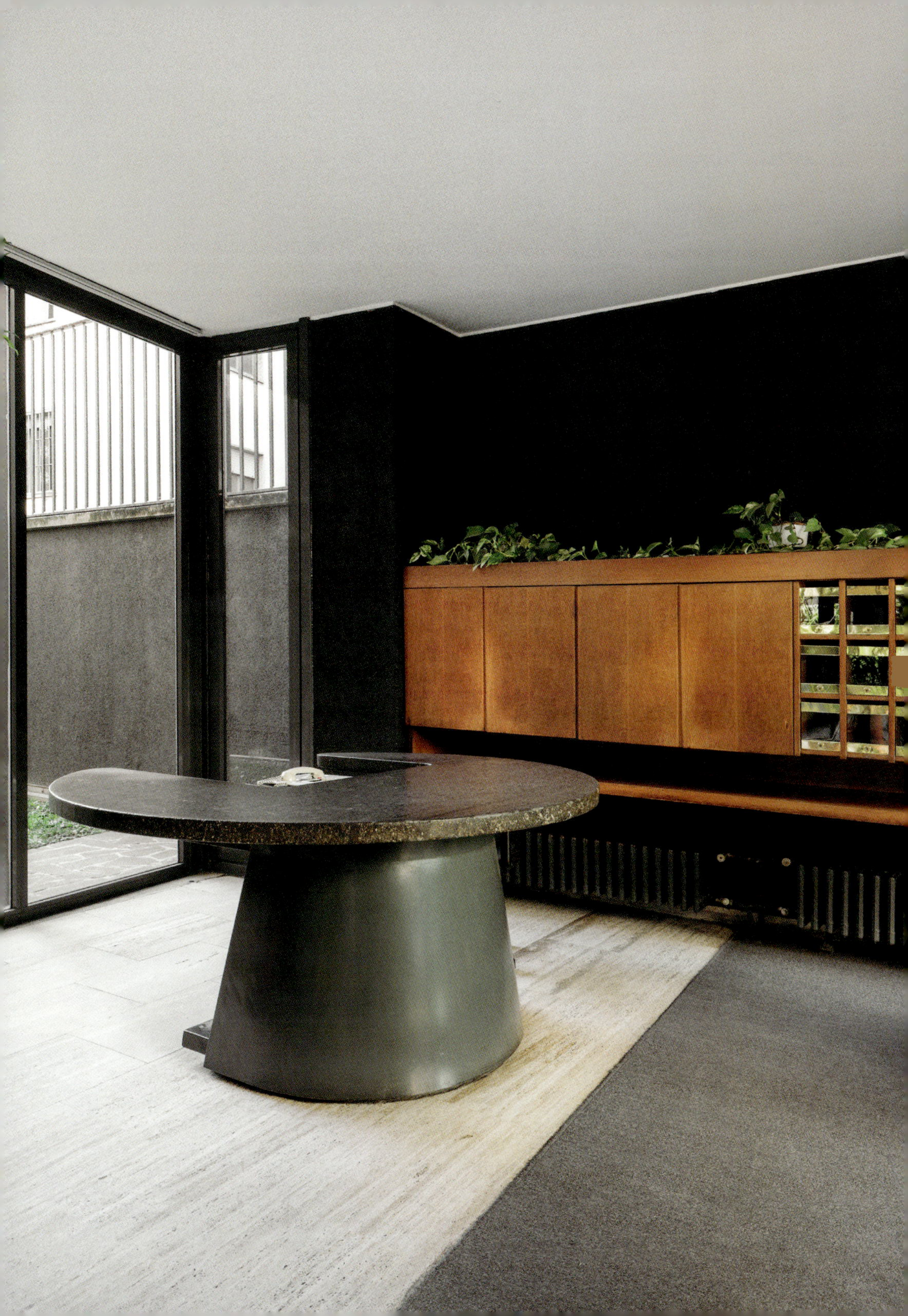

via Eugenio Vaina 2 · Giuseppe Invitti, 1934–37

Pendant lamp by Venini.

floor: Terrazzo *tiles made of Bardiglio, Rosso Levanto and other gray limestones and marbles*

wall: Occhialino Valcamonica limestone and white marble

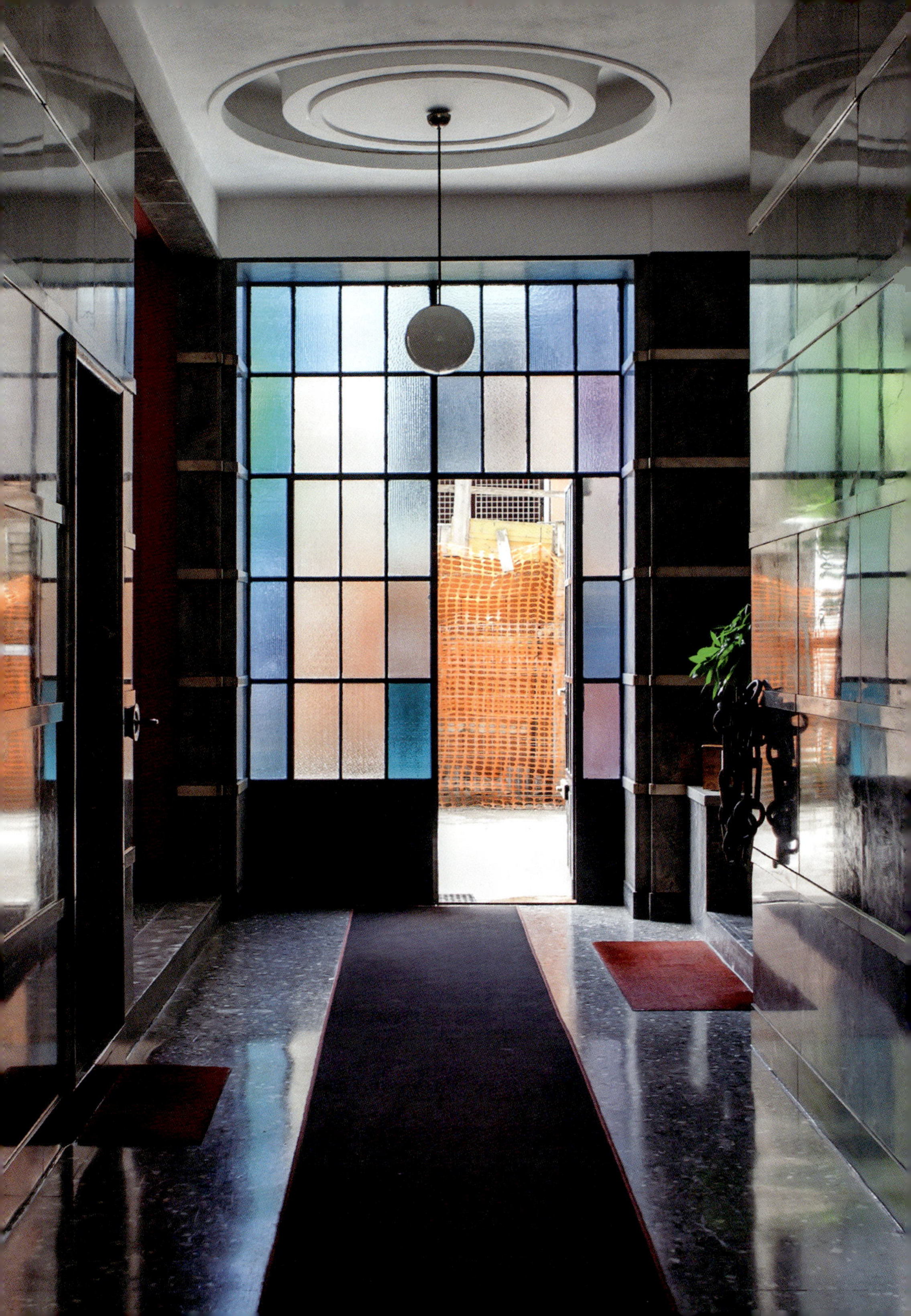

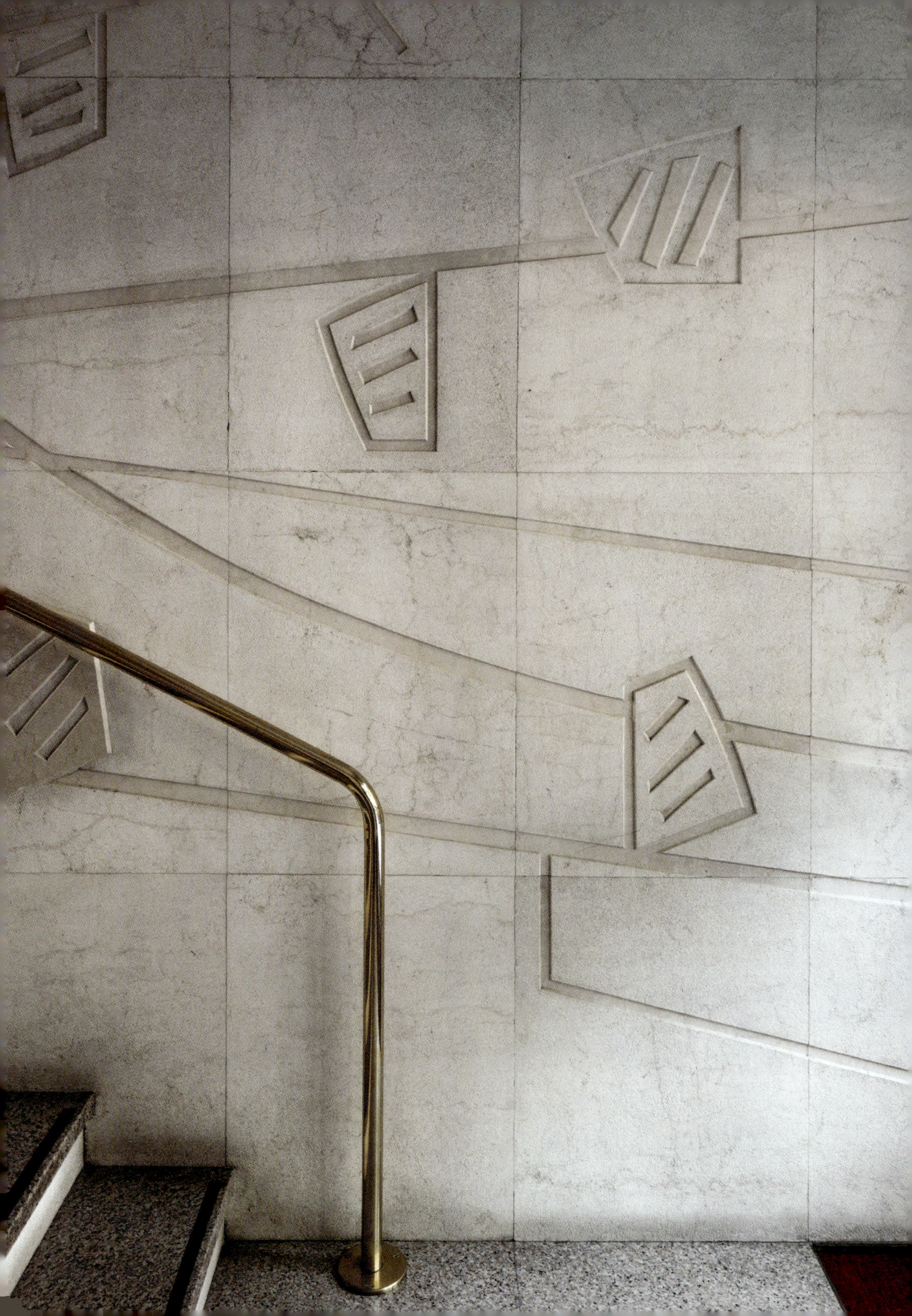

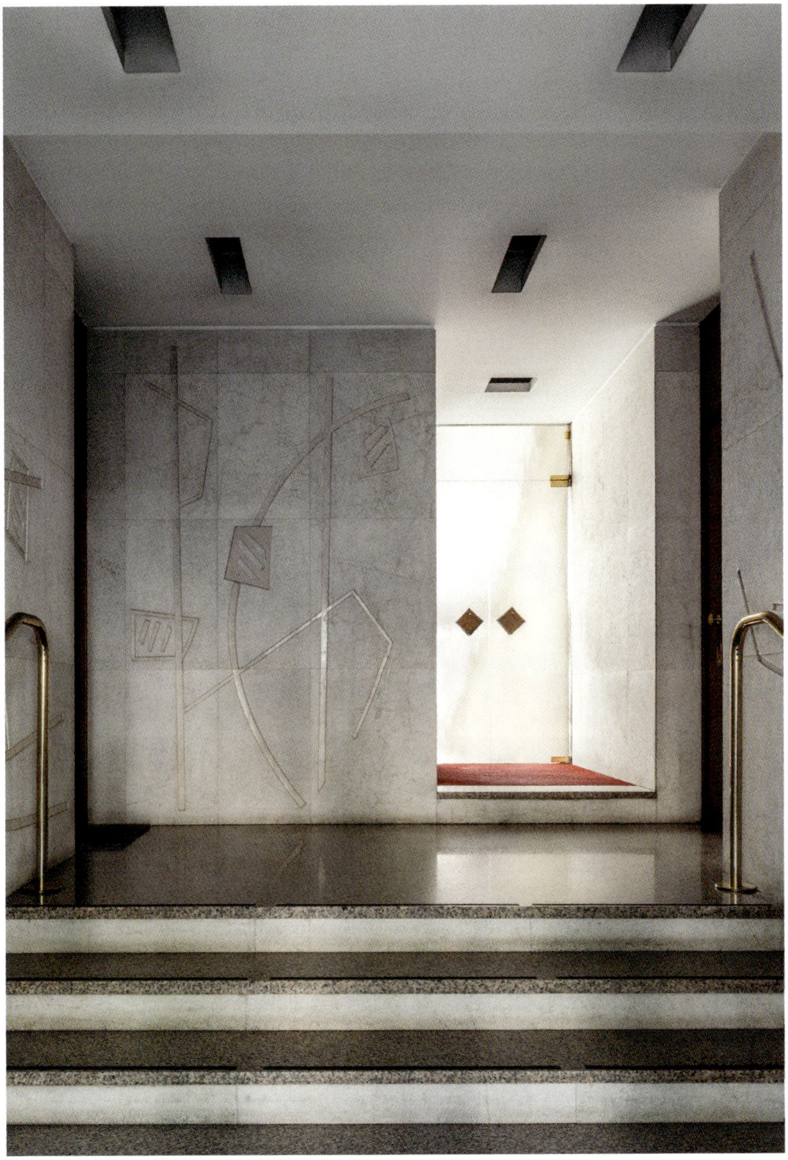

viale Lazio 24 · Gigi Ghò

floor: Rosa Baveno granite · stairs: Rosa Baveno granite and Botticino limestone · walls: Botticino limestone

ROSA VALTOCE

A metamorphic marble extracted from the same vein as Marmo di Candoglia, the deposit was reserved by Galeazzo Visconti, Lord of Milan, in the fourteenth century for the building and restoration of Milan Cathedral. Rosa Valtoce, found on the opposite side of the valley, is very similar to this stone in color and texture, and can be locally striped with wavy veins, or plain. In the book-matched installation we see here, special attention was paid to the black veining and the cutting planes of the slabs in order to create a striped effect running parallel with the long sides.

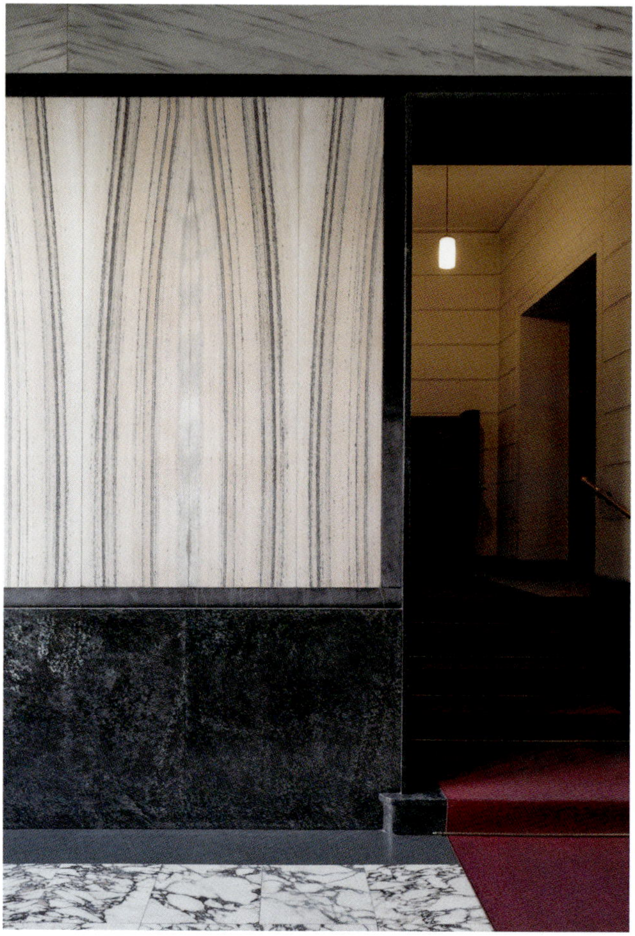

viale Lazio 21 · Gianfranco Arnaboldi, 1935–37

floor: Calcatta Viola, Verde Cemmo · base: serpentinite · walls: Rosa Valtoce marble, serpentinite

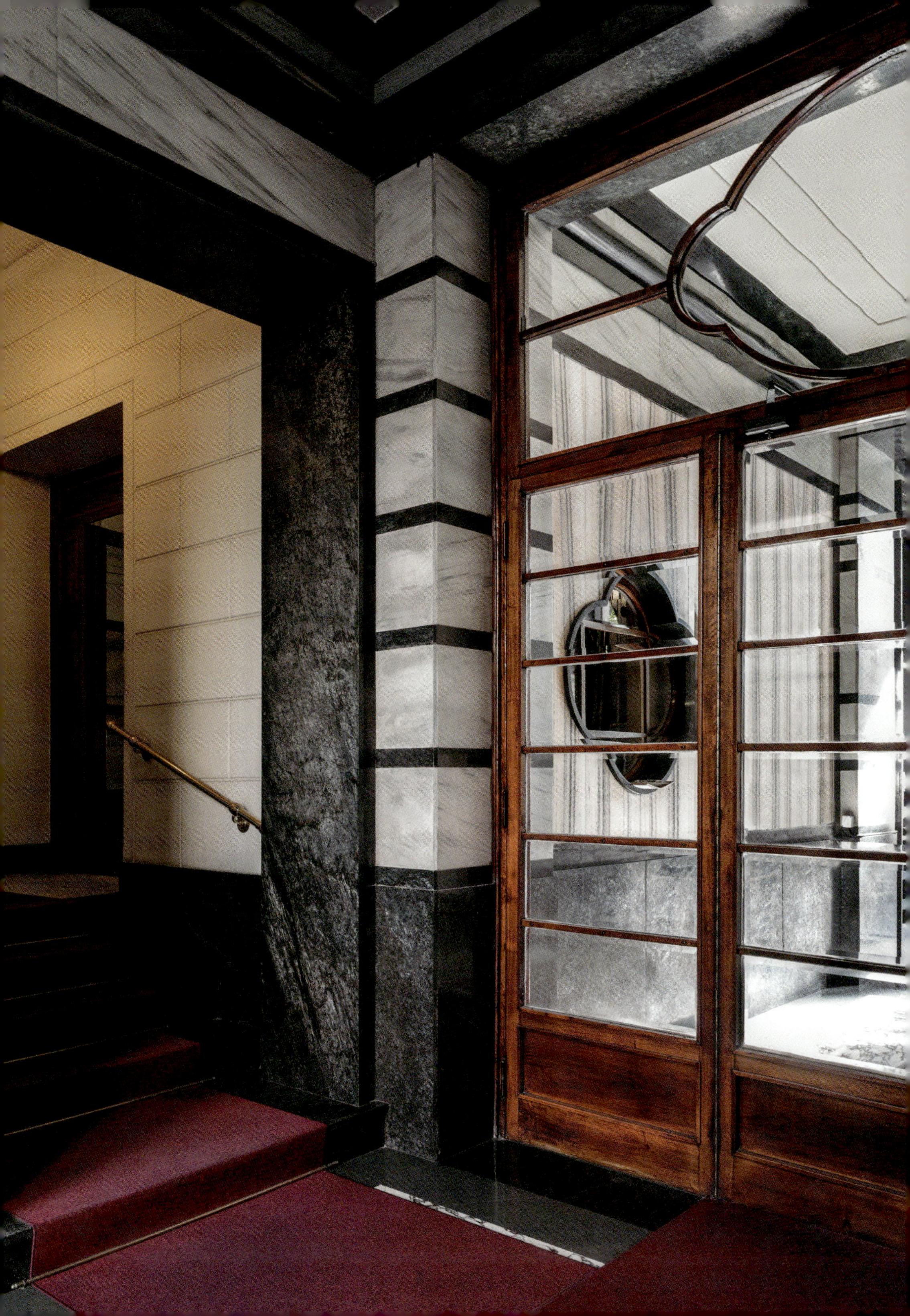

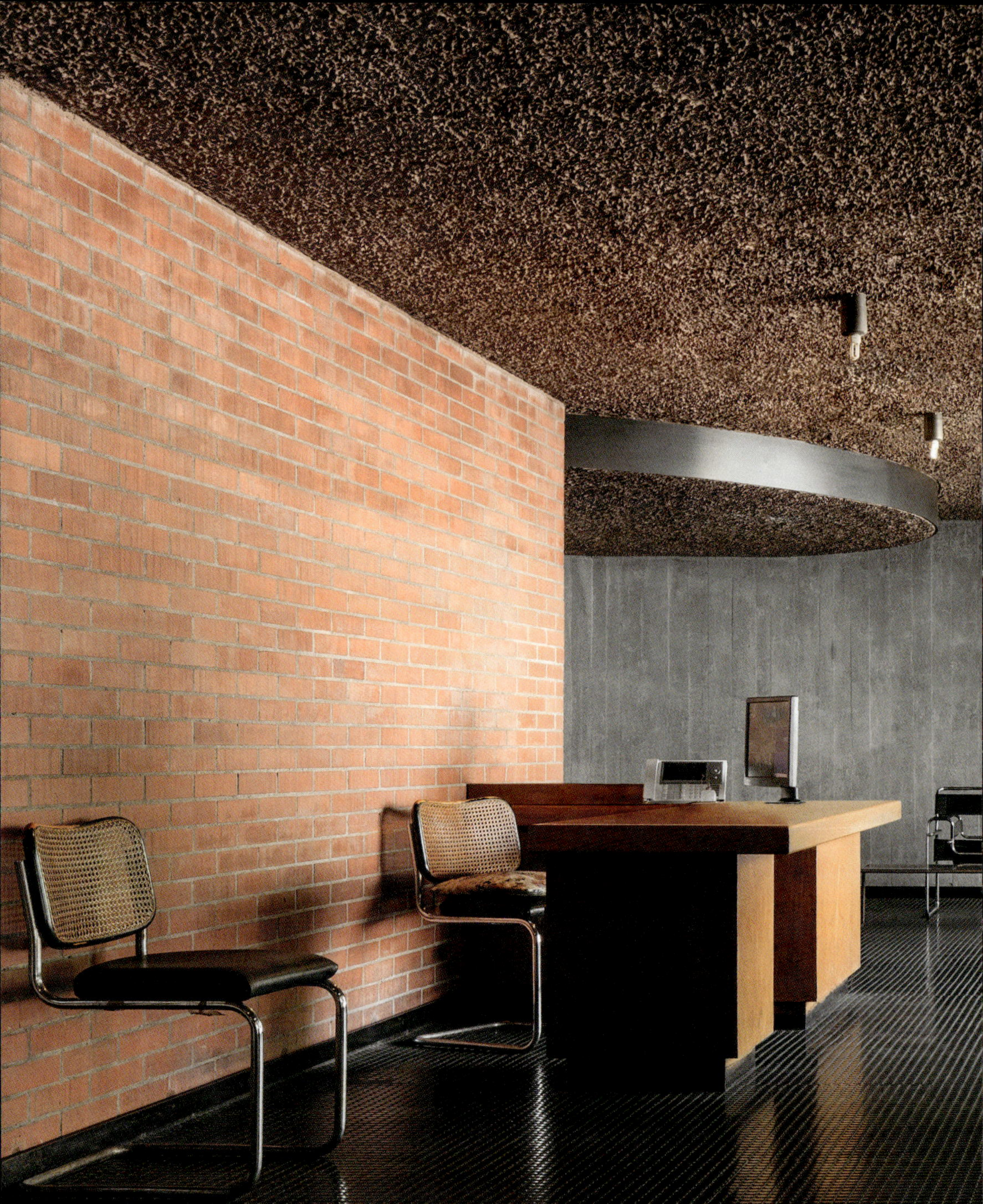

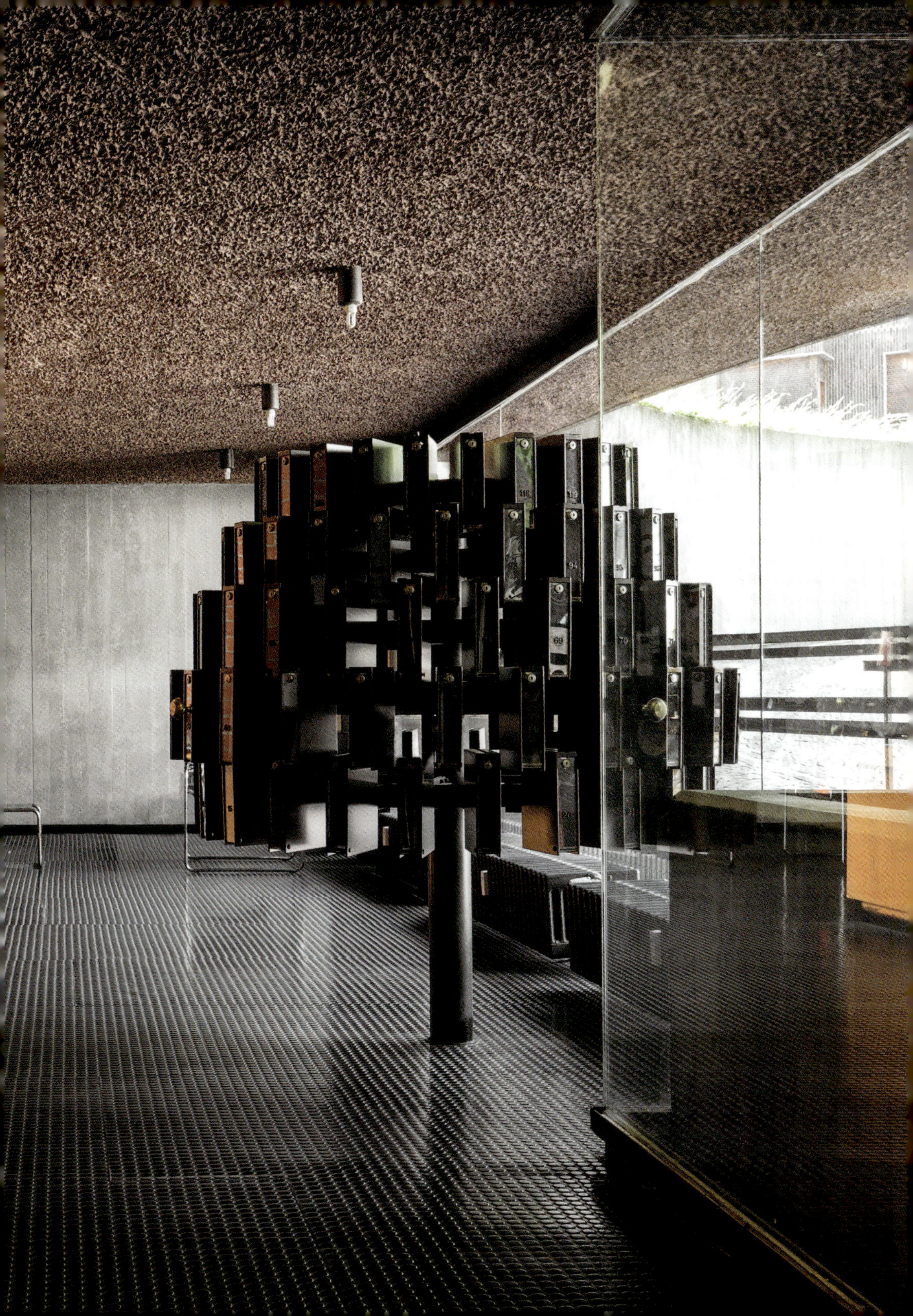

Previous spread:

via Lodovico Muratori 29 · Studio Passarelli, 1967–69

Lighting and freestanding rotating mailbox by Studio Passarelli.
Armchairs and coffee table by Marcel Breuer for Knoll.
Rubber floor by Pirelli.

This and following spread:

piazza Velasca 5, Torre Velasca · Studio BBPR, 1956–58

All lighting custom designed by Studio BBPR.

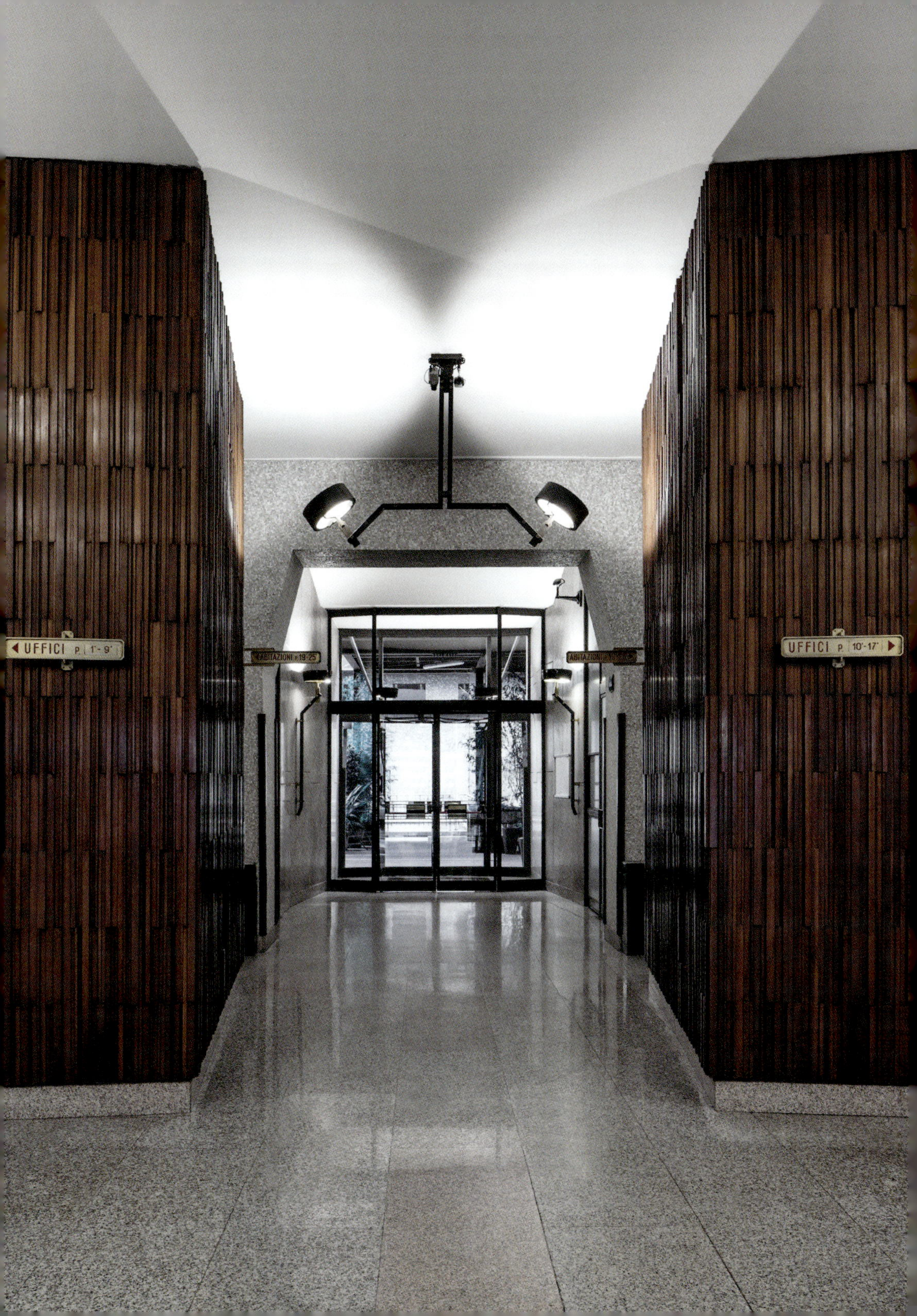

UFFICI P. 1°-9°
ABITAZIONI P. 19-25
UFFICI P. 10°-17°

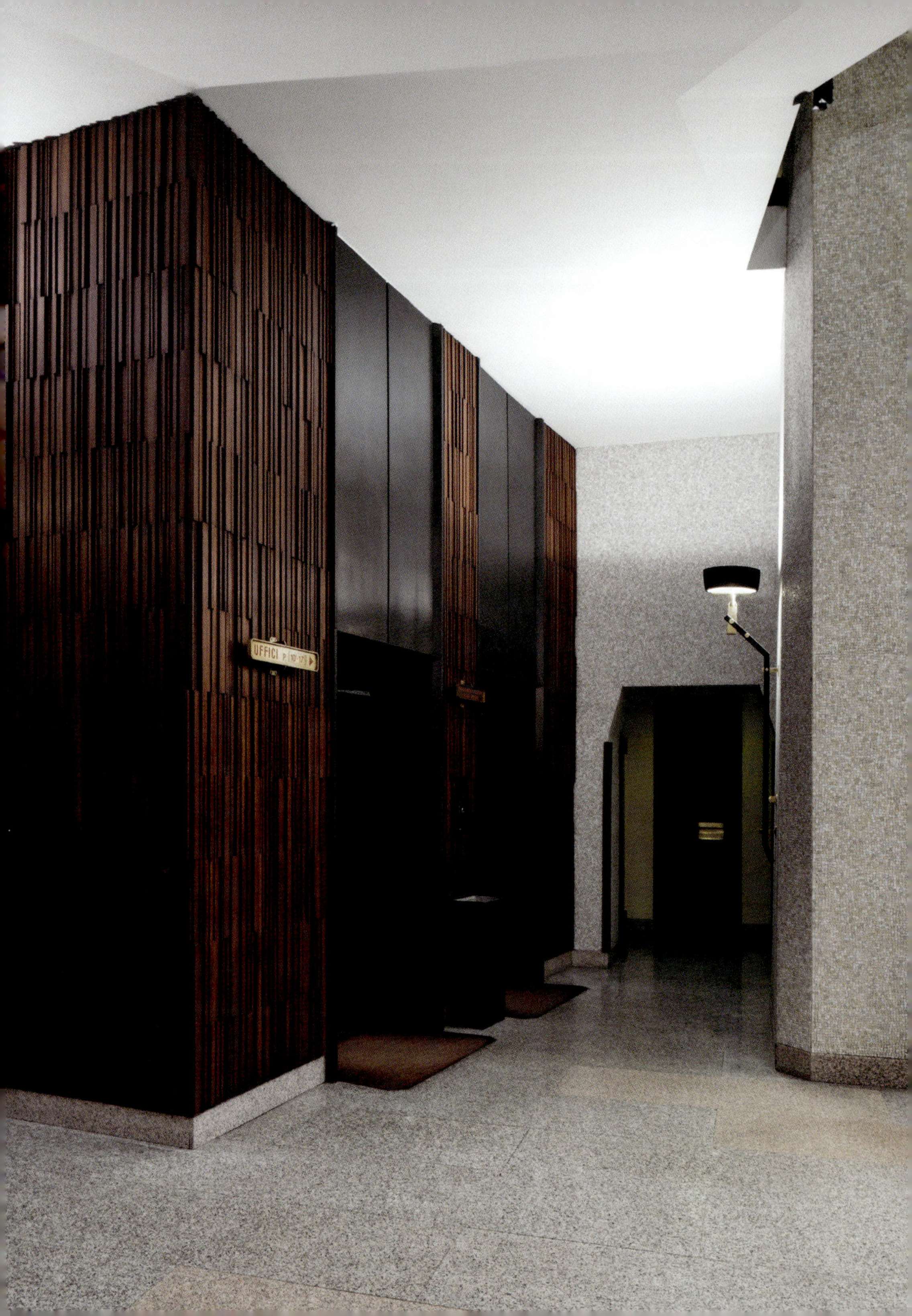
UFFICI P 10-17

BBPR's manifesto building, the Torre Velasca of 1958, with its haunting medieval allusions, was met at the time with both astonishment and hostility that have not abated to this day. Here the architects raise questions that they initially theorized about in the immediate aftermath of the war. These can be summed up in just one phrase: how do you build in the partially bombed-out historical city? The entrance and lobby of this early Milan high-rise was programmed around the dual function it served: that of part office and part residence. To this end, BBPR created ingenious circulations specifically catering to each space, be it domestic, office, or commercial. Materials are fastidiously selected, some neutral, others emphatic in equal measure. There are mosaic walls, granite floors, and black enameled panels near the elevator banks. Large sconces and chandeliers are engineered with striking tectonics. The design feature at the very core of the building is truly astonishing, composed as it is of an endless array of staggered strips of veneer that randomly overlap, recalling the primary dwellings of the ancient Lombards in a poetic metaphor.

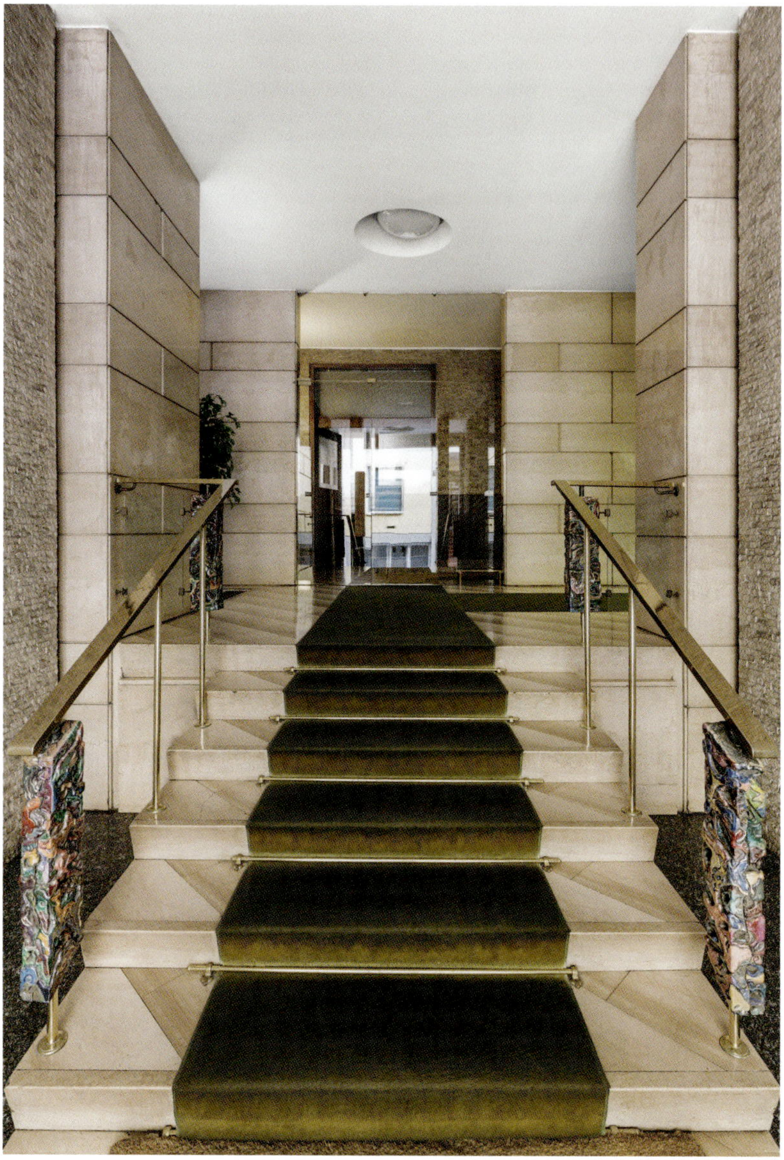

This spread and following spread:
via Santa Marta 19 · Gaetano Brusa, 1950–55
Ceramic wall tiles by Pietro Melandri.
Ceramic stair balustrades by Pietro Melandri.

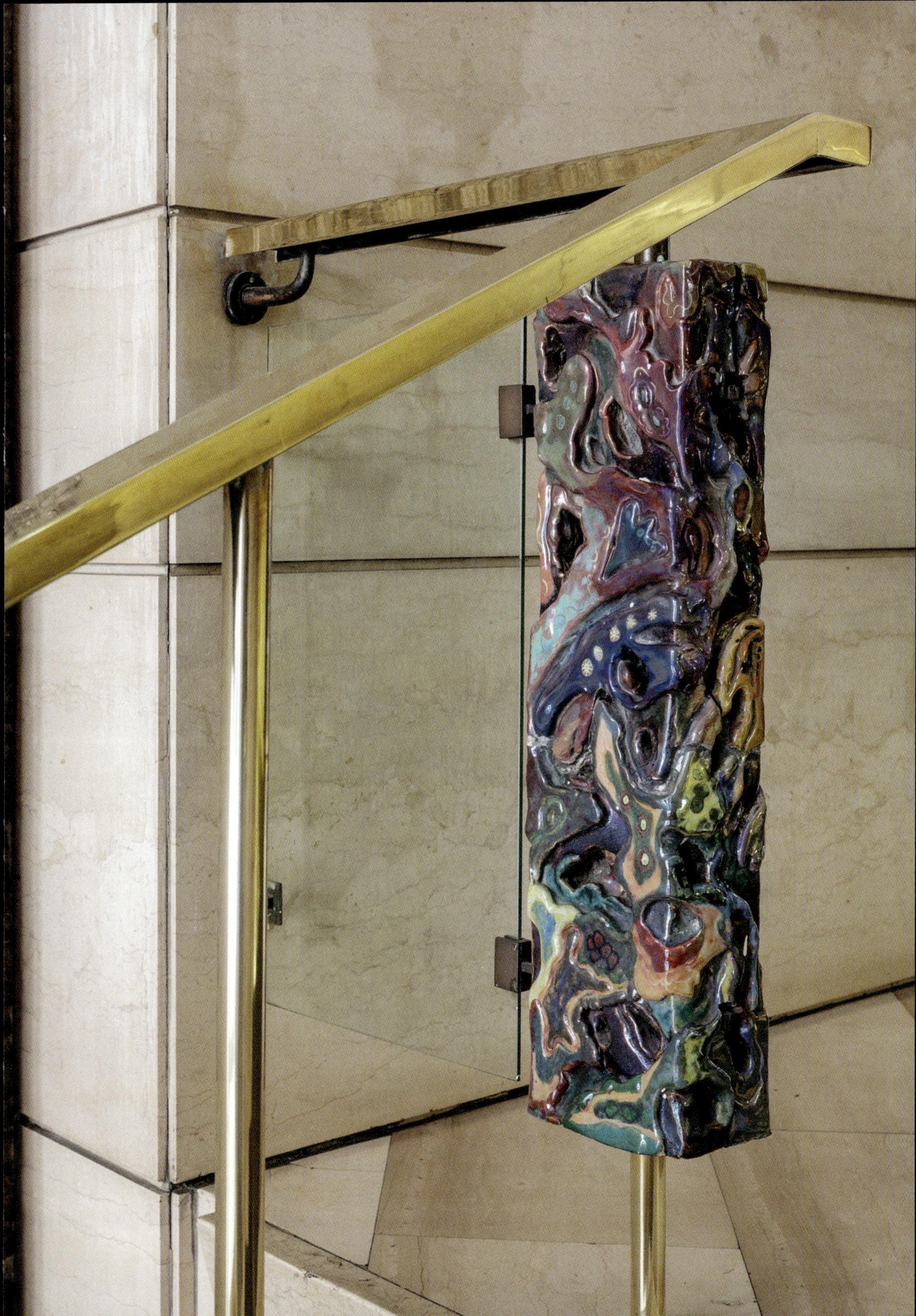

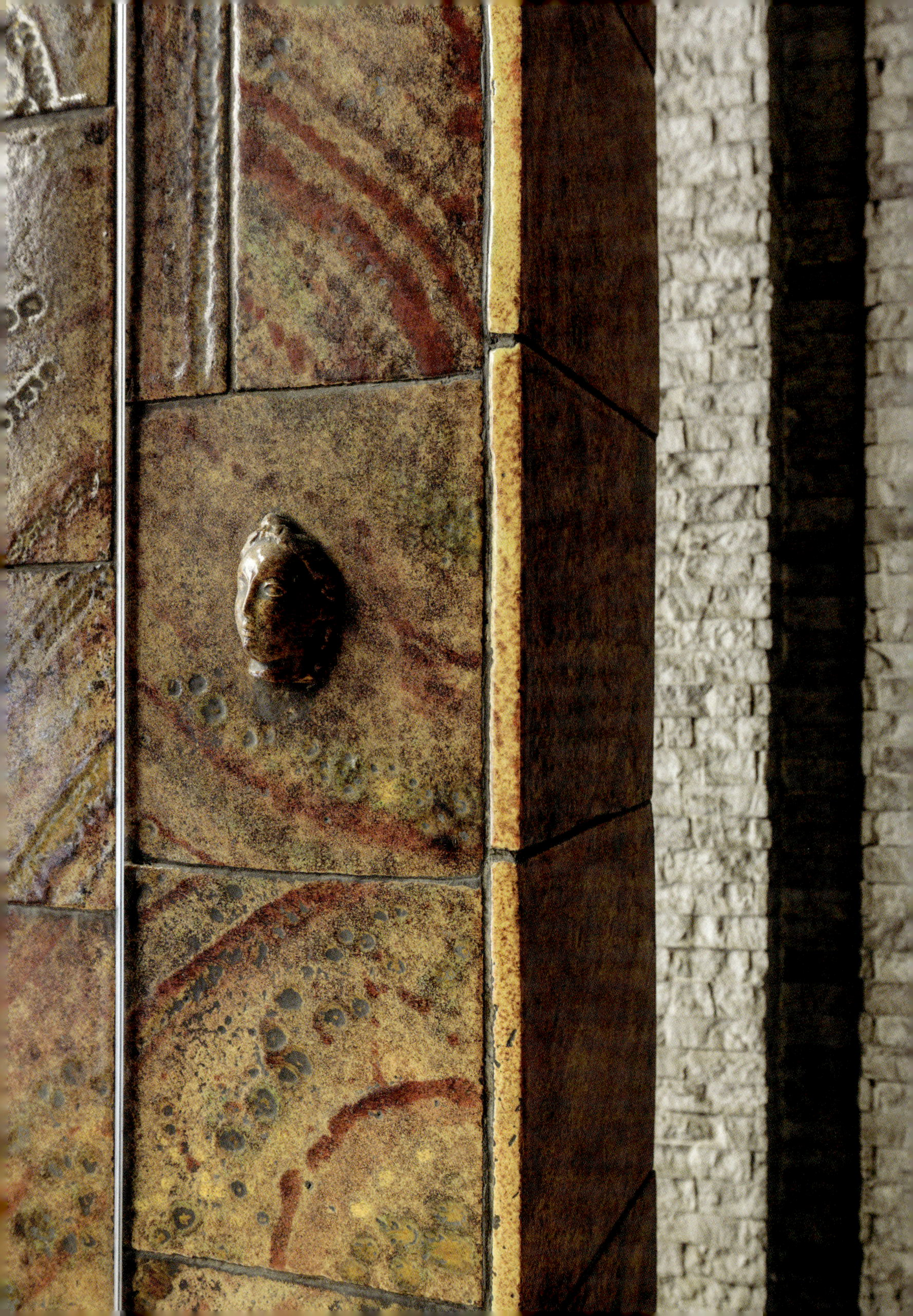

Lisa Hockemeyer

Ceramics Everywhere: An Italian Heritage

Harlequins, masks, and ships dancing on the waves of the sea, narrating the mythological world of the Mediterranean, its history, and popular culture, and vividly colored abstract art compositions are familiar structural and decorative "applied" art elements in Milanese postwar public and domestic interior decorating schemes. And more often than not they come in ceramics! In no other city in Italy did ceramic art and decoration play such an important role as it did in Milan. There, the use of artistic ceramics was characteristic for post-World War II reconstruction efforts and not only intrinsically linked to the collaborative efforts of a cultural avant-garde of architects, artists, and an enlightened public and private clientele, but synonymous with a newly reborn liberal and democratic society, too.

Ever since Antiquity and the Renaissance, ceramics have played a significant part, influencing every aspect of Italian private and civic life. A culturally instinctive use of the material and the often simultaneous manufacture by the same artist, craftsmen, or workshop of different product types, from utilitarian kitchen wares to artistic ornamental elements and architectural fittings, has contributed to the exceptional role ceramics have played in the shaping of Italy's material culture identity. The custom to integrate ceramic reliefs, mosaics, and sculptures of secular or religious content into internal or external architectural structures and interior decorating schemes was diffused widely and, despite some ups and downs, practiced throughout the centuries.

Following a general decline during the late eighteenth to mid-nineteenth century, a particularly strong revival of Italy's distinguished majolica tradition was reignited through the promotion of the applied and industrial art industries and attempts at educational reform at the end of the nineteenth century. New industries and the advent of modernity complemented the contemporary aesthetic canons of Art Nouveau and fostered the widespread application of ceramics as a decorative surface element notably in the form of colorful tile arrangements embellishing interiors or façades of important urban private and civic edifices, predominately in the upcoming affluent industrial cities of the north, Turin and Milan.

The aesthetic politics of the Fascist regime of the interwar years that followed, on the other hand, not only favored extensive public art schemes but a return to the ancient art of mural decoration, as well as materials and crafts and subject content, such as mythological themes, representative of national values. These guidelines contributed to the re-evaluation of the ceramic material for artistic ends, the breakdown of traditional boundaries between ceramists and artists, and fostered the inclusion of ceramic art in public, commercial, and private spaces and as exponents in national and international exhibitions. While the aesthetic directives of the Fascist regime of the interwar and war years helped significantly toward the inclusion of ceramic art in contemporary architectural schemes, the full potential of such synthesis came to the forefront only with the fall of Fascism, generating general artistic freedom and an explosion of creativity.

Artistic Ceramics at the Forefront of Milanese Reconstruction Efforts—During the immediate postwar years no other city in Italy communicated the optimistic spirit of reconstruction through the insertion of ceramic art better than Milan, where much of the city center and its symbols of religious, civic, and commercial prestige were heavily war-damaged and the reconstruction and the filling of bombed-out spaces became a priority to signal the re-awaking of a destroyed and defeated city. Appropriately, reconstruction efforts centered on the area near and around the most prestigious address in town, the Piazza del Duomo and in the adjacent Galleria Vittorio Emanuele II, the most prominent shopping arcade in all of Italy and one of the best known in the world.

As if wanting to dust away the signs of the war years with new and colorful ceramic art, it is close to the heart of the city that the largest concentration of avant-garde artistic ceramics adorning new and reconstructed historical architectural structures and interiors between 1947 and 1958 was to be found. There, many renowned architects, such as Melchiorre Bega, Marco Zanuso, Guglielmo Ulrich, the BBPR group, and Luciano Baldessari—all of whom had already worked together with ceramists and artists such as Pietro Melandri, Lucio Fontana, and others on architectural projects during the interwar years—inserted avant-garde artistic ceramics in the most distinguished commercial and retail interiors, such as the Motta café bar (1948–49), the Forst pub (1949), the prestigious Galtrucco fabric shop (1949), and Caffè Biffi (1957). Colorful, free-modeled bas-reliefs, table bases, structural columns, bar areas, and entire walls clad in two-colored abstract maiolica tiles, staircase balustrades, water fountains, door handles, and small and large-scale freestanding sculptures in ceramics were a common decorative feature contrasting with, and accentuating, the newly designed, strikingly modern interiors boasting clean-cut lines, the most modern materials, lighting systems, appliances, and gadgets.

The amalgamation of modern architectural structures with ceramic works of fine-art association, handmade by established artists and manufactured with traditional craft technologies, was not exclusive to spaces of commercial or retail purpose but applied to office blocks and residential buildings. The choice of ceramics as a decorative material in Milanese postwar public and domestic interior decorating schemes, including housing entrances, was neither arbitrary nor deliberate but fruit and expression of a distinctive postwar artistic, material, and ideological culture.

Ceramics were widely available, cheap, and durable, and devoid of any Fascist, monumental, or aristocratic overtones, rendering them politically inoffensive and ideal to symbolize a new, democratic, postwar Italy. Ceramics, already tried and tested throughout the centuries, also represented a highly suitable material for inserting color and sculpture into modern architecture and to apply a desired ideal of a synthesis of the arts propagated, among many others by the architect Gio Ponti and the Milanese avant-garde abstract art group Movimento Arte Concreta (MAC), headed by Gillo Dorfles and Bruno Munari. While Ponti restlessly sought to promote the collaboration between architects, artists, and craftsmen, the ideals proposed by MAC advocated the application of arts to architecture. Both had a significant influence on the widespread diffusion of architectural ceramics in Milan in the 1950s, and both are only but one reflection of the overall vibrating atmosphere that, fueled by the spirit of reconstruction and newly gained artistic freedom, marked Milan's postwar architectural undertakings, avant-garde artistic movements, and art gallery scene.

Perhaps no other artistic personality and art movement has contributed more to the revival and legitimization of ceramic art in Milan than Lucio Fontana and the Movimento Spaziale, which he founded in 1947. His affinity with clay and exploration of the experimental values of the material as part of his artistic-spatial research inspired many of the artists' and architects' work who gravitated around the enigmatic figure of Fontana, including the artist Fausto Melotti and the architects Ernesto Nathan Rogers, Enrico Peressutti, and Lodovico Barbiano di Belgiojoso, many of whose works are represented in this volume. The majority of their designs and creations and other ceramic interiors, supports, and appliances, which were once a familiar sight in Milanese shops, bars, restaurants, and residential interiors, have unfortunately been destroyed, removed, and displaced throughout the last decades, giving way to new fashions and interior aesthetic ideals. Their rarity today renders the ceramic decorated entrances represented in this volume ever more significant as they not only tell of a very special Italian relationship with clay, but are remnants of a bygone period when artistic ceramics were to be found just about everywhere. Above all, however, they are testimony to the artistic virtuosity representative of Milan's cultural avant-garde of architects, artists, and an enlightened public and private clientele during the postwar years.

Following spread:
via Santa Marta 19 · Gaetano Brusa, 1950–55
Ceramic wall bas-reliefs by Pietro Melandri.
floor and walls: Trani Serpeggiante limestone

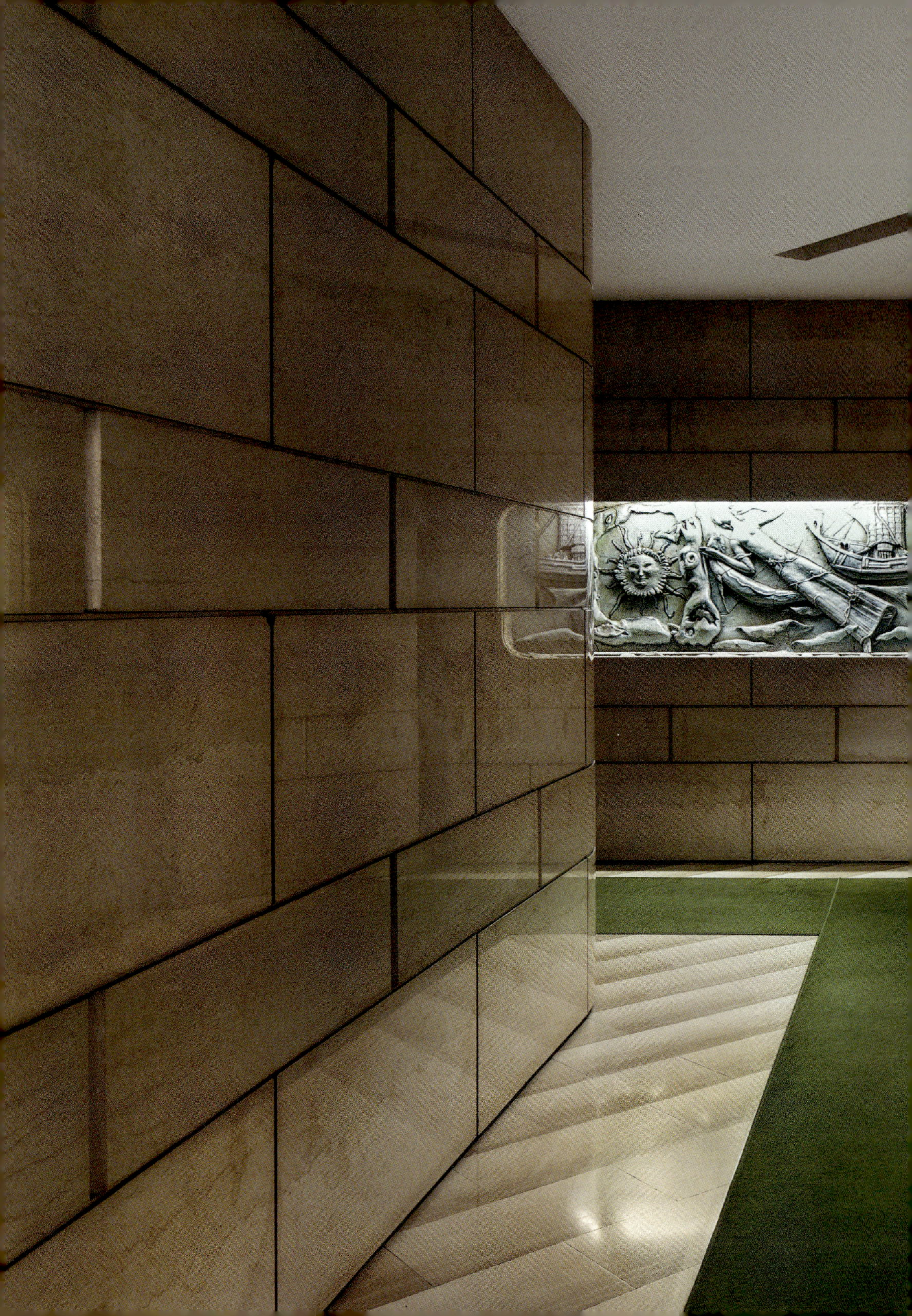

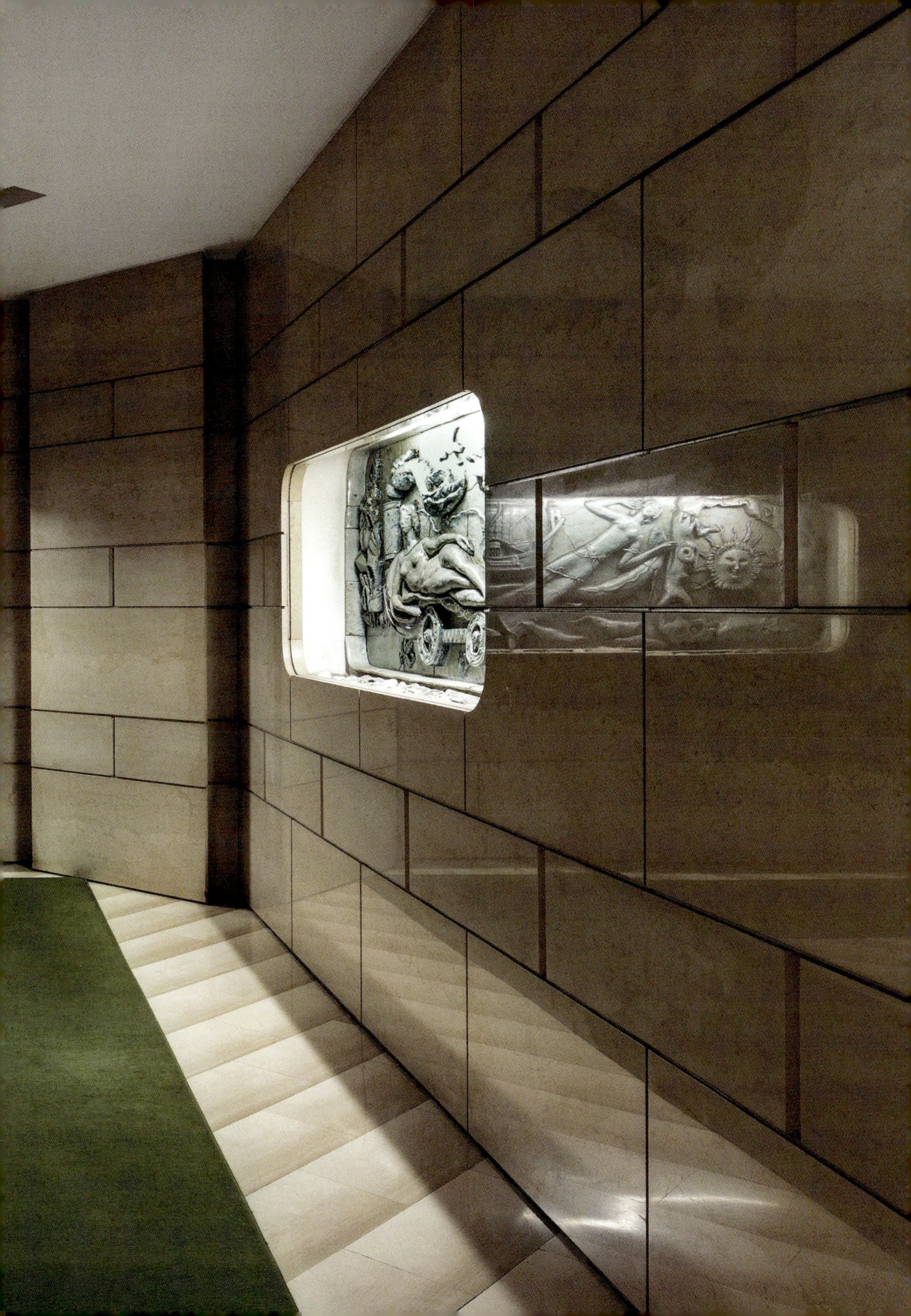

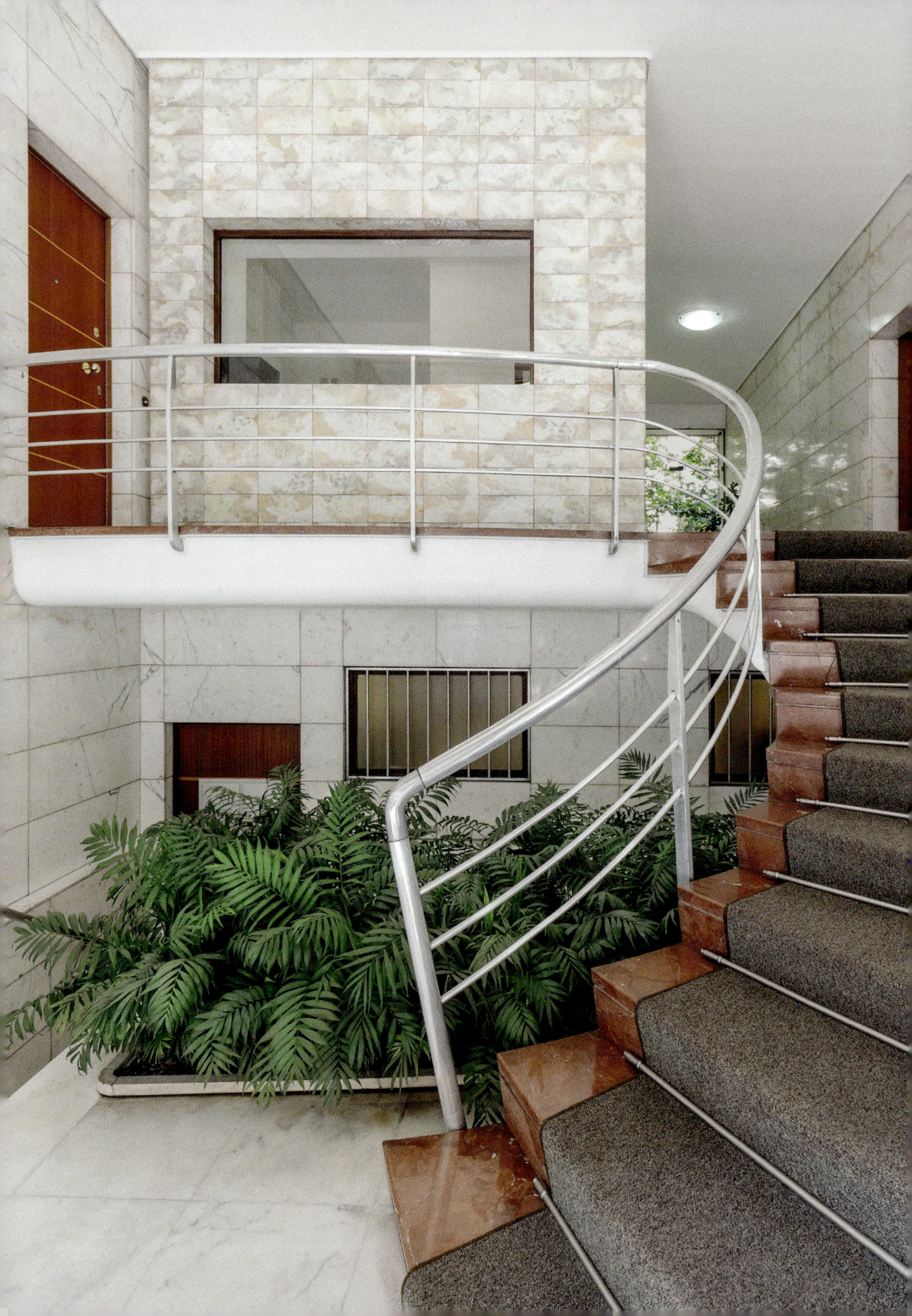

Lisa Hockemeyer

Ceramica dovunque: una tradizione italiana

Arlecchini, maschere, navi che danzano sulle onde a narrare il mondo mitologico mediterraneo, la sua storia e la sua cultura popolare, accanto a composizioni astratte dai colori vivacissimi, sono tutti elementi strutturali e ornamentali di arte "applicata" molto comuni negli schemi decorativi degli interni di edifici pubblici e privati nella Milano del dopoguerra. E più spesso che mai sono in ceramica! In nessun'altra città italiana l'arte della ceramica ha svolto un ruolo così importante come a Milano. Qui, l'utilizzo delle ceramiche artistiche ha connotato l'opera di ricostruzione del dopoguerra non solo in quanto intrinsecamente connesso all'impegno collaborativo di un'avanguardia di architetti, artisti e di una committenza illuminata sia pubblica che privata, ma anche come sinonimo di una società rinata ai valori umanistici e democratici.

Già dall'antichità e dal Rinascimento le ceramiche hanno avuto un'importanza significante in Italia, influenzando ogni aspetto della vita privata e pubblica del paese. L'uso culturalmente istintivo del materiale e la frequentemente simultanea manifattura da parte dello stesso artista, artigiano o laboratorio di tipi di prodotti molto diversi fra loro, dagli utensili da cucina a elementi ornamentali artistici e finiture architettoniche, hanno contribuito al ruolo eccezionale svolto dalla ceramica nel plasmare l'identità della cultura materiale italiana. L'usanza di integrare rilievi, mosaici e sculture in ceramica a tema secolare o religioso nelle strutture architettoniche interne o esterne e negli schemi decorativi degli interni è sempre stata diffusa ovunque e, pur con temporanei alti e bassi, praticata incessantemente attraverso i secoli.

Dopo un declino generale verificatosi tra la fine del Settecento e la metà del secolo successivo, verso la fine dell'Ottocento si è registrata una rinascita particolarmente spiccata della rinomata tradizione della maiolica italiana grazie alla promozione delle arti industriali e applicate e ai tentativi di varare una riforma dell'istruzione. Le nuove industrie e l'avvento della modernità, insieme ai canoni estetici dell'Art Nouveau che andavano sviluppandosi all'epoca, hanno alimentato la richiesta diffusa della ceramica come superficie decorativa, in particolare sotto forma di multicolori composizioni di piastrelle impiegate a scopo ornamentale per gli interni o per le facciate di importanti edifici cittadini, pubblici e privati, soprattutto nei centri urbani del Nord, come Milano e Torino, dove l'industria stava generando nuove ricchezze.

In seguito, la politica estetica del regime fascista negli anni fra le due guerre ha d'altro canto favorito non solo estensivi progetti di arte pubblica, ma anche un ritorno all'antica arte della decorazione muraria, così come di materiali, mestieri e soggetti rappresentativi dei valori nazionali, quali i temi mitologici. Queste linee guida hanno contribuito alla rivalorizzazione della ceramica come materiale impiegato in campo artistico, portando alla rottura dei tradizionali confini tra ceramisti e artisti e facilitando l'inclusione della ceramica in spazi pubblici, commerciali e privati nonché nelle mostre nazionali e internazionali. Se le direttive estetiche del fascismo hanno significativamente agevolato la presenza dell'arte ceramica nei progetti architettonici, le piene potenzialità di questa sintesi si sono rivelate soltanto dopo la caduta del regime, con la conseguente libertà di espressione artistica che ha generato una vera e propria esplosione creativa.

La ceramica artistica in prima linea nella ricostruzione postbellica di Milano – Negli anni dell'immediato dopoguerra nessuna città italiana ha saputo esprimere lo spirito ottimista della ricostruzione avvalendosi dell'arte ceramica meglio di Milano, dove gran parte del centro cittadino e dei suoi simboli di prestigio religioso, civico e commerciale aveva subito gravi danni durante la guerra, e l'urgenza di riempire gli spazi vuoti lasciati dalle bombe era divenuta il segnale della rinascita di una città piegata e distrutta. Gli sforzi ricostruttivi si sono dunque concentrati sulle aree attigue al cuore cittadino, piazza del Duomo con l'adiacente Galleria Vittorio Emanuele II, la più importante galleria di negozi di tutta Italia e una delle più conosciute al mondo.

Come a voler spazzare via le cicatrici degli anni di guerra con una nuova arte dai colori accesi, è nelle vicinanze del nucleo centrale della città che, tra il 1947 e il 1958, si è avuta la massima concentrazione di un impiego della ceramica artistica d'avanguardia nella decorazione di strutture architettoniche e interni nuovi e ricostruiti. Molti rinomati architetti, quali Melchiorre Bega, Marco Zanuso, Guglielmo Ulrich, il gruppo BBPR e Luciano Baldessari, ognuno dei quali aveva già collaborato in progetti architettonici con ceramisti e artisti come Pietro Melandri, Lucio Fontana e altri negli anni interbellici, introdussero ceramiche artistiche d'avanguardia negli interni di famosi locali commerciali, quali il Bar Motta (1948-49), la birreria Forst (1949), il prestigioso negozio di tessuti Galtrucco (1949) e il Caffè Biffi (1957). Variopinti bassorilievi, basi di tavoli, colonne, banconi e intere pareti rivestite di piastrelle in maiolica con fantasie astratte bicolori, balaustre di scale, fontane, maniglie e sculture in ceramica di tutte le dimensioni costituivano un tratto decorativo molto comune, che andava ad accentuare, spesso per contrasto, i nuovi interni dalle linee essenziali, realizzati con i più moderni materiali, sistemi illuminativi e accessori vari.

L'amalgama di strutture architettoniche moderne con opere in ceramica che rimandavano alle belle arti, fatte a mano da artisti famosi o prodotte con le tradizionali tecnologie artigiane, non era limitato agli spazi commerciali ma anche applicato all'edilizia residenziale e per uffici. La scelta della ceramica come materiale decorativo nella Milano del dopoguerra, negli interni di edifici sia pubblici che privati, tra cui gli ingressi dei palazzi, non era né arbitrario né soggettivo bensì il risultato e l'espressione di una ben riconoscibile cultura artistica, materiale e ideologica del dopoguerra.

La ceramica era disponibile ovunque, poco costosa e durevole, spogliata di ogni retorica fascista, monumentale o aristocratica così da renderla politicamente inoffensiva, e rappresentava dunque un mezzo ideale per simboleggiare una nuova Italia democratica. Già lungamente sperimentata nel corso di secoli, era anche un materiale molto adatto per introdurre il colore e la scultura nell'architettura contemporanea e per dare applicazione pratica a un ideale di sintesi delle arti auspicato da molti artisti, tra cui l'architetto Gio Ponti e il Movimento Arte Concreta (MAC), un gruppo d'avanguardia rivolto all'astrattismo capeggiato da Gillo Dorfles e Bruno Munari.

Se Ponti cercava instancabilmente di promuovere la collaborazione tra architetti, artisti e artigiani, gli ideali avanzati dal MAC si basavano sull'applicazione delle arti all'architettura. Entrambi esercitarono una forte influenza sull'ampia diffusione della ceramica architettonica nella Milano degli anni Cinquanta ed entrambi non furono che uno dei tanti riflessi di quell'atmosfera vibrante che, alimentata dallo spirito della ricostruzione e dell'appena riconquistata libertà artistica, segnò profondamente le imprese architettoniche, i movimenti artistici d'avanguardia e la scena delle gallerie d'arte del dopoguerra milanese.

Forse nessun'altra personalità o corrente artistica ha contribuito al ritorno alla ribalta e alla legittimazione dell'arte ceramica a Milano più di Lucio Fontana e del Movimento Spaziale, da lui fondato nel 1947. La sua affinità con l'argilla e l'esplorazione dei valori sperimentali del materiale come parte della sua ricerca artistico-spaziale ha ispirato numerosi lavori degli artisti e degli architetti che gravitavano intorno all'enigmatica figura di Fontana, tra cui l'artista Fausto Melotti e gli architetti Ernesto Nathan Rogers, Enrico Peressutti e Lodovico Barbiano di Belgiojoso, dei quali molte opere sono presenti in questo volume. La maggior parte dei loro progetti e delle loro creazioni, così come altre finiture, oggetti e supporti in ceramica un tempo familiari nei negozi, bar, ristoranti e interni residenziali di Milano, sono purtroppo andati distrutti, rimossi o rimpiazzati durante gli ultimi decenni, per lasciare il posto a nuove mode e nuovi ideali estetici applicati agli interni. La loro rarità rende dunque gli ingressi decorati in ceramica raffigurati in questo volume ancora più significativi, poiché essi non solo narrano la peculiare relazione italiana con questo materiale, ma sono vestigia di un tempo andato in cui le ceramiche artistiche si trovavano praticamente dovunque. Soprattutto, inoltre, sono la testimonianza del virtuosismo artistico rappresentativo di quella cultura avanguardistica di architetti, artisti e illuminati committenti pubblici e privati della Milano del dopoguerra.

Page 276 and following spread:
via Sant'Antonio Maria Zaccaria 3 · Gigi Ghò, 1951
Ceramic wall tiles by Fausto Melotti.
floor: Bianco Carrara marble · stairs: Rosso Collemandina limestone

Here we find two prominent Milanese artists, both former students of Adolfo Wildt, collaborating on a very sparse, but spatially dynamic entrance interior. Originally the chromatic effects of Fausto Melotti's glazed ceramic tiles were once further highlighted by Fontana's multicolored neon tubes in pale blue, white, and pink. Today all the tubes are white.

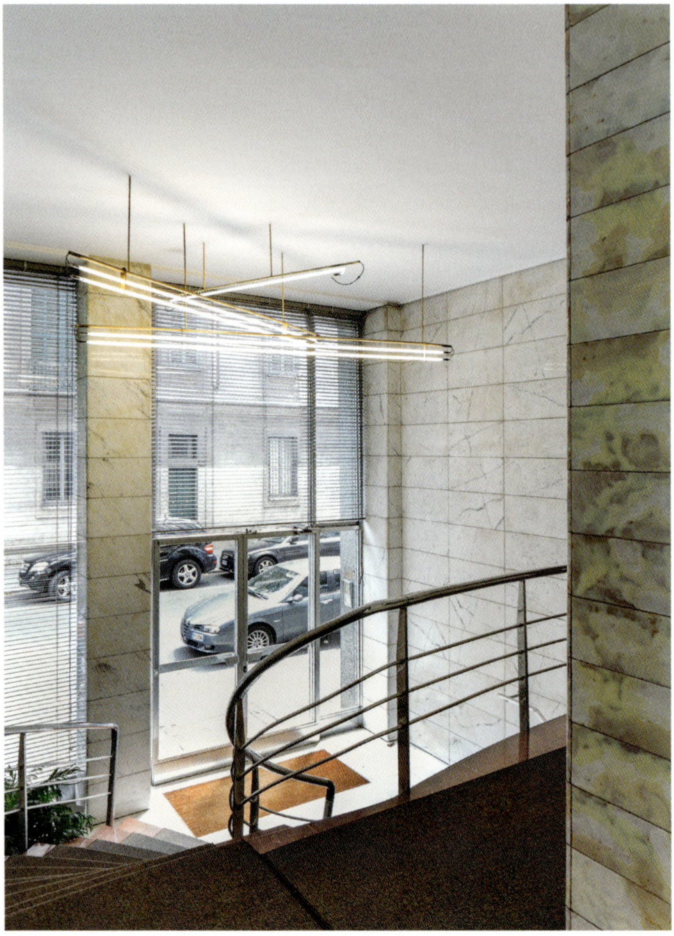

Neon ceiling sculpture by Lucio Fontana.
Ceramic wall tiles by Fausto Melotti.

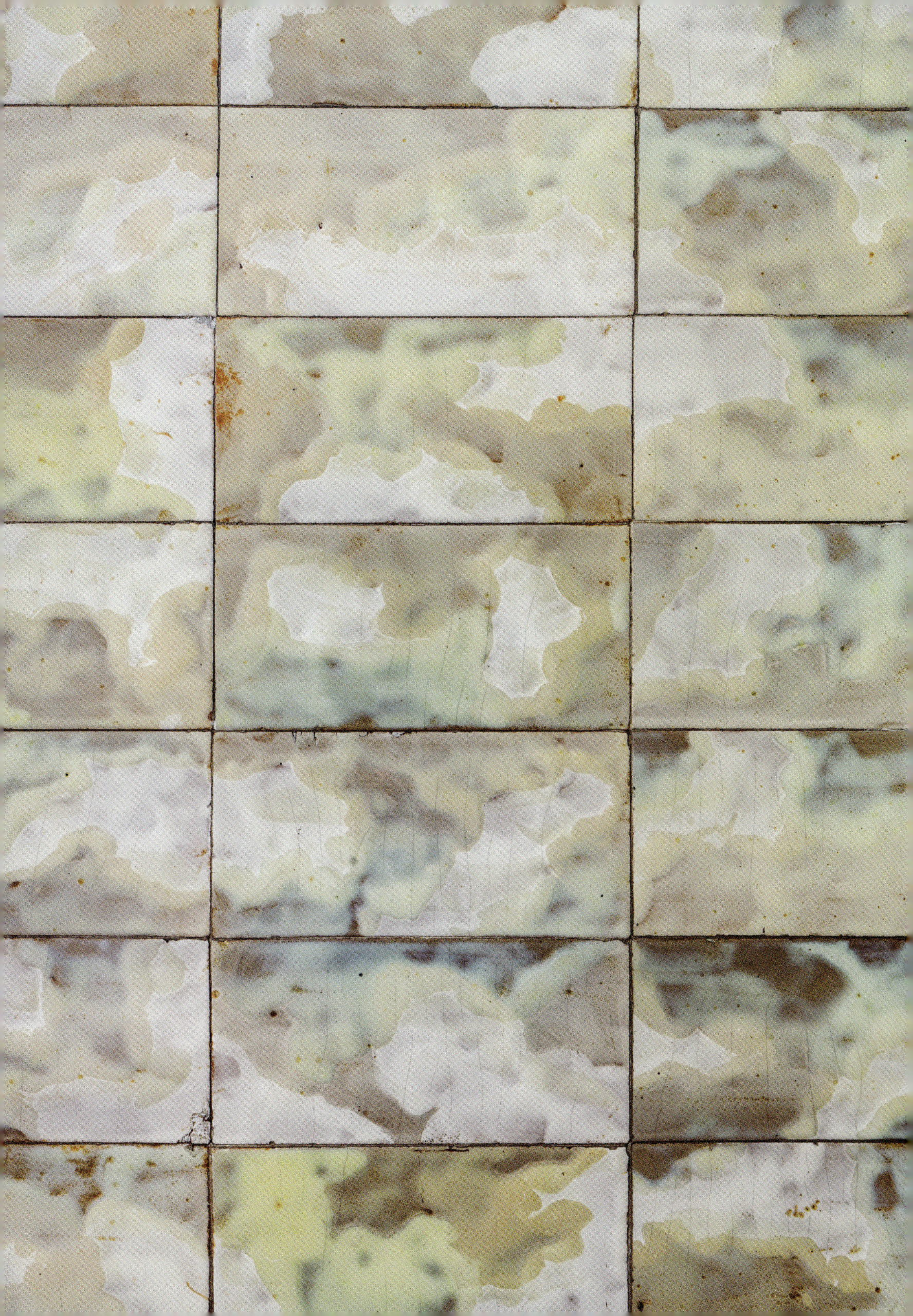

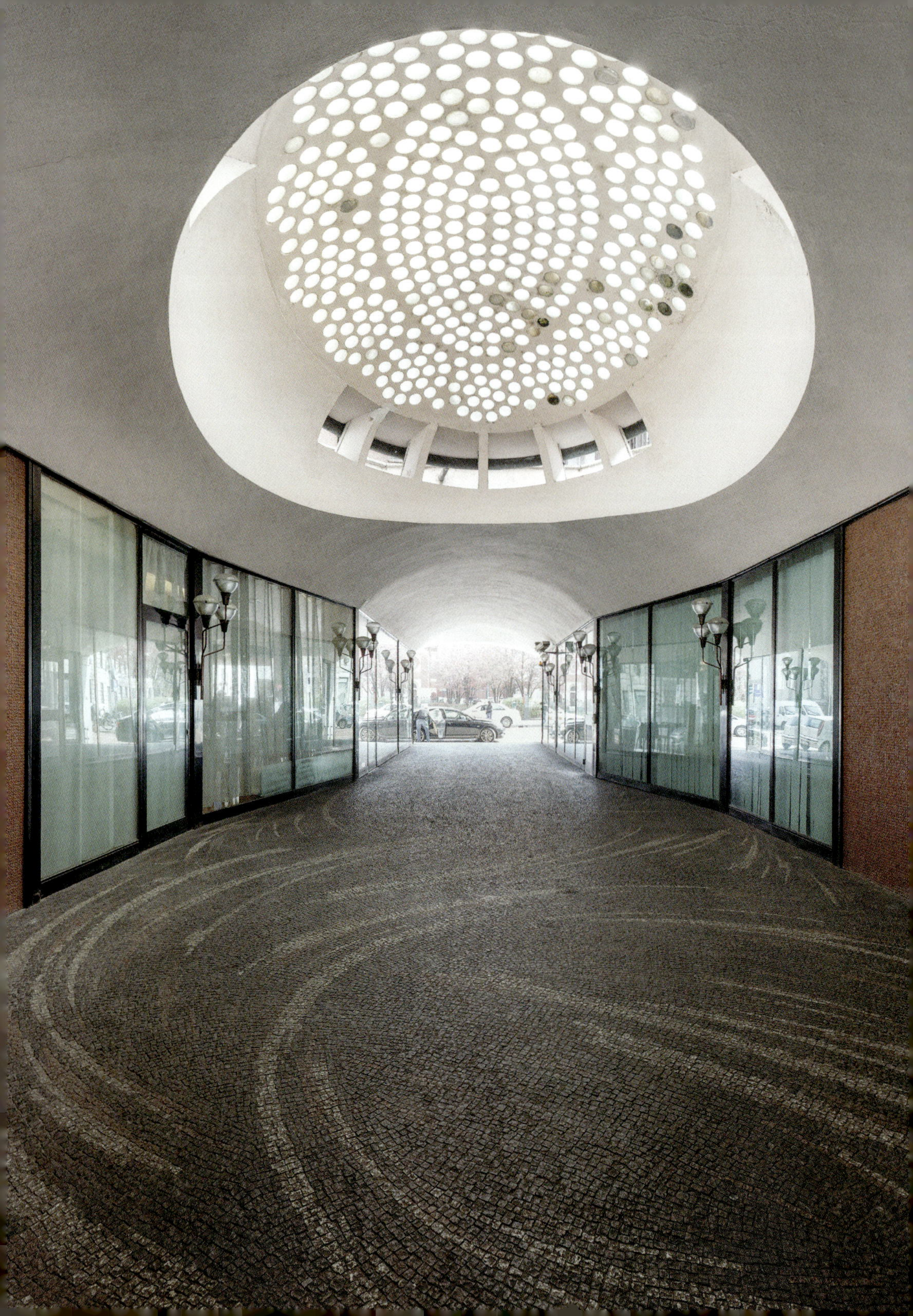

This entrance is in fact a passageway through the middle of a city block starting along Corso Italia. The floor pattern of mosaic tiles becomes tighter and more intricate as one walks further in, beyond the shops toward the private residential areas. The tilework was designed according to Caccia Dominioni's guidelines by one of his frequent collaborators, sculptor Francesco Somaini. The architect's concept evokes a river in an undulating cluster of streams that seems to channel the work of leading Italian Futurist Umberto Boccioni in order to generate fascinating effects underfoot, while ovoid arrays of circular glass bricks bring in daylight, and lamps inspired by historical Milan tramway lighting fixtures illuminate the way.

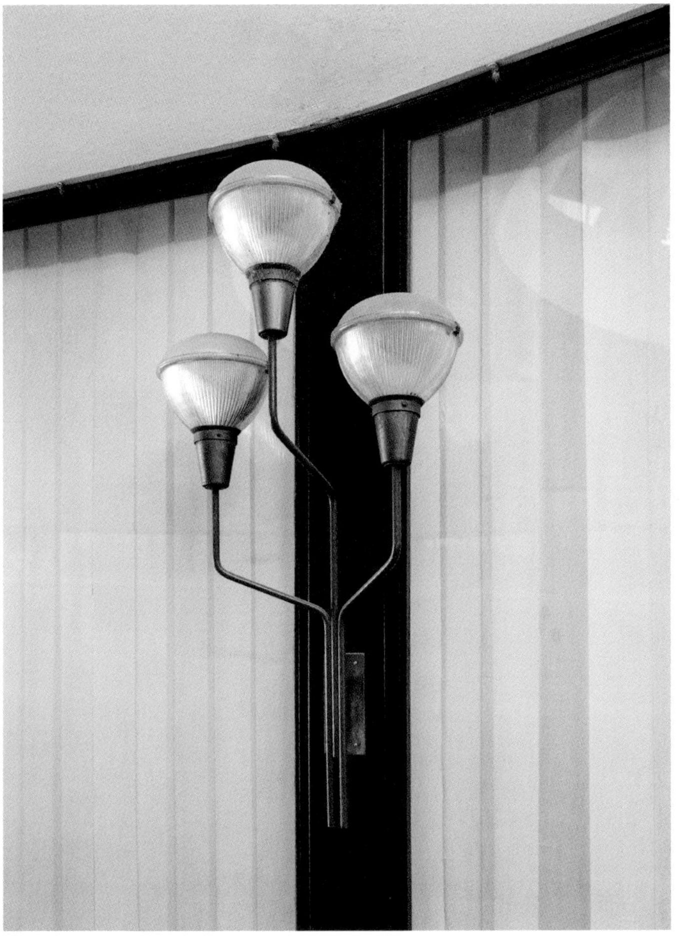

This and following spread:
corso Italia 22/1 & 22/2 · Luigi Caccia Dominioni, 1957–61
Floors by Francesco Somaini.
Sconces by Luigi Caccia Dominioni and Ignazio Gardella.

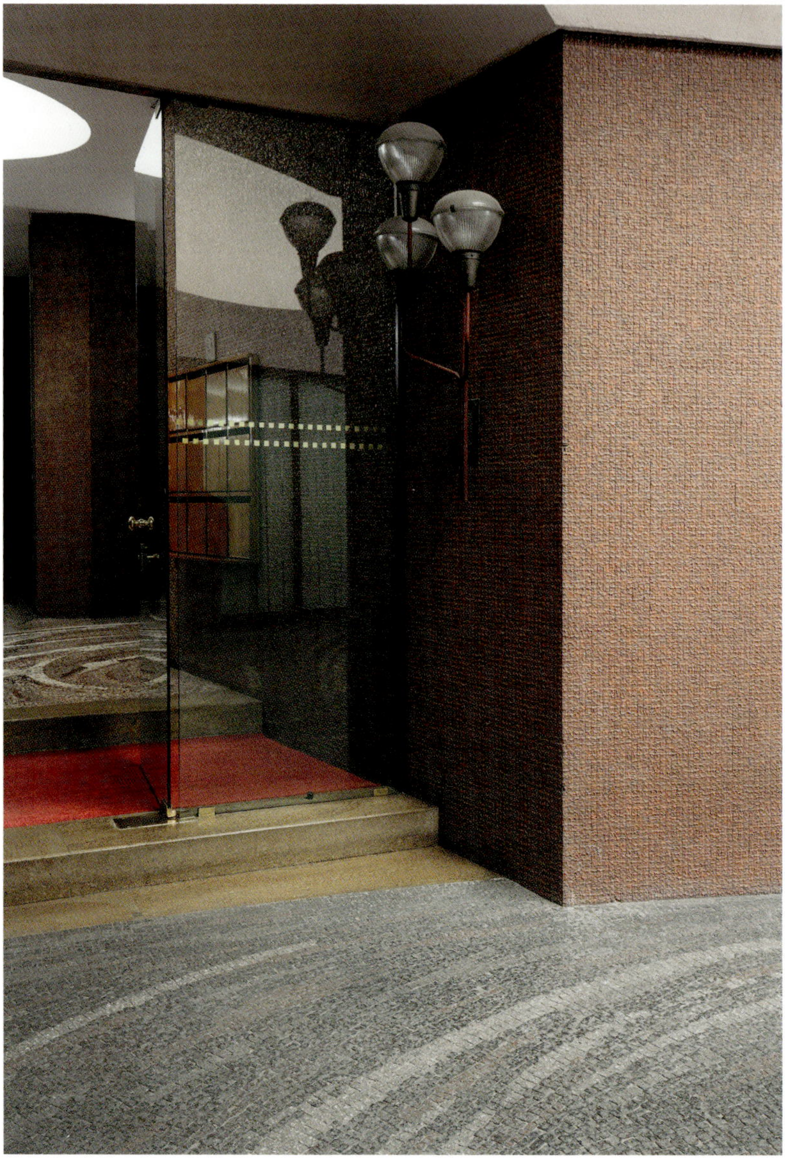

Floors by Francesco Somaini.
Sconces by Luigi Caccia Dominioni and Ignazio Gardella.

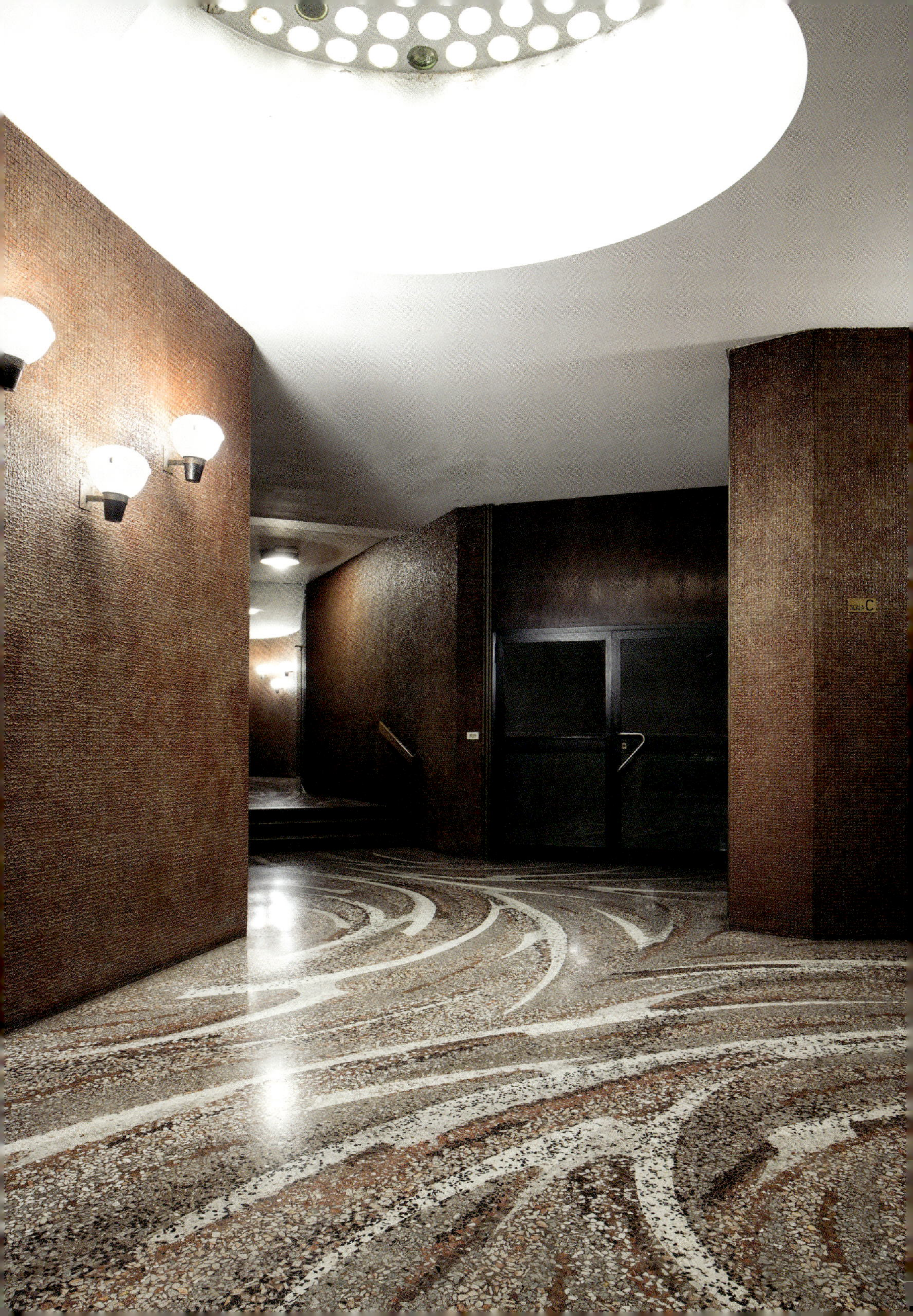
C

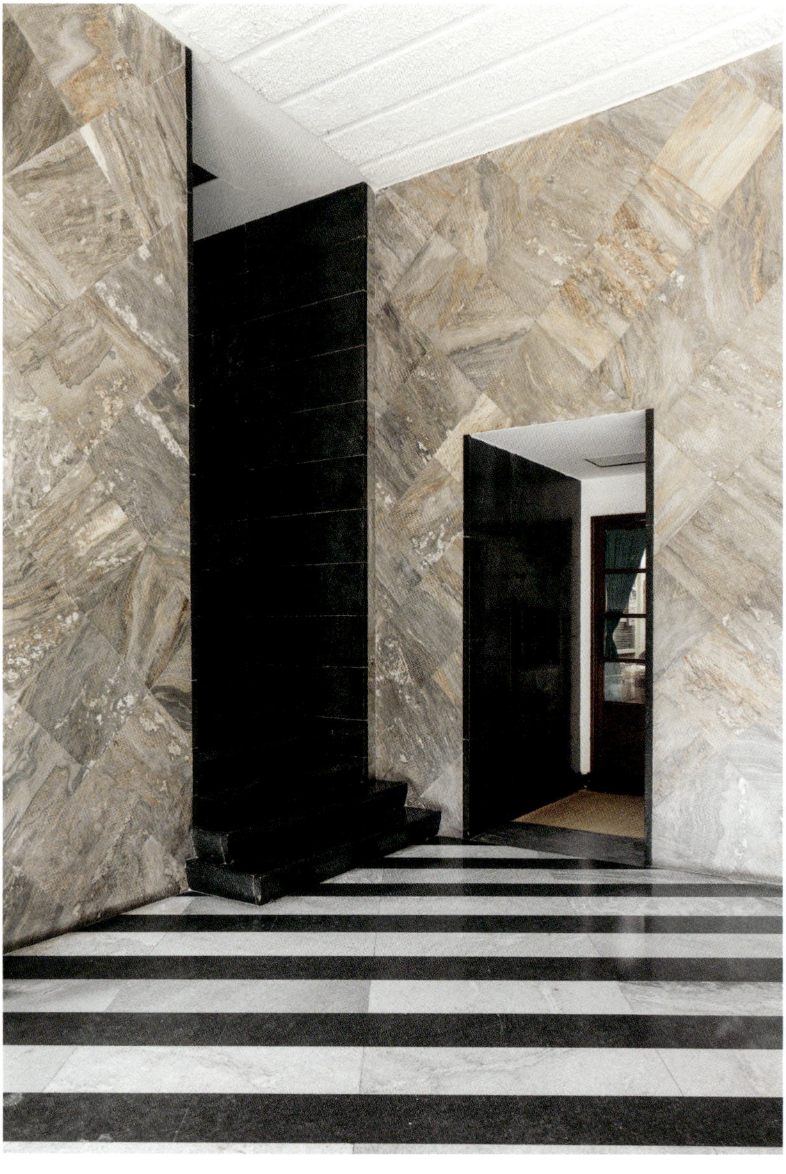

corso Italia 9 · Gio Ponti, 1934

Pendant lamp by Luigi Caccia Dominioni.
floor: Musso marble and serpentinite · walls: Crevola marble

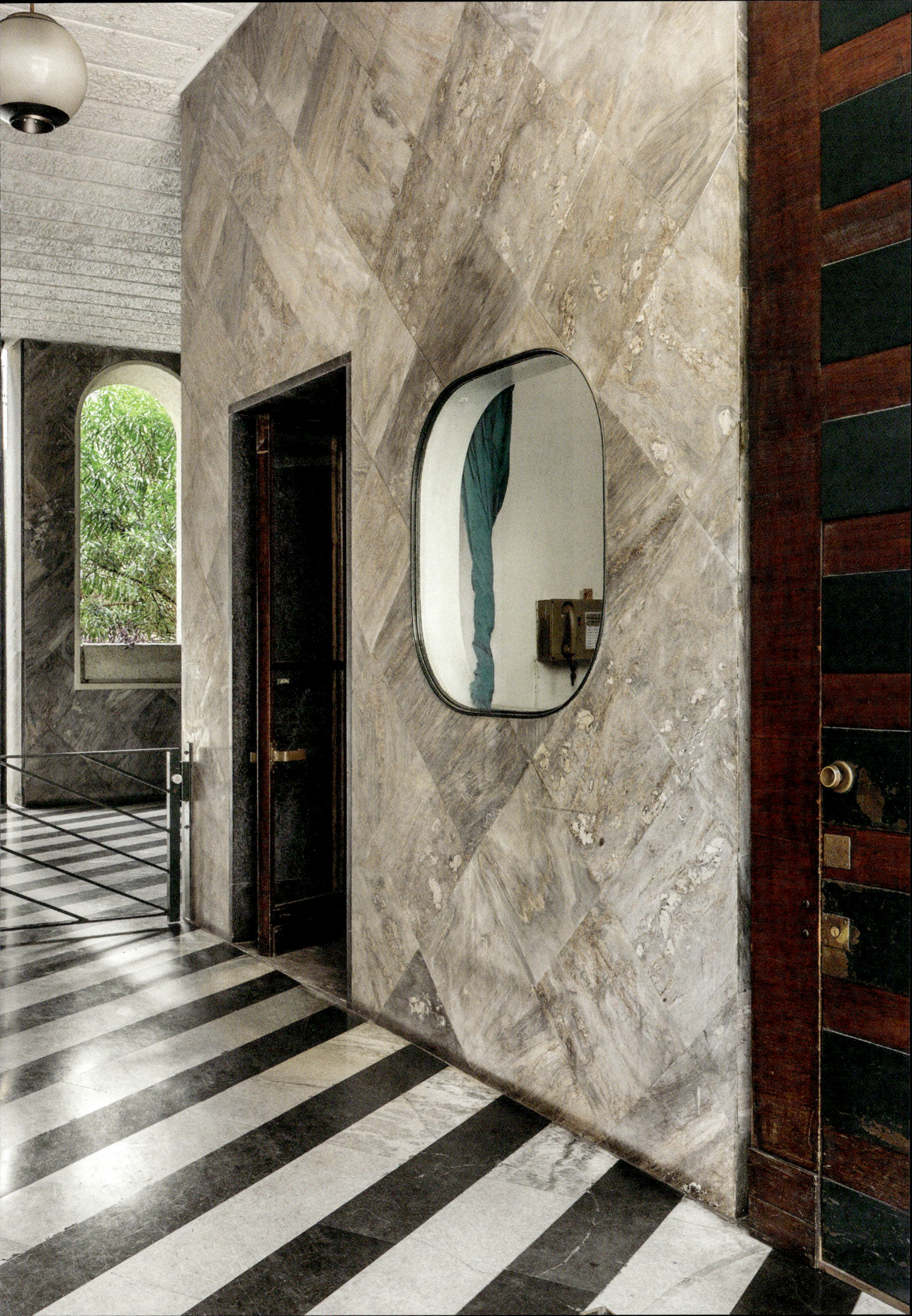

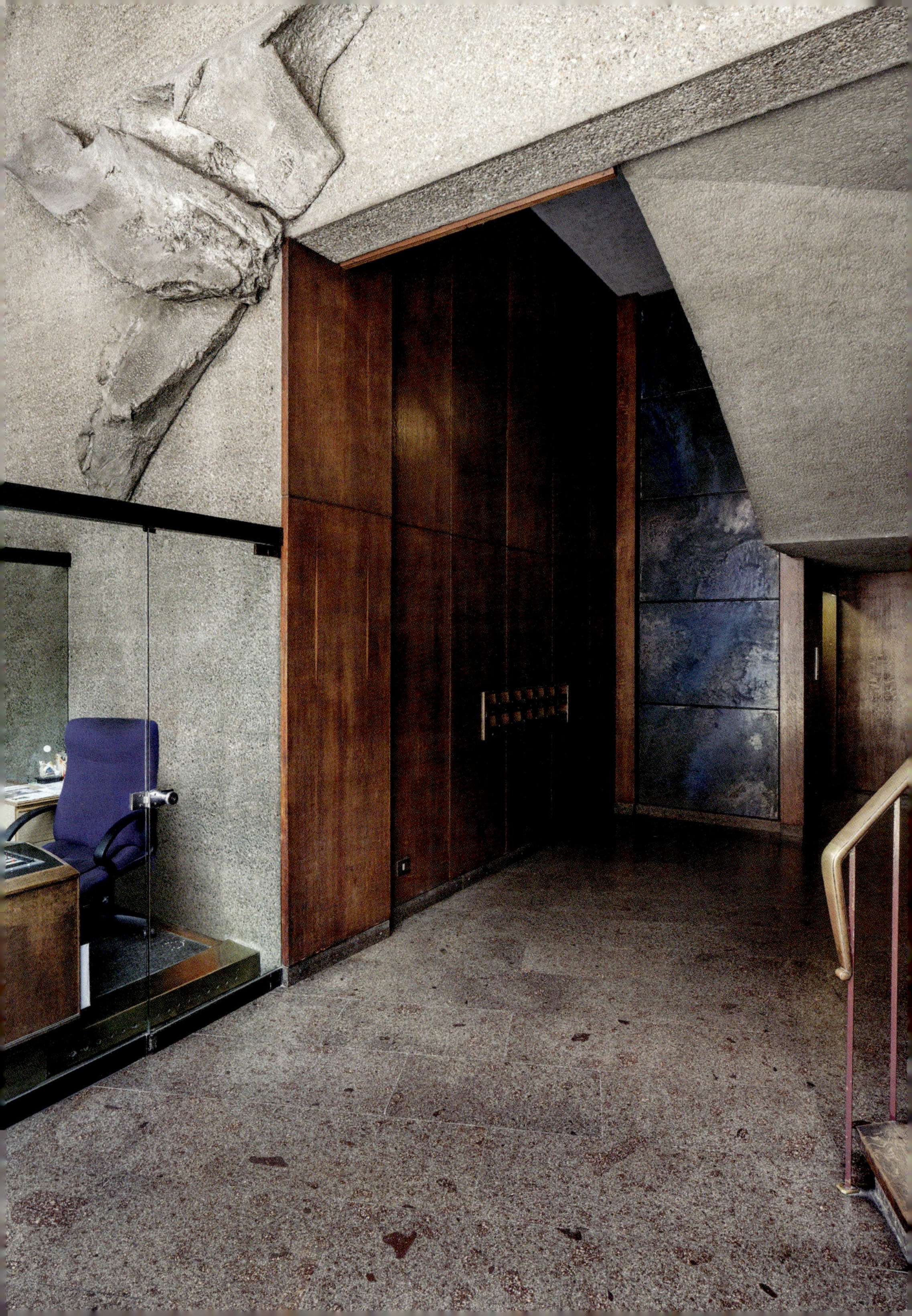

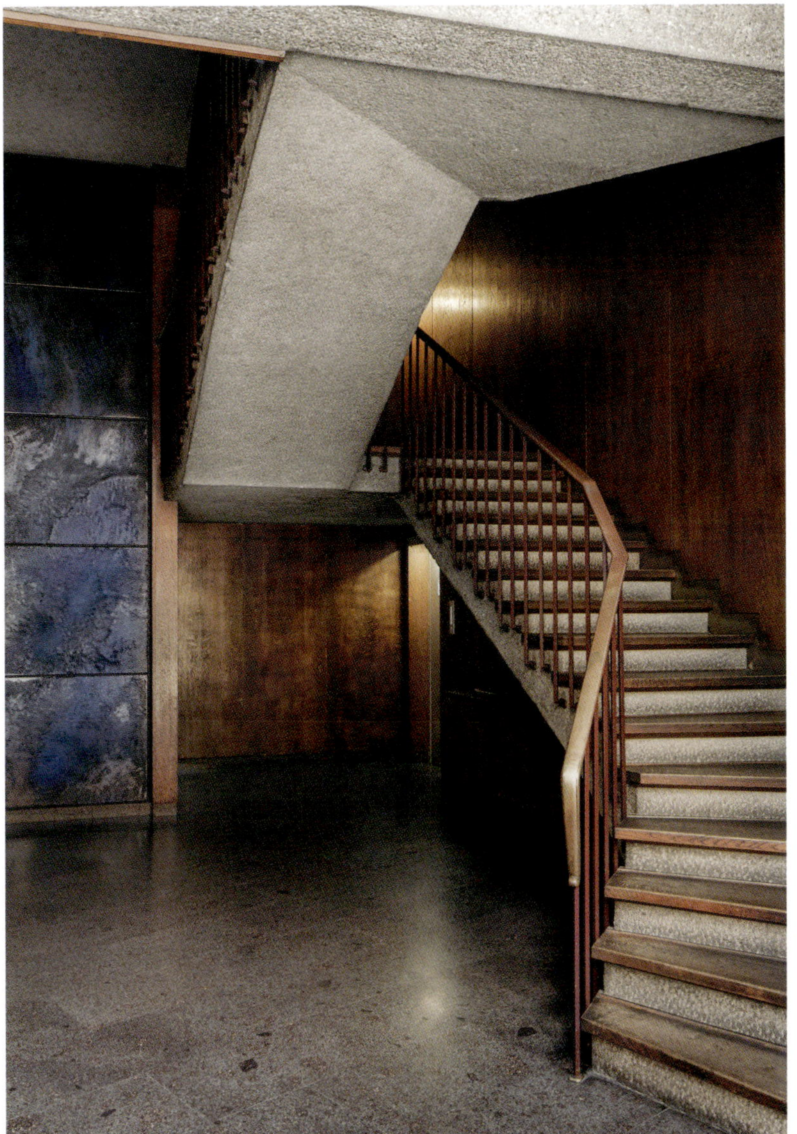

via Sambuco 15

Artwork by Enrico Ciuti, 1963.
floor: Sarda trachyte

via Giuseppe Prina 4 · Ugo Patetta, 1949–50

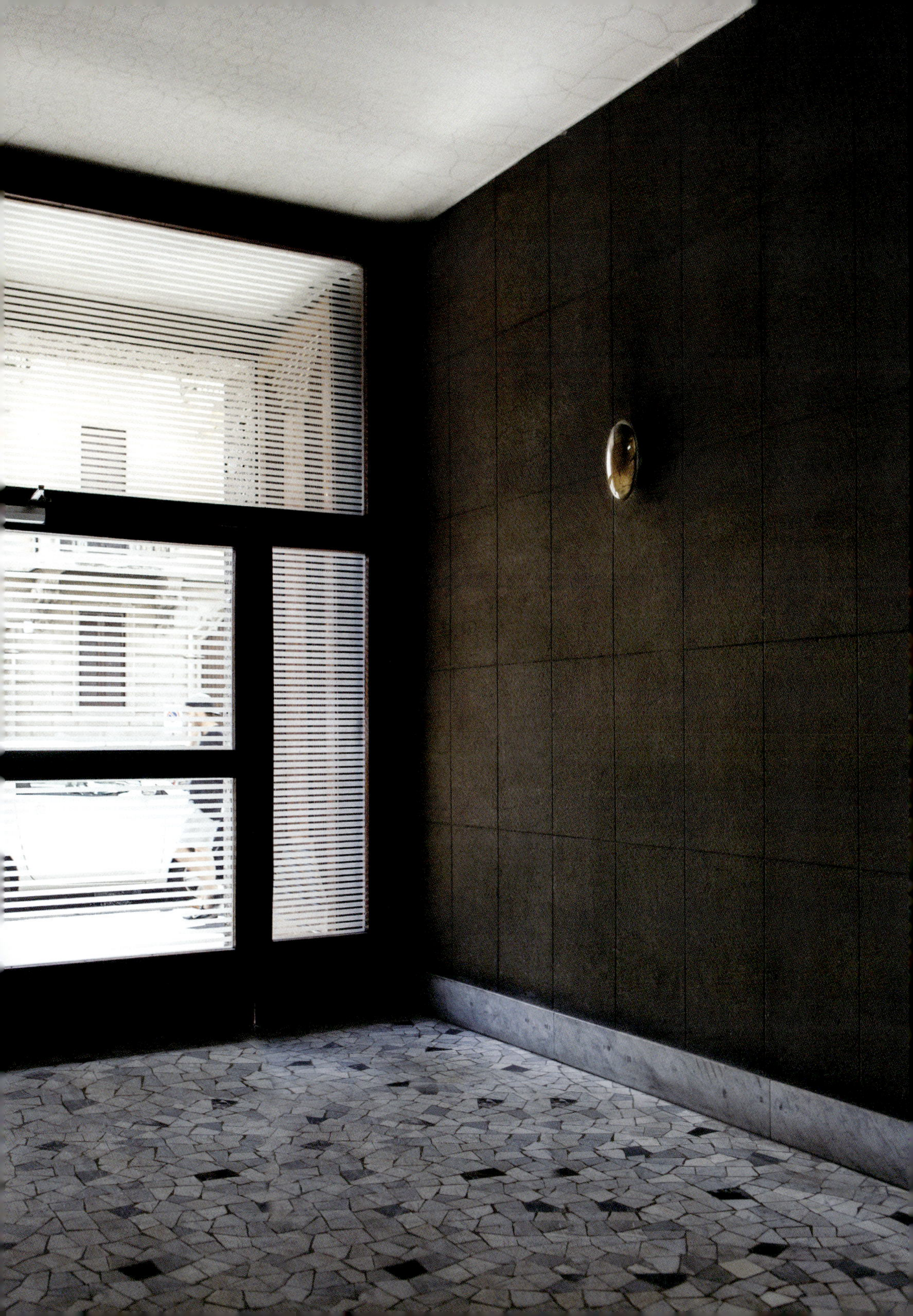

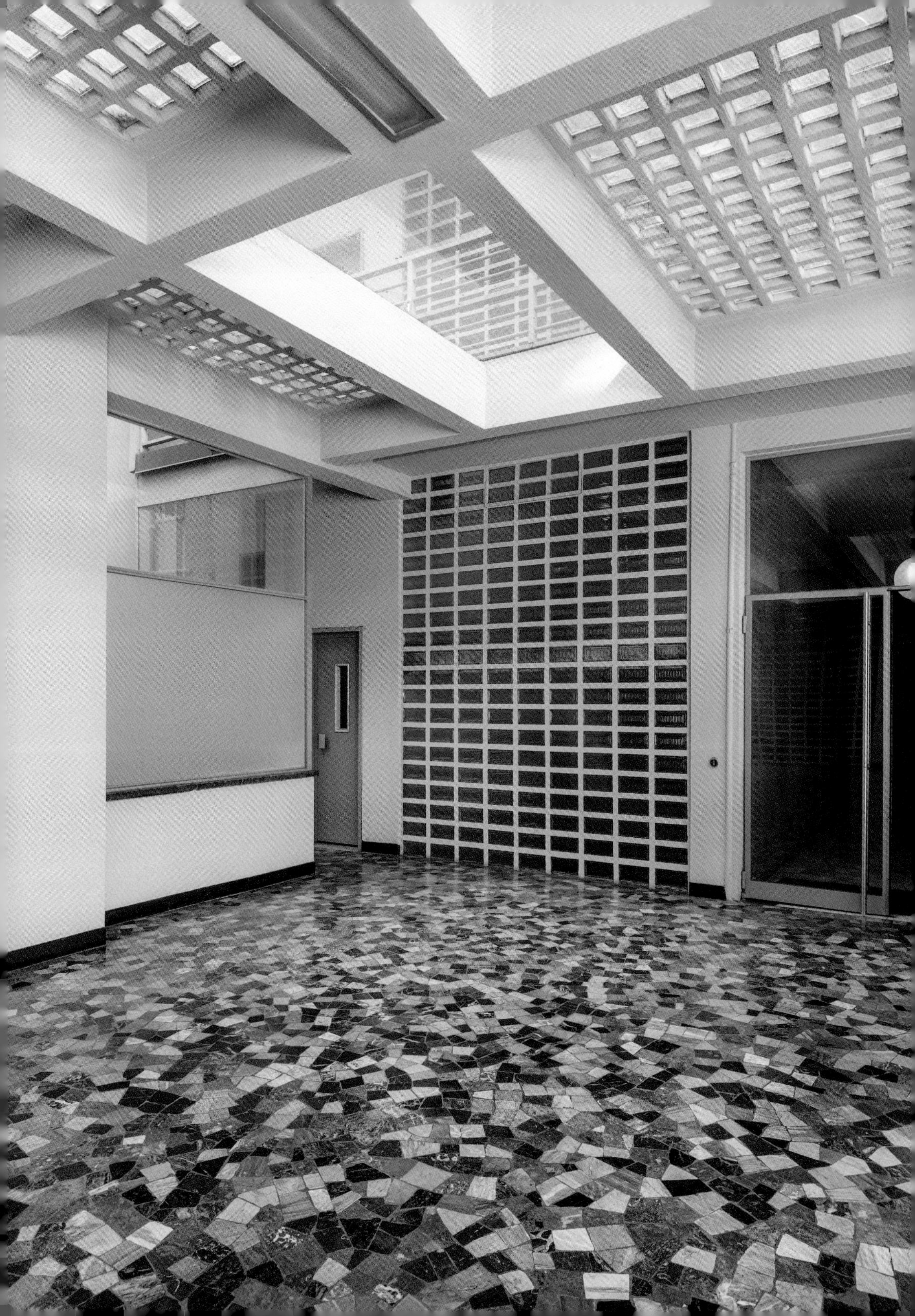

This and following spread:

corso Sempione 36, Casa Rustici · Pietro Lingeri, Giuseppe Terragni, 1934

Pendant lamp by Venini.

floor: Palladiana of several marbles and limestones *(page 295)*

floor: Carrara Statuario Venato marble

Another seminal work that represents a very different position in northern Italian modernism is the highly rigorous work of Giuseppe Terragni. Italy's preeminent Rationalist architect introduced his ideas of mystical geometries into a domestic realm in this large apartment block. The central entrance and lateral hallways are reduced to exacting volumes, derived from Terragni's investigations of the ancient Golden Section. The materials are kept simple, without recourse to decoration, save the terrazzo in the middle-room floor. Here the space is flooded with natural light through a complex ceiling, arranged in large gridded sections that are in turn embedded with smaller gridded glass blocks. The lateral hallways are delicately spectacular. There Terragni relies almost entirely on proportions and materials to articulate the pared-down environment surfaced in black, white, and gray marble panels. Gold also appears among other metal details, in a solitary pendant that beams a soft artificial glow from a Murano opaline glass sphere.

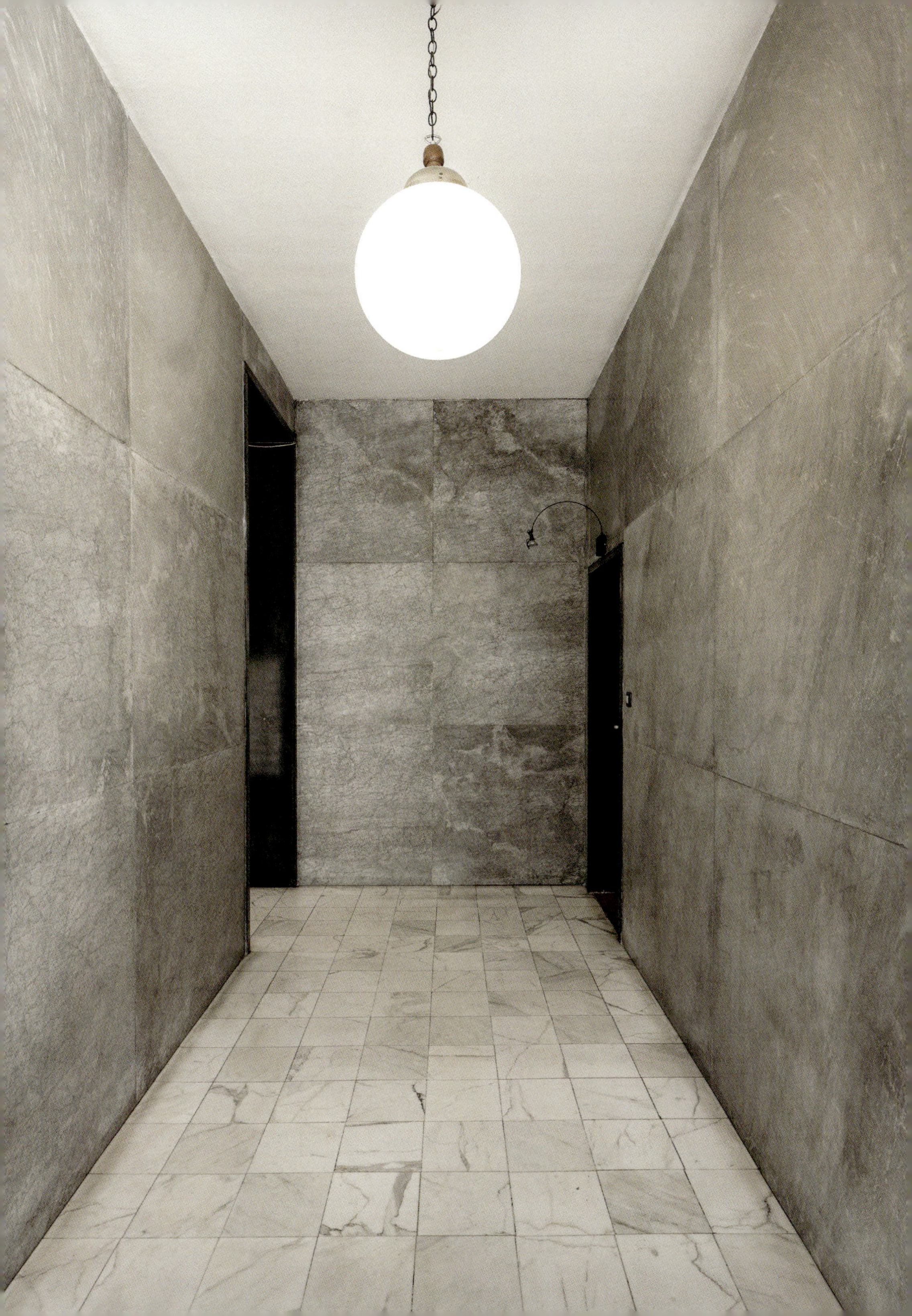

via Francesco Ferrucci 6 · Giovanni Novarese, 1960–61

floor: Serizzo Ghiandone granite · stairs and walls: Breccia Aurora limestone

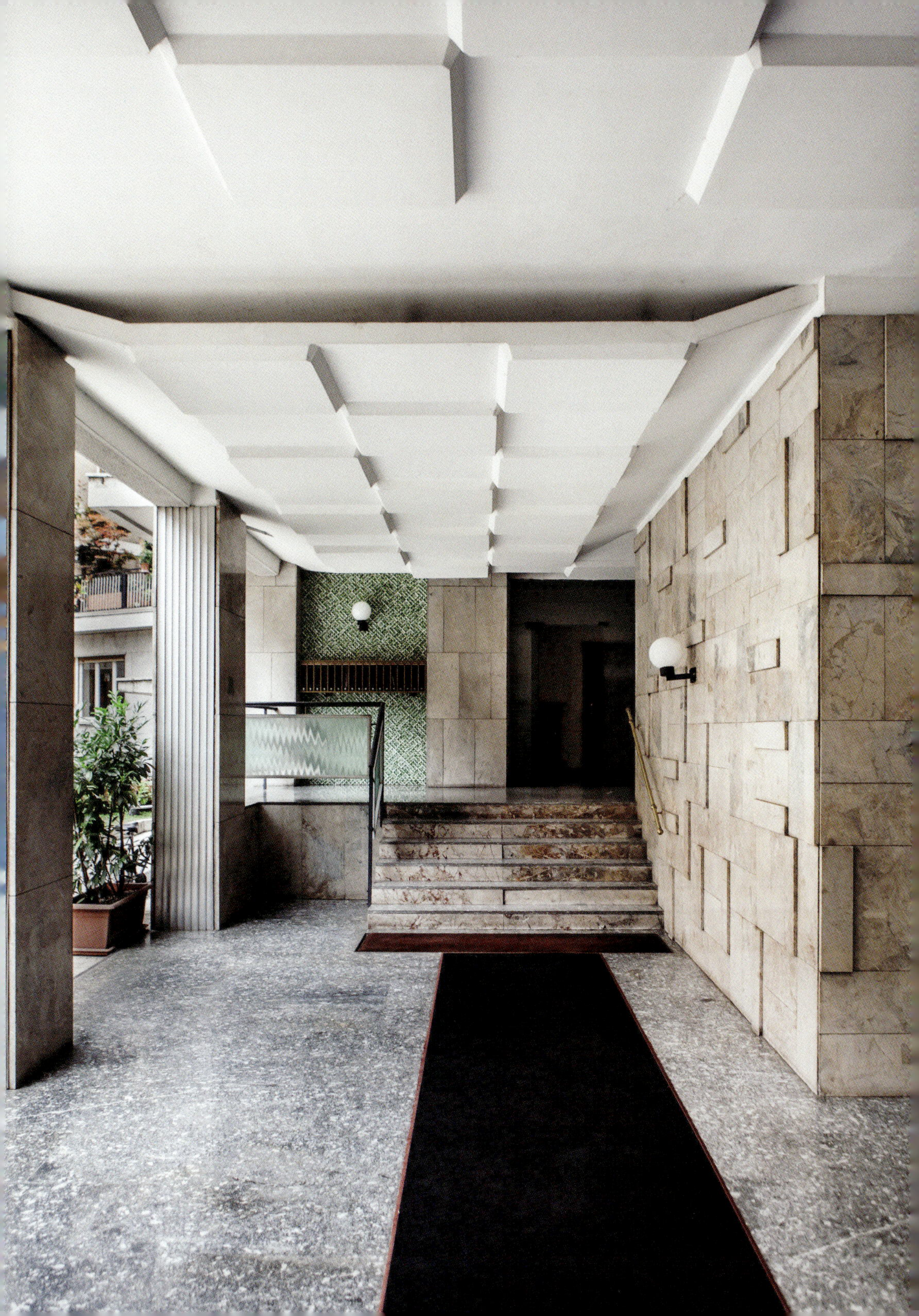

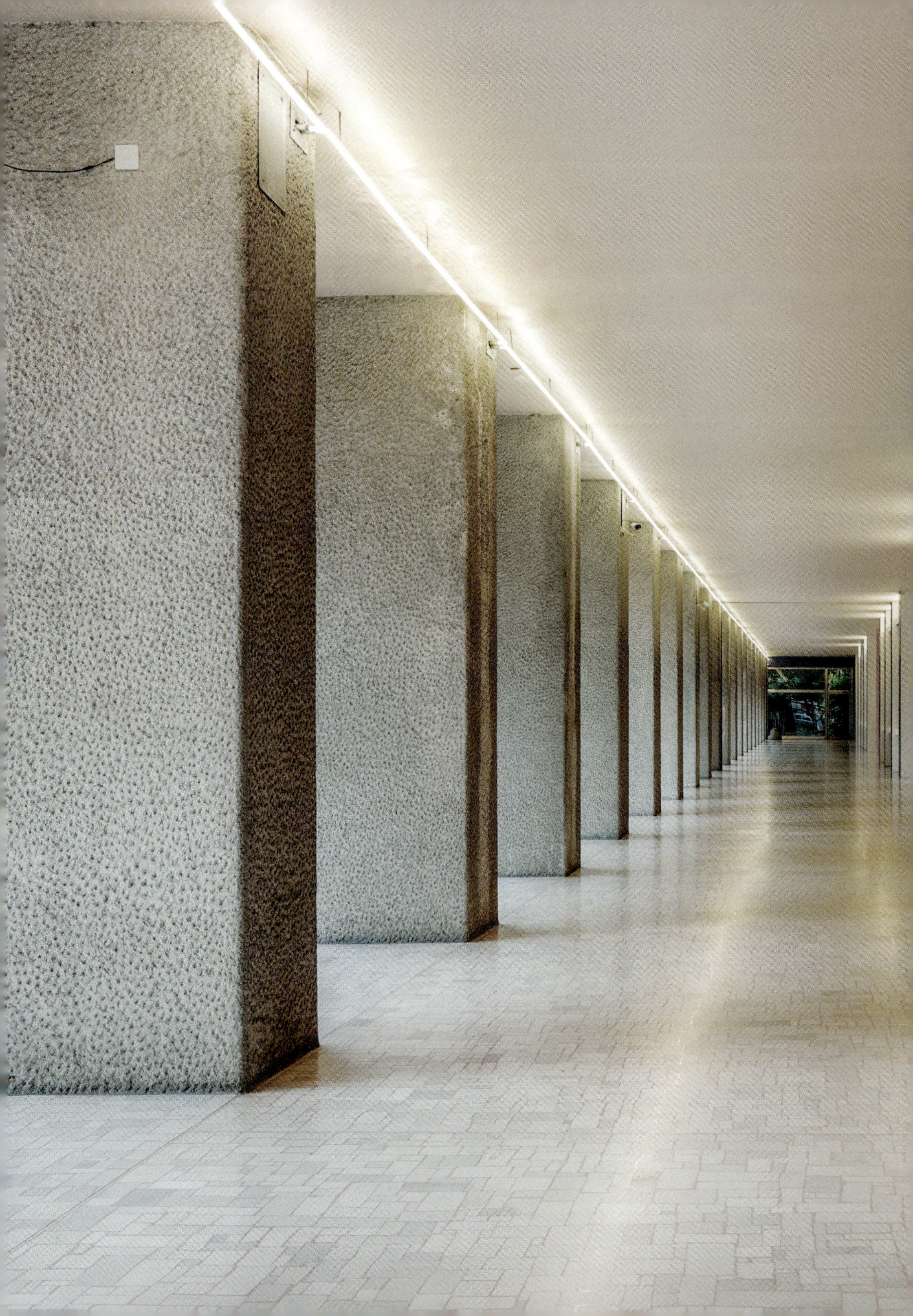

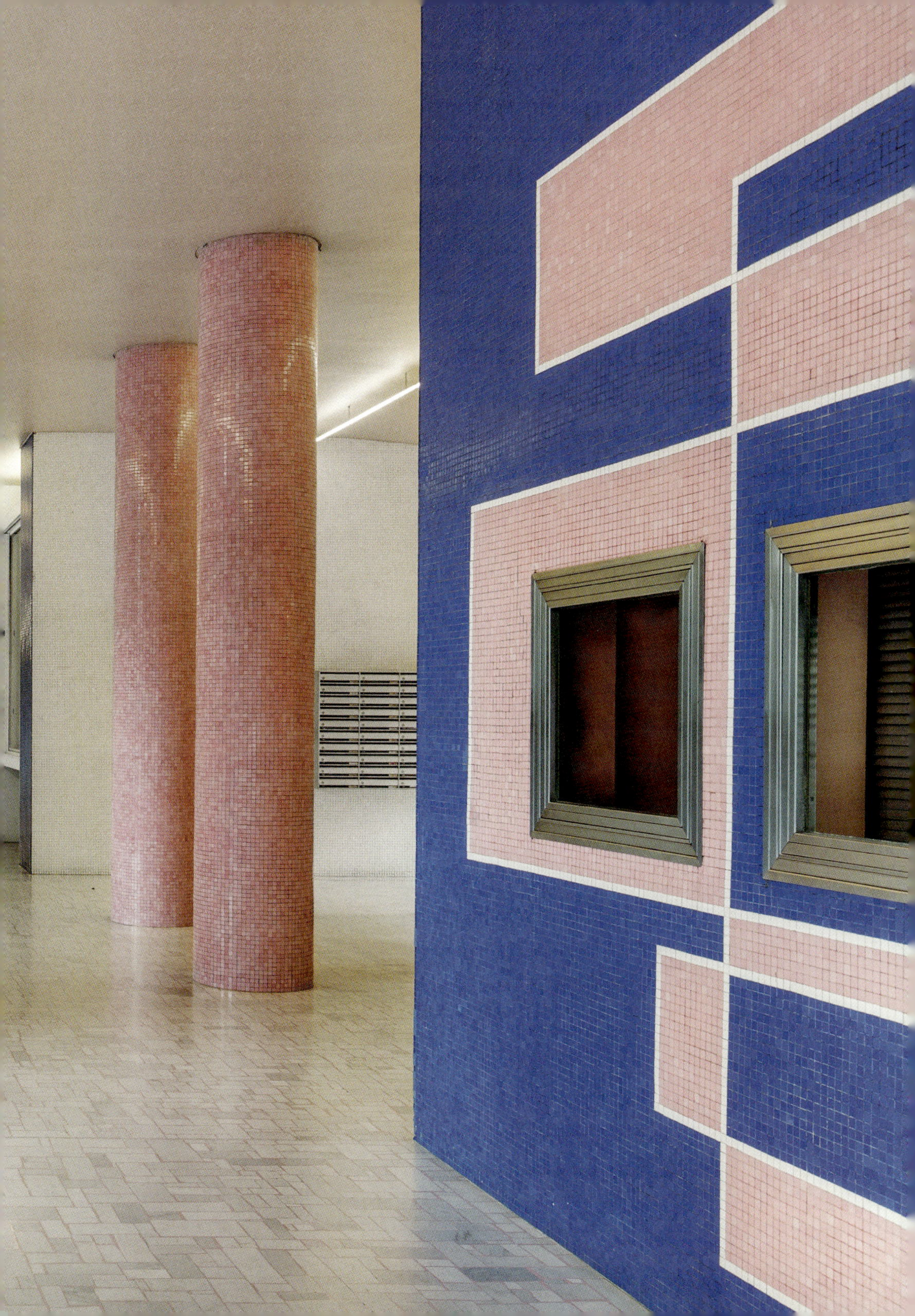

PALLADIAN FLOORING

A peculiar type of flooring that resembles mosaics and the mosaic technique, but is not a mosaic per se. Palladian flooring is created using fragments of stone slabs (of a single stone or of different types) or tiles with irregular shapes, edges, and sizes. These fragments can be installed in accordance with a specific, regular geometry, or randomly, or in simulation of specific patterns and motifs. Such floors were typical in the nineteenth and twentieth centuries, either for their beauty or because they were very cheap to install: for example, according to 1960 prices, one two-centimeter-thick slab of marble cost 2,600 lire per square meter, whereas fragments of the same type of two-centimeter-thick stone cost just 52 lire per square meter. This large difference in price has to do with the expense of manufacturing slabs on the one hand, and the abundant availability of fragments created during exploitation and manufacturing processes on the other—the fragments used in Palladian floors are industrial by-products. But what really made Palladian flooring affordable was the easy availability and low cost of highly skilled labor; from the 1970s onward, as the cost of labor grew, Palladian flooring became increasingly less economically sustainable, to the point where it is essentially no longer available.

This and previous spread:

corso Sempione 33, Palazzo Ina · Piero Bottoni, 1953–57

Wall mosaic by Piero Bottoni.

floor: geometrical and rectangular Palladiana of Bianco Carrara marble with pink joints

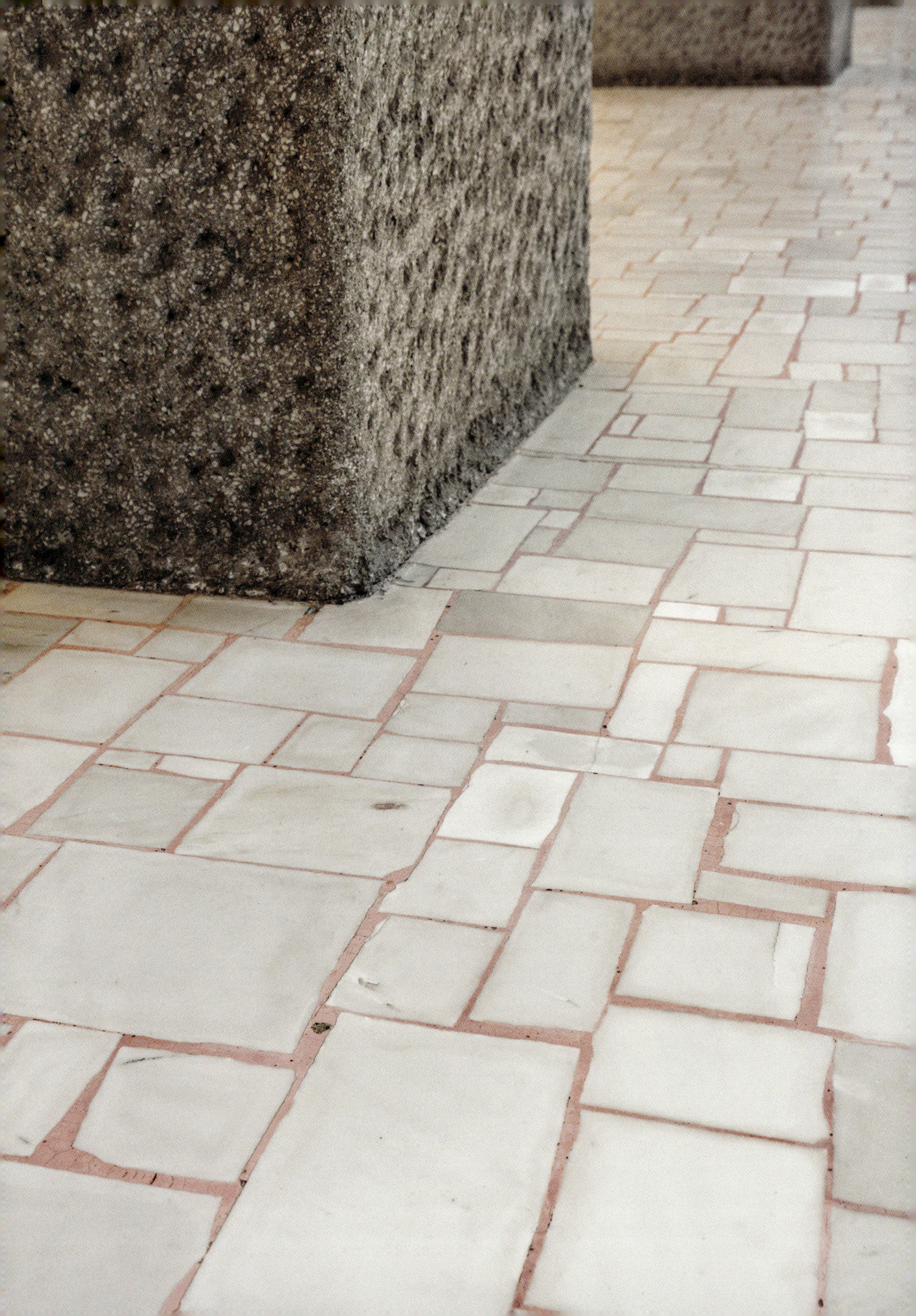

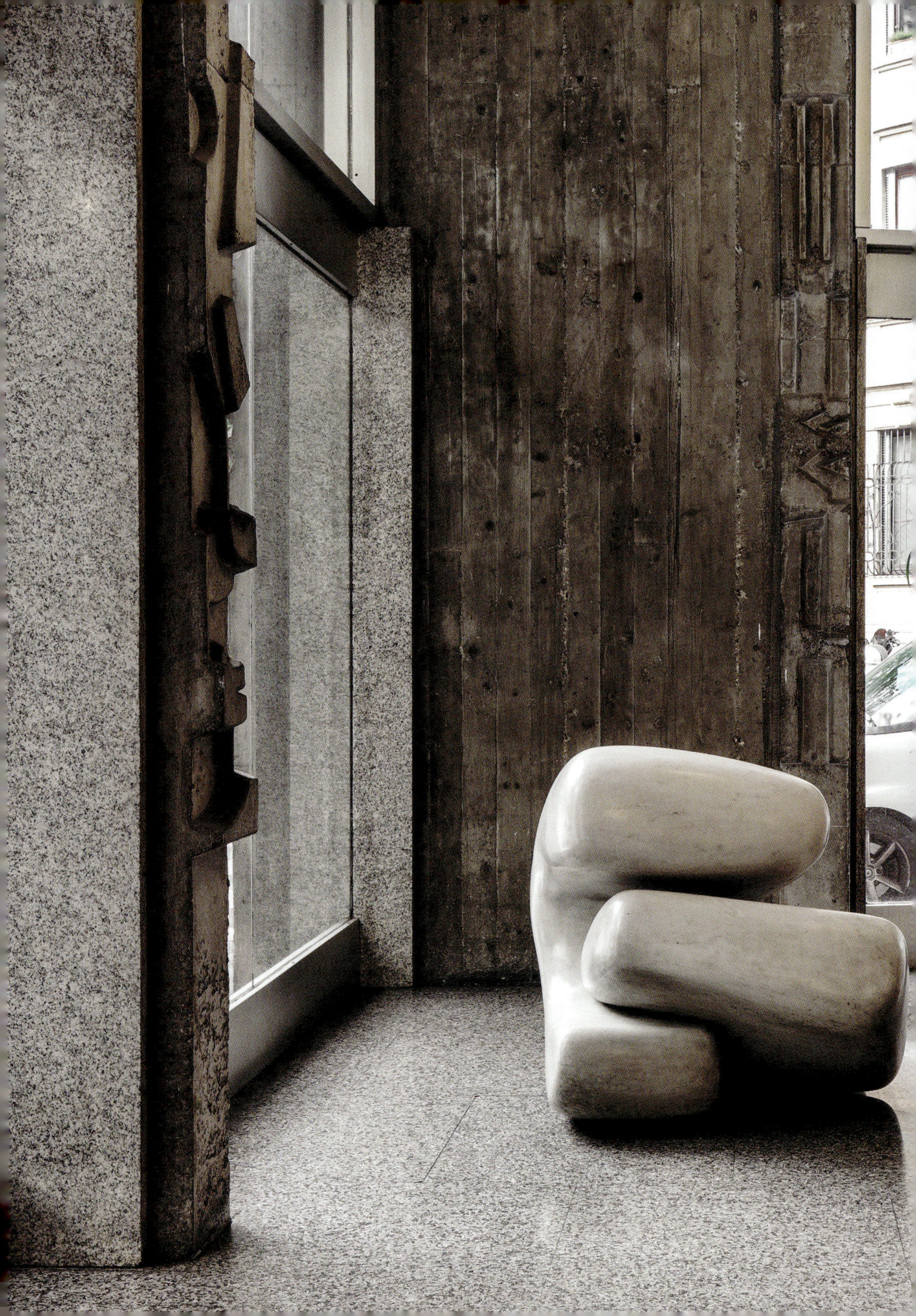

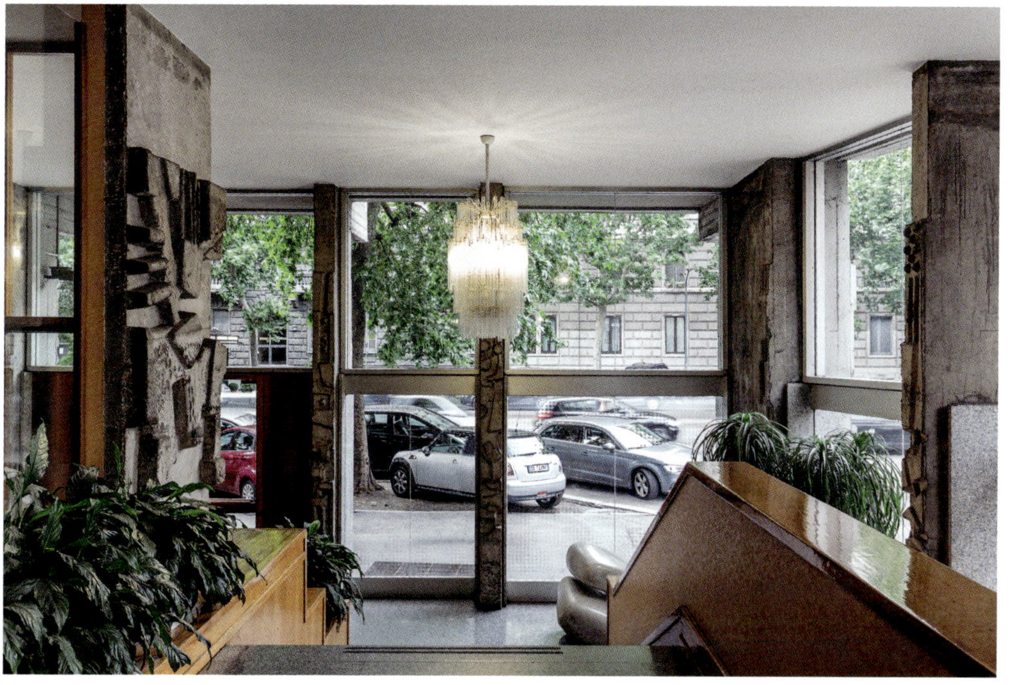

This and following spreads:
via Francesco Melzi d'Eril 29 · Ruggero Farina Morez, 1965
Cast-concrete pillars and panels and marble sculpture
Affinity *by Gino Cosentino.*
Armchairs by Osvaldo Borsani.
Chandeliers by Piero Toso for Barovier & Toso.
floor: Bianco Montorfano granite

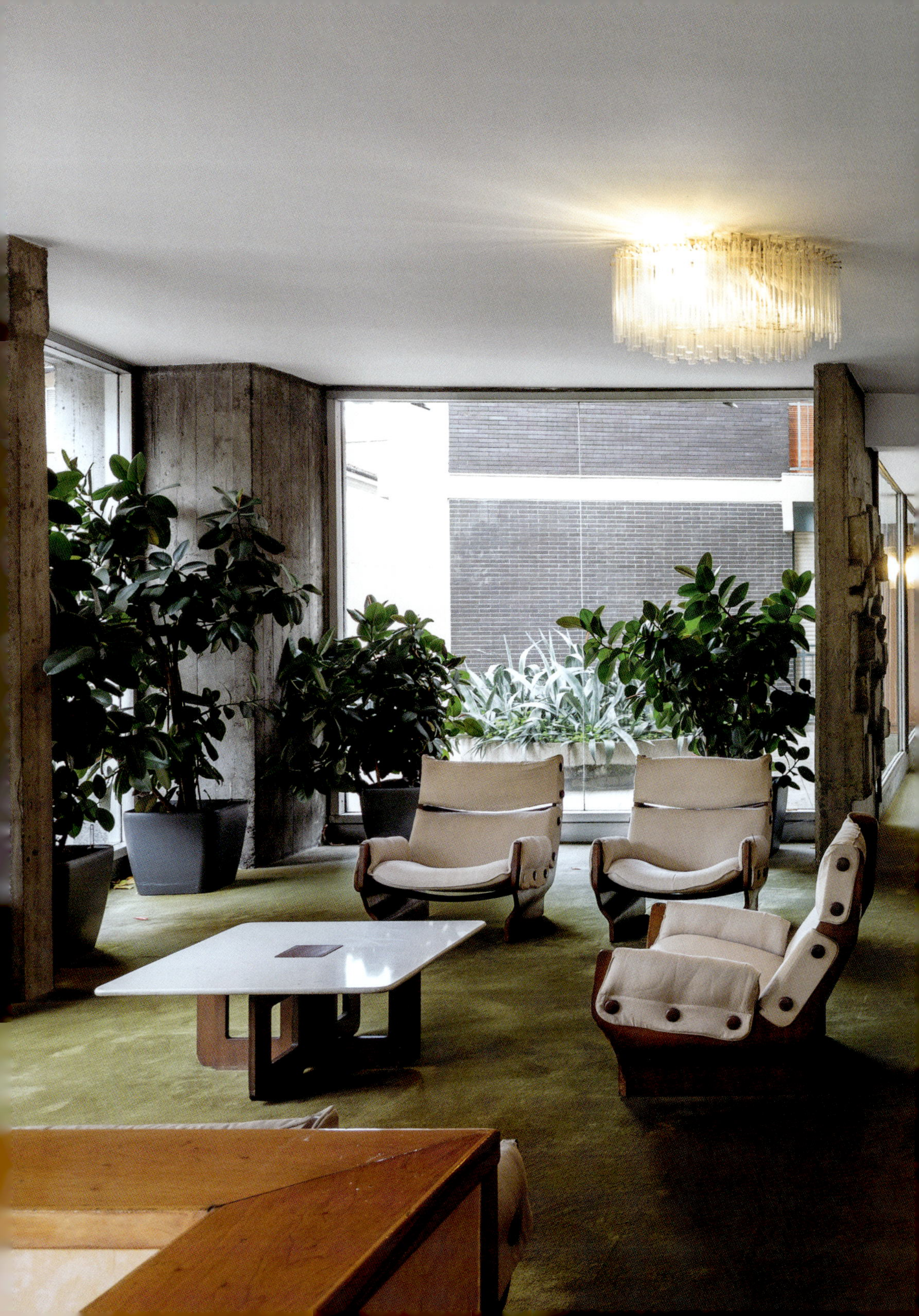

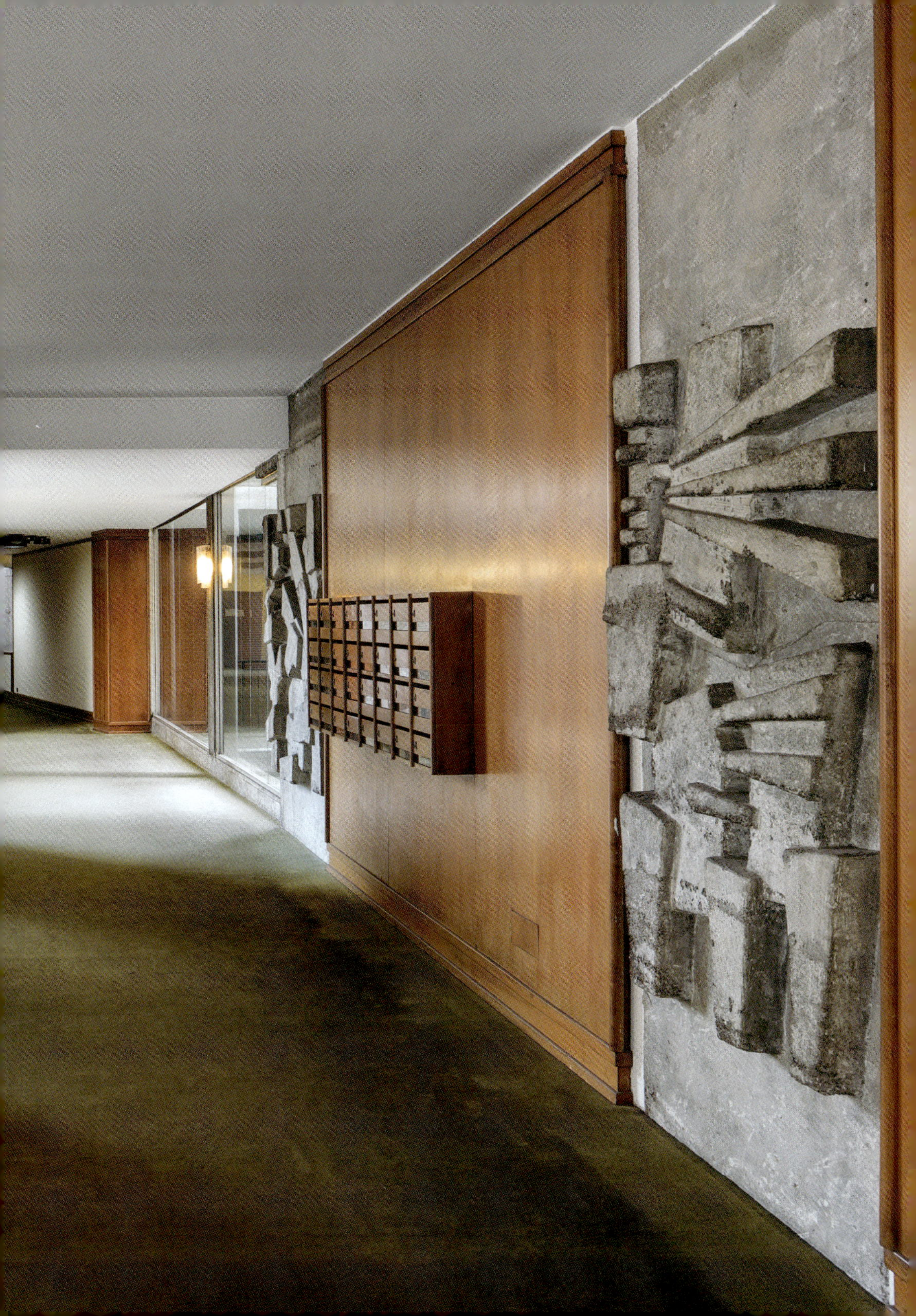

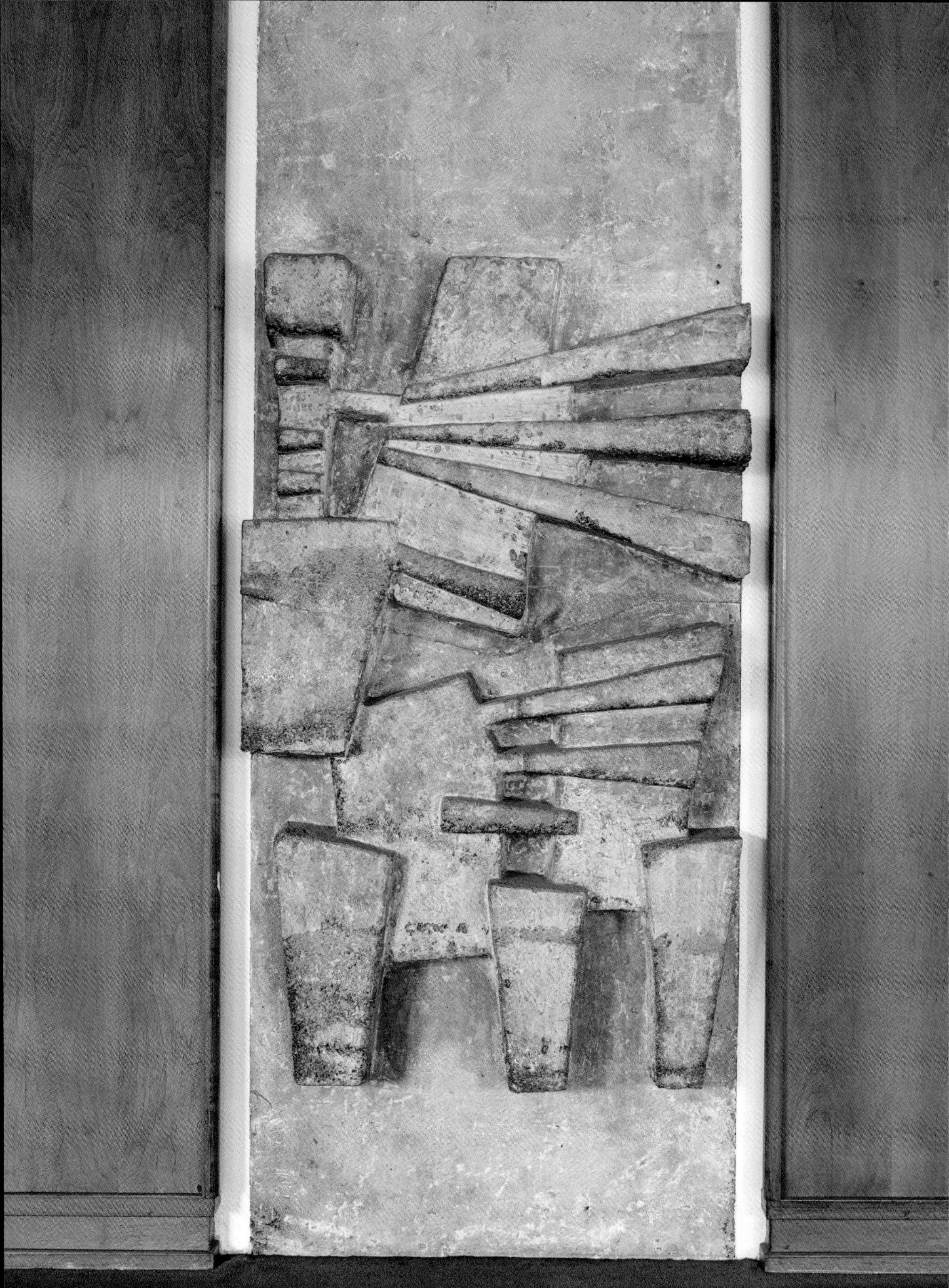

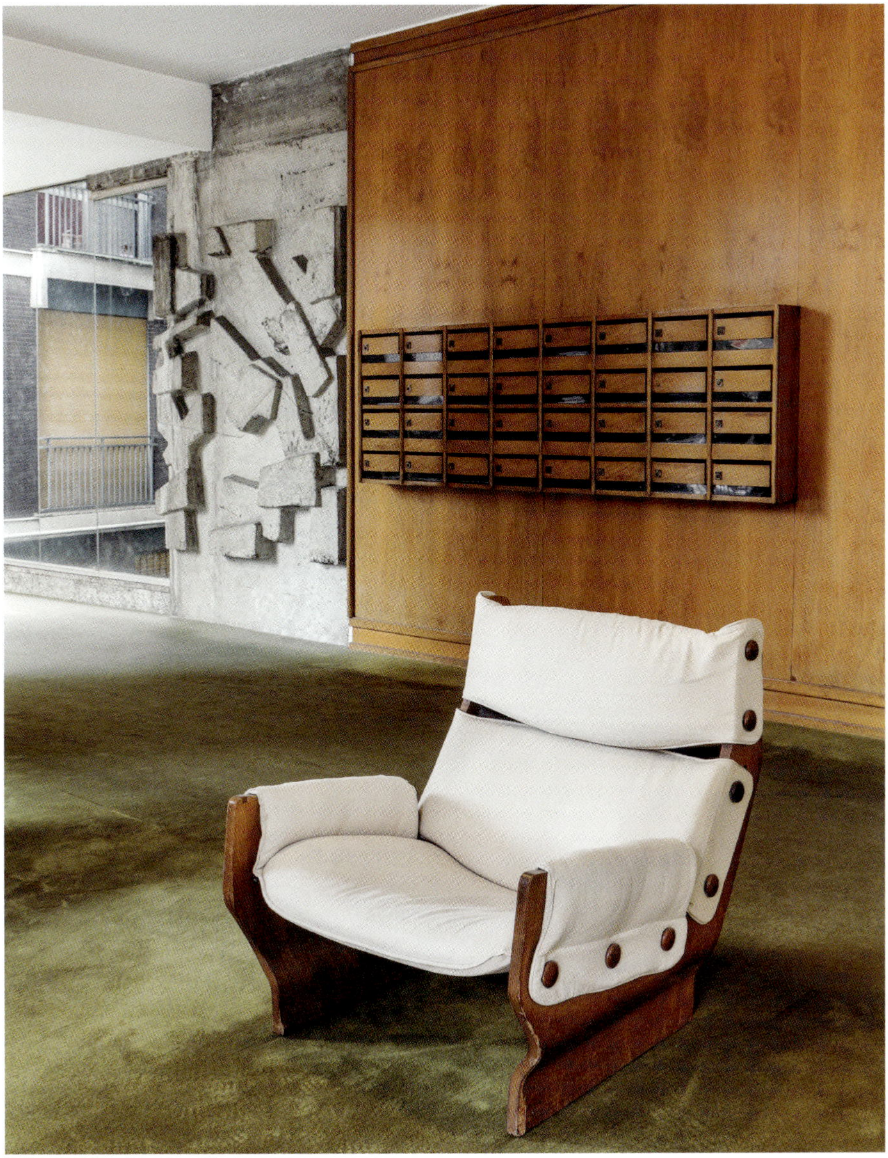

Cast-concrete panels by Gino Cosentino.
Armchair by Osvaldo Borsani.

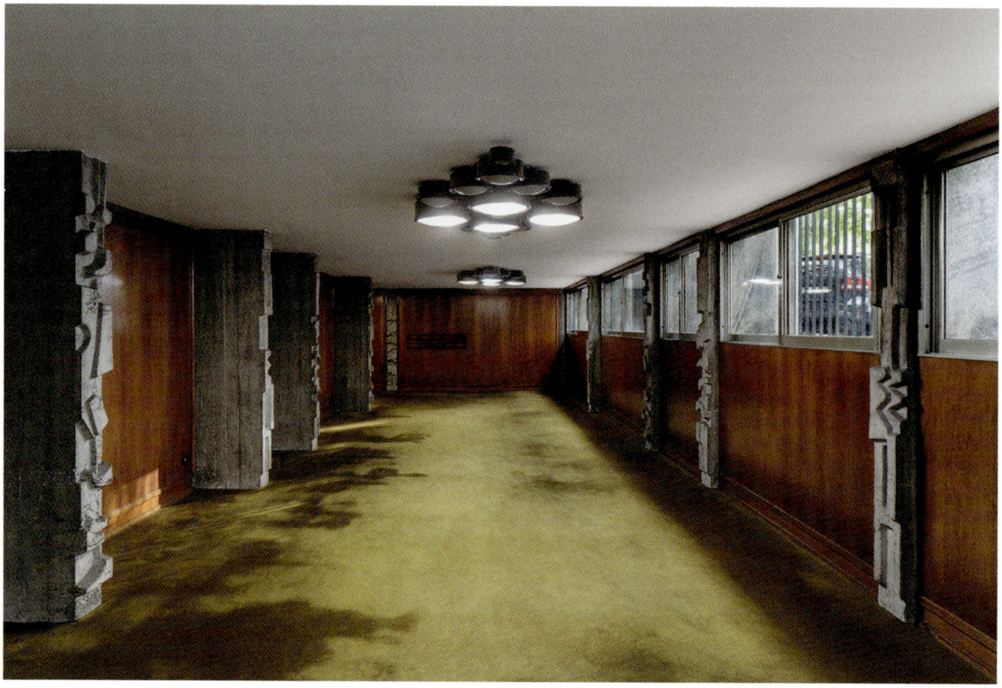

Throughout most of the twentieth century, Milan was a center for numerous manufacturers of lighting products. The architects of many of the city's buildings utilized their own designs in lighting, and this helped spur production in the growing companies. Many designs were used experimentally before entering larger production runs that were later to garner acclaim, critically and professionally. From the late 1950s, all the way to the 1970s, the city became the undisputed capital for advanced lighting design. The legacy continues in the vintage market, where museums and collectors vie for ownership of forward-thinking modern Milanese lighting.

Cast-concrete pillars by Gino Cosentino.
Ceiling lights by Studio BBPR.

Following spreads:
via Antonio Canova 39
floor: Nembro Rosato limestone · walls: Rosa Portogallo marble, New Imperial Red granite
sculpture: Bianco Carrara marble

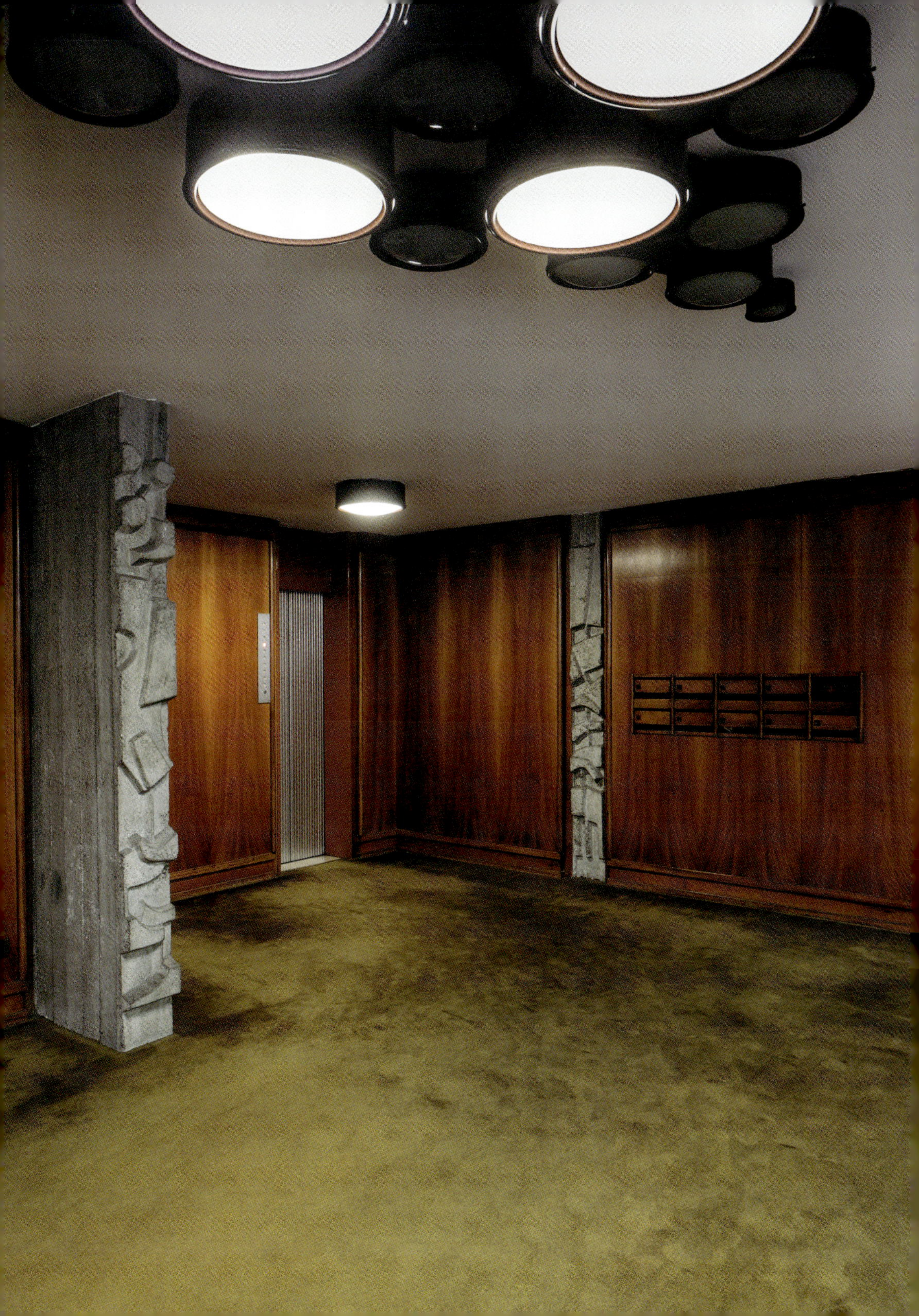

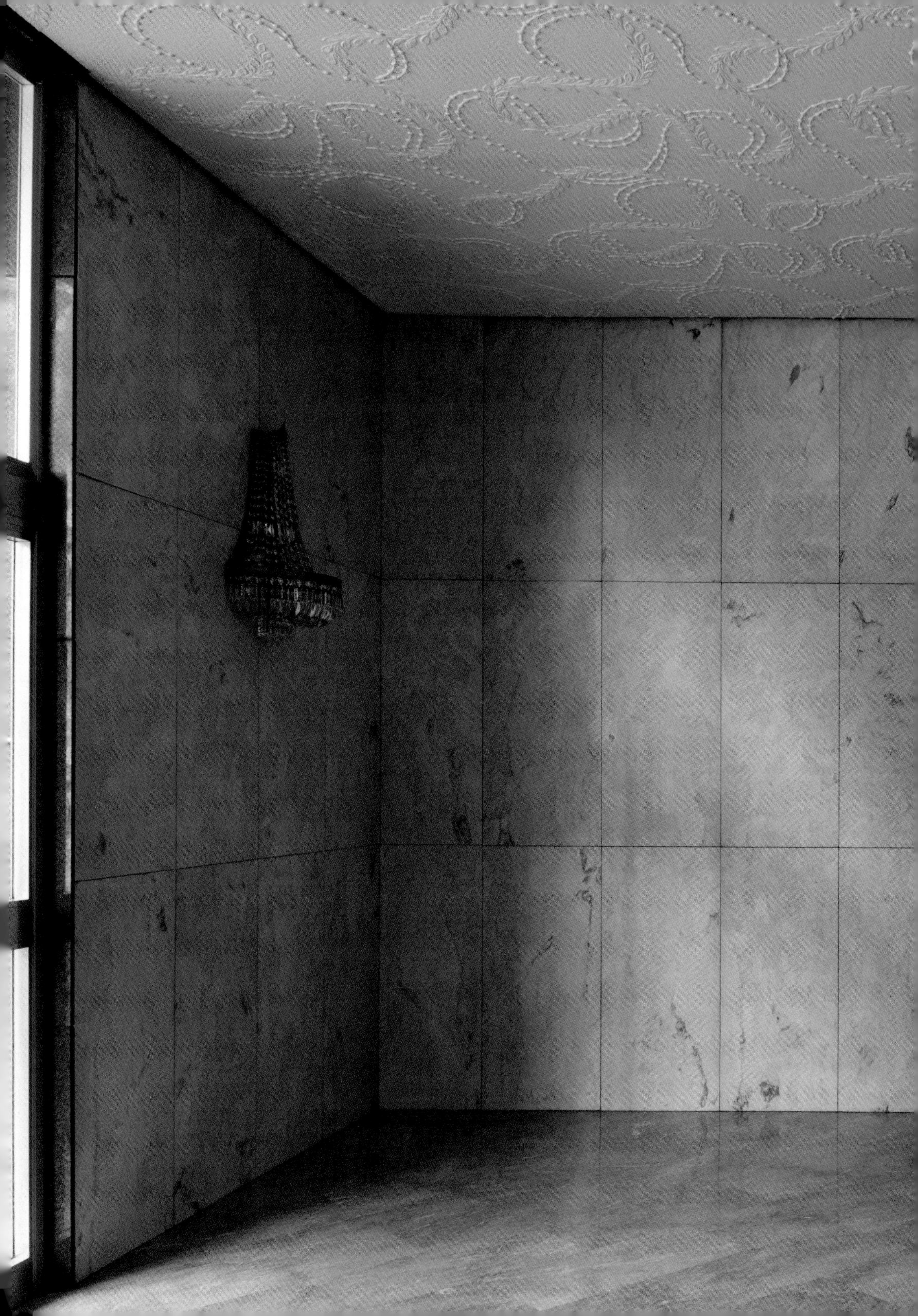

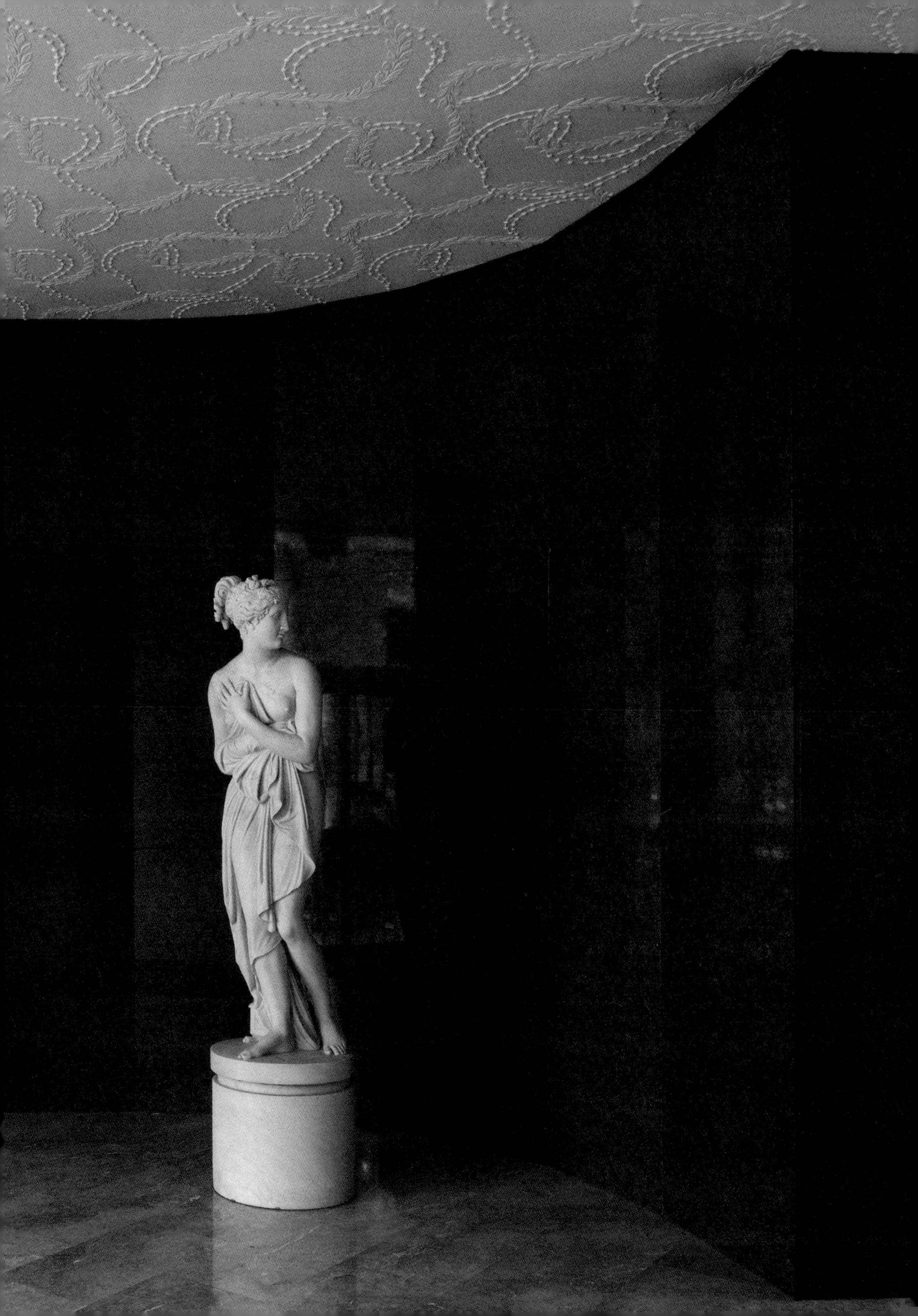

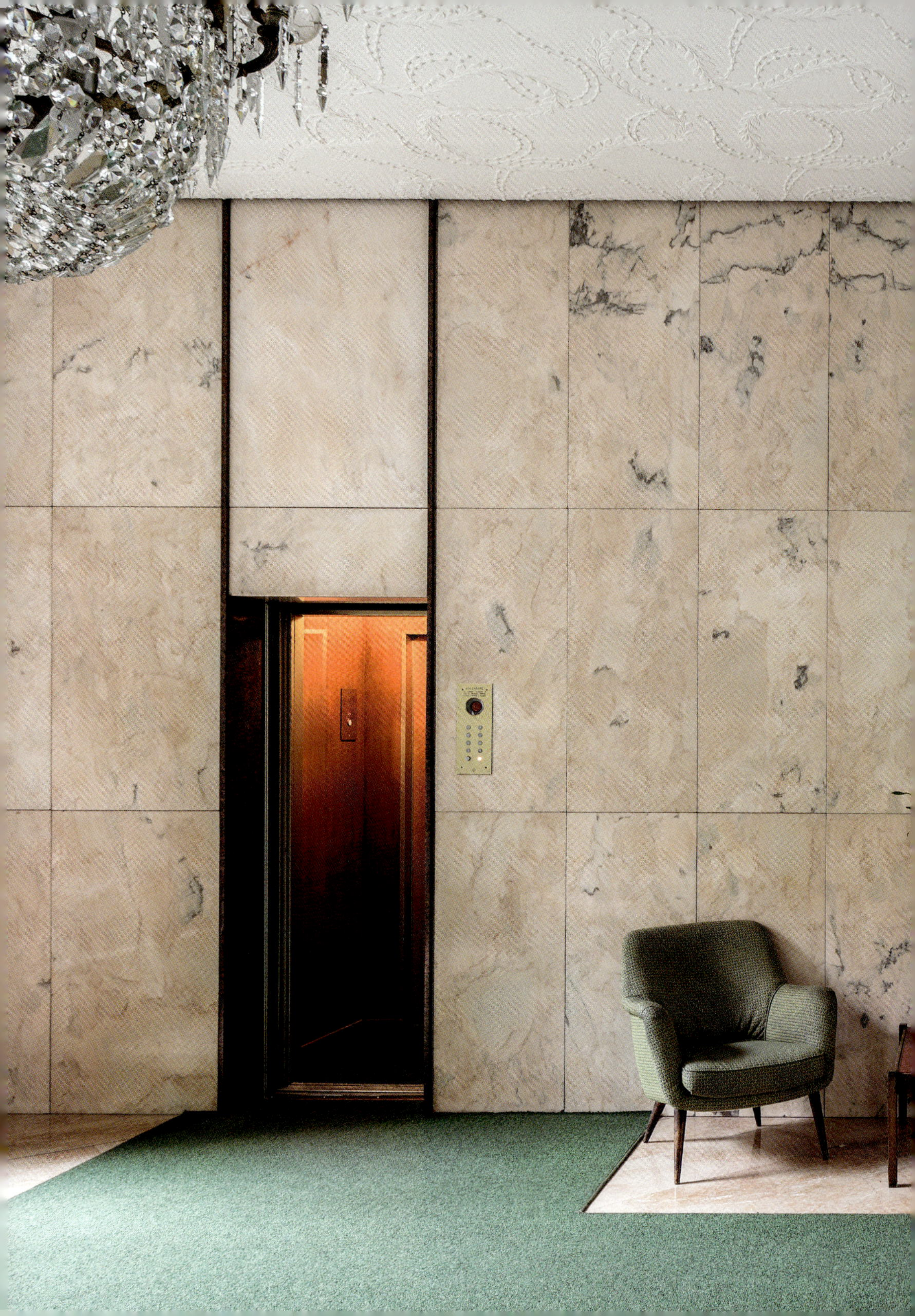

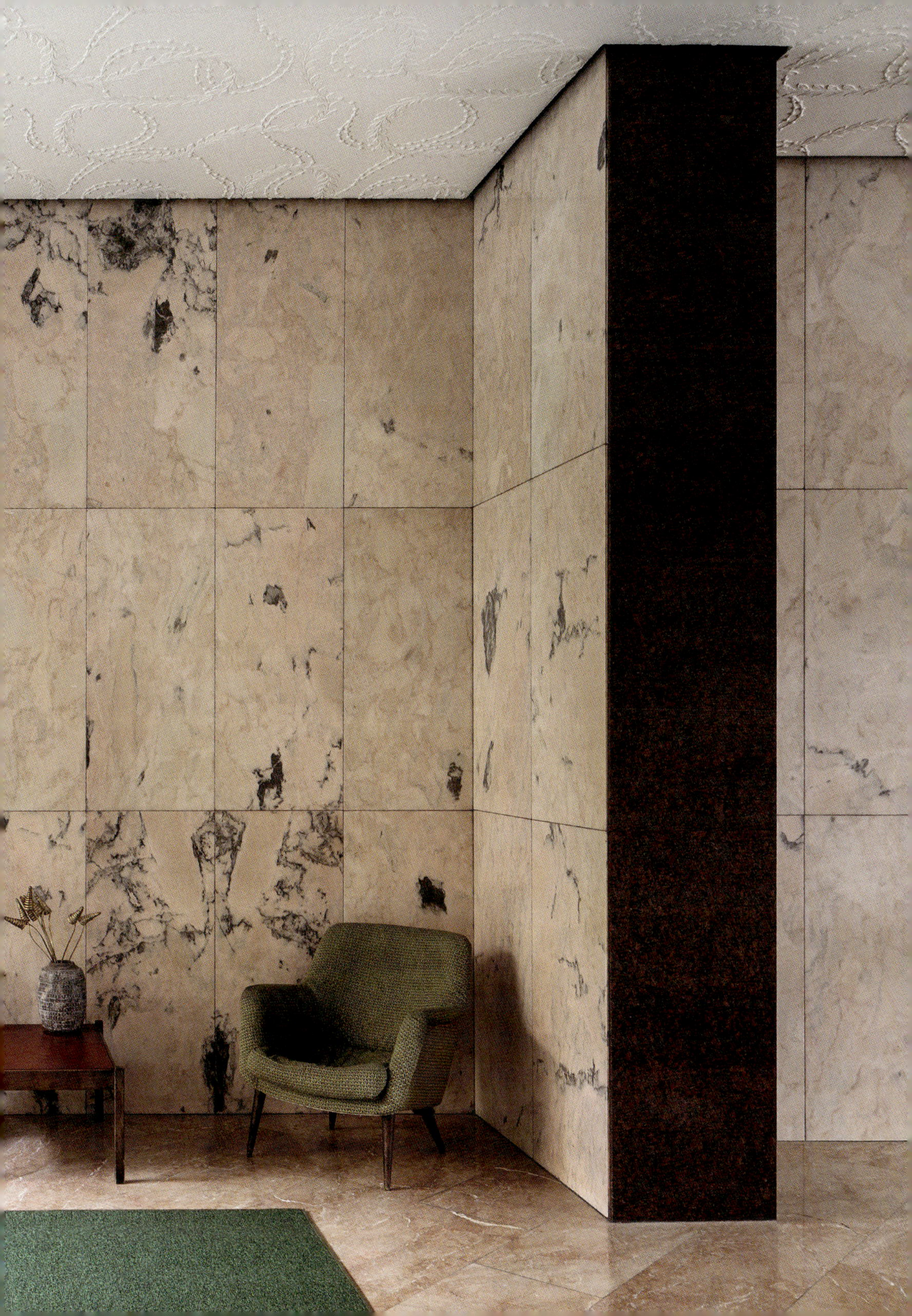

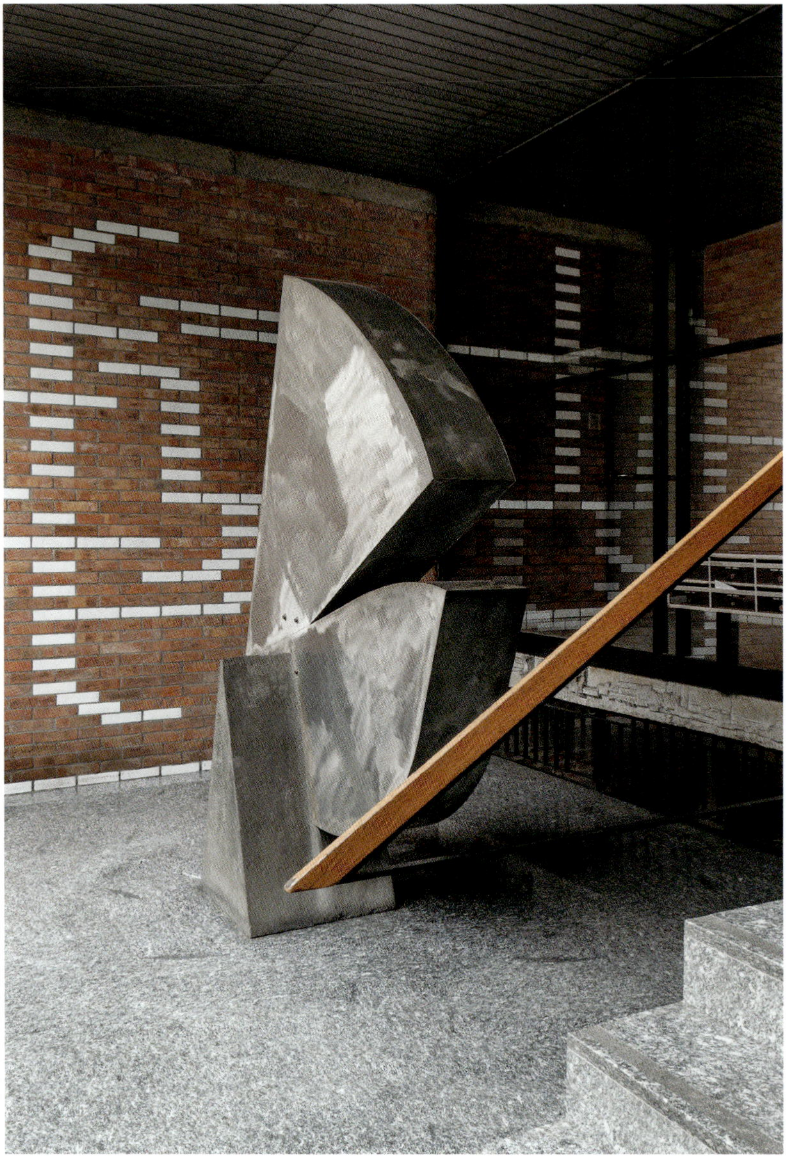

This and following spread:

via Antonio Canova 7A · Giandomenico Belotti, Sergio Invernizzi, Achille Boraschi, 1958–60

Metal and concrete sculpture by Gianfranco Pardi. Concrete reliefs by Arnoldo and Gio Pomodoro. Pendant lamps by Venini · floor and stairs: Serizzo granite

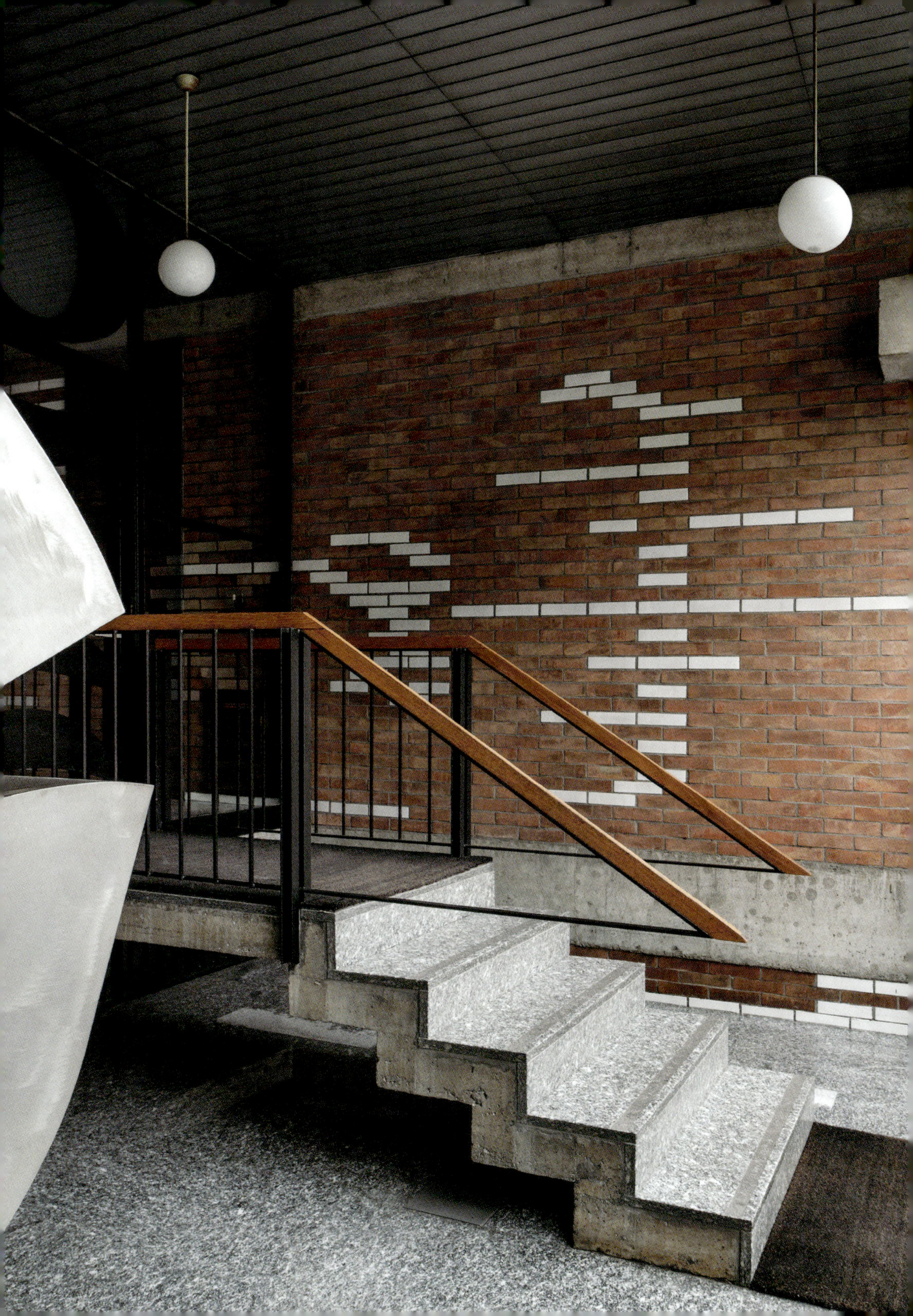

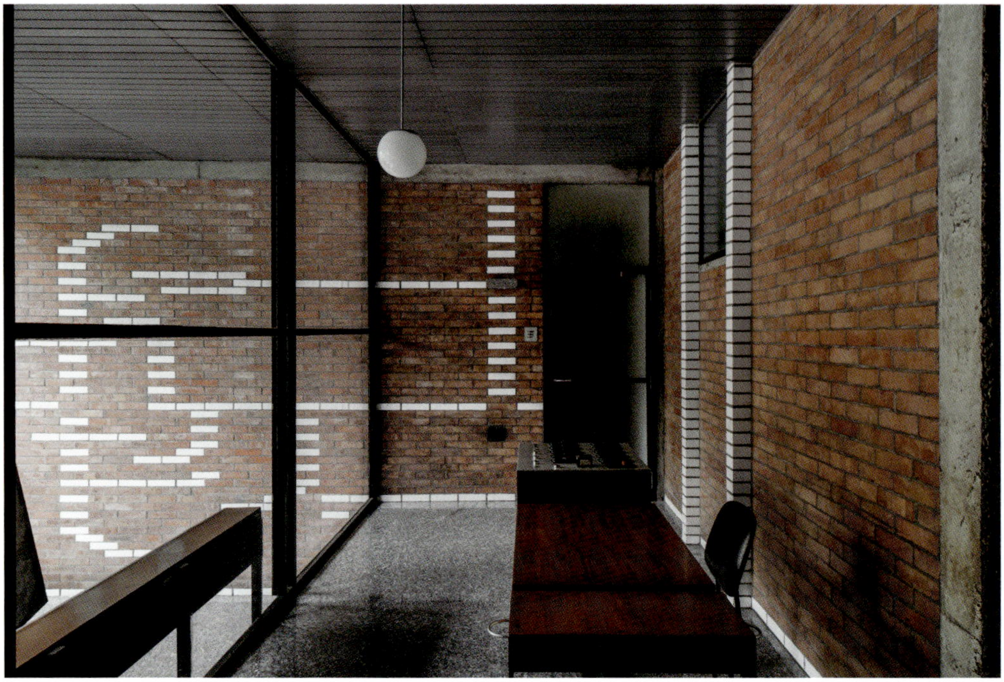

"[...] If we observe the most ancient monuments and churches of the city, we discover that Milan was a city built in 'bricks': red brickwork, in fact, dominates in the remains of the Roman city, in the medieval walls and in the façades of the Romanesque churches" (Veneranda Fabbrica del Duomo di Milano). The return of red brick as surface decoration for interior entrances begins in the late 1950s and reemerges on a larger scale in the 1970s. Here it is punctuated with seemingly random intervals of white glazed bricks. This entrance, along with the some elements of the building façade, is laden with the artwork of no less than three artists. In spite of being so numerous, the individual contributions stand well on their own. A paradoxical unity is achieved in the repertory of materials and surface textures that add up to a high point of Milanese architecture and art of its time; one that remains today as a testimonial of a creative period that emerged in reaction to the quest for synthesis that characterized the prewar period.

Door sculpture by Gio Pomodoro.
Pendant lamps by Venini.

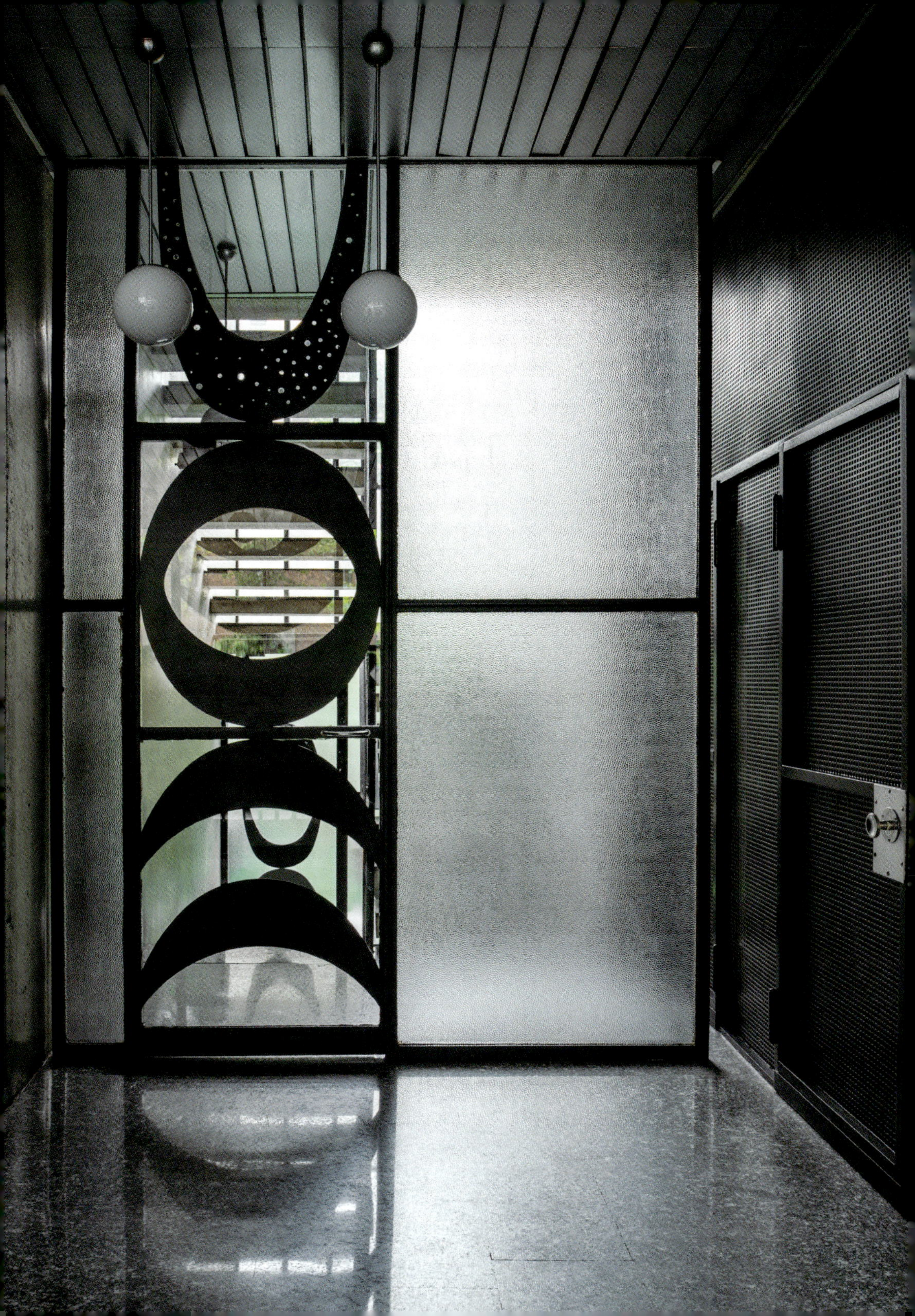

This and following spread:

via Giovanni Randaccio 9 · Gio Ponti, Emilio Lancia, 1925

Bronze sconces by Gio Ponti.

Large ornamental garden stoneware vases in flowing glaze by Gio Ponti for Manifattura Richard Ginori.

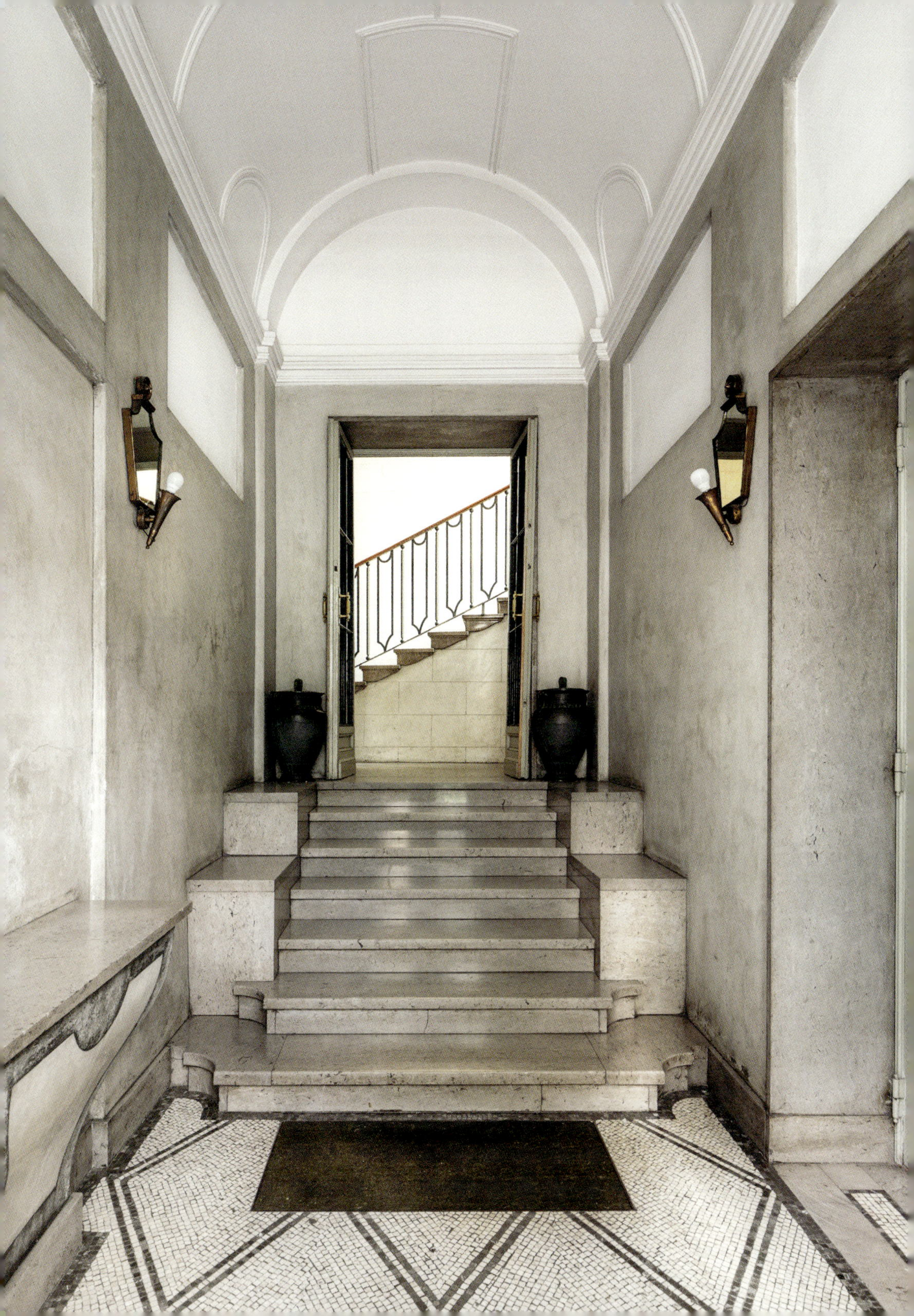

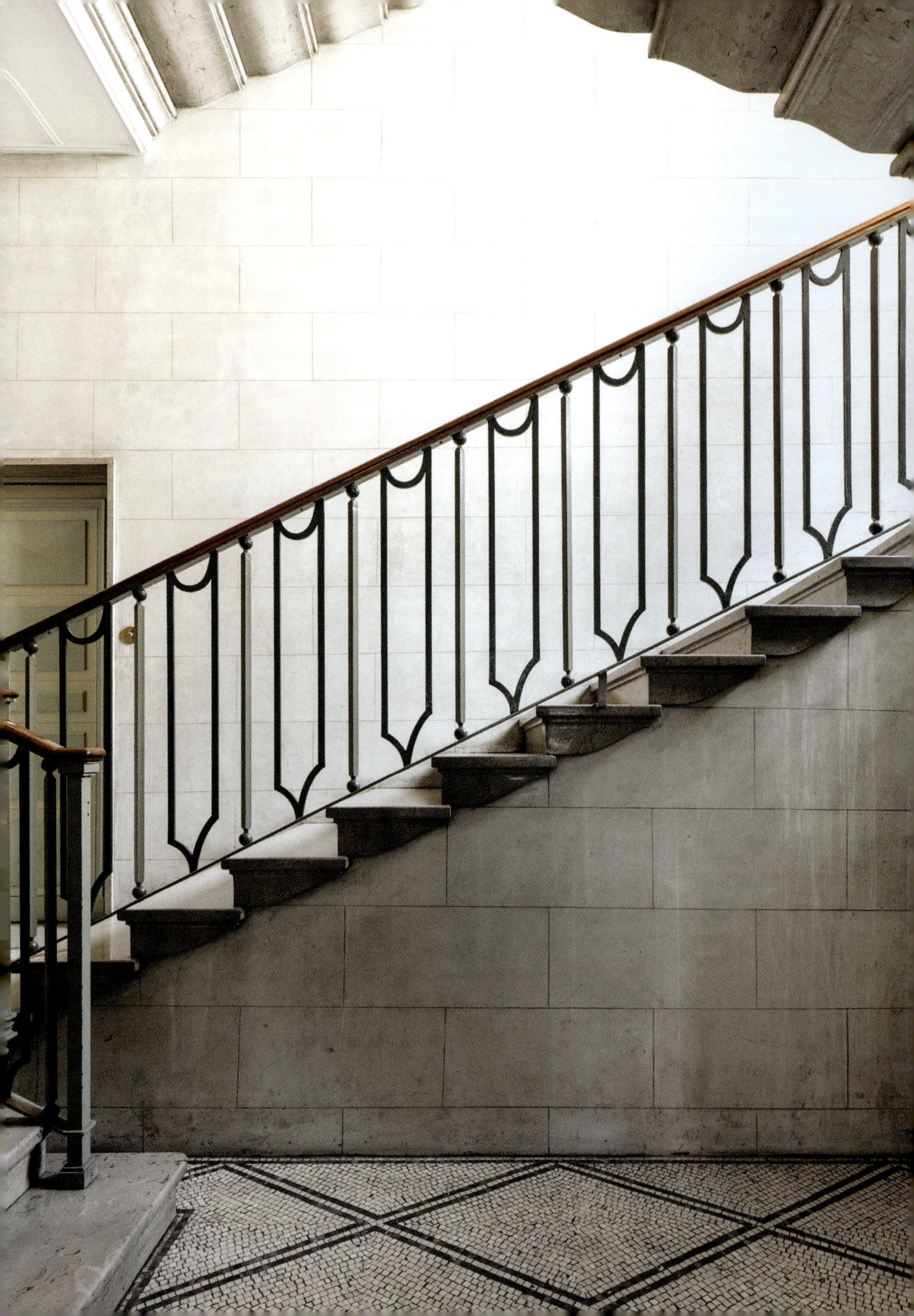

Designed in 1925, this is Gio Ponti's very first building. It shows the young architect with his own light, poetic touch at work in the then emerging Novecento idiom, which had been initiated in Milan by Giovanni Muzio. The façade with its obelisks and broken pediments is reminiscent of Galeazzo Alessi, a sixteenth-century Mannerist architect who introduced such elements into some of his best-known Milanese buildings. The interior is more restrained yet also plays with Mannerist codes: the stair risers are profiled to mimic cornices, while what appears to be bronze urns flanking the entrance portal are in fact ceramic pieces among many that Ponti designed at that time for large-scale production by the Richard Ginori china factory. In addition, the cartouche-shaped sconces later served as prototypes for some Fontana Arte production lines in the 1930s.

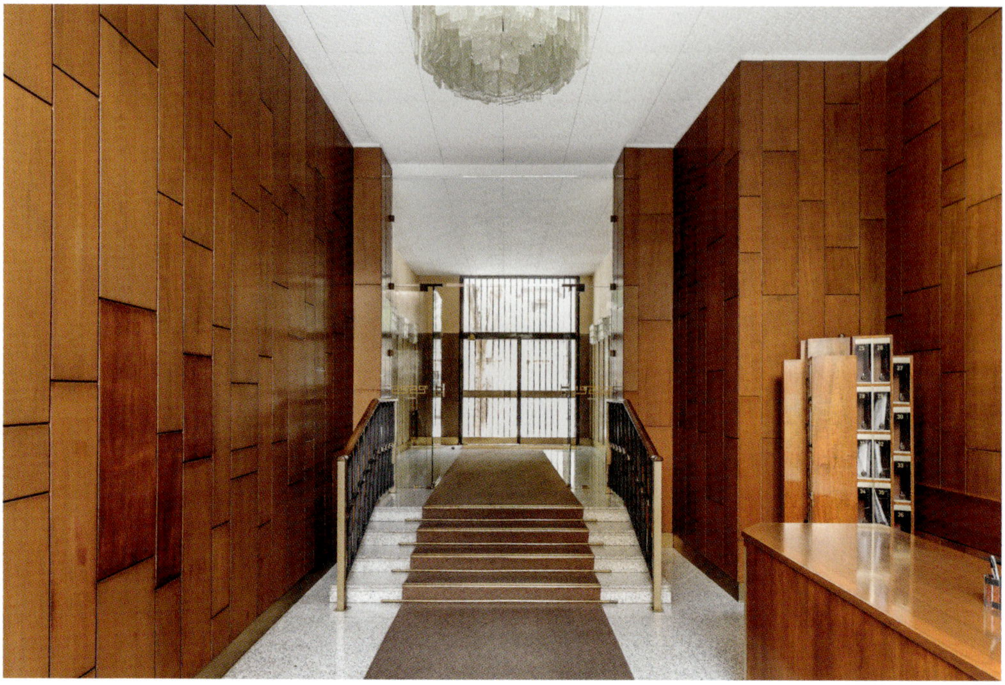

via Vincenzo Monti 41 · Luigi Mattioni, 1968

Murano chandelier and sconces by Mazzega.
Freestanding rotating mailbox by Luigi Mattioni.
floor: Bianco Montorfano granite

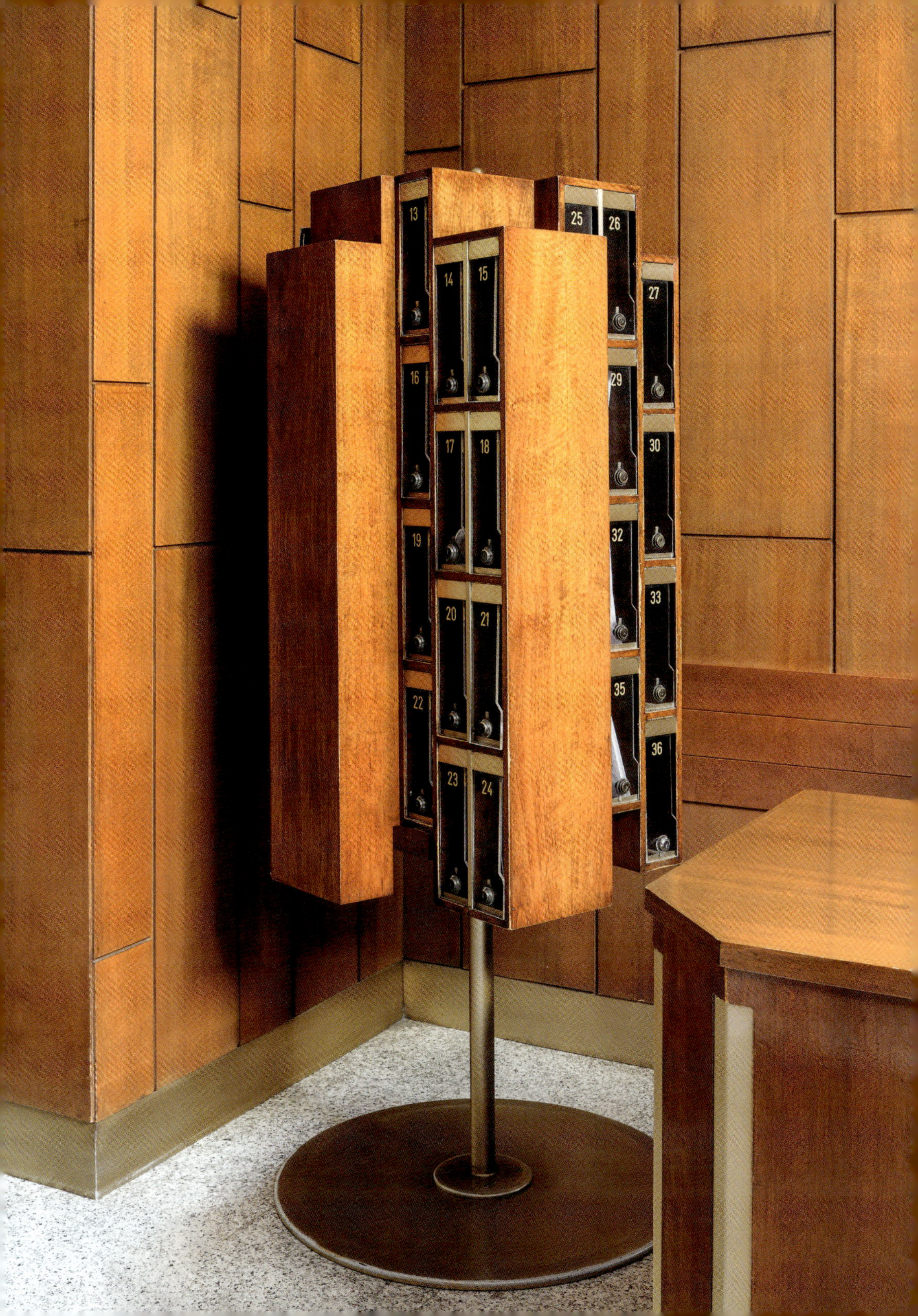
13
14
15
16
17
18
19
20
21
22
23
24
25
26
27
29
30
32
33
35
36

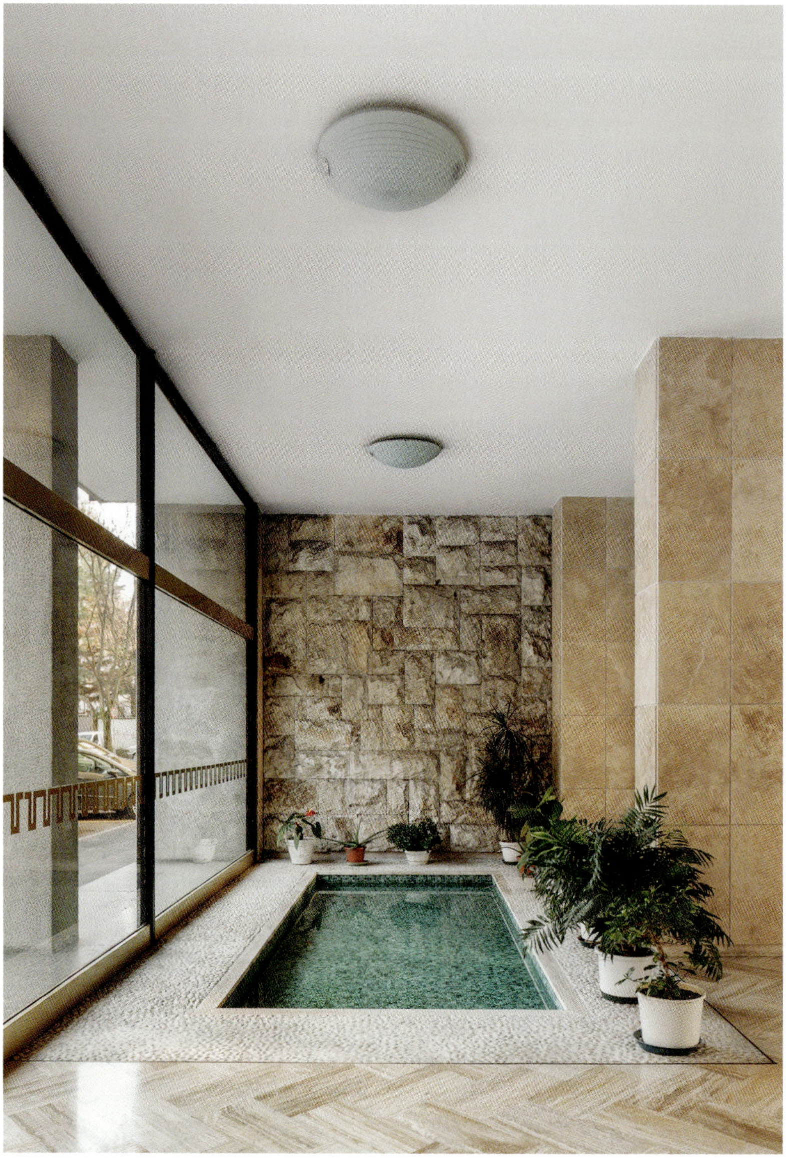

via Giacomo Griziotti 1

Ceramic tiles by Gio Ponti for Ceramica Joo.
floor: travertine · wall: travertine boulders

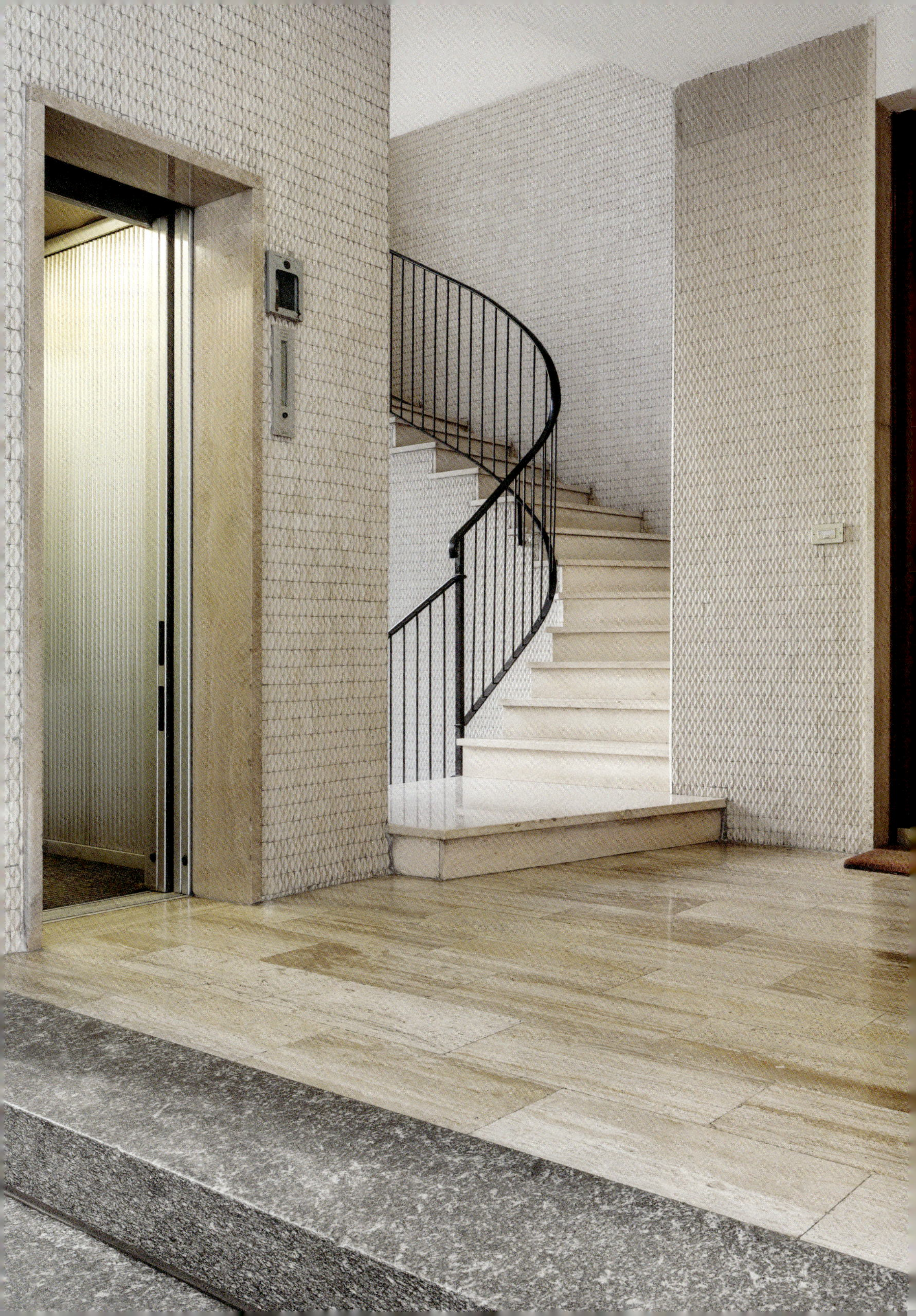

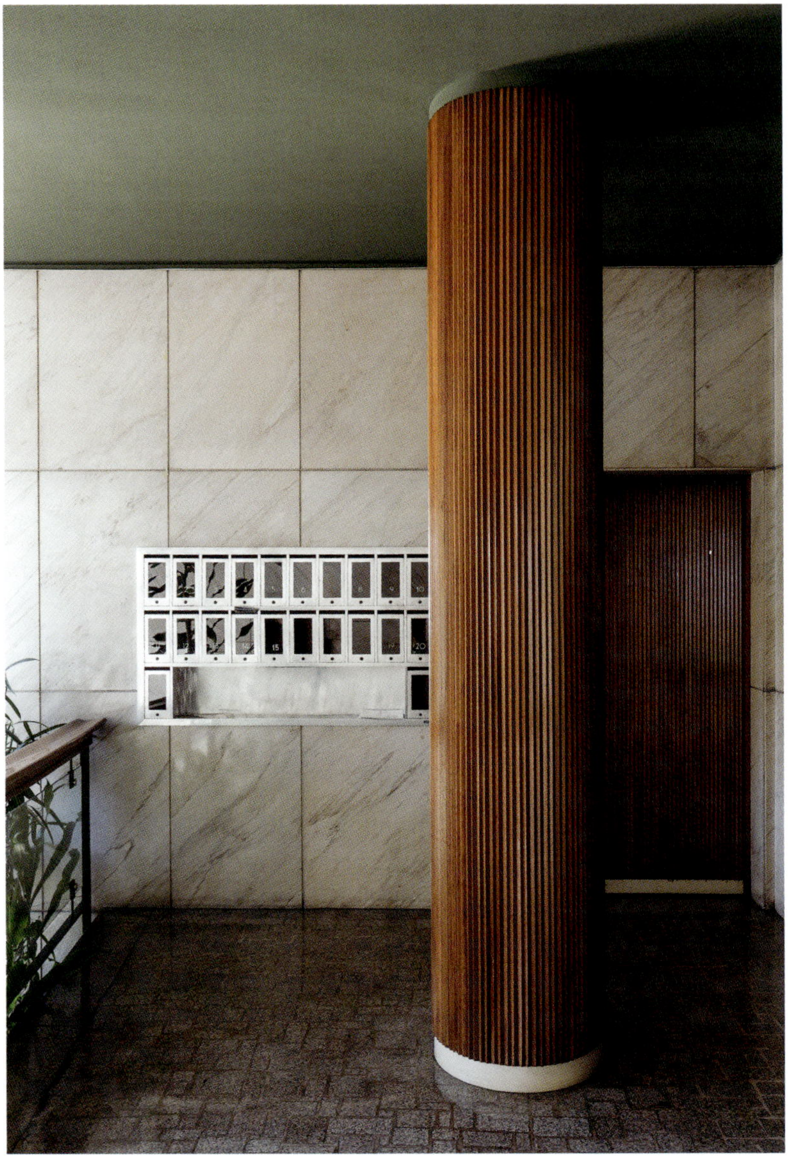

This and following spread:
via Uguccione da Pisa 6 · Giuseppe Barbieri, 1968
Chandelier by Gino Sarfatti.
floor: geometrical Palladiana of Rosa Baveno, geometrical Palladiana of red granite · stairs: Rosa Baveno granite

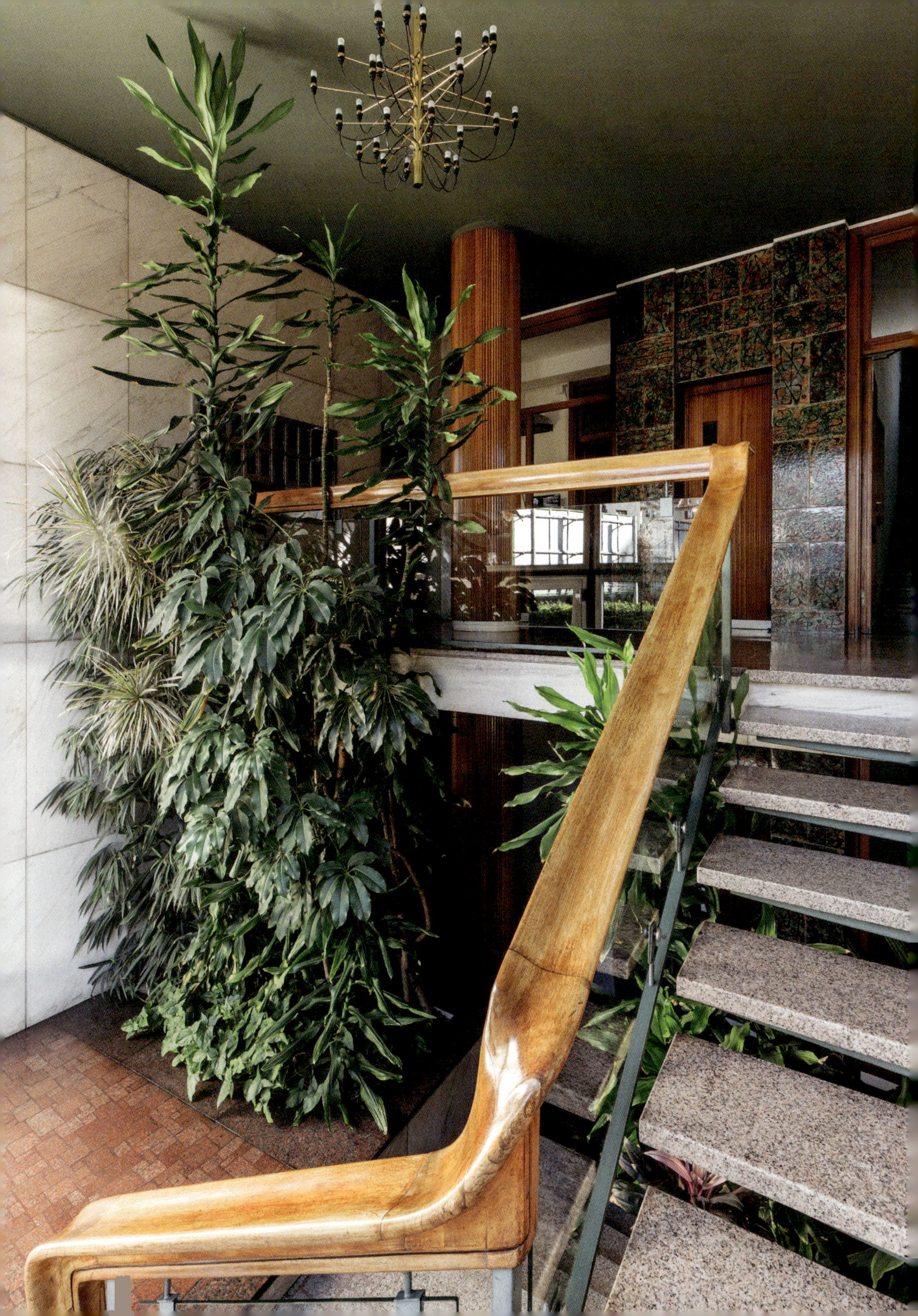

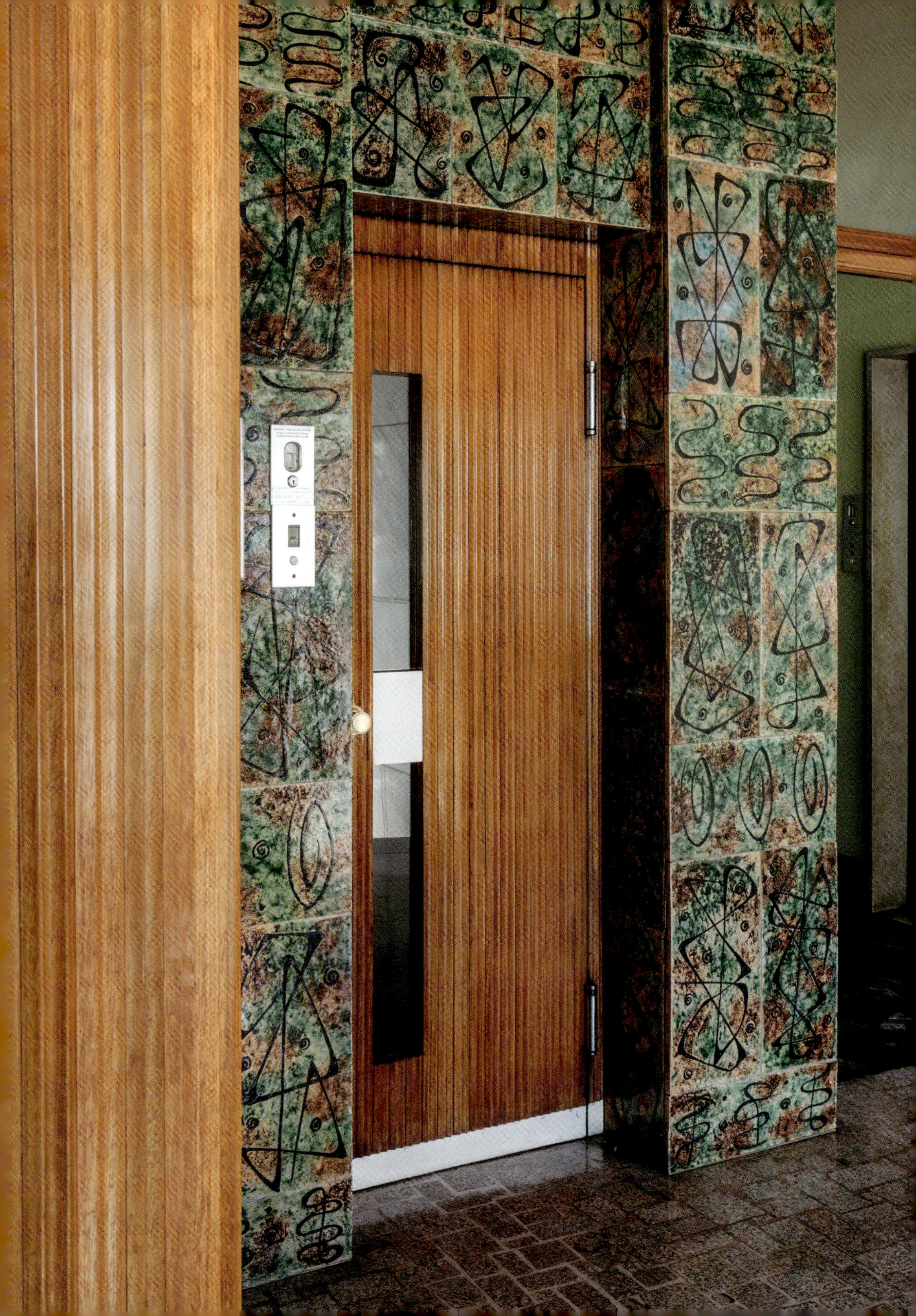

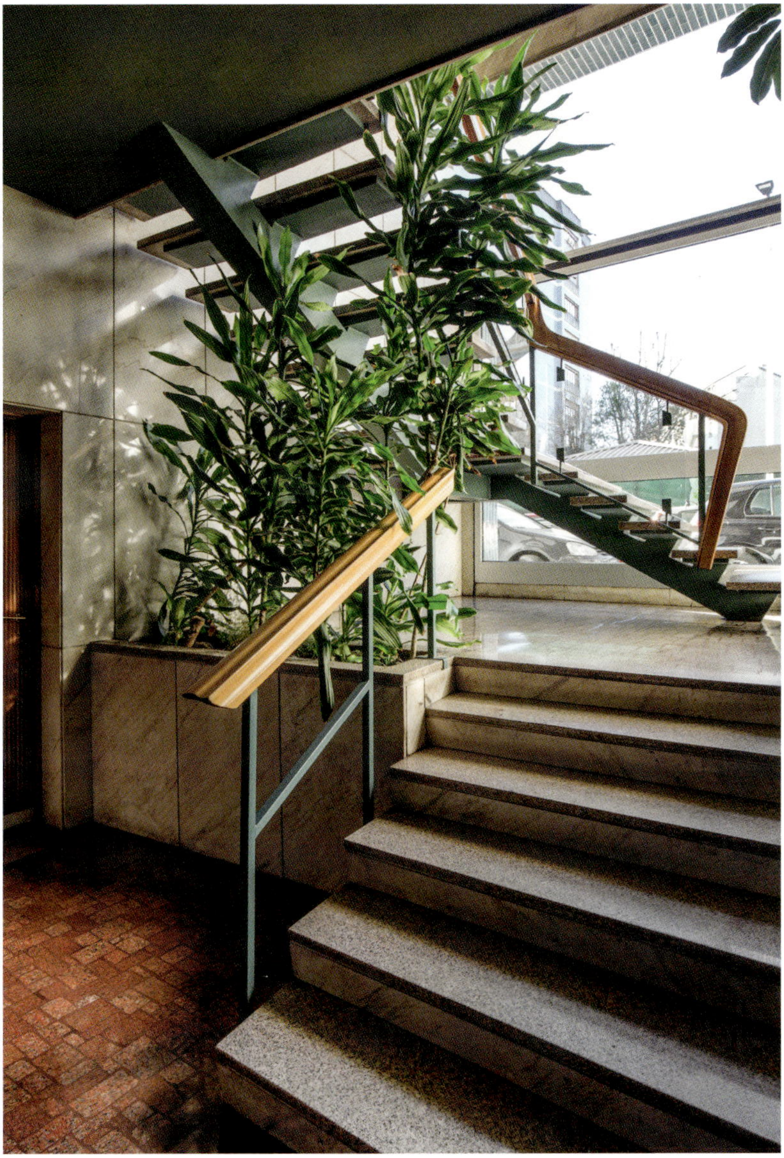

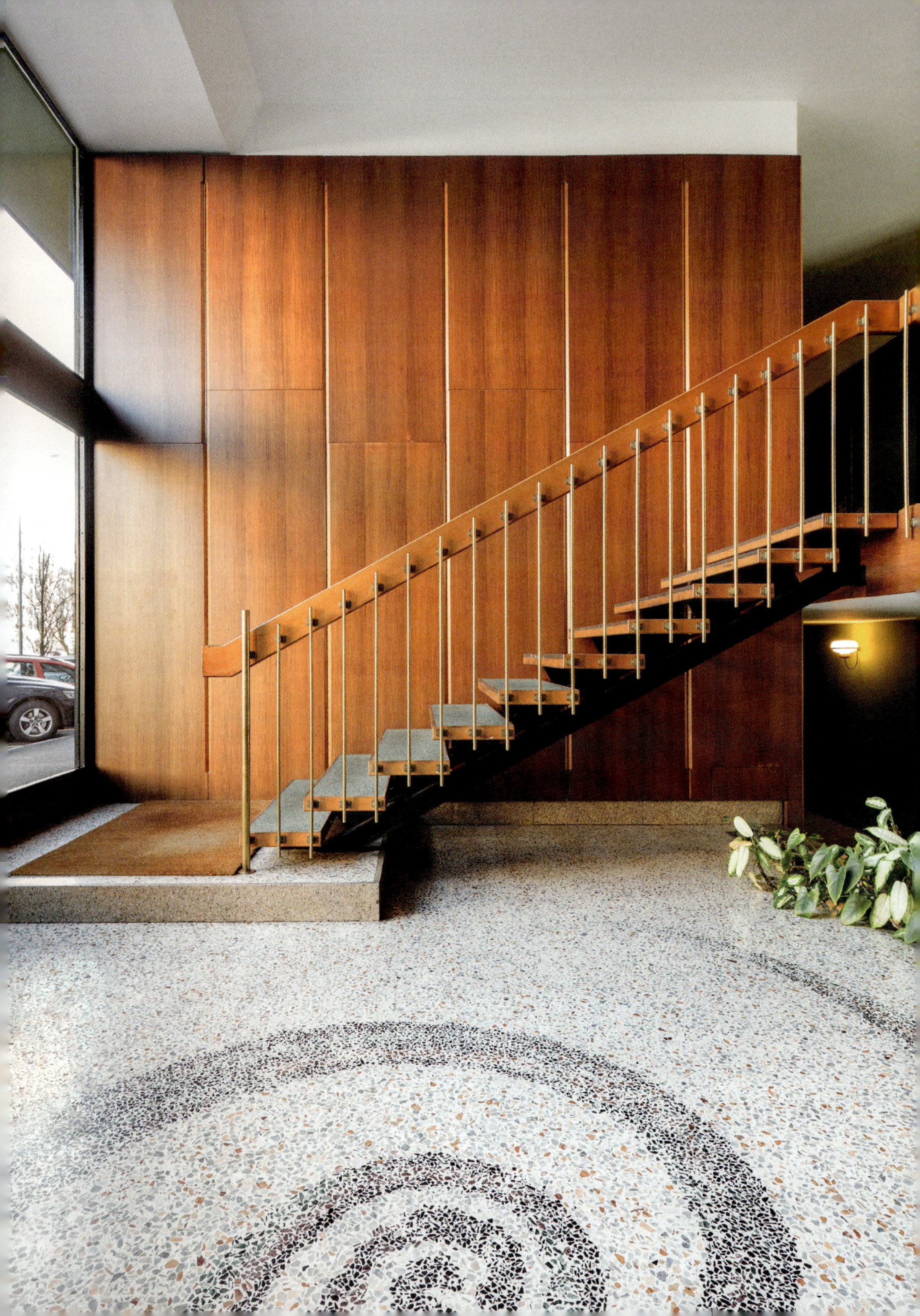

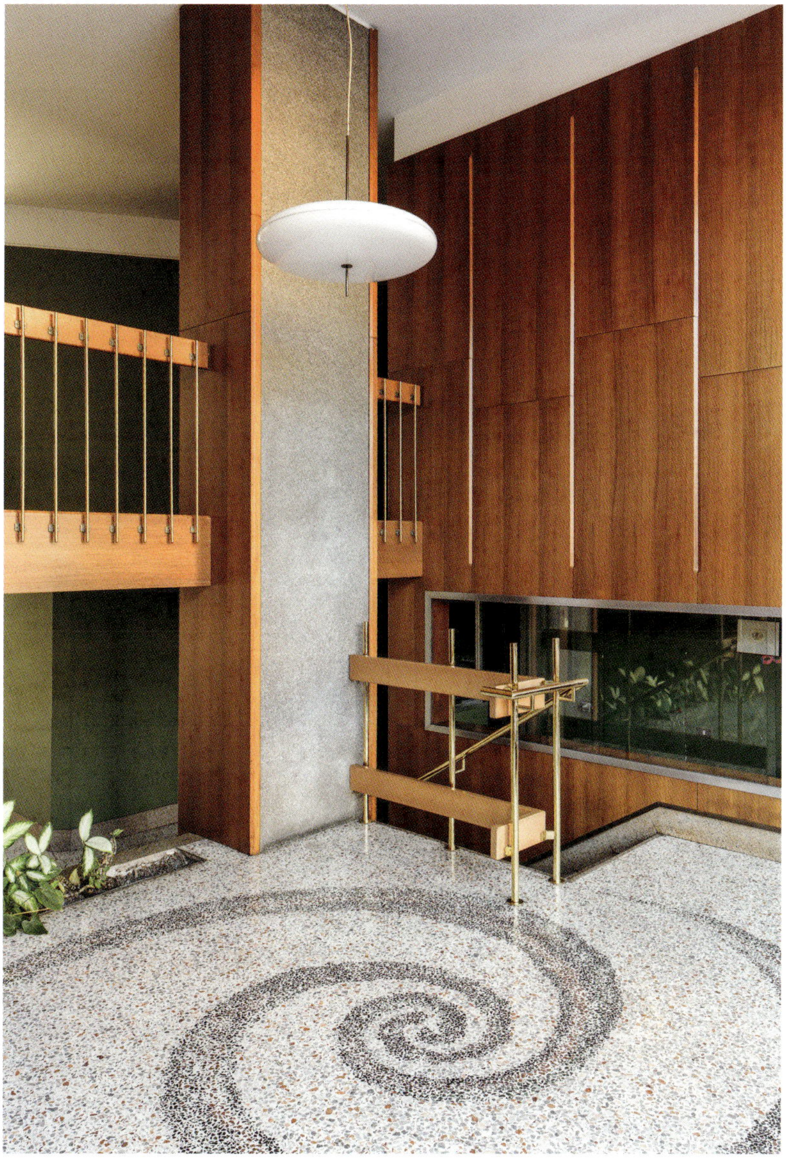

This and following spread:

via Gabriele Rossetti 19 · Gustavo Latis, Vito Latis, 1960

Pendant lamp and sconce by Gino Sarfatti.

Seminato *floor by Francesco Somaini.*

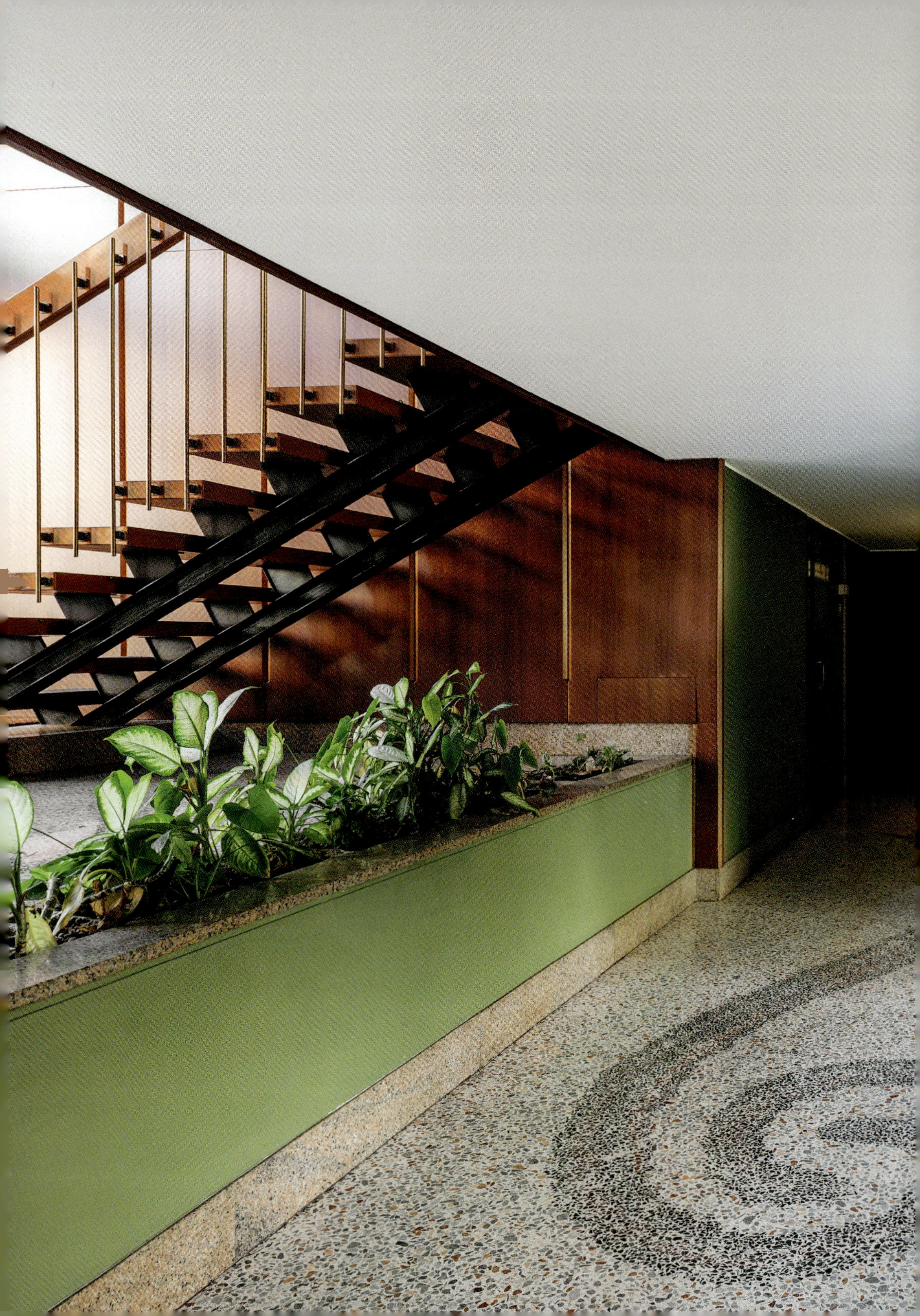

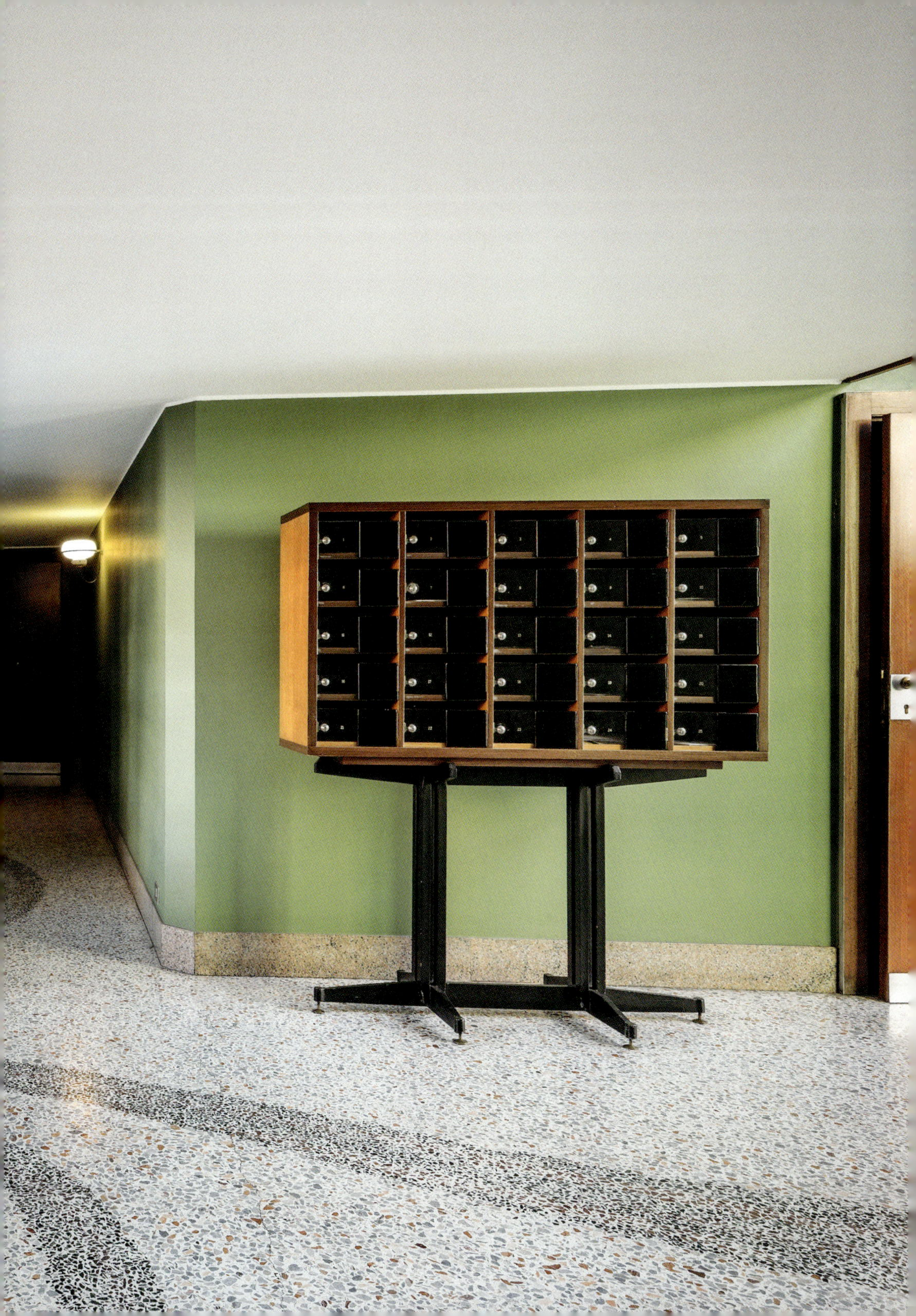

VERRUCANO LOMBARDO

A very durable Permian stone from the mountains of northern Bergamo and Brescia. No quarries are currently active; the stone has only ever been exploited intermittently.

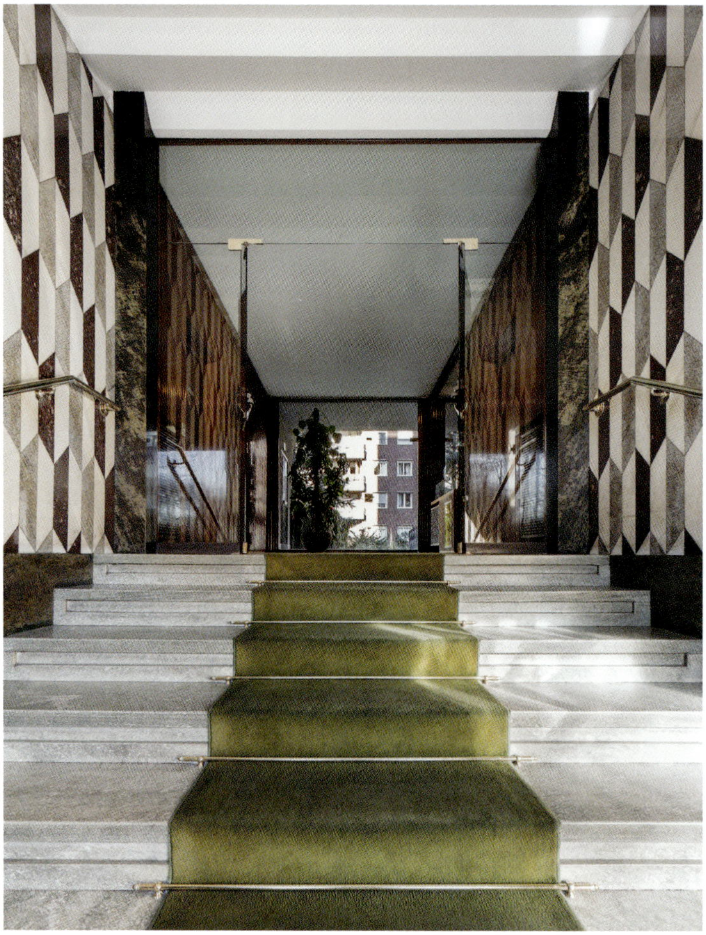

via Rita Tonoli 1 · Giovanni Muzio, 1956–65

floor: Musso marble and Verrucano Lombardo · walls: Bianco Lasa marble, Verrucano Lombardo, Montorfano granite, Serpentino Labrador

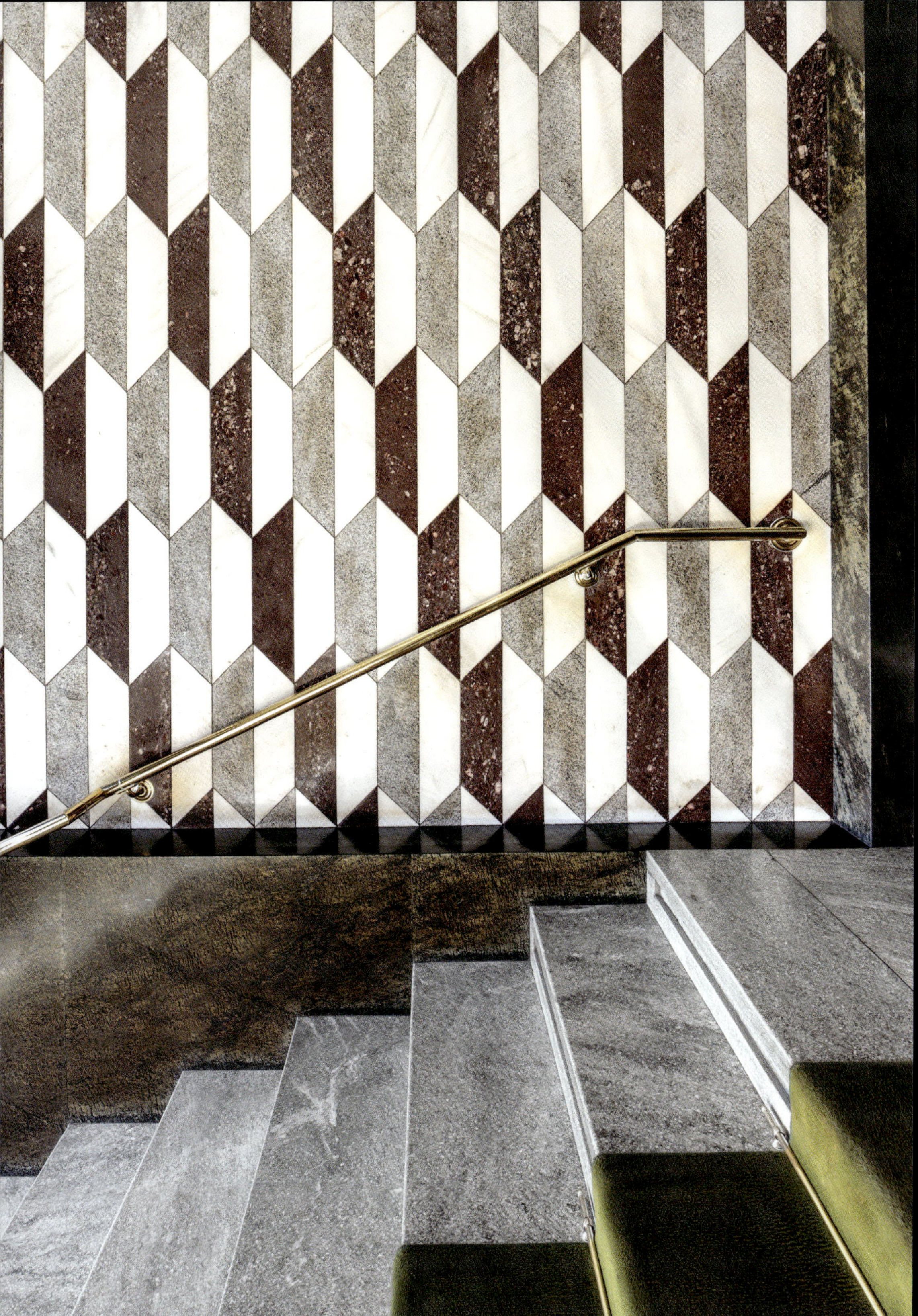

This and following spreads:
piazza VI Febbraio 10 · Renato Ferrari, 1934–36
base: serpentinite · cladding: Beola granite

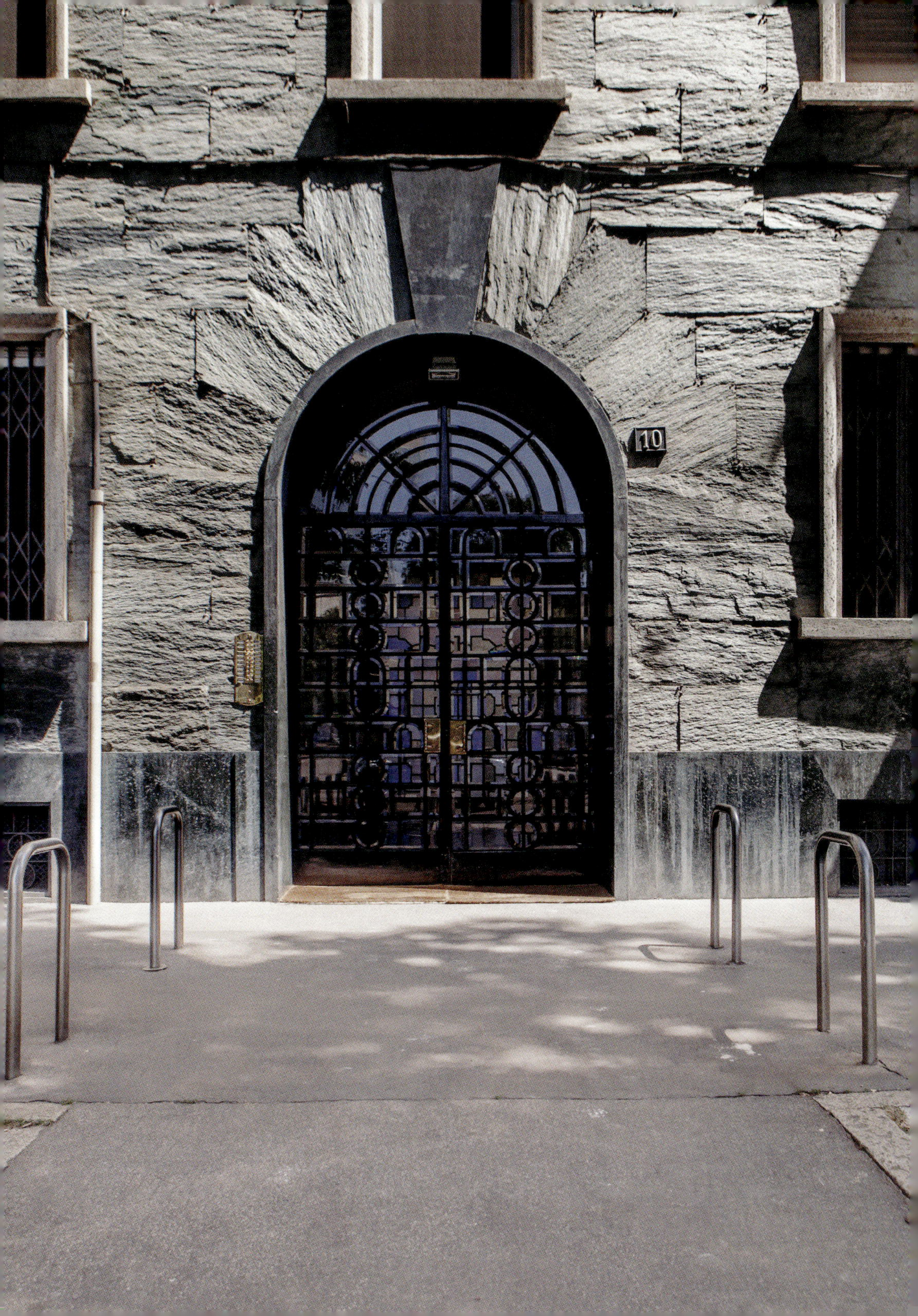
10

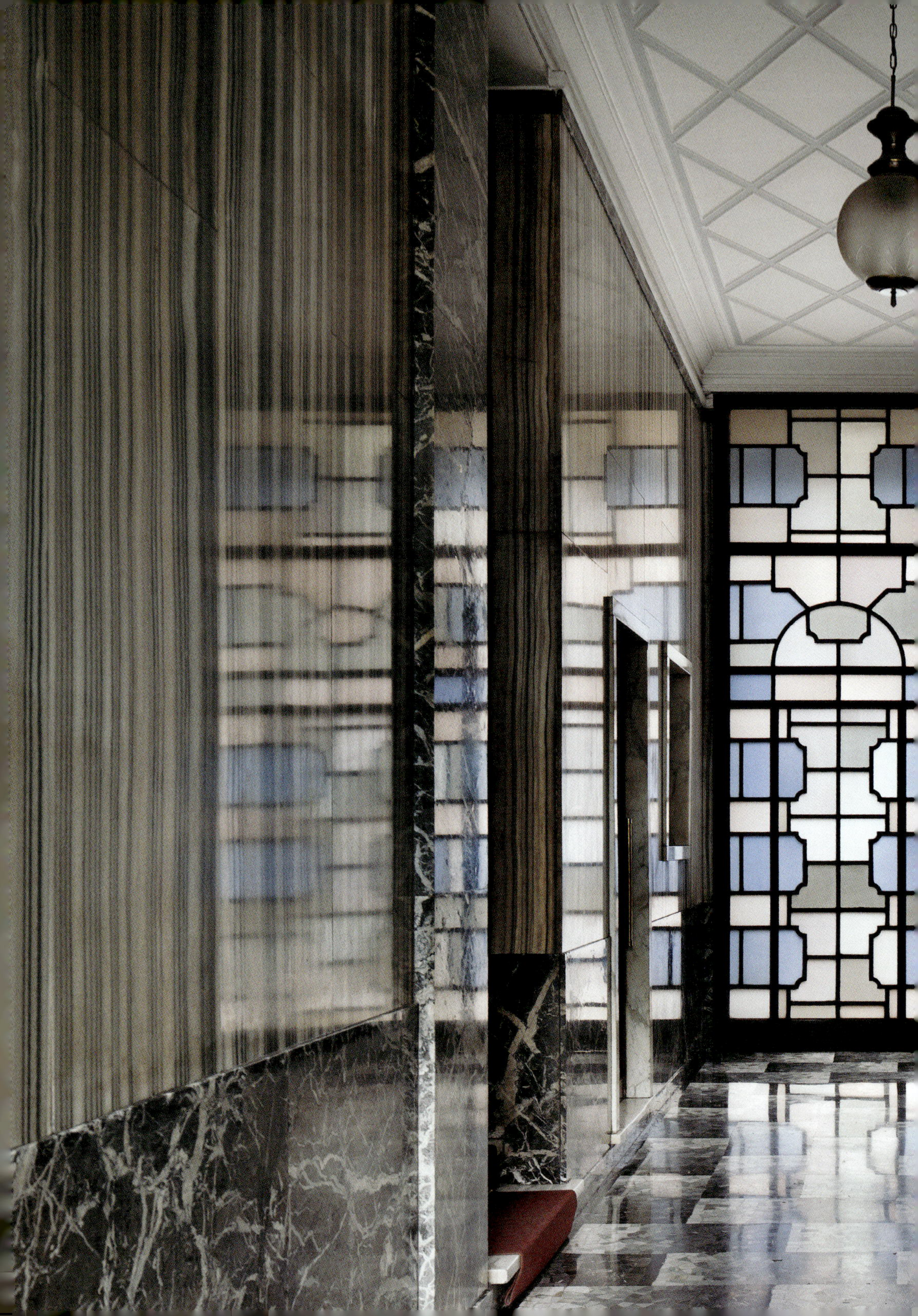

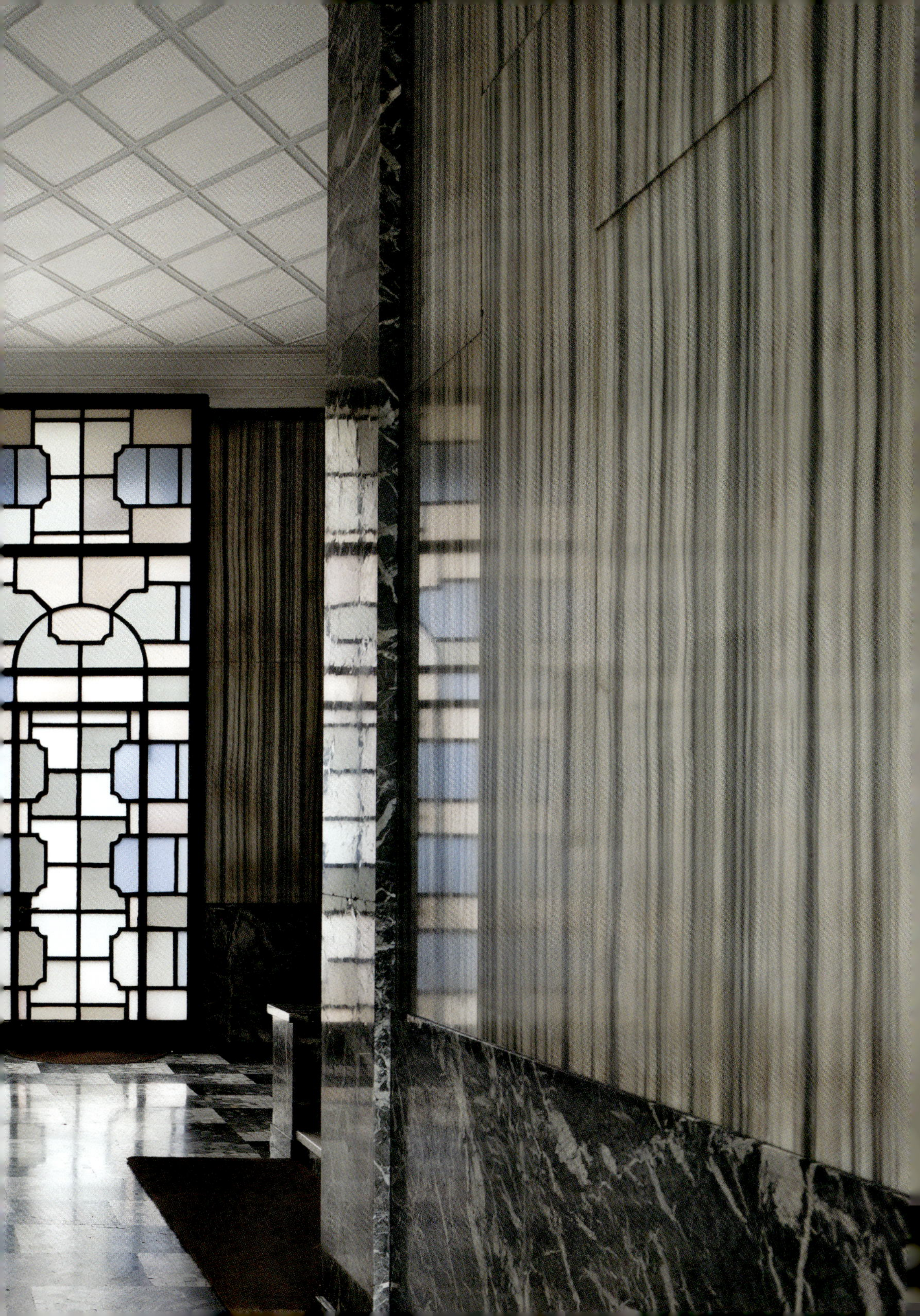

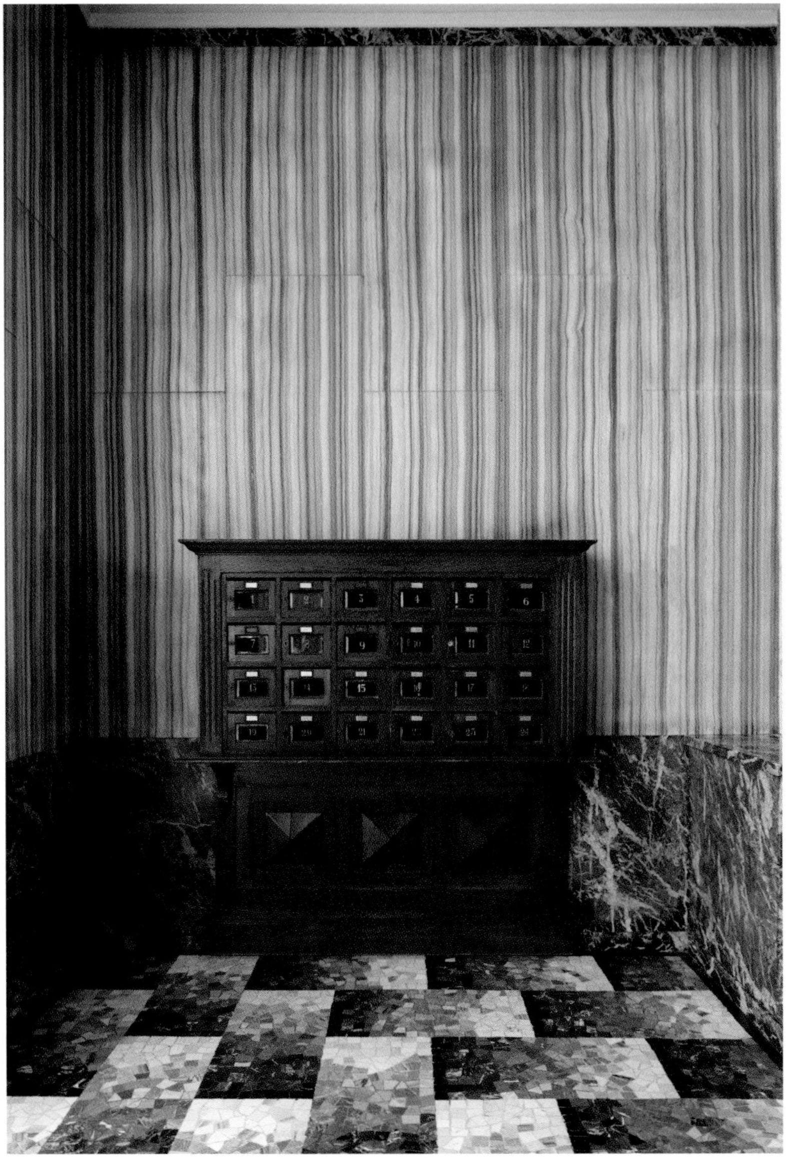

floor: Palladiana of white to gray and black marble and limestone arranged in a dégradé pattern
base: Grigio Carnico limestone · walls: Cipollino 900 marble, also known as Zebrino marble

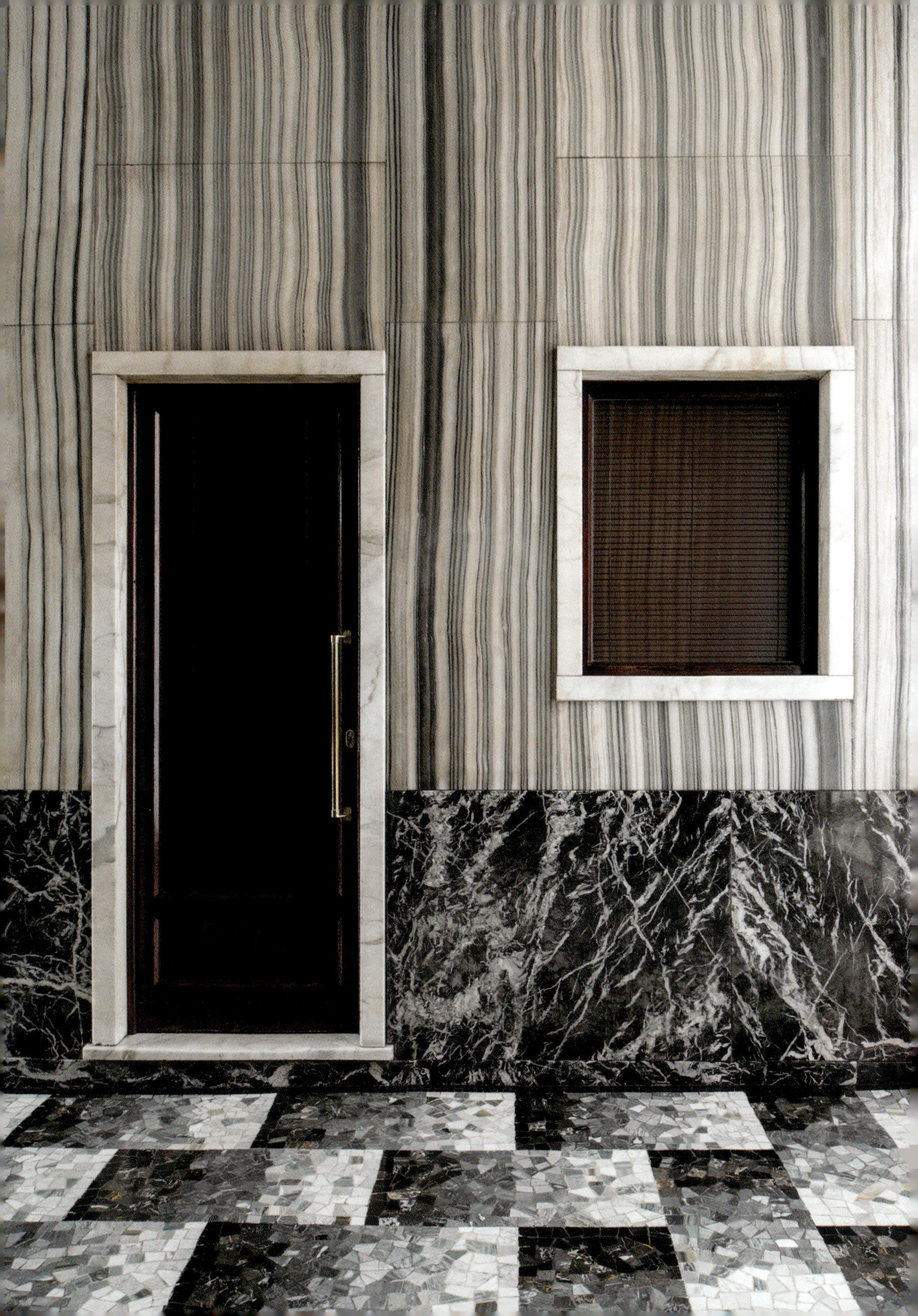

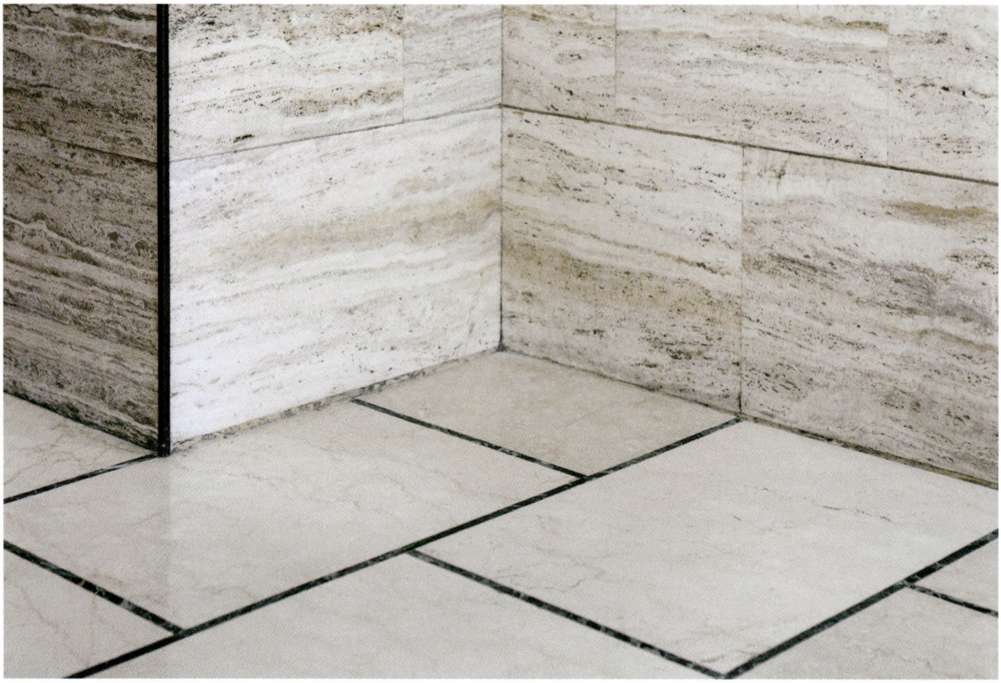

piazza VI Febbraio 16

floor: Botticino limestone with serpentinite joints · wall: Travertino Romano and wooden frames

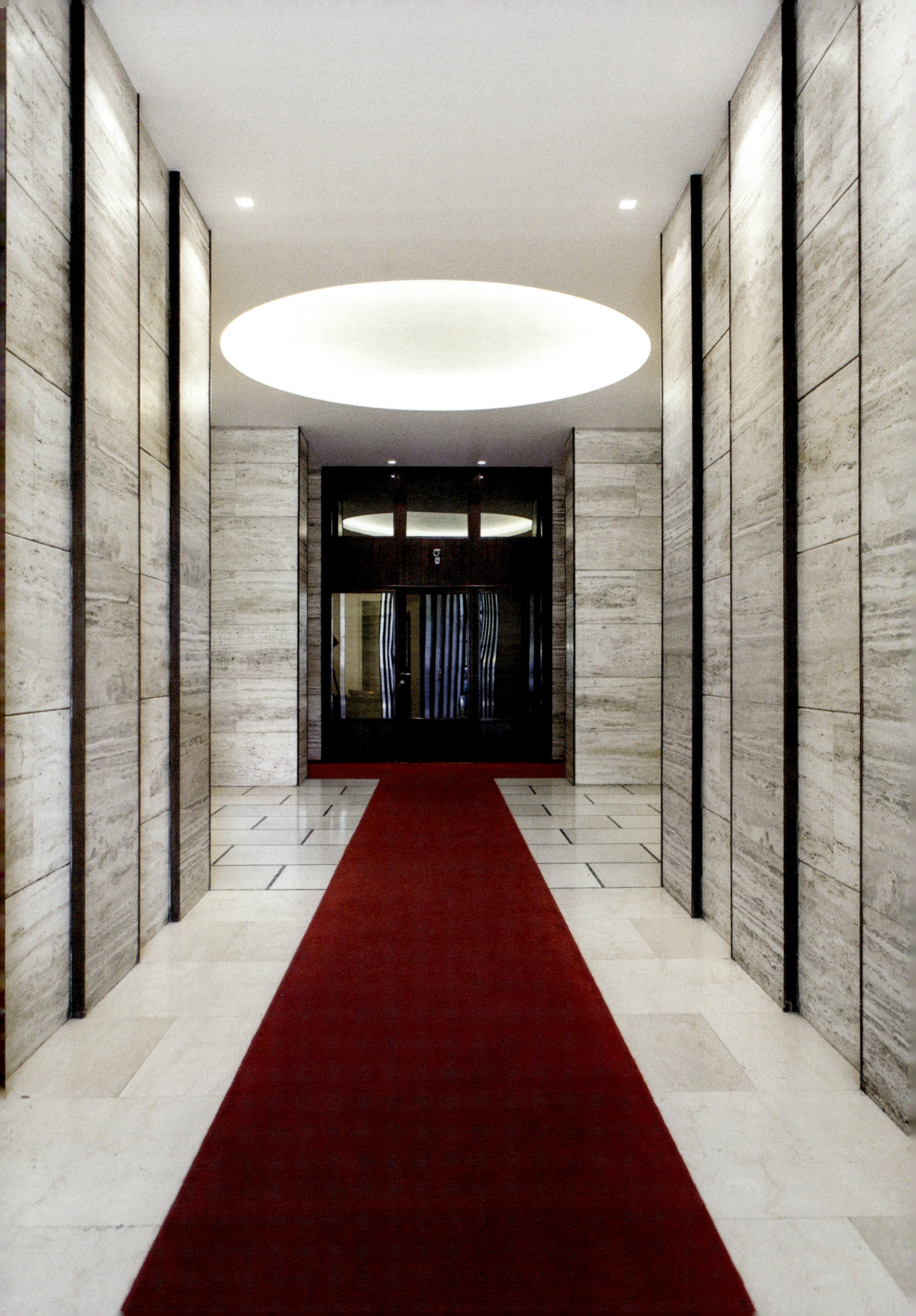

PIETRA DI VICENZA

An Eocene fossil-rich calcarenite quarried from the hills around Vicenza. Very soft and easy to carve, it naturally occurs in a range of colors, including ivory white, gray, and golden yellow. Easily available and workable, this stone has been exploited since ancient times, and was used extensively by Palladio in the sixteenth century for the construction of almost all his outstanding villas.

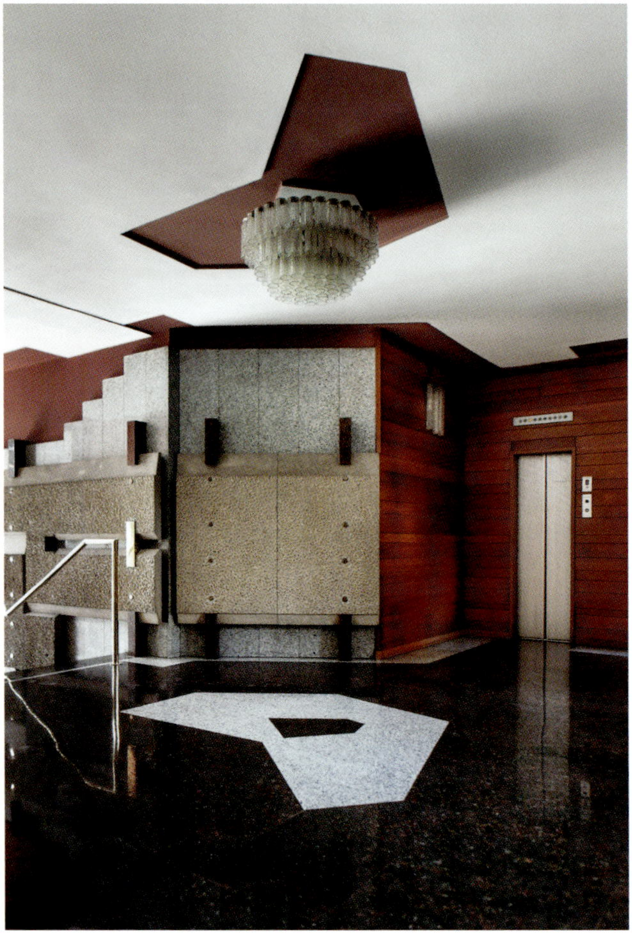

viale Severino Boezio 2

Chandelier and sconces by Aureliano Toso.

floor: red granite and Bianco Sardo granite · walls: Bianco Sardo granite · cladding panels: Pietra di Vicenza Gialla

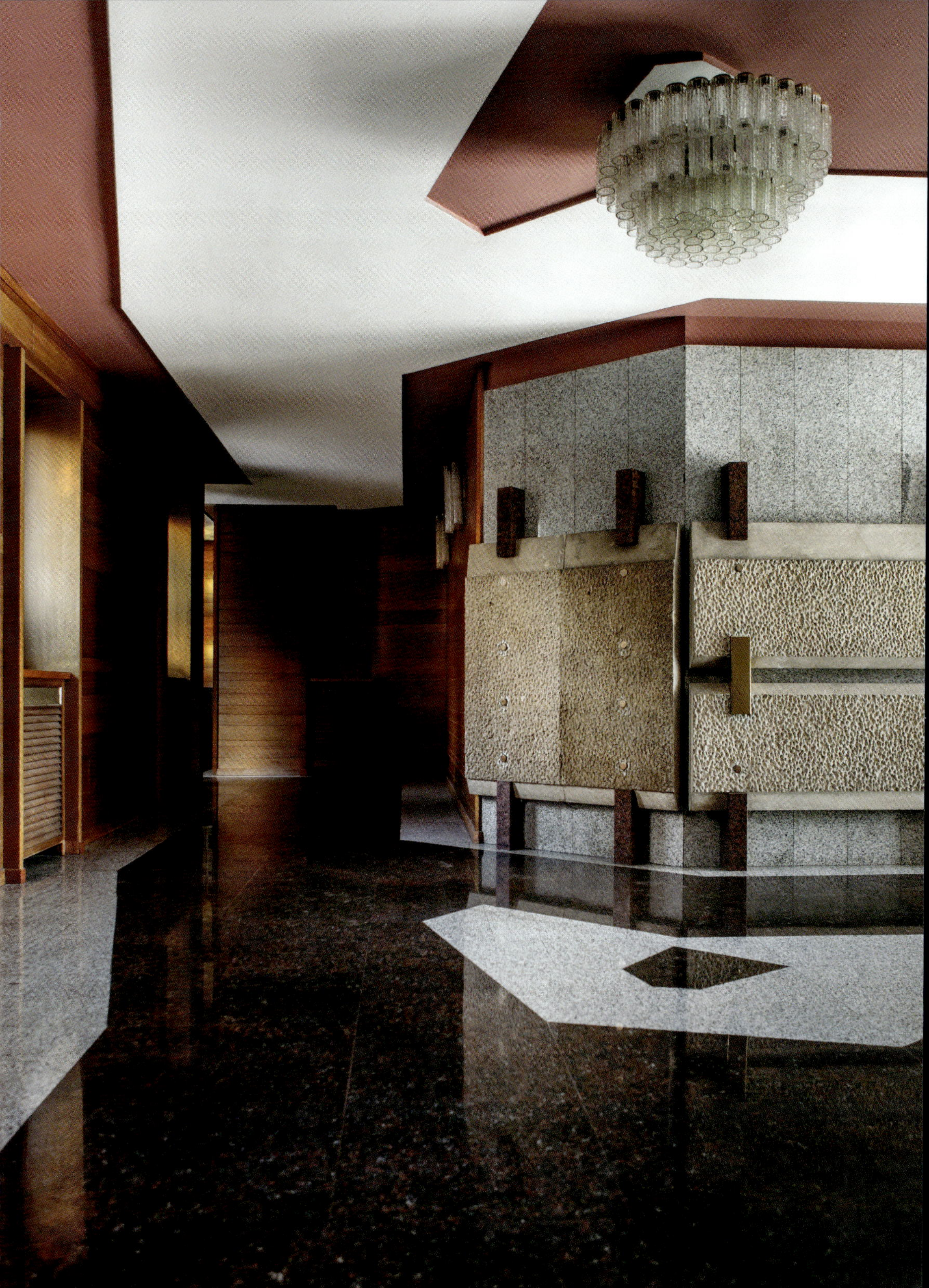

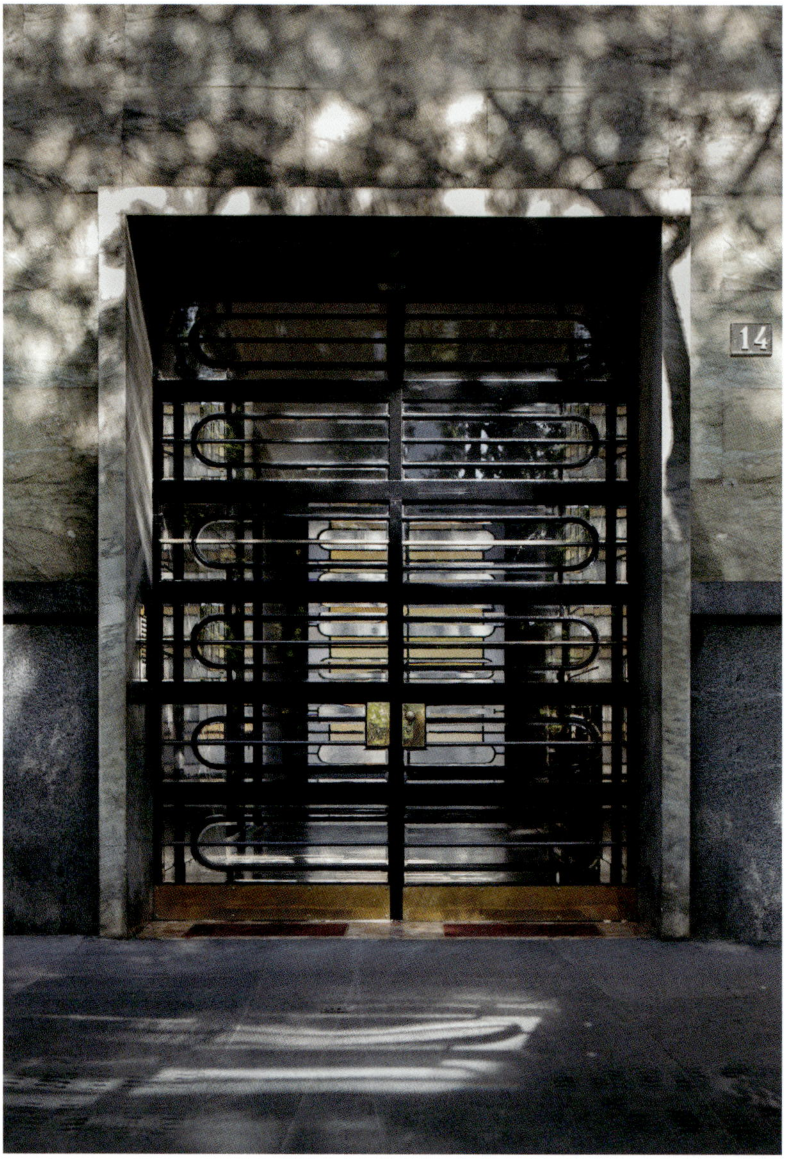

piazza VI Febbraio 14 · 1934

floor: Palladiana of several marbles and limestones · walls: Macchiavecchia limestone breccia and Magnaboschi

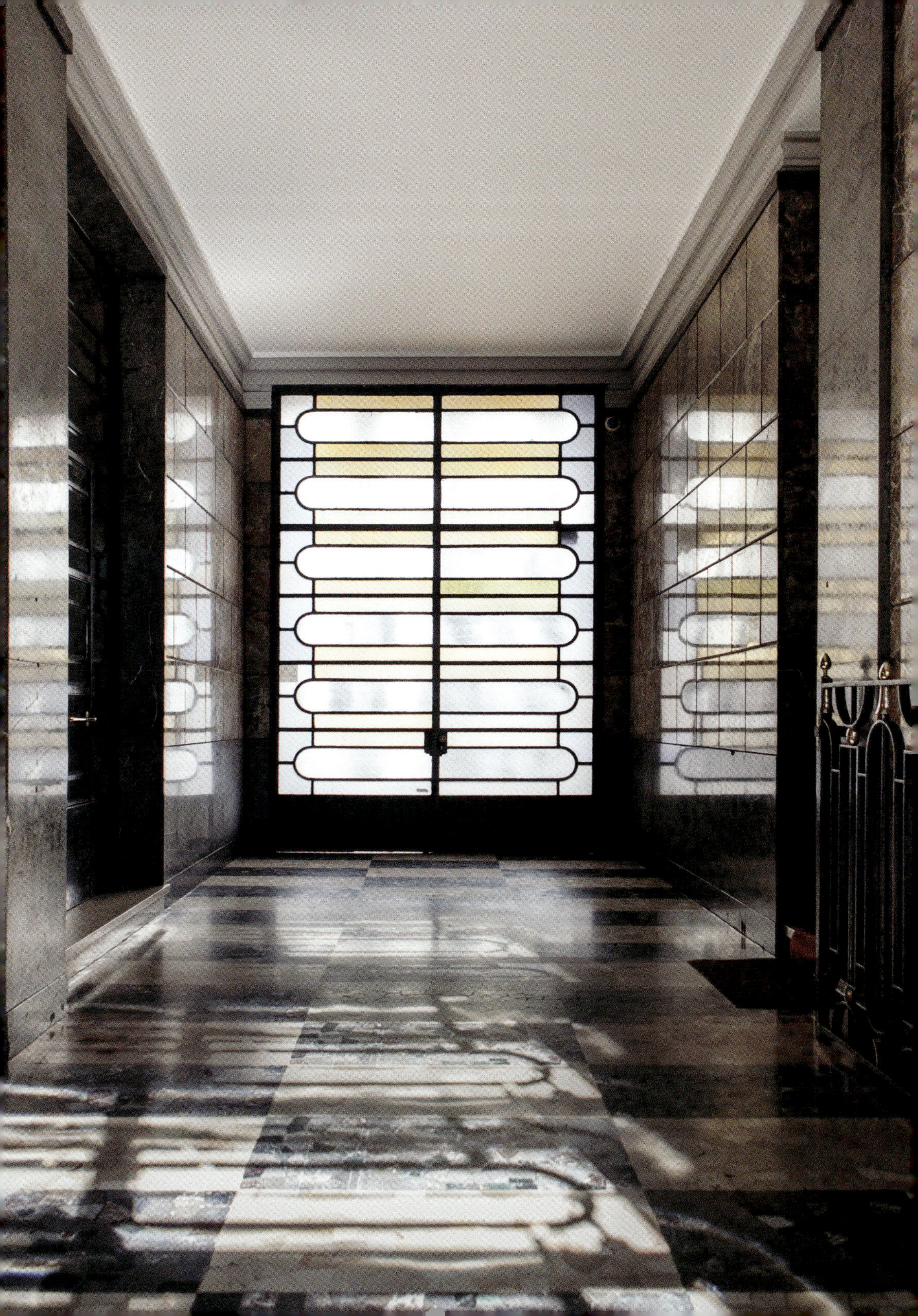

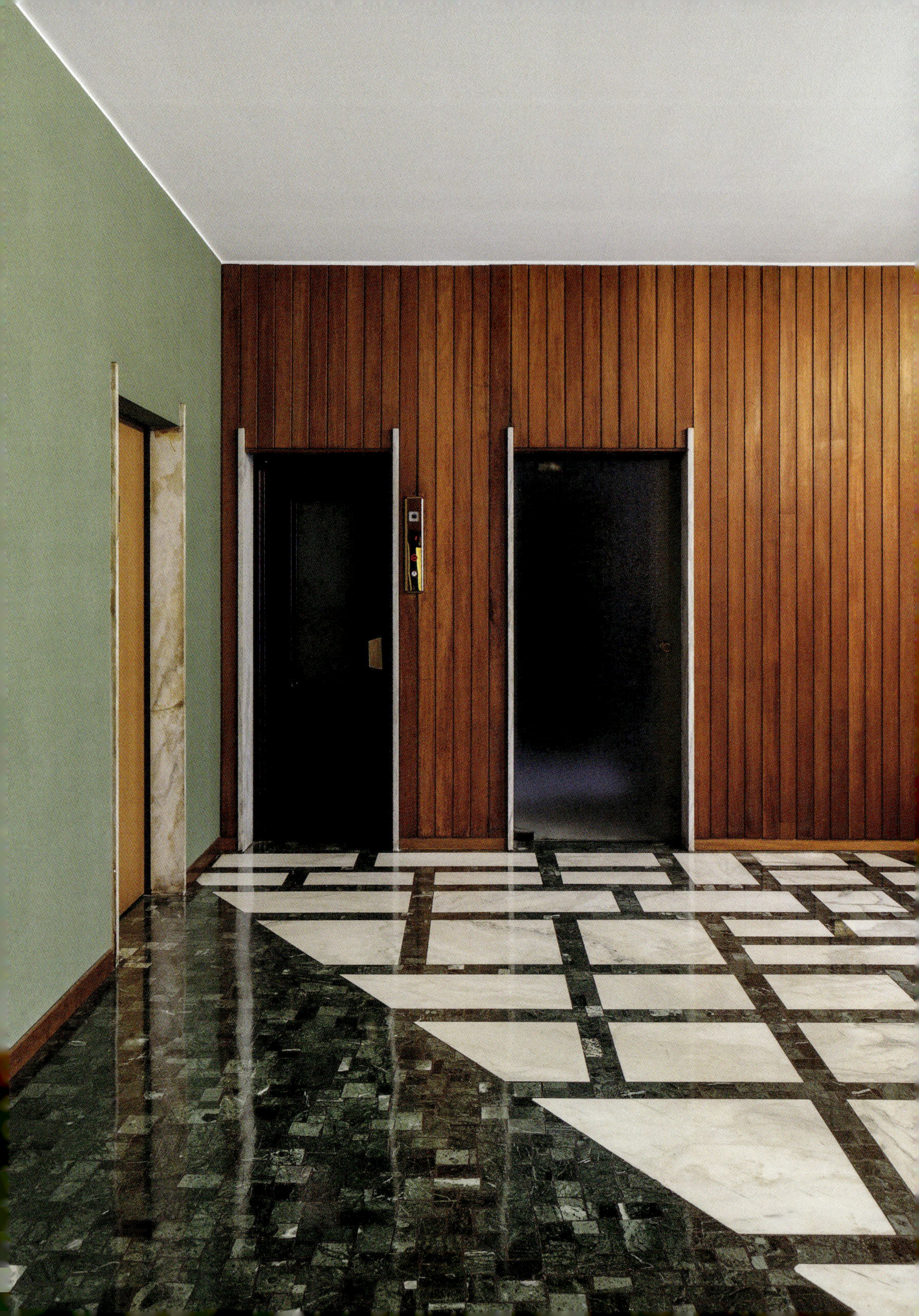

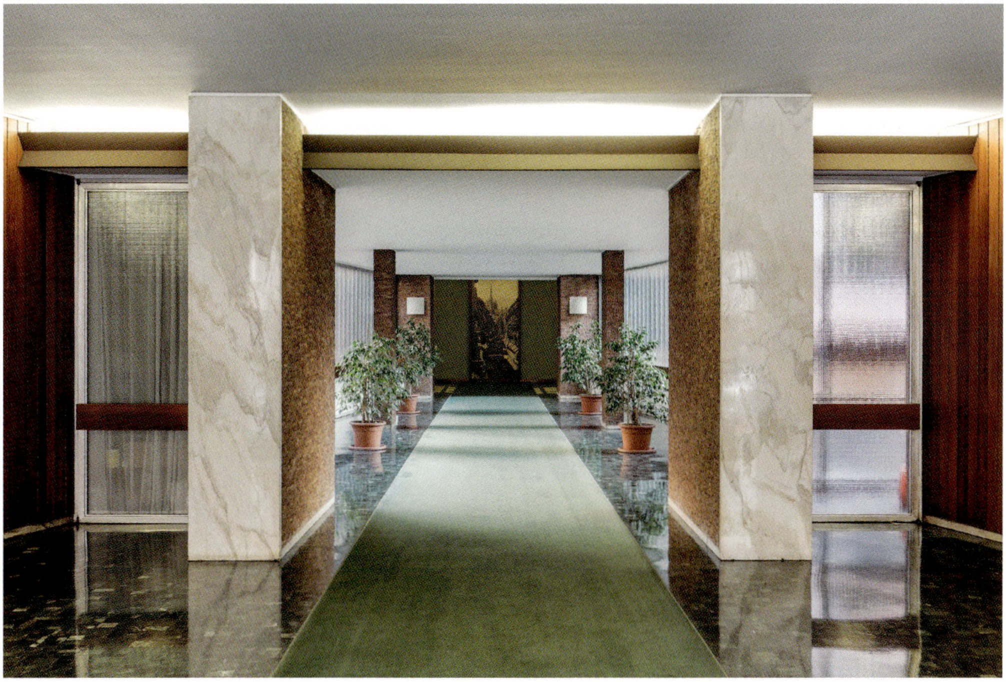

via Giovanni da Procida 6
floor: Bianco Carrara Arni marble, serpentinite, Palladiana of serpentinite

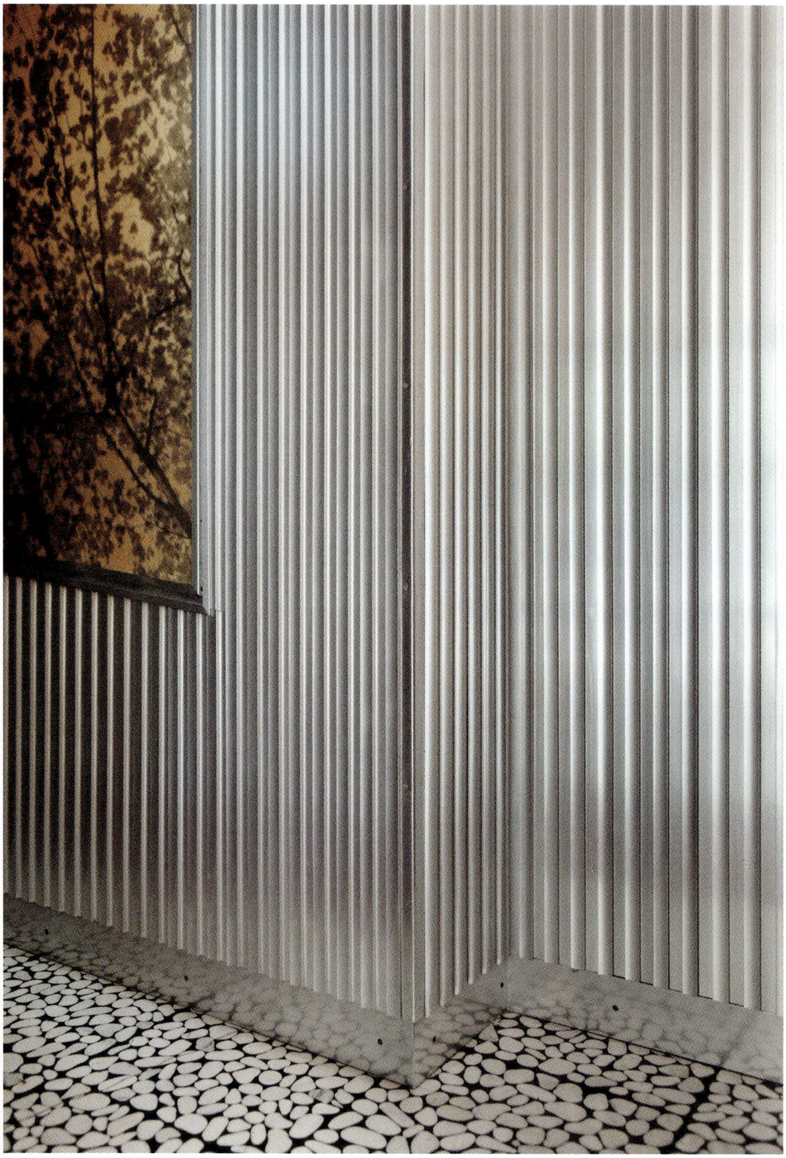

via Giacomo Boni 10

floor and stairs: Verde Alpi ophicalcite, white marble pebbles

Following spread:
via Moisè Loria 78 · Marcello Belleri, 1962–65

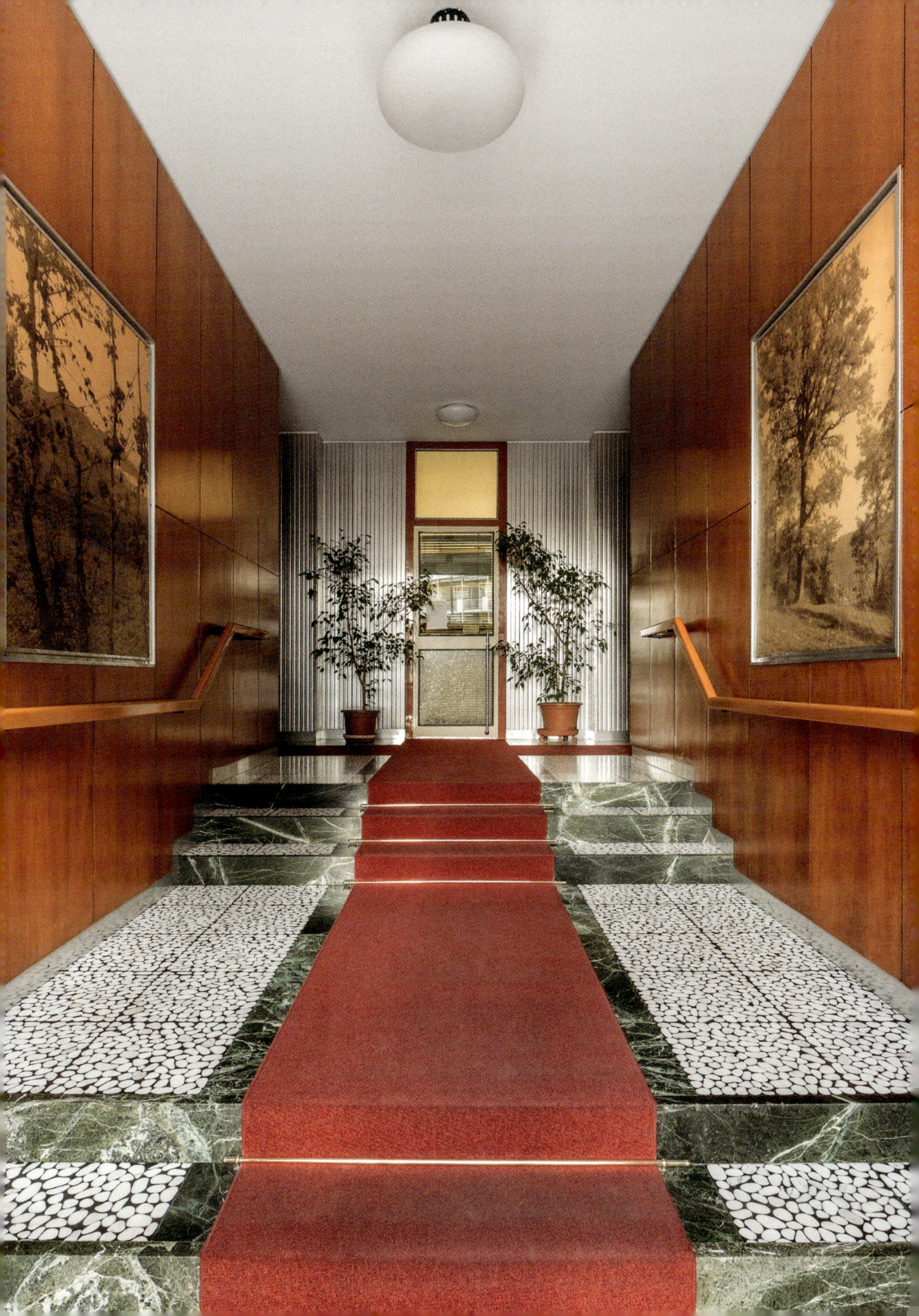

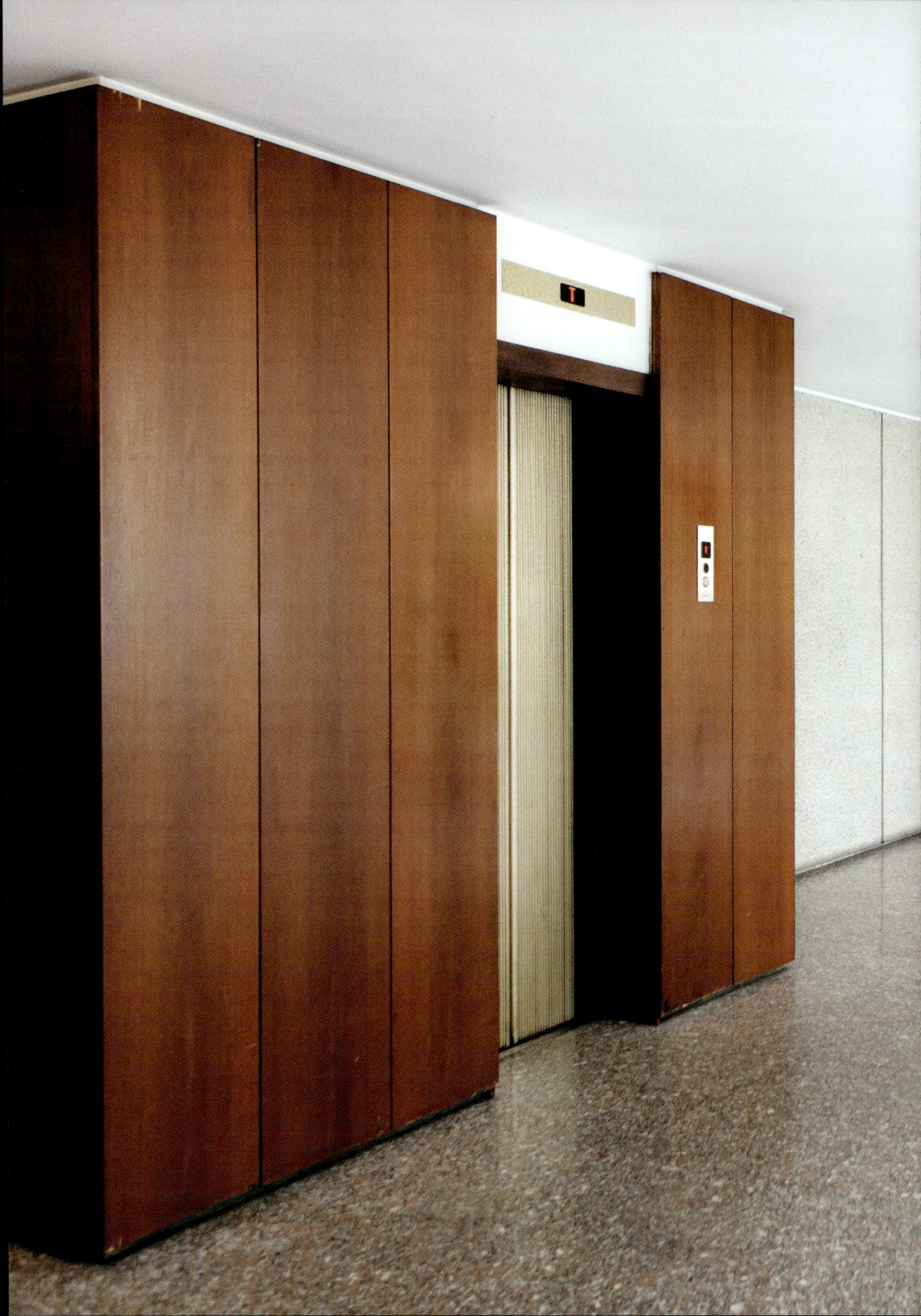

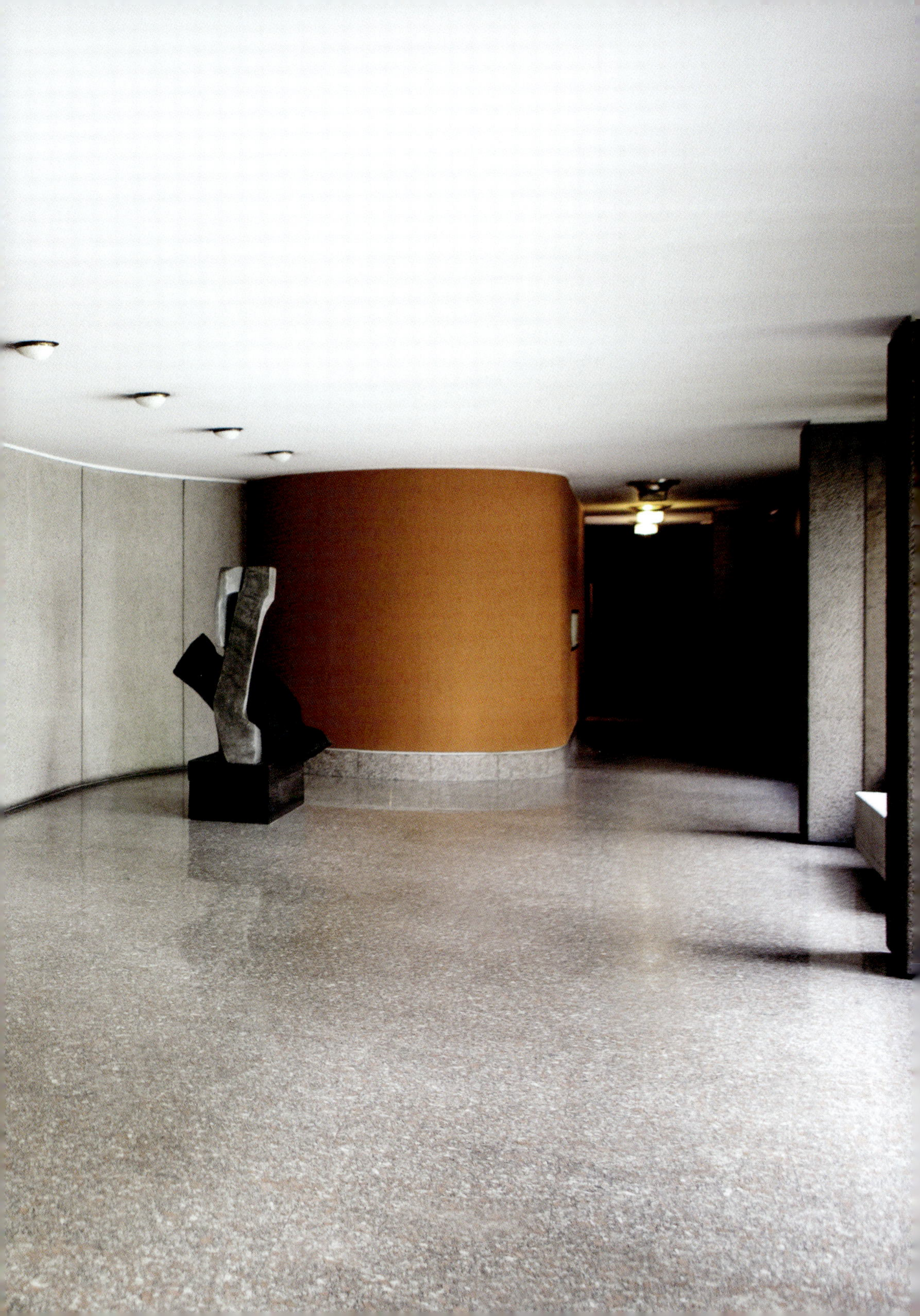

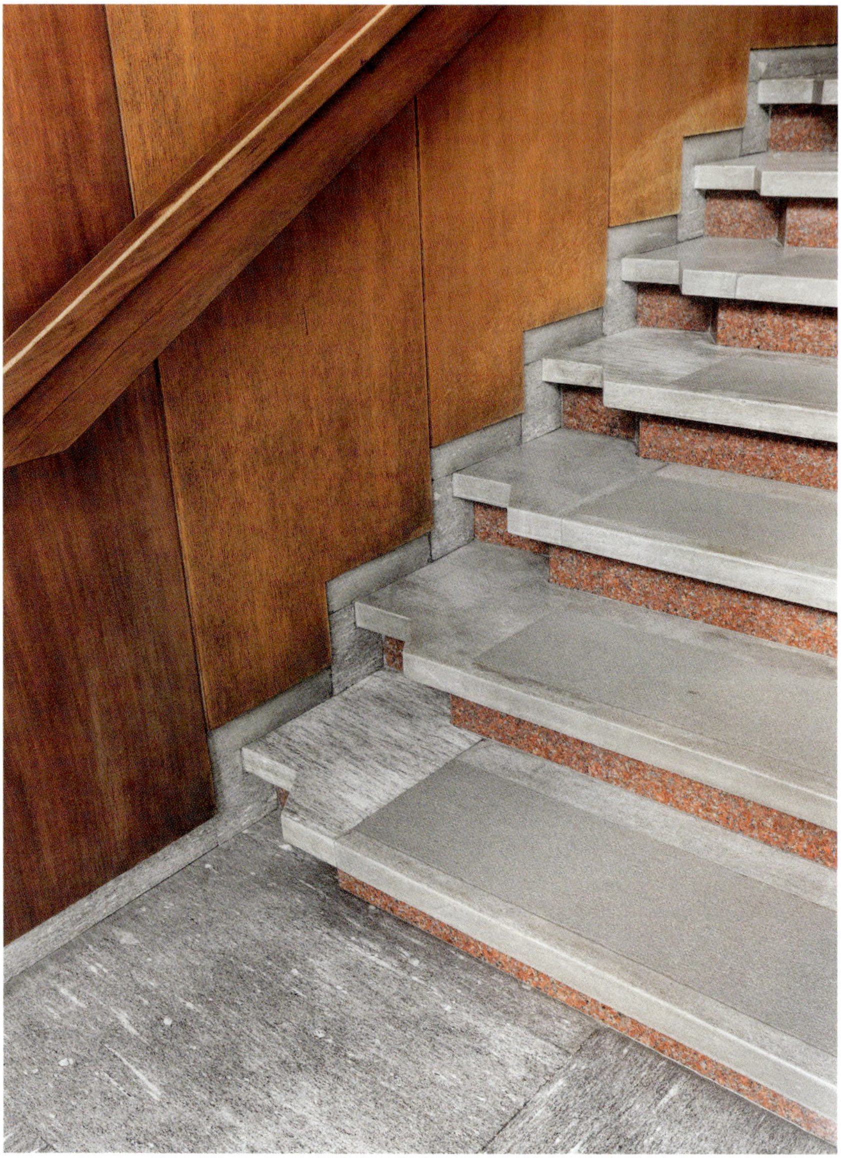

via Giuseppe Dezza 25 · Orlando Orlandi, Gianni Albricci, 1962–64

Sconces by Sergio Mazza for Artemide.
floor: Beola Ghiandonata · stairs: Beola Bianca granite, Rosso granite

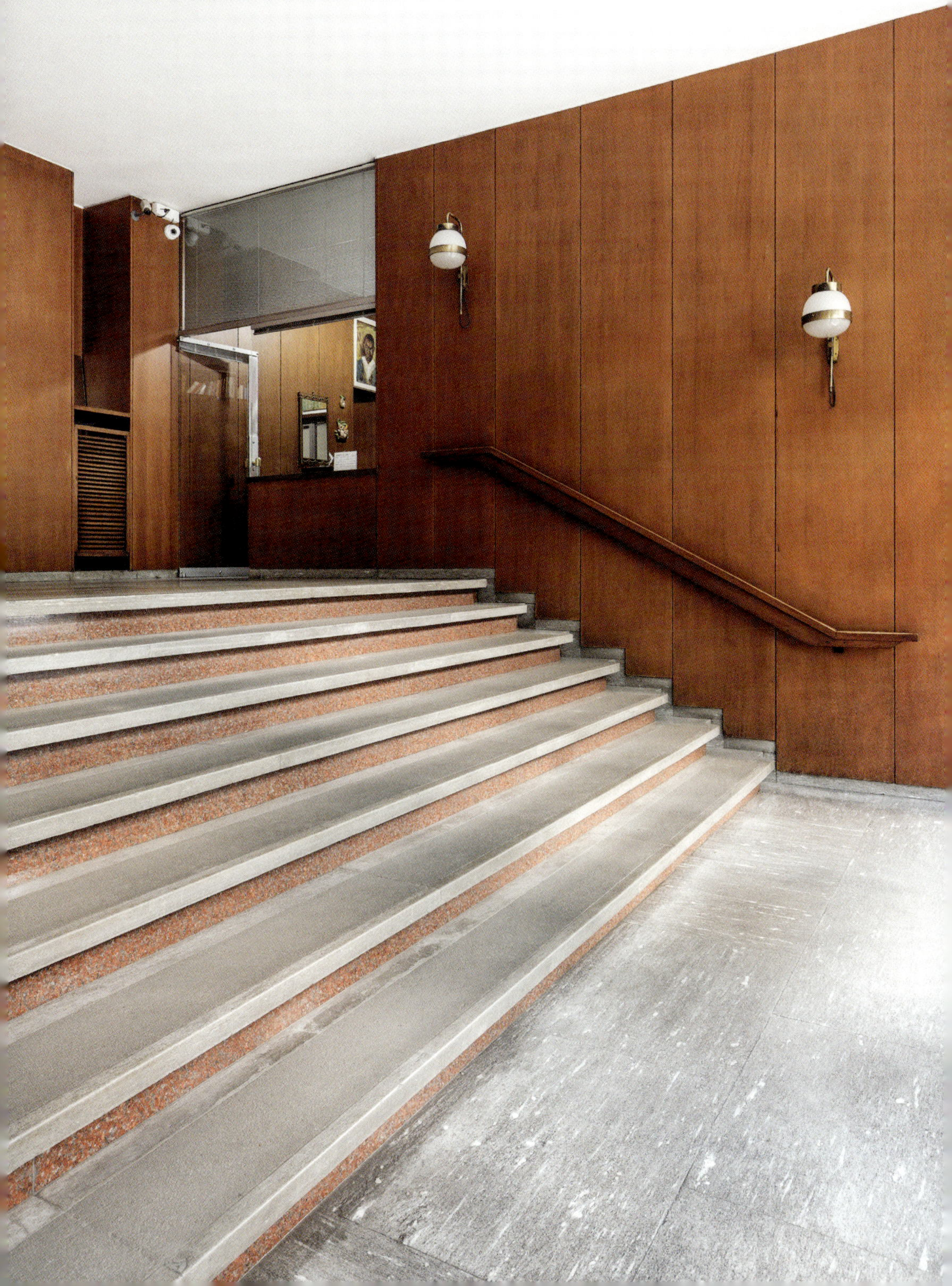

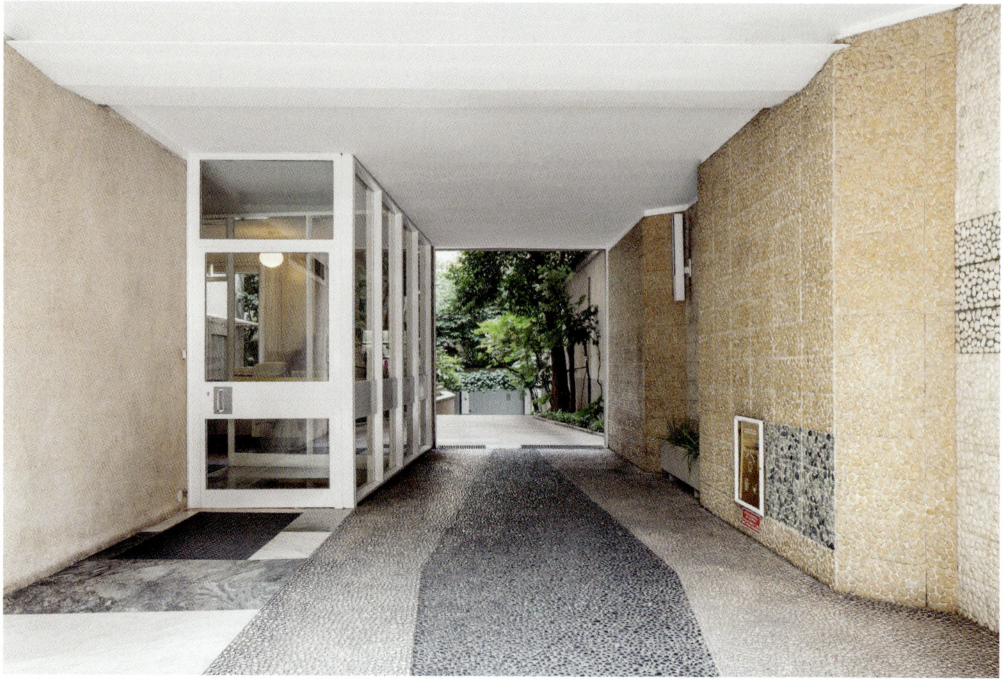

This and following spread:
via Giuseppe Dezza 49 · Gio Ponti, Antonio Fornaroli, Alberto Rosselli, 1952–56
Sconce, pebbled floor and wall by Gio Ponti.

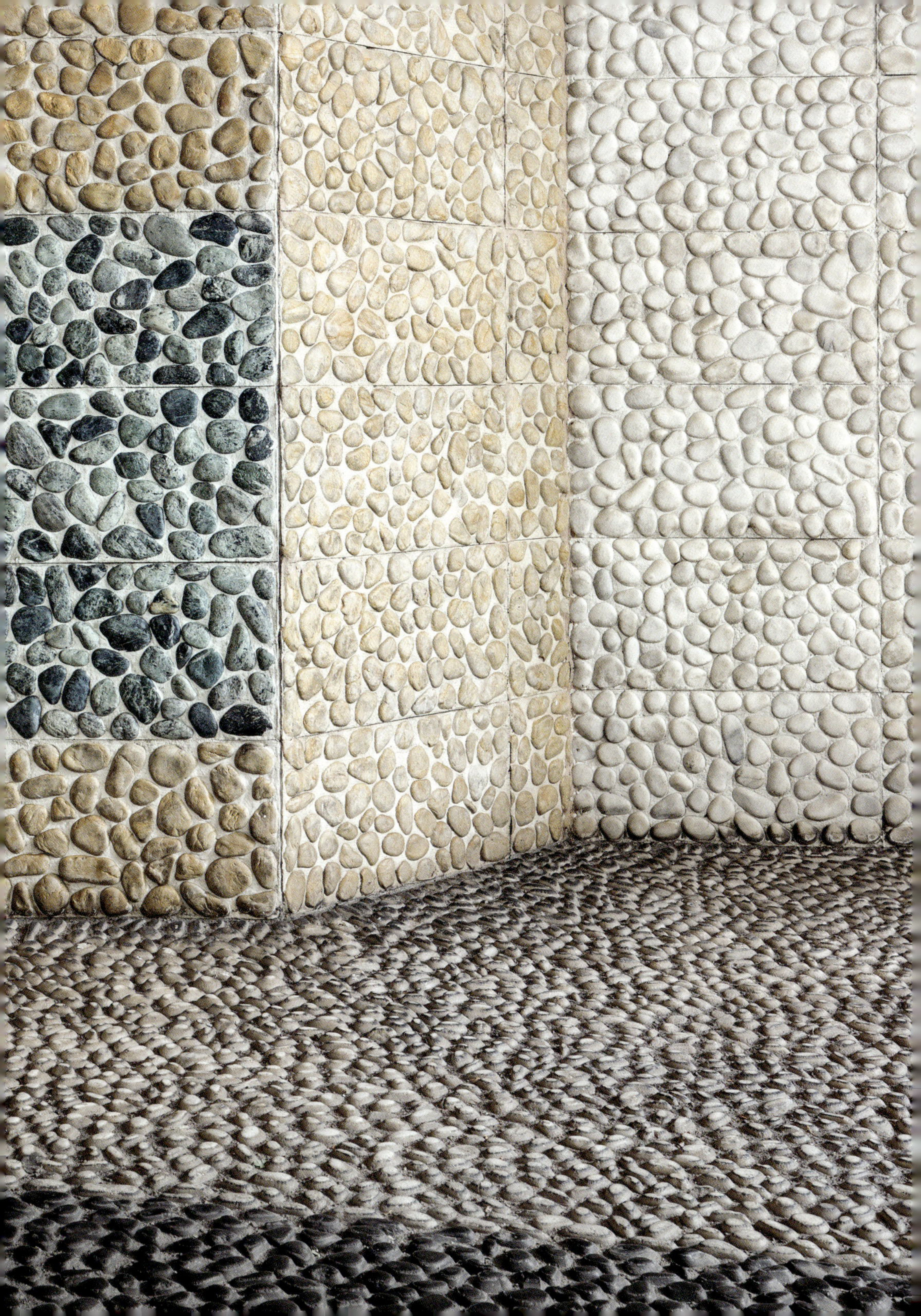

Sconce by Gio Ponti.
floor: serpentinite Verde Acceglio, Porta Santa limestone, Carrara Bardiglio marble, Carrara Bianco marble

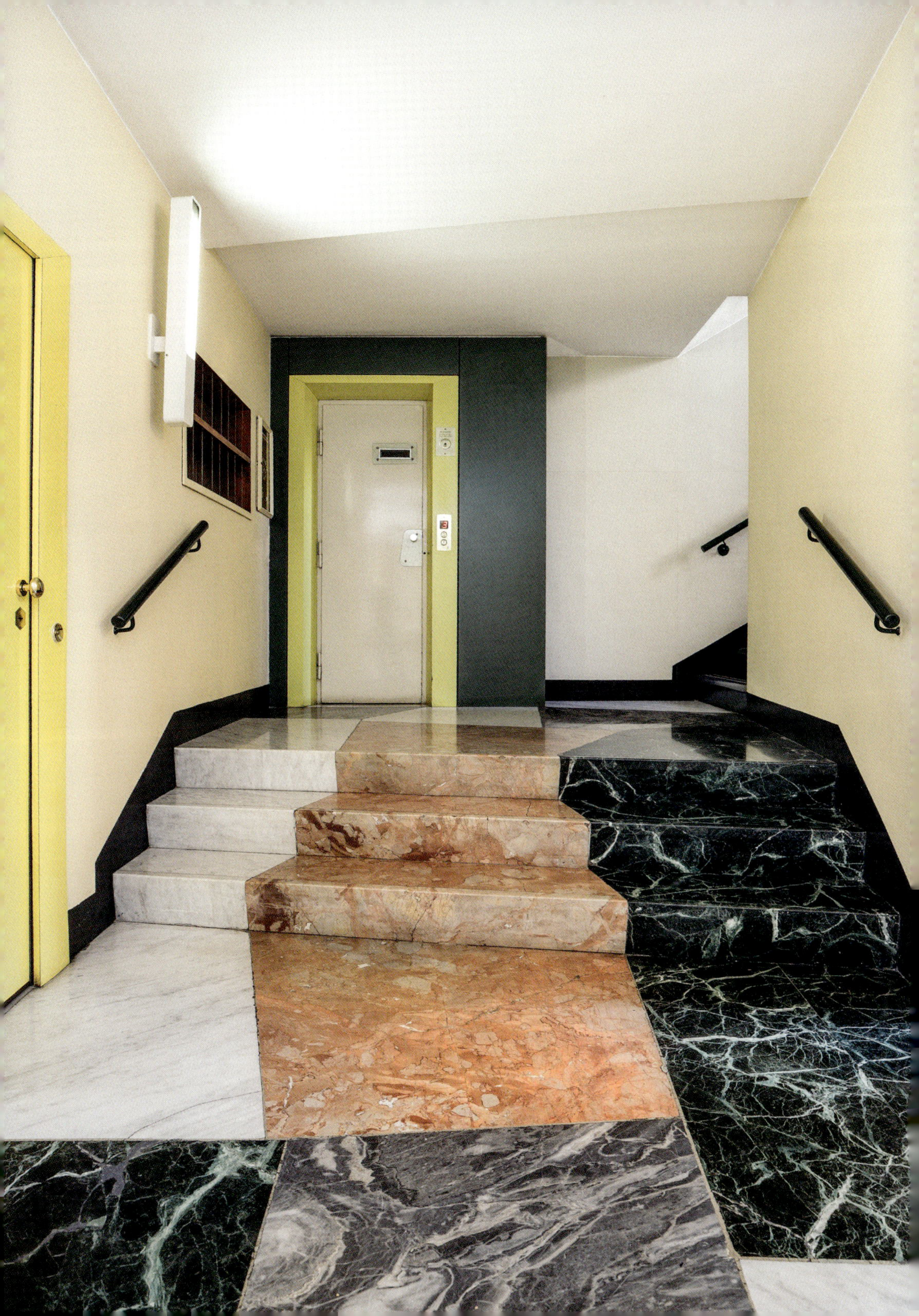

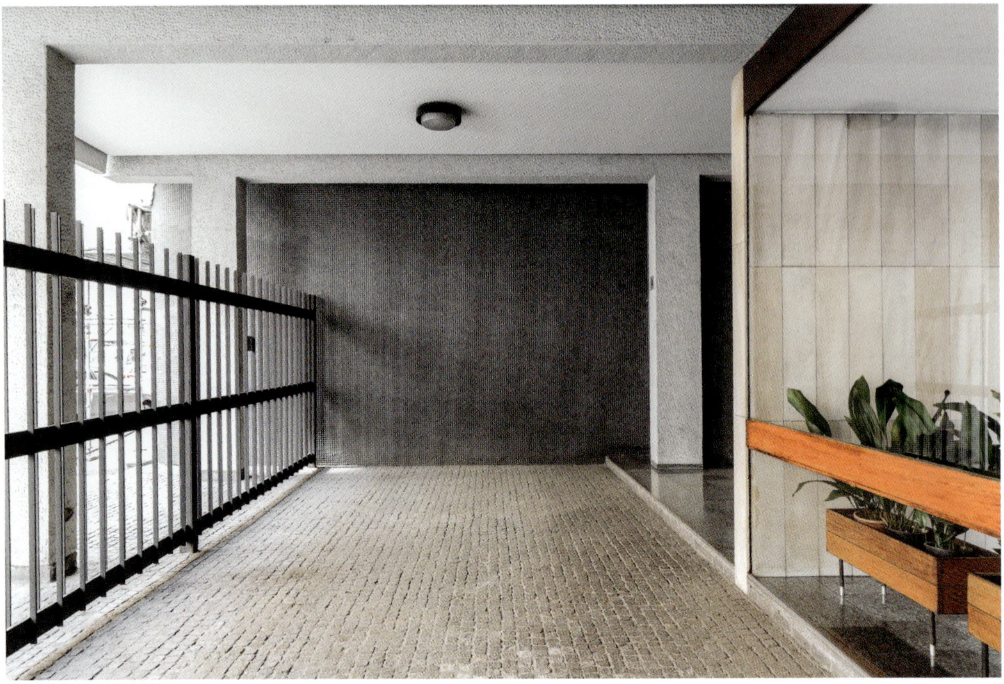

viale Coni Zugna 8

Ceiling lights by Gino Sarfatti.
Tiles by Gio Ponti.

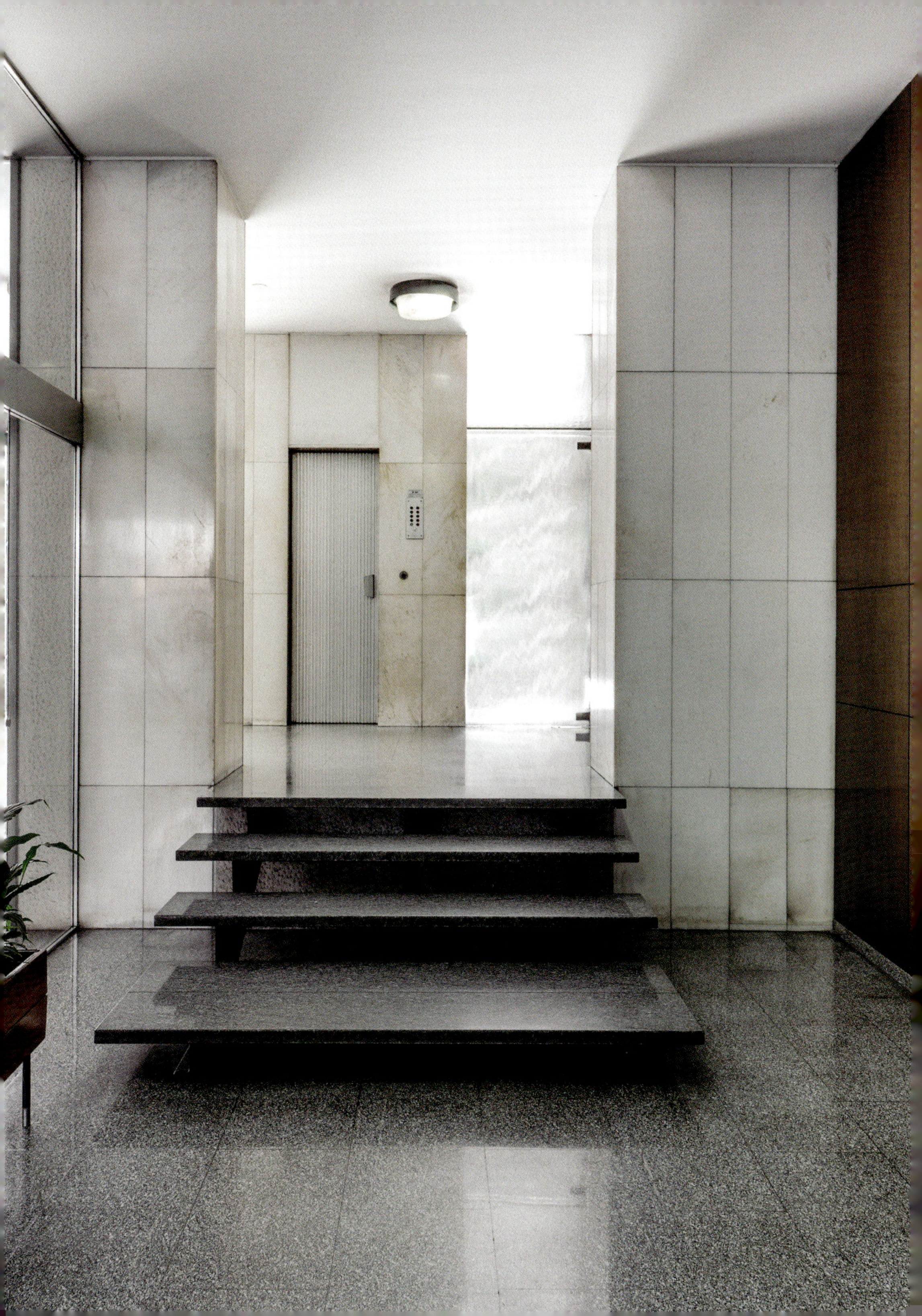

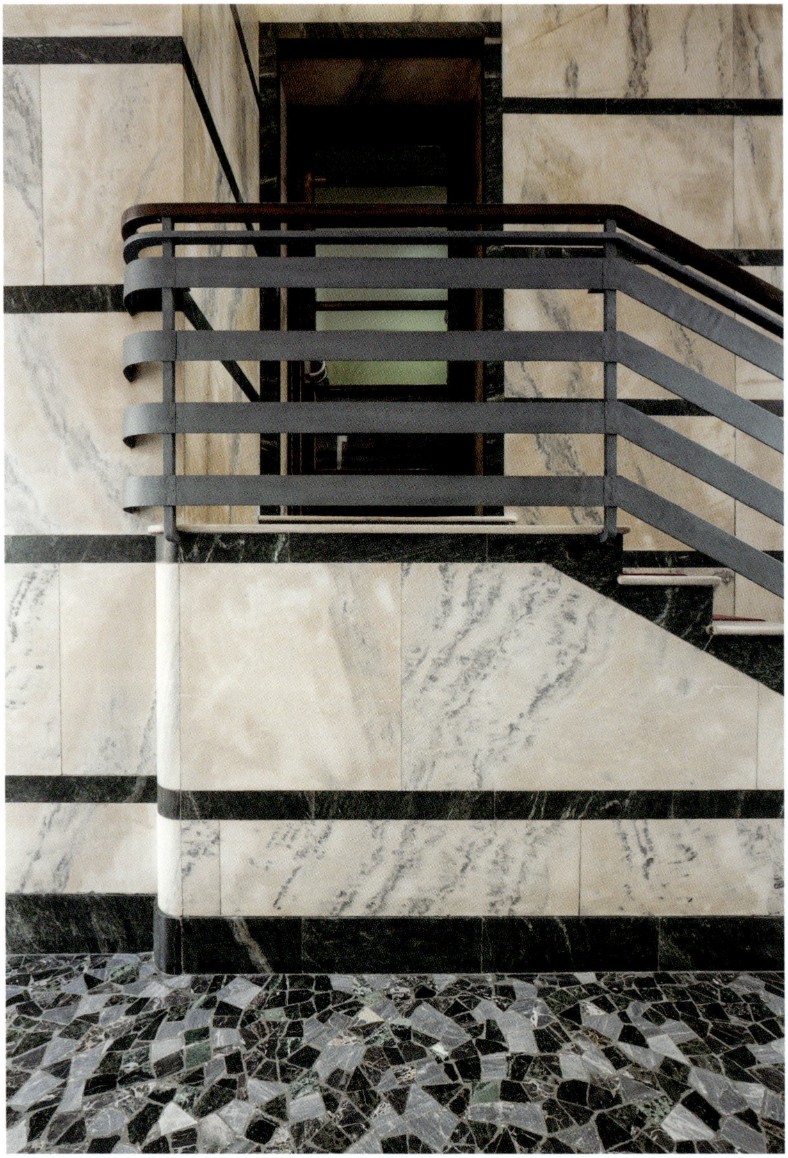

via Vincenzo Foppa 4 · Piero Portaluppi, 1933–34

walls: Lasa marble, serpentinite · floor: Palladiana of Bardiglio marble, Verde Levanto ophicalcite, Portoro limestone

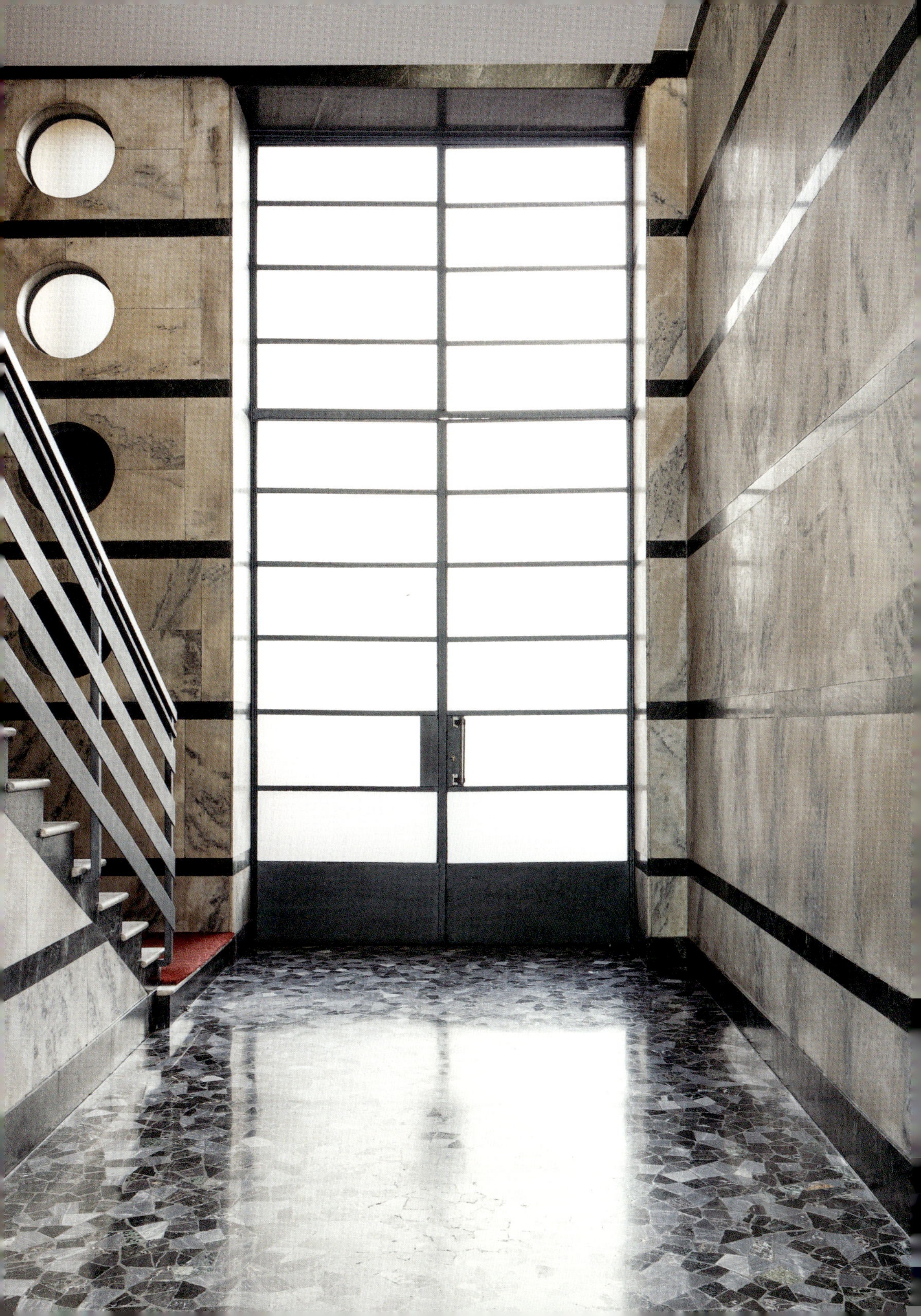

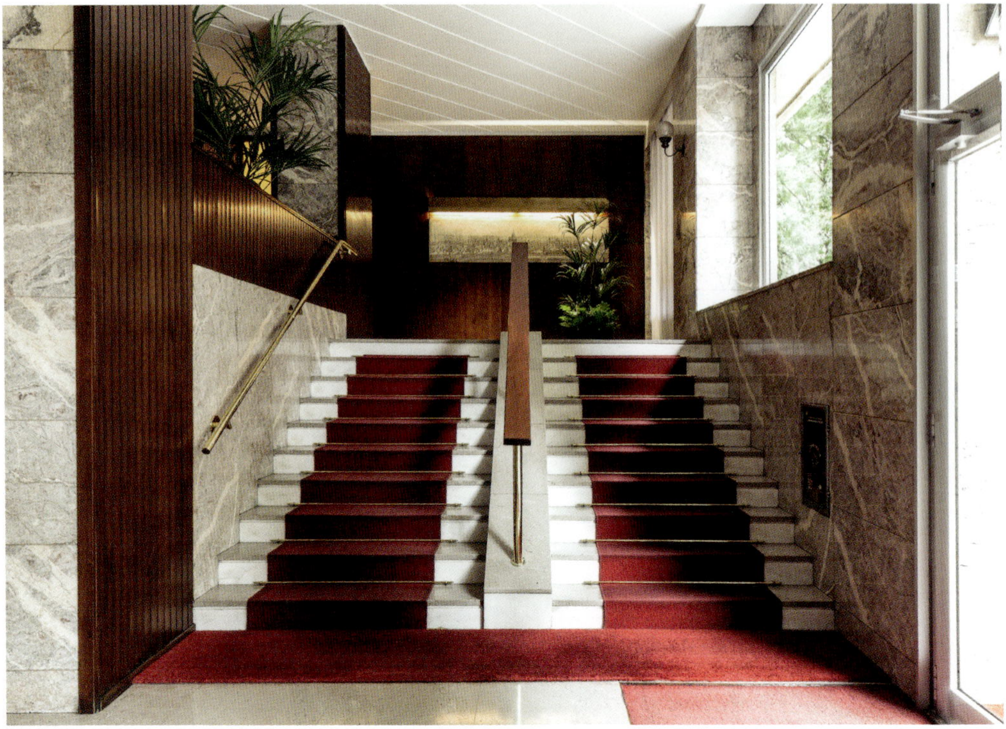

via San Vittore 36/1 · Cesare Donini, 1957

Sconce by Luigi Caccia Dominioni.

floor: Repen limestone · stairs: Repen limestone and Bianco Carrara marble · walls: Fior di Pesco Carnico marble

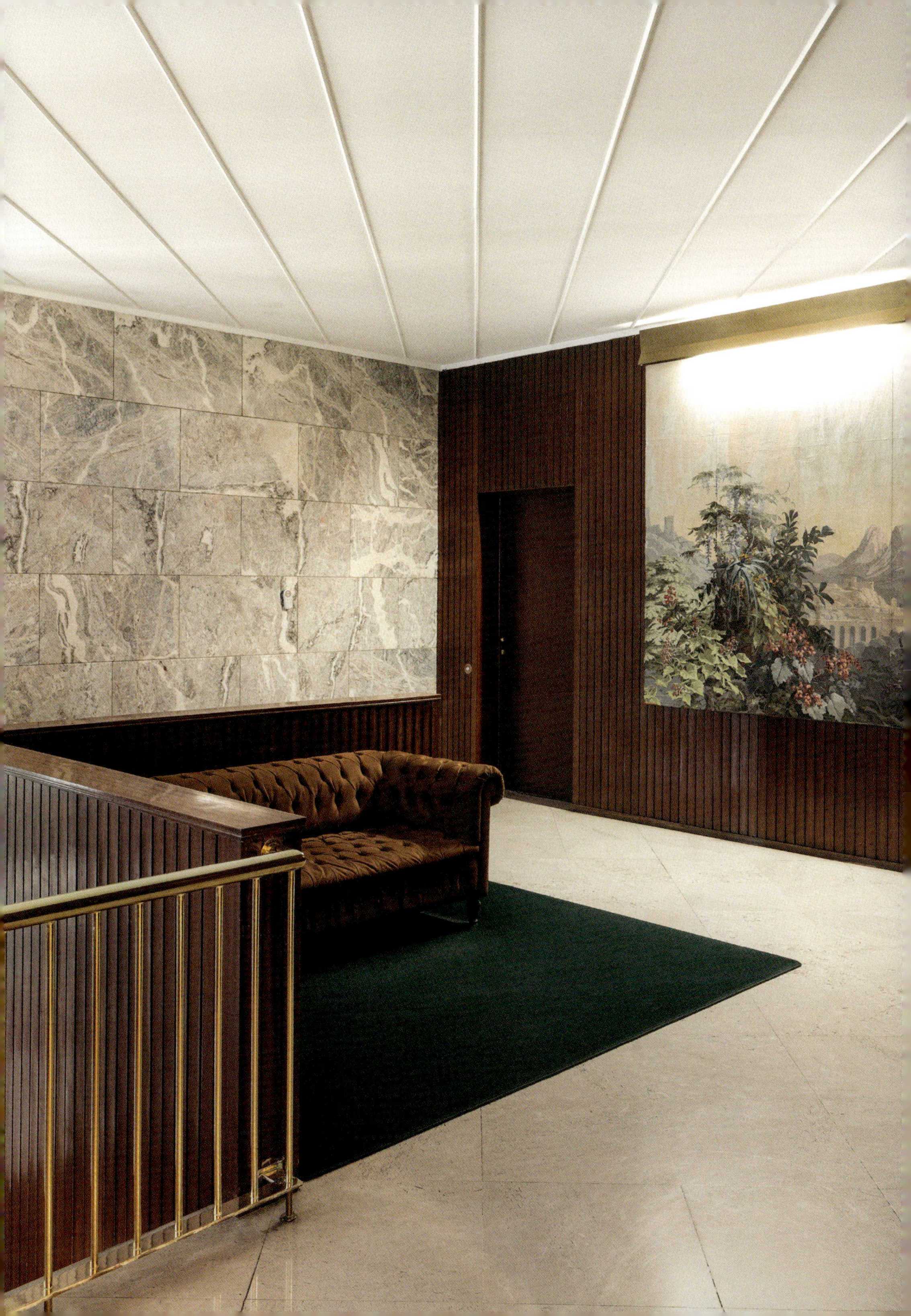

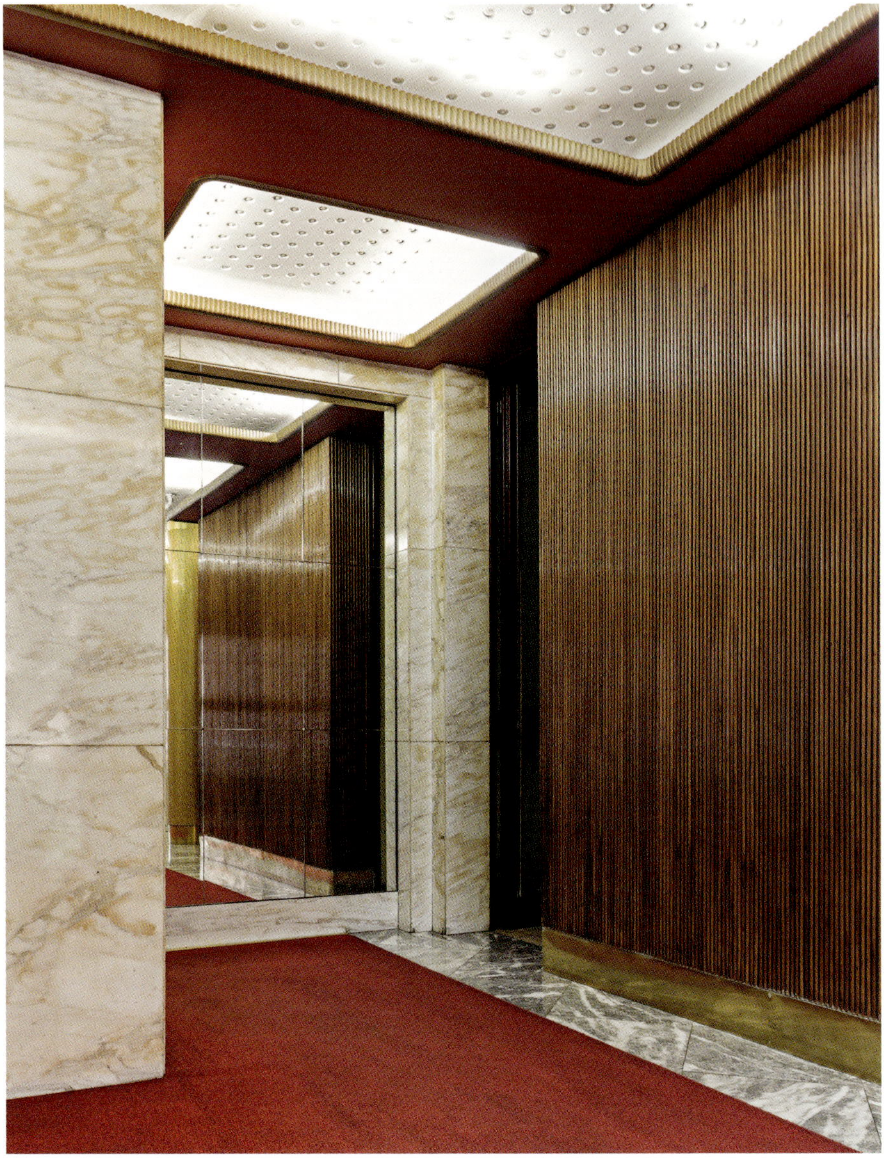

via Matteo Bandello 4/1 · Cesare Donini, 1953–56
floor: Fior di Pesco Carnico marble · walls: Arabescato Carrara marble

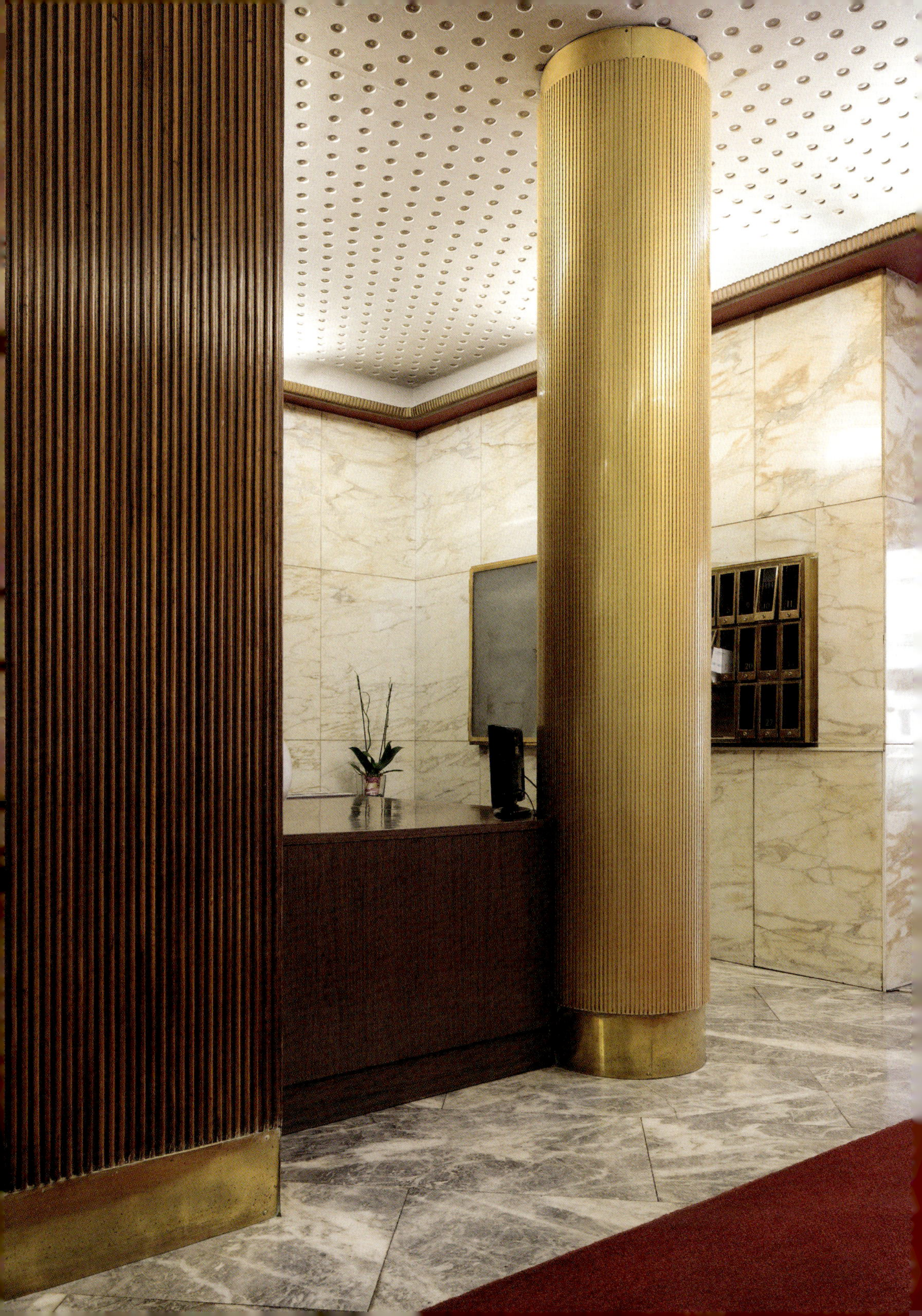

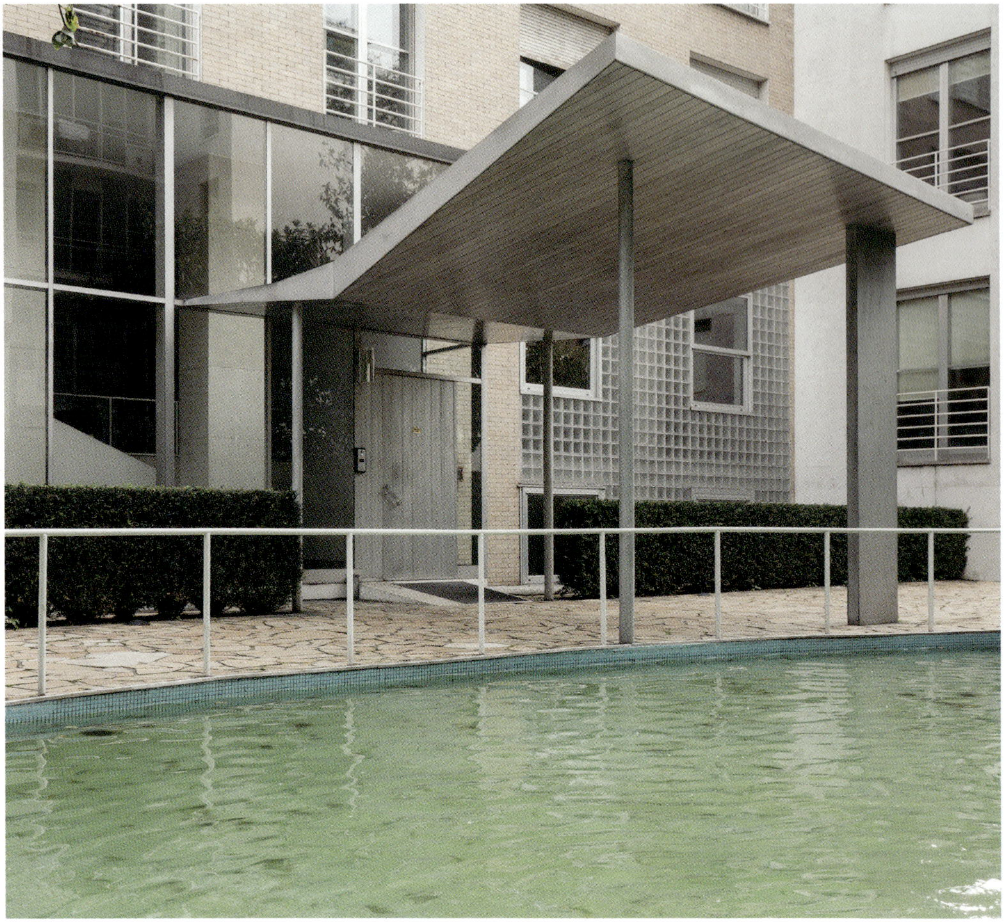

via Lanzone 7, Condominio XXI Aprile · Mario Asnago, Claudio Vender, 1950–53

Entrance canopy clad in sheet aluminum.
interior floor: Verde Alpi ophicalcite · stairs: Bianco Perlino limestone

Following spreads:
via San Vittore 45 · Giacinto Baldizzone, 1963–66
floor and stairs: Rosa Baveno granite

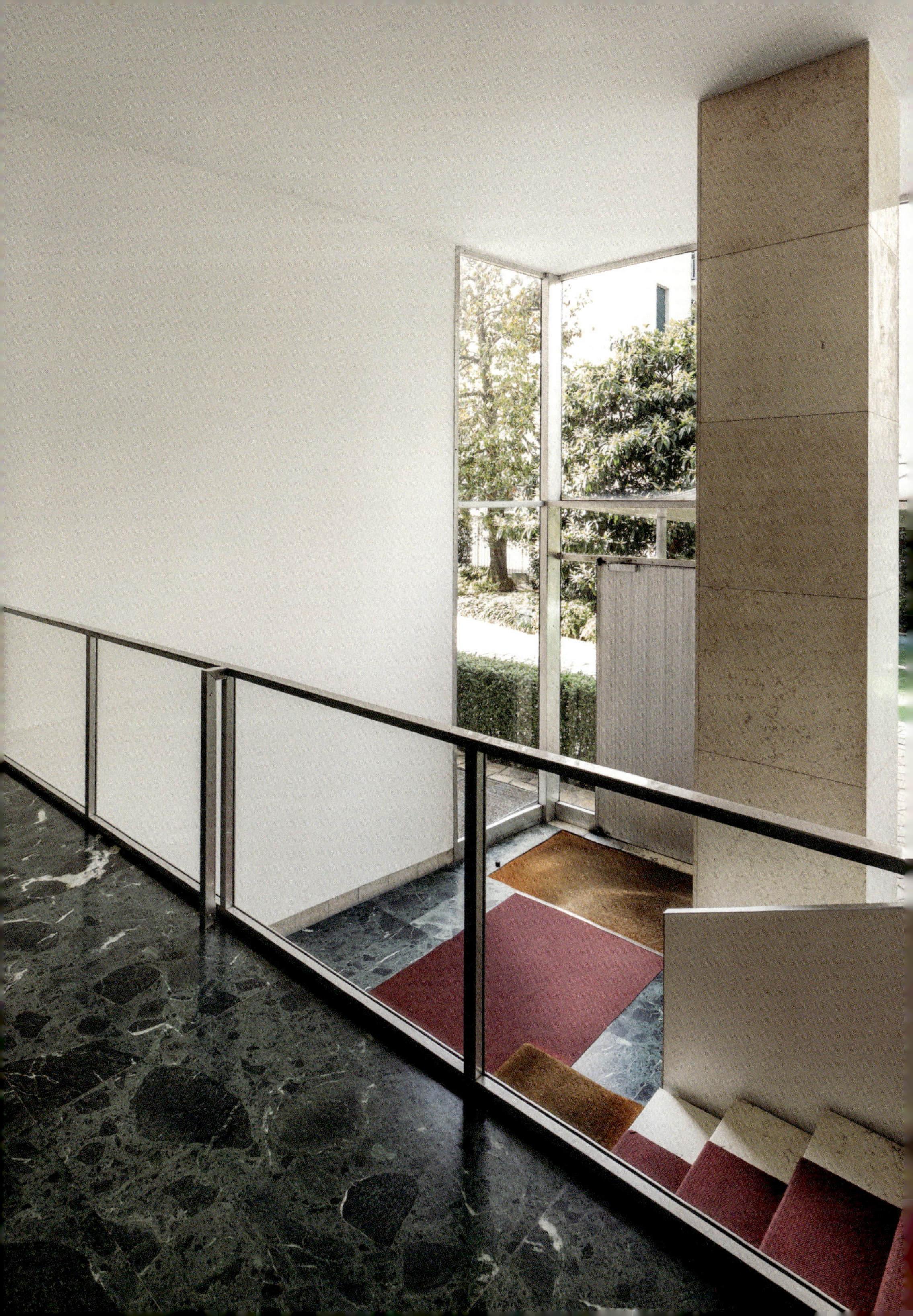

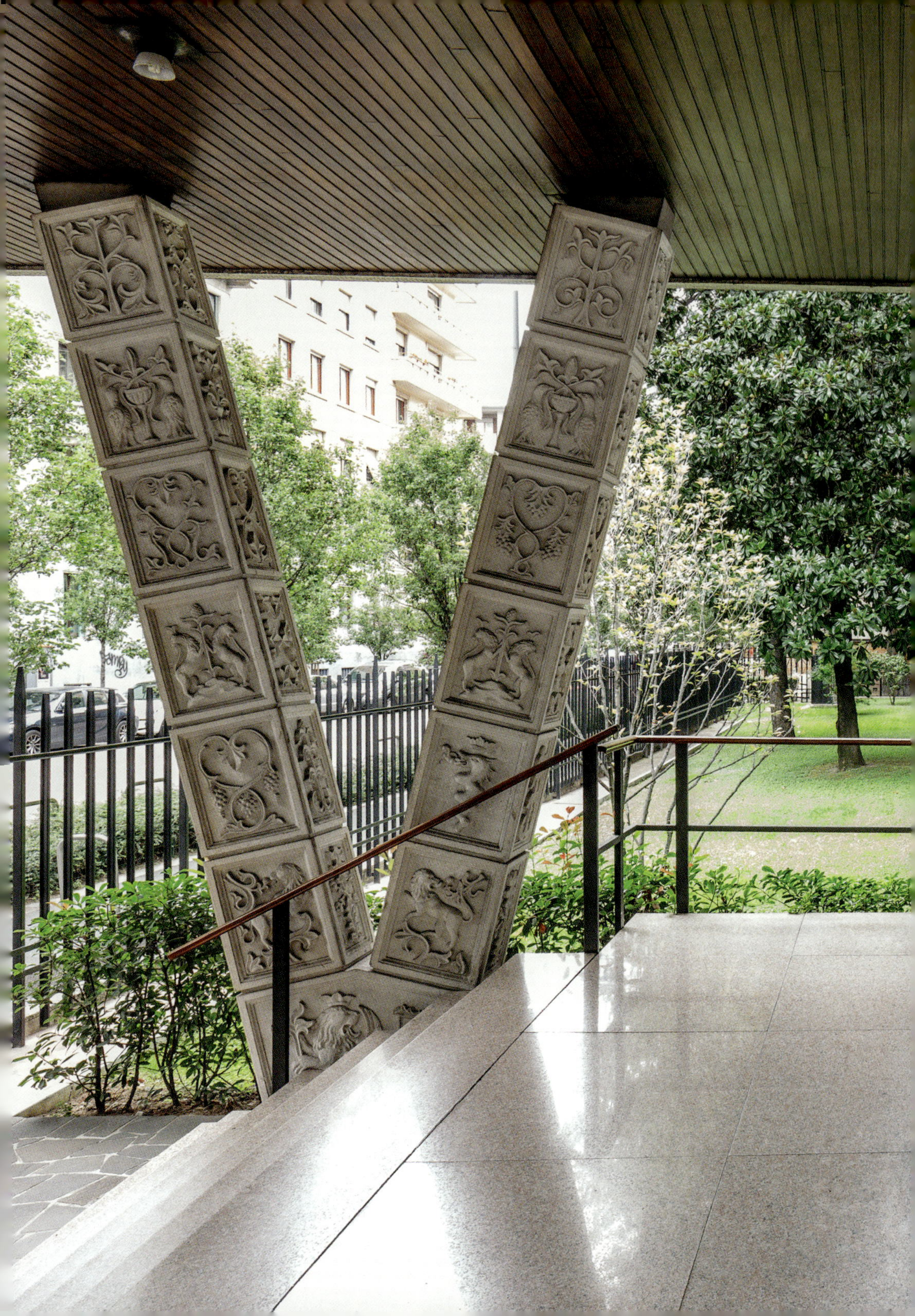

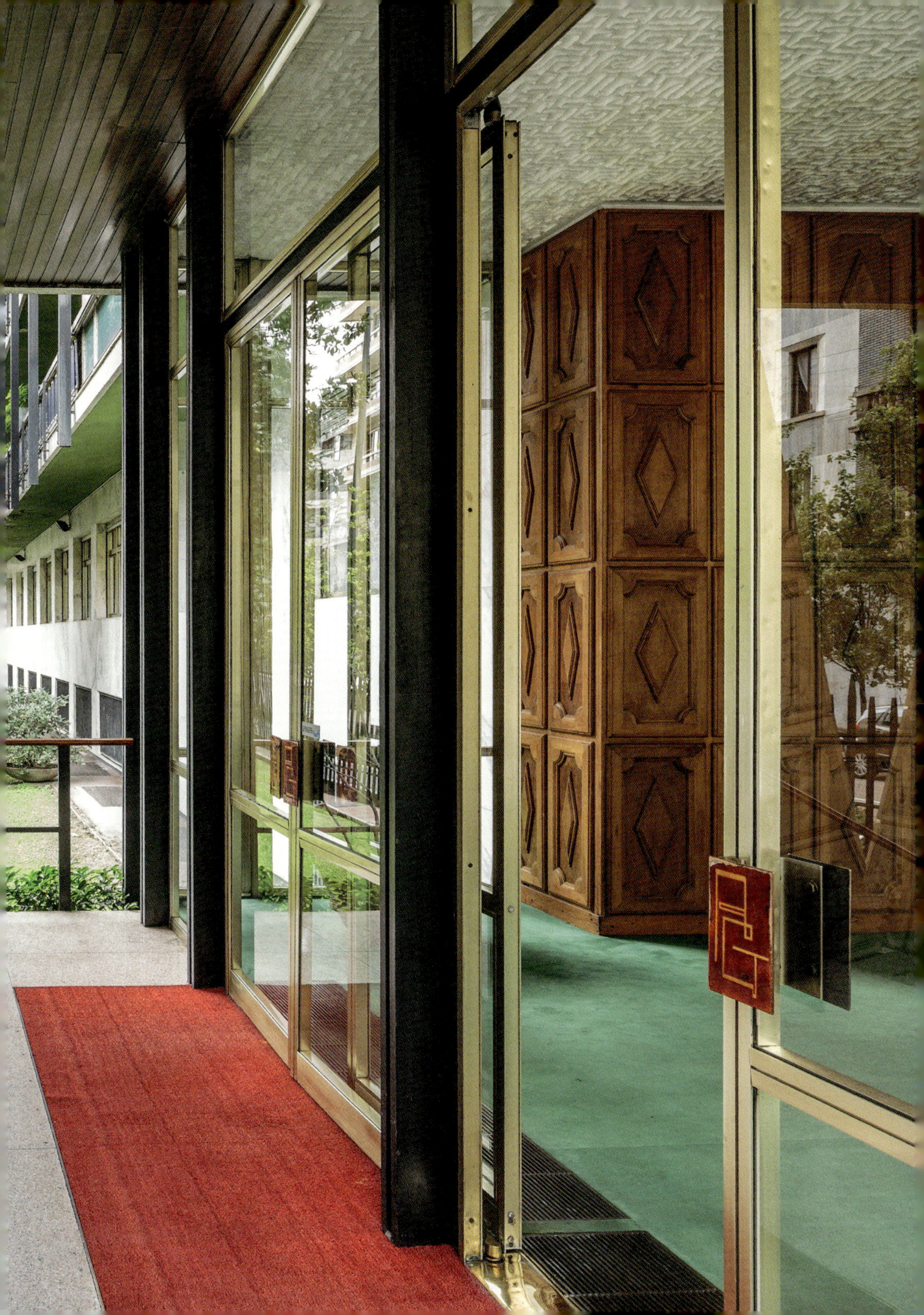

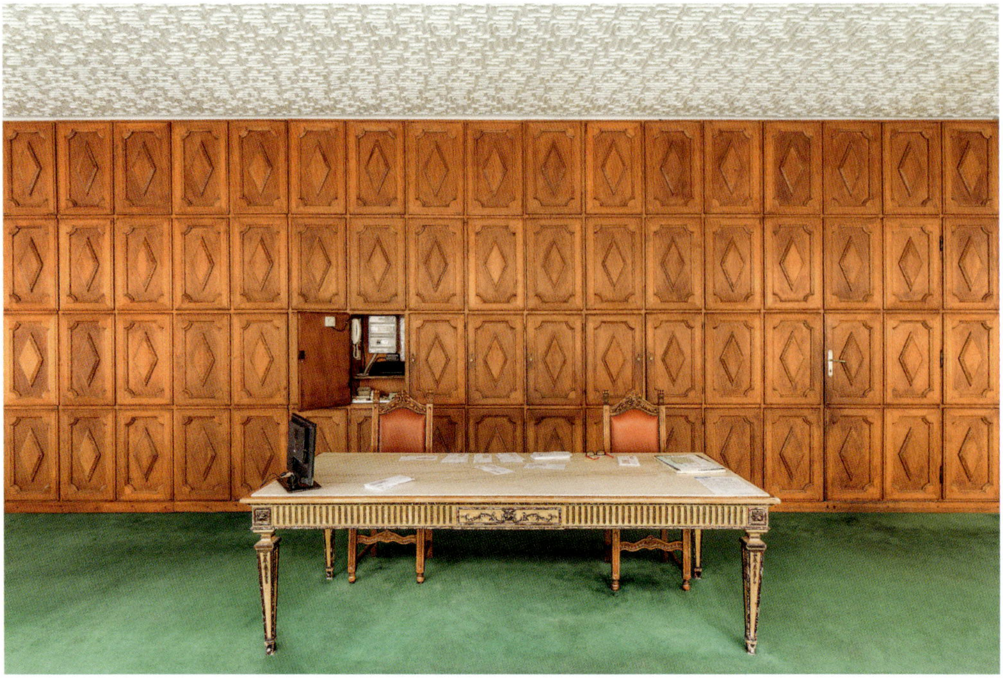

The departure point for interpreting this complex interior is the eclectic choice of combining a nineteenth-century Neoclassical reception desk with a pair of faux Renaissance chairs. As a result of this unorthodox combination diverse surface treatments come to the fore. All attempts at blending the edges are avoided, as all these planes abut one another, setting off a set of dizzying optical effects. Concrete molded panels, inset with diverse instances of Italian heraldry, envelop both the vertical and canted columns in an unsettling way. A certain amount of repose is found in the warm walnut paneling, set with attenuated diamond and emerald reliefs. Adding to the eclectic atmosphere are echoes of modern design tropes that alter the classical elements, seen in the abstracted meander pattern of the white plastered ceiling, as well as in the polychrome enameled door handles. An appropriate finishing touch is the use of the latest Venini Murano chandelier, with a cluster of small glass polyhedral pendants. Appropriating devices frequently seen in haute couture, the architect exhibits a knowing confidence in the way he handles the historical and modern codes, thereby achieving a success rarely seen outside his particular mid-century Milanese ambient.

Chandelier by Venini.
Wall cladding in walnut.

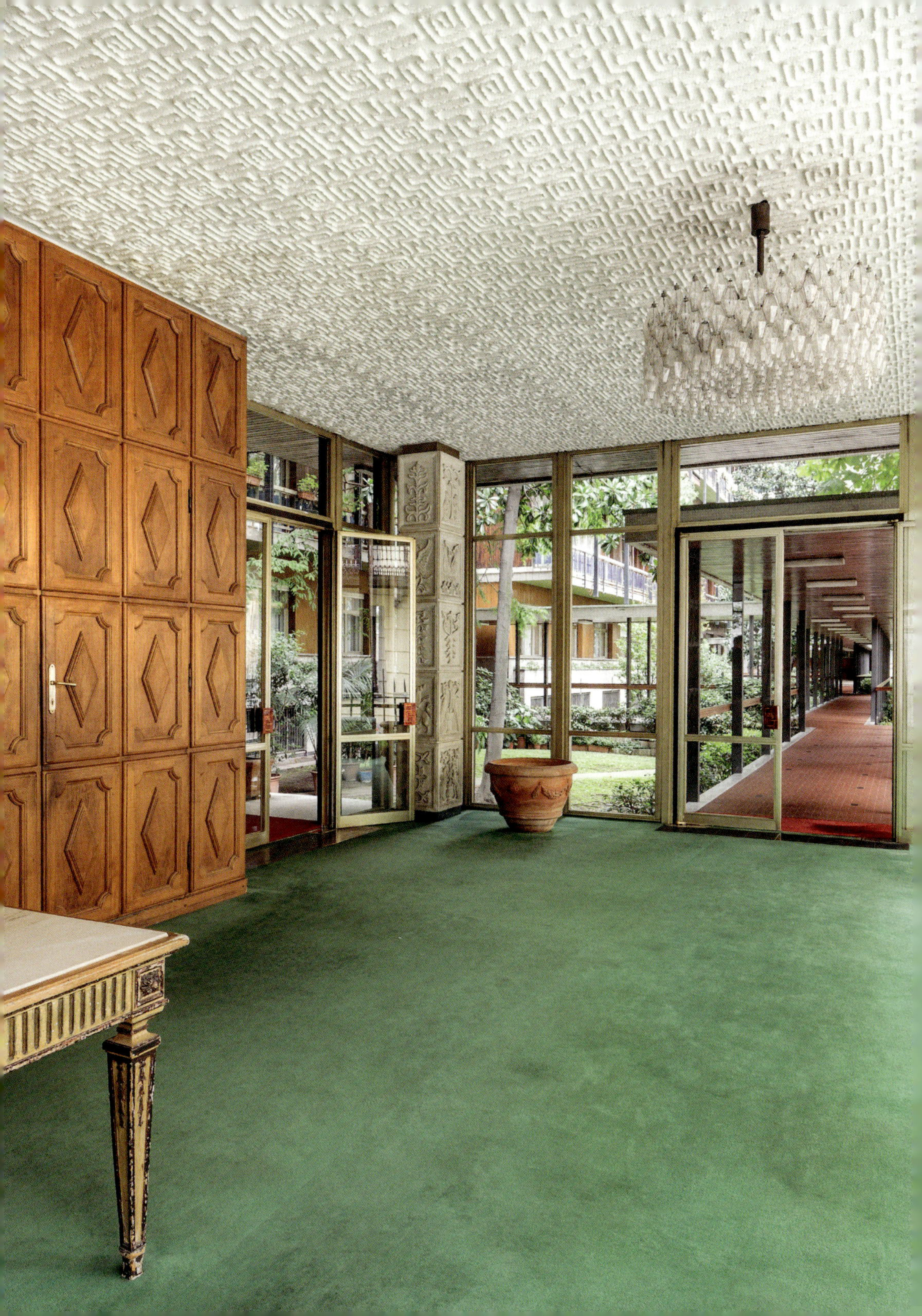

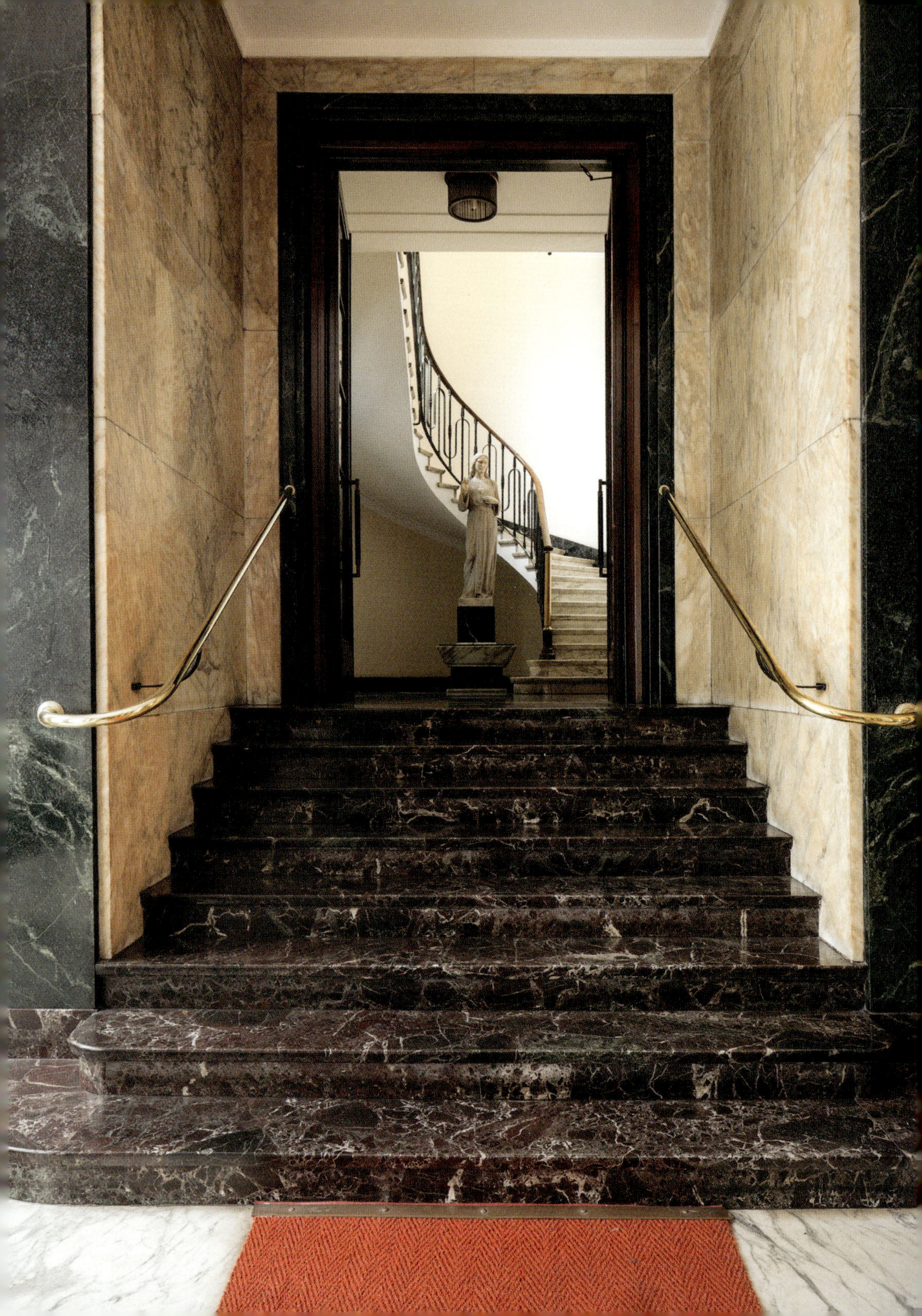

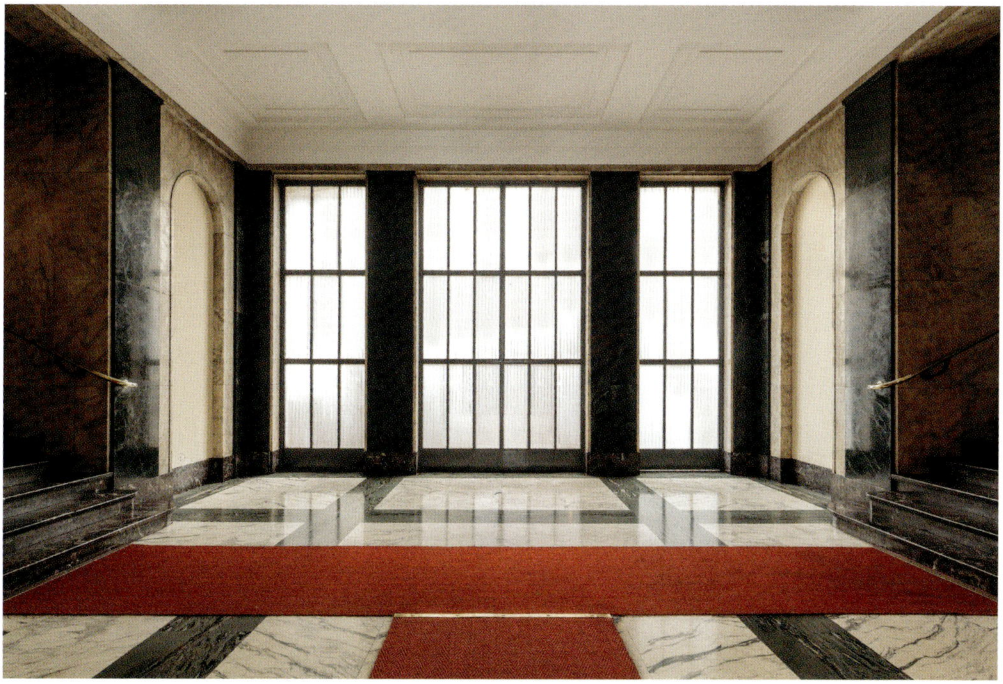

piazza Sant'Ambrogio 8

stairs: Rosso Levanto ophicalcite

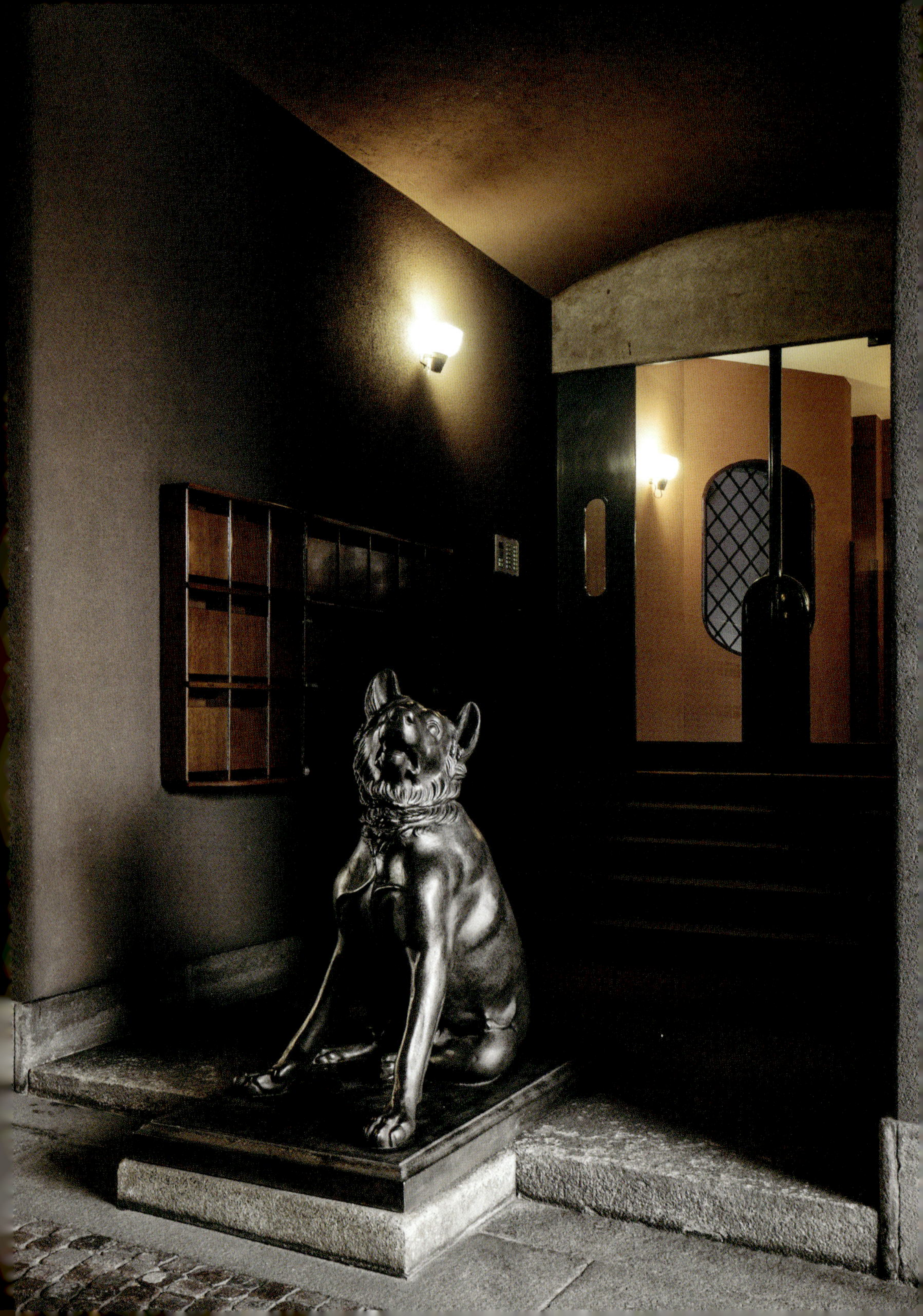

This and following spreads:

piazza Sant'Ambrogio 16, Casa Caccia Dominioni · Luigi Caccia Dominioni, 1947–49

Sconces by Luigi Caccia Dominioni and Ignazio Gardella.

floor: Trento Porphyry cobbles · exterior stairs and plinth: Montorfano granite

Immediately upon entering the hall of this grandiose private family palazzo in Piazza Sant'Ambrogio, one is confronted with a monumental pair of cast-iron Molossus dogs set on stone plinths that are wedged into the flanking steps leading to the facing twin entrances. These mythological creatures were ancient guard and hunting dogs, connected by history and legend to Alexander the Great. (Roman copies in marble of a Hellenistic bronze original can be found in the Vatican, the Uffizi, and the British Museum.) The left entrance door is marked with the crest of the noble Visconti family depicting a man eaten by a giant snake, which is part of Milan's coat of arms. Both the dogs and the crest were sourced by Luigi Caccia Dominioni specifically for the hallway and constitute two of the hermetic symbols placed at specific points in this important inaugural work. The palazzo was built in 1947 after the old family home was destroyed in a 1944 World War II bombing. Besides other functions, it served as both a residence and work studio for the architect from the mid-twentieth century until his death in 2016.

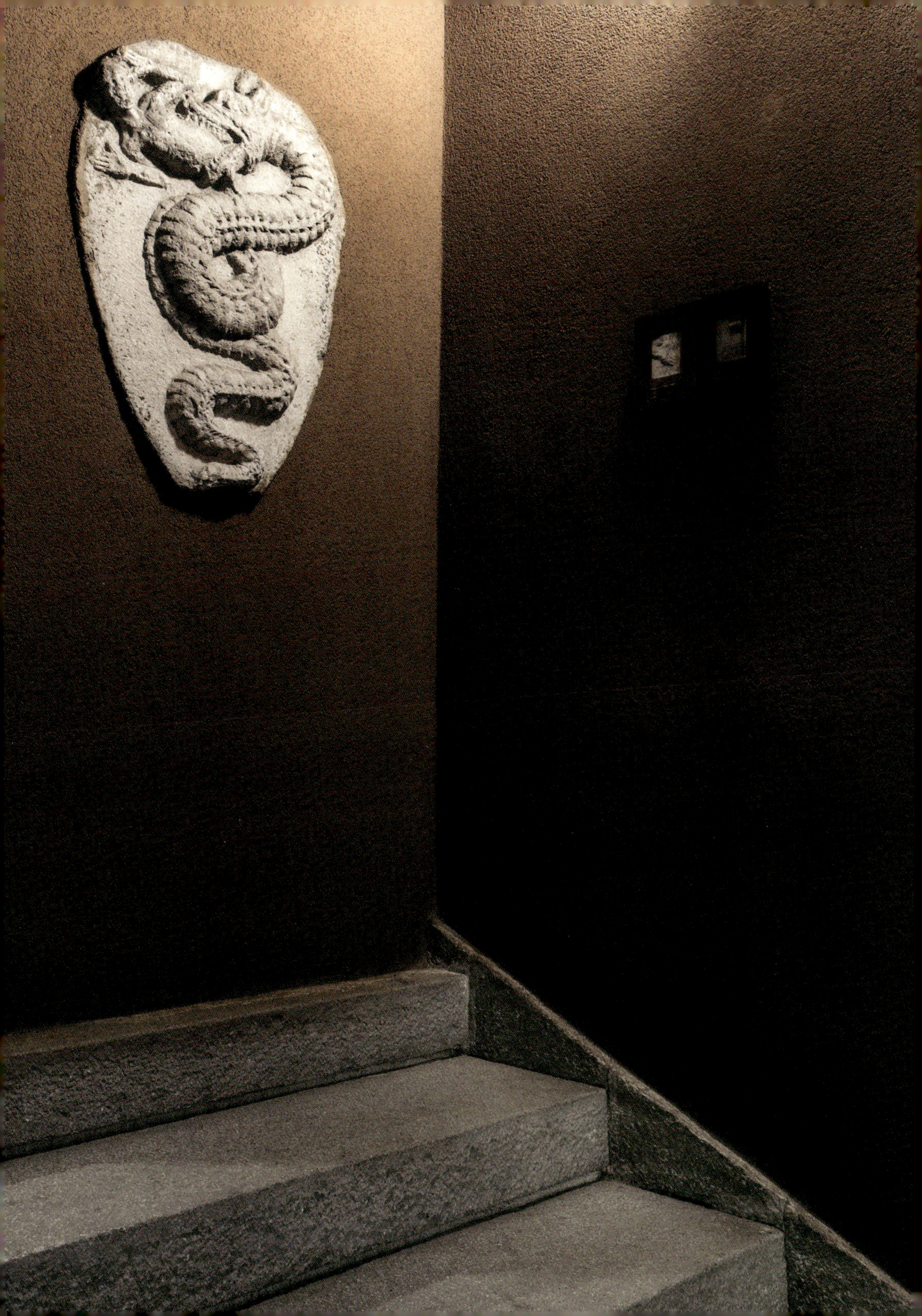

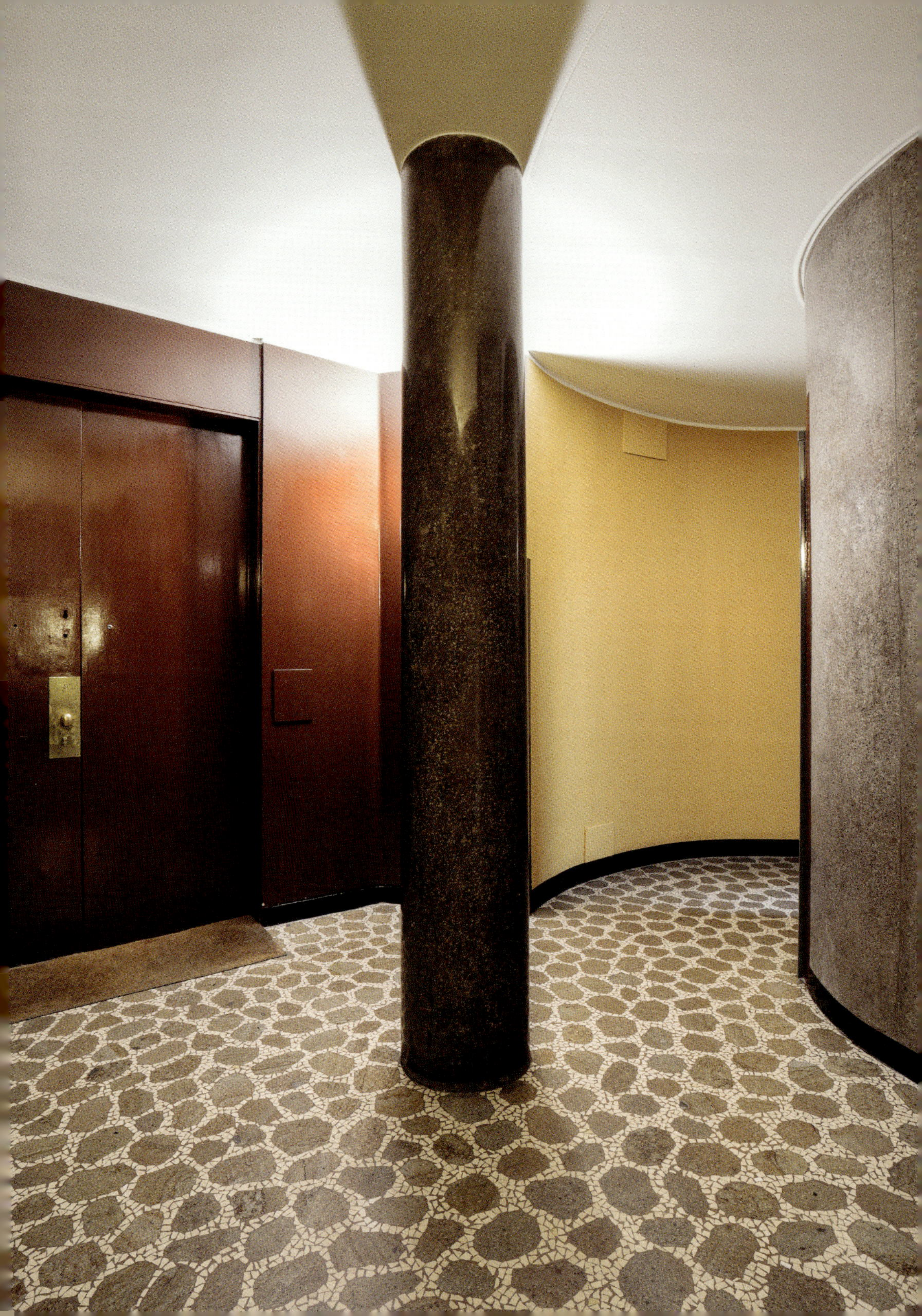

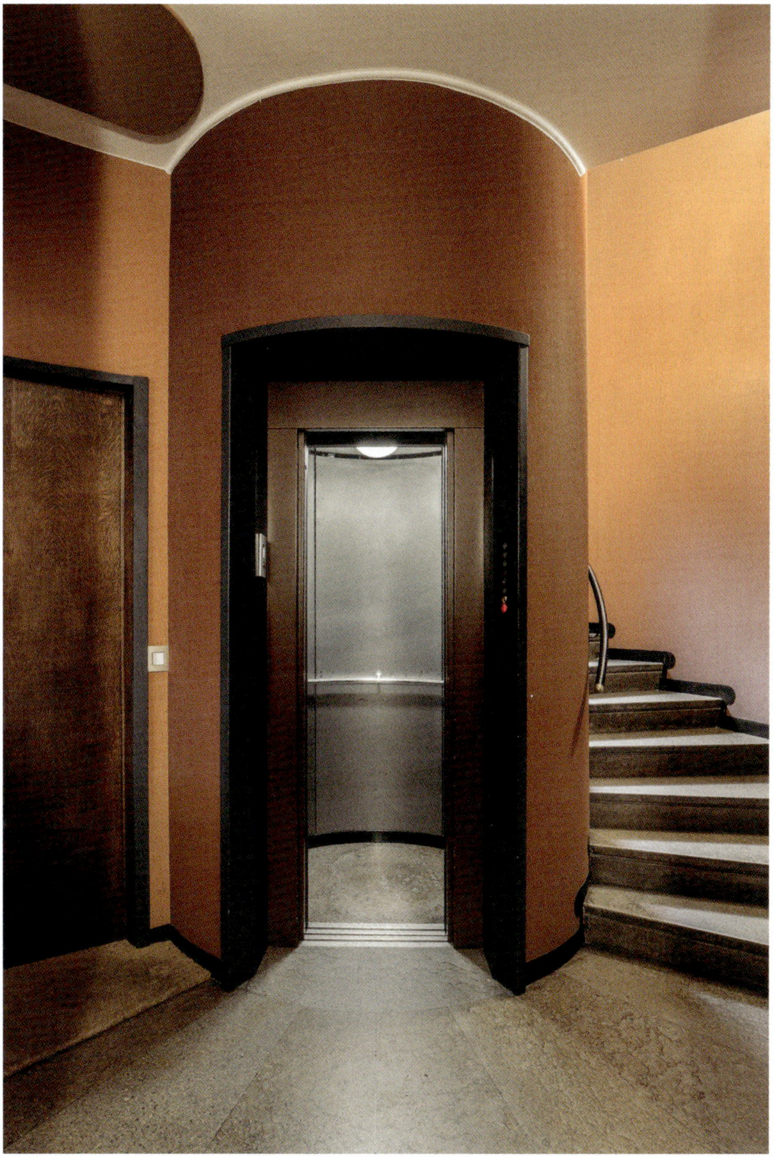

seminato floor: Trachite Zovonite a tinta calda and Carrara marbles
floor and stairs: Trachite Zovonite a tinta calda

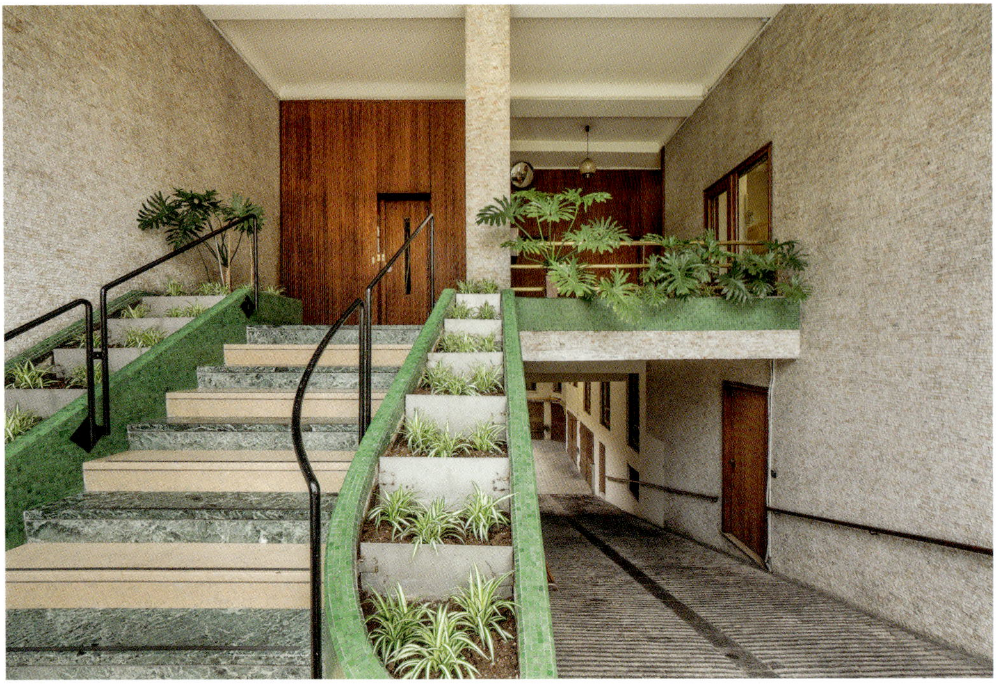

VERDE ALPI

Green is not a common color for stones, and so green marbles have always been both highly prized and valuable. The two traditional Italian green dimension stones are ophicaltcites (breccia-textured stones from Val d'Aosta, Piemonte, and the Levanto area) and serpentines (from Valmalenco). Val d'Aosta, a very short (fifty-kilometer) and narrow valley, has produced several different varieties that are now difficult to distinguish, as they were drawn from very small quarries and irregular boulders. Verde Issogne, Verde Issorie, Verde S. Denis, Verde Aver, Verde Frayé, Verde di Valtournanche, Verde Mongiove, Verde Mont Blanc, Verde Chatillon, Verde Plan Tressy, Verde Pineta, Verde Foresta, Verde Malachite or Challant, Verde Fontaine, Verde Florian, Verde di Pontey, Verde di Nus, Verde di Gressoney, and the like are all now simply known as Verde Alpi.

piazza Sant'Ambrogio 4 · Luigi Mattioni, 1950–52

Pendant lamp by Luigi Caccia Dominioni.

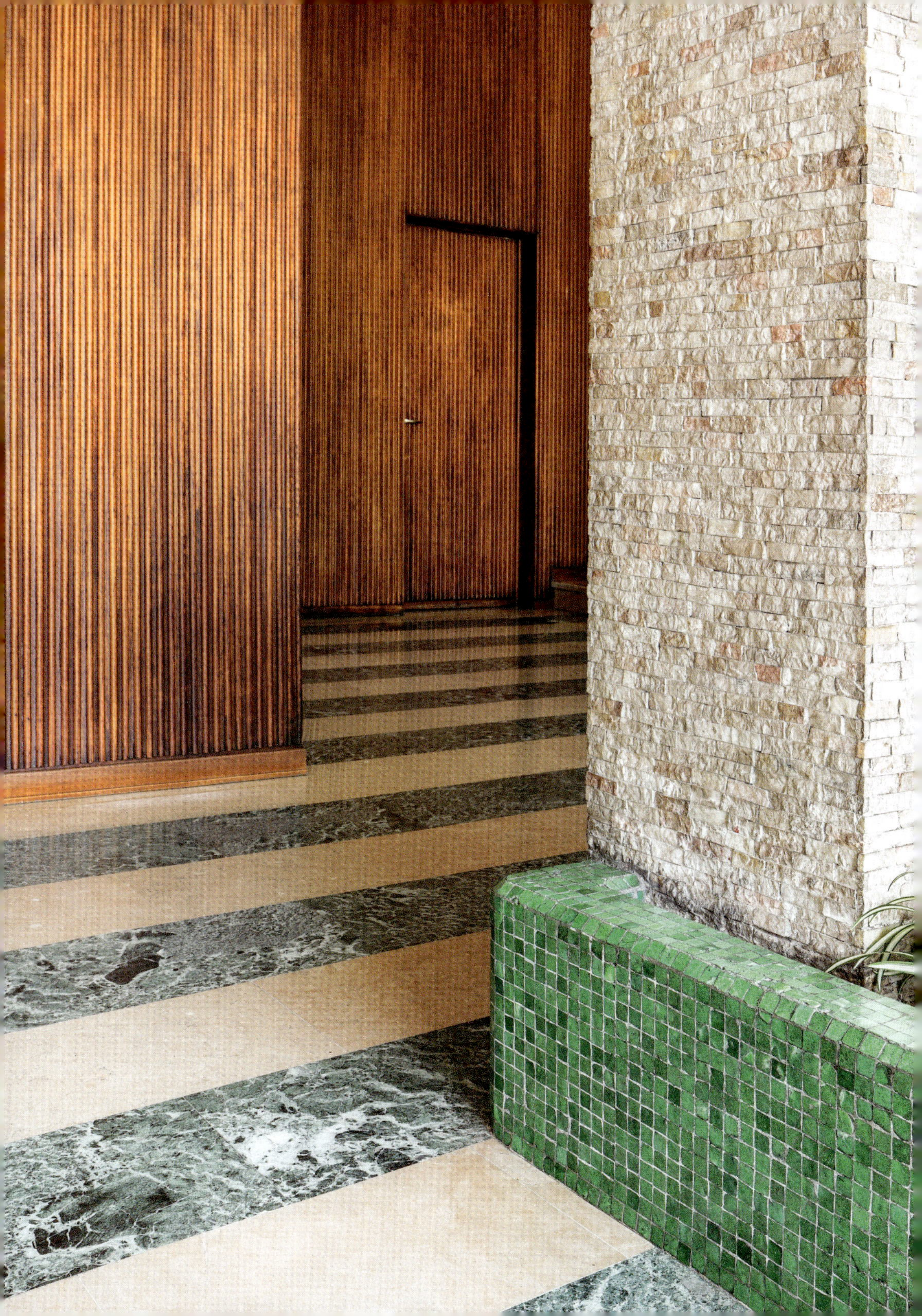

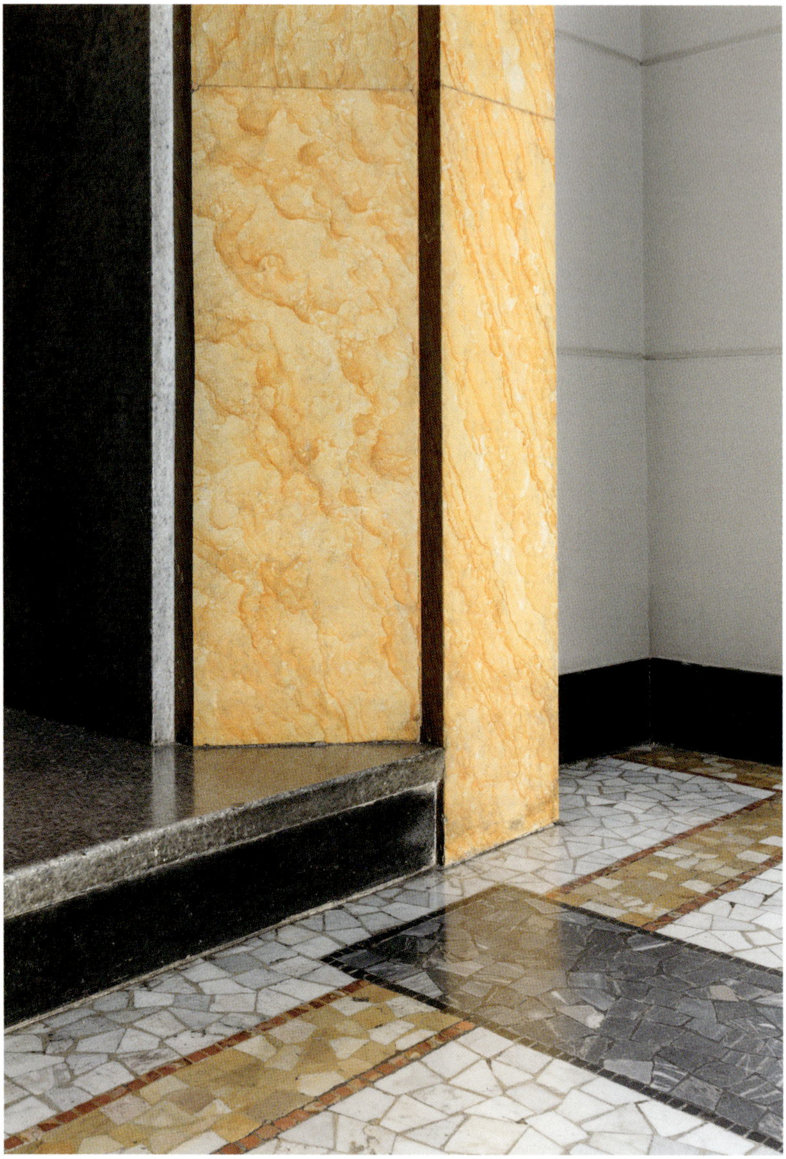

This and following spread:

via Aristide de Togni 14 · Pier Giulio Magistretti, 1934–36

Sconces by Ignazio Gardella.

doorframe: Giallo Mori limestone · floor: Palladiana of Bardiglio, Carrara, Giallo Siena marble, Giallo Torri, Giallo Mori, Musso marble

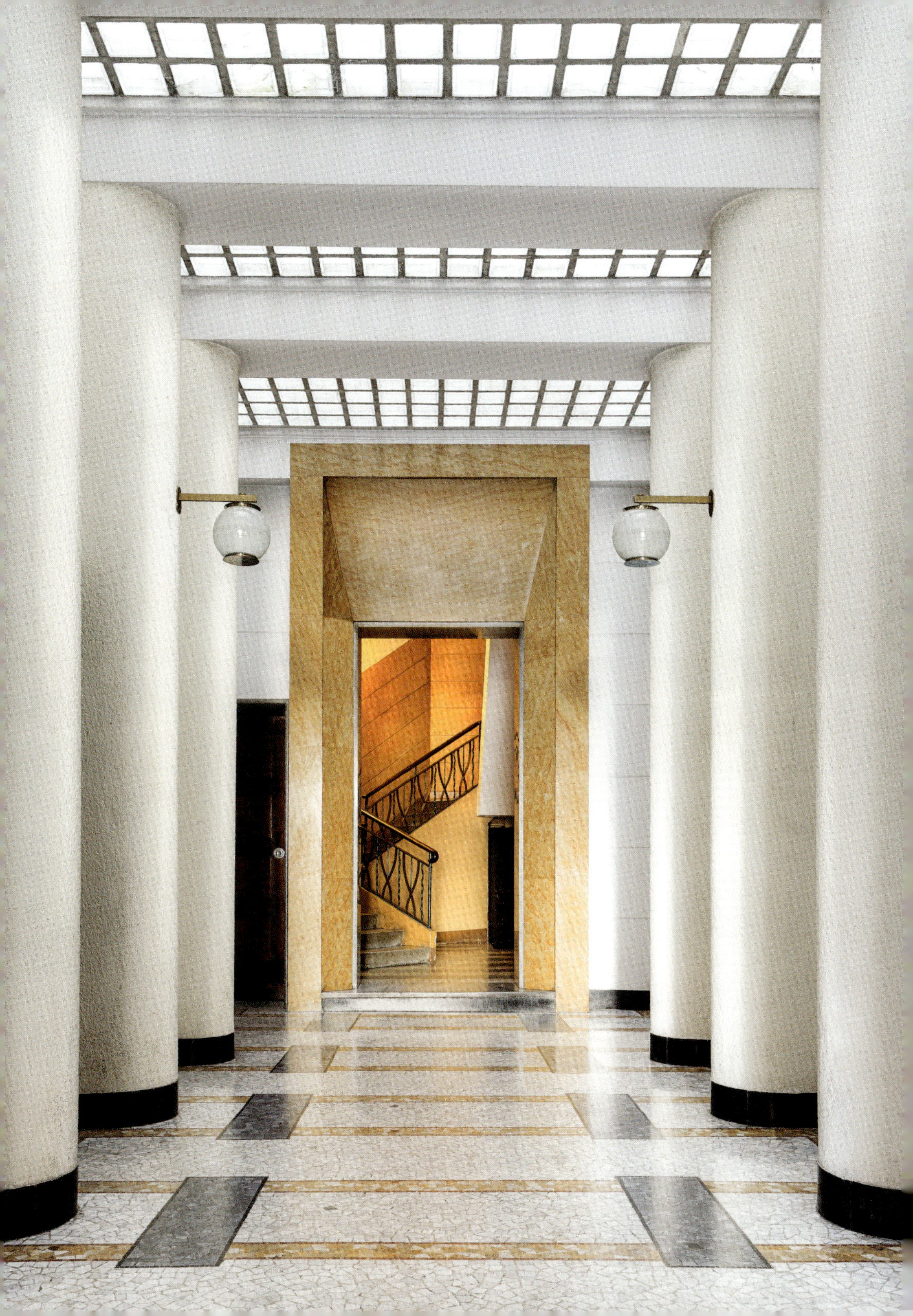

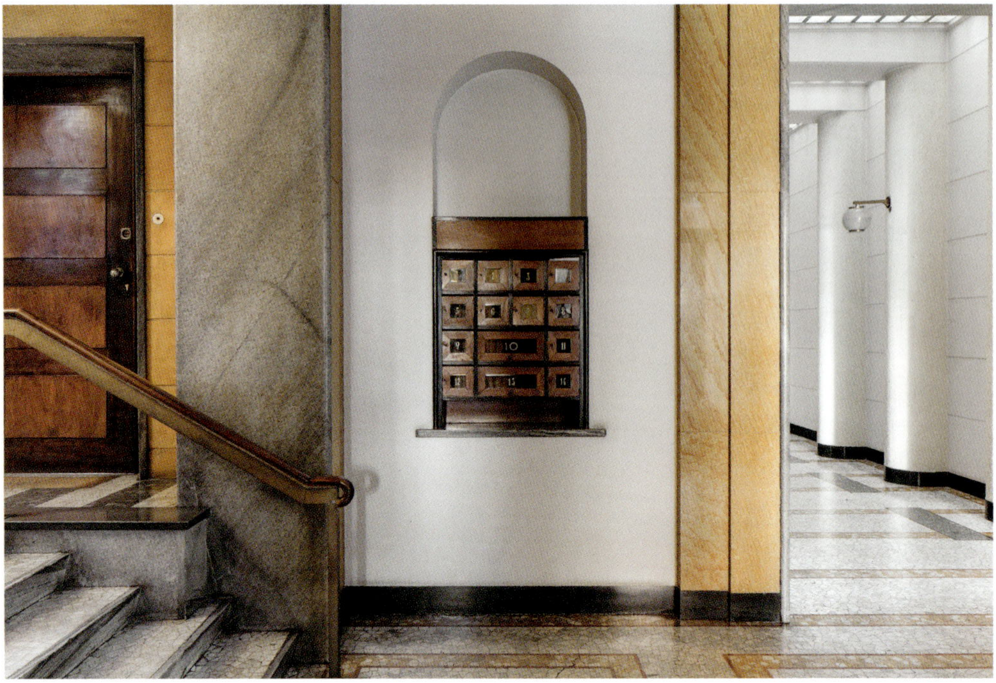

This is one of the most subtle and impressive entrance halls, created by a leading Milan architect of the 1930s: Pier Giulio Magistretti. A long, skylit colonnaded hall, leads to an exaggerated chamfered portal with a fastidiously detailed staircase bannister whose handrail is supported by a balustrade of stylized Roman numerals in the form of Xs. A color palette of grays, ochres, blacks, and whites strikes a sober tone contrasting with the voluptuous warmth of the walnut doors. Even though Ignazio Gardella's *doppio vetro* sconces were installed twenty years later, they strike an abstract classical note atop the columns.

Sconce by Ignazio Gardella.

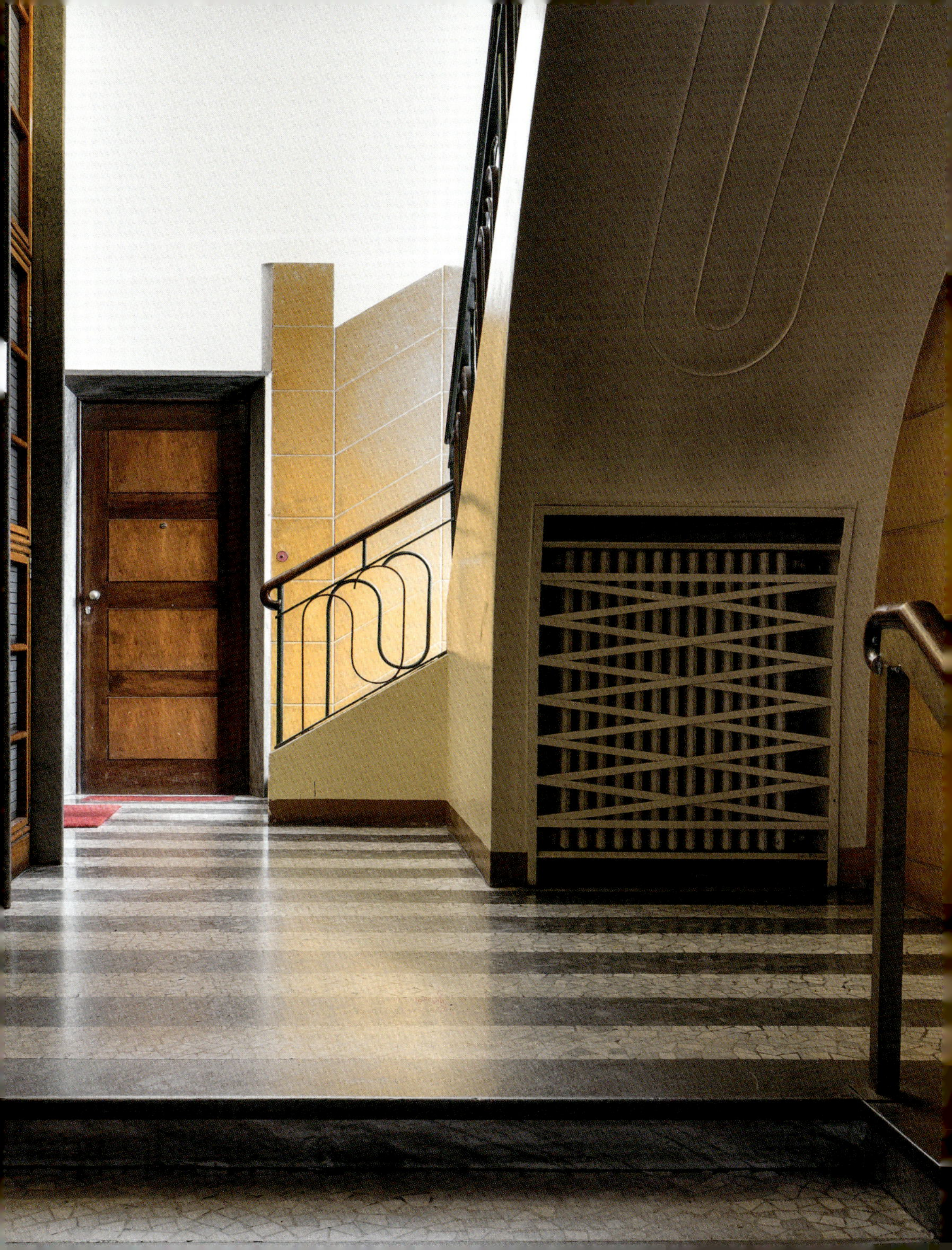

While submerged in the fluorescent green Challant marble environment, one still cannot fail to notice Piero Portaluppi's calling card rendered as a sculptural maquette in Carrara marble. This metaphysical 3-dimensional logo was placed at the entrance of the architect's studio.

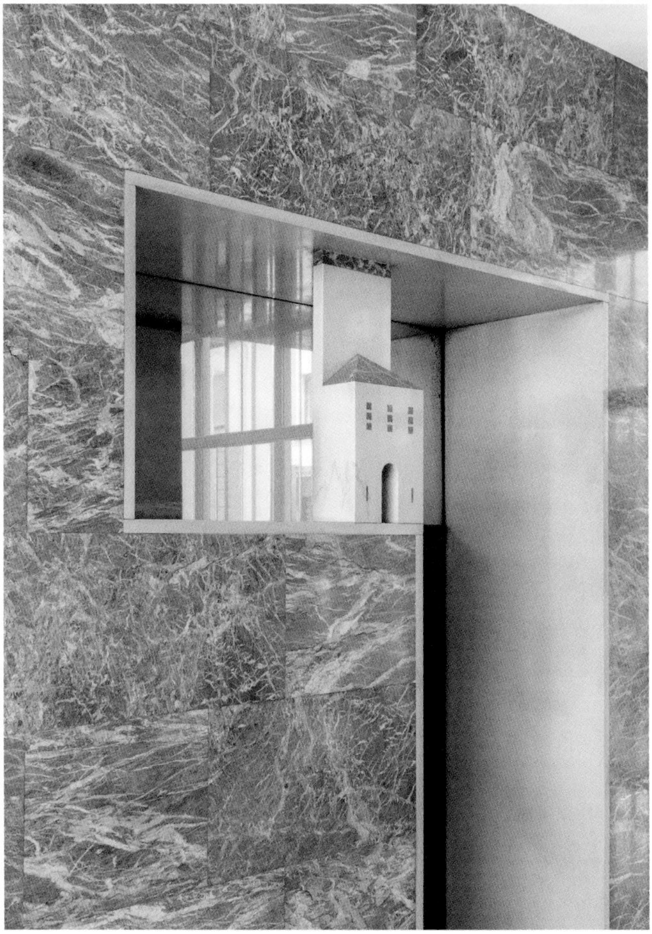

via Morozzo della Rocca 5, Casa Portaluppi · Piero Portaluppi, 1938–39

Architecture maquette by Piero Portaluppi.
stairs and walls: Verde Malachite, also known as Verde Challant, from Val d'Aosta

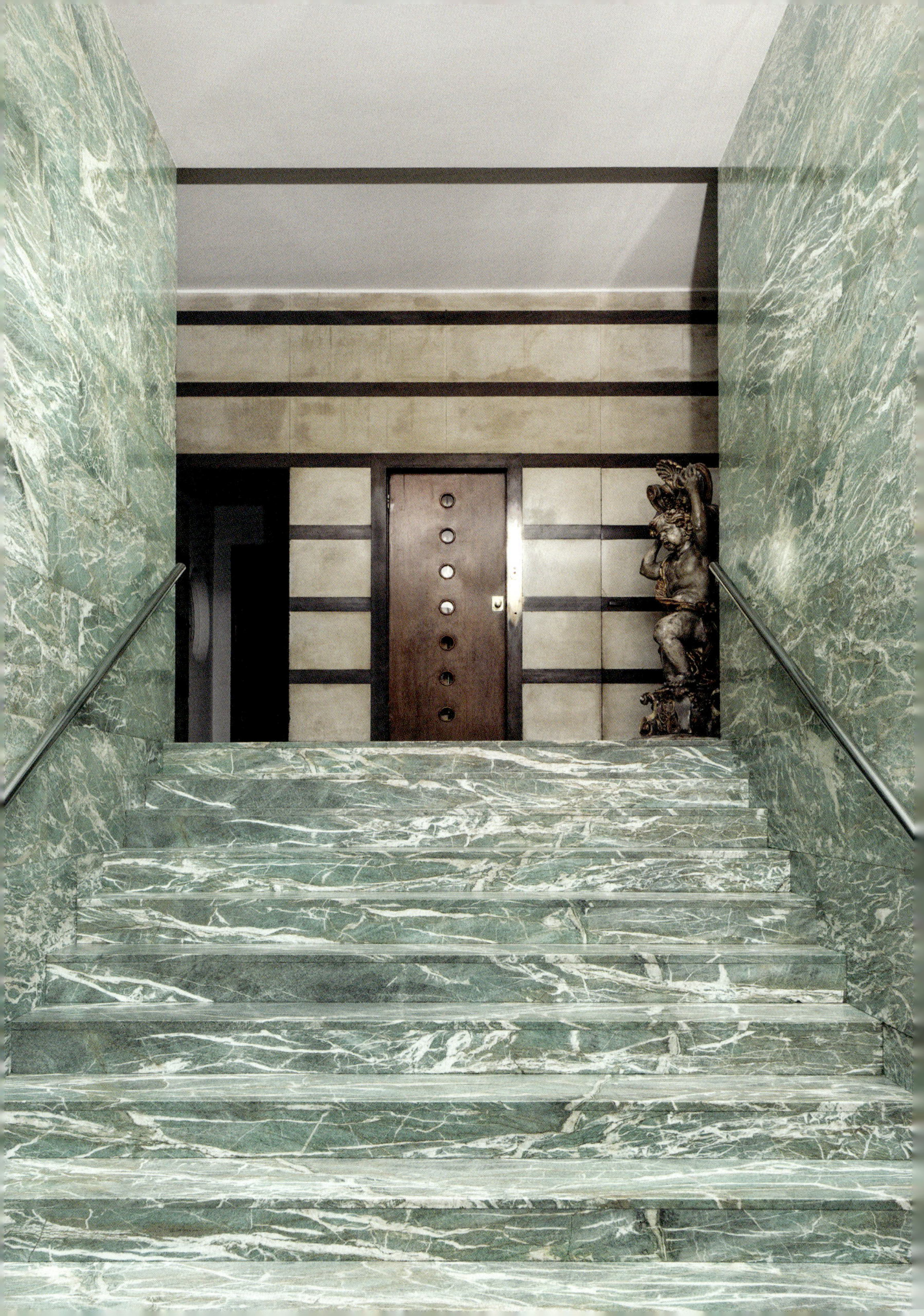

MARMO PALISSANDRO

A dolomitic marble from the Ossola and Lake Maggiore area. Straight or wavy veins sometimes run through this white marble. Here, special attention has been paid to the relationship between vein orientation and the cutting planes. This attention to detail creates a book-matched pattern on the walls of quite astonishing precision, and a checked pattern of alternating brown tiles with a striped effect (cut against the rift planes) and ivory-beige tiles with a homogeneous look (cut along the rift planes). The quarry is still active.

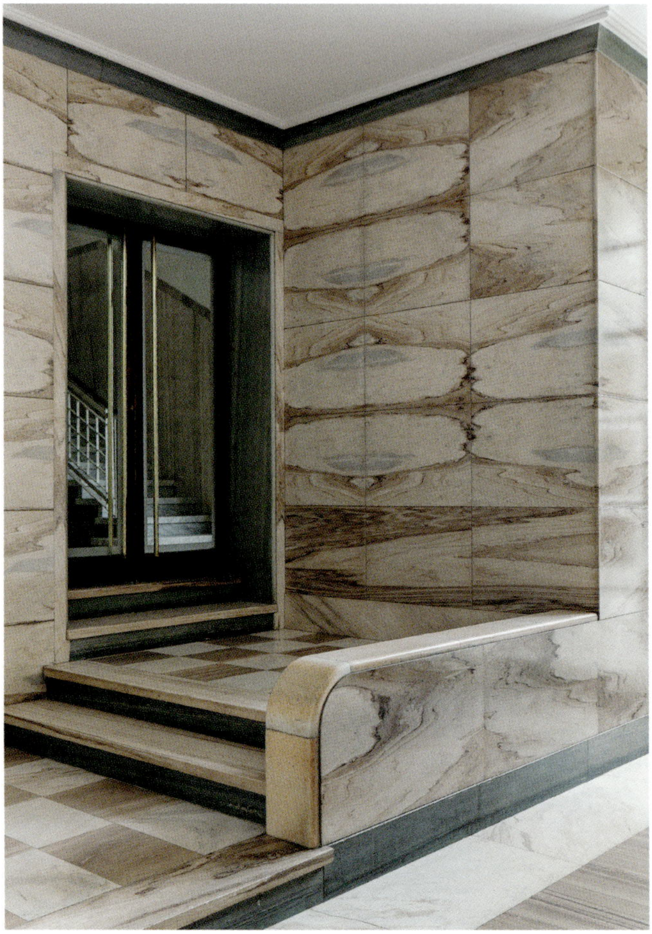

via Morozzo della Rocca 10 · Mario Uggè, 1935–37

floor: Palissandro marble, cross and vein cut · walls: Palissandro marble, book match · skirting: Carrara Bardiglio marble

Following spread:

via Matteo Bandello 5 · Romanini & Gilardi, 1937

floor and stairs: Breccia Aurora limestone · walls: Botticino limestone

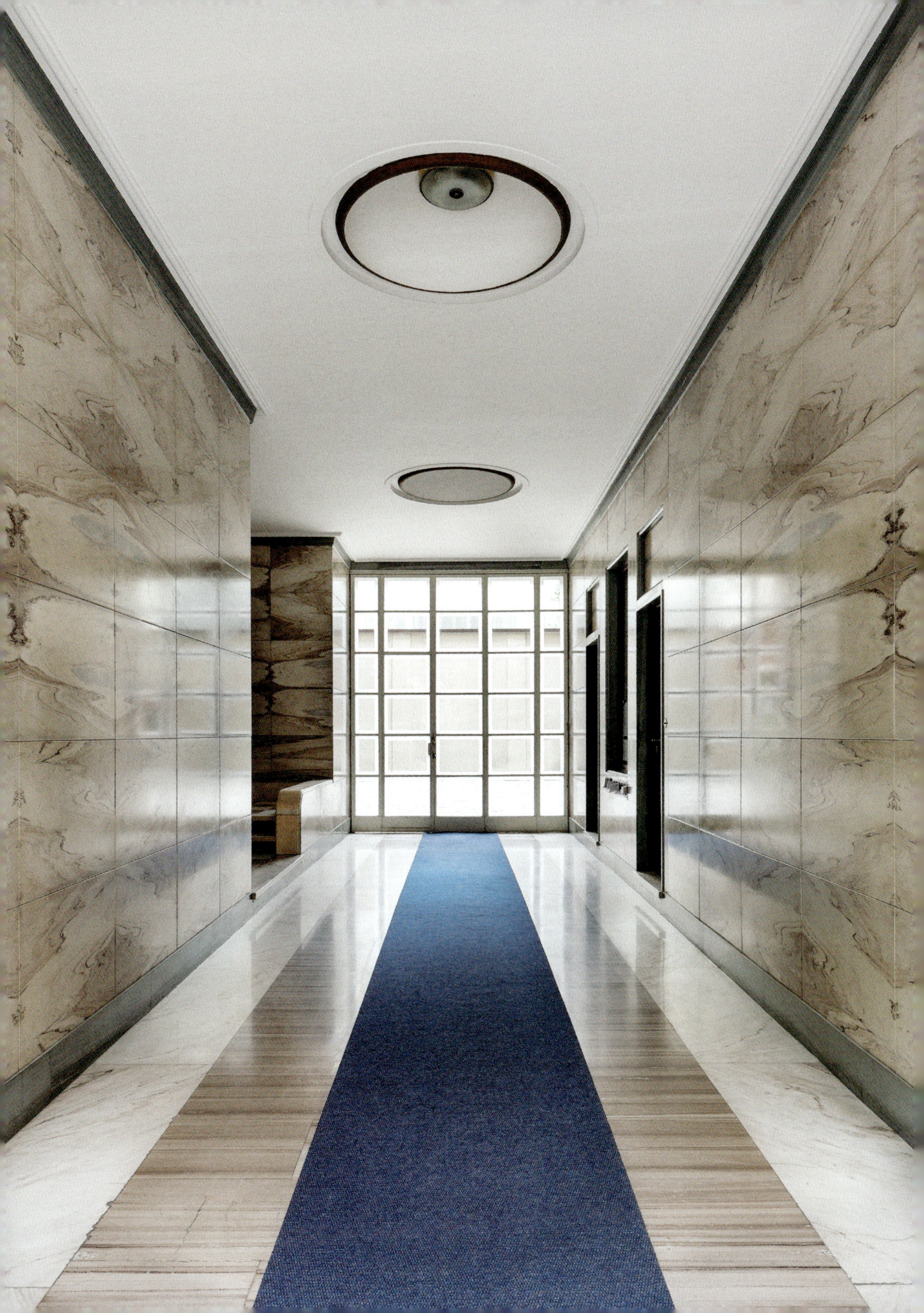

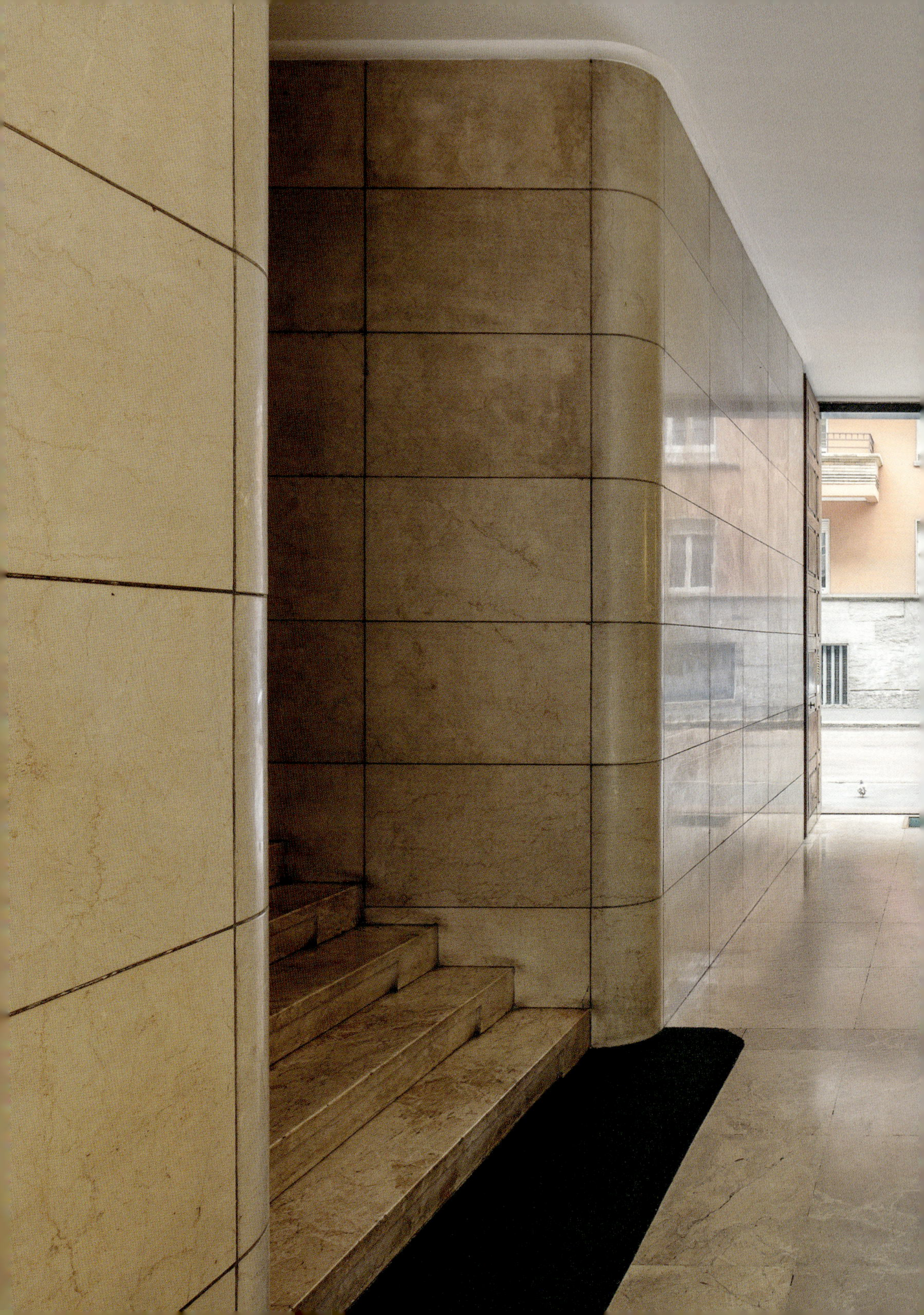

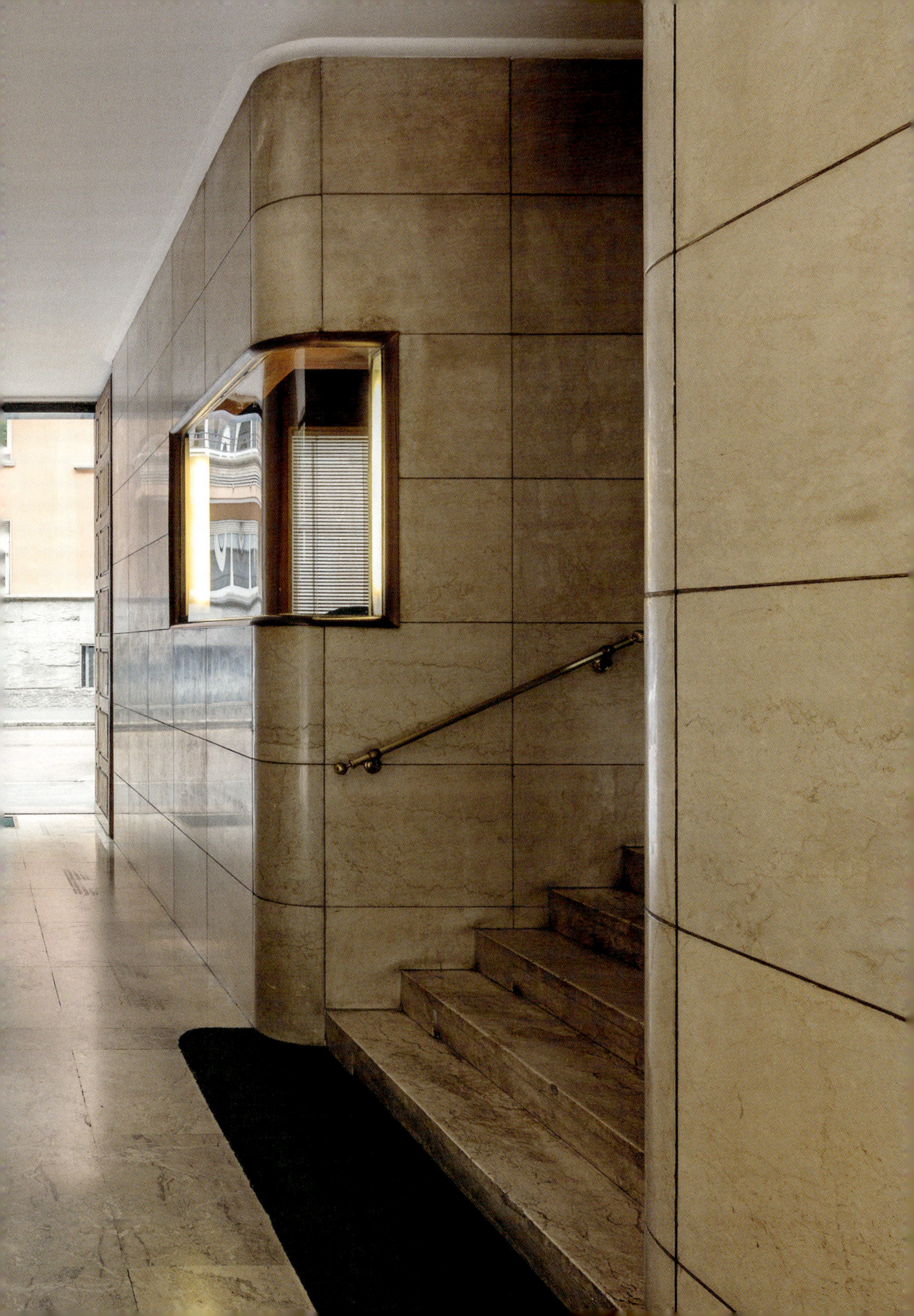

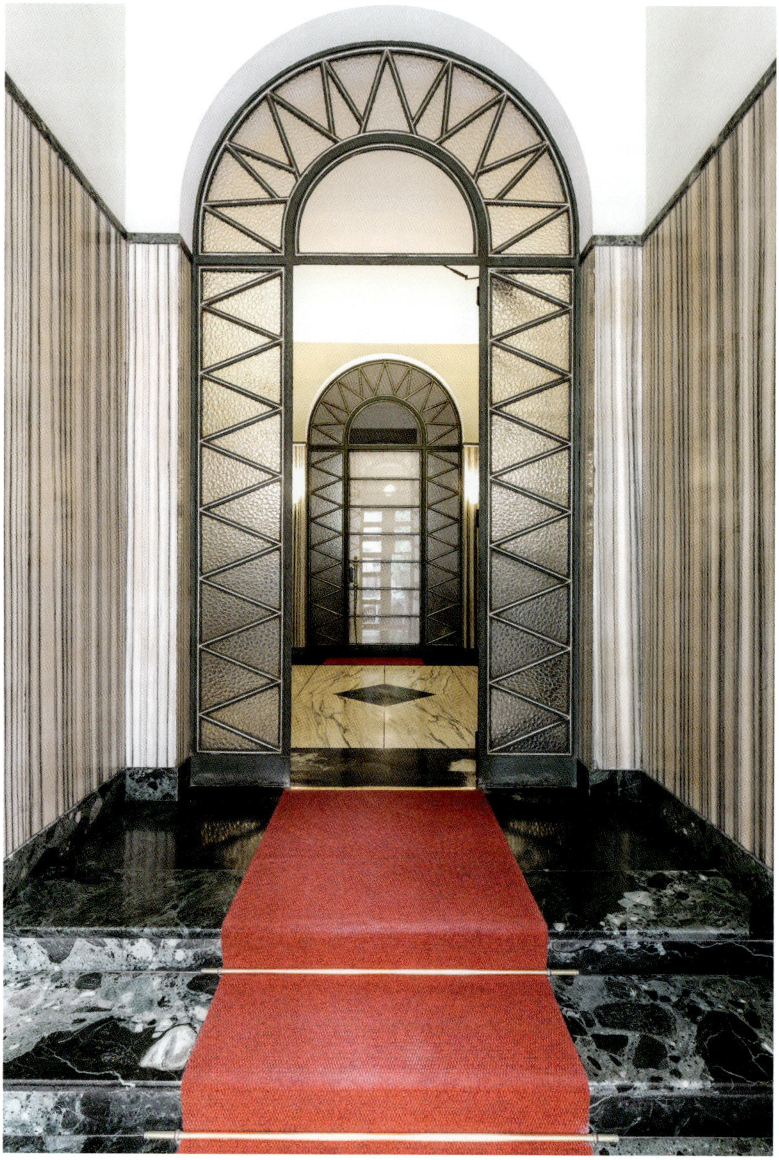

via San Vittore 32 · Vittorio Verganti, 1935–37

Textured tempered glass infill panels by Fontana Arte.

floor: Carrara Bianco Venato and Verde Alpi ophicalcite · walls: Cipollino 900 marble, also known as Zebrino marble

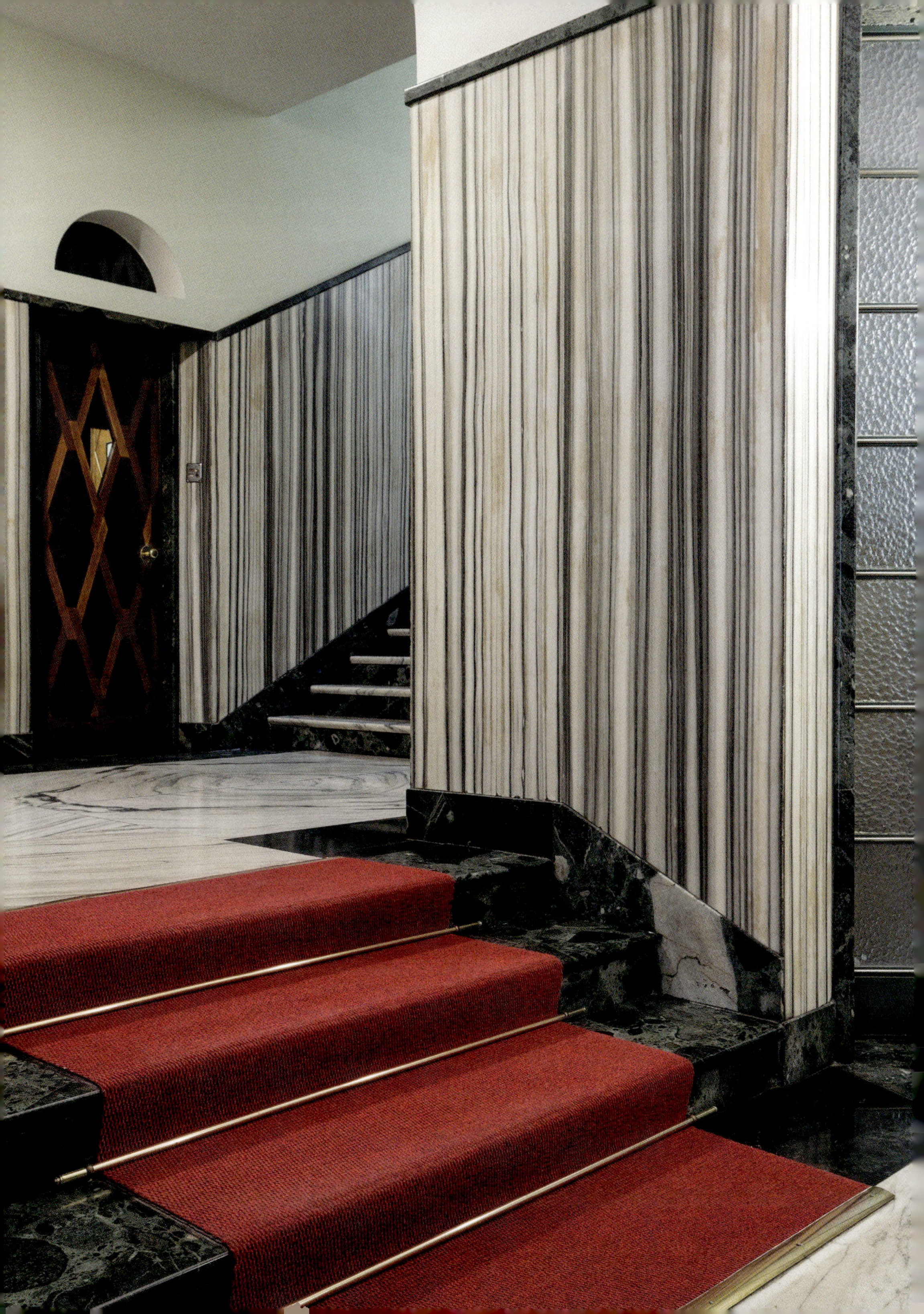

An encyclopedic use of all green marbles is set in the most Milanese of geometries: the octagon. This mystical geometric form appears in countless built structures throughout the ages in Milan, both in private and ecclesiastical spaces.

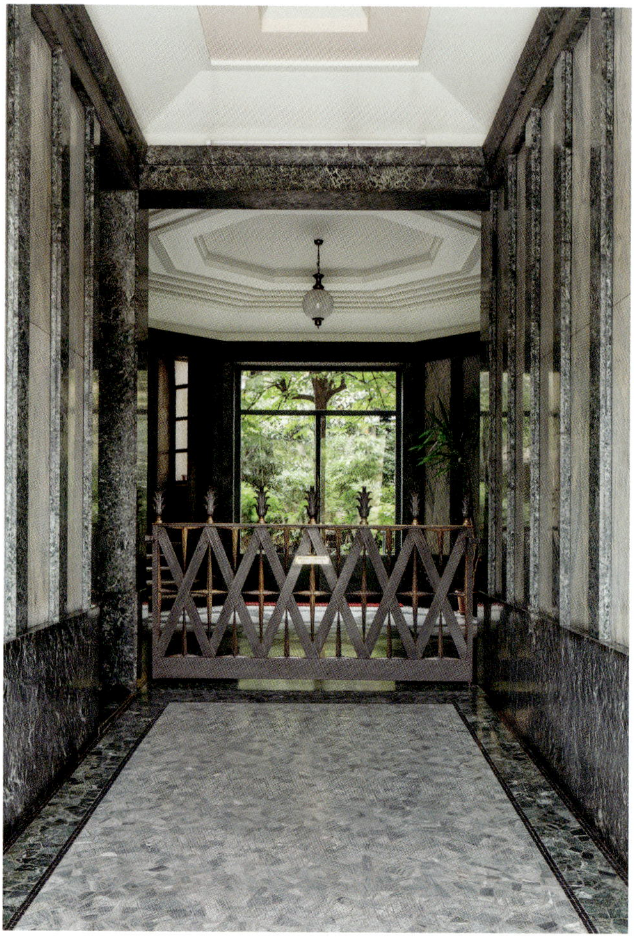

This and following spread:
via San Vittore 34 · Vittorio Verganti, 1935–37
floor: Palladiana of several marbles and serpentinite · walls: serpentinite and Cipollino Verde marble
stairs: Bianco Carrara Venato marble

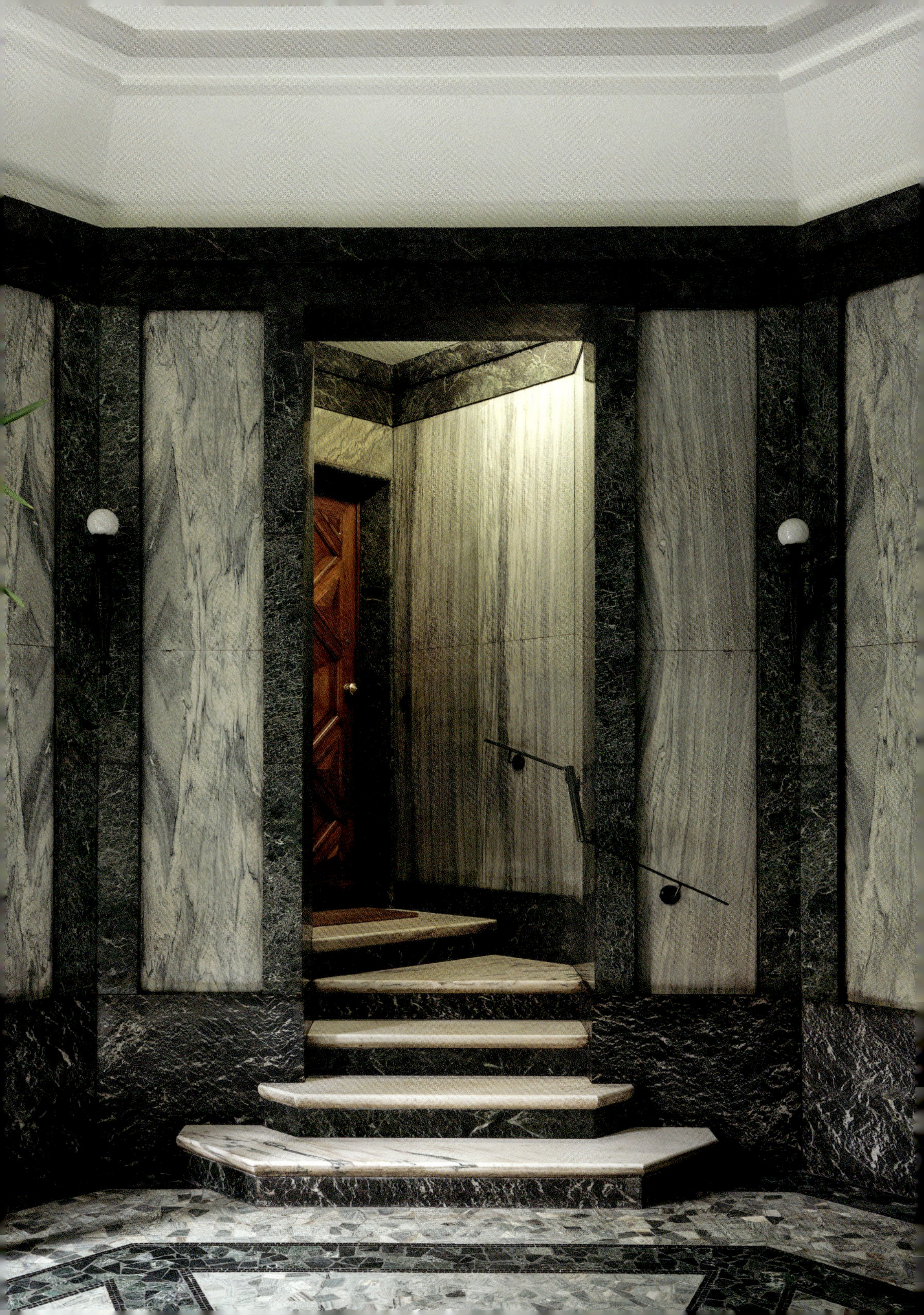

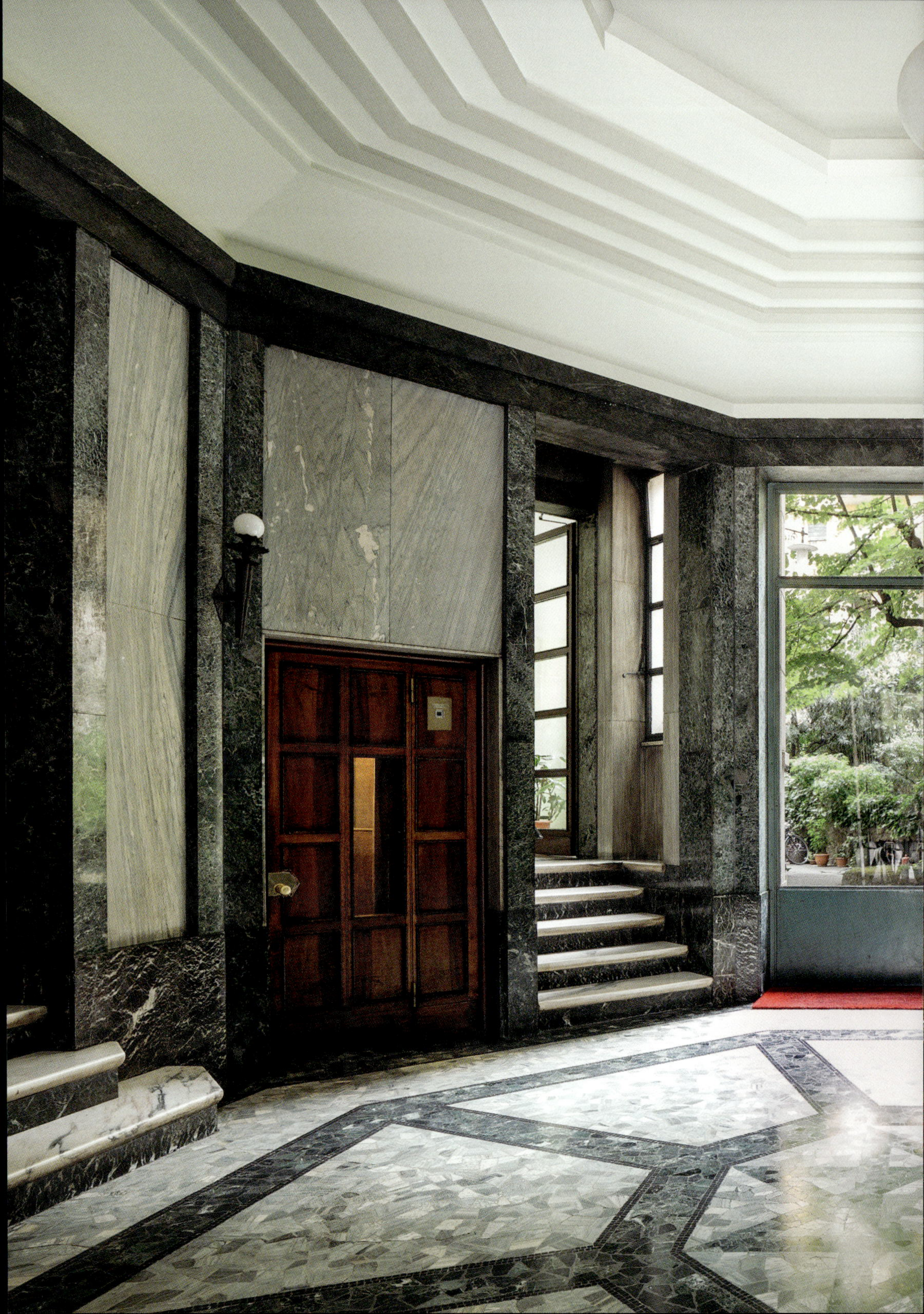

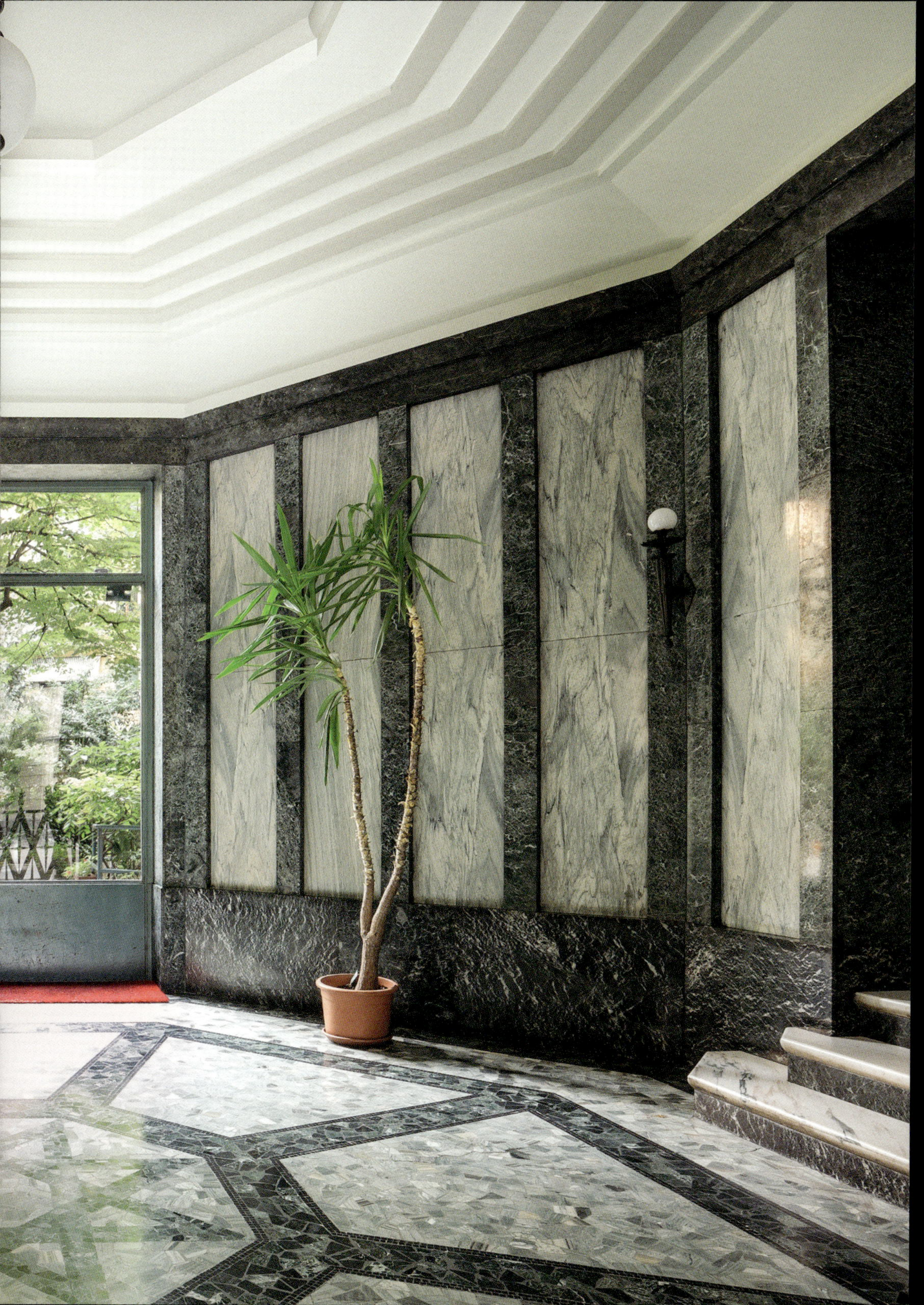

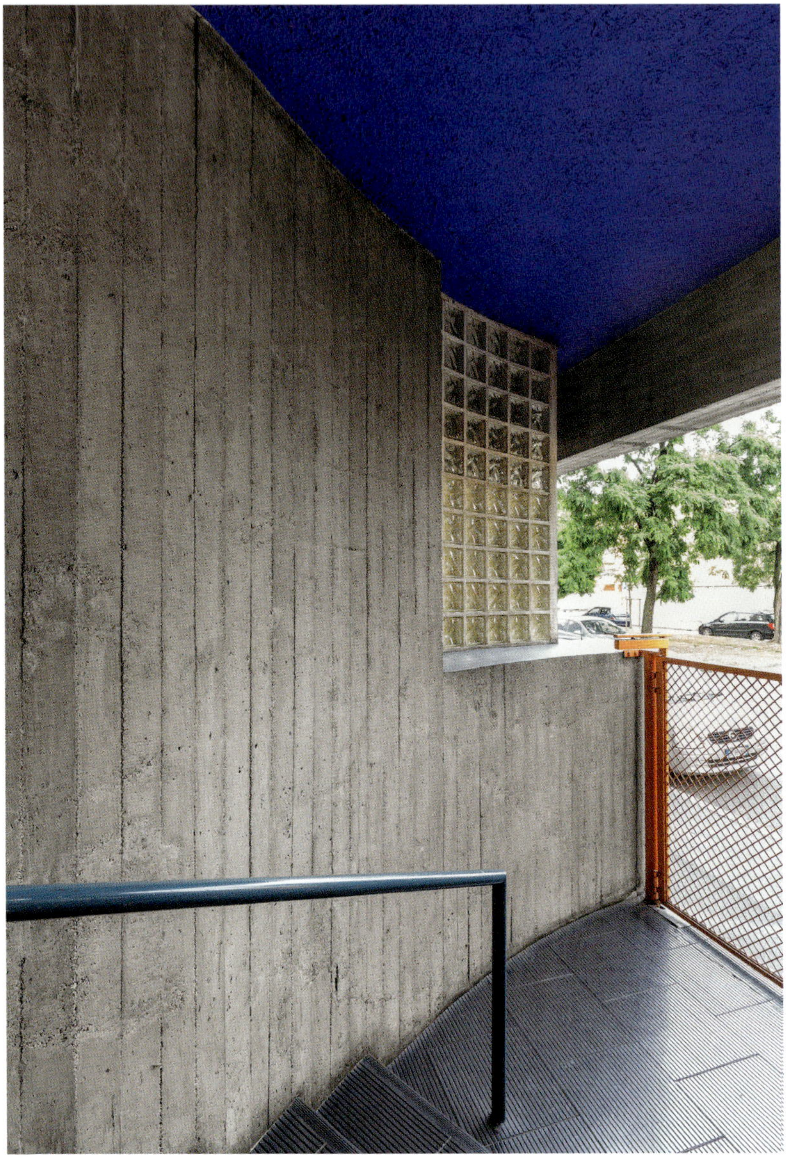

This and following spread:
via Paravia 37 · Umberto Riva, 1965

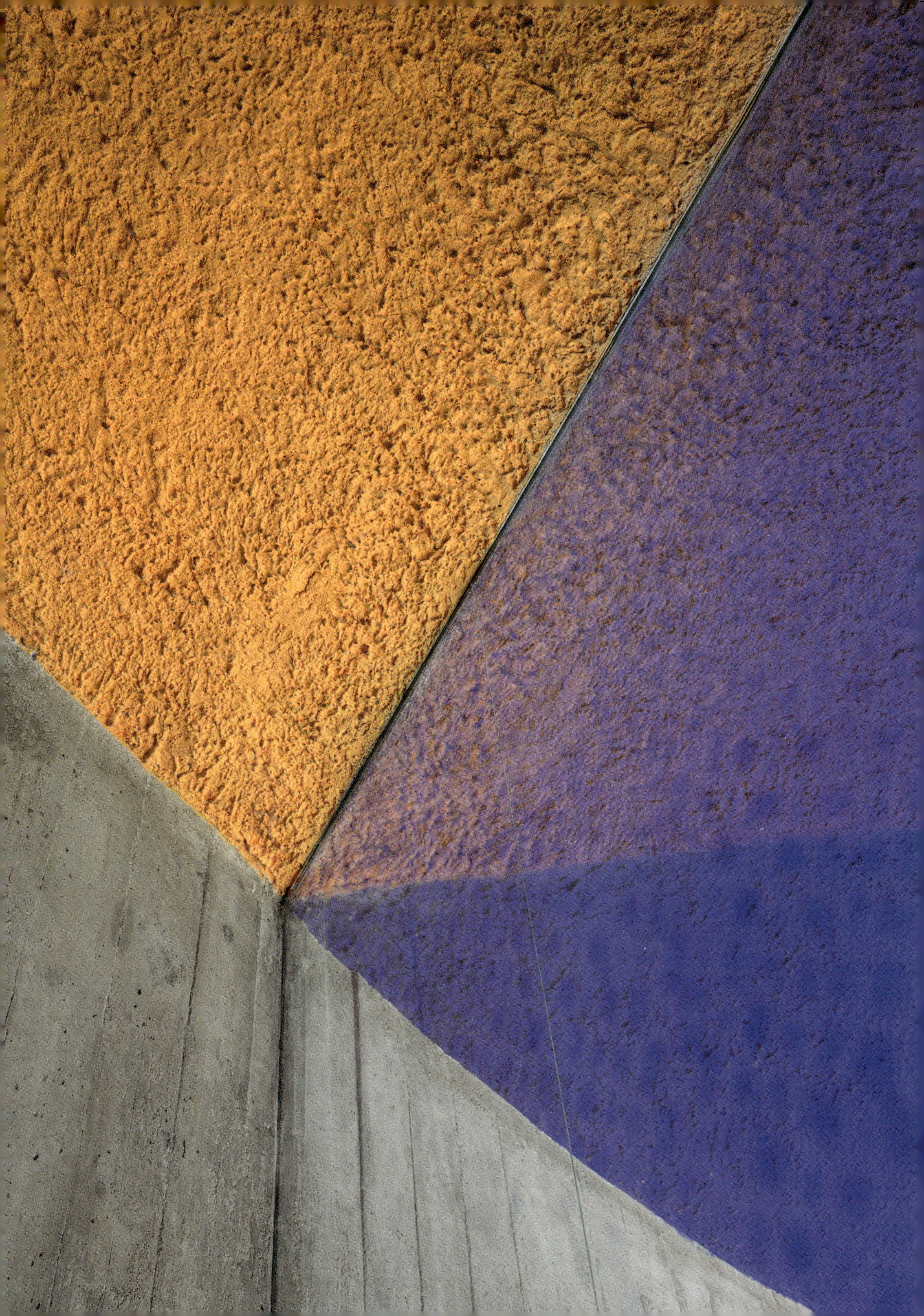

The enigmatic Umberto Riva, a former student of Carlo Scarpa, believes in an open text in architecture, eschewing complete images and definite forms. His is an architecture that privileges a sense of arrival rather than departure. Likewise this entrance, austere in materials but rich in subtle ideas about those materials, which are essential in expressing a poetics of organization. That achievement begins with a color coding of the ceilings: ultramarine blue for the outside entrance, abruptly transitioning beyond the threshold into a foyer with an ochre yellow ceiling. Here Riva has introduced elongated pendant lamps with a striking profile. This lighting source has the effect of throwing a yellow cast over the blue areas, toning down sharp contrasts, while providing a counterpoint to the ambient formal cohesion. It succeeds in intensifying the experience of a liminal situation, that is, the experience of arriving somewhere; that somewhere, as Riva suggests in interviews, is actually a space without a center.

Pendant lamps and enameled metal door handles by Umberto Riva.

Following spread:
via Enrico Falck 53, Gallaratese · Aldo Rossi, 1969–73

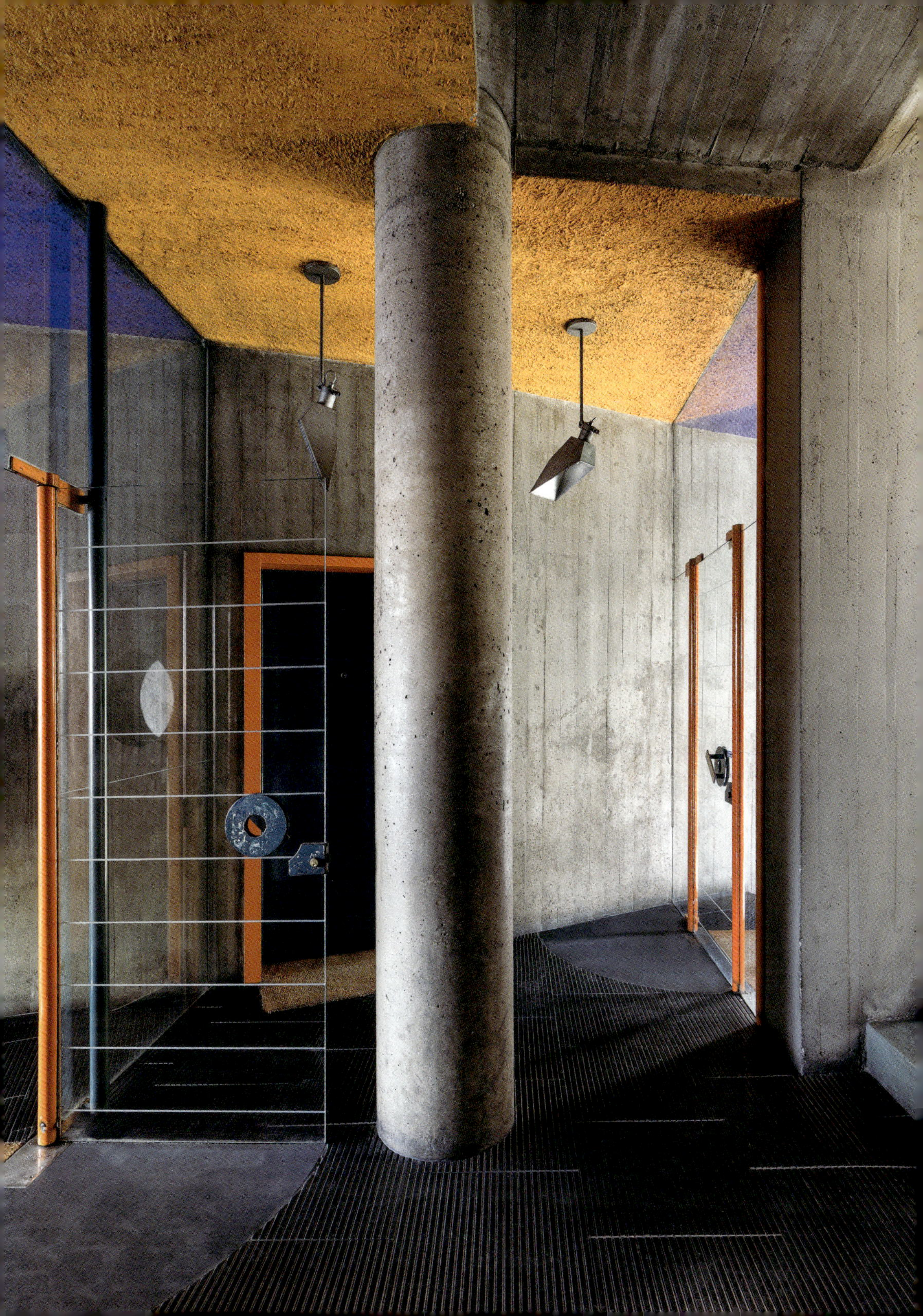

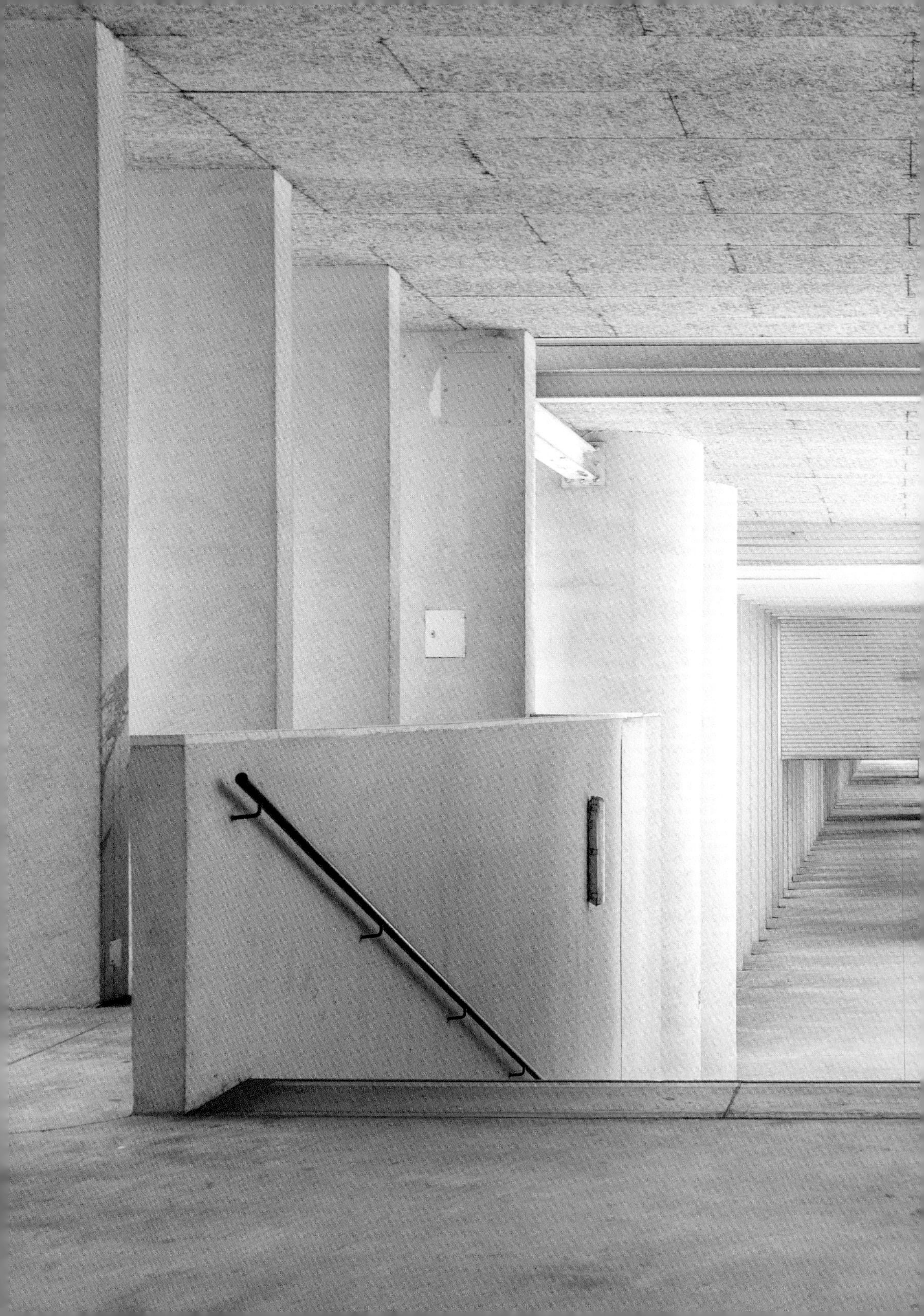

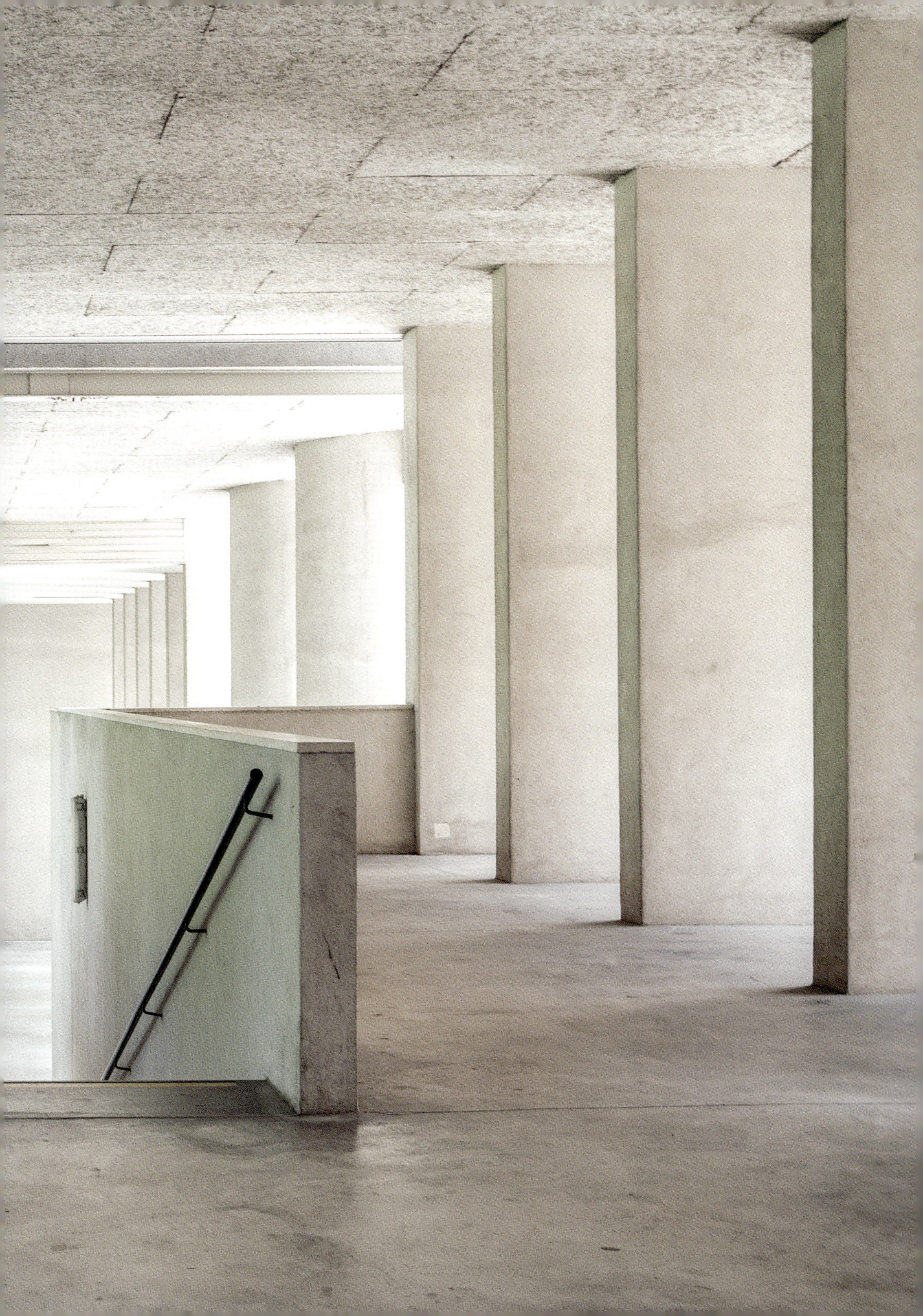

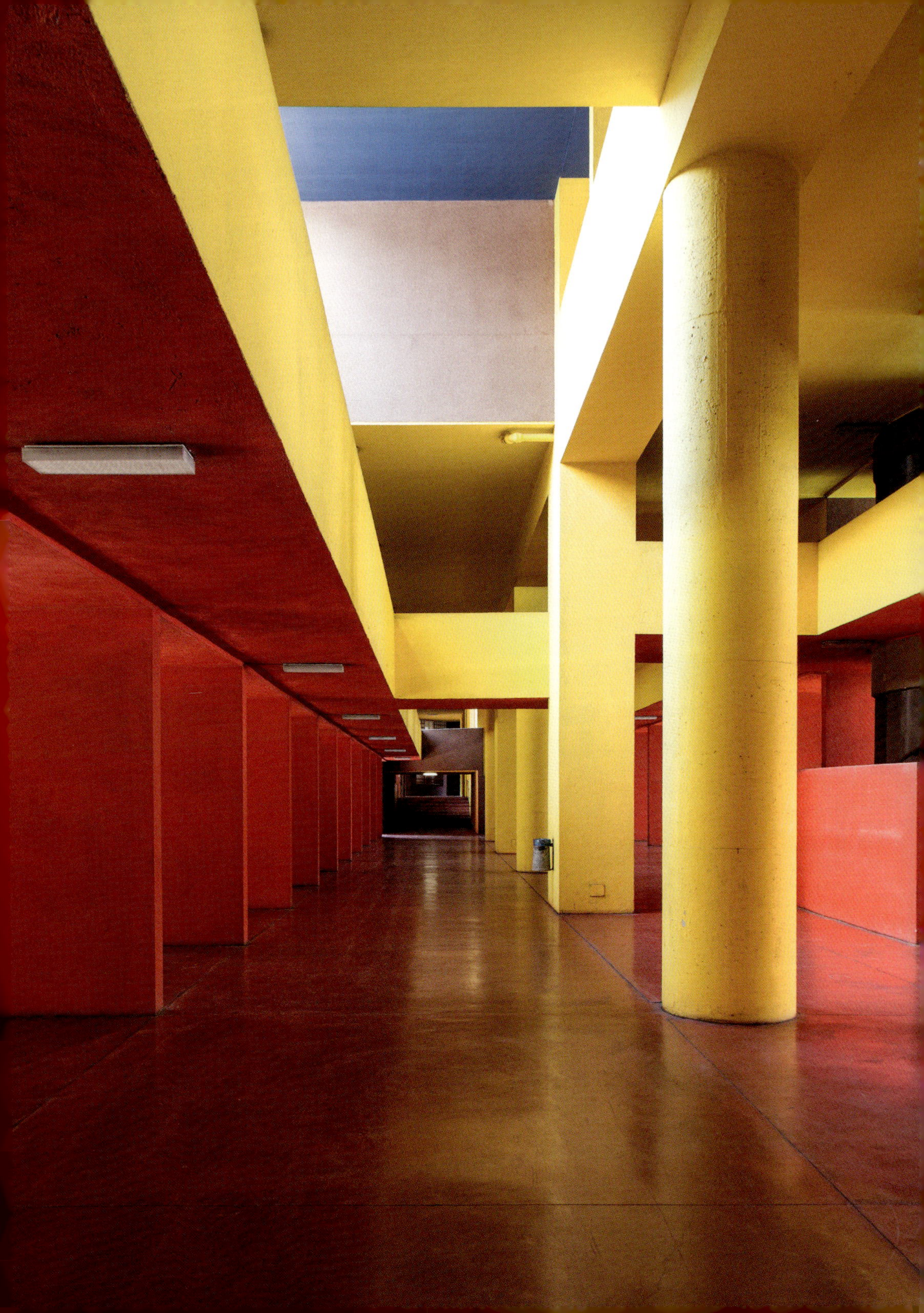

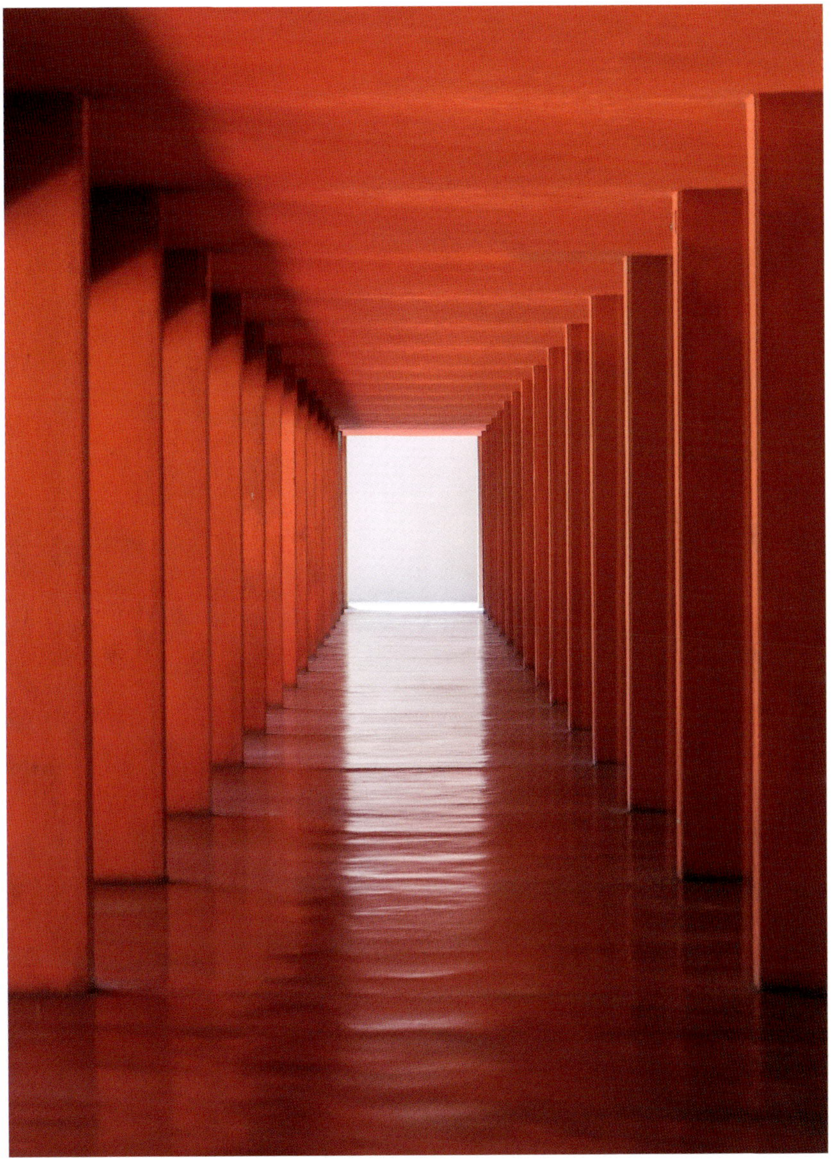

via Francesco Cilea 106, Gallaratese · Carlo Aymonino, 1967–74

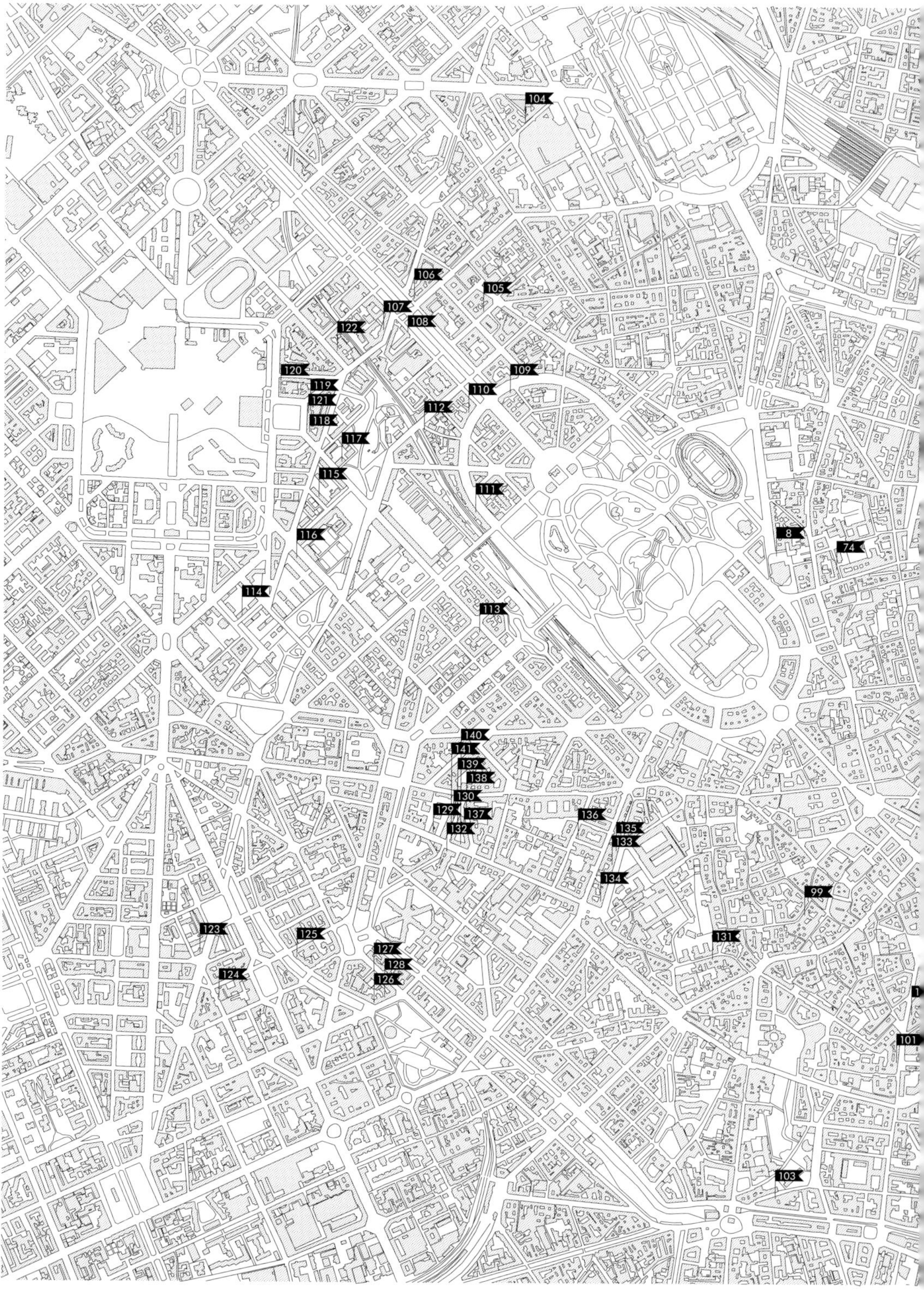
104
106
105
107
108
122
120
109
119
110
121
112
118
117
115
111
8
116
74
114
113
140
141
139
138
130
129
137
136
132
135
133
134
99
123
125
131
127
128
124
126
101
103

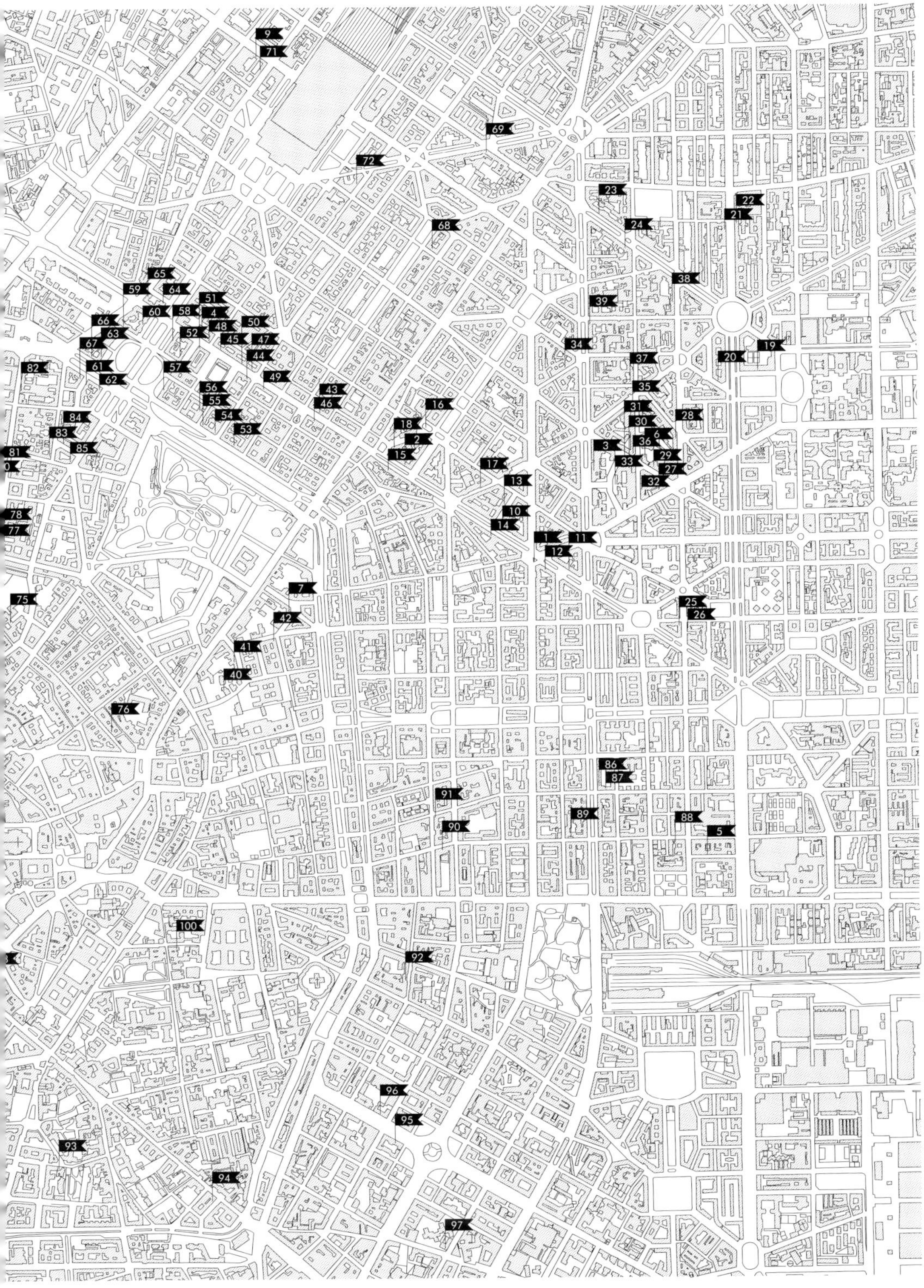
9
71
69
72
23
22
21
24
68
65
59
64
38
51
39
60
58
4
66
50
48
63
45
47
52
67
34
19
20
37
44
57
82
61
62
49
35
56
43
46
55
16
31
84
28
54
30
18
83
53
2
6
36
3
85
81
15
29
17
33
27
13
32
78
10
77
14
1
11
12
7
75
25
26
42
41
40
76
86
87
91
89
88
5
90
100
92
96
95
93
94
97

LOCATIONS / LUOGHI

INDEX OF ARCHITECTS, ARTISTS, DESIGNERS, AND MANUFACTURERS

Page numbers refer to photographs.

NOTES

Behind Closed Doors

1 By the 1910s, Milan's population had almost doubled the number registered early in the 1880s, and its urban fabric was swiftly spilling over the sixteenth-century Spanish walls that had historically retained it. Correspondingly, the late nineteenth century was characterized by intense urban growth prompted by the city's famous Beruto Plan (1885–89) and later redirected in the Pavia-Masera (1912) and Albertini Plans (1933), which more or less successfully governed frantic building activities while radically transforming the city's vehicular infrastructure.

2 Marzia Capello, "Palazzi privati nella prima metà del Settecento a Milano," *Arte Lombarda* 98/99 (1991): 155–159.

3 An interesting record of this condition was engraved probably between 1743 and 1750 by Marc'Antonio Dal Re in his *Vedute di Milano*, which features numerous façades of significant aristocratic palazzi. For more on the subject see Adele Mazzotta Buratti (ed.), *Milano nel settecento e le vedute architettoniche disegnate e incise da Marc'Antonio Dal Re* (Milan: Polifilo, 1976).

4 Lucio Gambi and Maria Cristina Gozzoli, *Le città nella storia d'Italia. Milano* (Rome-Bari: Laterza, 1982), 78, 157.

5 An in-depth account of the phenomenon can be found in Cino Zucchi, *L'Architettura dei cortili Milanesi 1535–1706* (Milan: Mondadori Electa, 1989).

6 These were the years of Milan's Borromeo bishops, when the city's civic culture gained much of its defining urban and societal traits. Under the stern motto *"humilitas nomini"* (in the name of humility), first San Carlo (1564–84) and later his cousin Federico Borromeo (1595–1631) were in fact sound protagonists of the Counter-Reformation, the former having participated in person in a number of sessions of the Council of Trent, the latter having applied its canons throughout the whole of his archbishopric. Architecturally speaking, Laura Gasparini notices how the arrival of the Borromeo in Milan curiously coincided with the "abandonment" of stone *bugnati*, classical orders, and other decorative apparatuses which would have previously embellished the façades of its palazzi (Marino, Cicogna, Medici, Omenoni) to the likes of contemporary aristocratic dwellings in other Italian cities. For more on the subject see Laura Giacomini, *Costruire una lauta dimora. Milano nell'età dei Borromeo* (1560–1631) (Benevento: Hevelius, 2007).

7 Here one may recall Heinrich Wölfflin's broader observations on the changing nature of the *cortile* in Cinquecento Rome, which was conceived as a space of both physical and visual transition in which boundless depth was achieved by means of distinct architectural or pictorial effects. Examples of these abound in the aforementioned Roman engravings of French scholar Paul Marie Letarouilly, who, symptomatically, dedicates a large part of his production to the description of "views into courtyards" through the very space of the *androne* (or the vestibule depending on the specific case). For more on the subject see Heinrich Wölfflin, *Renaissance and Baroque* (Ithaca: Cornell University Press, 1967).

8 Marzia Capello, "Palazzi privati nella prima metà del Settecento a Milano," degree thesis (1988–89), 155.

9 The façade is unglamorously clad in Ceppo di Gré, a gray stone typical of Milan's postwar architecture.

10 Fulvio Irace, "Condominio Milanese," in F. Irace, G. Basilico, and P. Roselli, *Milano moderna: architettura e città nell'epoca della ricostruzione* (Milan: Federico Motta, 1996), 50–58.

11 Cf. with Aldo Rossi, "La Costruzione della Città," in *Milano 70/70: un secolo d'arte, vol. 3: dal 1946 al 1970*, from May 30, 1972 , Museo Poldi Pezzoli, exhibition catalogue (Milan: Monolito, 1971); translated in Adam Caruso and Helen Thomas (eds.), *Asnago Vender and the Construction of Modern Milan* (Zurich: gta Verlag, 2014), 23.

The Discreet Charm of the Entryway

1 On the *portici* of Bologna, see F. Bocchi, *I Portici di Bologna e l'edilizia civile medievale* (Bologna, 1990); on the *portego* and *androne* of Venetian palazzi, see D. Howard, *Architectural History of Venice* (New Haven/London: Yale University Press, 1990), 34ff; on the palace stairs of Naples, R. Wittkower, *Art and Architecture in Italy 1600–1750* (New Haven/London: Yale University Press, 1999), III, 21–23; F. Ballabio,

"Snails and Hawkwings," *AA Files 69* (London: Architectural Association, 2014), 107–117.

2 Cf. P. Bourdieu, *Distinction, A Social Critique of the Judgment of Taste*, translated by Richard Nice (Cambridge, MA/London: Harvard University Press, 1984).

3 Manolo De Giorgi, "The Custodian's Vestibule," *Domus* 985 (November 2014); Luca Rubino, "Androni," *Domus* (March 31, 2015); Stefano Poli, "Signorile, cinque local con servizi: Gio Ponti sull'area ex-Bianchi. Via Plinio," in B. Bonomo, F. De Pieri, G. Caramellino, F. Zanfi (eds.), *Storie di case. Abitare l'Italia del boom* (Rome: Donzelli, 2013) 289–291. Although it does not single out the Milanese *ingressi* for analysis, see the perceptive studies of transitional spaces by Irene Guida, Corridoi (Macerata: Quodlibet, 2014) and Robin Evans, "Figures, Doors, and Passageways," in Id., *Translations from Drawing to Building and Other Essays* (Cambridge, MA: MIT Press, 1997).

4 On ceramic cladding as a sign of social mobility associated with "*lusso*" in postwar Milanese apartment buildings, see Poli, "Signorile: cinque locali piu servizi," op. cit., 282–283; Adam Caruso and Helen Thomas (eds.), *Asnago Vender and the Construction of Modern Milan* (Zurich: gta Verlag, 2014), 65ff.

5 Piero Bottoni, *Antologia di edifici moderni in Milano* (Milan: Editoriale Domus, 1954), 153ff, no. 40.

6 Thomas Schumacher, *Giuseppe Terragni. Danteum* (New York: Princeton Architectural Press, 2004).

7 De Giorgi, "The Custodian's Vestibule," op. cit.

8 P. Farina, "Casa Berri-Menegalli," in Lorenzo Capellini (ed.), *Milano. Allemandi's Architectural Guide* (Turin: Allemandi & C., 1998), no. 138, 191.

9 Cf. M. Tafuri, *Architecture and Utopia, Design and Capitalist Development* (Cambridge, MA: MIT Press, 1976), 1.

10 S. Freud and J. Breuer, *Studies on Hysteria* (London: Hogarth Press, 1895/1995). For further iconographic material relating to the history of hysteria, see Georges Didi-Huberman, *The Invention of Hysteria* (trans. Alisa Hartz) (Cambridge, MA: MIT Press, 2003).

11 M. Foucault, "Of Other Spaces: Utopias and Heterotopias," *Diacritics* 16 (1) (Spring 1986), 22–27.

12 Andreani, who trained both as a sculptor and an architect, had studied sculpture with Wildt at the Brera in 1927.

13 On the role of the *concetto* in Baroque art and architecture, see Wittkower, *Art and Architecture in Italy*, op. cit. I, 19ff.

14 Chiara Baglione, "Cronaca di un progetto. Palazzo Fidia a Milano," in *Casabella 706–707* (December 2002–January 2003) 75–86; M. Grandi, A. Pracchi, *Milano. Guida all'architettura moderna, L'architettura del Novecento* (Bologna: Zanichelli, 1980), 145, 156; Roberto Dulio and Mario Lupano, *Aldo Andreani Architetto: Visioni, costruzioni, immagini 1887–1971* (Milan: Electa, 2015), 33, 81.

15 This sculpture had been attributed to Wildt until Paola Mola, in 1995, shifted the attribution to Andreani: see P. Mola, "Miscellenea Wildtiana," Arte Lombarda 113, no. 115 (1995), 153–162. For further discussion see Dulio and Lupano, Aldo Andreani, op. cit., 166.

16 Athanasius Kircher, *Musurgia Universalis* (Rome, 1650), II, 303.

17 Bonomo et al., *Storie di case. Abitare l'Italia del boom*, op. cit.

18 M. Tafuri, *History of Italian Architecture 1944–1985* (trans. Jessica Levine) (Cambridge, MA: MIT Press, 1989), 67.

19 Caccia, interview 2013 quoted in my article, "The Caccia Effect. Milan's Hidden Master of Architecture and Design," *PIN-UP* 16 (Spring-Summer 2014), 214.

20 Sacha Craddock and James Cahill, *Angus Fairhurst* (London, 2009), 31.

21 Michelangelo Antonioni, in *Cronaca di un Amore* (*Story of a Love Affair*, 1950), makes the protagonist, played by Lucia Bose, an inhabitant of the Palazzo Fidia—a strategic move that drives home the fact that she belongs to the *haute-bourgeoisie*. On Antonioni's films and their Milanese sites, see F. Irace, "L'Architetto scultore che turbò i borghesi ma stregò Antonioni," *La Repubblica* (2015), 12/5.

NOTA

Dietro le porte chiuse

1 Negli anni Dieci del Novecento, la popolazione di Milano quasi raddoppiò rispetto al numero di persone registrate negli anni Ottanta del secolo precedente, e il tessuto urbano si espandeva velocemente al di fuori delle mura spagnole del sedicesimo secolo, che, storicamente, facevano da perimetro alla città stessa. Allo stesso modo, il tardo diciannovesimo secolo era stato caratterizzato da un intenso sviluppo urbano, stimolato dal famoso Piano Beruto (1885-89) e successivamente dai Piani Pavia-Masera (1912) e Albertini (1933), i quali controllarono più o meno soddisfacentemente le frenetiche attività costruttive mentre trasformarono radicalmente l'infrastruttura veicolare della città.

2 Marzia Capello, "Palazzi privati nella prima metà del Settecento a Milano", *Arte Lombarda* 98/99 (1991), pp. 155-159.

3 Un'interessante raccolta che illustra questa condizione è la serie di incisioni di Marc'Antonio Dal Re, *Vedute di Milano*, realizzate tra il 1743 e il 1750, le quali raffigurano numerose facciate dei principali palazzi nobiliari. Approfondimenti sul tema in Adele Mazzotta Buratti (a cura di), *Milano nel Settecento e le vedute architettoniche disegnate e incise da Marc'Antonio Dal Re* (Milano: Polifilo, 1976).

4 Lucio Gambi e Maria Cristina Gozzoli, *Le città nella storia d'Italia*. Milano (Roma-Bari: Laterza, 1982), pp. 78, 157.

5 Approfondimenti sul tema in Cino Zucchi, *L'Architettura dei cortili milanesi 1535-1706* (Milano: Mondadori Electa, 1989).

6 Questi erano gli anni del vescovato dei Borromeo, quando la cultura civica della città ottenne molti dei suoi tratti distintivi sociali e urbani. Sotto l'austero motto "humilitas nomini" (nel nome dell'umiltà), prima san Carlo (1564-84) e successivamente suo cugino Federico Borromeo (1595-1631) furono ferrei sostenitori e protagonisti della Controriforma, alla quale il primo partecipò in maniera diretta attendendo di persona alle diverse sessioni del Concilio di Trento, e della quale il secondo applicò i canoni nel suo arcivescovado. Dal punto di vista architettonico, Laura Gasparini osserva come l'arrivo dei Borromeo a Milano abbia curiosamente coinciso con l'"abbandono" dei bugnati di pietra, gli ordini classici, e degli altri apparati decorativi che previamente avevano abbellito le facciate dei palazzi di Milano (Marino, Cicogna, Medici, Omenoni) così come quelle di altri importanti centri italiani. Approfondimenti sul tema in Laura Giacomini, *Costruire una lauta dimora. Milano nell'età dei Borromeo (1560-1631)* (Benevento: Hevelius, 2007).

7 Qui si possono ricordare le osservazioni di Heinrich Wölfflin sui cambiamenti che delinearono il cortile cinquecentesco a Roma. Secondo Wölfflin, questo veniva concepito come uno spazio di transizione tanto fisico che visivo in cui il ricercato senso di profondità veniva raggiunto per mezzo di effetti sia architettonici che pittorici. Esempi di questi mezzi abbondano nelle incisioni romane dello storico francese Paul-Marie Letarouilly, che, sintomaticamente, dedica gran parte della sua produzione alla descrizione di "viste dei cortili" attraverso lo spazio dell'androne (o vestibolo a seconda del caso specifico). Per approfondimenti cfr. Heinrich Wölfflin, *Renaissance and Baroque* (Ithaca: Cornell University Press, 1967).

8 Marzia Capello, "Palazzi privati nella prima metà del Settecento a Milano", tesi di laurea (1988-89), p. 155.

9 La cui facciata è banalmente ricoperta in Ceppo di Gré, una pietra grigia tipica dell'architettura milanese postbellica.

10 Fulvio Irace, "Condominio milanese", in Id., Gabriele Basilico e Paolo Rosselli, *Milano moderna: architettura e città nell'epoca della ricostruzione* (Milano: Federico Motta, 1996), pp. 50-58.

11 Cfr. Aldo Rossi, "La costruzione della città", in *Milano 70/70: un secolo d'arte, vol. 3: dal 1946 al 1970*, catalogo della mostra (Milano, Museo Poldi Pezzoli, dal 30 maggio 1972) (Milano: Monolito, 1971); tradotto in Adam Caruso e Helen Thomas (a cura di), *Asnago Vender and the Construction of Modern Milan* (Zurigo: gta Verlag, 2014), p. 23.

Il fascino discreto della soglia

1 Sui portici di Bologna, cfr. Francesca Bocchi (a cura di), *I portici di Bologna e l'edilizia civile medievale* (Bologna: Grafis, 1990); sul portego e l'androne nei palazzi veneziani, cfr. Deborah Howard, *Architectural History of Venice* (New

Haven/London: Yale University Press, 1990), pp. 34 sgg.; sugli scaloni dei palazzi barocchi napoletani, Rudolf Wittkower, *Art and Architecture in Italy 1600-1750* (New Haven/London: Yale University Press, 1999), III, pp. 21-23; Fabrizio Ballabio, "Snails and Hawkwings", *AA Files 69* (London: Architectural Association, 2014), pp. 107-117.

2 Cfr. Pierre Bourdieu, *Distinction, A Social Critique of the Judgment of Taste*, trad. di Richard Nice (Cambridge, MA/London: Harvard University Press, 1984).

3 Manolo De Giorgi, "The Custodians's Vestibule", *Domus* 985 (novembre 2014); Luca Rubino, "Androni", *Domus* (31 marzo 2015); Stefano Poli, "Signorile, cinque locali più servizi: Gio Ponti sull'area ex Bianchi. Via Plinio, Milano", in Bruno Bonomo, Filippo De Pieri, Gaia Caramellino, Federico Zanfi (a cura di), *Storie di case. Abitare l'Italia del boom* (Roma: Donzelli, 2013), pp. 289-291. Sebbene non analizzino gli ingressi milanesi, sono molto utili per comprenderne la logica di transizione le discussioni di Irene Guida, *Corridoi* (Macerata: Quodlibet, 2014) e Robin Evans, "Figures, Doors, and Passageways", in Id., *Translations from Drawing to Building and Other Essays* (Cambridge, MA: MIT Press, 1997).

4 Sul *Klinker* come segno di lusso nell'edilizia altoborghese milanese cfr. Poli, "Signorile: cinque locali più servizi", op. cit., pp. 282-283; Adam Caruso e Helen Thomas, *Asnago Vender and the Construction of Modern Milan* (Zurigo: gta Verlag, 2014), pp. 65 sgg.

5 Piero Bottoni, *Antologia di edifici moderni in Milano* (Milano: Editoriale Domus, 1954), pp. 153 sgg., n. 40.

6 Thomas Schumacher, *Giuseppe Terragni. Danteum* (New York: Princeton Architectural Press, 2004).

7 De Giorgi, "The Custodians's Vestibule", op. cit.

8 P. Farina, "Casa Berri-Meregalli", in Lorenzo Capellini (a cura di), *Milano. Guida di Architettura* (Torino: Allemandi & c., 1990), nn. 138, 191.

9 Cfr. Manfredo Tafuri, *Architecture and Utopia, Design and Capitalist Development* (Cambridge, MA: MIT Press, 1976), 1.

10 Sigmund Freud e Josef Breuer, *Studies on Hysteria* (London: Hogarth Press, 1895/1955). Per approfondimenti iconografici sulla storia dell'isteria, cfr. Georges Didi-Huberman, *The Invention of Hysteria*, trad. di Alisa Hartz (Cambridge, MA: MIT Press, 2003).

11 Michel Foucault, "Of Other Spaces: Utopias and Heterotopias", *Diacritics* 16 (1) (primavera 1986), pp. 22-27.

12 Andreani, che aveva una formazione sia come scultore che come architetto, aveva studiato scultura con Wildt a Brera nel 1927.

13 Sul ruolo del "concetto" nell'arte e nell'architettura barocche, cfr. Wittkower, *Art and Architecture in Italy*, op. cit., I, pp. 19 sgg.

14 Chiara Baglione, "Cronaca di un progetto. Palazzo Fidia a Milano", in *Casabella* 706-707 (dicembre 2002-gennaio 2003), pp. 75-86; Maurizio Grandi e Attilio Pracchi, *Milano. Guida all'architettura moderna, L'architettura del Novecento* (Bologna: Zanichelli, 1980), pp. 145, 156; Roberto Dulio e Mario Lupano, *Aldo Andreani Architetto: Visioni, costruzioni, immagini 1887-1971* (Milano: Electa, 2015), pp. 33, 81.

15 Questa scultura era stata attribuita a Wildt fino alle ricerche di Paola Mola, che, nel 1995, ne ha riferito l'attribuzione ad Andreani: cfr. P. Mola, "Miscellenea Wildtiana", *Arte Lombarda* 113, n. 115 (1995), pp. 153-162. Cfr. anche la discussione in Dulio e Lupano, *Aldo Andreani*, op. cit., p. 166.

16 Athanasius Kircher, *Musurgia Universalis* (Roma, 1650), II, p. 303.

17 Bonomo et al., *Storie di case. Abitare l'Italia del boom*, op. cit.

18 Manfredo Tafuri, *History of Italian Architecture 1944-1985*, trad. di Jessica Levine (Cambridge, MA: MIT Press, 1989), p. 67.

19 Luigi Caccia Dominioni, intervista del 2013 citata alla fine del mio saggio, "The Caccia Effect. Milan's Hidden Master of Architecture and Design", *PIN-UP* 16 (primavera-estate 2104), p. 214.

20 Sacha Craddock e James Cahill, *Angus Fairhurst* (London: Philip Wilson Publishers Ltd, 2009), p. 31.

21 Michelangelo Antonioni, in *Cronaca di un amore* (1950), fa della protagonista, interpretata da Lucia Bosè, una dei residenti di Palazzo Fidia, una scelta strategica per sottolinearne l'appartenenza al ceto altoborghese. Sui film di Antonioni e le loro ambientazioni milanesi, cfr. anche Fulvio Irace, "L'architetto scultore che turbò i borghesi ma stregò Antonioni", *La Repubblica* (12 maggio 2015).

PHOTO CREDITS

MATTHEW BILLINGS
6, 51, 54, 55, 62–63, 66–67, 69, 125, 126, 127, 128, 129, 130, 131, 135, 138, 139, 142, 165, 166–167, 168, 169, 172, 173, 174, 175, 179, 221, 228, 229, 257, 291, 297, 337, 342, 343, 344, 345, 346, 347, 352–353

DELFINO SISTO LEGNANI
11, 12, 18, 38, 43, 46, 70, 71, 72–73, 75, 76, 77, 78, 79, 83, 84, 85, 87, 89, 90–91, 92, 93, 94, 97, 98, 99, 100, 101, 102, 103, 108–109, 118, 119, 120, 122–123, 194–195, 196, 197, 198, 199, 200–201, 203, 204, 211, 216, 217, 231, 232, 235, 236, 237, 239, 254, 255, 262–263, 268, 269, 270, 274–275, 276, 280, 281, 282, 283, 284, 285, 286, 287, 288, 289, 292, 295, 298–299, 301, 302, 303, 304–305, 306, 307, 308, 309, 319, 320, 322, 323, 324, 325, 326, 327, 328, 329, 330, 331, 332–333, 334, 335, 338–339, 340, 341, 348, 349, 350, 351, 354, 355, 356, 357, 359, 360, 361, 362, 363, 364, 365, 366, 367, 368, 369, 370–371, 372, 373, 374, 375, 376, 379, 380, 381, 382, 383, 384, 385, 386, 387, 388, 389, 390, 391, 392–393, 394, 395, 396, 397, 398–399, 400, 401, 403, 404–405, 406

PAOLA PANSINI
2, 4, 8, 24–25, 26, 31, 34, 52, 53, 56, 57, 58–59, 61, 64, 65, 80–81, 104–105, 106, 107, 110, 111, 113, 114, 116–117, 132–133, 136–137, 140, 141, 143, 144–145, 146, 147, 148–149, 151, 153, 154–155, 156, 157, 158–159, 160, 161, 162, 163, 170, 171, 176, 177, 181, 183, 184–185, 186, 188–189, 190, 191, 193, 208–209, 214–215, 219, 222, 223, 224, 225, 226–227, 241, 243, 245, 246, 247, 248, 249, 251, 252, 253, 258, 259, 260, 261, 265, 266, 310–311, 312–313, 314, 315, 316, 317

Front cover / Copertina
via Aristide de Togni 14
Pier Giulio Magistretti, 1934–36
Sconces by Ignazio Gardella.
floor: Palladiana of Bardiglio, Carrara, Giallo Siena, Giallo Torri, Giallo Mori, Musso marble · doorframe: Giallo Mori limestone
Photography / Fotografia: Delfino Sisto Legnani

Back cover / Retro di copertina
viale Vittorio Veneto 20
Achille Luigi Ferraresi, 1952–57
Sconce by Venini.
Ceramic door handles by Ceramica San Paolo, Venice.
floor: Botticino limestone and Verona Rosso limestone
wall: Botticino limestone
Photography / Fotografia: Paola Pansini

p. 2
piazza Maria Adelaide di Savoia 2
Giuseppe Roberto Martinenghi, 1935
floor: Zandobbio dolostone · skirting: San Benedetto limestone · walls: Giallo Reale limestone

ZANDOBBIO DOLOSTONE
A Jurassic dolomitic rock, white or pinkish-white in color, polishable and durable, and very finely grained. First exploited by the Romans, it continues to be quarried to this day in Zandobbio (Province of Bergamo).

p. 4
viale Regina Giovanna 7 · Vincenzo d'Alo, 1935
Pendant lamp by Luigi Caccia Dominioni.
floor: Palladiana of several marbles and limestones
base: Bardiglio marble · walls: Arabescato Carrara marble

ACKNOWLEDGEMENTS

My gratitude goes to Nicola Russi and Francesco Maria Cerroni, whose #ingressimilano, as well as their urban knowledge of Milan, provided the basis for this project.

Thank you to Francesco Martelli, Tommaso Bonfanti, and the entire team at Cittadella degli Archivi del Comune di Milano. Without your tireless efforts many of the architects' names and years of construction would have not been discovered.

Special thanks for your support and advice:
Fabrizio Ballabio, Katia Bey-Habedank, Matthew Billings, Carmen Brunner, Alessandra Cartella, Roberto Dulio, Angela Ehling, Philipp Hinz, Lisa Hockemeyer, Brian Kish, Florian Kobler, Delfino Sisto Legnani, Michele Occelli, Paola Pansini, Federico Perugini, Stefano Pilati, Livia Shamir, Daniel Sherer, Grazia Signori, Penny Sparke, Nicoletta Dalfino Spinelli, Benedikt Taschen, Marlene Taschen, Wolfgang Tillmans, Malte Wrede

Additional thanks:
Valentina Angeloni, Alessandro Benetti, Nini Bonavoglia, Bianca Bottero, Laura Bragalini, Marco Bruzzone, Edward Buchanan, Giacomo Bugini (Marmi Bugini), Felix Burrichter, Antonio and Daria Caccia Dominioni, Paolo Campiglio, Marco Cappelletti, Luca Cipelletti, Melania Dalle Grave, Etienne Descloux, Marte Eknæs, Tobias Engelschall, Yusuf Etiman, Andrea Faraguna, Matteo Foschi, Francesca Gavin, Alessandro Giovannelli and Marketa Luhanova (Giovannelli e Associati), Rosy Head, Tori Herbert, Salvatore Licitra (Gio Ponti Archives), Ian MacDonald, Patrick McGraw, Federico Martelli, Mauro Morales, Giovanni Muzio, Donato Nereo, Alessandro Neroni, Alessandro Padoan (Fragile Milano), Emil Rebek, Camillo Remuzzi (Remuzzi Marmi), Giulio Savoia (Essegi Marmi), Klaus Jürgen Schmidt, Gabriele Solazzi, Lilo Viehweg, Stephan Wilke, Will Yates-Johnson, Niklas Bildstein Zaar, Fabio Zambernardi, Cino Zucchi

IMPRINT

Editing, curatorship, and design:
Karl Kolbitz, Berlin

© Photographs:
Matthew Billings
Delfino Sisto Legnani
Paola Pansini

© Texts:
Fabrizio Ballabio
Lisa Hockemeyer
Brian Kish
Daniel Sherer
Grazia Signori
Penny Sparke

Design identification:
Brian Kish, New York

Material identification:
Angela Ehling Sc.D. (Geol), Berlin
Grazia Signori Sc.D (Geol), Bergamo

Archival researcher:
Federico Perugini, Milan

Graphic design:
Nicoletta Dalfino Spinelli, Berlin

Map design:
Livia Shamir, Milan

Post-production:
Matthew Billings:
Caroline Prange, Berlin
Delfino Sisto Legnani:
Delfino Sisto Legnani and Melania Dalle Grave, Milan
Paola Pansini: Paola Pansini and Tiziano Reguzzi, Milan

Text edit:
Brian Kish:
Franklin Boué, New York
Karl Kolbitz:
Michele Occelli, London
Grazia Signori:
Kyriacos Karseras, Athens

Ringrazio le portinaie e i portinai di Milano.
Thank you to all the concierges of Milan.

Italian translation (Karl Kolbitz, Penny Sparke, Lisa Hockemeyer):
Giuliana Olivero, Turin

Printed in Bosnia-Herzegovina
ISBN 978-3-7544-0126-2

Hohenzollernring 53
D-50672 Köln
taschen.com